American Stories

W. E. B. Du Bois was an African American activist and author. He helped found the National Association for the Advancement of Colored People (NAACP) and wrote *The Souls of Black Folk*, which portrayed the challenges faced by American blacks in their struggle to achieve equality.

American Stories
A History of the United States

THIRD EDITION
Volume 2, Since 1865

H. W. Brands
University of Texas

R. Hal Williams
Southern Methodist University

T. H. Breen
Northwestern University

Ariela J. Gross
University of Southern California

Boston   Columbus   Indianapolis   New York   San Francisco   Upper Saddle River
Amsterdam   Cape Town   Dubai   London   Madrid   Milan   Munich   Paris   Montréal   Toronto
Delhi   Mexico City   São Paulo   Sydney   Hong Kong   Seoul   Singapore   Taipei   Tokyo

Editor-in-Chief: Dickson Musslewhite
Executive Editor: Ed Parsons
Program Manager: Seanna Breen
Editorial Assistant: Ariel Puccio
Director of Marketing: Brandy Dawson
Executive Marketing Manager: Wendy Albert
Marketing Assistant: Cristina Liva
Senior Managing Editor: Ann Marie McCarthy
Senior Project Manager: Cheryl Keenan
Procurement Manager: Mary Fischer
Procurement Specialist: Mary Ann Gloriande
Senior Art Director: Maria Lange
Interior Design: Red Kite Project

Cover Design: Maria Lange/Red Kite Project
Cover Illustration: Paul Chung
Cover Art: W.E.B. Du Bois-Library of Congress Prints
and Photographs Division [LC-USZ62-16767]
Director of Media & Assessment: Brian Hyland
Digital Media Manager: Michael Halas
Media Project Manager: Elizabeth Roden
Composition and Full-Service Project Management:
PreMediaGlobal USA Inc. / Nancy Kincade

Text Font: 10.5/13 Minion ProRegular

Credits and acknowledgments borrowed from other sources and reproduced, with permission, in this textbook appear on appropriate page within text or on pages C1-C2.

Library of Congress Cataloging-in-Publication Data
Brands, H. W.
   American stories : a history of the United States / H.W. Brands, University of Texas; T.H. Breen, Northwestern University; R. Hal Williams, Southern Methodist University; Ariela J. Gross, University of Southern California. — Third Edition.
      pages cm
   ISBN-13: 978-0-205-95842-9 (pbk. : combined volume)
   ISBN-10: 0-205-95842-7 (pbk. : combined volume)
   [etc.]
   1. United States—History—Textbooks. I. Breen, T. H. II. Williams, R. Hal (Richard Hal), — III. Gross,
      Ariela Julie. IV. Title.
   E178.B813 2014
   973—dc23

                                                    2013025594

Volume 2:
ISBN-10: 0-205-96203-3
ISBN-13: 978-0-205-96203-7

Combined Volume:
ISBN-10: 0-205-96204-1
ISBN-13: 978-0-205-96204-4

Volume 1:
ISBN-10: 0-205-96202-5
ISBN-13: 978-0-205-96202-0

PEARSON

Brief Contents

Note: The icons listed here and throughout this book lead to learning resources on MyHistoryLab.

⊙ Video Series

✳ Explore ...

Maps

Figures

Tables

New to this Edition

Teachers familiar with previous editions of *American Stories* will find that this third edition expands impressively on its predecessors. The major changes include:

Personalize Learning With New MyHistoryLab

This text features full **integration with the new MyHistoryLab**—a rich resource that delivers proven results in helping students succeed, provides engaging experiences that personalize learning, and comes from a trusted partner with educational expertise and a deep commitment to helping students and instructors achieve their goals.

- The **Pearson eText**, with a new streamlined design for tablet devices, lets students access *American Stories* anytime, anywhere, and any way they want—and they can listen to and download every chapter. Section tabs on the margin of every page make the text much easier to navigate. The new Pearson eText is now fully interactive and links to all the learning resources in the MyLab.
- **Chapter launcher videos** introduce students to the material, helping to engage them even before they begin reading the chapter. Each chapter has a 15-minute segment, comprised of a three-minute overview and three four-minute videos on specific topics. The videos are featured on the second page, directly after the chapter opener.
- In the new **MyHistoryLibrary with audio**, students can read, listen to, annotate, download, and print over 200 of the most commonly assigned primary source documents. These documents can also be annotated by instructors.
- With the new **History Explorer**, students visualize and analyze historical evidence in a powerful mapping resource. The modules cover topics from English Colonization to the Civil Rights Movement, and each contains an assignable exercise with automated assessment. They are also featured in every chapter of the text in a special box.
- The new **automated writing assessment engine** allows students to further explore key topics by responding to them in essay form. The system offers ten formal prompts on standard topics like the American Revolution, the Lewis and Clark expedition, and the New Deal. Each assignment is based on one of MyHistoryLab's engaging **Author Video Lectures**.
- A **personalized study plan** for each student, based on Bloom's Taxonomy, promotes critical thinking skills and helps students succeed in the course and beyond.
- **Assessment** tied to videos, applications, and chapters enables instructors and students to track progress and get immediate feedback. Instructors will be able to find the best resources for teaching their students.
- **MyHistoryLab icons** are paired with images in the text for more thorough integration between the book and online resources.

- The new **Instructor's eText** makes it easier than ever for instructors to access subject-specific resources for class preparation. Housed within MyHistoryLab, it serves as the hub for all available instructor resources—including the new MyHistoryLab Instructor's Guide.
- The new **MyHistoryLab Instructor's Guide** outlines the basic steps for registering and building a course in MyHistoryLab and describes the key resources and assignments available for each chapter of *American Stories*.
- The **Class Preparation Tool** collects the best class presentation resources in one convenient online destination. Resources include PowerPoint slides, streaming audio and video, audio clips for class tests and quizzes, and all illustrations for creating interactive lectures.

Engage Students and Improve Critical Thinking

- **Chapter introductory vignettes**
- **Chapter images, maps, and figures** are bigger, visually interesting, and informative. Photographs and pieces of fine art encapsulate emotional and historical meaning. Captions provide valuable information that allows for a fuller understanding of the people who lived the American story.
- **Quick Check Questions** give students the opportunity to review as they read, leading to a more complete understanding of chapter content.

Support Instructors

- **Learning Objective questions** highlight the important issues and themes. Each is linked to one of the chapter's main sections, and they are all emphasized in the chapter overview.
- **Key Terms** throughout the chapters highlight important topics as they are introduced.
- The **thematic timeline** ending each chapter reinforces the essential points of the narrative.

A Note to my Fellow Teachers

H. W. Brands I've been teaching American history for thirty years now, and in that time I've noticed something. Our students come to our classrooms with increasingly varied backgrounds. Some students are better prepared, having taken A.P. courses and acquired a solid grounding in historical facts, interpretations, and methods. Other students arrive less well prepared. Many of these are international students; some are students for whom English is a second or third language. Some of these, and some others, simply never took American history in high school.

Different students require different methods of teaching. Students well versed in American history do best with a book that presupposes their preparation and takes them beyond it. Students for whom the subject is new or otherwise challenging are more likely to succeed with a book that focuses on essential themes, and offers features designed to facilitate the learning process. Any textbook can be intimidating, as even my best students have reminded me over the years. For that reason, whatever reduces the intimidation factor can help students succeed.

This is the philosophy behind *American Stories: A History of the United States*. A single purpose has motivated the creation of this book: to enhance the accessibility of American history and thereby increase students' chances of success. This goal is what brought me to the classroom, and it's one I think I share with you. If *American Stories: A History of the United States* contributes to achieving this goal, we all—teachers and students—will be the winners.

Approach and Themes

The most frequent complaint I get from students regarding history textbooks is that the mass of information is overwhelming. This complaint provided the starting point for *American Stories*, which differs from standard textbooks in two fundamental respects.

First, we reduced the number of topics covered, only retaining the essential elements of the American story. We surveyed over five hundred instructors from across the country to find out what topics were most commonly covered in a typical survey classroom. Once we received the results, we culled the most commonly taught topics and selected them for inclusion in *American Stories*.

Second, we integrated a variety of study aids into the text. These were originally developed with the assistance of Dr. Kathleen T. McWhorter and Debby Kalk. Kathleen is a professor and author with more than 40 years of experience who specializes in developmental reading, writing, composition, and study skills. Debby is an instructional designer and author with more than 20 years of experience producing materials. With the help of both Kathleen and Debby, *American Stories* is the first college-level U.S. history survey completely designed to meet the needs of the instructor and the student.

Beyond this, *American Stories* places great emphasis on a compelling narrative. We—I and my fellow authors—have used significant incidents and episodes to reflect the dilemmas, the choices, and the decisions made by the American people as well as by their leaders. Our story of the American past includes the major events that have shaped the nation. We examine the ways in which the big events influenced the lives of ordinary people. How did the American Revolution alter the fortunes and prospects of men, women, and children around the country? What was it like for blacks and whites to live in a plantation society?

Each chapter begins with a vignette that launches the narrative of that chapter and identifies its themes. Some of the vignettes have special meaning for the authors. The vignette that opens Chapter 26 , on the Great Depression of the 1930s, reminds me of the stories my father used to tell about his experiences during that trying decade. His family wasn't nearly as hard hit as many in the 1930s. Like Pauline Kael, he was a college student and like her, he saw how hard it was for many of his classmates to stay in school. He himself was always working at odd jobs, trying to make ends meet. Times were hard, yet he learned the value of a dollar—something he impressed on me as I was growing up.

By these means and others, I and my fellow authors have attempted to bring history to life for students. We believe that while history rarely repeats itself, the story of the American past is profoundly relevant to the problems and challenges facing the nation today.

Pedagogical Features

The pedagogical elements in *American Stories* have been carefully constructed to be accessible to students and to support a better, deeper understanding of U.S. history. These elements fall into two categories, Textual Pedagogy that appears throughout the main body of each chapter, and Study Resources collected at the ends of chapters.

- **Textual Pedagogy** Each chapter follows a consistent pedagogy that maximizes student learning. *Spotlight Questions* in the chapter openers preview the main idea for each major section and provide a framework for the entire chapter. As a reminder to students, these questions are repeated in the margins after each major section. *Quick Check Questions* follow each subsection for immediate reinforcement. *Key Terms* are highlighted throughout each chapter and are defined in the text's glossary. *MyHistoryLab Icons* appear alongside important figures and photos, identifying additional resources that students may find in the program. (See below for more on *MyHistoryLab*.)

- **Study Resources** Each chapter concludes with series of study resources. A chapter *Timeline* surveys the chronology of key events with page references for easy look-up of information. The *Chapter Review* connects back to the Spotlight Questions, providing brief answers that summarize the main points of each section.

A Final Word

My fellow authors and I, with the assistance of the professionals at Pearson, have devoted a great deal of effort to making a textbook of which we are all very proud. Our goal with *American Stories* is to convey our excitement for history to our students in the most accessible manner possible. We've done what we can toward this goal, but we realize that our success depends on you, the classroom instructors. Our job is to make your job easier. All of us—authors and instructors—are in this together. So keep up the good work, and thanks!

A Note to Students: Tips for Studying History

Every autumn for many years I have taught an introductory course in American history. Over that time I've appreciate the value of devoting the first class session to the fundamentals of studying and learning. Different students have different learning styles, but the experiences of the many students I've taught have convinced me that certain general techniques produce good results.

I always tell students that these techniques aren't the only way to study; they may have their own methods. But I also tell them that these techniques have worked for a lot of students in the past, and might work for them. Here they are:

1. **History is a *story***, not just an assortment of facts. The connections are critical. How do the events and people you are reading or hearing about relate to one another? This is what historians want to know.

   Therefore:

   Find the story line, the plot. Identify the main characters, the turning points. How did the story turn out? Why did it turn out that way and not some other?

2. **Dates matter, but order matters more.** Students often get the idea that history is all about dates. It's not. It's about what caused what (as in a story: see Rule 1 above). Dates are useful only in that they help you remember what happened before what else. This is crucial, because the thing that came first might have caused, or at least influenced, the thing that came later.

   Therefore:

   Concentrate on the order of events. If you do, the dates will fall into place by themselves.

3. **History takes time** —to happen, and to learn. History is a story. But like any richly detailed story, it can take time to absorb.

   Therefore:

   Spread out your studying. If you have three hours of reading to do, do it over three days for an hour a day. If you have a test coming up, give yourself two weeks to study, allocating a half hour each day. You'll learn more easily; you'll retain more. And you'll have a better chance to enjoy the story.

4. **History's stories are both spoken and written.** That's why most classes involve both lectures and readings.

   Therefore:

   Read the assigned materials before the corresponding lectures. It's tempting not to—to let the reading slide. But resist the temptation. Advance reading makes the lectures far more understandable—and far more enjoyable.

5. **Less is more,** at least in note-taking. Not every word in the text or lecture is equally important. The point of notes is to distill a chapter or a lecture into a smaller, more manageable size.

   Therefore:

   Hit the high points. Focus on where the text and lecture overlap. Write down key phrases and words; don't write complete sentences. And if you are using a highlighter on a book, be sparing.

6. **History is a twice-told tale.** History is both what happened and how we've remembered what happened. Think of your first exposure to a particular historical topic as history *happening*, and your second exposure as history *being remembered*. An awareness of both is necessary to making the history stick in your head.

Therefore:

Take a rest after reading a chapter or attending a lecture. **Then go back and review.** Your class notes should not be comprehensive (see Rule 5), but as you go back over them, you will remember details that will help you fill out your notes. While you are reviewing a chapter, ask yourself what your notes on the chapter mean, and why you highlighted this particular phrase or that.

To summarize, when approaching a history course:

- **Find the story line.**
- **Concentrate on the order of events.**
- **Spread out your studying.**
- **Read the assignments before the lectures.**
- **Hit the high points in taking notes.**
- **Take a rest, then review.**

A final suggestion: Allow enough time for this course so you aren't rushed. If you give yourself time to get into the story, you'll come to enjoy it. And what you enjoy, you'll remember.

Best wishes,

H. W. Brands

H. W. Brands Henry William Brands was born in Oregon, went to college in California, sold cutlery across the American West, and earned graduate degrees in mathematics and history in Oregon and Texas. He taught at Vanderbilt University and Texas A&M University before joining the faculty at the University of Texas at Austin, where he is the Dickson Allen Anderson Centennial Professor of History. He writes on American history and politics, with books including *The Man Who Saved the Union*, *Traitor to His Class*, *Andrew Jackson*, *The Age of Gold*, *The First American*, and *TR*. Several of his books have been bestsellers; two, *Traitor to His Class* and *The First American*, were finalists for the Pulitzer Prize. He lectures frequently on historical and current events, and can be seen and heard on national and international television and radio programs. His writings have been translated into Spanish, French, German, Russian, Chinese, Japanese, Korean, and Ukrainian.

T. H. Breen T. H. Breen, currently the William Smith Mason Professor of American History at Northwestern University and the James Marsh Professor At-Large at the University of Vermont, received his Ph.D. from Yale University. He founded Northwestern's Kaplan Center for the Humanities and the Chabraja Center for Historical Studies. Breen's major books include *The Character of the Good Ruler: A Study of Puritan Political Ideas in New England* (1974); *Puritans and Adventurers: Change and Persistence in Early America* (1980); *Tobacco Culture: The Mentality of the Great Tidewater Planters on the Eve of Revolution* (1985); with Stephen Innes *"Myne Owne Ground": Race and Freedom on Virginia's Eastern Shore* (1980), and *Marketplace of Revolution* (2004). His *Imagining the Past* (1989) won the 1990 Historic Preservation Book Award. His most recent book is *American Insurgents: American Patriots: The Revolution of the People* (2010). In addition to receiving several awards for outstanding teaching at Northwestern, Breen has been the recipient of research grants from the American Council of Learned Societies, the Guggenheim Foundation, Institute for Advanced Study (Princeton), National Humanities Center, and Huntington Library. He has served as the Fowler Hamilton Fellow at Christ Church, Oxford University (1987–1988), the Pitt Professor of American History and Institutions, Cambridge University (1990–1991), the Harmsworth Professor of American History at Oxford University (2000–2001), and was a recipient of the Humboldt Prize (Germany). He is currently completing a book tentatively titled *Washington's Appeal: How a Presidential Journey Transformed American Political Culture*.

Ariela J. Gross Ariela Gross is John B. and Alice R. Sharp Professor of Law and History, and Co-Director of the Center for Law, History and Culture, at the University of Southern California. She has been a visiting Professor at Tel Aviv University, the École des Hautes Études en Sciences Sociales, the Université de Paris 8, and Kyoto University. Her most recent book, *What Blood Won't Tell: A History of Race on Trial in America* (Harvard University Press, 2008, ppb. 2010), a Choice Outstanding Academic Title for 2009, was awarded the J. Willard Hurst Prize for outstanding scholarship in sociolegal history by the Law and Society Association, the Lillian Smith Book Award for a book that illuminates the people and problems of the South, and the American Political Science Association's award for the best book on race, ethnicity, and politics. Gross is also the author of *Double Character: Slavery and Mastery in the Antebellum Southern Courtroom* (Princeton University Press, 2000; ppb., University of Georgia

Press, 2006), and numerous articles and book chapters. Her research has been supported by a Guggenheim Fellowship, a Frederick J. Burkhardt Fellowship from the American Council of Learned Societies, and an NEH Long-Term Fellowship at the Huntington Library.

R. Hal Williams R. Hal Williams is professor of history emeritus at Southern Methodist University. He received his A.B. from Princeton University in 1963 and his Ph.D. from Yale University in 1968. His books include *The Democratic Party and California Politics, 1880–1896 (1973)*; *Years of Decision: American Politics in the 1890s (1978)*; *The Manhattan Project: A Documentary Introduction to the Atomic Age (1990)*; and *Realigning America: McKinley, Bryan, and the Remarkable Election of 1896 (2010)*. A specialist in American political history, he taught at Yale University from 1968 to 1975 and came to SMU in 1975 as chair of the Department of History. From 1980 to 1988, he served as dean of Dedman College, the school of humanities and sciences, and then as dean of Research and Graduate Studies. In 1980, he was a visiting professor at University College, Oxford University. Williams has received grants from the American Philosophical Society and the National Endowment for the Humanities, and he has served on the Texas Committee for the Humanities. He is currently working on a biography of James G. Blaine, the late-nineteenth-century speaker of the House, secretary of state, and Republican presidential candidate.

Acknowledgments

All of us are grateful to our families, friends, and colleagues for their support and encouragement. Jo Ann Argersinger and Peter Argersinger would like in particular to thank Margaret L. Aust, Rody Conant, Lizzie Gilman, and Ann Zinn; William Barney thanks Pamela Fesmire and Rosalie Radcliffe; Virginia Anderson thanks Fred Anderson, Kim Gruenwald, Ruth Helm, Eric Hinderaker, and Chidiebere Nwaubani; and David Goldfield thanks Frances Glenn and Jason Moscato.

Supplementary Instructional Materials

FOR INSTRUCTORS	FOR STUDENTS
MyHistoryLab www.myhistorylab.com **Save Time. Improve Results.** MyHistoryLab is a dynamic website that provides a wealth of resources geared to meet the diverse teaching and learning needs of today's instructors and students. MyHistoryLab's many accessible tools will encourage students to read their text and help them improve their grade in their course.	**MyHistoryLab** www.myhistorylab.com **Save Time. Improve Results.** MyHistoryLab is a dynamic website that provides a wealth of resources geared to meet the diverse teaching and learning needs of today's instructors and students. MyHistoryLab's many accessible tools will encourage you to read your text and help you improve your grade in your course.
Instructor's Resource Center www.pearsonhighered.com/irc This website provides instructors with additional text-specific resources that can be downloaded for classroom use. Resources include the Instructor's Resource Manual, PowerPoint presentations and the test item file. Register online for access to the resources for *American Stories*.	**www.coursemart.com** CourseSmart eTextbooks offer the same content as the printed text in a convenient online format—with highlighting, online search, and printing capabilities. You **save 60% over the list price** of the traditional book.
Instructor's Resource Manual Available for download at **www.pearsonhighered.com/irc**, the Instructor's Resource Manual contains chapter outlines, detailed chapter overviews, lecture outlines, topics for discussion, and information about audio-visual resources.	**Books à la Carte** These editions feature the exact same content as the traditional printed text in a convenient, three-hole-punched, loose-leaf version at a discounted price—allowing you to take only what you need to class. You'll **save 35% over the net price** of the traditional book.
Test Item File Available for download at **www.pearsonhighered.com/irc**, the Test Item File contains more than 1,500 multiple-choice, identification, matching, true-false, and essay test questions and 10–15 questions per chapter on the maps found in each chapter.	**Library of American Biography Series** www.pearsonhighered.com/educator/series/Library-of-American-Biography/10493.page Pearson's renowned series of biographies spotlighting figures who had a significant impact on American history. Included in the series are Edmund Morgan's *The Puritan Dilemma: The Story of John Winthrop*, B. Davis Edmund's *Tecumseh and the Quest for Indian Leadership*, J. William T. Youngs, *Eleanor Roosevelt: A Personal and Public Life*, and John R. M. Wilson's *Jackie Robinson and the American Dilemma*.
PowerPoint Presentations Available for download at **www.pearsonhighered.com/irc**, the PowerPoints contain chapter outlines and full-color images of maps, figures, and images.	**American Stories: Biographies in United States History** This two-volume collection of sixty-two biographies provides insight into the lives and contributions of key figures as well as ordinary citizens to American history. Introductions, pre-reading questions, and suggested resources helps students connect the relevance of these individuals to historical events. Volume 1 **ISBN-10: 0131826549 ISBN-13: 9780131826540**; Volume 2 **ISBN-10: 0131826530 ISBN-13: 9780131826533**

(continued)

FOR INSTRUCTORS	FOR STUDENTS
MyTest www.pearsonmytest.com MyTest is a powerful assessment generation program that helps instructors easily create and print quizzes and exams. Questions and tests can be authored online, allowing instructors ultimate flexibility and the ability to efficiently manage assessments anytime, anywhere! Instructors can easily access existing questions and edit, create, and store using simple drag-and-drop and Word-like controls.	**Penguin Valuepacks** www.pearsonhighered.com/penguin A variety of Penguin-Putnam texts is available at discounted prices when bundled with *American Stories, 5/e*. Texts include Benjamin Franklin's *Autobiography and Other Writings*, Nathaniel Hawthorne's *The Scarlet Letter*, Thomas Jefferson's *Notes on the State of Virginia*, and George Orwell's *1984*.
Retrieving the American Past (**www.pearsoncustom .com, keyword search | rtap**) Available through the Pearson Custom Library, the *Retrieving the American Past* (RTAP) program lets you create a textbook or reader that meets your needs and the needs of your course. RTAP gives you the freedom and flexibility to add chapters from several best-selling Pearson textbooks, in addition to *American Stories, 3/e* and/or 100 topical reading units written by the History Department of Ohio State University, all under one cover. Choose the content you want to teach in depth, in the sequence you want, at the price you want your students to pay.	**A Short Guide to Writing About History, 7/e** Written by Richard Marius, late of Harvard University, and Melvin E. Page, Eastern Tennessee State University, this engaging and practical text helps students get beyond merely compiling dates and facts. Covering brief essays and the documented resource paper, the text explores the writing and researching processes, identifies different modes of historical writing, including argument, and concludes with guidelines for improving style. **ISBN-10: 0205673708; ISBN-13: 9780205673704**
	Longman American History Atlas This full-color historical atlas designed especially for college students is a valuable reference tool and visual guide to American history. This atlas includes maps covering the scope of American history from the lives of the Native Americans to the 1990s. Produced by a renowned cartographic firm and a team of respected historians, the Longman American History Atlas will enhance any American history survey course. **ISBN: 0321004868; ISBN-13: 9780321004864**

MyHistoryLab

An online homework, tutorial, and assessment program, MyHistoryLab offers immersive content, tools, and experiences to engage students and help them succeed.

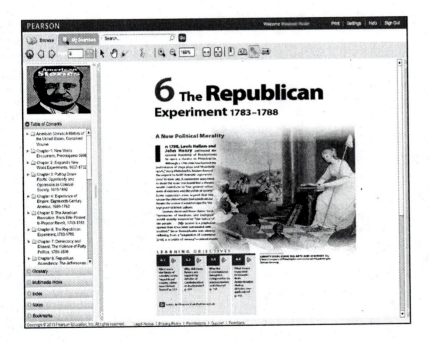

Pearson eText with Audio

Contained within MyHistoryLab, the Pearson eText enables students to access their textbook online—through laptops, iPads, and tablets. Download the free Pearson eText app to use on tablets. Students may also listen to their text with the Audio eText.

New MyHistoryLibrary

A new release of Pearson's MyHistoryLibrary contains more than 200 of the most commonly assigned primary source documents, delivered through Pearson's powerful eText platform. Each reading may also be listened to in the Audio eText companion.

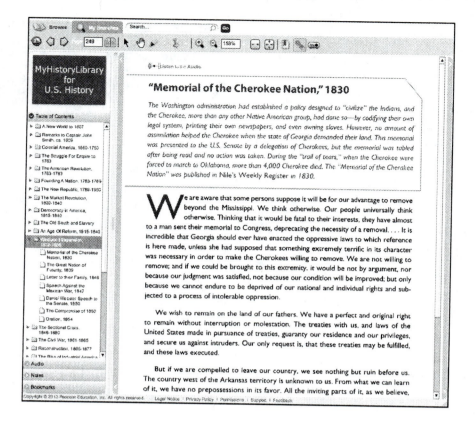

MyHistoryLab Video Series:

Key Topics in US History

This comprehensive video series helps students get up-to-speed on key topics. Correlated to the chapters of *American Stories*, each video unit reviews key topics of the period, readying students to get the most from the text narrative. The videos feature seasoned historians reviewing the pivotal stories of our past, in a lively format designed to engage and inform.

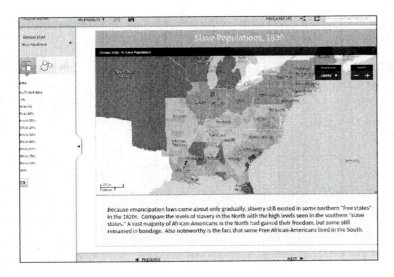

Explorer

This path-breaking new application in MyHistoryLab enables students to use dynamic maps to understand pivotal events and topics. A unique Explorer application is correlated to each chapter of *American Stories*.

Writing Space

MyHistoryLab Writing Space provides the best way to develop and assess concept mastery and critical thinking through writing. Use Writing Space to create, track, and grade writing assignments, access writing resources, and exchange meaningful, personalized feedback quickly and easily. Plus, Writing Space includes integrated access to Turnitin, the global leader in plagiarism prevention.

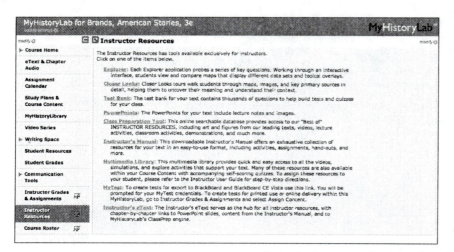

Key Supplements and Customer Support

Annotated Instructor's eText

Contained within MyHistoryLab, the *Annotated Instructor's eText* for your Pearson textbook leverages the powerful Pearson eText platform to make it easier than ever for you to access subject-specific resources for class preparation. The *AI eText* serves as the hub for all instructor resources, with chapter-by-chapter links to PowerPoint slides, content from the Instructor's Manual, and to *MyHistoryLab's* ClassPrep engine, which contains a wealth of history content organized for classroom use.

Instructor's Manual

The Instructor's Manual for your Pearson textbook contains chapter overviews, discussion questions, and suggested assignments for each chapter, including both general and text-specific content. It also contains a MyHistoryLab syllabus and suggestions for integrating MyHistoryLab into your course.

PowerPoint Presentations

Strong PowerPoint presentations make lectures more engaging for students. Correlated to the chapters of your Pearson textbook, each presentation includes a full lecture script, discussion questions, a wealth of images and maps, and links to the full array of MyHistoryLab media.

MyTest Test Bank

Containing a diverse set of multiple choice and essay questions, the MyTest test bank supports a variety of assessment strategies. The large pool of multiple choice questions for each chapter includes factual, conceptual, and analytical questions, so that instructors may assess students on basic information as well as critical thinking.

Customer Support

Pearson's dedicated team of local representatives will work with you not only to choose course materials but also to integrate them into your class and assess their effectiveness. Moreover, live support for MyHistoryLab users, both educators and students, is available 24/7.

American Stories
A History of the United States

THIRD EDITION
Volume 2, Since 1865

16 The Agony of Reconstruction 1865–1877

Robert Smalls and Black Politicians During Reconstruction

During the Reconstruction period immediately following the Civil War, African Americans struggled to become equal citizens of a democratic republic. Remarkable black leaders won public office. Robert Smalls of South Carolina was perhaps the most famous and widely respected southern black leader of the era.

Born a slave in 1839, Smalls was allowed as a young man to live and work independently, hiring his own time from a master who may have been his half brother. Smalls worked as a sailor and trained himself to be a pilot in Charleston Harbor. When the Union navy blockaded Charleston in 1862, Smalls, who was working on a Confederate steamship called the *Planter*, saw a chance to win his freedom. At three o'clock in the morning on May 13, 1862, when the white officers were ashore, he took command of the vessel and its slave crew, sailed it out of the fortified harbor, and surrendered it to the Union navy. Smalls immediately became a hero to antislavery northerners

LEARNING OBJECTIVES

16.1 📶	16.2 📶	16.3 📶	16.4 📶
What conflicts arose consecutively involving President Lincoln and then President Johnson and Congress during Reconstruction? p. 355	What problems did southern society face during Reconstruction? p. 363	Why did Reconstruction end? p. 369	Who benefited and who suffered from the reconciliation of the North and South? p. 372

ROBERT SMALLS With the help of several black crewmen, Robert Smalls—then twenty-three years old—commandeered the *Planter*, a Confederate steamship used to transport guns and ammunition, and surrendered it to the Union vessel, USS *Onward*. Smalls provided distinguished service to the Union during the Civil War and after the war went on to become a successful politician and businessman.

From Chapter 16 of *American Stories: A History of the United States*, Third Edition. H. W. Brands, R. Hal Williams, T. H. Breen and Ariela J. Gross Copyright © 2015 by Pearson Education, Inc. All rights reserved.

 Listen to Chapter 16 on MyHistoryLab

👁 Watch the Video Series on MyHistoryLab

Learn about some key topics related to this chapter with the *MyHistoryLab Video Series: Key Topics in U.S. History.*

1 **Reconstruction and Its Missed Opportunities: 1865–1877** This video introduces critical issues that arose during the post-Civil War period known as Reconstruction, when the former Confederacy was reincorporated into the United States and the freed slaves received their first taste of U.S. citizenship. The video examines the conflicts between Congress and Presidents Lincoln, Andrew Johnson, and Ulysses S. Grant over the goals of Reconstruction, especially the passage of constitutional amendments to protect the rights of freedmen and the expansion of federal government institutions to rebuild the South and integrate it into the nation.

 Watch on **MyHistoryLab**

The Amendments of Freedom In the years after the Civil War, Congress passed the Thirteenth, Fourteenth, and Fifteenth amendments to the Constitution, ending slavery, guaranteeing citizenship, and extending voting rights. This video reveals how these constitutional changes were enacted to protect the citizenship and rights of African Americans. Despite the efforts of Radical Republicans, however, southern states passed the Black Codes and engaged in other repressive measures that lasted generations. **2**

Watch on **MyHistoryLab**

3 **Presidential Reconstruction** This video explains the way Abraham Lincoln approached Presidential Reconstruction as the reincorporation of armed rebels into the Union, rather than as the aftermath of a civil war. This allowed him to use broad war powers as commander-in-chief to control the definition and progress of Reconstruction. Radical Republicans in Congress hoped to extend federal power even more broadly to remake Southern society, empowering the former slaves, but Lincoln's successor, Andrew Johnson, by contrast, sought to pardon former Confederate planters as quickly as possible and readmit the southern states to the Union with few conditions. The clash between Johnson and Congress led to his impeachment.

 Watch on **MyHistoryLab**

The Compromise of 1877 Reconstruction came to an end in the South with the Compromise of 1877, a political deal in which Republican Rutherford B. Hayes was awarded electoral victory over Democrat Samuel Tilden in the contested Presidential election of 1876, on the understanding that Hayes would withdraw the remaining federal troops from the states of the former confederacy. This video examines the Compromise of 1877, sometimes known as "The Great Betrayal," because it closed off the possibilities for the freed slaves to achieve full citizenship for another hundred years. **4**

Watch on **MyHistoryLab**

who were seeking evidence that the slaves were willing and able to serve the Union. The *Planter* became a Union army transport, and Smalls was made its captain after being commissioned as an officer. During the remainder of the war, he rendered conspicuous and gallant service as captain and pilot of Union vessels off the coast of South Carolina.

Like other African Americans who fought for the Union, Smalls had a distinguished political career during Reconstruction, serving in the South Carolina constitutional convention, the state legislature, and the U.S. Congress. He was also a shrewd businessman and owned extensive properties in Beaufort, South Carolina, and its vicinity. The electoral organization Smalls established was so effective that he controlled local government and was elected to Congress even after the election of 1876 had placed the state under the control of white conservatives bent on depriving blacks of political power. Organized mob violence defeated him in 1878, but he bounced back to win a contested congressional election in 1880. He did not leave the House of Representatives for good until 1886, when he lost another contested election.

To defeat him, Smalls's white opponents charged that he had a hand in the corruption that was allegedly rampant in South Carolina during Reconstruction. But careful historical investigation shows that he was, by the standards of the time, an honest and responsible public servant. In the South Carolina convention of 1868 and in the state legislature, he championed free and compulsory public education. In Congress, he fought for federal civil rights laws. Not especially radical on social questions, he sometimes bent over backward to accommodate what he regarded as the legitimate interests and sensibilities of South Carolina whites. Like other middle-class black political leaders in Reconstruction-era South Carolina, he can perhaps be faulted for not doing more to help poor blacks gain access to land of their own. But in 1875, he sponsored congressional legislation that opened for purchase at low prices the land in his own district that the federal government had confiscated during the war. As a result, blacks soon owned three-fourths of the land in the Beaufort area.

Robert Smalls spent the later years of his life as U.S. collector of customs for the port of Beaufort, a beneficiary of the patronage that the Republican Party continued to provide for a few loyal southern blacks. But the loss of real political clout for Smalls and men like him was a tragic consequence of the fall of Reconstruction.

For a few years, black politicians such as Robert Smalls exercised more power in the South than they would for another century. But political developments on the national and regional stage made Reconstruction "an unfinished revolution," promising but not delivering true equality for newly freed African Americans. National party politics; shifting priorities among northern Republicans; white southerners' commitment to white supremacy, which was backed by legal restrictions and massive extralegal violence against blacks, all combined to stifle the promise of Reconstruction.

Yet during the Reconstruction era, American society was transformed—new ways of organizing labor and family life, new institutions within and outside the government, and new ideologies about the role of institutions and government in social and economic life. Many of the changes begun during Reconstruction would revolutionize American life.

The President versus Congress

16.1 What conflicts arose consecutively involving President Lincoln and then President Johnson and Congress during Reconstruction?

Reconstructing the Union after the South's defeat was one of the most difficult challenges American policymakers ever faced. The Constitution provided no firm guidelines, for the Framers had not anticipated that the country would divide into warring sections. After emancipation became a northern war aim, a new issue compounded the problem: How far should the federal government go to secure freedom and civil rights for 4 million former slaves?

The debate led to a major political crisis. Advocates of a minimal Reconstruction policy favored quickly restoring the Union with no protection for the freed slaves except prohibiting slavery. Proponents of a more radical policy demanded guarantees that "loyal" men would displace the Confederate elite in power and that blacks would acquire basic rights of American citizenship as preconditions for readmitting the southern states. The White House favored the minimal approach. Congress came to endorse the more radical and thoroughgoing form of Reconstruction. The resulting struggle between Congress and the chief executive was the most serious clash between two branches of government in the nation's history.

Wartime Reconstruction

Tension between the president and Congress over how to reconstruct the Union began during the war. Preoccupied with achieving victory, Lincoln never set forth a final and

Ten Percent Plan Reconstruction plan proposed by President Abraham Lincoln as a quick way to readmit the former Confederate States. It called for pardon of all southerners except Confederate leaders, and readmission to the Union for any state after 10 percent of its voters signed a loyalty oath and the state abolished slavery.

Radical Republicans
Congressional Republicans who insisted on black suffrage and federal protection of civil rights of African Americans.

Wade-Davis Bill In 1864, Congress passed the Wade-Davis bill to counter Lincoln's Ten Percent Plan for Reconstruction. The bill required that a majority of a former Confederate state's white male population take a loyalty oath and guarantee equality for African Americans. President Lincoln pocket-vetoed the bill.

Quick Check

In what ways did Congress thwart Presidential Reconstruction?

comprehensive plan to bring rebellious states back into the fold. But he favored a lenient and conciliatory policy toward southerners who would give up the struggle and repudiate slavery. In December 1863, he issued a Proclamation of Amnesty and Reconstruction, which offered a full pardon to all southerners (except certain Confederate leaders) who would take an oath of allegiance to the Union and accept emancipation. This **Ten Percent Plan** provided that once ten percent or more of the voting population of any occupied state had taken the oath, they could set up a loyal government. By 1864, Louisiana and Arkansas, states that Union troops occupied, had established Unionist governments. Lincoln's policy was meant to shorten the war. He hoped to weaken the southern cause by making it easy for disillusioned or lukewarm Confederates to switch sides and support emancipation by insisting that the new governments abolish slavery.

Congress was unhappy with Lincoln's Reconstruction experiments and in 1864 refused to seat the Unionists that Louisiana and Arkansas elected to the House and Senate. A minority of congressional Republicans—the strongly antislavery **Radical Republicans**—favored protection for black rights (especially black male suffrage) as a precondition for readmitting southern states. But a larger group of congressional moderates opposed Lincoln's plan because they did not trust the repentant Confederates who would play a major role in the new governments. Congress also believed the president was exceeding his authority by using executive powers to restore the Union. Lincoln operated on the theory that secession, being illegal, did not place the Confederate states outside the Union in a constitutional sense. Since individuals and not states had defied federal authority, the president could use his pardoning power to certify a loyal electorate, which could then function as the legitimate state government.

After refusing to recognize Lincoln's ten percent governments, Congress passed a Reconstruction bill of its own in July 1864. Known as the **Wade–Davis Bill**, it required that 50 percent of the voters take a loyalty oath before the restoration process could begin. Once this had occurred, those who could swear they had never willingly supported the Confederacy could vote in an election for delegates to a constitutional convention. The bill did not require black suffrage, but it gave federal courts the power to enforce emancipation. Faced with this attempt to nullify his own program, Lincoln exercised a pocket veto by refusing to sign the bill before Congress adjourned. He said that he did not want to be committed to any single Reconstruction plan. The bill's sponsors responded angrily, and Lincoln's relations with Congress reached their low point.

Congress and the president remained stalemated on the Reconstruction issue for the rest of the war. During his last months in office, however, Lincoln showed a willingness to compromise. He tried to obtain recognition for the governments he had nurtured in Louisiana and Arkansas but seemed receptive to setting other conditions—perhaps including black suffrage—for readmitting those states in which wartime conditions had prevented execution of his plan. However, he was assassinated before he made his intentions clear, leaving historians to speculate whether his quarrel with Congress would have been resolved. Given Lincoln's record of flexibility, the best bet is that he would have come to terms with the majority of his party.

Andrew Johnson at the Helm

Andrew Johnson, the man an assassin's bullet suddenly made president, attempted to put the Union back together on his own authority in 1865. But his policies set him at odds with Congress and the Republican Party and provoked the most serious crisis in the history of relations between the executive and legislative branches of the federal government.

Johnson's background shaped his approach to Reconstruction. Born in poverty in North Carolina, he migrated to eastern Tennessee, where he worked as a tailor. Lacking formal schooling, he was illiterate until adult life. Entering politics as a Jacksonian Democrat, his railing against the planter aristocracy made him the spokesman for Tennessee's non-slaveholding whites and the most successful politician in the state. He advanced from state legislator to congressman to governor and then the U.S. Senate in 1857.

In 1861, Johnson was the only senator from a Confederate state who remained loyal to the Union and continued to serve in Washington. But his Unionism and

✳ Explore Reconstruction on MyHistoryLab

HOW DID RECONSTRUCTION AFFECT AFRICAN AMERICANS IN THE SOUTH?

In 1865, at the end of the Civil War, the United States was at a crossroads. The Thirteenth Amendment to the Constitution had freed the slaves of the rebellious eleven states, but questions remained on how to implement the rights of the newly liberated African Americans. Further, leaders were divided on how to reintegrate the war-torn southern states back into the Union. Many white Southerners tried to continue their ways of life while freed African Americans struggled in a society built on segregation. Though the subsequent Fourteenth and Fifteenth Amendments theoretically extended the realm of equality for blacks, in the end, whites in the North and South saw to it that the promises of Reconstruction for African Americans went unfulfilled.

RECONSTRUCTION Much hope was placed in the policies of Reconstruction as this allegorical lithograph shows. The reconciliation between the North and South, however, would have a mixed legacy, especially for African Americans.

RECONSTRUCTION AMENDMENTS TO THE CONSTITUTION

Amendment	Summary	Date
Thirteenth	Abolishes slavery	December 6, 1865
Fourteenth	Ensures equal rights and protections to every person born or naturalized in the United States	July 9, 1868
Fifteenth	Prohibits the denial of the right of vote based on race	February 3, 1870

SOURCE: United States Constitution; Amendments 13 and 14 and 15

KEY QUESTIONS Use **MyHistoryLab** *Explorer* to answer these **questions:**

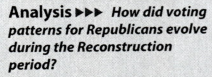

Analysis ▶▶▶ *How did voting patterns for Republicans evolve during the Reconstruction period?*

Chart voting patterns to understand reasons behind voting trends.

Comparison ▶▶▶ *How did literacy rates differ between African Americans and Euro-Americans in the South?*

Theorize how this might affect black disenfranchisement.

Response ▶▶▶ *What was the landholding situation for African Americans at the end of the nineteenth century?*

Map land tenure to see discrepancies with whites.

defense of the common people did not include antislavery sentiments. Nor was he friendly to blacks. In Tennessee, he had objected only to the fact that slaveholding was the privilege of a wealthy minority. He wished that "every head of family in the United States had one slave to take the drudgery and menial service off his family."

During the war, while acting as military governor of Tennessee, Johnson endorsed Lincoln's emancipation policy to destroy the power of the hated planter class rather than as recognition of black humanity. He was chosen as Lincoln's running mate in 1864 because a pro-administration Democrat, who was a southern Unionist in the bargain, would strengthen the ticket. No one expected this fervent white supremacist to become president. Radical Republicans initially welcomed Johnson's ascent to the nation's highest office. Their hopes made sense given Johnson's fierce loyalty to the Union and his apparent agreement with the Radicals that ex-Confederates should be severely treated. Unlike Lincoln, who had spoken of "malice toward none and charity for all," Johnson seemed likely to punish southern "traitors" and prevent them from regaining political influence. Only gradually did the deep disagreement between the president and the Republican congressional majority become evident.

The Reconstruction policy that Johnson initiated on May 29, 1865, created uneasiness among the Radicals, but most Republicans were willing to give it a chance. Johnson placed North Carolina, and eventually other states, under appointed provisional governors chosen mostly from among prominent southern politicians who had opposed the secession movement and had rendered no conspicuous service to the Confederacy. The governors were responsible for calling constitutional conventions and ensuring that only "loyal" whites could vote for delegates. Participation required taking the oath of allegiance that Lincoln had prescribed earlier. Confederate leaders and officeholders had to apply for individual presidential pardons to regain their political and property rights. Johnson made one significant addition to the list of the excluded: all those possessing taxable property exceeding $20,000 in value. He thus sought to prevent his longtime adversaries—the wealthy planters—from participating in the Reconstruction of southern state governments.

Thirteenth Amendment Ratified in 1865, it prohibits slavery and involuntary servitude.

Johnson urged the convention delegates to declare the ordinances of secession illegal, repudiate the Confederate debt, and ratify the **Thirteenth Amendment** abolishing slavery. After governments had been reestablished under constitutions meeting these conditions, the president assumed that the Reconstruction process would be complete and that the ex-Confederate states could regain their full rights under the Constitution.

The results of the conventions, which prewar Unionists and backcountry yeoman farmers dominated, were satisfactory to the president but troubling to many congressional Republicans. Delegates in several states approved Johnson's recommendations only grudgingly or with qualifications. Furthermore, all the constitutions limited suffrage to whites, disappointing the many northerners who hoped, as Lincoln had, that at least some African Americans—perhaps those who were educated or had served in the Union army—would be given the vote. Republican uneasiness turned to anger when the new state legislatures passed **Black Codes** restricting the freedom of former slaves. Especially troubling were vagrancy and apprenticeship laws that forced African Americans to work and denied them a free choice of employers. Blacks in some states could not testify in court on the same basis as whites and were subject to a separate penal code. The Black Codes looked like slavery under a new guise. More upsetting to northern public opinion in general was the election of prominent ex-Confederates to Congress in 1865.

Black Code Laws passed by southern states immediately after the Civil War to maintain white supremacy by restricting the rights of the newly freed slaves.

Johnson himself was partly responsible for these events. Despite his lifelong feud with the planter class, he was generous in granting pardons to members of the old elite who came to him, hat in hand, and asked for them. When former Confederate Vice President Alexander Stephens and other proscribed ex-rebels were elected to Congress even though they had not been pardoned, Johnson granted them special amnesty so they could serve.

The growing rift between the president and Congress came into the open in December, when the House and Senate refused to seat the recently elected southern delegations. Instead of recognizing the state governments Johnson had called into

THE AFTERMATH OF EMANCIPATION "Slavery Is Dead?" asks this 1866 cartoon by Thomas Nast. To the cartoonist, the Emancipation Proclamation of 1863 and the North's victory in the Civil War meant little difference to the treatment of the freed slaves in the South. Freed slaves convicted of crimes often endured the same punishments as had slaves—sale, as depicted in the left panel of the cartoon, or beatings, as shown on the right.

being, Congress established a joint committee to review Reconstruction policy and set further conditions for readmitting the seceded states.

Congress Takes the Initiative

The struggle over how to reconstruct the Union ended with Congress setting policy all over again. The clash between Johnson and Congress was a matter of principle and could not be reconciled. Johnson, an heir of the Democratic states' rights tradition, wanted to restore the prewar federal system as quickly as possible and without change except that states would not have the right to legalize slavery or to secede.

Most Republicans wanted guarantees that the old southern ruling class would not regain regional power and national influence by devising new ways to subjugate blacks. They favored a Reconstruction policy that would give the federal government authority to limit the political role of ex-Confederates and protect black citizenship.

Republican leaders—except for a few extreme Radicals such as Charles Sumner—lacked any firm conviction that blacks were inherently equal to whites. They did believe, however, that in a modern democratic state, all citizens must have the same basic rights and opportunities, regardless of natural abilities. Principle coincided with political expediency; southern blacks, whatever their alleged shortcomings, were likely to be loyal to the Republican party that had emancipated them and thus increase that party's power in the South.

Quick Check

Why did Northerners and Republicans grow uneasy and disillusioned with Johnson's approach to reconstruction?

Freedmen's Bureau Agency established by Congress in March 1865 to provide freedmen with shelter, food, and medical aid and to help them establish schools and find employment. The Bureau was dissolved in 1872.

The disagreement between the president and Congress became irreconcilable in early 1866, when Johnson vetoed two bills that had passed with overwhelming Republican support. The first extended the life of the **Freedmen's Bureau**—a temporary agency set up to provide relief, education, legal help, and assistance in obtaining land or work to former slaves. The second was a civil rights bill to nullify the Black Codes and guarantee to freedmen "full and equal benefit of all laws and proceedings for the security of person and property as is enjoyed by white citizens."

Johnson's vetoes shocked moderate Republicans. He succeeded in blocking the Freedmen's Bureau bill, although a modified version later passed. But his veto of the Civil Rights Act was overridden, signifying that the president was now hopelessly at odds with most of the legislators from what was supposed to be his own party. Congress had not overridden a presidential veto since Franklin Pierce was president in the early 1850s.

Johnson soon revealed that he intended to place himself at the head of a new conservative party uniting the few Republicans who supported him with a reviving Democratic party that was rallying behind his Reconstruction policy. In preparation for the elections of 1866, Johnson helped found the National Union movement to promote his plan to readmit the southern states to the Union without further qualifications. A National Union convention in Philadelphia called for electing men to Congress who endorsed the presidential plan for Reconstruction.

Meanwhile, the Republican majority on Capitol Hill, fearing that Johnson would not enforce civil rights legislation or that the courts would declare such laws unconstitutional, passed the **Fourteenth Amendment**. This, perhaps the most important of all the constitutional amendments, gave the federal government responsibility for guaranteeing equal rights under the law to all Americans. Section 1 defined national citizenship for the first time as extending to "all persons born or naturalized in the United States." The states were prohibited from abridging the rights of American citizens and could not "deprive any person of life, liberty, or property, without due process of law; nor deny to any person … equal protection of the laws." The amendment was sent to the states with the understanding that southerners would have no chance of being readmitted to Congress unless their states ratified it. (see Table 16.1).

Fourteenth Amendment Ratified in 1868, it provided citizenship to ex-slaves after the Civil War and constitutionally protected equal rights under the law for all citizens. Radical Republicans used it to enact a congressional Reconstruction policy in the former Confederate states.

The congressional elections of 1866 served as a referendum on the Fourteenth Amendment. Johnson opposed the amendment on the grounds that it created a "centralized" government and denied states the right to manage their own affairs; he also counseled southern state legislatures to reject it, and all except Tennessee followed his advice. But bloody race riots in New Orleans and Memphis weakened the president's case for state autonomy. These and other atrocities against blacks made it clear that the southern state governments were failing abysmally to protect the "life, liberty, or property" of the ex-slaves.

TABLE 16.1 RECONSTRUCTION AMENDMENTS, 1865–1870

Amendment	Main Provisions	Congressional Passage (2/3 majority in each house required)	Ratification Process (3/4 of all states required, including ex-Confederate states)
13	Slavery prohibited in United States	January 1865	December 1865 (27 states, including 8 southern states)
14	National citizenship; state representation in Congress reduced proportionally to number of voters disfranchised; former Confederates denied right to hold office; Confederate debt repudiated	June 1866	Rejected by 12 southern and border states, February 1867; Radicals make readmission of southern states hinge on ratification; ratified July 1868
15	Denial of franchise because of race, color, or past servitude explicitly prohibited	February 1869	Ratification required for re-admission of Virginia, Texas, Mississippi, Georgia; ratified March 1870

Johnson further hurt his cause by taking the stump on behalf of candidates who supported his policies. In his notorious "swing around the circle," he toured the nation, slandering his opponents in crude language and engaging in undignified exchanges with hecklers. Enraged by southern inflexibility and the antics of a president who acted as if he were still campaigning in the backwoods of Tennessee, northern voters repudiated the administration. The Republican majority in Congress increased to a solid two-thirds in both houses, and the Radical wing of the party gained strength at the expense of moderates and conservatives.

Quick Check
What events caused Congress to take the initiative in passing the Fourteenth Amendment?

Congressional Reconstruction Plan Enacted

Congress now implemented its own plan of Reconstruction. In 1867 and 1868, it nullified the president's initiatives and reorganized the South. Generally referred to as **Radical Reconstruction**, the measures actually represented a compromise between genuine Radicals and more moderate Republicans.

Radicals such as Senator Charles Sumner of Massachusetts and Congressmen Thaddeus Stevens of Pennsylvania and George Julian of Indiana wanted to reshape southern society before readmitting ex-Confederates to the Union. Their program of "regeneration before Reconstruction" required an extended period of military rule, confiscation and redistribution of large landholdings among the freedmen, and federal aid for schools to educate blacks and whites for citizenship. But most Republican congressmen found such a program unacceptable because it broke too sharply with American traditions of federalism and regard for property rights, and might take decades.

The First Reconstruction Act, passed over Johnson's veto on March 2, 1867, reorganized the South into five military districts. (see Map 16.1). But military rule would last for only a short time. Subsequent acts allowed for quickly readmitting any state that framed and ratified a new constitution providing for black suffrage. Ex-Confederates disqualified from holding federal office under the Fourteenth Amendment were

Radical Reconstruction The Reconstruction Acts of 1867 divided the South into five military districts. They required the states to guarantee black male suffrage and to ratify the Fourteenth Amendment as a condition of their readmission to the Union.

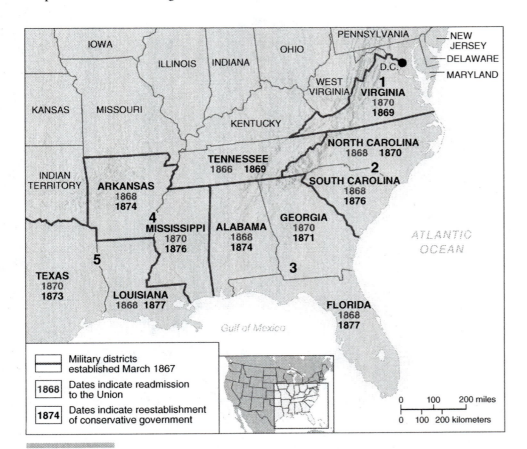

MAP 16.1 RECONSTRUCTION During the Reconstruction era, the southern state governments passed through three phases: control by white ex-Confederates; domination by Republican legislators, both white and black; and, finally, the regaining of control by conservative white Democrats.

prohibited from voting for delegates to the constitutional conventions or in the elections to ratify the conventions' work. Since blacks could participate in this process, Republicans thought they had ensured that "loyal" men would dominate the new governments. Radical Reconstruction was based on the dubious assumption that once blacks had the vote, they would be able to protect themselves against white supremacists' efforts to deny them their rights. The Reconstruction Acts thus signaled a retreat from the true Radical position that sustained federal authority was needed to complete the transition from slavery to freedom and prevent the resurgence of the South's old ruling class Most Republicans were unwilling to embrace centralized government and an extended period of military rule over civilians. Yet a genuine spirit of democratic idealism did give legitimacy and fervor to the cause of black male suffrage. Enabling people who were so poor and downtrodden to have access to the ballot box was a bold and innovative application of the principle of government by the consent of the governed. The problem was enforcing equal suffrage under conditions then existing in the postwar South.

The Impeachment Crisis

The first obstacle to enforcing Congressional Reconstruction was resistance from the White House. Johnson sought to thwart the will of Congress by obstructing the plan. He dismissed officeholders who sympathized with Radical Reconstruction and

Quick Check

What was "Radical Reconstruction", and how did it differ from previous plans?

THE PAROQUET OF THE WH—E HO—E.

IMPEACHED Andrew Johnson's successful defense against conviction in his impeachment case centered on his invocation of the Constitution to defend his presidential rights and powers. Impeached in 1868, Johnson escaped conviction by a single vote.

countermanded the orders of generals in charge of southern military districts who zealously enforced the new legislation. Conservative Democrats replaced Radical generals. Congress then passed laws to limit presidential authority over Reconstruction. The Tenure of Office Act required Senate approval for the removal of officials whose appointment had needed the consent of the Senate. Another measure limited Johnson's authority to issue orders to military commanders.

Johnson objected that the restrictions violated the constitutional doctrine of the separation of powers. When it became clear that the president was resolute in fighting for his powers and using them to resist establishing Radical regimes in the southern states, congressmen began to call for his impeachment. A preliminary effort foundered in 1867, but when Johnson tried to discharge Secretary of War Edwin Stanton—the only Radical in the cabinet—and persisted in his efforts despite the disapproval of the Senate, the pro-impeachment forces gained in strength.

In January 1868, Johnson ordered General Grant, who already commanded the army, to replace Stanton as head of the War Department. But Grant had his eye on the Republican presidential nomination and refused to defy Congress. General Lorenzo Thomas then agreed to serve. Faced with this violation of the Tenure of Office Act, the House impeached the president on February 24, and he went on trial before the Senate.

Because seven Republican senators broke with the party leadership and voted for acquittal, the effort to convict Johnson and remove him from office fell one vote short of the necessary two-thirds. This outcome resulted in part from a skillful defense. Attorneys for the president argued that the constitutional provision that a president could be impeached only for "high crimes and misdemeanors" referred only to indictable offenses and that the Tenure of Office Act did not apply to Stanton because Lincoln, not Johnson, had appointed him.

The core of the prosecution case was that Johnson had abused the powers of his office to sabotage congressional Reconstruction. Obstructing the will of the legislative branch, they claimed, was grounds for conviction even if no crime had been committed. The Republicans voting for acquittal could not endorse such a broad view of the impeachment power. They feared that removing a president for essentially political reasons would threaten the constitutional balance of powers and allow legislative supremacy over the executive.

Failure to remove Johnson from office embarrassed Republicans, but the episode did ensure that Reconstruction in the South would proceed as the majority in Congress intended. Johnson influenced the verdict by pledging to enforce the Reconstruction Acts, and he held to this promise during his remaining months in office. Unable to depose the president, the Radicals had at least neutralized his opposition to their program.

Quick Check

What Prompted Congress to initiate impeachment against Johnson, and what was the outcome of that action?

Reconstructing Southern Society

16.2 What problems did southern society face during Reconstruction?

The Civil War left the South devastated, demoralized, and destitute. Slavery was dead, but what this meant for future relationships between whites and blacks was unclear. Most southern whites wanted to keep blacks adrift between slavery and freedom—without rights, like the "free Negroes" of the Old South. Blacks sought to be independent of their former masters and viewed acquiring land, education, and the vote as the best means of achieving this goal. Thousands of northerners who went south after the war for materialistic or humanitarian reasons hoped to extend Yankee "civilization" to what they considered an unenlightened and barbarous region. For most of them, this meant aiding the freed slaves.

The struggle between these groups bred chaos, violence, and instability. This was scarcely an ideal setting for an experiment in interracial democracy, but one was attempted nonetheless. Its success depended on massive and sustained federal support. To the extent that this was forthcoming, progressive reform could be achieved. When it faltered, the forces of reaction and white supremacy were unleashed.

Reorganizing Land and Labor

The Civil War scarred the southern landscape and wrecked its economy. One devastated area—central South Carolina—looked to an 1865 observer "like a broad black streak of ruin and desolation." Atlanta, Columbia, and Richmond were gutted by fire. Factories were dismantled or destroyed. Railroads were torn up.

Investment capital for rebuilding was inadequate. The wealth represented by Confederate currency and bonds had melted away, and emancipation had divested the propertied classes of their most valuable and productive assets—the slaves. According to some estimates, the South's per capita wealth in 1865 was only about half what it had been in 1860.

Recovery could not begin until a new labor system replaced slavery. Most northerners and southerners assumed that southern prosperity still depended on cotton and that the plantation was the most efficient unit for producing the crop. Hindering efforts to rebuild the plantation economy were lack of capital, the conviction of southern whites that blacks would work only under compulsion, and the freedmen's resistance to labor conditions that recalled slavery.

Blacks preferred to determine their own economic relationships, and for a time they had reason to hope the federal government would support their ambitions. The freed slaves were, in effect, fighting a two-front war. Although they were grateful for federal aid in ending slavery, freed slaves' ideas about freedom often contradicted the plans of their northern allies. Many ex-slaves wanted to hold on to the family-based communal work methods that they used during slavery. Freed slaves in South Carolina, for example, attempted to maintain the family task system rather than adopt the individual piecework system northern capitalists pushed. Many ex-slaves opposed plans to turn them into wage laborers who produced exclusively for a market. Finally, freed slaves often wanted to stay on the land their families had spent generations farming rather than move elsewhere to occupy land as individual farmers.

While not guaranteeing all of the freed slaves' hopes for economic self-determination, the northern military attempted to establish a new economic base for them. General Sherman, hampered by the many black fugitives that followed his army on its famous march, issued an order in January 1865 that set aside the islands and coastal areas of Georgia and South Carolina for exclusive black occupancy on 40-acre plots. Furthermore, the Freedmen's Bureau was given control of hundreds of thousands of acres of abandoned or confiscated land and was authorized to make 40-acre grants to black settlers for three-year periods, after which they could buy at low prices. By June 1865, 40,000 black farmers were working on 300,000 acres of what they thought would be their own land.

But for most of them, the dream of "40 acres and a mule," or some other arrangement that would give them control of their land and labor, was not to be realized. President Johnson pardoned the owners of most of the land Sherman and the Freedmen's Bureau consigned to the ex-slaves, and Congress rejected proposals for an effective program of land confiscation and redistribution. Among the considerations prompting congressional opposition to land reform were a tenderness for property rights, fear of sapping the freedmen's initiative by giving them something they allegedly had not earned, and the desire to restore cotton production as quickly as possible to increase agricultural exports and stabilize the economy. Consequently, most blacks in physical possession of small farms failed to acquire title, and the mass of freedmen did not become landowners. As an ex-slave later wrote, "they were set free without a dollar, without a foot of land, and without the wherewithal to get the next meal even."

Despite their poverty and landlessness, ex-slaves were reluctant to settle down and commit themselves to wage labor for their former masters. Many took to the road, hoping to find something better. Some were still expecting land, but others were simply trying to increase their bargaining power. One freedman recalled that an important part of being free was that "we could move around [and] change bosses." By the end of 1865, many freedmen had still not signed up for the coming season; anxious planters feared that blacks were plotting to seize land by force. Within weeks, however, most holdouts signed for the best terms they could get.

One common form of agricultural employment in 1866 was a contract labor system. Under this system, workers committed themselves for a year in return for fixed wages, much of which was withheld until after the harvest. Since many planters drove hard bargains, abused their workers, or cheated them at the end of the year, the Freedmen's Bureau reviewed and enforced the contracts. But bureau officials had differing notions of what it meant to protect African Americans from exploitation. Some stood up for the rights of the freedmen; others served as allies of the planters.

An alternative capital–labor relationship—**sharecropping**—eventually replaced the contract system. First in small groups known as "squads" and later as individual families, black sharecroppers worked a piece of land for a fixed share of the crop, usually one-half. Credit-starved landlords liked this arrangement because it did not require much expenditure before the harvest, and the tenant shared the risks of crop failure or a fall in cotton prices.

African Americans initially viewed sharecropping as a step toward landownership. But during the 1870s, it evolved into a new kind of servitude. Croppers had to live on credit until their cotton was sold, and planters or merchants "provisioned" them at high prices and exorbitant interest. Creditors deducted what was owed to them out of the tenant's share of the crop. This left most sharecroppers with no net profit at the end of the year—and often with a debt they had to work off in subsequent years.

sharecropping After the Civil War, the southern states adopted a sharecropping system as a compromise between former slaves who wanted land of their own and former slave owners who needed labor. The landowners provided land, tools, and seed to a farming family, who in turn provided labor. The resulting crop was divided between them, with the farmers receiving a "share" of one-third to one-half of the crop.

Quick Check

What were the conflicting visions of the planters, the Freedmen's Bureau agents, and the freed slaves with regard to what a new labor system should look like?

((• Read **the** Document   Jourdan Anderson, Letter to His Former Master (1865)

SHARECROPPERS The Civil War brought emancipation to slaves, but the sharecropping system kept many of them economically bound to their employers. At the end of a year, the sharecropper tenants might owe most—or all—of what they had made to their landlord.

Black Codes: A New Name for Slavery?

While landless rural blacks were being reduced to economic dependence, those in towns and cities were living in an increasingly segregated society. The Black Codes of 1865 attempted to require separation of the races in public places and facilities; when federal authorities overturned most of the codes as violations of the Civil Rights Act of 1866, private initiative and community pressure often achieved the same end. In some cities, blacks resisted being consigned to separate streetcars by appealing to the military when it still exercised authority or by organizing boycotts. But they found it almost impossible to gain admittance to most hotels, restaurants, and other private establishments catering to whites. Although separate black, or "Jim Crow," cars were not yet the rule on railroads, African Americans were often denied first-class accommodations. After 1868, black-supported Republican governments required equal access to public facilities, but made little effort to enforce the legislation.

The Black Codes had other onerous provisions to control African Americans and return them to quasi-slavery. Most codes made black unemployment a crime, which meant blacks had to make long-term contracts with white employers or be arrested for vagrancy. Others limited the rights of African Americans to own property or engage in occupations other than those of servant or laborer. Congress, the military, and the Freedmen's Bureau set the codes aside, but vagrancy laws remained in force across the South.

Furthermore, private violence and discrimination against blacks continued on a massive scale, unchecked by state authorities. Whites murdered hundreds, perhaps thousands, of blacks during 1865–1866, and few perpetrators were brought to justice. Military rule was designed to protect former slaves from such violence and intimidation, but the task was beyond the capacity of the few thousand troops stationed in the South. When new constitutions were approved and states readmitted to the Union under the congressional plan in 1868, the problem became more severe. White opponents of Radical Reconstruction adopted systematic terrorism and mob violence to keep blacks from the polls.

The freed slaves, in the face of opposition from both their Democratic enemies and some Republican allies, tried to defend themselves by organizing their own militia groups and to assert their political rights. However, the militias were too weak to overcome the anti-Republican forces. And as the military presence was reduced, the new Republican regimes fought a losing battle against armed white supremacists.

Quick Check

What were the Black Codes, and how did they compare to the conditions of slavery?

Republican Rule in the South

Hastily organized in 1867, the southern Republican Party dominated the constitution-making of 1868 and the regimes it produced. The party was an attempted coalition of three social groups (which varied in their relative strength from state to state). One was the same class that was becoming the backbone of the Republican Party in the North—businessmen who wanted government aid for private enterprise. Many Republicans of this stripe were recent arrivals from the North—the so-called carpetbaggers—but some were scalawags, former Whig planters or merchants who were born in the South or had immigrated there before the war and now saw a chance to realize their dreams for commercial and industrial development.

Poor white farmers, especially those from upland areas where Unionist sentiment had been strong during the Civil War, were a second element in the original coalition. These owners of small farms expected the party to favor their interests at the expense of the wealthy landowners and pass special legislation when—as often happened in this period of economic upheaval—creditors attempted to seize their homesteads. Newly enfranchised blacks were the third group to which the Republicans appealed. Blacks formed most of the Republican rank and file in most states and were concerned mainly with education, civil rights, and landownership.

Under the best conditions, these coalitions would have been fragile. Each group had its own goals and did not fully support those of the others. White yeomen, for example, had a deep resistance to black equality. And for how long would essentially conservative businessmen support costly measures to elevate or relieve the lower classes of either race? In some states, astute Democrats exploited these divisions by appealing to disaffected white Republicans.

But during the relatively brief period when they were in power in the South—from one to nine years depending on the state—the Republicans chalked up notable achievements. They established (on paper at least) the South's first adequate systems of public education, democratized state and local government, and expanded public services and responsibilities.

As important as these social and political reforms were, they took second place to the Republicans' major effort—fostering economic development and restoring prosperity by subsidizing the construction of railroads and other internal improvements. But the policy of aiding railroads turned out to be disastrous, even though it addressed the region's real economic needs and was initially popular. Extravagance, corruption, and routes laid out in response to political pressure rather than on sound economic grounds increased public debt and taxation.

The policy did not produce the promised payoff of efficient, cheap transportation. Subsidized railroads went bankrupt, leaving the taxpayers holding the bag. When the Panic of 1873 brought many southern state governments to the verge of bankruptcy, and railroad building ended, it was clear the Republicans' "gospel of prosperity" through state aid to private enterprise had failed. Their political opponents, many of whom had favored such policies, now took advantage of the situation, charging that Republicans had ruined the southern economy.

In general, the Radical regimes failed to conduct public business honestly and efficiently. Embezzlement of public funds and bribery of state lawmakers or officials were common. State debts and tax burdens rose enormously, mainly because governments had undertaken heavy new responsibilities, but also because of waste and graft. The situation varied from state to state: Ruling cliques in Louisiana and South Carolina were guilty of much wrongdoing; Mississippi had a relatively honest and frugal regime.

Furthermore, southern corruption was not exceptional, nor was it a result of extending suffrage to uneducated African Americans, as critics of Radical Reconstruction have claimed. It was part of a national pattern during an era when private interests considered buying government favors as part of the cost of doing business, and politicians expected to profit by obliging them.

Many Reconstruction-era scandals started at the top. President Grant's first-term vice president, Schuyler Colfax of Indiana, was directly involved in the notorious Credit Mobilier scandal. Credit Mobilier was a construction company that actually served as a fraudulent device for siphoning off profits that should have gone to the stockholders of the Union Pacific Railroad, which had received massive federal land grants. Credit Mobilier distributed stock to influential congressmen, including Colfax before he became vice president, in order to keep Congress from inquiring into this shady arrangement. In 1875, during President Grant's second administration, his private secretary was indicted in a conspiracy to defraud the government of millions of dollars in liquor taxes, and his secretary of war was impeached for taking bribes. While there is no evidence that Grant profited personally from these misdeeds, he failed to take firm action against the wrongdoers and participated in covering up their crimes.

The new African American public officials were only minor participants in this rampant corruption. Although 16 blacks served in Congress—two in the Senate—between 1869 and 1880, only in South Carolina were blacks a majority of even one house of the legislature. Furthermore, no black governors were elected during Reconstruction (although Pinckney B. S. Pinchback was acting governor of Louisiana during 1872–1873). The biggest grafters were opportunistic whites. Businessmen offering bribes included members of the prewar gentry who were staunch opponents of Radical programs. Some black legislators went with the tide and accepted "loans" from railroad lobbyists who would pay most for their votes, but the same men would usually vote the will of their constituents on civil rights or education.

Quick Check

What were the three social groups that made up the southern Republican party?

Blacks served or supported corrupt and wasteful regimes because the alternative was dire. Although the Democrats, or Conservatives as they called themselves in some states, made sporadic efforts to attract African American voters, it was clear that if they won control, they would strip blacks of their civil and political rights. But opponents of Radical Reconstruction capitalized on racial prejudice and persuaded many Americans that "good government" was synonymous with white supremacy.

Contrary to myth, the few African Americans elected to state or national office during Reconstruction demonstrated on the average more integrity and competence than their white counterparts. Most were fairly well educated, having been free or unusually privileged slaves before the war. Among the most capable were Robert Smalls (whose career was described earlier); Blanche K. Bruce of Mississippi, elected to the U.S. Senate in 1874 after rising to prominence in the Republican party of his home state; Congressman Robert Brown Elliott of South Carolina, an adroit politician who was also a consistent champion of civil rights; and Congressman James T. Rapier of Alabama, who stirred the nation in 1873 with his appeals for federal aid to southern education and new laws to enforce equal rights for African Americans.

Claiming Public and Private Rights

The ways that freed slaves claimed rights for themselves were as important as party politics to the changing political culture of the Reconstruction South. Ex-slaves fought for their rights not only in negotiations with employers and in public meetings and convention halls, but also through the institutions they created and, perhaps most important, the households they formed.

Some ex-slaves used institutions formerly closed to them, like the courts, to assert rights they considered part of citizenship. Many ex-slaves rushed to formalize their

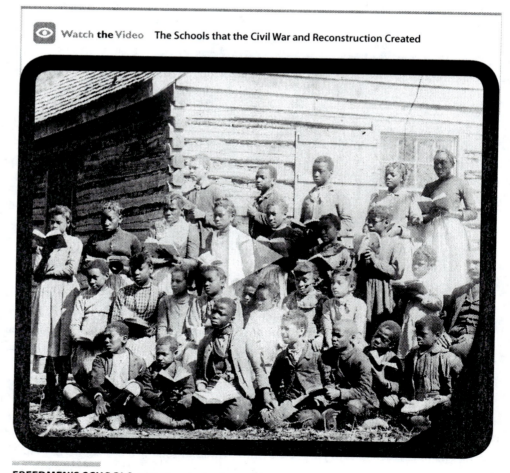

Watch the Video The Schools that the Civil War and Reconstruction Created

FREEDMEN'S SCHOOLS A Freedmen's school, one of the more successful endeavors the Freedmen's Bureau supported. The bureau, working with teachers from northern abolitionist and missionary societies, founded thousands of schools for freed slaves and poor whites.

marriages before the law, and they used their new status to fight for custody of children who had been taken from them under the apprenticeship provisions of the Black Codes. Ex-slaves sued white people and other blacks over domestic violence, child support, assault, and debt. Freed women sued their husbands for desertion and alimony and enlisted the Freedmen's Bureau to help them claim property from men. Immediately after the war, freed people created institutions that had been denied to them under slavery: churches, fraternal and benevolent associations, political organizations, and schools. Many joined all-black denominations such as the African Methodist Episcopal (AME) church, which provided freedom from white dominance and more congenial worship. Black women formed all-black chapters of organizations such as the Women's Christian Temperance Union and created their own women's clubs to oppose lynching and promote "uplift" in the black community.

A top priority for most ex-slaves was education for their children; the first schools for freed people were all-black institutions the Freedmen's Bureau and northern missionary societies established. Having been denied education during the antebellum period, most blacks viewed separate schooling as an opportunity rather than as a form of discrimination. However, these schools were precursors to the segregated public school systems first instituted by Republican governments. Only at city schools in New Orleans and the University of South Carolina were serious attempts made during Reconstruction to bring white and black students together in the same classrooms.

In many ways, African American men and women during Reconstruction asserted freedom in the "private" realm and the public sphere by claiming rights to their own families and building their own institutions. They did so despite the efforts of their former masters and the new government agencies to control their private lives and shape their new identities as husbands, wives, and citizens.

Quick Check

What new rights and institutions did free blacks create and use following emancipation?

Retreat from Reconstruction

16.3   Why did Reconstruction end?

The era of Reconstruction began to end almost before it got started. Although it was only three years after the end of the Civil War, the impeachment crisis of 1868 was the high point of popular interest in Reconstruction. That year, Ulysses S. Grant, a popular general, was elected president. Many historians blame Grant for the corruption of his administration and for the inconsistency and failure of his southern policy. He had neither the vision nor the sense of duty to tackle the difficult challenges the nation faced. From 1868 on, political issues other than southern Reconstruction moved to the forefront of national politics, and the plight of African Americans in the South receded in white consciousness.

Final Efforts of Reconstruction

The Republican effort to make equal rights for blacks the law of the land culminated in the **Fifteenth Amendment**. Passed by Congress in 1869 and ratified by the states in 1870, it prohibited any state from denying a male citizen the right to vote because of race, color, or previous condition of servitude. A more radical version, requiring universal manhood suffrage, was rejected partly because it departed too sharply from traditional federal–state relations. States therefore could still limit the suffrage by imposing literacy tests, property qualifications, or poll taxes allegedly applying to all racial groups; such devices would eventually be used to strip southern blacks of the right to vote. But the authors of the amendment did not foresee this. They believed it would prevent future Congresses or southern constitutional conventions from repealing or nullifying the provisions for black male suffrage included in the Reconstruction

Fifteenth Amendment Ratified in 1870, it prohibits the denial or abridgment of the right to vote by the federal or state governments on the basis of race, color, or prior condition as a slave. It was intended to guarantee African Americans the right to vote in the South.

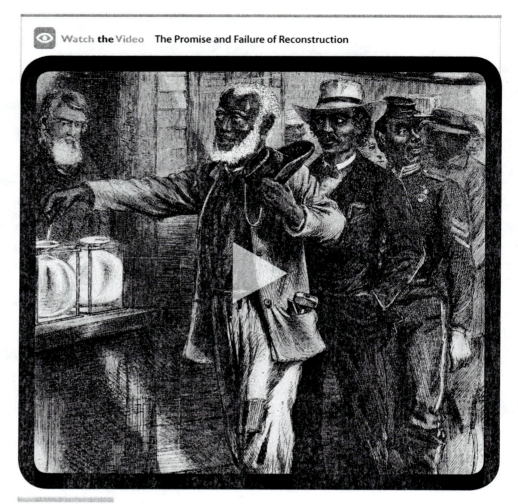

Watch the Video   The Promise and Failure of Reconstruction

AFRICAN AMERICAN VOTING *The First Vote*, drawn by A. H. Ward for *Harper's Weekly*, November 16, 1867.

Acts. A secondary aim was to enfranchise African Americans in northern states that still denied them the vote.

Many feminists were bitter that the amendment did not extend the vote to women. A militant wing of the women's rights movement, led by Elizabeth Cady Stanton and Susan B. Anthony, was so angered that the Constitution was being amended to, in effect, make gender a qualification for voting that they campaigned against ratification of the amendment. Other feminists led by Lucy Stone supported the amendment, saying this was "the Negro's hour" and that women could afford to wait a few years for the vote. This disagreement divided the woman suffrage movement for a generation.

The Grant administration was charged with enforcing the amendment and protecting black men's voting rights in the reconstructed states. Since survival of the Republican regimes depended on African American support, political partisanship dictated federal action, even though the North's emotional and ideological commitment to black citizenship was waning.

A Reign of Terror Against Blacks

Between 1868 and 1872, the **Ku Klux Klan** and other secret societies bent on restoring white supremacy by intimidating blacks who sought to exercise their political rights and were the main threat to Republican regimes. Founded in Tennessee in 1866, the Klan spread rapidly, adopting lawless and brutal tactics. A grassroots vigilante movement, not a centralized conspiracy, the Klan thrived on local initiative and support from whites of all social classes. Its secrecy, decentralization, popular support, and ruthlessness made it difficult to suppress. As soon as blacks had been granted the right to vote, hooded "night riders" began to visit the cabins of active Republicans. Some victims were only threatened. Others were whipped or murdered.

Quick Check

What did the Fifteenth Amendment provide, and who was left out of its protections?

Ku Klux Klan A secret terrorist society first organized in Tennessee in 1866. The original Klan's goals were to disfranchise African Americans, stop Reconstruction, and restore the prewar social order of the South. The Ku Klux Klan re-formed in the twentieth century to promote white supremacy and combat aliens, Catholics, and Jews.

Such methods were first used effectively in the presidential election of 1868. Grant lost in Louisiana and Georgia mainly because the Klan—or the Knights of the White Camellia, as the Louisiana variant was called—launched a reign of terror to prevent blacks from voting. In Louisiana, political violence claimed more than 1000 lives. In Arkansas, which Grant did carry, more than 200 Republicans, including a congressman, were killed.

Thereafter, Klan terrorism was directed mainly at Republican state governments. Virtual insurrections broke out in Arkansas, Tennessee, North Carolina, and parts of South Carolina. Republican governors called out the state militia to fight the Klan, but only the Arkansas militia brought it to heel. In Tennessee, North Carolina, and Georgia, Klan activities enabled Democrats to come to power by 1870.

During 1870–1871, Congress provided federal protection for black suffrage and authorized using the army against the Klan. The **Force Acts**, also known as the Ku Klux Klan acts, made interference with voting rights a federal crime and provided for federal supervision of elections. The legislation also empowered the president to call out troops and suspend the writ of habeas corpus to quell insurrection. During 1871–1872, the military or U.S. marshals arrested thousands of suspected Klansmen, and the writ was

Force Acts Designed to protect black voters in the South from the Ku Klux Klan in 1870–1871, these laws placed state elections under federal jurisdiction and imposed fines and punished those guilty of interfering with any citizen exercising his right to vote.

((• 📖 Read **the** Document   Albion W. Tourgee, Letter on Ku Klux Klan Activities (1870)

KU KLUX KLAN This 1868 photograph shows typical regalia of members of the Ku Klux Klan, a secret white supremacist organization. Before elections, hooded Klansmen terrorized African Americans to discourage them from voting.

suspended in nine counties of South Carolina that the Klan had virtually taken over. Although most of the accused Klansmen were never tried, were acquitted, or received suspended sentences, the enforcement effort did put a damper on hooded terrorism and ensure relatively fair and peaceful elections in 1872.

A heavy black turnout in these elections enabled the Republicans to hold on to power in most of the Deep South, despite Democratic-Conservative efforts to cut into the Republican vote by taking moderate positions on racial and economic issues. This setback prompted the Democratic-Conservatives to change their strategy and ideology. They stopped trying to take votes away from the Republicans by proclaiming support for black suffrage and government aid to business. Instead they began to appeal openly to white supremacy and the traditional Democratic and agrarian hostility to government promotion of economic development. They were thus able to attract part of the white Republican electorate, mostly small farmers.

This new strategy dovetailed with a resurgence of violence to reduce Republican, especially black Republican, voting. Its agents no longer wore masks but acted openly. They were effective because the northern public was increasingly disenchanted with federal intervention to prop up what were widely viewed as corrupt and tottering Republican regimes. Grant used force in the South for the last time in 1874 when an overt paramilitary organization in Louisiana, known as the White League, tried to overthrow a Republican government accused of stealing an election. When another unofficial militia in Mississippi instigated bloody race riots before the state elections of 1875, Grant refused the governor's request for federal troops. As a result, black voters were intimidated—one county registered only seven Republican votes where there had been a black majority of 2000—and Mississippi fell to the Democratic-Conservatives.

By 1876, partly because of Grant's hesitant and inconsistent use of presidential power, but mainly because the northern electorate would no longer tolerate military action to sustain Republican governments and black voting rights, Radical Reconstruction was collapsing.

Quick Check

How important was the Ku Klux Klan in influencing elections and policies in the South?

Reunion and The New South

16.4   Who benefited and who suffered from the reconciliation of the North and South?

The end of Radical Reconstruction in 1877 opened the way to a reconciliation of North and South. But the costs of reunion were high for less-privileged groups in the South. The civil and political rights of African Americans, left unprotected, were relentlessly stripped away by white supremacist regimes. Lower-class whites saw their interests sacrificed to those of capitalists and landlords. Despite the rhetoric hailing a prosperous "New South," the region remained poor and open to exploitation by northern business interests.

The Compromise of 1877

The election of 1876 pitted Rutherford B. Hayes of Ohio, a Republican governor untainted by the scandals of the Grant era, against Governor Samuel J. Tilden of New York, a Democratic reformer who had fought corruption in New York City. Honest government was apparently the electorate's highest priority. When the returns came in, Tilden had won the popular vote and seemed likely to win a narrow victory in the electoral college. But the returns from the three southern states the Republicans still controlled—South Carolina, Florida, and Louisiana—were contested. If Hayes were awarded these three states, plus one contested electoral vote in Oregon, Republican strategists realized, he would triumph in the electoral college by a single vote. (see Map 16.2).

The election remained undecided for months, plunging the nation into a political crisis. To resolve the impasse, Congress appointed a 15-member commission to determine who would receive the votes of the disputed states. Originally composed of seven Democrats, seven Republicans, and an independent, the commission fell under Republican control when the independent member resigned to run for the Senate and a Republican replaced him. The commission split along party lines and voted eight to seven to award Hayes all the disputed votes. But both houses of Congress still had to ratify the decision, and in the House, there was strong Democratic opposition. To ensure Hayes's election, Republican leaders struck an informal bargain with conservative southern Democrats that historians have dubbed the **Compromise of 1877**. What precisely was agreed to and by whom remains in dispute, but both sides understood that Hayes would be president and that southern blacks would be abandoned to their fate. President Hayes immediately ordered the army not to resist a Democratic takeover of state governments in South Carolina and Louisiana. Thus fell the last of the Radical governments. White Democrats firmly controlled the entire South. The trauma of the war and Reconstruction had destroyed the chances for renewing two-party competition among white southerners.

Election of 1876

	Uncontested Electoral Vote	Electoral Total		Popular Vote
REPUBLICAN Rutherford B. Hayes	165	185		4,036,298
DEMOCRATIC Samuel J. Tilden	184	184		4,300,590
GREENBACK Peter Cooper	—	—		81,737
	349			8,418,625

*Contested result settled by Special Election Commission in favor of Hayes.

MAP 16.2 ELECTION OF 1876

"Redeeming" a New South

The men who took power after Radical Reconstruction fell in one southern state after another are usually referred to as the **Redeemers**. Their backgrounds and previous loyalties differed. Some were members of the Old South's ruling planter class who had supported secession and now sought to reestablish the old order with as few changes as possible. Others, of middle-class origin or outlook, favored commercial and industrial interests over agrarian groups and called for a New South committed to diversified economic development. A third group consisted of professional politicians bending with the prevailing winds.

The Redeemers subscribed to no single coherent ideology but are best characterized as power brokers mediating among the dominant interest groups of the South to serve their own political advantage. The "rings" that they established on the state and county levels were analogous to the political machines developing at the same time in northern cities.

Redeemers did, however, endorse two basic principles: laissez-faire and white supremacy. Laissez-faire could unite planters, frustrated at seeing direct state support going to businessmen, and capitalist promoters, who realized that low taxes and freedom from government regulation were even more advantageous than state subsidies. The Redeemers responded only to privileged and entrenched interest groups, especially landlords, merchants, and industrialists, and offered little or nothing to tenants, small farmers, and working people. As industrialization gathered steam in the 1880s, Democratic regimes became increasingly accommodating to manufacturing interests and hospitable to agents of northern capital who were gaining control of the South's transportation system and its extractive industries.

White supremacy was the rallying cry that brought the Redeemers to power. Once in office, they stayed there by charging that opponents of ruling Democratic cliques were trying to divide "the white man's party" and open the way for a return to "black domination." Appeals to racism also deflected attention from the economic grievances of groups without political clout.

The new governments were more economical than those of Reconstruction, mainly because they drastically cut appropriations for schools and other public services. But they were scarcely more honest—embezzlement and bribery remained rife.

Compromise of 1877 Compromise struck during the contested presidential election of 1876, in which Democrats accepted the election of Rutherford B. Hayes (Republican) in exchange for the withdrawal of federal troops from the South and the end of Reconstruction.

Redeemers A loose coalition of prewar Democrats, Confederate veterans, and Whigs who took over southern state governments in the 1870s, supposedly "redeeming" them from the corruption of Reconstruction. They shared a commitment to white supremacy and laissez-faire economics.

Quick Check

Which principles divided, and which united, the new "Redeemer" governments?

Jim Crow laws Segregation laws enacted by southern states after Reconstruction.

The Redeemer regimes of the late 1870s and 1880s neglected small white farmers. Whites, as well as blacks, were suffering from the notorious crop lien system, which gave local merchants who advanced credit at high interest during the growing season the right to take possession of the harvested crop on terms that buried farmers deeper and deeper in debt. As a result, many whites lost title to their homesteads and were reduced to tenancy. When a depression of world cotton prices added to the burden of a ruinous credit system, agrarian protesters began to challenge the ruling elite, first through the Southern Farmers' Alliance of the late 1880s and then by supporting its political descendant—the Populist party of the 1890s (see Chapter 20).

The Rise of Jim Crow

The new order imposed the greatest hardships on African Americans. The dark night of racism fell on the South. From 1876 to 1910, southern states imposed restrictions on black civil rights known as **Jim Crow laws**. The term "Jim Crow" came from an antebellum minstrel show figure first popularized by Thomas "Daddy" Rice, who blackened his face and sang a song called "Jump Jim Crow." By the 1850s, Jim Crow was a familiar figure in minstrel shows, and had become a synonym for a black person in popular white speech. It was a short step to referring to segregated railroad cars for black people as Jim Crow cars. While segregation and disfranchisement began as informal arrangements in the immediate aftermath of the Civil War, they culminated in a legal regime of separation and exclusion that took firm hold in the 1890s. (see Chapter 19).

The rise of Jim Crow in the political arena was especially bitter for southern blacks who realized that only political power could ensure other rights. The Redeemers promised, as part of the understanding that led to the end of federal intervention in 1877, that they would respect the rights of blacks as set forth in the Fourteenth and Fifteenth Amendments. Governor Wade Hampton of South Carolina pledged that the new regimes would not reduce African Americans to second-class citizenship. But when blacks tried to vote Republican in the "redeemed" states, they encountered violence and intimidation. "Bulldozing" African American voters remained common in state elections during the late 1870s and early 1880s; those blacks who withstood the threat of losing their jobs or being evicted from tenant farms if they voted for the party of Lincoln were visited at night and literally whipped into line. The message was clear: Vote Democratic, or vote not at all.

Furthermore, white Democrats now controlled the electoral machinery and manipulated the black vote by stuffing ballot boxes, discarding unwanted votes, or reporting fraudulent totals. Some states imposed complicated voting requirements to discourage black participation. Full-scale disfranchisement did not occur until literacy tests and other legalized obstacles to voting were imposed from 1890 to 1910, but by then, less formal and comprehensive methods had already made a mockery of the Fifteenth Amendment.

Nevertheless, blacks continued to vote freely in some localities until the 1890s; a few districts, like the one Robert Smalls represented, even elected black Republicans to Congress during the immediate post-Reconstruction period. The last of these, Representative George H. White of North Carolina, served until 1901. His farewell address eloquently conveyed the agony of southern blacks in the era of Jim Crow (strict segregation):

> These parting words are in behalf of an outraged, heart-broken, bruised, and bleeding but God-fearing people, faithful, industrious, loyal people—rising people, full of potential force.... The only apology that I have to make for the earnestness with which I have spoken is that I am pleading for the life, the liberty, the future happiness, and manhood suffrage of one-eighth of the entire population of the United States.

Conclusion: Henry McNeal Turner and The "Unfinished Revolution"

The career of Henry McNeal Turner sums up the bitter side of the black experience in the South during and after Reconstruction. Born free in South Carolina in 1834, Turner became a minister of the AME Church just before the Civil War. During the war, he

Quick Check

What aspects of southern society did the Jim Crow Laws regulate?

HENRY MCNEAL TURNER Turner, who was born in freedom, became a bishop of the African Methodist Episcopal Church and was elected to the Georgia legislature.

recruited African Americans for the Union army and served as chaplain for black troops. After the war, he went to Georgia to work for the Freedmen's Bureau but encountered racial discrimination from white officers and left government service for church work and Reconstruction politics. Elected to the 1867 Georgia constitutional convention and to the state legislature in 1868, he was one of many black clergymen who became leaders among the freedmen. But whites won control of the Georgia legislature and expelled all the black members. As the inhabitant of a state in which blacks never gained the power that they achieved in other parts of the South, Turner was one of the first black leaders to see the failure of Reconstruction as the betrayal of African American hopes for citizenship.

Becoming a bishop of the AME Church in 1880, Turner emerged as the era's leading proponent of black emigration to Africa. Because he believed that white Americans would never grant blacks equal rights, Turner became an early advocate of black nationalism and a total separation of the races. Emigration became popular among southern blacks, who were especially hard hit by terror and oppression just after the end of Reconstruction. Still, most blacks in the nation as a whole and even in Turner's own church refused to give up the hope of eventual equality on American soil. But Bishop Turner's anger and despair were the understandable responses of a proud man to how he and his fellow African Americans had been treated in the post–Civil War period.

By the late 1880s, the wounds of the Civil War were healing, and white Americans were seized by the spirit of sectional reconciliation and their common Americanism. But whites could reunite only because northerners had tacitly agreed to give southerners a free hand to reduce blacks to servitude. The "outraged, heart-broken, bruised, and bleeding" African Americans of the South paid the heaviest price for sectional reunion.

Chapter Review

The President Versus Congress

16.1 What conflicts arose consecutively involving President Lincoln and then President Johnson and Congress during Reconstruction? p. 355

Both Lincoln and Johnson had their own notions of how Reconstruction should be governed. Radical Republicans who sought more protection for black rights challenged Lincoln's Ten Percent Plan. Later, when Johnson hesitated to renew the Freedmen's Bureau and fight the Black Codes, Congress passed the Fourteenth Amendment to ensure equal rights to all Americans.

Reconstructing Southern Society

16.2 What problems did southern society face during Reconstruction? p. 363

The immediate problems facing the South were economic and physical devastation, and providing for the mass of freed slaves. While former slaveholders hoped to reduce ex-slaves to conditions not unlike slavery, northern Republicans wanted to reorganize southern land and labor on a northern free-labor model. Freedmen's Bureau agents emphasized that ex-slaves had to sign contracts and work for wages. The freed slaves hoped instead to own land. Sharecropping was a compromise.

Retreat from Reconstruction

16.3 Why did Reconstruction end? p. 369

Although intended to protect civil rights, the Fifteenth Amendment allowed states to limit local suffrage through difficult voting prerequisites. Further, the Ku Klux Klan intimidated black voters and representation. By 1876, these tactics had defeated the Republicans in most southern states and Reconstruction was nearly dead.

Reunion and the New South

16.4 Who benefited and who suffered from the reconciliation of the North and South? p. 372

Reunion came at the expense of African Americans. The Compromise of 1877 restored autonomous government in the South to resolve the 1876 election. The North would no longer enforce unpopular civil rights, allowing the Redeemers to bring back laissez-faire economics and restore white supremacy through the Jim Crow laws.

Timeline

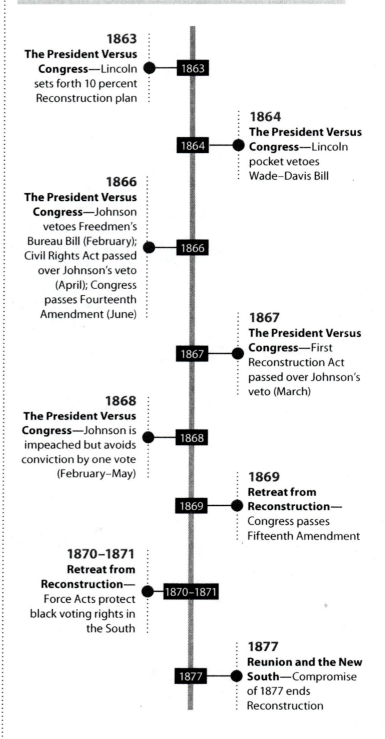

1863
The President Versus Congress—Lincoln sets forth 10 percent Reconstruction plan

1863

1864
The President Versus Congress—Lincoln pocket vetoes Wade–Davis Bill

1864

1866
The President Versus Congress—Johnson vetoes Freedmen's Bureau Bill (February); Civil Rights Act passed over Johnson's veto (April); Congress passes Fourteenth Amendment (June)

1866

1867
The President Versus Congress—First Reconstruction Act passed over Johnson's veto (March)

1867

1868
The President Versus Congress—Johnson is impeached but avoids conviction by one vote (February–May)

1868

1869
Retreat from Reconstruction—Congress passes Fifteenth Amendment

1869

1870–1871
Retreat from Reconstruction—Force Acts protect black voting rights in the South

1870–1871

1877
Reunion and the New South—Compromise of 1877 ends Reconstruction

1877

17 The West Exploiting an Empire 1849–1902

Lean Bear's Changing West

I n 1863, federal Indian agents took a delegation of Cheyenne, Arapaho, Comanche, Kiowa, and Plains Apache to visit the eastern United States, hoping to impress them with the power of the white man. The visitors were, in fact, impressed. In New York City, they stared at the tall buildings and crowded streets, so different from the wide-open plains to which they were accustomed. They visited the museum of the great showman Phineas T. Barnum, who in turn put them on display; they even saw a hippopotamus.

In Washington, they met President Abraham Lincoln. Lean Bear, a Cheyenne chief, assured Lincoln that Indians wanted peace but were worried about the numbers of white people who were pouring into their country. Lincoln swore friendship, said the Indians would be better off if they began to farm, and promised to do his best to keep the peace. But, he said, smiling at Lean Bear, "You know it is not always possible for any father to have his children do precisely as he wishes them to do."

Lean Bear, who had children of his own, understood what Lincoln said, at least in a way. A year later, back on his own lands, he watched federal troops, Lincoln's "children," approach his camp. Wearing a peace medal that

LEARNING OBJECTIVES

17.1 (((	17.2 (((	17.3 (((	17.4 (((
What were the challenges of settling the country west of the Mississippi? p. 379	How did white Americans crush the culture of the Native Americans as they moved west? p. 380	Why did Americans and others move to the West? p. 387	Why was the West a bonanza of dreams and get-rich-quick schemes? p. 391

LITTLE BIG HORN This pictogram by Oglala Sioux Amos Bad Heart Bull is a Native American version of the Battle of the Little Bighorn, also known as Custer's Last Stand.

(((Listen to **Chapter 17** on **MyHistoryLab**

◉ Watch the Video Series on MyHistoryLab

Learn about some key topics related to this chapter with the
MyHistoryLab Video Series: Key Topics in U.S. History.

1 Conquest of the West By the early 1900s the culture and political organization of the indigenous populations living west of the Appalachian Mountains had been virtually annihilated. In 1800 there were as many as 600,000 such people in the US; by 1900, the population had been reduced to about 250,000, most living on small reservations. Through policies such as The Homestead Act in 1862, the US government encouraged and facilitated westward expansion. Westward moving white Americans, and Chinese and Japanese moving east converged with Mexican immigrants to populate the western frontier of the United States. Laws including the Chinese Seclusion Act limited the legal rights of immigrants and emphasized the prevailing view by the US government of the superiority of whites over non-whites.

◉ Watch on MyHistoryLab

The Dawes Act Congress to passed the Dawes Act in 1887. This video examines how the law sought to change Indian relations by ending the reservation system and assimilating Native Americans. The Dawes Act also allowed the U.S. government to purchase Indian land considered in excess of real needs, leaving tribes with an "allotment" and so opening more land up for white settlement.

2

Watch on MyHistoryLab ◉

3 Chinese Exclusion Act This video looks at the Chinese Exclusion Act, the federal law signed by President Chester A. Arthur in 1882 that allowed the United States to suspend Chinese immigration for a host of reasons, from depressing wages to preventing race riots.

◉ Watch on MyHistoryLab

The Gold Rush The California Gold Rush of the 1840s and '50s promised great wealth to thousands of immigrants, but often failed to deliver. This video reveals how most of the prospectors who came to California after the discovery of gold failed to make their fortune and eventually traded their dreams of wealth for a wage in the mining industry.

4

Watch on MyHistoryLab ◉

Lincoln had given him, Lean Bear rode slowly toward the troops to again offer his friendship. When he was 20 yards away, they opened fire, then rode closer and fired again and again into his fallen body.

As Lean Bear had feared, in the last three decades of the nineteenth century, a flood of settlers ventured into the vast lands across the Mississippi River. Prospectors searched for "pay dirt," railroads crisscrossed the continent, eastern and foreign capitalists invested in cattle and land bonanzas, and farmers took up the promise of free western lands. In 1867, Horace Greeley, editor of the New York *Tribune,* told New York City's unemployed: "If you strike off into the broad, free West, and make yourself a farm from Uncle Sam's generous domain, you will crowd nobody, starve nobody, and neither you nor your children need evermore beg for something to do."

With the end of the Civil War in 1865, white Americans again claimed a destiny to expand across the continent. In the process, they crushed the culture of the Native Americans and ignored the contributions of people of other races, such as Chinese miners and laborers and Mexican herdsmen. As millions moved west, the states of Colorado, Washington, Montana, North and South Dakota, Idaho, Wyoming, and Utah were carved out of the lands across the Mississippi. By 1900, only Arizona, New Mexico, and Oklahoma remained as territories.

The West became a great colonial empire, harnessed to eastern capital and tied increasingly to national and international markets. Its raw materials, sent east by wagon, train, and ship, helped fuel eastern factories. Westerners' economies relied heavily on the federal government, which subsidized their railroads, distributed their land, and spent millions of dollars for the upkeep of soldiers and Indians.

By the 1890s, the lands west of the Mississippi had changed substantially. In place of buffalo and unfenced vistas, there were cities and towns, health resorts, homesteads, sheep ranches, and, in the arid regions, the beginnings of the irrigated agriculture that would reshape the West in the twentieth century. Ghost towns, abandoned farms, and the scars in the earth left by miners and farmers spoke to the less favorable side of settlement. As the new century dawned, the West had become a place of conquest and exploitation, as well as a mythic land of cowboys and quick fortunes.

Beyond the Frontier

17.1 What were the challenges of settling the country west of the Mississippi?

The line of white settlement had reached the edge of the Missouri timber country by 1840. Beyond lay an enormous land of rolling prairies, parched deserts, and rugged, majestic mountains. Emerging from the timber country, travelers first encountered the Great Plains—treeless, nearly flat, an endless "sea of grassy hillocks" extending from the Mississippi River to the Rocky Mountains.

Running from Alaska to central New Mexico, the Rockies presented a formidable barrier, and most travelers crossed the northern passes, emerging in the desolate basin of present-day southern Idaho and Utah. On the west, the lofty Cascades and Sierra Nevada held back rainfall; beyond was the temperate Pacific coast.

Few rivers cut through the Plains; those that did raged in the winter and trickled in the summer. Rainfall usually did not reach 15 inches a year, not enough to support extensive agriculture. There was little lumber for homes and fences, and the tools of

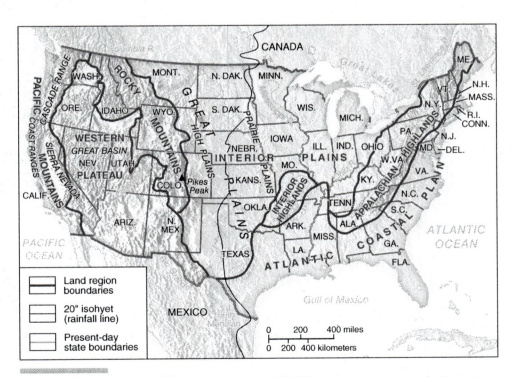

MAP 17.1 PHYSIOGRAPHIC MAP OF THE UNITED STATES In the Great Plains and Rocky Mountains, the topography, altitudes, crops, and climate—especially the lack of rain west of the rainfall line shown here—led to changes in mode of settlement, which had been essentially uniform from the Atlantic coast through Kentucky, Ohio, and Missouri. The traditional rectangular land surveys and quarter-section lots could not accommodate Great Plains conditions.

eastern settlement—the cast-iron plow, the boat, and the ax—were virtually useless on the tough and treeless Plains soil. "East of the Mississippi," historian Walter Prescott Webb noted, "civilization stood on three legs—land, water, and timber; west of the Mississippi not one but two of these legs were withdrawn—water and timber—and civilization was left on one leg—land" (see Map 17.1).

Crushing the Native Americans

17.2 How did white Americans crush the culture of the Native Americans as they moved west?

When Greeley urged New Yorkers to move west and "crowd nobody," he—like almost all white Americans—ignored the fact that many people already lived there. At the close of the Civil War, Native Americans inhabited nearly half the United States. By 1880, they had been driven onto smaller and smaller reservations and were no longer an independent people. A decade later, even their culture had crumbled under white domination.

In 1865, nearly 250,000 Native Americans lived in the western half of the country. Tribes such as the Winnebago, Menominee, Cherokee, and Chippewa were resettled there, forced out of their eastern lands by advancing white settlement. Other tribes were native to the region. In the Southwest were the Pueblo groups, including the Hopi, Zuni, and Rio Grande Pueblos. Peaceful farmers and herders, they had built up complex traditions around a settled way of life.

More nomadic were the Camp Dwellers, the Jicarilla Apache and Navajo, who roamed Arizona, New Mexico, and western Texas. The Navajo herded sheep and produced beautiful ornamental silver, baskets, and blankets. Fierce fighters, Apache horsemen were feared by whites and fellow Indians across the southwestern Plains.

Farther west were the tribes that inhabited present-day California. Divided into many small bands, they eked out a difficult existence living on roots, grubs, berries, acorns, and small game. In the Pacific Northwest, where fish and forest animals made life easier, the Klamath, Chinook, Yurok, and Shasta tribes developed a rich civilization. They built plank houses and canoes, worked extensively in wood, and evolved a complex social and political organization.

By the 1870s, most of these tribes had been destroyed or beaten into submission. The powerful Ute, crushed in 1855, ceded most of their Utah lands to the United States and settled on a small reservation near the Great Salt Lake. The Navajo and Apache fought back fiercely, but between 1865 and 1873, they too were confined to reservations. The Native Americans of California succumbed to the contagious diseases whites carried during the Gold Rush of 1849. Miners burned their villages, and by 1880, fewer than 20,000 Indians lived in California.

Life of the Plains Indians

In the mid-nineteenth century, nearly two-thirds of the Native Americans lived on the Great Plains. The Plains tribes included the Sioux of present-day Minnesota and the Dakotas; the Blackfoot of Idaho and Montana; the Cheyenne, Crow, and Arapaho of the central Plains; the Pawnee of western Nebraska; and the Kiowa, Apache, and Comanche of present-day Texas and New Mexico.

Nomadic and warlike, the Plains Indians depended on the buffalo and horse. The modern horse, first brought by Spanish explorers in the 1500s, spread north from Mexico onto the Plains, and by the 1700s, horses had changed the Plains Indians' way of life. The Plains tribes gave up farming almost entirely and hunted the buffalo on horseback, ranging widely over the rolling plains. The men became superb warriors and horsemen, among the best light cavalry in the world.

HALCYON DAYS After the buffalo was killed, women skinned the hide, cut up the meat, and then cured the hide, as shown in the painting *Halcyon Days* by George Catlin. Women also decorated the tepees and preserved the meat by drying it in the sun.

Migratory in culture, the Plains Indians formed tribes of several thousand people but lived in smaller bands of 300 to 500. The bands followed and lived off the buffalo. Buffalo provided food, clothing, and shelter; the Indians, unlike later white hunters, used every part of the animal. The meat was dried or "jerked" in the hot Plains air. The skins made tepees, blankets, and robes. Buffalo bones became knives; tendons were made into bowstrings; horns and hooves were boiled into glue. Buffalo "chips"—dried manure—were burned as fuel.

The Plains tribes divided labor tasks according to gender. Men hunted, traded, supervised ceremonial activities, and cleared ground for planting. They usually held the positions of authority, such as chief or medicine man. Women were responsible for childrearing and artistic activity. They also did the camp work, grew vegetables, prepared buffalo meat and hides, and gathered berries and roots. In most tribes, women played an important role in political, economic, and religious activities. Among the Navajo and Zuni, kinship descended from the mother's side, and Navajo women were in charge of most of the family's property. In tribes such as the Sioux, there was little difference in status. Men were respected for hunting and war, women for their artistic skills with quill and paint.

Quick Check

What characterized the life of the Plains Indians?

Searching for an Indian Policy

Before the Civil War, Americans used the land west of the Mississippi as "one big reservation." The government named the area "Indian Country," moved eastern tribes there with firm treaty guarantees, and in 1834 prohibited any white person from entering Indian country without a license.

This changed in the 1850s. Wagon trains wound their way to California and Oregon, miners pushed into western goldfields, and there was talk of a transcontinental railroad. To clear the way for settlement, the federal government in 1851 abandoned the "one big reservation" in favor of a new policy of concentration. For the first time, it assigned definite boundaries to each tribe. The Sioux, for example, were given the Dakota country north of the Platte River, the Crow a large area near the Powder River, and the Cheyenne and Arapaho the Colorado foothills between the North Platte and Arkansas Rivers for "as long as waters run and the grass shall grow."

The concentration policy lasted only a few years. Accustomed to hunting widely for buffalo, many Native Americans refused to stay within their assigned areas. White settlers poured into Indian lands, then called on the government to protect them. Indians were pushed out of Kansas and Nebraska in the 1850s, even as white reformers fought to hold those territories open for free blacks. In 1859, gold miners moved into the Pikes Peak country, touching off warfare with the Cheyenne and Arapaho.

In 1864, tired of the fighting, the two tribes asked for peace. Certain that the war was over, Chief Black Kettle led his 700 followers to camp on Sand Creek in southeastern Colorado. Early on the morning of November 29, 1864, Colorado militia led by Colonel John M. Chivington attacked the sleeping group. "Kill and scalp all, big and little," Chivington told his men. "Nits make lice." Black Kettle tried to stop the ambush, raising first an American flag and then a white flag. Neither worked. Men, women, and children were clubbed, stabbed, and scalped.

The Chivington massacre set off angry protests in Colorado and the East. Congress appointed an investigating committee, and the government concluded a treaty with the Cheyenne and Arapaho, condemning "the gross and wanton outrages." Still, the two tribes had to surrender their Sand Creek reservation in exchange for lands elsewhere. The Kiowa and Comanche were also ousted from areas they had been granted "forever" only a few years before. As the Sioux chief Spotted Tail said, "Why does not the Great Father put his red children on wheels so that he can move them as he will?"

Before long, the powerful Sioux were on the warpath in the great Sioux War of 1865–1867. Again, an invasion of gold miners touched off the war, which flared even more intensely when the federal government announced plans to connect the various mining towns by building the Bozeman Trail through the heart of the Sioux hunting grounds in Montana. Red Cloud, the Sioux chief, determined to stop the trail. In December 1866, he lured an army column under Captain William J. Fetterman deep into the wilderness, ambushed it, and wiped out all 82 soldiers in Fetterman's command.

The Fetterman massacre, coming so soon after the Chivington massacre, sparked a debate over Indian policy. Like the policy itself, the debate reflected differing white views of the Native Americans. In the East, some reform, humanitarian, and church groups wanted a humane peace policy, directed toward educating and "civilizing" the tribes. Many white people, in the East and West, questioned this approach, convinced that Native Americans were savages unfit for civilization. Westerners, of course, had reason to fear Indian attacks, and the fears often fed on wild rumors of scalped settlers and besieged forts. As a result, Westerners in general favored firm control over the Native Americans, including swift punishment of any who rebelled.

In 1867, the peace advocates won the debate. Halting construction on the Bozeman Trail, Congress created a Peace Commission of four civilians and three generals to end the Sioux War and eliminate the causes of Indian wars. The Peace Commissioners agreed that only one policy offered a permanent solution: "small reservations" to isolate the Native Americans on distant lands, teach them to farm, and "civilize" them.

((• Read the Document   **Chief Red Cloud, Speech After Wounded Knee (1890)**

RED CLOUD Red Cloud was chief of the Oglala Teton Sioux. He was an important leader who opposed white incursions into Native American lives and territory, although he openly advocated peace whenever possible and did not support the more violent actions of Crazy Horse and his followers.

The Kiowa, Comanche, Cheyenne, and Arapaho agreed to the plan in 1867, the Sioux in 1868. The policy was extended beyond the Plains, and the Ute, Shoshone, Bannock, Navajo, and Apache also accepted small reservations (see Map 17.2).

Quick Check

How did American policy toward the Indians evolve in these years?

Final Battles on the Plains

Few Native Americans settled peacefully into life on the new reservations. The reservation system not only changed their age-old customs; it impoverished and isolated them. Young warriors and minor chiefs denounced the treaties and drifted back to the open countryside. In late 1868, warfare broke out again, and it took more than a decade of violence to beat the Indians into submission.

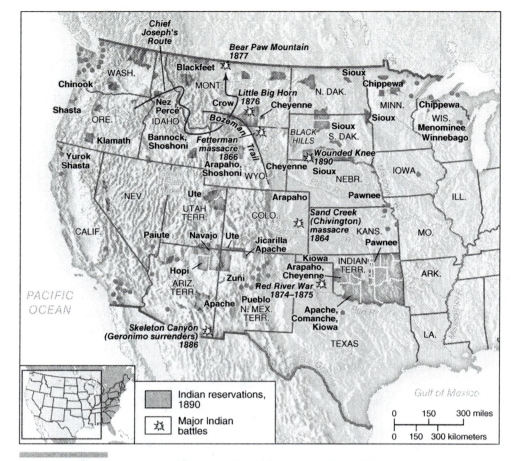

MAP 17.2 NATIVE AMERICANS IN THE WEST: MAJOR BATTLES AND RESERVATIONS "They made us many promises, more than I remember, but they never kept but one; they promised to take our land, and they took it." So said Red Cloud of the Oglala Sioux, summarizing Native American–white relations in the 1870s.

On the northern Plains, fighting resulted from the Black Hills Gold Rush of 1875. As prospectors tramped across Native American hunting grounds, the Sioux gathered to stop them. They were led by Rain-in-the-Face, the great war chief Crazy Horse, and the famous medicine man Sitting Bull. The army sent troops after the Indians, but one column, under flamboyant Lieutenant Colonel George Armstrong Custer, pushed recklessly ahead, eager to claim the victory. On the morning of June 25, 1876, thinking he had a small band of Native Americans surrounded in their village on the banks of the Little Bighorn River in Montana, Custer divided his column and took 265 men toward it. Instead of a small band, he had stumbled on the main Sioux camp, with 2,500 warriors. It was the largest Native American army ever assembled in the United States.

By mid-afternoon Custer and his men were dead. Custer was largely responsible for the loss, but "Custer's Last Stand" set off a nationwide demand for revenge. Within months, the Sioux were surrounded and beaten, 3000 of them surrendering in October 1876. Sitting Bull and a few followers who had fled to Canada gave up in 1881.

The Sioux War ended major Indian warfare in the West, but occasional outbreaks still recurred. In 1890, many of the Teton Sioux of South Dakota, bitter and starving, turned to the **Ghost Dances**, rites that grew from a vision of a Paiute messiah named Wovoka. The dances, Wovoka said, would bring back Native American lands and make the whites disappear. All Native Americans would unite, the earth would be covered with dust, and a new earth would come upon the old. The buffalo would return in great herds.

The army intervened to stop the dancing, touching off violence that killed Sitting Bull and other warriors. Frightened Native Americans fled southwest to join other Ghost Dancers under the aging chief Big Foot. The Seventh Cavalry, Custer's old regiment, caught up with Big Foot's band and took them to the army camp on Wounded Knee Creek in South Dakota. A Native American, it is thought, fired the first shot, but the army's new machine guns, firing a shell a second, shredded tepees

Ghost Dances A religious movement that arose in the late nineteenth century under the prophet Wavoka, a Paiute Indian. Its followers believed that dances and rites would cause white men to disappear and restore lands to the Native Americans. The U.S. government outlawed the Ghost Dances, and army intervention to stop them led to the **Wounded Knee Massacre**.

and people. In the infamous **Wounded Knee Massacre**, about 200 men, women, and children were killed in the snow.

The End of Tribal Life

The final step in Indian policy came in the 1870s and 1880s. Reformers had long argued against segregating the Native Americans on reservations, urging instead that the nation assimilate them individually into white culture. "Assimilationists" wanted to use education, land policy, and federal law to eradicate tribal society.

Congress began to adopt the policy in 1871 when it stopped making treaties with Native American tribes. Since tribes were no longer separate nations, they lost many of their political and judicial functions, and the power of the chiefs was weakened.

While Congress worked to break down the tribes, educators trained young Native Americans to adjust to white culture. In 1879, 50 Pawnee, Kiowa, and Cheyenne youths were brought to the new Carlisle Indian School in Carlisle, Pennsylvania. Other Native American schools soon opened, including the Haskell Institute in Kansas and numerous day schools on the western reservations. The schools taught students to fix machines and farm; they forced young Indians to trim their long hair and made them

Quick Check

What were the final battles on the Plains?

Wounded Knee Massacre In December 1890, troopers of the Seventh Cavalry, under orders to stop the **Ghost Dance** religion among the Sioux, took Chief Big Foot and his followers to a camp on Wounded Knee Creek in South Dakota. It is uncertain who fired the first shot, but 200 Native Americans were killed.

Watch the Video   **Sioux Ghost Dance**

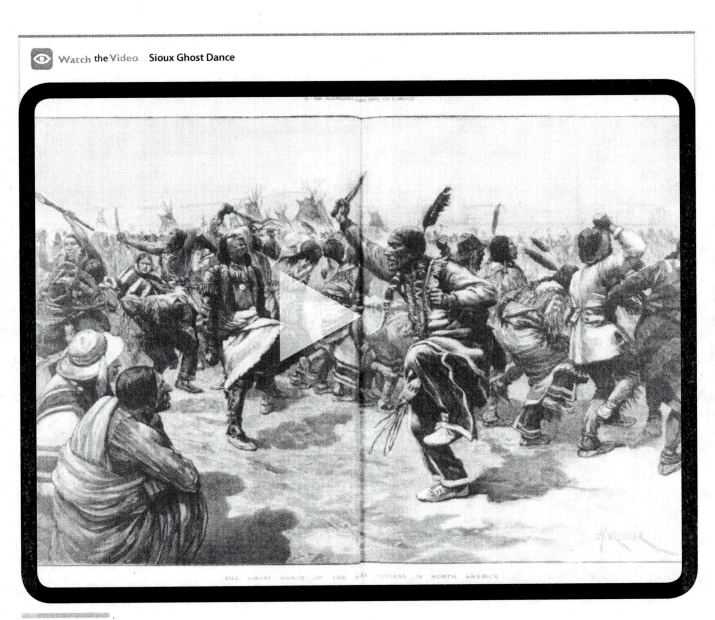

THE GHOST DANCE This wood engraving from 1891 depicts a group of Sioux dancers performing, most likely, one of their last ghost dances before the arrest of the warrior chief Sitting Bull.

speak English, banned wearing tribal paint or clothes, and forbade tribal ceremonies and dances. "Kill the Indian and save the man," said Richard H. Pratt, the army officer who founded the Carlisle School.

Land ownership was the final and most important link in the new policy. Native Americans who owned land, it was thought, would become responsible, self-reliant citizens. Deciding to give each Native American a farm, Congress in 1887 passed the **Dawes Severalty Act**, the most important legal development in Indian–white relations in more than three centuries.

To end tribal life, the Dawes Act divided tribal lands into small plots for distribution among members of the tribe. Each family head received 160 acres, single adults 80 acres, and children 40 acres. Once the land was distributed, any surplus was sold to white settlers, with the profits going to Native American schools.

Through the Dawes Act, 47 million acres of land were distributed to Native Americans and their families, but many Native Americans knew little about farming. Their tools were rudimentary, and in Plains Indians' culture, men had not ordinarily participated in farming. In 1934, the government returned to the idea of tribal land ownership, but by then 138 million acres of Indian land had shrunk to 48 million acres, half of which was barren.

The final blow to tribal life was the virtual extermination of the buffalo, the Plains Indians' chief resource and the basis for their unique way of life. The killing began in the 1860s as the transcontinental railroads pushed west, and it stepped up as settlers found they could harm the Indians by wiping out the buffalo. "Kill every buffalo you can," an army officer said. "Every buffalo dead is an Indian gone." Then, in 1871, a Pennsylvania tannery discovered that buffalo hides made valuable leather. Professional hunters such as William F. "Buffalo Bill" Cody swarmed across the Plains, killing millions of the beasts.

Between 1872 and 1874, professional hunters slaughtered 3 million buffalo a year. By 1883, the buffalo were almost gone. When the government set out to produce the famous "buffalo nickel," the designer had to go to the Bronx Zoo in New York City to find a buffalo.

Dawes Severalty Act Legislation passed by Congress in 1887 that aimed to break up traditional Indian life by promoting individual land ownership. It divided tribal lands into small plots that were distributed among members of each tribe. Provisions were made for education and eventual citizenship. The law led to corruption and exploitation and weakened tribal culture.

BUFFALO HUNTING Huge buffalo herds grazing along railroads in the West frequently blocked passing trains. Passengers often killed for sport, shooting at the beasts with "no intention of using or removing the animal carcasses."

By 1900, only 250,000 Native Americans lived in the United States. (There had been 600,000 within the limits of the present-day United States in 1800, and more than 5 million in 1492, when Columbus first set foot in the New World.) Most of the Indians lived on reservations. Many lived in poverty. Alcoholism and unemployment were growing problems, and Native Americans, no longer able to live off the buffalo, became wards of the state. They lost their cultural distinctiveness. Once possessors of the entire continent, they had been crowded into smaller and smaller areas, overwhelmed by the demand to become settled, literate, and English-speaking. "Except for the internment of the West Coast Japanese during World War II," said historian Roger L. Nichols, "Indian removal is the only example of large-scale government-enforced migration in American history. For the Japanese, the move was temporary; for the Indians it was not."

Even as the Native Americans lost their identity, they entered the romantic folklore of the West. Dime novels, snapped up by readers young and old, told tales of Indian fighting on the Plains. "Buffalo Bill" Cody turned it all into a profitable business. Beginning in 1883, his Wild West Show played to millions of viewers in the United States, Canada, and Europe for more than three decades. It featured Plains Indians chasing buffalo, performing a war dance, and attacking a settler's cabin. In 1885, Sitting Bull himself, victor over Custer at the Battle of the Little Bighorn, performed in the show.

Quick Check

What events and measures ended tribal life?

Settlement of the West

17.3 Why did Americans and others move to the West?

Between 1870 and 1900, white—and some African, Hispanic, and Asian-Americans—settled the 430 million acres west of the Mississippi; they took over more land than Americans had occupied in all the years before 1870.

People moved west for many reasons. Some sought adventure; others wanted to escape the drab routine of factory or city life. Many moved to California for their health. The Mormons settled Utah to escape religious persecution. Others followed the mining camps, the advancing railroads, and the farming and cattle frontier.

Whatever the specific reason, most people moved west to better their lot. On the whole, their timing was good, for as the nation's population grew, so did demand for the livestock and the agricultural, mineral, and lumber products of the expanding West. Contrary to older historical views, the West did not act as a major "safety valve," an outlet for social and economic tensions. The poor and unemployed could not afford to move there and establish farms.

Men and Women on the Overland Trail

The first movement west aimed not for the nearby Plains but for California and Oregon on the continent's far shore. It started in the **Gold Rush of 1849**, and in the next three decades, perhaps 500,000 people made the long journey over the **Overland Trail**, a network of trails leading west. Some walked; others rode horses alone or in small groups. About half joined great caravans, numbering 150 wagons or more, that inched across the 2000 miles between the Missouri River and the Pacific coast.

More often than not, men made the decision to make the crossing, but, except for the stampedes to the mines, migration was usually a family affair. Wives were consulted, though in some cases they had little choice. They could either go along or live alone at home. While many women regretted leaving family and friends,

Gold Rush of 1849 Prospectors made the first gold strikes along the Sierra Nevada Mountains in California in 1849, touching off a mining boom that set the pattern for subsequent strikes in other regions.

Overland Trail The route from the Mississippi Valley to the Pacific Coast in the last half of the nineteenth century.

they agreed to the trip, sometimes as eagerly as the men. Most people traveled in family groups, including in-laws, grandchildren, aunts, and uncles. As one historian has said, "The quest for something new would take place in the context of the very familiar."

Individuals and wagon trains set out from points along the Missouri River. During April, travelers assembled in camp just across the Missouri River, waiting for the new grass to ripen into forage. They packed and repacked the wagons and elected the trains' leaders, who would set the line of march, look for water and campsites, and impose discipline. Some trains adopted detailed rules, fearing a lapse into savagery in the wild lands across the Missouri. "Every man to carry with him a Bible and other religious books, as we hope not to degenerate into a state of barbarism," one agreement said.

Setting out in early May, travelers divided the route into manageable portions. The first leg of the journey followed the Platte River west to Fort Kearney in central Nebraska Territory, a distance of about 300 miles. From a distance, the white-topped wagons seemed driven by a common force, but, in fact, internal discipline broke down almost immediately. Arguments erupted over the pace of the march, the choice of campsites, the number of guards to post, whether to rest or push on. Elected leaders quit; new ones were chosen. Every train was filled with individualists, and as the son of one train captain said, "If you think it's any snap to run a wagon train of 66 wagons with every man in the train having a different idea of what is the best thing to do, all I can say is that some day you ought to try it."

Men, women, and children had different tasks on the trail. Men concerned themselves almost entirely with hunting, guard duty, and transportation. They rose at 4 A.M. to hitch the wagons, and after breakfast began the day's march. At noon, they stopped and set the teams to graze. After the midday meal, the march continued until sunset. Then, while the men relaxed, the women fixed dinner and the next day's lunch, and the children kindled the fires, fetched water, and searched for wood or other fuel. Walking 15 miles a day, in searing heat and mountain cold, travelers were exhausted by late afternoon.

For women, the trail was lonely, and they worked to exhaustion. Some adjusted their clothing to the harsh conditions, adopting the new bloomer pants, shortening their skirts, or wearing "wash dresses"—so called because they had shorter hemlines that did not drag on the wet ground on washday. Other women continued to wear their long dresses, thinking bloomers "indecent." Both men and women carried firearms in case of Indian attacks, but most emigrants saw few Indians en route.

What they often did see was trash, miles of it, for the wagon trains were an early example of the impact of migration and settlement on the western environment. On the Oregon and other trails, travelers sidestepped mounds of garbage, tin cans, furniture, cooking stoves, kegs, tools, and clothing discarded by people who had passed through before.

The first stage of the journey was deceptively easy, and travelers usually reached Fort Kearney by late May. The second leg led another 300 miles up the Platte River to Fort Laramie on the eastern edge of Wyoming Territory. The heat of June had dried the grass, and there was no wood. Anxious to beat the early snowfalls, travelers rested a day or two at the fort, then hurried on to South Pass, 280 miles to the west, the best route through the forbidding Rockies. It was now mid-July, but the mountain nights were so cold that ice formed in the water buckets.

Beyond South Pass, some emigrants turned south to the Mormon settlements on the Great Salt Lake, but most headed 340 miles north to Fort Hall on the Snake River in Idaho. It took another three months to cover the remaining 800 miles. California-bound travelers followed the Humboldt River through the summer heat of Nevada. Well into September, they began the final arduous push: first, a 55-mile stretch of desert; then 70 difficult miles up the eastern slopes of the Sierra Nevada, laboriously hoisting wagons over massive outcrops of rock; and finally the last 100 miles down the western slopes to the welcome sight of California's Central Valley in October.

Under the best conditions the trip took six months, 16 hours a day, dawn to dusk, of grueling labor. Walking halfway across the continent was no easy task, a never-to-be-forgotten experience for those who did it. The wagon trains, carrying the dreams of thousands of individuals, reproduced society in small focus: individualistic, hopeful, mobile, divided by age and gender roles, apprehensive, yet willing to strike out for the distant and new.

Quick Check

What was life like on the Overland Trail?

Land for the Taking

As railroads pushed west in the 1870s and 1880s, locomotive trains replaced wagon trains, but the shift was gradual, and until the end of the century, emigrants often combined both modes of travel. Early railroad transportation was expensive, and the average farm family could not afford to buy tickets and ship supplies. Many Europeans traveled by rail to designated outfitting places and then proceeded west with wagons and oxen.

Traffic flowed in all directions, belying the image of a simple "westward" movement. Many people did go west, of course, but others, such as migrants from Mexico, became westerners by moving north, and Asian Americans moved eastward from the Pacific coast. Whatever their route, they all ended up in the meeting ground of cultures that formed the modern West.

Why did they come? "The motive that induced us to part with the pleasant associations and the dear friends of our childhood days," explained Phoebe Judson, an early emigrant, "was to obtain from the government of the United States a grant of land that 'Uncle Sam' had promised to give to the head of each family who settled in this new country." A popular camp song reflected the same motive:

Come along, come along—don't be alarmed,
Uncle Sam is rich enough to give us all a farm.

Read the Document   **Homestead Act of 1862**

HOMESTEAD ACT Between 1862 and 1890, the government gave away 48 million acres under the Homestead Act of 1862. A law of great significance, it gave 160 acres of land to anyone who would pay a $10 registration fee and pledge to live on the land, cultivating it for five years.

Uncle Sam owned about one billion acres of land in the 1860s, much of it mountain and desert unsuited for agriculture. By 1900, land laws had distributed half of it. Between 1862 and 1890, the government gave away 48 million acres to western farmers, sold about 100 million acres to private citizens and corporations, granted 128 million acres to railroad companies to tempt them to build across the unsettled West, and sold huge tracts to the states.

The **Homestead Act of 1862** gave 160 acres of land to anyone who would pay a $10 registration fee and pledge to live on the land and cultivate it for five years. The offer set off a mass migration of land-hungry Europeans, dazzled by a country that gave its land away. Americans also seized on the act's provisions, and between 1862 and 1900, nearly 600,000 families claimed free homesteads under it.

Yet the Homestead Act did not work as Congress had hoped. Few farmers and laborers had the cash to move to the frontier, buy farm equipment, and wait out the year or two before the farm became self-supporting. Tailored to the timber and water conditions of the East, the act worked less well in the semiarid West. In the fertile valleys of the Mississippi, 160 acres provided a generous farm. A farmer on the Great Plains needed either a larger farm for dry farming or a smaller one for irrigation.

Speculators made ingenious use of the land laws. Sending agents in advance of settlement, they moved along choice river bottoms or irrigable areas, accumulating large holdings to be held for high prices. In the arid West, where control of water meant control of the surrounding land, shrewd ranchers plotted their holdings accordingly. In Colorado, one cattleman, John F. Iliff, owned only 105 small parcels of land, but by placing them around the few water holes, he effectively dominated a 6000-square-mile empire.

Water, in fact, became a dominant issue, since much of the trans-Mississippi West received less than 20 inches of rainfall annually. People speculated in water as if it were gold and planned great irrigation systems in Utah, eastern Colorado, and California's Central Valley to "make the desert bloom."

Irrigators received a major boost in 1902 when the **National Reclamation Act (Newlands Act)** set aside most of the proceeds from the sale of public lands in 16 western states to finance irrigation projects in the arid states. Dams, canals, and irrigation systems channeled water into dry areas, creating a "hydraulic" society that was rich in crops and cities (such as Los Angeles and Phoenix), but ever thirstier and in danger of outrunning the precious water on which it all depended.

As beneficiaries of government land grants for railway construction, the railroad companies were the West's largest landowners. Eager to have immigrants settle on the land they owned near the railroad right-of-way, and eager to boost their freight and passenger business, the companies sent agents to the East and Europe.

In all, half a billion acres of western land were given or sold to speculators and corporations. Only 600,000 homestead patents were issued, covering 80 million acres. Thus, only one acre in every nine grants initially went to individual pioneers, the intended beneficiaries of the nation's largesse. Two-thirds of all homestead claimants before 1890 failed to farm their new land.

The Spanish-Speaking Southwest

In the nineteenth century, almost all Spanish-speaking people in the United States lived in California, Arizona, New Mexico, Texas, and Colorado. Their numbers were small—California had only 8086 Mexican residents in 1900—but the influence of their culture and institutions was large. In some respects, the southwestern frontier was more Spanish American than Anglo American.

Pushing north from Mexico, the Spanish gradually established the present-day economic structure of the Southwest. They brought with them techniques of mining, stock raising, and irrigated farming. After winning independence in the 1820s, the

Mexicans brought new laws and ranching methods as well as chaps and the burro. Both Spanish and Mexicans created the legal framework for distributing land and water. They gave large grants of land to communities for grazing, to individuals as rewards for service, and to the Native American pueblos.

In southern California, the Californios, descendants of the original colonizers, began after the 1860s to lose their vast landholdings to drought and mortgages. As they died out, Mexican Americans continued the Spanish–Mexican influence. In 1880, one-fourth of the residents of Los Angeles County were Spanish speaking.

Throughout the Southwest, the Spanish–Mexican heritage shaped society. Men headed the families and dominated economic life. Women had substantial economic rights (though few political ones) and enjoyed a status their English American counterparts lacked. Wives kept full control of property acquired before their marriage and held half title to all property in a marriage, which later caused many southwestern states to pass community property laws.

The Spanish–Mexican heritage also fostered a modified economic caste system, a strong Roman Catholic influence, and the Spanish language. Continuous immigration from Mexico kept language and cultural ties strong. Spanish names and customs spread, even among Anglos. David Starr Jordan, arriving from Indiana in 1891 to become the first president of Stanford University in California, bestowed Spanish names on streets, houses, and a dormitory. Spanish was the region's first or second language. Confronted by Sheriff Pat Garrett in 1881 in a darkened room, New Mexico's famous outlaw Billy the Kid died asking, "Quién es? Quién es?" ("Who is it? Who is it?").

Quick Check

In what ways did the Spanish–Mexican heritage of the Southwest shape its development?

The Bonanza West

17.4   Why was the West a bonanza of dreams and get-rich-quick schemes?

Between 1850 and 1900, waves of newcomers swept across the trans-Mississippi West. There were riches for the taking, hidden in gold-washed streams, spread lushly over grass-covered prairies, or in the gullible minds of greedy newcomers. The nineteenth-century West took shape in the search for mining, cattle, and land bonanzas that drew eager settlers from around the world.

As with all bonanzas, the consequences in the West were uneven growth, boom-and-bust economic cycles, and wasted resources. Society seemed constantly in the making. People moved here and there, following river bottoms, gold strikes, railroad tracks, and other opportunities. "Instant cities" arose. San Francisco, Salt Lake City, and Denver were the most spectacular examples, but every cow town and mining camp witnessed similar spurts of growth. Boston needed more than two centuries to attract 300,000 people; San Francisco did the same in a little more than 20 years.

Many westerners had left home to get rich quickly, and they adopted institutions that reflected that goal. The West was an idea as well as a region, and the idea molded westerners as much as they molded it.

The Mining Bonanza

Mining was the first important magnet to attract people to the West. Many hoped to "strike it rich" in gold and silver, but at least half the newcomers had no intention of working in the mines. Instead, they provided food, clothing, and services to the thousands of miners.

�֎ Explore the New Economy of the West, 1850–1893 on MyHistoryLab

WHAT NEW ECONOMIC PATTERNS EMERGED IN THE WEST?

The second half of the 1800s brought quick expansion of the United States into the West. Railroads quickly spread across the region which created a giant national marketplace that stretched from coast to coast. The federal government established post offices through the West to help further connect the nation. Settlers streamed from the East in search of cheap land on which to raise their crops and livestock. Around railroad hubs, cities emerged to which farmers brought their agricultural products to be sold and often shipped off to the East and elsewhere to be sold as the West became an important agricultural region of the United States.

MOVING WEST This patriotic lithograph, titled "Across the Continent – Westward the Course of Empire Takes Its Way," represents the expansion into the American West made possible by the nation's first transcontinental railway, which was completed in 1869.

GROWING POPULATION IN THE WEST

	1860	1890
Montana	N/A	142,924
Idaho	N/A	88,548
Wyoming	N/A	62,555
Colorado	34,277	413,249
New Mexico	93,516	160,282
Arizona	N/A	88,243
Utah	40,273	210,779
Nevada	6,857	47,355
Washington	11,594	357,232
Oregon	52,465	317,704
California	379,994	1,213,398

SOURCE: "United States Resident Population by State", http://lwd.dol.state.nj.us/labor/lpa/census/1990/poptrd1.htm.

KEY QUESTIONS Use **MyHistoryLab** *Explorer* to answer these **questions:**

Cause ▶▶▶ *How did railroad expansion shape population growth in the West?*

Map the growth of the railroad network and the development of western towns and cities.

Analysis ▶▶▶ *How did western agriculture develop during the late 1800s?*

Map the importance of agricultural commodities produced in the West.

Response ▶▶▶ *How did the federal government's presence manifest itself as settlers moved west?*

Trace the spread of post offices.

The California Gold Rush of 1849 set the pattern for subsequent mining booms. Individual prospectors made the first strikes, discovering gold along streams flowing westward from the Sierra Nevada. To get the gold, they used **placer mining**, which required little skill, technology, or capital. A placer miner needed only a shovel, a washing pan, and a good claim. As the placers gave out, much gold remained, but it was locked in quartz or buried deep in the earth. Mining became an expensive business, far beyond the reach of the average miner.

Large corporations moved in to dig the deep shafts and finance costly equipment. Quartz mining required heavy rock crushers, mercury vats to dissolve the gold, and large retorts to recapture it. Eastern and European financiers took control, labor became unionized, and mining towns took on some of the characteristics of the industrial city. Individual prospectors meanwhile dashed on to the next find. Unlike other frontiers, the mining frontier moved from west to east, as the original California miners—the "yonder-siders"—hurried eastward in search of the big strike.

In 1859, fresh strikes near Pikes Peak in Colorado and in the Carson River Valley of Nevada set off wild migrations—100,000 miners were in Pikes Peak country by June 1859. The gold there quickly played out, but the Nevada find uncovered a thick bluish black ore that was almost pure silver and gold. A quick-witted drifter named Henry T. P. Comstock talked his way into partnership in the claim, and word of the **Comstock Lode**—a fabulous mine with ore worth $3,876 a ton—flashed over the mountains.

Thousands of miners climbed the Sierra Nevada that summer; but the biggest strike was yet to come. In 1873, John W. Mackay and three partners formed a company to dig deep into the mountain, and at 1167 feet they hit the Big Bonanza, a seam of gold and silver more than 54 feet wide. It was the richest discovery in the history of mining. Between 1859 and 1879, the Comstock Lode produced gold and silver worth $306 million. Most of it went to financiers and corporations. Mackay became the richest person in the world.

In the 1860s and 1870s, important strikes were made in Washington, Idaho, Nevada, Colorado, Montana, Arizona, and Dakota. Miners flocked from strike to strike, and new camps and mining towns sprang up overnight (see Map 17.3).

The final fling came in the Black Hills rush of 1874 to 1876. The army had tried to keep miners out of the area, the heart of the Sioux hunting grounds, and even sent a scientific party under Colonel George Armstrong Custer to disprove the rumors of gold and stop the miners' invasion. Instead, Custer found gold all over the hills, and the rush was on. Miners, gamblers, desperadoes, and prostitutes flocked to Deadwood, the most lawless of all the mining camps. There, Martha Jane Canary—a crack shot who, as Calamity Jane, won fame as a scout and teamster—fell in love with "Wild Bill" Hickok. Hickok himself—a western legend who had tamed Kansas cow towns, killed an unknown number of men, and toured in Buffalo Bill's Wild West Show—died in Deadwood, shot in the back of the head. He was 39 years old.

17.1

17.2

17.3

17.4

placer mining Mining that included using a shovel and washing pan to separate gold from the ore in streams and riverbeds. Placer miners worked as individuals or in small groups.

Comstock Lode Discovered in 1859 near Virginia City, Nevada, this ore deposit was the richest discovery in the history of mining. Named after T. P. Comstock, the deposit produced silver and gold worth more than $306 million.

Read the Document   John Lester, "Hydraulic Mining" (1873)

MAP 17.3 **MINING REGIONS OF THE WEST** Gold and silver mines dotted the West, drawing settlers and encouraging political organization.

393

Towns such as Deadwood, in the Dakota Territory; Virginia City, Nevada; Leadville, Colorado; and Tombstone, Arizona, demonstrated a new development process in the frontier experience. The farming frontier had developed naturally in a rural setting. On the mining frontier, the germ of a city—the camp—appeared almost simultaneously with the first "strike." Periodicals, the latest fashions, theaters, schools, literary clubs, and lending libraries came quickly to the camps, providing civilized refinements not available on other frontiers. Urbanization also created the need for municipal government, sanitation, and law enforcement.

A simple democracy governed mining camps. Soon after a strike, the miners organized a mining "district" and adopted rules governing behavior in it. Rules regulated the size and boundaries of claims, established procedures for settling disputes, and set penalties for crimes. Petty criminals were banished; serious offenders were hanged. For a major dispute, the whole camp gathered, chose legal counsel for both sides, and heard the evidence. If all else failed, miners formed secret vigilance committees to hang a few offenders as a lesson to the rest. Early visitors to the mining country were struck by how miners, solitary and competitive, joined together, founded a camp, and created a society.

The camps were mostly male, made up of "men who can rough it" and a few "ladies of spirit and energy." In 1870, men outnumbered women in the mining districts by more than two to one; there were few children. Prostitutes followed the camps around the West, and a "respectable" woman was a curiosity. Some women worked claims, but more often they took jobs as cooks, housekeepers, and seamstresses—for wages considerably higher than in the East.

In most camps, between one-quarter and one-half of the population was foreign born. The lure of gold drew many Chinese, Chileans, Peruvians, Mexicans, French, Germans, and English. Experienced miners, the Latin Americans brought valuable mining techniques. At least 6000 Mexicans joined the California rush of 1849, and by 1852, there were 25,000 Chinese in California. Painstakingly, the Chinese profitably worked claims others had abandoned. In the 1860s, almost one-third of the miners in the West were Chinese.

Hostility often surfaced against foreign miners, particularly the French, Latin Americans, and Chinese. Riots against Chinese laborers occurred in the 1870s and 1880s in Los Angeles, San Francisco, Seattle, Reno, and Denver. Responding to pressure, Congress passed the **Chinese Exclusion Act of 1882**, which suspended immigration of Chinese laborers for ten years. The number of Chinese in the United States fell drastically.

By the 1890s, the early mining bonanza was over. All told, the western mines contributed billions of dollars to the economy. They had helped finance the Civil War and industrialization. The vast boost in silver production from the Comstock Lode changed the relative value of gold and silver, the base of American currency. Disputes over the currency affected politics and led to the famous "battle of the standards" in the presidential election of 1896 (see Chapter 20).

The mining frontier populated portions of the West and sped up its political organization. Nevada, Idaho, and Montana were granted early statehood because of mining. Merchants, editors, lawyers, and ministers moved with the advancing frontier, establishing permanent settlements. Women in the mining camps helped foster family life and raised the moral tone by campaigning against drinking, gambling, and prostitution. But the industry also left painful scars in the form of invaded Indian reservations, pitted hills, and ghost towns.

Chinese Exclusion Act of 1882 Legislation passed in 1882 that excluded Chinese immigrants for ten years and denied U.S. citizenship to Chinese nationals. It was the first U.S. exclusionary law aimed at a specific racial group.

Quick Check

What were the characteristics of the mining industry?

The Cattle Bonanza

"There's gold from the grass roots down," said California Joe, a guide in the gold districts of Dakota in the 1870s, "but there's more gold from the grass roots up." Ranchers began to recognize the potential of the vast western grasslands. The Plains

CHARLES M. RUSSELL, COWBOY CAMP DURING ROUNDUP, C. 1885–1887 Artist Charles Russell here documents the cowboys' activities during the annual spring roundup. Before setting off on the long trek to drive cattle to market, the cowboys had to rope and break in horses that might have gone wild over the winter.

were covered with buffalo or grama grass, a wiry variety with short, hard stems. Cattle thrived on it.

For 20 years after 1865, cattle ranching dominated the "open range," a vast fenceless area from the Texas Panhandle north into Canada. The techniques of the business came from Mexico. Long before American cowboys moved herds north, their Mexican counterparts, the *vaqueros*, developed the essential techniques of branding, roundups, and roping. The cattle themselves, the famous Texas longhorns, also came from Mexico. Spreading over the grasslands of southern Texas, the longhorns multiplied rapidly. Although their meat was coarse and stringy, they fed a nation hungry for beef at the end of the Civil War.

The problem was getting the beef to eastern markets, and Joseph G. McCoy, a livestock shipper from Illinois, solved it. To market Texas beef, McCoy conceived the idea of taking the cattle to railheads in Kansas. He talked first with the president of the Missouri Pacific, who ordered him out of his office, and then with the head of the Kansas Pacific, who laughed at the idea. McCoy finally signed a contract in 1867 with the Hannibal and St. Joseph Railroad. Searching for an appropriate rail junction, he settled on the sleepy Kansas town of Abilene, "a very small, dead place," he remembered, with about a dozen log huts and one nearly bankrupt saloon.

In September 1867, McCoy shipped the first 20 cars of longhorn cattle. By the end of the year, 1000 carloads had followed, all headed for Chicago markets. In 1870, 300,000 head of Texas cattle reached Abilene, followed the next year—the peak year— by 700,000 head. The Alamo Saloon, crowded with tired cowboys at the end of the drive, employed 75 bartenders, working three eight-hour shifts.

The profits were enormous. Drivers bought cheap Texas steers for $4 a head and sold them for $30 or $40 a head at the northern railhead. The most famous trail, the Chisholm, ran from southern Texas through Oklahoma Territory to Ellsworth and Abilene, Kansas, on the Kansas Pacific Railroad. Dodge City, Kansas, became the prime shipping center between 1875 and 1879 (see Map 17.4).

MAP 17.4 CATTLE TRAILS Cattle raised in Texas were driven along the cattle trails to the northern railheads where trains carried them to market.

Cowboys pushed steers northward in herds of 2000–3000. Novels and films have portrayed the cowboys as white, but at least a quarter of them were black, and possibly another quarter were Mexicans. A typical crew on the trail north might have eight men, half of them black or Mexican. Most of the trail bosses were white; they earned about $125 a month.

Like miners, cattlemen lived beyond the formal reach of the law. So they established their own. Before each drive, Charles Goodnight drew up rules governing behavior on the trail. A cowboy who shot another was hanged on the spot. Ranchers adopted rules for cattle ownership, branding, roundups, and drives, and they formed associations to enforce them. The Wyoming Stock Growers' Association, the largest and most formidable, had 400 members owning 2 million cattle; its reach extended into Colorado, Nebraska, Montana, and the Dakotas. Throughout this vast territory, the "laws" of the association were often the law of the land.

By 1880, more than 6 million cattle had been driven to northern markets. But the era of the great cattle drive was ending. Farmers were planting wheat on the old buffalo ranges; barbed wire, a recent invention, cut across the trails and divided up the big ranches. Mechanical improvements in slaughtering, refrigerated transportation, and cold storage modernized the industry. Ranchers bred the Texas longhorns with heavier Hereford and Angus bulls, and as the new breeds proved profitable, more and more ranches opened on the northern ranges. Stories of vast profits attracted outside capital. Large investments transformed ranching into big business, often controlled by absentee owners and subject to new problems.

By 1885, however, experienced cattle ranchers were growing alarmed. The winter of 1885–1886 was cold, and the following summer was one of the hottest on record. Water holes dried up; the grass turned brown. Beef prices fell.

The winter of 1886–1887 was one of the worst in western history. Temperatures dropped to 45 degrees below zero, and cattle that once would have saved themselves by drifting ahead of the storms came up against the new barbed wire fences. Herds jammed together, pawing the frozen ground or stripping bark from trees in search of food. Tens of thousands of cattle died. In the spring of 1887, when the snows thawed, ranchers found carcasses piled up against the fences.

The melting snows did, however, produce lush grass for the survivors. The cattle business recovered, but it took different directions. Outside capital, so plentiful in the boom years, dried up. Ranchers began fencing their lands, reducing their herds, and growing hay for winter food.

The last roundup on the northern ranges took place in 1905. Ranches grew smaller, and some ranchers, at first in the scrub country of the Southwest, then on the Plains themselves, switched to raising sheep. By 1900, there were nearly 38 million sheep west of the Missouri River, far more than there were cattle.

Ranchers and sheepherders fought to control the grazing lands, but they had one problem in common: The day of the open range was over. Homesteaders, armed with barbed wire and new strains of wheat, were pushing onto the Plains.

Quick Check

What characterized the growth of the cattle business in these years?

The Farming Bonanza

Like miners and cattle ranchers, millions of farmers moved into the West after 1870 to seek crop bonanzas and new ways of life. Some realized their dreams; many fought just to survive.

Between 1870 and 1900, farmers cultivated more land than ever before in American history. They peopled the Plains from the Dakotas to Texas, pushed the Indians out of their last sanctuary in Oklahoma, and poured into the basins and foothills of the Rockies. By 1900, the western half of the nation contained almost 30 percent of the population, compared to less than 1 percent in 1850.

Unlike mining, farm settlement often followed predictable patterns, taking population from states east of the settlement line and moving westward. Crossing the Mississippi, farmers settled first in western Iowa, Minnesota, Nebraska, Kansas, Texas, and South Dakota. The movement slumped during the depression of the 1870s, but then a new wave of optimism carried thousands more west. Years of above-average rainfall convinced farmers that the Dakotas, western Nebraska and Kansas, and eastern Colorado were the "rain belt of the Plains." Between 1870 and 1900, the population on the Plains tripled.

Some newcomers were blacks who had fled the South, fed up with beatings and murders, crop liens, and the Black Codes that institutionalized their subordination. In 1879, about 6000 African Americans known as the **Exodusters** left Louisiana, Mississippi, and Texas to establish new and freer lives in Kansas, the home of John Brown and the Free-Soil campaigns of the 1850s. Once there, they farmed or worked as laborers; women worked in the fields alongside the men or cleaned houses and took in washing to make ends meet. All told, the Exodusters homesteaded 20,000 acres of land, and though they met prejudice, it was less extreme than they had known in the South.

Other African Americans moved to Oklahoma, thinking they might establish the first African American state. Whether headed for Oklahoma or Kansas, they picked up and moved in sizable groups based on family units; they took with them the customs

Exodusters A group of about 6000 African Americans who left Louisiana, Mississippi, and Texas in 1879, for freer lives as farmers or laborers in Kansas.

they had known, and in their new homes, they were able, for the first time, to enjoy some measure of self-government.

For blacks and whites alike, farming on the Plains presented new problems. There was little surface water, and wells ranged between 50 and 500 feet deep. Well drillers charged up to $2 a foot. Taking advantage of the steady Plains winds, windmills brought the water to the surface, but they too were expensive, and until 1900, many farmers could not afford them. Lumber for homes and fences was also scarce.

Unable to afford wood, farmers often started out in dreary sod houses. Cut into 3-foot sections, the thick prairie sod was laid like brick, with space for two windows and a door. Since glass was scarce, cloth covered the windows; a blanket was hung from the ceiling to make two rooms. Sod houses were small, provided little light and air, and were impossible to keep clean. Rain water seeped through the roof. But a sod house cost only $2.78 to build.

Outside, the Plains environment tested the men and women who moved there. In the winters, savage storms swept the open grasslands. Ice caked on the cattle until their heads were too heavy to hold up. Summer temperatures stayed near 110 degrees for weeks. Fearsome rainstorms, building in the heat, beat down the young corn and wheat. Summers also brought grasshoppers in clouds so huge they shut out the sun. The grasshoppers ate everything in sight: crops, clothing, mosquito netting, tree bark, even plow handles. In 1874, they ate everything on the Plains "but the mortgage," as one farmer said, from Texas to the Dakotas.

Farmers adopted new techniques to meet these conditions. Most importantly, they needed cheap and effective fencing material, and in 1874, Joseph F. Glidden, a farmer from De Kalb, Illinois, provided it with the invention of barbed wire. By 1883, his factory was turning out 600 miles of barbed wire every day, and farmers were buying it faster than it could be produced. Barbed wire fences helped them pen their own stock in and keep other animals out.

Discontent on the Farm

Touring the farming areas in the 1860s, Oliver H. Kelley, a clerk in the U.S. Department of Agriculture, was struck by the drabness of rural life. In 1867, he founded the **National Grange of the Patrons of Husbandry**, known simply as the Grange. The Grange provided social, cultural, and educational activities for its members. Its constitution banned involvement in politics, but Grangers often ignored the rules and supported railroad regulation and other measures.

The Grange grew rapidly during the depression of the 1870s, and by 1875, it had more than 800,000 members in 20,000 local Granges. Most were in the Midwest and South. The Granges set up cooperative stores, grain elevators, warehouses, insurance companies, and farm machinery factories. Many of these failed, but the organization made its mark. Picking up where the Grange left off, groups such as the Farmers' Alliance, with branches in both the South and West, attracted followers.

Like the cattle boom, the farming boom ended abruptly after 1887. A severe drought that year cut harvests, and more droughts in 1889 and 1894 wiped out thousands of new farmers on the western Plains. Between 1888 and 1892, more than half the population of western Kansas left. Angry and restless farmers complained about declining crop prices, rising railroad rates, and heavy mortgages.

Although many farmers were unhappy, the peopling of the West in those years transformed American agriculture. The states beyond the Mississippi became the nation's garden. California sent fruit, wine, and wheat to eastern markets. Under the Mormons, Utah flourished with irrigation. Texas beef stocked the country's tables, and vast wheat fields, stretching to the horizon, covered Minnesota, the

Quick Check

What was farming like on the Plains?

National Grange of the Patrons of Husbandry Founded by Oliver H. Kelly in 1867, the Grange sought to relieve the drabness of farm life by providing a social, educational, and cultural outlet for its members. It also set up grain elevators, cooperative stores, warehouses, insurance companies, and farm machinery factories.

Dakotas, Montana, and eastern Colorado. All produced more than Americans could consume. By 1890, American farmers were exporting large amounts of wheat and other crops.

Farmers became more commercial and scientific. They needed to know more and work harder. Mail-order houses and rural free delivery diminished their isolation and tied them ever closer to the national future. "This is a new age to the farmer," said a statistician in the Department of Agriculture in 1889. "He is now, more than ever before, a citizen of the world."

17.1
17.2
17.3
17.4

Quick Check

Why were so many farmers unhappy in the last decades of the nineteenth century, and what did they try to do about it?

The Final Fling

As the West filled in with people, pressure mounted to open the last Indian territory, Oklahoma, to settlers. In March 1889, Congress forced the Creek and Seminole tribes, which had been moved into Oklahoma in the 1820s, to surrender their rights to the land. President Benjamin Harrison announced the opening of the Oklahoma District as of noon, April 22, 1889.

On the morning of April 22, nearly 100,000 people lined the Oklahoma borders. At noon, the starting flag dropped. Bugles and cannon signaled the opening of the "last" territory. Horsemen lunged forward; overloaded wagons collided and overturned. By sunset, settlers claimed 12,000 homesteads, and the 1.92 million acres of the Oklahoma District were officially settled. The "Boomers" (those who waited for the signal) and "Sooners" (those who had jumped the gun) reflected the speed of western settlement. "Creation!" a character in Edna Ferber's novel *Cimarron* declared. "Hell! That took six days. This was done in one. It was History made in an hour—and I helped make it."

Quick Check

Who were the "Boomers," and Who were the "Sooners"?

Conclusion: The Meaning of the West

Between the Civil War and 1900, the West witnessed one of the greatest migrations in history. With the Native Americans driven into smaller and smaller areas, farms, ranches, mines, and cities took over the vast lands from the Mississippi to the Pacific. The 1890 census noted that for the first time in American history, "there can hardly be said to be a frontier line." Picking up the theme, Frederick Jackson Turner, a young historian at the University of Wisconsin, examined its importance in an influential 1893 paper, "The Significance of the Frontier in American History."

"The existence of an area of free land," Turner wrote, "its continuous recession, and the advance of American settlement westward, explain American development." It shaped customs and character; gave rise to independence, self-confidence, and individualism; and fostered invention and adaptation. Historians have modified **Turner's thesis** by pointing to frontier conservatism and imitativeness, the influence of racial groups, and the persistence of European ideas and institutions. Most recently, they have shown that family and community loomed as large as individualism on the frontier; men, women, and children played much the same roles as they had back home.

Rejecting Turner almost completely, a group of "new Western historians" has advanced a different and complex view of the West, and one with few heroes and heroines. Emphasizing the region's racial and ethnic diversity, these historians stress the role of women as well as men, trace struggles between economic interests instead of fights between gunslingers, and question the impact of development on the environment. White English-speaking Americans, they suggest, could be said to have conquered the West rather than settled it.

The West, in this view, was not settled by a wave of white migrants moving west across the continent (Turner's "frontier") but by a set of waves—Anglo, Mexican

Turner's thesis Put forth by historian Frederick Jackson Turner in 1893, this thesis asserted that the existence of a frontier and its settlement had shaped American character; given rise to individualism, independence, and self-confidence; and fostered the American spirit of invention and adaptation. Later historians modified the thesis by pointing out the environmental and other consequences of frontier settlement, the federal government's role in peopling the West, and the clash of races and cultures that took place on the frontier.

Read the Document The Significance of the Frontier in American History (1893)

FREDERICK JACKSON TURNER During a gathering of historians at the World's Columbian Exhibition in Chicago in 1893, Frederick Jackson Turner presented an essay titled "The Significance of the Frontier in American History." Turner's article, also known as the Frontier Thesis, argued that the settlement of the frontier made the American nation unique. Turner credited the frontier's settlement as the primary force in shaping the nation's democratic institutions.

American, African American, Asian American, and others—moving in many directions and interacting with each other and with Native American cultures to produce the modern West. Nor did western history end in 1890 as Turner would have it. Instead, migration, development, and economic exploitation continued into the twentieth and twenty-first centuries, illustrated by the fact that many more people moved to the West after 1900 than before.

In the nineteenth, twentieth, and twenty-first centuries, there can be no doubt that the image of the frontier and the West influenced American development. Western lands attracted European, Latin American, and Asian immigrants, adding to the society's talent and diversity. The mines, forests, and farms of the West fueled the economy, sent raw materials to eastern factories, and fed the growing cities. Though defeated in warfare, the Native Americans and Mexicans influenced art, architecture, law, and western folklore. The West was the first American empire, and it profoundly affected the American mind and imagination.

Chapter Review

Beyond the Frontier

17.1 What were the challenges of settling the country west of the Mississippi? p. 379

West of the Mississippi River, settlers encountered new conditions, including vast treeless plains and towering mountain ranges. Above all, they left behind the water and timber on which they had depended in the East, forcing them to devise new ways to deal with the different challenges.

Crushing the Native Americans

17.2 How did white Americans crush the culture of the Native Americans as they moved west? p. 380

Native Americans had a complex culture suited to the various environments in which they lived. The U.S. government and white settlers employed various methods—political, military, legal, and cultural—to oust the Indians from their lands, "civilize" them, and contain and control them.

Settlement of the West

17.3 Why did Americans and others move to the West? p. 387

Americans moved west for many reasons, including a desire to get rich, seek religious freedom, and improve health. The federal government helped out with generous land laws and laws favoring irrigation in the arid West. In the Southwest, a proud culture took shape around Spanish laws and customs, involving water, the rights of women, and the sale, ownership, and use of land.

The Bonanza West

17.4 Why was the West a bonanza of dreams and get-rich-quick schemes? p. 391

The West attracted many people seeking a better economic life. Many failed, but others found bonanzas in mining, cattle ranching, and farming. In many of these areas, western development paralleled trends in the rest of the nation: larger and larger businesses, new uses for technology, and the employment of outside capital.

Timeline

1849
Bonanza West—Gold Rush to California — 1849

1862 — **1862**
Settlement—Homestead Act encourages western settlement

1867
Beyond the Frontier—Horace Greeley urges easterners to "Go West, young man"; National Grange of the Patrons of Husbandry (the Grange) founded to enrich farmers' lives — 1867

1867–1868 — **1867–1868**
Native Americans—Policy of "small reservations" for Indians adopted

1876
Native Americans—Sioux defeat and kill Custer at Battle of the Little Bighorn, Montana (June) — 1876

1887 — **1887**
Native Americans—Dawes Severalty Act makes Indians individual landowners

1889
Settlement—Oklahoma Territory opened to settlement — 1889

1890 — **1890**
Native Americans—Teton Sioux massacred at Battle of Wounded Knee, South Dakota (December)

1893
Meaning of the West—Historian Frederick Jackson Turner analyzes closing of the frontier — 1893

1902 — **1902**
Settlement—National Reclamation Act (the Newlands Act)

18 The Industrial Society 1850–1901

A Machine Culture

I n 1876, Americans celebrated their first century of independence. Survivors of a recent civil war, they observed the centenary proudly and self-consciously, in song and speech, and above all in a grand Centennial Exposition held in Philadelphia, Pennsylvania.

Spread over hundreds of acres, the exposition occupied 180 buildings and attracted 9 million visitors, about one-fifth of the country's population. Significantly, it focused more on the present than the past. Fairgoers strolled through exhibits of life in colonial times, then hurried off to the main attractions: machines, inventions, and products of the new industrial era. They saw linoleum, a new, easy-to-clean floor covering made of linseed oil and canvas. For the first time, they tasted root beer, supplied by a young druggist named Charles Hires, and the exotic banana, wrapped in foil and selling for a dime. They saw their first bicycle, an awkward high-wheeled contraption with solid tires.

A Japanese pavilion generated widespread interest in that country's culture. A

LEARNING OBJECTIVES

18.1	18.2	18.3	18.4	18.5
What enabled the United States to build an industrial economy? p. 405	What were the main characteristics of the new steel and oil industries? p. 411	Why were the new methods of advertising so important? p. 417	Who were the wage earners in the new economy? p. 418	How did wage earners organize in this period, and what demands did they make? p. 421

THE CORLISS ENGINE A "mechanical marvel" at the Centennial Exposition of 1876, the Corliss engine was a prime example of the giantism the public admired.

SOURCE: Art Resource/The Metropolitan Museum of Art.

Listen to Chapter 18 on MyHistoryLab

👁 Watch the Video Series on MyHistoryLab

Learn about some key topics related to this chapter with the *MyHistoryLab Video Series: Key Topics in U.S. History.*

1 **The Transcontinental Railroad** This video surveys the construction and realization of the Transcontinental Railroad, which linked the Atlantic and Pacific coasts, as well as the enormous influences that railroads had on changing the life and economy of the United States in the nineteenth century.

👁 Watch on MyHistoryLab

The Gilded Men Robber Barons or Captains of Industry? In this video industrialists, financiers, and other capitalists of the late nineteenth century are profiled. Not only did these men build industrial empires and make the United States a dominant economic power, they consolidated wealth in ways never before seen in human history. **2**

Watch on MyHistoryLab 👁

3 **The Making of a Consumer Culture** This video looks at the Second Industrial Revolution and the consumer culture it brought with it. This included new gadgets, labor saving devices, ready-to-wear clothes, fast food, and many other conveniences. The new system of consumer credit and the many kinds of retail outlets, such department stores, dime stores, and mail order catalogs, are also examined.

👁 Watch on MyHistoryLab

Knights of Labor This video assesses the importance of the Knights of Labor, the first attempt to organize workers on a massive scale in the United States. Strikes and the disastrous Haymarket Riot Affair, however, doomed the Knights as many in American society came to see organized labor as dangerous and unpatriotic. **4**

Watch on MyHistoryLab 👁

women's building, the first one ever in a major exposition, displayed paintings and sculpture by women artists, and textile machinery staffed by female operators.

Machinery was the focus of the entire exposition, and Machinery Hall was the most popular building. Here were the products of an ever-improving civilization. Long lines waited to see the telephone, Alexander Graham Bell's new device. ("My God, it talks!" the emperor of Brazil exclaimed.) Thomas A. Edison displayed recent inventions, while nearby, machines turned out bricks, chewing tobacco, and other products. Fairgoers saw the first public display of the typewriter, Elisha Otis's new elevator, and the Westinghouse railroad air brake.

But above all, they crowded around the mighty Corliss engine, the exposition's focal point. A giant steam engine, its twin vertical cylinders towered almost four stories high, dwarfing everything else in Machinery Hall. Alone, it supplied power for the 8000 other machines, large and small, on the exposition grounds. Poorly designed, the Corliss was soon obsolete, but it captured the nation's imagination. It symbolized swift movement toward an industrial and urban society. John Greenleaf Whittier, the aging poet from rural New England, likened it to the snake in the biblical Garden of Eden and refused to see it.

As Whittier feared, the United States was fast becoming an industrial society. Developments earlier in the century laid the basis, but the most spectacular advances in industrialization came during the three decades after the Civil War. At the start of the war in 1861, the country lagged behind industrializing nations such as Britain, France, and Germany. By 1900, its manufacturing output exceeded that of its three European rivals combined. Over the same years, cities grew, technology advanced, and farm production rose. Developments in manufacturing, mining, agriculture, transportation, and communications changed society.

In this change, railroads, steel, oil, and other industries, all shaped by the hands of labor, played a leading role. Many Americans welcomed the new directions. The Corliss awed the novelist William Dean Howells when he visited the Exposition. Howells preferred the machine to the artworks on display: "It is in these things of iron and steel that the national genius most freely speaks."

Industrial Development

18.1   What enabled the United States to build an industrial economy?

American industry owed its remarkable growth to several considerations. It fed on an abundance of natural resources: coal, iron, timber, petroleum, waterpower. An iron manufacturer likened the nation to "a gigantic bowl filled with treasure." Labor was also abundant, drawn from American farm families and the European immigrants who flocked to American mines, cities, and factories. Nearly 8 million immigrants arrived in the 1870s and 1880s; another 15 million came between 1890 and 1914—large figures for a nation whose population in 1900 was about 76 million.

The burgeoning population led to expanded markets, which new devices such as the telegraph and telephone helped to exploit. The growing cities devoured goods, and the railroads linked the cities together and opened a national market. Within its boundaries, the United States had the largest free trade market in the world, while tariff barriers protected its producers from outside competition.

Expansive market and labor conditions buoyed the confidence of European and American investors, who provided large amounts of capital. Technological progress doomed some older industries (tallow, for example) but increased productivity in others (like kerosene), and created entirely new ones like electric lights. Inventions such as the harvester and the combine strengthened the agricultural base, on which industrialization depended.

Eager to promote economic growth, government at all levels—federal, state, and local—gave manufacturers money, land, and other resources. The American system of government also provided stability, commitment to private property, and, initially at least, a reluctance to regulate industry. Unlike their European counterparts, American manufacturers faced few legal or social barriers. Their main domestic rivals, the southern planters, had lost power in the Civil War.

In this atmosphere, entrepreneurs flourished. Taking steps crucial for industrialization, they organized, managed, and assumed the financial risks of the new enterprises. Admirers called them captains of industry; foes labeled them robber barons. To some degree, they were both—creative *and* acquisitive. If sometimes they seemed larger than life, it was because they dealt in concepts, distances, and quantities often unknown to earlier generations.

Industrial growth was not simple, steady, or inevitable. It involved human decisions and entailed social benefits and costs. Growth varied from industry to industry and from year to year. It was concentrated in the Northeast, where in 1890 more than 85 percent of America's manufactured goods originated. The more sparsely settled West provided raw materials. The South, although making gains in the manufacture of iron, textiles, and tobacco, had to rebuild after wartime devastation.

Still, industry developed quickly. Between 1865 and 1914, the real gross national product—the total monetary value of all goods and services produced in a year, with prices held stable—grew at more than 4 percent a year, increasing about eightfold overall. As Robert Higgs, an economic historian, noted, "Never before had such rapid growth continued for so long."

An Empire on Rails

Genuine revolutions are rare, but a major one occurred in the nineteenth century: a revolution in transportation and communications. When the century began, people traveled and communicated much as they had for centuries before; when it ended, the railroad, the telegraph, the telephone, and the steamship had wrought enormous changes.

The steamship sliced in half the time it took to cross the Atlantic and introduced new regularity in moving goods and passengers. The telegraph, flashing messages almost instantaneously along miles of wire (400,000 miles of it in the early 1880s), transformed communications, as did the telephone a little later. But the railroad worked the largest changes of all. Along with Bessemer steel, it was the century's most significant technical innovation.

Advantages of the Railroad

The railroad dramatically affected economic and social life. Economic growth would have occurred without it, of course; canals, inland steamboats, and the country's superb system of interior waterways already provided the outlines of an effective transportation network. But the railroad contributed advantages all its own.

Those advantages included more direct routes, greater speed, safety, and comfort than other modes of land travel, more dependable schedules, a larger volume of traffic, and year-round service. A day's travel on stagecoach or horseback might cover 50 miles. The railroad covered 50 miles in about an hour, 700 miles in a day. It went where canals and rivers did not go—directly to the loading platforms of factories or across the arid West. As construction crews pushed tracks onward, vast areas opened for settlement.

Consequently, American railroads differed from European ones. In Europe, railroads were usually built between cities and towns that already existed; they carried mostly the same goods that earlier forms of transportation had. American railroads did that and more: They often created the towns they then served. They carried cattle from Texas, fruit from Florida, and goods that had never been carried before.

Linking widely separated cities and villages, the railroad ended the relative isolation and self-sufficiency of the country's "island communities." It tied people together, brought in outside products, fostered interdependence, and encouraged economic specialization. The railroad made possible a national market and thus pointed the way toward mass production and mass consumption, two hallmarks of twentieth-century society. It also pointed the way toward business development.

A railroad corporation, far-flung and complex, was a new kind of business. It stretched over thousands of miles, employed thousands of people, dealt with countless customers, and required an unprecedented scale of organization and decision making. Railroad managers never met most of their customers or even many of their employees. This created new problems in marketing and labor relations. Year by year, railroad companies consumed large quantities of iron, steel, coal, lumber, and glass, stimulating growth and employment in numerous industries.

No wonder the railroad captured so completely the country's imagination. For nearly a hundred years—the railroad era lasted through the 1940s—children gathered at depots, paused in the fields to wave as the fast express flashed by, listened at night to far-off whistles, and wondered what lay down the tracks. They lived in a world grown smaller.

Quick Check

What advantages did the railroad have over earlier forms of transportation?

Building the Empire

When Robert E. Lee surrendered at Appomattox in 1865, the country already had 35,000 miles of track, and much of the railroad system east of the Mississippi was in place. Farther west, the rail network stood poised on the edge of settlement. Although the Civil War had reduced southern railroads to shambles, the United States had nearly as much railroad track as the rest of the world combined.

After the Civil War, rail construction boomed. From 35,000 miles in 1865, the network expanded to 193,000 miles in 1900—more than in all Europe, including Russia. Mileage peaked at 254,037 miles in 1916, just before the industry began its long decline into the mid-twentieth century (see Figure 18.1).

Building such an empire took vast amounts of capital. American and European investors provided some of the money; government supplied the rest. The federal government loaned nearly $65 million to a half dozen western railroads and donated millions of acres of the public domain.

Almost 90 percent of the federal land grants lay in 20 states west of the Mississippi. Federal land grants helped build 18,738 miles of track, less than 8 percent of the system. The land was frequently distant and difficult to market. Railroad companies sold it to raise cash, but more often they used it as security for bonds or loans.

Beyond doubt, the grants of cash and land promoted waste and corruption. The companies built fast and wastefully, eager to collect government subsidies for each mile of track they laid. The grants also enabled railroads to build into territories that the government had pledged to the Indians, thus contributing to the destruction of Indian life.

Yet the grants probably worked more benefits than evils. As Congress had hoped, the grants stimulated railroad building across the rugged, unsettled West, where the railroads' revenues would not repay their construction for years. Farmers, ranchers, and merchants poured into the newly opened areas, boosting the value of government-owned and private land. The grants seemed necessary in a nation that, unlike most of Europe, expected private enterprise to build the railroads. In return for government aid, Congress required the railroads to carry government freight, troops, and mail at reduced rates—saving the government almost $1 billion between 1850 and 1945. In no other cases of federal subsidies to carriers—canals, highways, and airlines—did Congress exact specific benefits in return.

Quick Check

How did the railroad empire grow?

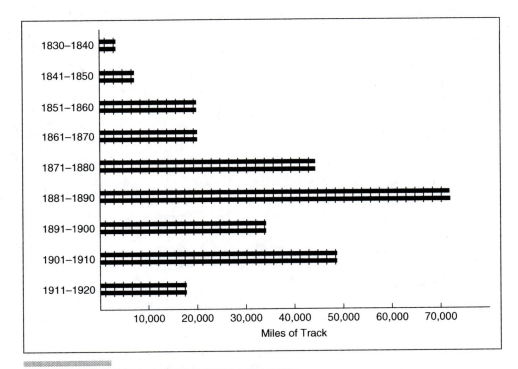

FIGURE 18.1 RAILROAD CONSTRUCTION, 1830–1920

SOURCE: U.S. Bureau of the Census, *Historical Statistics of the United States, Colonial Times to 1970*, Bicentennial Edition, Washington, D.C., 1975.

Linking the Nation via Trunk Lines

The early railroads may seem to have linked different regions, but in fact they did not. Built with little regard for through traffic, they were designed more to protect local interests than to tap outside markets. Many extended less than 50 miles. To avoid cooperating with other lines, they adopted conflicting schedules, built separate depots, and, above all, used different gauges. Gauges, the distance between the rails, ranged from 4 feet 8.5 inches, which became the standard, to 6 feet. Without special equipment, trains of one gauge could not run on tracks of another.

The Civil War showed the value of fast long-distance transportation, and after 1865, railroad managers worked to provide it. In a burst of consolidation, the large companies swallowed the small; integrated rail networks became a reality. Railroads also adopted standard schedules, signals, and equipment and finally, in 1886, the standard gauge.

In the Northeast, four great **trunk lines** took shape, all intended to link eastern seaports with the Great Lakes and western rivers. Like a massive river system, trunk lines drew traffic from dozens of tributaries (feeder lines) and carried it to major markets. The Baltimore and Ohio (B&O), which reached Chicago in 1874, was one; the Erie Railroad, which ran from New York to Chicago, was another. The Erie competed with the New York Central Railroad, the third trunk line, and Cornelius Vanderbilt, its multimillionaire owner from the shipping business.

J. Edgar Thomson and Thomas A. Scott built the fourth trunk line, the Pennsylvania Railroad, which initially ran from Philadelphia to Pittsburgh and eventually extended to New York City, Chicago, and Washington, D.C.

In the war-damaged South, however, consolidation took longer. As Reconstruction waned, northern and European capital rebuilt and integrated the southern lines, especially during the 1880s, when rail construction in the South led the nation. By 1900, five large systems connected the South's major cities and farming and industrial regions and tied them to a national transportation network.

Over that rail system, passengers and freight moved in relative speed, comfort, and safety. Automatic couplers, air brakes, refrigerator cars, dining cars, heated cars, electric switches, and stronger locomotives transformed railroad service. George Pullman's lavish sleeping cars became popular on overnight routes.

In November 1883, the railroads even changed time. Ending the country's crazy-quilt jumble of local times that caused scheduling nightmares, the American Railway Association divided the country into four time zones and adopted the modern system of standard time. Congress took 35 years longer; it finally adopted standard time in 1918, during World War I (see Map 18.1).

Rails Across the Continent

The dream of a transcontinental railroad, linking the Atlantic and Pacific Oceans, had always been lost to sectional quarrels over the route. In 1862 and 1864, with the South out of the picture, Congress moved to build the first transcontinental railroad. It chartered the Union Pacific Railroad Company to build westward from Nebraska and the Central Pacific Railroad Company to build eastward from California.

Construction began simultaneously at Omaha and Sacramento in 1863, lagged during the war, and became a race after 1865, each company vying for land, loans, and markets. General Grenville M. Dodge, a tough Union army veteran, was construction chief for the Union Pacific. Charles Crocker, a former Sacramento dry goods merchant, led the Central Pacific crews. Dodge organized 10,000 workers, many of them ex-soldiers and Irish immigrants. Pushing rapidly westward, his crews were attacked by Native Americans defending their lands, but he had the advantage of building over flat prairie.

Crocker had to contend with the high Sierra Nevada along California's eastern border. He decided that Chinese laborers worked best and hired 6,000 of them, most brought directly from China. "I built the Central Pacific," Crocker boasted, but the Chinese crews in fact did the work. Under the most difficult conditions, they dug, blasted, and pushed their way slowly east.

trunk lines Four major railroad networks that emerged after the Civil War to connect the eastern seaports to the Great Lakes and western rivers. They reflected the growing integration of transportation across the country that helped spur large-scale industrialization.

Quick Check

How did the railroad tie the nation together?

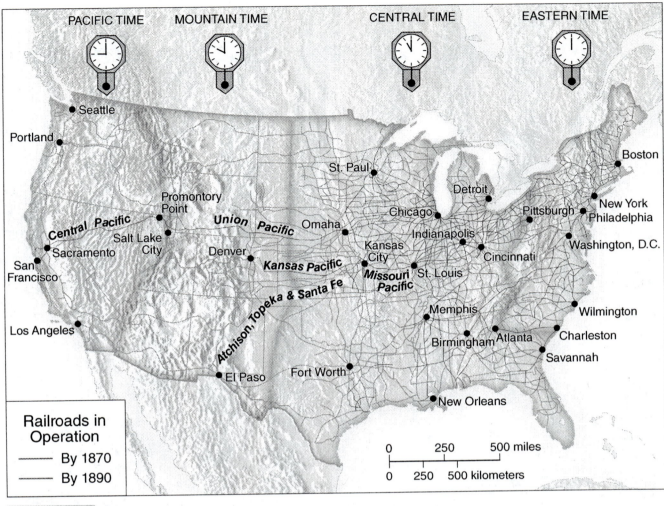

MAP 18.1 RAILROADS, 1870 AND 1890 In the last quarter of the nineteenth century, railroads expanded into Texas, the far Southwest, and the Northwest, carrying settlers, businesses, and government to the far-flung areas.

On May 10, 1869, the two lines met at Promontory, Utah, near the northern tip of the Great Salt Lake. Dodge's crews had built 1,086 miles of track, Crocker's 689. The Union Pacific and Central Pacific presidents hammered in a golden spike (both missed it on the first try), and the dreamed-of connection was made. The telegraph flashed the news east and west, setting off celebrations. A photograph was taken, but it left out the Chinese who had worked so hard to build the road; they were asked to step aside.

The transcontinental railroad symbolized American unity and progress. Along with the Suez Canal in Egypt, completed the same year, it helped knit the world together. Three more railroads reached the coast in 1883: the Northern Pacific, running from Minnesota to Oregon; the Atchison, Topeka, and Santa Fe, connecting Kansas City and Los Angeles; and the Southern Pacific, running from San Francisco and Los Angeles to New Orleans.

Quick Check

What characterized the building and completion of the transcontinental railroads?

Problems of Growth

Overbuilding during the 1870s and 1880s caused problems for the railroads. Competition was severe, and managers fought desperately for traffic. They offered special rates and favors: free passes for large shippers; low rates on bulk freight, carload lots, and long hauls; and, above all, rebates—secret discounts below published rates. Rate wars convinced managers that ruthless competition helped no one. They tried to arrange pooling agreements, sharing traffic to control competition, but none of these agreements survived the pressures of competition.

Railroad owners next tried to consolidate. Through purchase, lease, and merger, they gobbled up competitors and built "self-sustaining systems" that dominated entire regions. But many of the systems, expensive and unwieldy, collapsed in the economic

THE MEETING OF THE CENTRAL PACIFIC AND UNION PACIFIC RAILROADS After the last spike was hammered in at Promontory, Utah, the pilots of the two locomotives exchanged champagne toasts. The chief engineers of the two lines are shaking hands. Absent from the photograph are the Chinese laborers who helped build the railroad.

Panic of 1893, which led to a depression that paralyzed the country (see Chapter 20). By mid-1894, a quarter of the railroads were bankrupt, including such legendary names as the Erie, B&O, Santa Fe, Northern Pacific, and Union Pacific.

Needing money, the railroads turned to bankers, who finally imposed order. J. Pierpont Morgan, head of the New York investment house of J. P. Morgan and Company, took the lead. Massively built, with eyes so piercing they seemed like the headlights of an onrushing train, Morgan was the most powerful figure in American finance. He liked efficiency, combination, and order. He disliked "wasteful" competition.

After 1893, Morgan and other bankers refinanced ailing railroads and took control of the industry. Fixed costs and debt were cut, new stock was issued to provide capital, rates were stabilized, rebates and competition were eliminated, and control was vested in a "voting trust" of handpicked trustees. Between 1894 and 1898, Morgan reorganized—critics said "Morganized"—the Southern Railway, the Erie, the Northern Pacific, and the B&O. By 1900, he was a dominant figure in American railroading.

As the new century began, the railroads had pioneered the patterns most other industries followed. Seven giant systems controlled nearly two-thirds of the mileage. They in turn answered to a few investment banks such as the House of Morgan. For good and ill, a national transportation network, centralized and relatively efficient, was now in place.

Quick Check

What problems did railroads face as they grew?

An Industrial Empire

18.2 What were the main characteristics of the new steel and oil industries?

The new industrial empire was based on a number of dramatic innovations, including steel, oil, and inventions of all kinds that transformed ordinary life. Steel was as important as the railroads. Harder and more durable than other kinds of iron, steel changed manufacturing, agriculture, transportation, and architecture. It permitted construction of longer bridges, taller buildings, stronger railroad track, deadlier weapons, better plows, heavier machinery, and faster ships. Made in great furnaces by strong men, it symbolized the tough, often brutal, nature of industrial society. From the 1870s onward, steel output became the worldwide measure of industrial progress, and nations vied for leadership in steel production (see Figure 18.2).

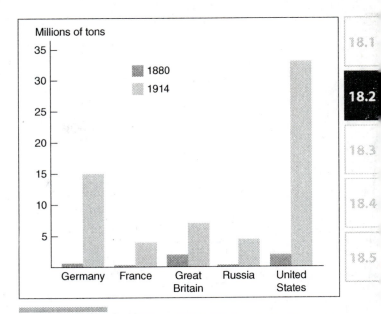

FIGURE 18.2 INTERNATIONAL STEEL PRODUCTION, 1880–1914

The Bessemer process, developed in the late 1850s by Henry Bessemer in England and independently by William Kelly in the United States, increased steel production. Bessemer and Kelly discovered that a blast of air forced through molten iron burned off carbon and other impurities, resulting in more uniform and durable steel. The discovery transformed the industry. Earlier methods produced amounts a person could lift. A Bessemer converter handled 5 tons of molten metal at a time. The mass production of steel was now possible.

Carnegie and Steel

Bessemer plants demanded extensive capital investment, abundant raw materials, and sophisticated techniques. Using chemical and other processes, the plants also required research departments, which became critical components of American industries. Costly to build, Bessemer plants limited entry into the industry to the few who could afford them.

Great steel districts arose in Pennsylvania, Ohio, and Alabama—in each case around large coal deposits that fueled the huge furnaces. Pittsburgh became the center of the industry. Its giant mills employed thousands of workers. Output soared. In 1874, the United States produced less than half the amount of pig iron, which was used to make steel, that Britain produced. By 1900, it produced four times as much as Britain.

Like the railroads, steel companies grew larger and larger. In 1880, only nine companies could produce more than 100,000 tons a year. By the early 1890s, several companies exceeded 250,000 tons, and two—including the great Carnegie Steel Company—produced more than 1 million tons a year. As operations expanded, managers needed more complex skills. Product development, marketing, and consumer preferences became important.

Andrew Carnegie became the master of the industry. Born in Scotland, he came to the United States in 1848 at age 12. Settling near Pittsburgh, he worked as a bobbin boy in a cotton mill, earning $1.20 a week. He soon took a job in a telegraph office, where in 1852 his hard work and skill caught the eye of Thomas A. Scott of the Pennsylvania Railroad. Starting as Scott's personal telegrapher, Carnegie spent 12 years with the Pennsylvania, a training ground for managers. By 1859, he had become a divisional superintendent. He was 24 years old.

Rich from shrewd investments, Carnegie plunged into the steel industry in 1872. He attracted able partners and subordinates such as Henry Clay Frick and Charles M. Schwab, whom he drove hard and paid well. Although he had written articles defending the rights of workers, Carnegie kept the wages of the laborers in his mills low and disliked unions. With the help of Frick, he crushed a violent strike at his Homestead works near Pittsburgh in 1892 (see p. 466).

In 1878, Carnegie won the steel contract for the Brooklyn Bridge. During the next decade, as city building boomed, he converted the huge Homestead works to making structural beams and angles, which went into the New York City elevated railway, the first skyscrapers, and the Washington Monument. In 1900, Carnegie Steel alone produced more steel than Britain. Employing 20,000 people, it was the largest industrial company in the world.

In 1901, Carnegie sold it. Believing that wealth brought social obligations, he wanted to devote his time to philanthropy. He found a buyer in J. Pierpont Morgan, who had put together several steel companies, including Federal Steel, Carnegie's chief rival. In mid-1900, when a price war loomed between the two interests, Morgan decided to buy Carnegie out. In January 1901, Morgan told Charles M. Schwab: "Go and find his price." Schwab cornered Carnegie on the golf course; Carnegie listened. The next day he handed Schwab a note, asking for almost a half billion dollars. Morgan glanced at it and said, "I accept this price."

Drawing other companies into the combination, Morgan created the United States Steel Corporation on March 3, 1901. The new firm was capitalized at $1.4 billion, the first billion-dollar company. It absorbed more than 200 other companies, employed 168,000 people, produced 9 million tons of iron and steel a year, and controlled three-fifths of the country's steel business. Soon other giants also appeared, including Bethlehem Steel, Republic Steel, and National Steel. By 1900, steel products—rare just 30 years before—had altered the landscape. Huge firms, investment bankers, and professional managers dominated the industry.

Quick Check

What were the main characteristics of the growth of the steel industry?

Rockefeller and Oil

Petroleum also changed the economic and social landscape, although mostly after 1900. Distilled into oil, it lubricated the machinery of the industrial age. There seemed little use for gasoline (the internal combustion engine had only just been developed). But kerosene, another major distillate of petroleum, brought inexpensive illumination into almost every home. Whale oil, cottonseed oil, and even tallow candles were so expensive to burn that many people went to bed at nightfall. Kerosene lamps opened the evenings to activity, altering the patterns of life.

Like other changes in these years, the oil boom happened quickly. In 1859, Edwin L. Drake drilled the first oil well near Titusville in northwest Pennsylvania, and "black gold" fever struck. Chemists soon discovered ways to transform petroleum into lubricating oil, grease, paint, wax, varnish, naphtha, and paraffin. A world market in oil arose.

At first, the industry was chaotic. Early drillers and refiners produced for local markets. Since drilling wells and even erecting refineries cost little, competition flourished. Output and prices fluctuated, with devastating effect.

A young merchant from Cleveland named John D. Rockefeller imposed order on the industry. "I had an ambition to build," he recalled. Beginning in 1863 at age 24, he built the Standard Oil Company, a corporate titan. Like Morgan, Rockefeller considered competition wasteful, small-scale enterprise inefficient, and consolidation vital. Methodically, he absorbed or destroyed competitors. As ruthless as Carnegie, he lacked the steel master's charm.

Rockefeller triumphed over his competitors by marketing high-quality products at the lowest unit cost. But he also employed other, less savory methods. He threatened rivals and bribed politicians. He used spies to harass competitors' customers. Above all, he extorted railroad rebates that lowered his transportation costs and undercut competitors. By 1879, he controlled 90 percent of the country's oil-refining capacity.

((• ▮▮ Read the Document Andrew Carnegie, "Wealth," *North American Review* (1889)

STEEL MANUFACTURING The machinery dwarfs the workers in this colored engraving of steel making using the Bessemer process at Andrew Carnegie's Pittsburgh steel works. Men worked 12 hours a day in the blazing heat and deafening roar of the machines.

Vertically integrated, Standard Oil owned wells, timberlands, barrel and chemical plants, refineries, warehouses, pipelines, and fleets of tankers and oil cars. Its marketing organization was the model for the industry. Standard exported oil to Asia, Africa, and South America; its 5-gallon kerosene tin, like Coca-Cola bottles and cans of a later era, was familiar in the most distant parts of the world.

To manage it all, the company developed a new business organization, the **trust**, which had profound significance for American business. In 1881, Samuel C. T. Dodd,

trust A device to centralize and make more efficient the management of diverse and far-flung business operations. It allowed stockholders to exchange their stock certificates for trust certificates, on which dividends were paid. John D. Rockefeller organized the first major trust, the Standard Oil Trust, in 1882.

KING OF A NEW INDUSTRY John D. Rockefeller, satirized in a 1901 *Puck* cartoon, is enthroned on oil, the base of his empire; other holdings gird his crown.

Standard's attorney, set up the Standard Oil Trust. Its nine trustees were empowered "to hold, control, and manage" all Standard's properties. Stockholders exchanged their stock for trust certificates, on which dividends were paid. On January 2, 1882, the first modern trust was born. As Dodd intended, it immediately centralized control of Standard's far-flung empire.

Competition almost disappeared; profits soared. A trust movement swept the country. Industries with similar problems—whiskey, lead, and sugar, among others—followed Standard's example. The word *trust* became synonymous with monopoly, amid vehement protests from the public. *Antitrust* became a watchword for a generation of reformers, from the 1880s through the era of Woodrow Wilson. But Rockefeller's purpose had been *management* of a monopoly, not monopoly itself, which he had already achieved.

Other companies organized their own trusts, including American Sugar Refining, the Northern Securities Company, and the National Biscuit Company. Merger followed merger. By 1900, 1 percent of the nation's companies controlled more than one-third of its industrial production.

In 1897, Rockefeller retired with nearly $900 million, but for Standard Oil and petroleum in general, the most expansive period was yet to come. The great oil pools of Texas and Oklahoma had not yet been discovered. Plastics and other oil-based synthetics were in the future. The country had only four usable automobiles. The day of the gasoline engine, automobile, and airplane lay just ahead.

Quick Check

How did John D. Rockefeller transform the oil industry?

The Business of Invention

"America has become known the world around as the home of invention," boasted the commissioner of patents in 1892. It had not always been so; until the late nineteenth century, the country had imported most of its technology. Then an extraordinary group of inventors and tinkerers—"specialists in invention," as Thomas A. Edison, the most famous of them all, called them—began to study the world around them. Some of their inventions gave rise to new industries; a few changed the quality of life.

In the very act of inventing, Edison and others drew on a deeper "invention," a realization that people could mold nature to their own ends. As a result, the number of patents issued to inventors soared. During the 1850s, fewer than 2000 patents were issued each year. By the 1880s and 1890s, the figure reached more than 20,000 a year. Between 1790 and 1860, the U.S. Patent Office issued just 36,000 patents; in the 1890s alone, it issued more than 200,000.

Some of the inventions transformed communications. In 1866, Cyrus W. Field improved the transatlantic cable linking the telegraph networks of Europe and the United States. By the early 1870s, land and submarine cables ran to Brazil, Japan, and the China coast; by the 1890s, they reached Africa and spread across South America. Diplomats and business leaders in Washington and New York could now "talk" to their counterparts in Berlin or Hong Kong. Even before the telephone, the cables quickened the pace of foreign affairs, revolutionized journalism, and allowed businesses to expand and centralize.

The typewriter (1867), stock ticker (1867), cash register (1879), calculating machine (1887), and adding machine (1888) facilitated business transactions. High-speed spindles, automatic looms, and electric sewing machines transformed the clothing industry, which for the first time in history turned out ready-made clothes for the masses. In 1890, the Census Bureau first used machines to sort and tabulate data on punched cards, a portent of a new era of information storage and processing.

In 1879, George Eastman patented a process for coating gelatin on photographic dry plates, which led to celluloid film and motion pictures. By 1888, he was marketing the Kodak camera, which weighed 35 ounces, took 100 exposures, and cost $25. Even though early Kodaks had to be returned to the factory, camera and all, for film developing, they revolutionized photography. Now almost anyone could snap a picture.

Other innovations changed the diet. There were new processes for flour, canned meat and vegetables, condensed milk, and even beer (from an offshoot of Louis Pasteur's discoveries about bacteria). Packaged cereals appeared on breakfast tables. Refrigerated railroad cars, ice-cooled, brought fresh fruit from Florida and California to all parts of the country. In the 1870s, Gustavus F. Swift, a Chicago meat packer, hit on the idea of using the cars to distribute meat nationwide. Setting up "disassembly" factories to butcher meat (Henry Ford later copied them for his famous automobile "assembly" lines (see Chapter 25), Swift started an "era of cheap beef."

📖 Read the Document   **Thomas Edison, "The Success of the Electric Light" (1880)**

THOMAS EDISON In the late 1870s, the electric light and power transfer were only at the invention stage, having been explored unsuccessfully by a number of inventors. At that time Thomas Edison, with his ideas and proven analytical abilities, undertook the problem. It was Edison's interest in technological systems that led him to a general system of incandescent lighting in the fall of 1878. In this photograph, Edison demonstrates another new invention, the phonograph.

No innovation, however, rivaled the importance of the telephone and the use of electricity for light and power. The telephone was the work of Alexander Graham Bell, a shrewd and genial Scot who settled in Boston in 1871. Interested in the problems of the deaf, Bell experimented with ways to transmit speech electrically. He eventually developed electrified metal disks that, like the human ear, converted sound waves to electrical impulses and back again. On March 10, 1876, he transmitted the first sentence over a telephone: "Mr. Watson, come here; I want you." Later that year, he exhibited the new device to excited crowds at the Centennial Exposition.

In 1878—when a telephone was installed in the White House—the first telephone exchange opened in New Haven, Connecticut. Fighting off competitors who challenged the patent, the young Bell Telephone Company dominated the growing industry. By 1895, there were about 310,000 phones; a decade later, there were 10 million—about one for every ten people. American Telephone and Telegraph Company, formed by the Bell interests in 1885, became another vast holding company, consolidating more than 100 local systems.

If the telephone dissolved communication barriers as old as the human race, Thomas Alva Edison, the "Wizard of Menlo Park," invented processes and products of comparable significance. Born in 1847, Edison had little formal education, although he was an avid reader. Like Carnegie, he went into the new field of telegraphy. Tinkering in his spare time, he made improvements, including a telegraph capable of sending four messages over a single wire. Gathering specialists to work on specific problems, Edison built the first modern research laboratory at Menlo Park, New Jersey. It may have been his most important invention.

The laboratory, Edison promised, would turn out "a minor invention every ten days and a big thing every six months or so." In 1877, it turned out a big thing, the phonograph. Those unable to afford a phone, Edison thought, could record their voices for replay from a central telephone station. Using tin foil wrapped around a grooved, rotating cylinder, he shouted the verses of "Mary Had a Little Lamb" and then listened in awe as the machine played them back. "I was never so taken aback in all my life," he said. "Everybody was astonished. I was always afraid of things that worked the first time." For the first time in history, people could listen again and again to a favorite symphony or a song. The phonograph made human experience repeatable in a way never before possible.

In 1879 came an even larger triumph, the incandescent lamp. Sir Joseph William Swan, an English inventor, had already experimented with the carbon filament, but Edison set out to do nothing less than change light. A trial-and-error inventor, he tested 1,600 materials before producing the carbon filament he wanted. Then he devised a complex system of conductors, meters, and generators to distribute electricity to homes and businesses.

With the backing of J. P. Morgan, Edison organized the Edison Illuminating Company and built the Pearl Street power station in New York City, the testing ground of the new apparatus. On September 4, 1882, as Morgan and others watched, Edison threw a switch and lit the house of Morgan, the stock exchange, the *New York Times*, and other buildings. A *Times* reporter marveled that writing stories in the office at night "seemed almost like writing in daylight." By 1900, 2,774 power stations were lighting 2 million electric lights around the country. In a nation alive with light, the habits of centuries changed. A flick of the switch lit homes and factories at any hour of the day or night.

Electricity could light a lamp or illuminate a skyscraper, pull a streetcar or drive a railroad, run a sewing machine or power an assembly line. Transmitted easily over long distances, it freed factories and cities from dependence on water power or coal. Electricity, in short, brought a revolution.

Frank J. Sprague, a young engineer, electrified the Richmond, Virginia, streetcar system in 1887. Other cities followed. Electric-powered subway systems opened in Boston in 1897 and New York City in 1904. Overhead wires and third rails made urban transportation quieter, faster, and cleaner. Buried under pavement or strung from pole to pole, wires of every description—trolley, telephone, and power—marked the birth of the modern city.

Quick Check

What were the most important inventions of the years between 1870 and 1900?

The Sellers

18.3 Why were the new methods of advertising so important?

The increased output of the industrial age alone was not enough to ensure huge profits. The products still had to be sold, and that gave rise to a new "science" of marketing. Some business leaders—such as Swift in meatpacking, James B. Duke in tobacco, and Rockefeller in oil—built their own marketing organizations. Others relied on retailers, merchandising techniques, and advertising to convince consumers to buy.

In 1867, businesses spent about $50 million on advertising. In 1900, they spent more than $500 million, and the figure was increasing rapidly. The rotary press (1875) churned out newspapers and introduced a new era in newspaper advertising. Bringing producer and consumer together, nationwide advertising was the final link in the national market. From roadside signs to newspaper ads, it pervaded American life.

The idea of consumption became prominent. R. H. Macy in New York, John Wanamaker in Philadelphia, and Marshall Field in Chicago turned the department store into a national institution. There people could browse (a new concept) and buy. Innovations in pricing, display, and advertising helped customers develop wants they did not know they had. In 1870, Wanamaker took out the first full-page newspaper ad, and Macy, an aggressive advertiser, touted "goods suitable for the millionaire at prices in reach of the millions."

In a similar fashion, Sears, Roebuck and Montgomery Ward sold to rural customers through mail-order catalogs—a means of selling that depended on effective transportation and a high level of customer literacy. As a traveler for a dry goods firm, Aaron Montgomery Ward had seen an unfulfilled need among rural westerners. He started the mail-order trend in 1872 with a one-sheet price list offered from a Chicago loft. By 1884, he offered almost 10,000 items in a 240-page catalogue.

Richard W. Sears also entered the mail-order business, starting with watches and jewelry. In the 1880s, he moved to Chicago and with Alvah C. Roebuck founded Sears, Roebuck and Company. Sears sold anything and everything, prospering in a business that relied on mutual trust between unseen customers and distant distributors. Sears catalogs, soon more than 500 pages thick, exploited four-color illustration and other new techniques. By the early 1900s, Sears distributed 6 million catalogs annually.

Advertising, brand names, chain stores, and mail-order houses brought Americans into a national market. Even as the country grew, a homogeneity of goods bound it together, touching cities and farms, East and West, rich and poor. There was a common language of consumption. Americans had become a community of consumers, surrounded by goods unavailable a few decades before, and able to purchase them. They had learned to make, want, and buy.

The Wage Earners

18.4 Who were the wage earners in the new economy?

Although entrepreneurs were important, the labor of millions of men and women built the new industrial society. In their individual stories, nearly all unrecorded, lay much of the achievement, drama, and pain of these years.

In some respects, their lot improved during the last quarter of the nineteenth century. Real wages rose, working conditions got better, and the workers' influence in national affairs increased. Workers also benefited from expanding health and educational services.

Working Men, Working Women, Working Children

Still, life was hard. Before 1900, most wage earners worked at least ten hours a day, six days a week. If skilled, they earned about 20 cents an hour; if unskilled, half that. On average, workers earned between $400 and $500 a year. To live decently, a family of four needed about $600. Construction workers, machinists, government employees, printers, clerical workers, and western miners made more than the average. Eastern coal miners, agricultural workers, garment workers, and unskilled factory hands made less.

There were few holidays or vacations and little respite from the grueling routine. Safety standards were low, and accidents were common—more common, in fact, than in any other industrial nation in the world. On the railroads, one in every 26 workers was injured and one in every 399 was killed each year. Thousands suffered without knowing why from chronic illness, victims of dust, chemicals, and other pollutants at their jobs. In the early 1900s, Dr. Alice Hamilton established a link between jobs and disease, but meanwhile, illness weakened or struck down many a breadwinner.

The breadwinner might be a woman or a child; both worked in increasing numbers. In 1870, about 15 percent of women over the age of 16 were employed for wages; in 1900, 20 percent were. Of 303 occupations in the 1900 census, women were represented in 296. The textile industry was their largest employer. Between 1870 and 1900, the number of working children more than doubled. In 1900, one out of every ten girls and one out of every five boys between the ages of 10 and 15 held jobs.

So many children were in the labor force that when people spoke of child labor, they often meant boys and girls under the age of 14. Boys were paid little enough, but girls made even less. Girls, it was argued, were headed for marriage; those who worked were just doing so to help out their families. "We try to employ girls who are members of families," a box manufacturer said, "for we don't pay the girls a living wage in this trade."

Most working women were young and single. Many began working at 16 or 17, worked a half dozen years or so, married, and quit. In 1900, only 5 percent of all married women were employed outside the home, although 25 percent of married African American women worked, usually on southern farms or as low-paid laundresses or servants. As clerical work expanded, women learned new skills such as typing and stenography. Moving into formerly male occupations, they became secretaries, bookkeepers, typists, telephone operators, and clerks in the new department stores.

A few women—very few—became ministers, lawyers, and doctors. Arabella Mansfield, admitted to the Iowa bar in 1869, was the country's first woman lawyer. But change was slow. In the 1880s, law schools still were refusing to admit women because they "had not the mentality to study law." Most women in the professions became nurses, schoolteachers, and librarians. These fields became "feminized": Most workers were women, a few men took the management roles, and most men left for other jobs, lowering the profession's status.

In most jobs, status and pay were divided unequally between men and women. Many of both sexes thought a woman's place was in the home. When employed in factories, women tended to occupy jobs that were viewed as natural extensions of household activity. They made clothes and textiles, food products, cigars, tobacco, and shoes. In the garment industry, which employed many women, they were the sewers and finishers, doing jobs that paid less; men were the higher-paid cutters and pressers.

In general, adults earned more than children, the skilled more than the unskilled, native-born more than foreign-born, Protestants more than Catholics or Jews, and whites more than blacks or Asians. On average, women made a little more than half as much as men, according to contemporary estimates. Some employers defended the differences—the foreign born, for example, might not speak English—but most simply reflected biases against race, creed, or gender. In the industrial society, white, native-born Protestant men—the bulk of the male population—reaped the greatest rewards.

NEW JOBS FOR WOMEN As demand for workers grew, women took over many of the duties formerly performed by men. Despite their performance in the workplace, however, the women were usually overseen by male supervisors.

Chinese Exclusion Act Legislation passed in 1882 that excluded Chinese immigrants for ten years and denied U.S. citizenship to Chinese nationals. It was the first U.S. exclusionary law aimed at a specific racial group.

Quick Check

What were conditions like for working men, women, and children?

Blacks labored on the fringes, usually in menial jobs. The last hired and first fired, they earned less than other workers at almost every level of skill. On the Pacific coast, the Chinese—and later the Japanese—lived in enclaves and suffered from discrimination. In 1882, the **Chinese Exclusion Act** prohibited the immigration of Chinese workers for ten years.

Culture of Work

18.5 How did wage earners organize in this period, and what demands did they make?

Among almost all groups, industrialization shattered age-old patterns, including work habits and the culture of work. As Herbert G. Gutman, a social historian, noted, it made people adapt "older work routines to new necessities and strained those wedded to premodern patterns of labor." Adaptation was difficult and often demeaning. Virtually everyone endured it, and newcomers repeated the experiences of those who came before.

Men and women fresh from farms were not accustomed to the factory's disciplines. Now they worked indoors rather than out, paced themselves to the clock rather than the sun, and followed the needs of the market rather than the natural rhythms of the seasons. They had supervisors, hierarchies, and strict rules.

As industries grew larger, work became more impersonal. Machines displaced skilled artisans, and the unskilled tended the machines for employers they never saw. Workers picked up and left their jobs with startling frequency. Factories drew on a churning, mobile labor supply. Historian Stephan Thernstrom, who studied the census records, found that only about half the people recorded in any census still lived in the same community ten years later: "The country had an enormous reservoir of restless and footloose men, who could be lured to new destinations when opportunity beckoned."

There was also economic and social mobility. The rags-to-riches stories of Horatio Alger had always celebrated it. Careers of men such as Andrew Carnegie—the impoverished immigrant boy who made good—seemed to confirm it. The actual record was more limited. Most business leaders came from well-to-do or middle-class families of old American stock. Of 360 iron and steel barons in Pittsburgh, Carnegie's own city, only five fit the Carnegie characteristics, and one of those was Carnegie himself. Still, if few workers became steel magnates, many workers made progress during their lifetimes. Thernstrom discovered that a quarter of the manual laborers rose to middle-class positions. Working-class children were even more likely to move up the ladder.

The chance for advancement played a vital role in American industrial development. It gave workers hope, wedded them to the system, and tempered their response to the appeal of labor unions and working-class agitation. Few workers rose from rags to riches, but many rose to better jobs and higher status.

Labor Unions

Weak throughout the nineteenth century, labor unions never included more than 2 percent of the total labor force or more than 10 percent of industrial workers. To many workers, unions seemed "foreign," radical, and out of step with the American tradition of individual advancement. Craft, ethnic, and other differences fragmented the labor force, and its extraordinary mobility made organization difficult. Employers opposed unions. "I have always had one rule," said an executive of U.S. Steel. "If a worker sticks up his head, hit it."

As the national economy emerged, however, so did national labor unions. In 1869, Uriah S. Stephens and Philadelphia garment workers founded the Noble and Holy Order of the Knights of Labor, known simply as the **Knights of Labor**. A secret fraternal order, it grew slowly, until Terence V. Powderly, the new Grand Master Workman elected in 1879, ended the secrecy and began to recruit aggressively. The Knights welcomed everyone who "toiled," regardless of skill, creed, sex, or color. Unlike most unions, it organized women workers, and at its peak, it had 60,000 black members.

Knights of Labor Founded in 1869, this labor organization pursued broad reform and practical issues such as improved wages and hours. The Knights welcomed all laborers regardless of race, gender, or skill.

Harking back to the Jacksonians (see Chapter 10), the Knights set the "producers" against monopoly and special privilege. As members they excluded only "nonproducers"—bankers, lawyers, liquor dealers, and gamblers. Since employers were "producers," they could join; and since workers and employers had common interests, the Knights maintained that workers should not strike. The order's platform included the eight-hour day and the abolition of child labor, but more often it focused on uplifting, utopian reform. Powderly, the eloquent and idealistic leader, spun dreams of a new era of harmony and cooperation.

In March 1885, ignoring Powderly's dislike of strikes, Knights in St. Louis, Kansas City, and other cities won a victory against Jay Gould's Missouri Pacific Railroad, and membership increased. But in 1886, the wily Gould crushed the Knights on the Texas and Pacific Railroad. This defeat punctured the union's growth and revealed the ineffectiveness of its national leaders. Tens of thousands of unskilled laborers deserted the ranks. The Haymarket Riot turned public sympathy against unions like the Knights. By 1890, the order had shrunk to 100,000 members. A few years later, it was virtually defunct.

Even as the Knights waxed and waned, a more enduring organization emerged. Founded in 1886, the **American Federation of Labor (AFL)** was a loose alliance of national craft unions. It organized only skilled workers along craft lines, avoided politics, and worked for specific practical objectives. "I have my own philosophy and my own dreams," said Samuel Gompers, its founder and longtime president, "but first and foremost I want to increase the workingman's welfare year by year."

Born in a London tenement in 1850, Gompers was a child of the union movement. Settling in New York, he worked as a cigar maker, participated in union activities, and experimented with socialism and working-class politics. As leader of the AFL, he adopted a pragmatic approach to labor's needs. Gompers accepted capitalism and did not argue for fundamental changes in it. For labor he wanted simply a recognized place within the system and more of the rewards.

Unlike Powderly, Gompers and the AFL assumed that most workers would remain workers throughout their lives. The goal was to improve lives in "practical" ways: higher wages, shorter hours, and better working conditions. The AFL reassured employers. As a trade union, it would use the strike and boycott, but only for limited gains. If treated fairly, the AFL would provide a stable labor force. It would not oppose monopolies and trusts, as Gompers said, "so long as we obtain fair wages."

By the 1890s, the AFL was the most important labor group in the country. Gompers remained its president, except for one year, until his death in 1924. By then, the AFL included almost one-third of the country's skilled workers. Most workers—skilled and unskilled—remained unorganized, but Gompers and the AFL had become a significant force.

The AFL either ignored or opposed women workers. Only two of its national affiliates—the Cigar Makers' Union and the Typographical Union—accepted women members; others prohibited them outright. Gompers himself complained that women workers undercut the pay scales for men.

The AFL did not forbid blacks from joining, but member unions used high initiation fees, technical examinations, and other means to discourage black membership. The AFL's informal exclusion practices were a sorry record, but Gompers defended his policy toward blacks, women, and the unskilled by pointing to the dangers unions faced. Only by restricting membership, he argued, could the union succeed.

Labor Unrest

Workers adjusted to the factory age in various ways. To the dismay of managers and "efficiency" experts, employees often dictated the pace and quality of their work and set the tone of the workplace. Friends and relatives of newly arrived immigrants found jobs for them, taught them how to deal with factory conditions, and humanized the workplace.

American Federation of Labor (AFL) Founded by Samuel Gompers in 1886, the AFL organized skilled workers by craft and pursued specific practical objectives, such as higher wages, shorter hours, and better working conditions. The AFL avoided politics, and while it did not expressly forbid blacks and women from joining, it used exclusionary practices to keep them out.

Quick Check

What was the history of the Knights of Labor and the American Federation of Labor during the late nineteenth century?

Workers also formed their own institutions to deal with their jobs. Overcoming differences of race or ethnic origin, they often helped each other. They joined social or fraternal organizations. Their unions offered companionship, news of job openings, and insurance plans for sickness, accident, or death. Workers went to the union hall to play cards or pool, sing union songs, and hear older workers tell of past labor struggles. Unions provided food for sick members. There were dances, picnics, and parades. Unions also argued for higher wages.

Many employers, however, believed in an "iron law of wages" in which supply and demand, not their workers' welfare, dictated wages. Employers wanted a docile labor force and would often fire union members, hire scabs to replace strikers, and obtain court injunctions to quell strikes. The injunction, which forbade workers to interfere with their employers' business, was used to break the great Pullman Strike of 1894, and the Supreme Court upheld use of the injunction in 1895.

As employers' attitudes hardened, strikes and violence broke out. The United States had the greatest number of violent confrontations between capital and labor in the industrial world. Between 1880 and 1900, more than 23,000 strikes involved 6.6 million workers (see Map 18.2). The great railroad strike of 1877 paralyzed railroads from West Virginia to California, resulted in the deaths of more than 100 workers, and required federal troops to suppress it.

The worst incident took place at Haymarket Square in Chicago, where workers had been campaigning for an eight-hour workday. In May 1886, police shot and killed two workers in a strike at the McCormick Harvester works. The next evening, May 4, labor leaders called a protest meeting at Haymarket Square near downtown Chicago. The meeting was peaceful, even dull. About 3,000 people attended. Police ordered them to disperse, but someone threw a bomb that killed one policeman and fatally wounded six others. Police fired into the crowd and killed four people.

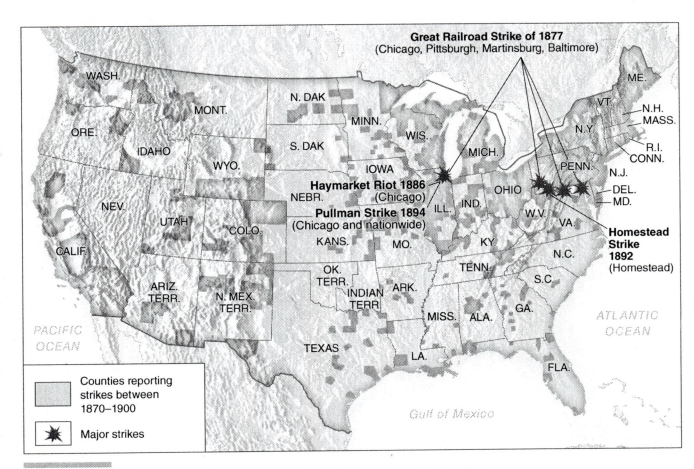

MAP 18.2 LABOR STRIKES, 1870–1900 More than 14,000 strikes occurred in the 1880s and early 1890s, involving millions of workers.

THE RIOT IN HAYMARKET SQUARE In the rioting that followed the bomb explosion in Haymarket Square in Chicago, seven police officers and five workers died and more than 60 officers were wounded, many of them by fellow police.

The authorities never discovered who threw the bomb, but many Americans—not just business leaders—demanded action against labor "radicalism." Cities strengthened their police forces and armories. Eight Chicago anarchists were convicted of murder. Although there was no evidence of their guilt, four were hanged, one committed suicide, and three remained in jail until the governor pardoned them in 1893. Linking labor and anarchism in the public mind, the Haymarket Riot weakened the labor movement because the public associated labor with anarchism.

Violence again broke out in the unsettled conditions of the 1890s. In 1892, Carnegie and Henry Clay Frick, Carnegie's partner and manager, cut wages nearly 20 percent at the Homestead steel plant. The Amalgamated Iron and Steel Workers, an AFL affiliate, struck. Frick locked the workers out of the plant. The workers surrounded it, and Frick hired an army of Pinkerton detectives to drive them off. But workers pinned the Pinkertons down with gunfire and forced them to surrender. Three detectives and ten workers died in the battle.

A few days later, the governor of Pennsylvania ordered the state militia to impose peace at Homestead. On July 23, an anarchist named Alexander Berkman, who was not one of the strikers, walked into Frick's office, shot him twice, and stabbed him. Incredibly, Frick survived. In late July, the Homestead works reopened under military guard. In November, the strikers gave up.

Events like the **Homestead Strike** troubled many Americans who wondered whether the benefits of industrialization might carry too heavy a price in social upheaval,

Homestead Strike In July 1892, wage-cutting at Andrew Carnegie's Homestead Steel Plant in Pittsburgh provoked a violent strike in which three company-hired detectives and ten workers died. Using ruthless force and strikebreakers, company officials broke the strike and destroyed the union.

class tensions, and outright warfare. Most workers did not share in the immense profits of the industrial age, and as the nineteenth century ended, some rebelled against the inequity.

Quick Check

What major strikes occurred between the 1870s and the 1890s?

18.1

18.2

18.3

18.4

18.5

Conclusion: Industrialization's Benefits and Costs

In the half century after the Civil War, the United States became an industrial nation—the leading one in the world. On one hand, industrialization meant "progress," growth, world power, and in some sense, fulfillment of the American promise of abundance. National wealth grew from $16 billion in 1860 to $88 billion in 1900; wealth per capita more than doubled. For the bulk of the population, the standard of living—a particularly American concept—rose.

But industrialization also meant rapid change, social instability, exploitation of labor, and growing disparity in income between rich and poor. Industry flourished, but control rested in fewer and fewer hands. Maturing quickly, the young system became a new corporate capitalism: giant businesses, interlocking in ownership, managed by a new professional class, and selling an expanding variety of goods in an increasingly controlled market. As goods spread through society, so did a sharpened, aggressive materialism. Workers felt the strains of the shift to a new social order.

In 1902, a well-to-do New Yorker named Bessie Van Vorst decided to see what it was like to work for a living in a factory. Disguising herself in coarse woolen clothes,

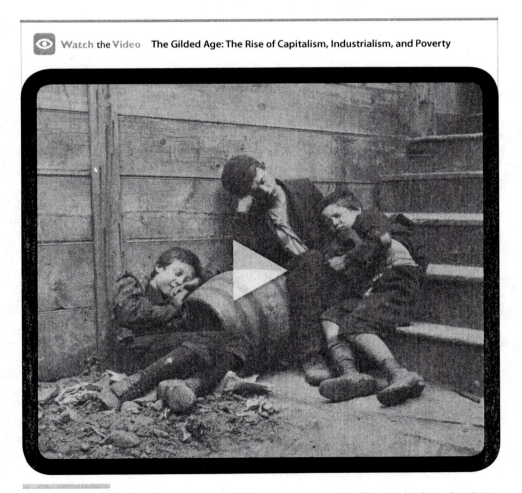

 Watch the Video **The Gilded Age: The Rise of Capitalism, Industrialism, and Poverty**

THE GILDED AGE The Gilded Age is associated with an enormous expansion of American industry, American manufacturing, and the growth of the factory system. It was also the moment when it became increasingly clear that large numbers of Americans would be wage laborers for life.

✴ Explore Labor Strikes and Disputes on MyHistoryLab

HOW DID LABOR UNREST MANIFEST ITSELF AS INDUSTRIALIZATION SPREAD?

Industrialization swept across the United States in the late 1800s. Though agriculture still employed most Americans, more and more people found work in industry—frequently in cities—wherever factories appeared given such factors as entrepreneurship, investment, technology, markets, and, importantly, labor supply. The factories often made their owners quite wealthy, but workers could face long hours, low wages, and poor working conditions. Labor organization such as the Knights of Labor expanded, representing the interests of workers, though racial division undermined labor solidarity in certain areas of the country. When labor disputes broke out, workers turned to the strike and other forms of work stoppage to advance their interests, often prompting employers to respond with violence.

RIOTS IN CHICAGO The police charge rioters in old Haymarket Square on the night of May 4th.

MAJOR LABOR STRIKES AND WORK STOPPAGES, 1880S–1890S

Event	Location	Year
Great Railroad Strike	Chicago, Pittsburgh, Martinsburg, Baltimore	1877
Haymarket Riot	Chicago	1886
Homestead Strike	Homestead	1892
Pullman Strike	Chicago, nationwide	1894

KEY QUESTIONS Use MyHistoryLab *Explorer* to answer these questions:

Comparison ▶▶▶ *Where was labor unrest most pronounced?*

Explore possible reasons for geographic differences.

Cause ▶▶▶ *How did factors such as urbanization and wage levels affect labor activity?*

Chart these patterns based on census data.

Consequence ▶▶▶ *How did the spread of Knights of Labor assemblies relate to the geographic distribution of different U.S. industries?*

Consider the reasons behind this relationship.

a shabby felt hat, a cheap piece of fur, and an old shawl and gloves, she obtained a job in a Pittsburgh canning factory. Van Vorst worked ten hours a day, six days a week, including four hours on Saturday afternoons when she and the other women, on their hands and knees, scrubbed the tables, stands, and factory floor. For that she earned $4.20 a week, $3 of which went for food.

Van Vorst was lucky—when she tired of the life, she went back to her home in New York. The working men and women around her were less fortunate. They stayed on the factory floor, and, by dint of their labor, created the new industrial society.

Chapter Review

Industrial Development

18.1 What enabled the United States to build an industrial economy? p. 405

The United States had an abundance of natural resources, plentiful labor from Europe and American farms, numerous inventions, a national market, prolific capital, favorable government policies, and entrepreneurs who saw the possibilities in developing a national economy.

An Industrial Empire

18.2 What were the main characteristics of the new steel and oil industries? p. 411

In the late nineteenth century, an industrial empire took shape, centered around steel and oil, leading to the importance of the automobile in the twentieth century. The result was larger and more complex business organizations and greater concentrations of wealth, capital, and control by a relatively few individuals and companies.

The Sellers

18.3 Why were the new methods of advertising so important? p. 417

Advertising, a relatively new industry, helped to sell the goods of the new industrial economy. Americans learned to buy goods they did not even know they wanted. When bored or troubled, they went to a store—today's mall—to shop.

The Wage Earners

18.4 Who were the wage earners in the new economy? p. 418

The hard work of millions of men and women built the new factory society. Their work was grueling and often dangerous. Men, women, and children often worked for low wages in unsafe conditions.

Culture of Work

18.5 How did wage earners organize in this period, and what demands did they make? p. 421

Laborers faced many challenges in the new economy, including work that followed the clock, bigger industries, machines, and wages. Unions formed, including the American Federation of Labor (AFL), which still exists. Labor unrest for better wages and safer working conditions took peaceful forms, but also resulted in violence that disturbed other Americans.

Timeline

1859
Industrial Development—First oil well drilled near Titusville, Pennsylvania

1869
Empire on Rails—Transcontinental railroad completed at Promontory, Utah; Knights of Labor organize

1876
Industrial Development—Alexander Graham Bell invents the telephone; Centennial Exposition held in Philadelphia

1877
The Wage Earner—Railroads cut workers' wages, leading to bloody and violent strikes

1879
An Industrial Empire—Thomas A. Edison invents the incandescent lamp

1882
An Industrial Empire—Rockefeller's Standard Oil Company becomes the nation's first trust

1886
Culture of Work—Samuel Gompers founds the American Federation of Labor (AFL); Violent labor protest erupts in Haymarket Riot in Chicago; **An Industrial Empire**—Railroads adopt standard gauge; they introduced standard time zones three years earlier

1892
Culture of Work—Workers strike at the Homestead steel plant in Pennsylvania

19 Toward an Urban Society 1877–1900

The Overcrowded City

One day around **1900**, Harriet Vittum, a settlement house worker in Chicago, went to help a young Polish girl who lived in a nearby slum. The girl, aged 15, had discovered she was pregnant and had taken poison. An ambulance was on the way, and Vittum rushed over to do what she could.

She raced up three flights of stairs to the floor where the girl and her family lived. Pushing open the door, she found the father, male boarders, and small boys asleep on the kitchen floor. In the next room, the mother was also on the floor among women boarders and small children. Another building was so close Vittum could reach out the window and touch it.

The girl lay in a third room, along with two more children who were asleep. Vittum thought about the girl's life in the crowded tenement. Should she even try to save her and bring her back "to the misery and hopelessness of the life she was living in that awful place"?

LIFE IN THE SLUMS The kitchen of a tenement apartment was often a multipurpose room. Here the tenement dwellers prepared and ate their meals; the room might also serve as a workroom, and sleeping quarters for one or more members of the family.

SOURCE: The Museum of the City of New York/Art Resource, NY.

LEARNING OBJECTIVES

19.1	19.2	19.3	19.4
Why did cities in the United States grow between 1880 and 1900? p. 431	How did the growth of American cities affect social, cultural, and political life? p. 438	Why did Jim Crow laws spread across the South after the end of Reconstruction? p. 446	How did life in the growing cities lead to ideas of reform? p. 448

Listen to Chapter 19 on MyHistoryLab

From Chapter 19 of *American Stories: A History of the United States*, Third Edition. H. W. Brands, R. Hal Williams, T. H. Breen and Ariela J. Gross Copyright © 2015 by Pearson Education, Inc. All rights reserved.

Watch the Video Series on MyHistoryLab

Learn about some key topics related to this chapter with the *MyHistoryLab Video Series: Key Topics in U.S. History*

1 **An Urban Society** The early 19th century was characterized by a level of urban growth unmatched in world history. This period saw dramatic shifts in social stratification. Large numbers of new immigrants, rural whites, and rural African-American moved to city centers such as Atlanta, Memphis and Louisville seeking economic opportunities and social enrichment. Reform movements would eventually take on severe urban overcrowding, the need for efficient mass transportation, and child welfare standards. Racial tension culminated in what became known as Jim Crow laws, which institutionalized segregation between blacks and whites and thedisenfranchised the black population.

 Watch on MyHistoryLab

The New American City The growth of industry during the Gilded Age went hand-in-hand with the expansion of urban centers in the Northeastern and Midwestern United States. U.S. cities remained attractive destinations for immigrants as well as for newcomers from the country's rural regions who wished to take advantage of the greater economic opportunities that urban life afforded. However, as this video makes clear, these new opportunities created challenges and ultimately changed the face of American cities forever.

Watch on MyHistoryLab **2**

3 **Boss Tweed** This video profiles the life and career of Democratic politician William M. Tweed, whose Tammany Hall political machine ran New York City during the 1860s. "Boss" Tweed was eventually indicted on corruption charges, but not before overseeing, and profiting handsomely from, the creation of many of the services that came to be central to civic government.

 Watch on MyHistoryLab

Plessy v. Ferguson Despite the Emancipation Proclamation and the Thirteenth, Fourteenth, and Fifteenth amendments, discrimination and racial segregation became increasingly powerful forces in the decades following the Civil War. This video provides an assessment of the case of *Plessy v. Ferguson* (1896), which tested the discrimination laws of Louisiana. The Supreme Court decided in the case that segregation was acceptable so long as "separate, but equal" facilities were provided and, in doing so, validated the Jim Crow laws of the South.

Watch on MyHistoryLab **4**

The young girl died, and Vittum often retold her story. It was easy to see why. The girl's life in the slum, the children on the floor, the need for boarders to make ends meet, the way the mother and father collapsed at the end of a workday that began before sunup—all reflected the lives of millions in America's cities.

Vittum and people like her were responding to the challenges of the nation's burgeoning cities. People poured into cities in the late nineteenth century, lured by glitter and excitement, by friends and relatives who were already there, and, above all, by the opportunities for jobs and higher wages. Between 1860 and 1910, the rural population of the United States almost doubled, but the number of people living in cities increased sevenfold. Little of the increase came from natural growth, since urban families had high rates of infant mortality, a declining fertility rate, and a high death rate from injury and disease. Many of the newcomers came from rural America, many more from Europe, Latin America, and Asia. In the 1880s, in one of the most significant migrations in American history, thousands of African Americans began to move from the rural South to northern cities. By 1900, New York, Baltimore, Philadelphia, Chicago, Washington, D.C., and other cities had large black communities. Yet to come was the even greater black migration during World War I.

Two major forces reshaped American society between 1870 and 1920: industrialization and urbanization, the headlong rush of people from their rural roots into the modern urban environment. In these years, cities grew upward and outward, attracting millions of newcomers and influencing politics, education, entertainment, and family life. By 1920, they had become the center of American economic, social, and cultural life.

The Lure of the City

19.1 Why did cities in the United States grow between 1880 and 1900?

Between 1870 and 1900, the city—like the factory—became a symbol of a new America. Drawn from farms, small towns, and foreign lands, newcomers swelled the population of older cities and created new ones almost overnight. At the beginning of the Civil War in 1861, only one-sixth of the American people lived in cities of 8,000 people or more. By 1900, one-third did; by 1920, one-half.

Growth was explosive. Thousands of years of history had produced only a handful of cities with more than 500,000 in population. In 1900, the United States had six such cities, including three—New York, Chicago, and Philadelphia—with populations greater than 1 million.

Skyscrapers and Suburbs

As it did to so many things in these years, a revolution in technology transformed the city. Beginning in the 1880s, the age of steel and glass produced the skyscraper, and the streetcar produced the suburbs and new residential patterns.

On the eve of the change, American cities were a crowded jumble of small buildings. Church steeples soared above the roofs of factories and office buildings. Buildings were

THE WAINWRIGHT BUILDING The Wainwright Building (1890) in St. Louis, Missouri, was designed by Chicago architect Louis Sullivan. The 10-story red brick office building was one of the first skyscrapers in the world and had many of the modern design features found in Sullivan's buildings of this period.

usually made of masonry, and since the massive walls had to support their own weight, they could only be a dozen or so stories tall. But steel frames and girders allowed buildings to go higher and higher. "Curtain walls," which concealed the steel framework, were no longer load-bearing; they were pierced by many windows that let in fresh air and light.

To a group of talented Chicago architects, the new trends were a springboard for innovative forms. The leaders of the movement were John Root and Louis H. Sullivan, both of whom were attracted by the chance to rebuild Chicago after a great fire destroyed much of the city in 1871. Noting that the fire had fed on fancy exterior ornamentation in buildings, Root developed a plain, stripped-down style, bold in mass and form—the keynotes of modern architecture. He had another important insight: In an age of business, the office tower, more than a church or government building, symbolized the society, and he designed office buildings that embodied, as he said, "the ideas of modern business life: simplicity, stability, breadth, dignity."

Sullivan had studied at the Massachusetts Institute of Technology (MIT) and in Paris before settling in Chicago. In 1886, at age 30, he began work on the Chicago Auditorium, one of the last great masonry buildings. "Then came the flash of imagination which saw the single thing," he later said. "The trick was turned; and there swiftly came into being something new under the sun." Sullivan's "flash of imagination"—skyscrapers—changed the urban skyline.

Electric elevators, first used in 1871, carried passengers upward in the new skyscrapers. During the same years, streetcars, another innovation, transformed urban life by carrying people outward.

Cities were no longer largely "walking cities," confined to a radius of two or three miles, the distance a person might walk. Streetcar systems extended the city's radius and changed the urban habitat. Cable lines, electric surface lines, and elevated rapid transit brought shoppers and workers into central business districts and sped them home. For a modest five-cent fare with a free transfer, the mass transit systems fostered commuting, and widely separated business and residential districts sprang up. The middle class moved farther and farther out to the leafy greenness of the suburbs.

As the middle class left the cities, the immigrants and working class poured in. They turned the older brownstones, row houses, and workers' cottages into the slums of the central city. In the cities of the past, classes and occupations had been thrown together; without streetcars and subways, they had no other choice. The streetcar city, sprawling and specialized, became a more fragmented and stratified society with middle-class residential rings surrounding a business and working-class core.

Quick Check

How did life in the cities change between 1870 and 1900?

Tenements and the Problems of Overcrowding

In the shadow of the skyscrapers, grimy rows of tenements crowded people into cramped apartments in the central city. In the late 1870s, architect James E. Ware won a competition for tenement design with the "dumbbell tenement." Seven or eight stories high, the dumbbell tenement packed about 30 four-room apartments on a 25-by-100-foot lot. Between 4 and 16 families lived on a floor with two toilets in the hall of each floor. Narrowed at the middle, the tenement was shaped like a giant dumbbell.

In 1890, nearly half the dwellings in New York City were tenements. That year, more than 1.4 million people lived on Manhattan Island, one of whose wards had a population density of 334,000 people per square mile. Many people lived in alleys and basements so dark they could not be photographed until flashlight photography was invented in 1887. Exploring the city, the novelist William Dean Howells inhaled "the stenches of the neglected street . . . [and] the yet fouler and dreadfuller poverty smell which breathes from the open doorways."

Howells smelled more than poverty. In the 1870s and 1880s, cities stank. One problem was horse manure, hundreds of tons of it a day in every city. Another was the outdoor toilet or privy, "a single one of which," said a leading authority on public health, "may render life in a whole neighborhood almost unendurable in the summer."

Baltimore smelled "like a billion polecats," recalled H. L. Mencken, who grew up there. Said one New York City resident, "The stench is something terrible." Another wrote that "the stink is enough to knock you down." In 1880, the Chicago *Times* said that a "solid stink"

✳ Explore the Settlement in the United States, 1900, on MyHistoryLab

A SHIFTING POPULATION A group of passengers on the deck of USS *Amsterdam*

WHAT CHARACTERIZED U.S. POPULATION PATTERNS IN 1900?

By 1900, a major change had occurred across the continent: The states and territories of the continental United States had expanded from the Atlantic to the Pacific and its population had spread with it. However, large sections of the country were still sparsely populated, even though the historian Frederick Jackson Turner declared in 1893 that the American frontier was closed. As the frontier had been an important part of the American identity, this thesis of the "closing of the frontier" raised questions about what the new character of the nation would become. Regardless, large cities had grown in certain regions of the country and clear differences in their racial demographics marked the population patterns of the United States by 1900.

The 10 largest cities in the U.S., 1800

The 10 largest cities in the U.S., 1900

KEY QUESTIONS   Use **MyHistoryLab** *Explorer* to answer these **questions:**

Comparison ▶▶▶ *What were the population densities of various U.S. regions?*

Conceptualize what these densities meant for the frontier thesis.

Choices ▶▶▶ *Where had members of major immigrant communities settled by 1900?*

Theorize why immigrants and immigrant communities might cluster together.

Cause ▶▶▶ *In what parts of the United States were African Americans concentrated at this point?*

Speculate about what factors explained this pattern in 1900.

Quick Check

What were the main challenges
of life in the overcrowded city?

pervaded the city. "No other word expresses it so well as stink. A stench means something finite. Stink reaches the infinite and becomes sublime in the magnitude of odiousness."

Cities dumped their wastes into the nearest body of water, then drew drinking water from the same site. Many built purified waterworks but could not keep pace with spiraling growth. In 1900, fewer than one in ten city dwellers drank filtered water. Factories, the pride of the era, polluted the urban air.

Crime was another problem. The nation's homicide rate nearly tripled in the 1880s, much of the increase coming in the cities. Slum youths formed street gangs with names such as the Hayes Valley Gang in San Francisco and the Baxter Street Dudes, the Daybreak Boys, and the Alley Gang in New York. After remaining constant for decades, the suicide rate rose steadily between 1870 and 1900, according to a study of Philadelphia. Alcoholism also rose, especially among men, though studies have shown that for working-class men, the urban saloon was as much a gathering spot as a place to drink. Nonetheless, in 1905, Chicago had as many saloons as grocery stores, meat markets, and dry goods stores combined.

Strangers in a New Land

While some of the new city dwellers came from farms and small towns, many more came from abroad. Most came from Europe, where unemployment, food shortages, and threats of war sent millions fleeing across the Atlantic to make a fresh start. Often they knew someone already in the United States, a friend or relative who had written them about jobs and freer lives in a new land.

The immigration figures were staggering. Between 1877 and 1890, more than 6.3 million people entered the United States. In 1882 alone, almost 789,000 people came. By 1890, about 15 percent of the population, 9 million people, were foreign born.

Most newcomers were job seekers. Nearly two-thirds were males, most between the ages of 15 and 40. Most were unskilled laborers who settled on the East Coast. In 1901, the Industrial Relocation Office was established to relieve overcrowding in eastern cities; opening Galveston, Texas, as a port of entry, it attracted Russian Jews to Texas and the Southwest. But most immigrants preferred the shorter, more familiar journey to New York. Entering through Ellis Island in New York harbor, as four in every ten immigrants did, most of them crowded into northern and eastern cities, settling among others of their nationality or religion.

Cities had increasingly large foreign-born populations. In 1900, four-fifths of Chicago's population was foreign born or of foreign-born parentage, two-thirds of Boston's, and one-half of Philadelphia's. New York City, where most immigrants arrived and many stayed, had more Italians than Naples, more Germans than Hamburg, and twice as many Irish as Dublin. Four out of five New York City residents in 1890 were of foreign birth or foreign parentage (see Map 19.1).

new immigrants Starting in the 1880s, immigration into the United States began to shift from northern and western Europe to southern and eastern Europe. These new immigrants were mostly poor, non-Protestant, and unskilled; they tended to stay in close-knit communities and retain their language, customs, and religions. Between 1880 and 1910, approximately 8.4 million of these so-called new immigrants came to the United States.

Beginning in the 1880s, immigration shifted away from northern and western Europe, the chief source of immigration for more than two centuries. More and more immigrants now came from southern and eastern Europe: Italy, Greece, Austria–Hungary, Poland, and Russia. Between 1880 and 1910, approximately 8.4 million people came from these lands (see Figure 19.1). The **new immigrants** tended to be Catholics or Jews rather than Protestants. Like their predecessors, most were unskilled rather than skilled, and they often spoke "strange" languages. Most were poor and uneducated; they clung to their native customs, languages, and religions in close-knit communities.

More than any previous group, the so-called new immigrants troubled mainstream society. Could they be assimilated? Did they share "American" values? Such questions preoccupied groups like the American Protective Association, a midwestern anti-Catholic organization that expanded in the 1890s and worked to limit or end immigration.

Anti-Catholicism and anti-Semitism flared up again, as they had in the 1850s. The Immigration Restriction League, founded in 1894, demanded a literacy test for immigrants from southern and eastern Europe. Congress passed such a law in 1896, but President Grover Cleveland vetoed it as violating the country's traditions.

Quick Check

What drew the river of immigrants
to the United States?

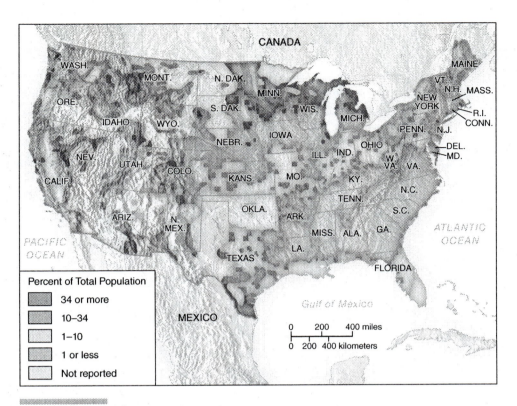

MAP 19.1 FOREIGN-BORN POPULATION, 1890 Immigrants tended to settle in regions where jobs were relatively plentiful or conditions were similar to those in their homelands. Cities of the Northeast, Midwest, and West offered job opportunities, while land available for cultivation drew immigrant farmers to the plains and prairies of the nation's midsection.

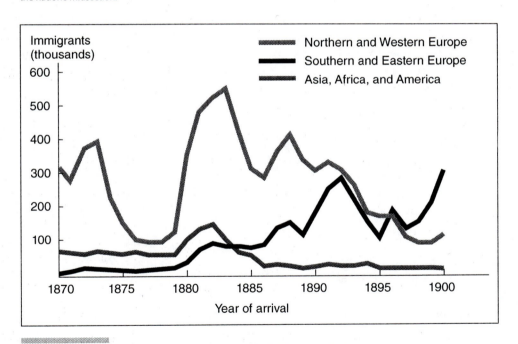

FIGURE 19.1 IMMIGRATION TO THE UNITED STATES, 1870–1900

Note: For purposes of classification, "Northern and Western Europe" includes Great Britain, Ireland, Scandinavia, the Netherlands, Belgium, Luxembourg, Switzerland, France, and Germany. "Southern and Eastern Europe" includes Poland, Austria–Hungary, Russia and the Baltic States, Romania, Bulgaria, European Turkey, Italy, Spain, Portugal, and Greece. "Asia, Africa, and America" includes Asian Turkey, China, Japan, India, Canada, the Caribbean, Latin America, and all of Africa.

SOURCE: U.S. Bureau of the Census, *Historical Statistics of the United States, Colonial Times to 1970,* Bicentennial Edition, Washington, D.C., 1975

Immigrants and the City

Industrial capitalism—the world of factories, foremen, and grimy machines—tested the immigrants and their families. Many immigrants came from peasant societies where life proceeded according to outdoor routine and age-old tradition. In their new city homes, they found new freedoms and confinements, a different language, and novel customs and expectations. Historians have only recently begun to discover the remarkable ways in which they learned to adjust.

Like the native-born, most immigrant families were nuclear in structure—two parents and their children. Though variations occurred from group to group, men's and women's roles were also similar to those in native families: Men were wage earners; women were housekeepers and mothers. However, immigrants tended to marry at a later age than natives and to have more children, which worried nativists opposed to immigration.

Immigrants shaped the city as much as it shaped them. Most of them tried to retain their traditional culture for themselves and their children while adapting to life in their new country. To do this, they spoke their native language, practiced their religion, read their own newspapers, and established parochial or other schools. They observed traditional holidays and formed myriad social organizations to maintain ties within the group.

Immigrant associations—every city had many of them—offered fellowship in a strange land. They helped newcomers find jobs and homes; they provided services such as unemployment insurance and health insurance. In a Massachusetts textile town, the Irish Benevolent Society said, "We visit our sick, and bury our dead." Some groups were no larger than a neighborhood; others spread nationwide. In 1914, the Deutsch-Amerikanischer Nationalbund (German-American National Association), the largest of the associations, had more than 2 million members in dozens of cities and towns. Many women belonged to and participated in the immigrant associations' work. There were also groups exclusively for women, such as the Polish Women's Alliance, the Society of Czech Women, and the National Council of Jewish Women.

Every major city had dozens of foreign-language newspapers. The first newspaper in the Lithuanian language appeared in the United States, not in Lithuania. Eagerly read, the papers not only carried news of the homeland but also reported on local ethnic leaders, told readers how to vote and become citizens, and gave practical tips on adjusting to life in the United States.

The church and the school were the most important institutions in every immigrant community. Eastern European Jews established synagogues and religious schools wherever they settled; they taught Hebrew and raised their children in a heritage they did not want to leave behind. Among such groups as the Irish and the Poles, the Roman Catholic Church provided spiritual and educational guidance. In parish schools, Polish priests and nuns taught Polish American children about Polish as well as American culture in the Polish language.

Church, school, and fraternal societies shaped how immigrants adjusted to life in America. By preserving language, religion, and heritage, they also shaped the country itself.

Quick Check

In what specific ways did immigrants respond to the American city?

Urban Political Machines

Closely connected with urban growth was the emergence of the powerful city political machine. As cities grew, lines of responsibility in city governments became hopelessly confused, increasing the opportunity for corruption and greed. Burgeoning populations required streets, buildings, and public services; immigrants needed even more services. In this situation, political party machines flourished.

The machines traded services for votes. A strong leader—the "boss"—tied together a loose network of ward and precinct captains, each of whom looked after his local constituents. In New York, "Honest" John Kelly, Richard Croker, and Charles F. Murphy led Tammany Hall, the famous Democratic party organization that dominated city politics from the 1850s to the 1930s. Other bosses included "Hinky Dink" Kenna and "Bathhouse John" Coughlin in Chicago, James McManes in Philadelphia, and Christopher A. Buckley—the notorious "Blind Boss," who used an exceptional memory for voices to make up for his failing eyesight—in San Francisco.

William M. Tweed, head of the famed Tweed Ring in New York, provided the model for them all. Nearly six feet tall, weighing almost 300 pounds, Tweed rose through the ranks of Tammany Hall. He served in turn as city alderman, member

"THAT'S WHAT'S THE MATTER."

Boss Tweed. "As long as I count the Votes, what are you going to do about it? say?"

BOSS TWEED This political cartoon skewers the success of political bosses, such as the depicted Boss (William) Tweed of New York, to manipulate the political process and use patronage to enrich themselves and retain political power in various cities during this period.

of Congress, and New York State assemblyman. A warm, cultured man, he moved easily between the rough back alleys of New York and the parlors and clubs of the city's elite. Behind the scenes, he headed a ring that plundered New York for tens of millions of dollars.

The role of the political bosses can be overemphasized. Power structures in the turn-of-the-century city involved many people and institutions. Banks, real estate investors, insurance companies, architects, and engineers, among others, played roles in governing the city. Many city governments were remarkably successful. With populations that in some cases doubled every decade, city governments provided water and sewer lines, built parks and playgrounds, and paved streets. They gave Boston the world's largest public library and New York City the Brooklyn Bridge and Central Park, two of the finest achievements in city planning and architecture of any era. By the 1890s, New York also had 660 miles of water lines, 464 miles of sewers, and 1,800 miles of paved streets, far more than comparable cities in Europe.

Why did voters keep the bosses in power? The answers are complex, but two reasons were skillful political organization and the fact that immigrants and others made up the bosses' constituency. Most immigrants had little experience with democratic government and proved easy prey for well-oiled machines. However, the bosses stayed in power mostly because they paid attention to the needs of the least privileged city voters. They offered valued services in an era when neither government nor business lent a hand.

If an immigrant, tired and bewildered after crossing the ocean, came looking for a job, bosses like Tweed or Buckley found him one in city offices or local businesses. If a family's breadwinner died or was injured, the bosses donated food and clothing and saw the family through the crisis.

Most bosses became wealthy; they were not Robin Hoods who took from the rich to give to the poor. They also took for themselves. Reformers occasionally ousted them. Tweed fell from power in 1872, "Blind Boss" Buckley in 1891, Croker in 1894. But the reformers rarely stayed in power. Drawn mainly from the middle and upper classes, they did not understand the needs of the poor.

"What tells in holdin' your grip on your district," Tammany's George Washington Plunkitt once said, "is to go right down among the poor families and help them in the different ways they need help. . . . It's philanthropy, but it's politics, too—mighty good politics. . . . The poor are the most grateful people in the world."

Quick Check

What role did politicians play
in American cities?

Social and Cultural Change, 1877–1900

19.2 How did the growth of American cities affect social, cultural, and political life?

The rise of cities and industry between 1877 and the 1890s affected all aspects of American life. Customs changed; family ties loosened. Factories turned out consumer goods, and the newly invented cash register rang up record sales. Public and private educational systems burgeoned, illiteracy declined, life expectancy increased. While many people worked harder just to survive, others had more leisure time. The roles of women and children changed, and the family took on functions it had not had before. Thanks to technological advances, news flashed across the oceans, and for the first time in history, people read of the day's events in distant lands in their daily newspapers.

The population continued to grow. In 1877, the country had 47 million people. In 1900, it had nearly 76 million. Nine-tenths of the population was white; just under one-tenth was black. There were 66,000 American Indians, 108,000 Chinese, and 148 Japanese. The bulk of the white population, most of whom were Protestant, came from the so-called Anglo-Saxon countries of northern Europe: Britain, Germany, and Scandinavia. WASPs—white Anglo-Saxon Protestants—dominated American society.

Though the rush to the cities was about to begin, most people in 1877 still lived on farms or in small towns. Their lives revolved around the farm, the church, and the general store. In 1880, nearly 75 percent of the population lived in communities of fewer than 2500 people. In 1900, despite city growth, 60 percent still did. The average family in 1880 had three children, dramatically fewer than in 1800. Life expectancy was about 43 years. By 1900, improved health care and sanitation had raised it to 47 years. For blacks and other minorities, who often lived in unsanitary rural areas, life expectancy was only 33 years.

Meals tended to be heavy, and so did people. Even breakfast had several courses and could include steak, eggs, fish, potatoes, toast, and coffee. Food was cheap. Families ate fresh homegrown produce in the summer and "put up" their fruits and vegetables for the long winters. Toward the end of the century, eating habits changed. Packaged breakfast cereals became popular; fresh fruit and vegetables came in on fast trains from Florida and California; and commercially canned food became safer and cheaper. The newfangled icebox, cooled by blocks of ice, kept food fresher and added new treats such as ice cream.

Medical science was undergoing a revolution. Louis Pasteur's discovery that germs cause infection and disease created the new science of microbiology and led the way to new vaccines and other preventive measures. But tuberculosis, typhoid, diphtheria, and pneumonia—all now curable—were still the leading causes of death. Infant mortality gradually declined between 1877 and 1900, but a great drop did not come until after 1920.

There were few hospitals and no hospital insurance. Most patients stayed at home, although medical practice, especially surgery, expanded rapidly. Once brutal and dangerous, surgery became relatively safe and painless. Anesthetics—ether and chloroform—eliminated pain, and antiseptics helped prevent postoperative infections. Antiseptic practices at childbirth reduced puerperal fever, an infection that for centuries had killed women and newborns. The new science of psychology began to explore the mind, hitherto uncharted. William James, a leading American psychologist and philosopher, laid the foundations of modern behavioral psychology, which stressed the importance of the environment on human development.

Manners and Mores

Victorian morality, its name derived from the British queen who reigned from 1837 to 1901, set the tone for the era. The code prescribed strict standards of dress, manners, and sexual behavior. It was both obeyed and disobeyed and reflected the tensions of a generation whose moral standards were changing.

In 1877, children were to be seen and not heard. They spoke only when spoken to, listened rather than chattered—or at least that was the rule. Older boys and girls were often chaperoned, although they could always find moments alone. They played post office and spin the bottle; they puffed cigarettes behind the barn. Journalist William Allen White recalled his boyhood high jinks. He and his friends smeared their naked bodies with mud and leaped out in full view of passing trains. Counterbalancing such youthful exuberance was pride in virtue and self-control. "Thank heaven I am absolutely pure," Theodore Roosevelt, the future president, wrote in 1880 after proposing to Alice Lee. "I can tell Alice everything I have ever done."

Middle-class gentlemen dressed in heavy black suits, derby hats, and white shirts with paper collars. Women wore tight corsets, long dark dresses, and black shoes reaching well above the ankles. As with so many things, styles changed dramatically toward 1900, spurred in part by new sporting fads such as golf, tennis, and bicycling, which required looser clothing. By the 1890s, a middle-class woman wore a tailored suit or a dark skirt and a blouse, called a shirtwaist, modeled after men's shirts. Her skirts still draped about the ankles, but she increasingly removed or loosened the corset, the dread device that squeezed internal organs into fashionable 18-inch waistlines.

Religious and patriotic values were strong. A center of community life, the church often set the tenor for family and social relationships. In the 1880s, eight out of ten church members were Protestants; most of the rest were Roman Catholics.

With slavery abolished, reformers turned their attention to new moral and political issues. One group, known as the **Mugwumps**, worked to end corruption in politics. Other zealous reformers campaigned for prohibiting the sale of intoxicating liquors, hoping to end the social evils that stemmed from drunkenness. In 1874, women who advocated total abstinence from alcoholic beverages formed the **Women's Christian Temperance Union (WCTU)**. Frances E. Willard was president of the group from 1879 until her death in 1898. By then, the WCTU had 500,000 members.

Leisure and Entertainment

In the 1870s, people rose early. They washed from a pitcher and bowl in the bedroom. After dressing and eating, they went to work and school. Without refrigerators, housewives marketed almost daily. In the evening, families gathered in the "second parlor" or living room, where the children did their lessons, played games, sang around the piano, and listened to that day's verse from the Bible.

Mugwumps Educated and upper-class reformers who crusaded for lower tariffs, limited federal government, and civil service reform. They were best known for helping elect Grover Cleveland president in 1884.

Women's Christian Temperance Union (WCTU) This organization campaigned to end drunkenness and the social ills that accompanied it. By 1898, it had 10,000 branches and 500,000 members. The WCTU illustrated the role women played in politics and reform long before they won the right to vote.

Quick Check

What was the nature of Victorian morality?

Cards, dominoes, backgammon, chess, and checkers were popular. Many homes had a packet of "author cards" that required knowledge of books, authors, and quotations. The latest fad was the stereopticon or "magic lantern," which brought three-dimensional life to art, history, and nature. Like author cards and other games, it was both instructional and entertaining.

Sentimental ballads such as "Silver Threads Among the Gold" (1873) remained the most popular musical form, but the insistent syncopated rhythms of ragtime reflected the influence of the new urban culture. By the time Scott Joplin's "Maple Leaf Rag" (1899) popularized ragtime, critics complained that "a wave of vulgar, filthy, and suggestive music has inundated the land." Classical music flourished. The New England Conservatory (1867), the Cincinnati College of Music (1878), and the Metropolitan Opera (1883) were new sources of civic pride; New York, Boston, and Chicago launched first-rate symphony orchestras between 1878 and 1891.

Fairs, horse races, balloon ascensions, bicycle tournaments, and football and baseball contests attracted avid fans. The popularity of organized spectator sports between 1870 and 1900 reflected both the rise of the city and new uses of leisure. Baseball's first professional team, the Cincinnati Red Stockings, appeared in 1869, and baseball soon became the preeminent national sport. Fans sang songs about it ("Take Me Out to the Ballgame"), wrote poems about it ("Casey at the Bat"), and made up riddles about it ("What has 18 feet and catches flies?"). Modern rules were adopted. Umpires were designated to call balls and strikes; catchers wore masks and chest protectors and moved closer to the plate instead of staying back to catch the ball on the bounce. Fielders had to catch the ball on the fly rather than on one bounce in their caps. By 1890, professional baseball games were drawing crowds of 60,000. In 1901, the American League was organized. Two years later the Boston Red Sox beat the Pittsburgh Pirates in the first modern World Series.

In 1869, Princeton and Rutgers played the first intercollegiate football game. Soon, other schools picked up the sport. By the 1890s, crowds of 50,000 or more attended the most popular contests. Basketball, invented in 1891, gained a large following.

As gas and electric lights brightened the night, and streetcars crisscrossed city streets, leisure habits changed. Delighted with the new technology, people took advantage of an increasing variety of things to do. They stayed home less often. New York City's first electric sign—"Manhattan Beach Swept by Ocean Breezes"—appeared in 1881. At night people filled the streets on their way to the theater, vaudeville shows, and dance halls or just out for a stroll.

Quick Check

In a period of increasing leisure, what did people do in their free time?

Changes in Family Life

Industrialization and urbanization were changing family relationships. On the farm, parents and children worked more or less together, and the family was a producing unit. In factories and offices, family members rarely worked together. In working-class families, mothers, fathers, and children separated at dawn and returned, exhausted, at dark.

Late-nineteenth-century working-class families, like that of the young Polish girl that Harriet Vittum saw, often lived in complex household units—taking in relatives and boarders to pay the rent. As many as one-third of all households contained people who were not members of the immediate family. Although the daily routine separated its members, working-class families tended to retain strong family ties, cemented by the need to survive in the industrial economy.

Middle-class wives and children, however, became increasingly isolated from the world of work, and the middle-class family became more self-contained. Older children spent more time in adolescence, and formal schooling lengthened. Families took in fewer apprentices and boarders. By 1900, more middle-class offspring lived with their parents into their late teens and twenties than do today.

Fewer middle-class wives participated directly in their husbands' work. As a result, they and their children occupied what contemporaries called a "separate sphere of domesticity," set apart from the masculine sphere of income-producing work. The family home became a "walled garden," a retreat from the crass materialism of the outside world. Middle-class fathers began to move their families out of the city to the suburbs, commuting to work on the new streetcars, leaving wives and children at home and school.

The middle-class family had once functioned in part to transmit a craft or skill, arrange marriages, and care for dependent kin. As these functions declined, the family took on new emotional and ideological responsibilities. In a society that worried about the weakening hold of other institutions, the family became an important means of social control.

Magazines such as the *Ladies' Home Journal*, which started in 1889, glorified motherhood and the home, and its articles and ads featured women as homebound, child-oriented consumers. While society's leaders praised the value of homemaking, housewives' status declined under the factory system, which emphasized money rewards and devalued household labor.

Underlying these changes was one of the modern world's most important trends, a decline in fertility rates that lasted from 1800 to 1939. Though blacks, immigrants, and rural dwellers had more children than white native-born city dwellers, the trend affected all classes and races; among white women, the birthrate fell from seven in 1800 to just over four in 1880 to about three in 1900. People everywhere tended to marry later and to have fewer children.

Since contraceptives were not yet widely used, the decline reflected abstinence and a conscious decision to postpone or limit families. Some women decided to devote greater attention to fewer children, others to pursue careers. The number of young unmarried women working for wages, attending school, delaying marriage, or not marrying at all increased, while rates of illegitimacy and premarital pregnancy declined.

The decline in fertility largely stemmed from people's responses to social and economic forces, the rise of cities and industry. Couples decided to have fewer children, and the result reshaped American society.

Quick Check

How did the process of urbanization affect the family?

Changing Views: A Growing Assertiveness Among Women

In and out of the family, self-sufficient women, employed in factories, telephone exchanges, or offices, were increasingly entering the workforce. Most were single and worked because they had to rather than chose to.

Many regarded this "new woman" as a corruption of the ideal vision of the American woman, in which man worshiped "a diviner self than his own," innocent, helpless, and good. Women were to be better than the world around them. They were brought up, said Ida Tarbell, a leading political reformer, "as if wrongdoing were impossible to them."

Views changed, albeit slowly. One important change occurred in the legal codes, particularly in the common law doctrine of *femme couverte*. Under that doctrine, wives were their husbands' chattel; they could not legally control their own earnings, property, or children unless they had a specific contract before marriage. By 1890, many states had revised the doctrine to allow wives control of their earnings and inherited property. The new laws also recognized divorced women's rights to custody or joint custody of their children. Although divorce was still not socially acceptable, divorce rates more than doubled during the last third of the century. By 1905, one in 12 marriages ended in divorce.

In the 1870s and 1880s, more women were asserting their own humanness. They fought for the vote, lobbied for equal pay, and sought self-fulfillment. The new interest in psychology and medicine strengthened their causes. Charlotte Perkins Gilman, author of *Women and Economics* (1898), argued that the ideal of womanly "innocence" actually meant ignorance. In medical and popular literature, menstruation, sexual intercourse, and childbirth were becoming discussed as natural functions instead of taboo topics. For example, Edward Bliss Foote's *Plain Home Talk of Love,*

Quick Check

In what ways did women respond to life in the urban-industrial society?

National American Woman Suffrage Association Founded by Susan B. Anthony in 1890, this organization worked to secure women the right to vote. It stressed careful organization and peaceful lobbying.

Civil Rights Cases A group of cases in 1883 in which the Supreme Court ruled that the Fourteenth Amendment barred state governments from discriminating on the basis of race but did not prevent private individuals or organizations from doing so. The ruling dealt a major blow to efforts to protect African Americans.

Plessy v. Ferguson A Supreme Court case in 1896 that established the doctrine of "separate but equal." The Court applied it to schools in *Cumming v. County Board of Education* (1899). The doctrine was finally overturned in 1954, in *Brown v. Board of Education of Topeka*.

Marriage, and Parentage, a bestseller between the 1880s and 1900, challenged Victorian notions that sexual intercourse was unhealthy and intended solely to produce children.

Women espoused causes with new fervor. Susan B. Anthony, a veteran of many reform campaigns, tried to vote in the 1872 presidential election and was fined $100, which she refused to pay. In 1890, she helped form the **National American Woman Suffrage Association** to work for the enfranchisement of women.

Educating the Masses

Continuing a trend that stretched back a century, childhood was becoming a more distinct time of life. Adolescence—the special nature of the teenage years—was still only a vague concept, but the role of children was changing. Less and less were children perceived as "little adults," valued for the financial gain they might bring the family. Now children were to grow, learn, and be nurtured rather than rushed into adulthood.

As a result, schooling became more important, and universal education for American children came closer than ever before. By 1900, 31 states and territories (out of 51) had made school compulsory, though most required attendance only until age 14. In 1870, there were only 160 public high schools; in 1900, there were 6000. Illiteracy declined from 20 percent to just over 10 percent of the population. Still, even in 1900, the average adult had only five years of schooling.

Educators saw the school as the primary means to train people for life and work in an industrializing society. Hence teachers focused on basic skills—reading and mathematics—and on values—obedience and attentiveness to the clock. Most schools had a highly structured curriculum, built around discipline and routine. In 1892, Joseph Rice, a pediatrician, toured 1200 classrooms in 36 cities. In a typical classroom, he reported, the atmosphere was "damp and chilly," the teacher strict. "The unkindly spirit of the teacher is strikingly apparent; the pupils, being completely subjugated to her will, are silent and motionless." One teacher asked her pupils, "How can you learn anything with your knees and toes out of order?"

School began early; boys attended all day, but girls often stayed home after lunch, since they were thought to need less learning. Many children dropped out of school, and not just to earn money. Helen Todd, a factory inspector in Chicago, found young girls working in a hot, stuffy attic. When she asked why they were not in school, Tillie Isakowsky, who was 14, said, "School! School is de fiercest t'ing youse kin come up against. Factories ain't no cinch, but schools is worst." Todd asked 500 children whether they would go to school or work in a factory if their families did not need the money—412 preferred the factory.

The South lagged far behind in education. The average family size was about twice as large as in the North, and a greater proportion of the population lived in isolated rural areas. State and local authorities mandated fewer weeks in the average school year, and many southern states refused to adopt compulsory education laws. Most important, southerners insisted on maintaining segregated school systems—North Carolina and Alabama in 1876, South Carolina and Louisiana in 1877, Mississippi in 1878, and Virginia in 1882. Supreme Court decisions in the 1880s and 1890s upheld the legality of segregation. In the **Civil Rights Cases** (1883), the Court ruled that the Fourteenth Amendment barred state governments from discriminating on account of race but did not prevent private individuals or organizations from doing so. In **Plessy v. Ferguson (1896)**, the Court established the "separate but equal" doctrine and upheld a Louisiana law requiring different seating in railroad cars for whites and blacks. In *Cumming v. County Board of Education* (1899), the Court approved the creation of separate schools for whites, even if there were no comparable schools for blacks. Segregated schooling added a devastating financial burden to education in the South.

Southern school laws often implied that the schools would be "separate but equal," and they were often separate but rarely equal. Black schools were usually dilapidated, and black teachers were paid considerably less than white teachers. In 1890, only 35 percent of black children attended school in the South; 55 percent of white children did. That year nearly two-thirds of the country's black population was illiterate.

Educational techniques changed after the 1870s. Educators paid more attention to early elementary education, a trend that placed young children in school and helped the growing number of mothers who worked outside the home. The kindergarten movement, started in St. Louis in 1873, spread across the country. In kindergartens, 4- to 6-year-olds learned by playing, not by keeping their knees and toes in order. For older children, social reformers advocated "practical" courses in manual training and homemaking.

Quick Check

In what ways did ideas about education change during these years?

Higher Education

Nearly 150 new colleges and universities opened between 1880 and 1900. The Morrill Land Grant Act of 1862 gave the states land to establish colleges to teach "agriculture and the mechanic arts." The act fostered 69 "land-grant" institutions, including the great state universities of Wisconsin, California, Minnesota, and Illinois.

Private philanthropy, born of the large fortunes of the industrial age, also spurred growth in higher education. Leland Stanford gave $24 million to endow Stanford University on his California ranch, and John D. Rockefeller, founder of the Standard Oil Company, gave $34 million to found the University of Chicago. Other industrialists established Cornell (1865), Vanderbilt (1873), and Tulane (1884).

As colleges expanded, their function changed, and their curriculum broadened. No longer did they exist primarily to train young men for the ministry. They moved away from the classical curriculum of rhetoric, mathematics, Latin, and Greek toward "reality and practicality," as President David Starr Jordan of Stanford University said. MIT, founded in 1861, focused on science and engineering.

Women still had to fight for educational opportunities. Some formed study clubs, an important movement that spread rapidly between 1870 and 1900. Club members read Virgil and Chaucer, studied history and architecture, and discussed women's rights.

Clubs sprang up almost everywhere there were women: in Caribou, Maine; Tyler, Texas; and Leadville, Colorado—as well as San Francisco, New York, and Boston. Although they were usually small, study clubs sparked interest in education among women and their daughters and contributed to a rapid rise in the number of women entering college in the early 1900s.

Before the Civil War, only three private colleges admitted women to study with men. After the war, educational opportunities increased for women. Women's colleges opened, including Vassar (1861), Wellesley (1870), Smith (1871), Bryn Mawr (1885), Barnard (1889), and Radcliffe (1894). The land-grant colleges of the Midwest, open to women from the outset, spurred a nationwide trend toward coeducation, although some physicians, such as Harvard Medical School's Dr. Edward H. Clarke in his popular *Sex in Education* (1873), argued that the strain of learning made women sterile. By 1900, women made up about 40 percent of college students, and four out of five colleges admitted them.

Fewer opportunities existed for African Americans and other minorities. Jane Stanford encouraged the Chinese who had worked on her husband's Central Pacific Railroad to apply to Stanford University, but that was unusual. Most colleges did not accept minority students, and only a few applied. W.E.B. Du Bois, the brilliant African American sociologist and civil rights leader, attended Harvard in the late 1880s but found the social life of Harvard Yard closed to him. Disdained

📖 Read the Document   Morrill Act (1862)

J. Morrill

HON. JUSTIN S. MORRILL

JUSTIN SMITH MORRILL The Morrill Land Grant Act of 1862 gave large grants of land to the states for the establishment of colleges to teach "agriculture and the mechanic arts." The act, sponsored by U.S. Representative Justin Smith Morrill of Vermont, facilitated the creation of 69 "land-grant" institutions, including the state universities of California, Minnesota, Wisconsin, and Illinois.

and disdainful, he "asked no fellowship of my fellow students." Chosen as one of the commencement speakers, Du Bois picked as his topic "Jefferson Davis," the president of the Confederacy, treating it, said an onlooker, with "an almost contemptuous fairness."

Most black students turned to black colleges such as the Hampton Normal and Industrial Institute in Virginia and the Tuskegee Institute in Alabama. Whites who favored manual training for blacks often supported these colleges. Booker T. Washington, an ex-slave, put his educational ideas into practice at Tuskegee, which opened in 1881. Washington began Tuskegee with limited funds, four run-down buildings, and only 30 students; by 1900, it was a model industrial and agricultural school. Spread over 46 buildings, it offered instruction in 30 trades to 1400 students.

Washington stressed patience, manual training, and hard work. "The wisest among my race understand," he said in an acclaimed speech to a white audience at the Atlanta

Cotton States Exposition in 1895, "that the agitation of questions of social equality is the extremest folly." Blacks should focus on economic gains; they should go to school, learn skills, and work their way up the ladder: "No race can prosper till it learns that there is as much dignity in tilling a field as in writing a poem. It is at the bottom of life we must begin, and not at the top." Southern whites should help out, he said, because they would then have "the most patient, faithful, law-abiding, and unresentful people that the world has seen."

Washington's philosophy became known as the Atlanta Compromise, and many whites and some blacks welcomed it. Acknowledging white domination, it called for slow progress through self-improvement, not through lawsuits or agitation. Rather than fighting for equal rights, blacks should acquire property and show they were worthy of their rights. But Washington did believe in black equality. He worked behind the scenes to organize black voters and lobby against harmful laws. In his own way, he bespoke a racial pride that contributed to the rise of black nationalism in the twentieth century.

Du Bois wanted a more aggressive strategy. Born in Massachusetts in 1868, the son of poor parents, he studied at Fisk University in Tennessee and the University of Berlin in Germany before attending Harvard. Unable to find a teaching job in a white college, he took a low-paying research position at the University of Pennsylvania. He had no office but did not need one. Du Bois used the new discipline of sociology, which emphasized factual observation in the field, to study the condition of blacks.

((• Read the Document   W.E.B. du Bois, The Talented Tenth (1903)

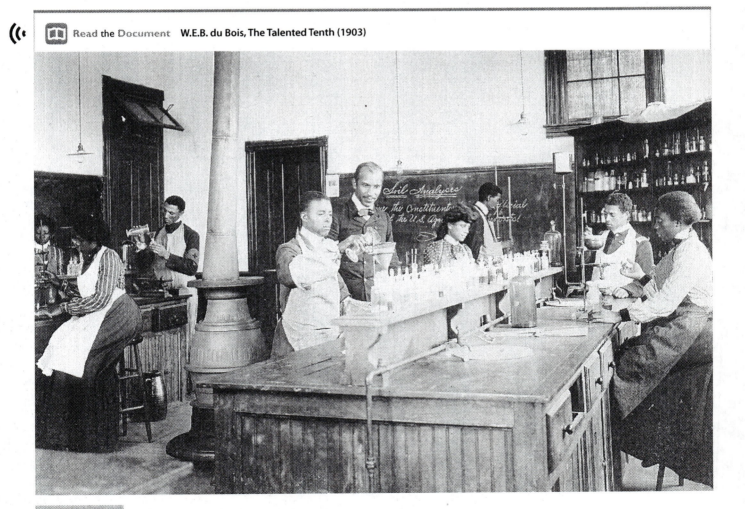

EDUCATIONAL OPPORTUNITIES FOR AFRICAN AMERICANS Booker T. Washington, who served as the first president of Tuskegee Institute, advocated work efficiency and practical skills as keys to advancement for African Americans. Students like these at Tuskegee studied academic subjects and received training in trades and professions.

Notebook in hand, he examined crime in Philadelphia's black seventh ward. He interviewed 5000 people, mapped and classified neighborhoods, and produced *The Philadelphia Negro* (1898). The first study of the effect of urban life on blacks, it cited a wealth of statistics, all suggesting that crime in the ward stemmed not from inborn degeneracy but from the environment in which blacks lived. Change the environment, and people would change, too; education was a good way to go about it.

In *The Souls of Black Folk* (1903), Du Bois openly attacked Booker T. Washington and the philosophy of the Atlanta Compromise. He urged African Americans to aspire to professional careers, fight for their civil rights, and get a college education. Calling for integrated schools with equal opportunity for all, Du Bois urged blacks to educate their "talented tenth," a highly trained intellectual elite, to lead them.

Du Bois was not alone in promoting careers in the professions. Throughout higher education there was increased emphasis on professional training, particularly in medicine, dentistry, and law. Enrollments swelled, even as standards of admission tightened. The number of medical schools in the country rose from 75 in 1870 to 160 in 1900, and the number of medical students—including more women—almost tripled. Nursing schools grew from only 15 in 1880 to 432 in 1900. Doctors, lawyers, and others became part of a growing middle class that shaped the concerns of the Progressive Era of the early twentieth century.

Although less than 5 percent of the college-age population attended college during 1877–1890, the new trends had great impact. A generation of men and women encountered new ideas that changed their views of themselves and society. Courses never before offered, such as Philosophy II at Harvard, "The Ethics of Social Reform," which students called "drainage, drunkenness, and divorce," heightened interest in social problems and the need for reform. Some students burned with a desire to cure society's ills. "My life began . . . at Johns Hopkins University," Frederic C. Howe, an influential reformer, recalled. "I came alive, I felt a sense of responsibility to the world, I wanted to change things."

Quick Check

What were the trends in higher education between the 1870s and 1900?

The Spread of Jim Crow

19.3 Why did Jim Crow laws spread across the South after the end of Reconstruction?

Though Washington and Du Bois differed widely in their views, both of them fought the growing restrictions on black civil rights known as Jim Crow laws (see Chapter 16). While segregation and disfranchisement began as informal arrangements in the immediate aftermath of the Civil War, they soon culminated in a legal regime of separation and exclusion that took firm hold in the 1890s.

Throughout the South, the new measures lent the sanction of law to a racial ostracism that included voting booths, churches, schools, housing, and jobs. Touching virtually all parts of life, they affected public transportation, hospitals, prisons, and asylums—even funeral homes and cemeteries.

A number of influences lay behind their rapid growth. By the 1870s, many northerners had lost interest in guarding the rights of blacks. Weariness with Civil War issues played a role in this trend, as did beliefs in Anglo-Saxon superiority and, after the Spanish–American War of 1898, the acquisition of colonial subjects—called, revealingly, "the white man's burden"—in Hawaii, Guam, Puerto Rico, and the Philippines.

As a result, the North and the federal government did little to stem the tide. Supreme Court decisions between 1878 and 1898 gutted the Reconstruction amendments and the legislation passed to enforce them, leaving blacks virtually defenseless against political and social discrimination (see Table 19.1).

TABLE 19.1 SUPREME COURT DECISIONS AFFECTING BLACK CIVIL RIGHTS, 1875–1900

Case	Effects of Court's Decisions
Hall v. DeCuir (1878)	Struck down Louisiana law prohibiting racial discrimination by "common carriers" (railroads, steamboats, buses). Declared the law a "burden" on interstate commerce, over which states had no authority.
United States v. Harris (1882)	Declared unconstitutional federal laws to punish crimes such as murder and assault. Declared such crimes to be the sole concern of local government. Ignored the frequent racial motivation behind such crimes in the South.
Civil Rights Cases (1883)	Struck down Civil Rights Act of 1875. Declared that Congress may not legislate on civil rights unless a state passes a discriminatory law. Declared the Fourteenth Amendment silent on racial discrimination by private citizens.
Plessy v. Ferguson (1896)	Upheld Louisiana statute requiring "separate but equal" accommodations on railroads. Declared that segregation is *not* necessarily discrimination.
Williams v. Mississippi (1898)	Upheld state law requiring a literacy test to qualify for voting. Refused to find any implication of racial discrimination in the law, although it permitted illiterate whites to vote if they "understood" the Constitution. Using such laws, southern states rapidly disfranchised blacks.

Most visible in areas like voting, Jim Crow laws soon penetrated nearly every aspect of southern life. In 1915, a South Carolina code banned textile factories from allowing laborers of different races to work together in the same room or to use the same entrances, exits, toilets, and drinking water. That year, Oklahoma required telephone companies to maintain separate phone booths for whites and blacks. North Carolina and Florida ordered separate textbooks for black and white children. Florida even required that the books be segregated while they were in storage. A New Orleans ordinance placed black and white prostitutes in separate districts of the city. There were Jim Crow Bibles for African American witnesses in Atlanta courts and Jim Crow elevators in Atlanta buildings.

Jim Crow laws expanded during the 1920s and 1930s. Mississippi segregated white and black patients in hospitals and mandated that nurses could tend only the sick of their own race. City ordinances required Jim Crow taxis in Jacksonville, Florida, in 1929; Birmingham, Alabama, in 1930; and Atlanta, Georgia, in 1940. In 1930, a Birmingham ordinance forbade blacks and whites from playing each other at dominoes or checkers.

Lynchings also spread. Between 1889 and 1899, an average of 187 blacks were lynched every year for alleged offenses against white supremacy. Many blacks (and whites) convicted of petty crimes were leased out to private contractors whose brutality rivaled that of the most sadistic slaveholders. The convict lease system enabled entrepreneurs, such as mine owners and lumber companies, to rent prisoners from the state and treat them as they saw fit. Unlike slaveowners, they suffered no loss when a forced laborer died from overwork.

Racism, of course, was not limited to the South, as race riots in East St. Louis, Illinois (1917), and Chicago (1919), among other events, attested. In 1903, the New York public school system banned *Uncle Tom's Cabin* from its reading lists, saying that Harriet Beecher Stowe's depiction of antebellum slavery "does not belong to today but to an unhappy period of our country's history, the memory of which it is not well to revive in our children." Encountering the racism of the North—far less brutal but racism nonetheless—blacks who had migrated there called it James Crow.

LYNCHING Perhaps no event better expresses the cruel and barbaric nature of the racism and white supremacy that swept the South after Reconstruction than lynching. Although lynchings were not confined to the South, most occurred there, and African American men were the most frequent victims. Here two men lean out of a barn window above a black man who is about to be hanged. Others below prepare to set on fire the pile of hay at the victim's feet. Lynchings were often public events, drawing huge crowds to watch the victim's agonizing death.

The Stirrings of Reform

19.4 How did life in the growing cities lead to ideas of reform?

social Darwinism Adapted by English social philosopher Herbert Spencer from Charles Darwin's theory of evolution, this theory held that the "laws" of evolution applied to human life, that change or reform therefore took centuries, and that the "fittest" would succeed in business and social relationships. It promoted competition and individualism, saw government intervention into human affairs as futile, and was used by the economic and social elite to oppose reform.

When Henry George, a leading reformer, asked a friend what could be done about political corruption in American cities, his friend replied: "Nothing! You and I can do nothing at all.... We can only wait for evolution. Perhaps in four or five thousand years evolution may have carried men beyond this state of things."

This stress on the slow pace of change reflected the doctrine of **social Darwinism**, which argued against the usefulness of reform, and was based on the writings of the English philosopher Herbert Spencer. In influential books, Spencer applied Charles Darwin's principles of natural selection to society. He combined biological evolution and sociology to develop a theory of "social selection" that tried to explain human progress. Like animals, society evolved, slowly, by adapting to the environment. The "survival of the fittest"—Spencer's term, not Darwin's—preserved the strong and weeded out the weak.

Social Darwinism had a number of influential followers in the United States, including William Graham Sumner, a professor of political and social science at Yale University. One of the country's best known academics, Sumner was forceful and eloquent. In writings such as *What Social Classes Owe to Each Other* (1883) and "The Absurd Effort to Make the World Over" (1894), he argued that government action to help the poor or weak interfered with evolution and sapped the species. Reform tampered with the laws of nature.

Social Darwinism's impact on American thinking has been exaggerated, but in the powerful hands of Sumner and others it did influence some journalists, ministers, and policymakers. Between 1877 and the 1890s, however, social Darwinism came under increasing attack. In religion, economics, politics, literature, and law, thoughtful people questioned established conditions and advocated reform.

Progress and Poverty

Read and reread, passed from hand to hand, Henry George's bestseller *Progress and Poverty* (1879) led to a more critical appraisal of American society in the 1880s and beyond. The book jolted traditional thought.

Disturbed by an economic depression in the 1870s and by labor upheavals such as the great railroad strikes of 1877 (see Chapter 18), George saw modern society—rich, complex, with material goods hitherto unknown—as sadly flawed: "The wealthy class is becoming more wealthy; but the poorer class is becoming more dependent. The gulf between the employed and the employer is growing wider; social contrasts are becoming sharper. . . ."

George proposed a simple solution. Land, he thought, formed the basis of wealth, and a few people could grow wealthy just because the price of their land rose. Since the rise in price did not result from any effort on their part, it represented an "unearned increment" that should be taxed for the good of society. A "single tax" on the increment, replacing all other taxes, would help equalize wealth and raise revenue to aid the poor. "Single-tax" clubs sprang up around the country, but George's solution, simplistic and unappealing, had much less impact than his analysis of the problem itself. He raised questions a generation of readers set out to answer.

Quick Check

What was Henry George's solution to economic inequity in the late nineteenth century?

New Currents in Social Thought

George's emphasis on the effects of deprivation in the social environment excited a young country lawyer in Ohio—Clarence Darrow. Unlike the social Darwinists, Darrow was sure that criminals were made and not born. They grew out of "the unjust condition of human life." In the mid-1880s, he left for Chicago and a 40-year career working to convince people that poverty lay at the root of crime. "There is no such thing as crime as the word is generally understood," he told startled prisoners in the Cook County jail. "If every man, woman, and child in the world had a chance to make a decent, fair, honest living there would be no jails and no lawyers and no courts."

Edward Bellamy also dreamed of a cooperative society that eradicated poverty, greed, and crime. A lawyer from western Massachusetts, Bellamy published *Looking Backward, 2000–1887* in 1887 and became a national reform figure overnight. The novel's protagonist, Julian West, falls asleep in 1887 and awakes in 2000 to find himself in a socialist utopia: The government owns the means of production, and citizens share the material rewards. Cooperation, not competition, is the watchword.

📖 Read the Document   Edward Bellamy, from "Looking Backward" (1887)

EDWARD BELLAMY Edward Bellamy was the author in 1887 of *Looking Backward, 2000–1887*. The book envisioned a nation cured of its social problems through the creation of a socialist utopia including the elimination of private competition and government ownership of industry.

Social Gospel Preached by urban Protestant ministers, the Social Gospel focused as much on improving the conditions of life on earth as on saving souls for the hereafter. Its adherents worked for child-labor laws and measures to alleviate poverty.

The world of *Looking Backward* had limits; it was regimented, paternalistic, and filled with the gadgets and material concerns of Bellamy's own day. But it enthralled readers. The book sold 10,000 copies a week, and its followers formed Nationalist Clubs to work for its objectives. By 1890, there were such clubs in 27 states, calling for the nationalization of public utilities and a wider distribution of wealth.

Despite these ideas, some Protestant sects stressed individual salvation and a better life in the next world, not in this one. Poverty was evidence of sinfulness; the poor had only themselves to blame. "God has intended the great to be great and the little to be little," said Henry Ward Beecher, the country's best known pastor. Wealth and destitution, suburbs and slums—all formed part of God's plan.

Challenging those traditional doctrines, churches in the 1880s began establishing missions in city slums. Living among the poor and homeless, urban missionaries grew impatient with religious doctrines that endorsed the status quo.

A religious philosophy known as the **Social Gospel** reflected many of the new trends. As the name suggests, the Social Gospel focused on society as well as individuals, on improving living conditions as well as saving souls. Sermons in Social Gospel churches called on church members to fulfill their social obligations, and adults met before and after the regular service to discuss social and economic problems. Children were excused from sermons, organized into age groups, and encouraged to make the church a center for social and religious activity. Soon churches included dining halls, gymnasiums, and even theaters.

The Settlement Houses

Like Tweed and other bosses, social reformers living in the urban slums appreciated the dependency of the poor; unlike them, they wanted to eradicate the conditions that underlay it. To do so, they formed **settlement houses** in the slums and lived in them to experience the problems they were trying to solve.

Youthful, idealistic, and mostly middle class, these social workers took as their model Toynbee Hall, founded in 1884 in the slums of east London to provide community services to the British poor. Stanton Coit, a moody and poetic graduate of Amherst College, was the first American to borrow the settlement house idea; in 1886, he opened the Neighborhood Guild on New York's Lower East Side. The idea spread. By 1900, there were more than 100 settlements in the country; five years later, more than 200, and by 1910, more than 400.

The settlements included Jane Addams's famous Hull House in Chicago (1889), Robert A. Woods's South End House in Boston (1892), and Lillian Wald's Henry Street Settlement in New York (1893). The reformers wanted to bridge the socioeconomic gap between rich and poor and bring education, culture, and hope to the slums. They sought to create in the heart of the city the values and sense of community of small-town America.

Many of the settlement workers were women, some of them college graduates, who found that society had little use for their talents and energy. Jane Addams, a graduate of Rockford College in Illinois, opened Hull House on South Halsted Street in the heart of the Chicago slums. Twenty-nine years old, forceful and winning, she intended "to share the lives of the poor" and humanize the industrial city. "American ideals," she said, "crumbled under the overpowering poverty of the overcrowded city."

Occupying an old, rundown house, Hull House stressed education, offering classes in elementary English and Shakespeare, lectures on ethics and the history of art, and courses in cooking, sewing, and manual skills. A pragmatist, Addams believed in investigating a problem and then doing something to solve it. Noting the lack of medical care in the area, she established an infant welfare clinic and free medical dispensary. Because the tenements lacked bathtubs, she installed showers in the basement of Hull House and built a bathhouse. Because there was no local library, she opened a reading room. Hull House eventually occupied a dozen buildings, sprawling over more than a city block.

Like settlement workers in other cities, Addams and her colleagues studied the immigrants in nearby tenements. Laboriously, they identified the background of every family in a one-third-square-mile area around Hull House. Finding people of 18 different nationalities, they taught them American history and the English language, yet Addams also encouraged them—through folk festivals and art—to preserve their own heritage.

But the settlement house movement had its limits. Although Hull House, one of the best, attracted 2000 visitors a week, this was still just a fraction of the 70,000 people who lived within six blocks of it. Immigrants sometimes resented the middle-class "strangers" who told them how to live. Dressed always in a brown suit and dark stockings, Harriet Vittum, the head resident of Chicago's Northwestern University Settlement (who told the story of the suicide victim at the beginning of this chapter), was known as "the police lady in brown." She once stopped a dance because it was too wild, and then was disgusted when the boys made "vulgar sounds with their lips." Though her attempts to help were sincere, in private Vittum called the people she was trying to help "ignorant foreigners, who live in an atmosphere of low morals . . . surrounded by anarchy and crime."

What new ideas did Henry George and others offer, and what effect did those ideas have?

19.4

settlement houses Located in poor districts, these community centers tried to soften the impact of urban life for immigrant and other families. Often run by young, educated women, they provided social services and a political voice for their neighborhoods. Chicago's Hull House, founded by Jane Addams in 1889, was the most famous of them.

((Read the Document   **Jane Addams, from** *Twenty Years at Hull House* **(1910)**

THE SETTLEMENT HOUSE, A REVOLUTION AND SOCIAL REFORM Jane Addams founded Chicago's Hull House in 1889. The settlement house provided recreational and day-care facilities; offered extension classes in academic, vocational, and artistic subjects; and, above all, sought to bring hope to poverty-stricken slum dwellers.

Quick Check

What were the causes and characteristics of the numerous settlement houses formed in these years?

Although Addams tried to offer programs for blacks, most white reformers did not, and after 1900, a number of black reformers opened their own settlements. Like the whites, they offered employment information, medical care, and recreational facilities, along with concerts, lectures, and other educational events. White or black, the settlement workers made important contributions to urban life.

A Crisis in Social Welfare

The depression of 1893 jarred the young settlement workers, many of whom had just begun their work. In cities and towns across the country, traditional methods of helping the needy foundered in the crisis. Churches, charity organization societies, and Community Chests did what they could, but their resources were limited, and they functioned on traditional lines. Many of them still tried to change rather than aid individual families, and people were often reluctant to call on them for help.

Gradually, a new class of professional social workers filled the need. Unlike the church and charity volunteers, these social workers wanted not only to feed the poor but to study their condition and alleviate it. Revealingly, they called themselves "case workers" and collected data on the income, housing, jobs, health, and habits of the poor. Prowling tenement districts, they gathered information about the number of rooms and occupants, ventilation, and sanitation of the buildings in tenement districts, putting together a fund of useful data.

Studies of the poor popped up everywhere. Du Bois carried out his pioneering study of urban blacks; Lillian Pettengill worked as a servant to see "the ups and downs of this particular dog-life from the dog's end of the chain." Others became beggars, miners, lumberjacks, and factory laborers.

William T. Stead, a prominent British editor, visited the Chicago World's Fair in 1893 and stayed to examine the city. He roamed the flophouses and tenements and dropped in at Hull House to drink hot chocolate and talk over conditions with Jane Addams. Later he wrote an influential book, *If Christ Came to Chicago* (1894), and in a series of mass meetings during 1893, he called for a civic revival. In response, Chicagoans formed the Civic Federation, a group of 40 leaders who aimed to make Chicago "the best governed, the healthiest city in this country." Setting up task forces for philanthropy, moral improvement, and legislation, they helped spawn the National Civic Federation (1900), a nationwide organization devoted to reforming urban life.

19.1

19.2

19.3

19.4

Quick Check

What effect did the panic and depression of the 1890s have on social thought?

Conclusion: The Pluralistic Society

"The United States was born in the country and moved to the city," historian Richard Hofstadter said. Much of that move occurred during the nineteenth century when the United States was the most rapidly urbanizing nation in the Western world. American cities bustled with energy; they absorbed millions of migrants from Europe and other parts of the world. That migration, and the urban growth that accompanied it, reshaped American politics and culture.

The 1920 census showed that, for the first time, most Americans lived in cities. By then, too, almost half the population was descended from people who had arrived after the American Revolution. As European, African, and Asian cultures met in the American city, a culturally pluralistic society emerged. Dozens of nationalities produced a culture whose members considered themselves Polish Americans, African Americans, and Irish Americans. The melting pot sometimes softened distinctions among the groups, but it only partially blended them into a unified society.

"Ah, Vera," said a character in Israel Zangwill's popular play *The Melting Pot* (1908), "what is the glory of Rome and Jerusalem where all nations and races come to worship and look back, compared with the glory of America, where all races and nations come to labour and look forward!" Critics scorned the play as "romantic claptrap," and indeed it was. But the metaphor of the melting pot depicted a new national image. In the decades after the 1870s, a jumble of ethnic and racial groups struggled for a place in society.

That society, it is clear, experienced a crisis between 1870 and 1900. Together, the growth of cities and the rise of industrial capitalism brought jarring change, the exploitation of labor, ethnic and racial tensions, poverty—and, for a few, wealth beyond imagination. There was often open warfare between capital and labor. As reformers struggled to mediate the situation, they turned to state and federal government to look after human welfare, a tendency the Supreme Court resisted. In the midst of the crisis, the depression of the 1890s added to the turmoil, straining American institutions. Tracing the changes wrought by waves of urbanization and industrialization, Henry George described the country as "the House of Have and the House of Want," almost a paraphrase of Abraham Lincoln's earlier metaphor of the "house divided" over slavery. The question was, Could this house, unlike that one, stand?

Chapter Review

The Lure of the City

19.1 Why did cities in the United States grow between 1880 and 1900? p. 431

American cities grew by leaps and bounds between 1880 and 1900. Among the reasons for the growth were the needs of an industrializing society; technological change in the form of electricity, elevators, steel beams, and other advances; and the arrival of millions of immigrants. Politically, city bosses retained power by responding to the needs of immigrants and other urban voters.

Social and Cultural Change, 1877–1900

19.2 How did the growth of American cities affect social, cultural, and political life? p. 438

The rapid growth of cities changed how Americans thought and acted. Cities opened up new areas of entertainment, employment, and behavior. They reshaped the family, brought more women into the workforce, and emphasized education.

The Spread of Jim Crow

19.3 Why did Jim Crow laws spread across the South after the end of the Reconstruction? p. 446

After Reconstruction ended in 1877, northern weariness with Civil War issues, a series of Supreme Court decisions, and growing racism led the federal government to stop trying to uphold civil rights legislation in the South. This enabled Southern states and cities to pass and enforce Jim Crow laws that mandated rigid separation between blacks and whites.

The Stirrings of Reform

19.4 How did life in the growing cities lead to ideas of reform? p. 448

Urban life, which forced many people close together, made social problems unprecedentedly visible. The city could not hide the contrasts between rich and poor, the dirtiness and dangers of factory life, and the woeful lot of millions of immigrants. Reformers argued for change. Some of them, like Jane Addams, opened urban settlement houses where they lived among the poor.

Timeline

1862
Social and Cultural Change—Morrill Land Grant gives land to states to establish colleges

1873
Social and Cultural Change—Nation's first kindergarten opens in St. Louis

1874
Social and Cultural Change—Women's Christian Temperance Union formed to crusade against evils of liquor

1879
Stirrings of Reform—Henry George analyzes urban problems in *Progress and Poverty*

1881
Stirrings of Reform—Booker T. Washington opens Tuskegee Institute in Alabama

1889
Stirrings of Reform—Jane Addams opens Hull House in Chicago

1890
Stirrings of Reform—National American Woman Suffrage Association formed

1894
Lure of the City—Immigration Restriction League formed to limit immigration from southern and eastern Europe

1896
Spread of Jim Crow—Supreme Court in *Plessy v. Ferguson* establishes constitutionality of "separate but equal" facilities

20 Political Realignments 1876–1901

Hardship and Heartache

n June 1894, Susan Orcutt, a young farm woman from western Kansas, wrote a letter to the governor of her state. She was desperate. The nation was in the midst of a devastating economic depression, and, like thousands of others, she had no money and nothing to eat. "I take my Pen In hand to let you know that we are Starving to death," she wrote. Hail had ruined the Orcutts' crops, and none of the household could find work. "My Husband went away to find work and came home last night and told me that we would have to Starve. [H]e has bin in ten countys and did not Get no work . . . . I havent had nothing to Eat today and It is three oclock[.]"

We do not know what happened to the Orcutts, but conditions were no better in the cities. "There are thousands of homeless and starving men in the streets," reported a Chicago journalist in the winter of 1893. "I have seen more misery in this last week than I ever saw in my life before." Charity societies and churches could not

WEALTH AND POVERTY Tiny children peddling newspapers and women domestics serving the rich— their meager earnings were desperately needed.

LEARNING OBJECTIVES

20.1 ((⋅	20.2 ((⋅	20.3 ((⋅	20.4 ((⋅	20.5 ((⋅	20.6 ((⋅
Why was there a stalemate between Republicans and Democrats until the mid-1890s? p. 457	What factors led to the formation and growth of the Farmers' Alliance and People's party? p. 462	What were the main political and labor effects of the panic and depression of the 1890s? p. 467	What changes in outlook did the panic and depression of the 1890s bring about? p. 470	Why was the presidential election of 1896 so important? p. 471	What did McKinley accomplish that placed the results of the 1896 election on a solid base? p. 475

From Chapter 20 of *American Stories: A History of the United States,* Third Edition. H. W. Brands, R. Hal Williams, T. H. Breen and Ariela J. Gross Copyright © 2015 by Pearson Education, Inc.

((⋅ **Listen to Chapter 20 on MyHistoryLab**

20.1

20.2

20.3

20.4

20.5

20.6

⊙ Watch the Video Series on MyHistoryLab

Learn about some key topics related to this chapter with the *MyHistoryLab Video Series: Key Topics in U. S. History.*

1 **Changing Political Landscape** As industrialization became entrenched in the United States, politicians felt pressure to resolve the tensions that arose between the financial interests of the working class and wealthy businessmen. The Sherman Anti-trust act of 1890 established federal jurisdiction over monopolies; but was also used as a way to control unions. The divide between workers and businessmen was reflected in a political debate as to whether the US dollar should be backed by gold or silver. Maintenance of a gold standard would have tended to control inflation and hence benefit creditors, while a silver standard would tend to deflate the dollar and stimulate growth.

⊙ Watch on MyHistoryLab

Populist Party During the 1890s, grievances and concerns of both the rural farm population and the urban working class led to the formation of a powerful new political party, the Populists, which championed currency reform, regulation of industry, and expanded, participatory democracy. This video examines the party's origins and issues, as well as its nomination of the Democratic candidate William Jennings Bryan as its candidate for president in the 1896 election. **2**

Watch on MyHistoryLab

3 **Financial Crisis** Between the Civil War and World War I and US economy was characterized by alternating periods of contraction and expansion, and periodic financial crises. This unstable financial environment produced calls for social reform and fear among property classes of social and political upheaval. The Pullman Strike of 1894 which spread to 27 states exemplified this instability. The unwillingness of President Cleveland, a Democrat, to address financial crisis by removing the country from the gold standard produced a long period of Republican dominance in Presidential politics.

⊙ Watch on MyHistoryLab

The Age of Reform This video profiles those reformers who confronted the abuses and inequalities of the so-called Gilded Age. They include author and social critic Mark Twain, politician and monetary reformer William Jennings Bryan, and Jacob Riis, an urban social reformer. Like factory workers, famers too organized themselves into cooperative organizations such as the Grangers to counter the abuses and price manipulations of railroad tycoons and commodity speculators. **4**

Watch on MyHistoryLab

handle the huge numbers who were in need. The records of the Massachusetts state medical examiner told a grim story:

K.R., 29   Suicide by drowning
Boston   October 2, 1896

Out of work and despondent for a long while. Body found floating in the Charles [River].

F.S., 29   Suicide by arsenic
Boston   January 1, 1896

Much depressed for several weeks. Loss of employment. At 7:50 A.M. Jan. 1, she called her father and told him she had taken poison and wished to die.

L.M., 38   Hanging suicide
E. Boston   October 15, 1895

20.1

20.2

20.3

20.4

20.5

20.6

Had been out of work for several weeks and was very despondent. Wife went to market at about 11 A.M. and upon returning at about 12 P.M. found him hanging from bedroom door. . . . Slipped noose about his neck and [fell] forward upon it.

R.N., 23   Suicide by bullet wound of brain

Boston   June 22, 1896

Out of work. Mentally depressed. About 3 P.M. June 21 shot himself in right temple. . . . Left a letter explaining that he killed himself to save others the trouble of caring for him.

Lasting until 1897, the depression was the decisive event of the decade. At its height, 3 million people were unemployed—20 percent of the workforce. The human costs were enormous, even among the well-to-do. "They were for me years of simple Hell," shattering "my whole scheme of life," said Charles Francis Adams, Jr., the descendant of two American presidents. "I was sixty-three years old and a tired man when at last the effects of the 1893 convulsion wore themselves out."

Like the Great Depression of the 1930s that gave rise to the New Deal, the depression of the 1890s had profound and lasting effects. Bringing to a head many of the tensions that had been building in the society, it increased rural hostility toward the cities, provoked a bitter fight over the currency, and changed attitudes to government, unemployment, and reform. There were outbreaks of war between capital and labor; farmers demanded a fairer share of economic and social benefits; the new immigrants came under attack. The depression of the 1890s changed the course of American history, as did another event of that decade: the war with Spain in 1898.

The impact of the depression changed American history. It led to a stronger impulse toward reform, a larger role for the presidency, help for farmers and laborers. The depression brought to fruition a realignment of the American political system that had been developing since the end of Reconstruction in 1877, establishing new patterns that gave rise to the Progressive Era and have endured into the twenty-first century.

Politics of Stalemate

20.1   Why was there a stalemate between Republicans and Democrats until the mid-1890s?

Politics fascinated late-nineteenth-century Americans. Political campaigns involved the whole community, even though in most states only men could vote. During the weeks before an election, there were rallies, parades, picnics, and torchlight processions. In the six presidential elections from 1876 to 1896, an average of almost 79 percent of the electorate voted, a higher percentage than before or after.

White males made up the bulk of the electorate; until after 1900, women could vote in national elections only in Wyoming, Utah, Idaho, and Colorado. The National Woman Suffrage Association sued for the vote, but in 1875, the Supreme Court (*Minor v. Happersett*) upheld the power of the states to deny them this right. Congress refused to pass a constitutional amendment for woman suffrage, and between 1870 and 1910, nearly a dozen states defeated referenda to grant women the vote.

Black men were also kept from the polls. In 1877, Georgia adopted the poll tax to make voters pay an annual tax for the right to vote. The technique, aimed at disfranchising impoverished blacks, quickly spread across the South.

In 1890, Mississippi required voters to be able to read and interpret the Constitution to the satisfaction of registration officials, all of them white. Such literacy tests, which the Supreme Court upheld in *Williams v. Mississippi* (1898), excluded poor white voters as well as blacks. To get around this, in 1898 Louisiana adopted the infamous "grandfather clause," which used a literacy test to disqualify black voters but permitted men who had failed the test to vote anyway if their fathers and grandfathers had voted before 1867—a time, of course, when no blacks could vote. The tactics worked. Black voters almost disappeared in the South. In 1896, there were 130,334 registered black voters in Louisiana; in 1904, there were 1342.

20.1

20.2

20.3

20.4

20.5

20.6

The Party Deadlock

The Civil War generation, the singular group of men who rose to power in the turbulent 1850s, still dominated politics in the 1870s and 1880s. In both North and South, they had ruled longer than most generations, aware that the war had set them apart. Five of the six presidents elected between 1865 and 1900 had served in the Civil War, as had many civic, business, and religious leaders. In 1890, over 1 million veterans of the Union army and hundreds of thousands of Confederates were still alive.

Party loyalties—rooted in Civil War traditions, ethnic and religious differences, and perhaps class distinctions—were strong. Voters clung to their old parties, shifts were infrequent, and there were relatively few "independent" voters. Although linked to the defeated Confederacy, the Democrats revived quickly after the war. They rested on a less sectional base than the Republicans. Identification with civil rights and military rule cut Republican strength in the South, but the Democratic party's principles of states' rights, decentralization, and limited government won supporters everywhere.

While Democrats wanted to keep government local and small, the Republicans pursued policies for the nation as a whole, in which government was an instrument to promote moral progress and material wealth. The Republicans passed the Homestead Act (1862), granted subsidies to the transcontinental railroads, and pushed other measures to encourage economic growth. They enacted legislation and constitutional amendments to protect civil rights. They advocated a high protective tariff as a tool of economic policy, to keep out foreign products while "infant industries" grew.

In national elections, 16 states, mostly in New England and the North, consistently voted Republican; 14 states, mostly in the South, consistently voted Democratic. A handful of "doubtful" states therefore could swing elections. These states—New York, New Jersey, Connecticut, Ohio, Indiana, and Illinois—received special attention during elections. Politicians lavished money and time on them; presidential candidates usually came from them. From 1868 to 1912, eight of the nine Republican presidential candidates and six of the seven Democratic candidates came from the "doubtful" states, especially New York and Ohio.

The two parties were evenly matched, and elections were closely contested. In three of the five presidential elections from 1876 to 1892, the victor won by less than 1 percent of the vote; in 1876 and 1888, the losing candidates actually had more popular votes than the winners but lost in the electoral college. Only twice during these years did one party control the presidency and both houses of Congress—the Republicans in 1888 and the Democrats in 1892.

Reestablishing Presidential Power

Andrew Johnson's impeachment in 1868, the scandals of the Grant administrations in the 1870s, and the controversy over the 1876 election weakened the presidency. In the 1880s and 1890s, presidents fought to reassert their authority. By 1900, under William McKinley, they had largely succeeded. The late 1890s, in fact, marked the birth of the modern powerful presidency.

The disputed election of 1876 clouded Rutherford B. Hayes' title to the presidency, but he soon began to reassert his authority (see Chapter 16). Hayes worked to reform the civil service, appointed reformers to high office, and ended military Reconstruction. Committed to the gold standard, a monetary system based on gold—the only basis, Hayes thought, of a sound currency—in 1878 he vetoed a bill calling for the partial coinage of silver. Congress passed the **Bland-Allison Silver Purchase Act**, requiring coinage of silver, over his veto.

James A. Garfield, a Union army hero and long-time member of Congress from Ohio, succeeded Hayes in 1881 (see Table 20.1). Winning by a handful of votes, he took office determined to unite the Republican party (which was split by personality differences and disagreements over the tariff and the South), lower the tariff to cut taxes, and assert American interests in Latin America. Garfield had looked forward to the presidency, yet within weeks he told friends, "My God! What is there in this place that a man should ever want to get into it?"

Quick Check

What were the characteristics of politics in the 1870s, 1880s, and 1890s?

Bland-Allison Silver Purchase Act This 1878 act called for the partial coinage of silver. Those favoring silver coinage argued that it would increase the money supply and help farmers and workers repay their debts. Opponents advocated a restricted money supply based solely on gold and pointed out that few other major countries accepted silver coinage. Congress passed the bill over President Rutherford B. Hayes's veto.

20.1

20.2

20.3

20.4

20.5

20.6

TABLE 20.1 THE ELECTION OF 1880

Candidate	Party	Popular Vote	Electoral Vote
Garfield	Republican	4,454,416	214
Hancock	Democrat	4,444,952	155
Weaver	Greenback	308,578	0

Office seekers, hordes of them, caused Garfield's anguish. Each wanted a government job and thought nothing of cornering the president on every occasion. Garfield planned to leave Washington on July 2, 1881, for a New England vacation. Walking toward his train, he was shot in the back by Charles J. Guiteau, a deranged lawyer and disappointed office seeker. Suffering through the summer, Garfield died on September 19, 1881, and Vice President Chester A. Arthur—an ally of Senator Roscoe Conkling from New York—became president.

Arthur was a better president than many had expected. In 1883, with his backing, Congress passed the **Pendleton Act** to reform the civil service. In part a reaction to Garfield's assassination, the act created a bipartisan Civil Service Commission to administer competitive examinations and appoint officeholders on the basis of merit. It laid the basis for the expansion of the civil service.

In the election of 1884, Grover Cleveland, the Democratic governor of New York, won a narrow victory (see Table 20.2). The first Democratic president since 1861, Cleveland reflected his party's desire to curtail federal activities. He vetoed more than two-thirds of the bills presented to him, more than all his predecessors combined.

In 1887, Cleveland committed himself and the Democratic party to lowering the tariff, "the vicious, inequitable, and illogical source of unnecessary taxation." The Republicans accused him of undermining American industries. In 1888, they nominated for the presidency Benjamin Harrison of Indiana, a defender of the tariff. Cleveland garnered 90,000 more popular votes than Harrison but carried only two northern states, Connecticut and New Jersey, and the South. Harrison won the electoral vote 233 to 168 (see Map 20.1).

Pendleton Act This 1883 law created a bipartisan Civil Service Commission to administer competitive exams for civil service jobs and appoint officeholders based on merit. It also outlawed compulsory political contributions from appointed officials.

Quick Check

How did each of the presidents from Rutherford B. Hayes to Benjamin Harrison work to regain the powers of his office, diminished during the impeachment of president Andrew Johnson?

Republicans in Power: The Billion-Dollar Congress

Despite Harrison's narrow margin, the election of 1888 was the most sweeping victory for either party in almost twenty years; it gave the Republicans the presidency and both houses of Congress. They had broken, it seemed, the party stalemate and become the majority party in the country.

Tariffs, Trusts, and Silver

As if a dam had burst, law after law poured out of the Republican Congress during 1890. The McKinley Tariff Act raised tariff duties about 4 percent, higher than ever before. A Dependent Pensions Act granted pensions to Union army veterans and their widows and children. The pensions were modest—$6 to $12 a month—but the number of pensioners doubled by 1893, when nearly one million people received about $160 million in pensions.

TABLE 20.2 THE ELECTION OF 1884

Candidate	Party	Popular Vote	Electoral Vote
Cleveland	Democrat	4,874,986	219
Blaine	Republican	4,851,981	182
Butler	Greenback	175,370	0
St. John	Prohibition	150,369	0

20.1

20.2

20.3

20.4

20.5

20.6

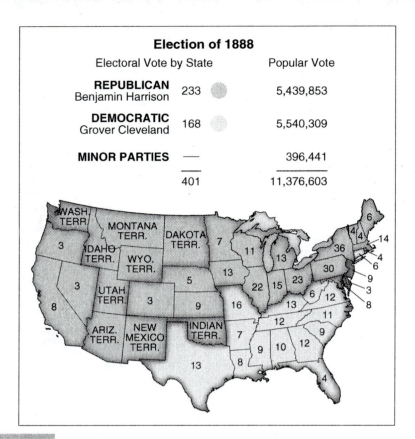

Election of 1888

	Electoral Vote by State		Popular Vote
REPUBLICAN Benjamin Harrison	233		5,439,853
DEMOCRATIC Grover Cleveland	168		5,540,309
MINOR PARTIES	—		396,441
	401		11,376,603

MAP 20.1 ELECTION OF 1888

Sherman Antitrust Act This 1890 act was the first major U.S. attempt to deal with the problem of the increasing size of business. It declared illegal "every contract, combination in the form of trust or otherwise, or conspiracy, in restraint of trade or commerce."

With little debate, the Republicans and Democrats joined in passing the **Sherman Antitrust Act**, the first federal attempt to deal with the problem of trusts and industrial growth (see Chapter 18). The act shaped all later antitrust policy. It declared illegal "every contract, combination in the form of trust or otherwise, or conspiracy, in restraint of trade or commerce." Experimental in nature, the act's terms were often vague, leaving precise interpretation to later experience and the courts.

The Sherman Antitrust Act made the United States virtually the only industrial nation to regulate business combinations. It tried to harness big business without harming it. Many members of Congress did not expect the new law to have much effect, and for a decade it did not. The Justice Department rarely filed suit under it, and in the first judicial interpretation of the law in 1895, the Supreme Court crippled it. Though the E. C. Knight Co. controlled 98 percent of sugar refining in the country, the Court sharply distinguished commerce from manufacturing, holding that the company, as a manufacturer, was not subject to the law. But judicial interpretations changed after 1900, and the Sherman Antitrust Act gained fresh power.

Sherman Silver Purchase Act An 1890 act that attempted to resolve the controversy over silver coinage by requiring the Treasury to purchase 4.5 million ounces of silver each month and issue legal tender (in the form of Treasury notes) for it. The act pleased opponents of silver because it did not call for free coinage; it pleased proponents of silver because it bought up most of the nation's silver production.

Another measure, the **Sherman Silver Purchase Act**, tried to solve the problem silver presented. Together with gold, silver had played a large role in currencies around the world. But by the mid-1800s, silver coinage had slipped into disuse. With the discovery of the great bonanza mines in Nevada (see Chapter 18), American silver production quadrupled between 1870 and 1890, glutting the world market, lowering the price of silver, and persuading many European nations to abandon silver coinage in favor of the scarcer metal, gold, and thus restrict the amount of money in circulation.

Support for silver coinage was especially strong in the South and West, where people thought it might inflate the currency, raise wages and crop prices, make it cheaper to repay debts, and challenge the power of the gold-oriented Northeast, which favored high prices for its manufactured goods. Eager to avert the so-called free coinage of silver, which would require the U.S. mints to buy all the silver available for coinage,

📖 Read the Document Workingman's Amalgamated Sherman Antitrust (1893)

20.1

20.2

20.3

20.4

20.5

20.6

THE BOSSES OF THE SENATE.

SHERMAN ANTITRUST ACT Congress passed the Sherman Antitrust Act in 1890, which authorized federal action against any "combination in the form of trust or otherwise, or conspiracy, in restraint of trade." Though the act was envisioned as a way to control big business, its wording was sufficiently vague as to allow the federal government to use this law against labor unions, which many people considered to be combinations.

President Harrison and other Republicans pressed for a compromise that took shape in the Sherman Silver Purchase Act of 1890.

The act directed the Treasury to purchase 4.5 million ounces of silver a month and issue legal tender in the form of Treasury notes in payment for it. This satisfied both sides. Opponents of silver were pleased that it did not include free coinage. Silverites were delighted that the monthly purchases would buy up most of the country's silver production. The Treasury notes, moreover, could be cashed for either gold or silver at a bank, a gesture toward a bimetallic coinage system based on silver and gold.

Quick Check

What were the three most important measures of the "Billion-Dollar Congress"?

The 1890 Elections

The Republican Congress of 1890 was one of the most important Congresses in American history. It passed a record number of laws that helped shape later policy and asserted the authority of the federal government to a degree the country would not then accept. Sensing the public unease, the Democrats labeled it the "Billion-Dollar Congress" for spending that much in appropriations and grants.

"This is a billion-dollar country," Speaker of the House Thomas B. Reed of Maine replied, but the voters disagreed. The 1890 elections crushed the Republicans, who lost 78 seats in the House. Political veterans went down to defeat, and new leaders vaulted into prominence. Nebraska elected a Democratic governor for the first time in its history. Iowa, once so staunchly Republican that an Iowa Republican had predicted that "Iowa will go Democratic when Hell goes Methodist," went Democratic in 1890.

Quick Check

Why were the 1890 elections among the most important midterm elections in American history?

20.1

20.2

20.3

20.4

20.5

20.6

THE BATTLE OF THE STANDARDS In this 1886 cartoon illustrating the silver standard versus gold standard controversy, Uncle Sam bicycles to national bankruptcy on an enormous silver dollar.

The Rise of the Populist Movement

20.2 What factors led to the formation and growth of the Farmers' Alliance and People's party?

National Farmers' Alliance and Industrial Union The Alliance sought to organize farmers in the South and West to fight for reforms that would improve their lot, including measures to overcome low crop prices, burdensome mortgages, and high railroad rates. The Alliance ultimately organized the People's (Populist) party.

The elections of 1890 drew attention to a fast-growing movement among farmers that came to be known as populism. That summer, thousands of farm families in the South and West met on campgrounds and picnic areas to socialize and discuss problems. They were weary of drought, mortgages, and low crop prices, and they listened to recruiters from the **National Farmers' Alliance and Industrial Union**, which promised united action to solve agricultural problems.

One thousand farmers a week were joining the Alliance; the Kansas Alliance alone claimed 130,000 members in 1890. The summer of 1890 became "that wonderful picnicking, speech-making Alliance summer," a time of fellowship and spirit farmers long remembered.

20.1
20.2
20.3
20.4
20.5
20.6

✳ Explore the Populist Movement on MyHistoryLab

WHAT IMPACT DID THE POPULIST MOVEMENT HAVE ON AMERICAN POLITICS?

THE POPULIST PARTY The short-lived Populist Party saw its candidate, William Jennings Bryan, nominated as the Democratic Party's candidate in the election of 1896. This pro-Republican caricature attempts to show how the Democrats had been swallowed by the orator's progressive message and political power.

In the last decades of the 1800s, farmers—especially those in the South and in the Plains states—faced serious difficulties. Crop prices had been depressed by commodity speculation and further aggravated by a drought between 1890 and 1896. The U.S. gold standard, too, restricted the supply of money. The minting of more silver coinage—"Free Silver"—was seen as a solution to farmers unable to pay their bills. The farmers began to look outside the established Democratic and Republican parties for candidates to voice their grievances, leading to the birth of a new movement, the Populist Movement. The new movement formed coalitions with urban labor unions and so increased their influence. This movement produced a new political party, the People's Party, which focused on a need for more government action in the regulation of the economy. The People's Party nominated James B. Weaver as its candidate for president in the election of 1892. Although he lost, his party won several Western states as well as various state and local offices. This partial victory and the depression of 1893 allowed the People's Party to expand and to gain power within the Democratic Party in the election of 1896. The People's Party made the Democratic nominee for president, William Jennings Bryan, its nominee for president. Bryan's loss to William J. McKinley would weaken and end the People's Party as a separate party. Its influence, however, would contribute to realignments in both the Republican and Democratic parties that exist to this day, notably in their shifts of voting support, regions of strength, and stances of policy. The Republicans, for example, would inherit some of the key issues of the People's Party. The Democratic Party would adopt its emphasis on the economically disadvantaged.

PRESIDENTIAL ELECTION RESULTS: 1892

Candidate	Popular Vote
Grover Cleveland (D)	5,551,833
Benjamin Harrison (R)	5,179,244
James B. Weaver (P)	1,041,028

PRESIDENTIAL ELECTION RESULTS: 1896

Candidate	Popular Vote
William McKinley (R)	7,108,480
William J. Bryan (D)	6,511,495

SOURCE: Library of Congress http://www.archives.gov/federal-register/electoral-college/scores.html#1892

KEY QUESTIONS Use MyHistoryLab *Explorer* to answer these questions:

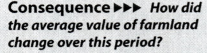

Consequence ▶▶▶ *How did the average value of farmland change over this period?*

Chart these changes to consider their impact on national politics.

Analysis ▶▶▶ *How did the People's Party fare in various elections?*

Consider the overall larger political influence of the People's Party.

Response ▶▶▶ *In what regions was support for the People's Party strongest?*

Map the geographical distribution of Populist support.

20.1

20.2

20.3

20.4

20.5

20.6

The Farm Problem

Farm discontent was a worldwide phenomenon between 1870 and 1900. The new means of transportation and communication enmeshed farmers everywhere in a complex international market they neither controlled nor entirely understood.

American farmers complained bitterly about declining prices for their products, rising railroad rates to ship them, and burdensome mortgages. Some of their grievances were valid. Farm profits were low; agriculture in general tends to produce low profits because the ease of entry into the industry fosters competition. But even though farmers received less for their crops, their purchasing power actually increased in these years.

The farmers' second grievance—rising railroad rates—was not entirely justified. Railroad rates actually fell during these years, benefiting shippers of all products. Farm mortgages, the farmers' third grievance, were common because many farmers mortgaged their property to expand their holdings or buy new machinery. While certainly burdensome, most mortgages were short, with a term of four years or less, after which farmers could renegotiate at new rates. The new machinery farmers bought enabled them to triple their output and increase their income.

Some farmers did have valid grievances, though many understandably exaggerated them. More important, many farmers felt their condition had declined, and this perception—as bitterly real as any actual fact—sparked a growing anger. Equally upsetting, everyone in the 1870s and 1880s seemed excited about factories, not farms. A literature of disillusionment described the drabness of farm life.

The Fast-Growing Farmers' Alliance

By the late 1880s, different farm societies had formed into two major organizations: the National Farmers' Alliance, located on the Plains west of the Mississippi and known as the Northwestern Alliance, and the Farmers' Alliance and Industrial Union, based in the South and known as the Southern Alliance.

Quick Check

What was the situation of farmers between 1870 and 1900?

📖 Read the Document   **Proceedings of the Thirteenth Session of the National Grange of the Patrons of Husbandry (1879)**

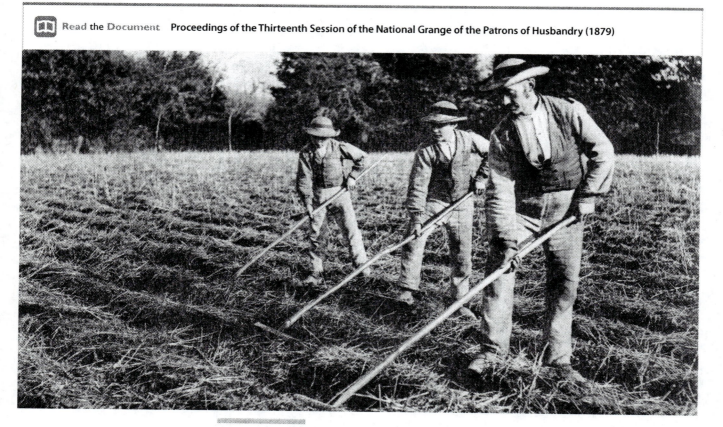

THE FARMERS' ALLIANCE The Alliance movement grew quickly in the late 1800s among discontented farmers. Pictured here, a farmer and his two sons pose as they tend to the hay fields.

20.1

20.2

20.3

20.4

20.5

20.6

The Southern Alliance spread rapidly across the South, where farmers were fed up with crop liens, depleted lands, and sharecropping. In 1890, the Southern Alliance claimed more than a million members. It welcomed the farmers' "natural friends"— country doctors, teachers, preachers, and mechanics. It excluded lawyers, bankers, cotton merchants, and warehouse operators.

The Southern Alliance published its own newspaper and distributed material to hundreds of local newspapers. In five years its lecturers spoke to 2 million farm families in 43 states and territories. It was "the most massive organizing drive by any citizen institution of nineteenth-century America."

Loosely affiliated with the Southern Alliance, a separate Colored Farmers' National Alliance and Cooperative Union enlisted black farmers in the South. Claiming more than 1 million members, it probably had about 250,000, but even that was sizable in an era when "uppity" blacks faced not merely hostility, but death. In 1891, black cotton pickers struck for higher wages in Tennessee. Led by Ben Patterson, a 30-year-old picker, they walked off several plantations. A posse hunted them down and, following violence on both sides, lynched 15 strikers, including Patterson. The abortive strike ended the Colored Farmers' Alliance.

((• 📖 Read the Document   **Mary E. Lease,** *The Populist Crusader* (1892)

MARY E. LEASE Populist Mary E. Lease advised farmers to "raise less corn and more hell." She also said, "if one man has not enough to eat three times a day and another man has $25 million, that last man has something that belongs to the first."

SOURCE: Everett Collection Inc./Alamy

20.1

20.2

20.3

20.4

20.5

20.6

On the Plains, the Northwestern Alliance, a smaller organization, was formed in 1880. Its objectives were similar to those of the Southern Alliance, but it disagreed with the Southerners' emphasis on secrecy, centralized control, and separate organizations for blacks. In 1889, the Southern Alliance changed its name to the National Farmers' Alliance and Industrial Union and persuaded the three strongest state alliances on the Plains—those in the Dakotas and Kansas—to join. Thereafter, it dominated the Alliance movement.

The Alliance mainly sponsored social and economic programs, but it turned early to politics. In the West, its leaders rejected both the Republicans and Democrats and organized their own party; in June 1890, Kansas Alliance members formed the first major People's party. The Southern Alliance resisted forming a new party lest it divide the white vote and undercut white supremacy. Instead, the Southerners followed leaders such as Benjamin F. "Pitchfork Ben" Tillman of South Carolina, who wanted to capture control of the dominant Democratic party.

The Alliance leadership was highly qualified. Thomas E. Watson, a talented orator and organizer, urged Georgia farmers, black and white, to unite against their oppressors. The president of the National Farmers' Alliance, Leonidas L. Polk, a former Confederate officer from North Carolina, believed in scientific farming and cooperative action. In Kansas, Mary E. Lease helped head a movement remarkably open to female leadership. A captivating speaker, she made 160 speeches during the summer of 1890, calling on farmers to resist Wall Street and the industrial East.

Meeting in Ocala, Florida, in 1890, the Alliance adopted the **Ocala Demands**, a platform the organization pushed as long as it existed. First and foremost, it demanded the creation of a "sub-treasury system," to allow farmers to store their crops in government warehouses. In return, they could claim Treasury notes for up to 80 percent of the local market value of the crop. They would repay this loan when the crops were sold. Farmers could thus hold their crops until they could get the best price. The Ocala Demands also urged the free coinage of silver, an end to protective tariffs and national banks, a federal income tax, the direct election of senators by voters instead of state legislatures, and tighter regulation of railroads.

The Alliance strategy worked well in the elections of 1890. In Kansas, the Alliance-related People's party elected four congressmen (out of eight) and a U.S. senator. Across the South, the Alliance won victories based on the "Alliance yardstick," a demand that Democratic candidates support Alliance measures. Alliance leaders claimed 38 Alliance supporters elected to Congress, with at least a dozen more pledged to Alliance principles.

Ocala Demands Adopted by the Farmers' Alliance in 1890 in Ocala, Florida, these demands became the organization's main platform. They called for a sub-treasury system to allow farmers to store their crops until they could get the best price, the free coinage of silver, an end to protective tariffs and national banks, a federal income tax, the direct election of senators by voters, and tighter regulation of railroads. (see People's party).

Quick Check

What were the Ocala Demands?

The People's Party

After the 1890 elections, Northern Alliance leaders wanted to form a national third party to promote reform. In July 1892, a convention in Omaha, Nebraska, formed the new **People's (or Populist) party**. Southern Alliance leaders finally joined, convinced that the Democrats exploited Alliance popularity but failed to adopt its reforms.

In the South, some Populists worked for a time to unite black and white farmers. "They are in the ditch just like we are," a white Texas Populist said. Blacks and whites served on Populist election committees, spoke from the same platforms, and ran on the same tickets. Populist sheriffs called blacks for jury duty, an unheard-of practice in the South.

For president, the Omaha convention nominated James B. Weaver of Iowa, a former congressman, Union army general, and third-party candidate for president in 1880. Weaver won 1,027,329 votes, the first third-party presidential candidate ever to attract more than a million, and 22 electoral votes, a measure of agrarian unrest. The Populists elected governors in Kansas and North Dakota, ten congressmen, five senators, and about 1500 state legislators.

Despite the Populists' victories, the election brought disappointment. Southern Democrats used intimidation, fraud, and manipulation to hold Weaver to less than a quarter of the vote in every southern state except Alabama. In most of the country, he lost heavily in urban areas except for mining towns in the Far West. He even failed to win over most farmers.

People's (or Populist) party This political party was organized in 1892 by farm, labor, and reform leaders, mainly from the Farmers' Alliance. It offered a broad-based reform platform reflecting the Ocala Demands. After 1896, it became identified as a one-issue party focused on free silver and gradually died away.

20.1

20.2

20.3

20.4

20.5

20.6

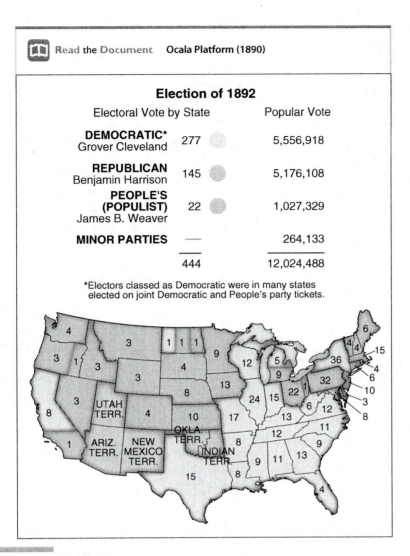

Read the Document   Ocala Platform (1890)

Election of 1892

	Electoral Vote by State	Popular Vote
DEMOCRATIC* Grover Cleveland	277	5,556,918
REPUBLICAN Benjamin Harrison	145	5,176,108
PEOPLE'S (POPULIST) James B. Weaver	22	1,027,329
MINOR PARTIES	—	264,133
	444	12,024,488

*Electors classed as Democratic were in many states elected on joint Democratic and People's party tickets.

MAP 20.2 ELECTION OF 1892

In 1892, many voters did switch parties, but they tended to realign with the Democrats rather than the Populists, whose platform on silver and other issues had little appeal among city dwellers or factory workers. Although the Populists ran candidates in the next three presidential elections, 1892 was their peak. Farmers' Alliance membership dropped. The organization, which was once the breeding ground of the People's party, was broken.

But while it lived, the Alliance was one of the most powerful protest movements in American history. Catalyzing the feelings of hundreds of thousands of farmers, it attempted to solve specific economic problems while advancing a larger vision of harmony and community, in which people who cared about each other were rewarded for what they produced.

Quick Check

What happened to the
People's party?

The Crisis of the Depression

20.3 What were the main political and labor effects of the panic and depression of the 1890s?

Economic crisis, however, not harmony and community, dominated the 1890s. Responding to the heady forces of industrialization, the American economy had expanded too rapidly in the 1870s and 1880s. Railroads had overbuilt, gambling on future growth. Companies had outgrown their markets; farms and businesses had borrowed heavily for expansion.

20.1

20.2

20.3

20.4

20.5

20.6

The Panic of 1893

The mood changed in mid-February 1893, when panic suddenly hit the New York stock market. In one day, investors dumped one million shares of the Philadelphia and Reading Railroad, and it went bankrupt. Investment dropped sharply in the railroad and construction industries, touching off the worst economic downturn to that point in the country's history.

Frightened, people sold stocks and other assets to buy gold. On April 22, the Treasury's gold reserve, which represented the government's commitment to the gold standard, fell below $100 million for the first time since the 1870s.

The news shattered business confidence—the stock market broke. On May 3, railroad and industrial stocks plummeted. Major firms went bankrupt. When the market opened on May 5, crowds filled its galleries, anticipating a panic. Within minutes, leading stocks plunged to record lows, and there was pandemonium on the floor and in the streets outside.

Banks cut back on loans. Unable to get capital, businesses failed at an average rate of two dozen a day in May. On July 26, the Erie Railroad, one of the leading names in railroading history, failed. August 1893 was the worst month. Across the country, factories and mines shut down. On August 15, the Northern Pacific Railroad went bankrupt; the Union Pacific and the Santa Fe soon followed. An estimated 2 million people, or nearly 15 percent of the labor force, were unemployed.

The year 1894 was even worse. The gross national product dropped again. By midyear, 3 million workers, one out of every five, were unemployed. A heat wave and drought struck the farm belt west of the Mississippi, creating conditions unmatched until the devastating Dust Bowl of the 1930s. Corn withered in the fields. The price of cotton fell below five cents a pound, far below the break-even point.

People became restless and angry. As one newspaper said in 1896: "On every corner stands a man whose fortune in these dull times has made him an ugly critic of everything and everybody." There was talk of revolution and bloodshed.

Quick Check

What were the causes of the depression of 1893?

The Pullman Strike

Pullman Strike Beginning in May 1894, this strike at the Pullman Palace Car Company near Chicago was one of the largest strikes in American history. Workers struck to protest wage cuts, high rents for company housing, and layoffs. The American Railway Union, led by Eugene V. Debs, joined the strike in June. Extending into 27 states and territories, it paralyzed the western half of the nation. President Grover Cleveland secured an injunction to break the strike on the grounds that it obstructed the mail, and sent federal troops to enforce it.

The great **Pullman strike**—one of the largest strikes in the country's history—began in May 1894 when the employees of the Pullman Palace Car Company struck to protest wage cuts and layoffs. On June 26, the American Railway Union (ARU) under Eugene V. Debs joined the strike by refusing to handle trains that carried Pullman sleeping cars.

Within hours, the strike paralyzed the western half of the nation. Grain and livestock could not reach markets. Factories shut down for lack of coal. The strike extended into 27 states and territories, tying up the economy and renewing talk of class warfare. In Washington, President Grover Cleveland, who had been reelected in 1892, decided to break the strike on the grounds that it obstructed delivery of the mail.

On July 2, he secured a court injunction against the ARU and ordered troops to Chicago, the center of the strike. When they arrived on the morning of Independence Day, the city was peaceful. Before long, however, violence broke out. Mobs, composed mostly of nonstrikers, overturned freight cars, looted, and burned. Restoring order, the army occupied railroad yards in Illinois, California, and other places. By late July, the strike was over; Debs was jailed for violating the injunction.

The Pullman strike had far-reaching consequences for the labor movement. Workers resented Cleveland's actions in the strike, particularly as it became apparent that he sided with the railroads. Upholding Debs's sentence in *In re Debs* (1895), the Supreme Court endorsed the use of the injunction in labor disputes, thus giving business and government an effective antilabor weapon that hindered union growth.

Quick Check

What were the three most important causes and events of the Pullman Strike?

A Beleaguered President

Building on the Democratic party's triumph in the midterm elections of 1890, Grover Cleveland decisively defeated James B. Weaver, and the incumbent president,

Benjamin Harrison, in 1892. He won by nearly 400,000 votes, a large margin for the era. The Democrats increased their strength in the cities and among working-class voters. For the first time since the 1850s, they controlled the White House and both branches of Congress.

The Democrats, it now seemed, had broken the party stalemate, but unfortunately for Cleveland, the Panic of 1893 struck almost as he took office. He blamed the Sherman Silver Purchase Act of 1890 for damaging business confidence, draining the Treasury's gold reserve, and causing the panic. The solution to the depression was simple: Repeal the act.

In June 1893, Cleveland summoned Congress into special session. British-ruled India had just closed its mints to silver. Mexico was now the only country with free silver coinage. The silverites pleaded for a compromise. But Cleveland pushed the repeal bill through Congress, and on November 1, 1893, he signed it into law. Always sure of himself, he had staked everything on a single measure—a winning strategy if he succeeded, a devastating one if he did not.

Repeal of the Sherman Silver Purchase Act was probably necessary. It responded to the realities of international finance, reduced the flight of gold out of the country, and, over the long run, boosted business confidence. But in the short term, it contracted the currency and led to deflation at a time when inflation might have helped. The stock market remained listless, businesses continued to close, unemployment spread, and farm prices dropped. "We are hourly expecting the arrival of the benevolent man who is to pay ten cents a pound for cotton," a Virginia newspaper said.

By discrediting the conservative Democrats who had dominated the party since the 1860s, the repeal battle of 1893 reshaped politics. It confined the Democratic party largely to the South, helped the Republicans become the majority party in 1894, and strengthened the silver Democrats in their bid for the presidency in 1896. It also focused national attention on the silver issue and thus intensified the sentiment for silver that Cleveland had intended to dampen. Repeal did not even solve the Treasury's gold problem. By January 1894, the reserve had fallen to $65 million. A year later, it was $44.5 million.

The Democrats' morale fell further when they failed to reduce the tariff. Despite their efforts, the Wilson-Gorman Tariff Act in August 1894 reduced duties only modestly. It also imposed a small income tax, a provision the Supreme Court overturned in 1895 (*Pollock v. Farmer's Loan and Trust Co.*). Few Democrats, including Cleveland, were pleased with the measure. The president let it become law without his signature.

Quick Check

How did President Grover Cleveland respond to the difficult events of the 1890s?

Breaking the Party Deadlock

The elections of 1894 crushed the Democrats. In the greatest defeat in congressional history, they lost 113 House seats, while the Republicans gained 117. In 24 states, not one Democrat was elected to Congress. Only one Democrat (Boston's John F. Fitzgerald, the grandfather of President John F. Kennedy) came from all of New England. The Democrats even lost some of the "solid South." In the Midwest, a crucial battleground, the party was virtually destroyed.

Wooing labor and the unemployed, the Populists gained in the South and West. Yet in a year in which thousands of voters switched parties, the People's party elected only four senators and four congressmen. Southern Democrats again used fraud and violence to keep the Populists' totals down. In the Midwest, the Populists won double the number of votes they had received in 1892, yet still attracted less than 7 percent of the vote. Across the country, the discontented tended to vote for the Republicans, not the Populists, a discouraging sign for the Populist party.

For millions of people, Grover Cleveland became a scapegoat for the country's economic ills. Fearing attack, he placed police barracks on the White House grounds. The Democratic party split. Southern and western Democrats deserted him.

The elections of 1894 broke the party deadlock that had existed since the 1870s. The Democrats lost, the Populists gained somewhat, and the Republicans became the

20.1

20.2

20.3

20.4

20.5

20.6

Quick Check

What was the outcome and significance of the midterm elections of 1894?

majority party in the country. In the midst of the depression, the Republican doctrines of activism and national authority, which voters had repudiated in 1890, became more attractive. As Americans became more accepting of the use of government power to regulate the economy and safeguard individual welfare, the way lay open to the reforms of the Progressive Era, the New Deal, and beyond.

Changing Attitudes

20.4   What changes in outlook did the panic and depression of the 1890s bring about?

The depression, brutal and far-reaching, did more than shift political alignments. Across the country, it undermined traditional views about government, the economy, and society. As men and women concluded that established ideas had failed to deal with the depression, they looked for new ones.

In prosperous times, Americans had thought of unemployment as a personal failure, affecting primarily the lazy and immoral. In the depression, such views were harder to hold. Everyone knew people who were both worthy and unemployed.

People debated issues they had long taken for granted. New and reinvigorated local institutions—discussion clubs, women's clubs, reform societies, university extension centers, church groups, farmers' societies—gave people a place to discuss alternatives to the existing order. Pressures for reform increased, and demand grew for government intervention to help the poor and unemployed.

Women and Children in the Labor Force

Women and children had been entering the labor force for years, and the depression accelerated the trend. As husbands and fathers lost their jobs, more women and children went to work. Even as late as 1901, well after the depression had ended, a study of working-class families showed that more than half the principal breadwinners were out of work. So many women and children worked that "Everybody Works But Father" was a popular song in 1905.

During the 1890s, the number of working women rose from 4 million to 5.3 million. To make ends meet, they took in boarders and worked as laundresses, cleaners, and domestics or in offices and factories. More black urban women than white worked to supplement their husbands' meager earnings. Men still dominated business offices, but during the 1890s, more employers noted that female labor was cheaper. The number of women telegraph and telephone operators nearly tripled during the decade. Women worked as clerks in the new five-and-tens and department stores, and as nurses; in 1900, 500,000 were teachers. They became stenographers and typists in offices.

The depression also caused more children to work. During the 1890s, the number of children in southern textile mills jumped more than 160 percent. Boys and girls under 16 years were nearly one-third of the mills' labor force. Youngsters of 8 and 9 years worked 12 hours a day for pitiful wages. However, most children worked in farming and on city streets as peddlers and shoe shiners.

Concerned about child labor, middle-class women in 1896 formed the League for the Protection of the Family, which called for compulsory education to get children out of factories and into classrooms. The Mothers Congress of 1896 gave rise to the National Congress of Parents and Teachers, the spawning ground of thousands of local Parent–Teacher Associations. The National Council of Women and the General Federation of Women's Clubs took up similar issues. By the late 1890s, the Federation had 150,000 members who worked for reforms in child welfare, education, and sanitation.

Quick Check

In what ways did the depression of the 1890s affect women and children?

Changing Themes in Literature

The depression also gave point to a growing movement in literature toward realism and naturalism. In the years after the Civil War, literature was often sentimental and unrealistic. Horatio Alger's novels about poor boys who succeeded through hard work, thrift, honesty, and luck attracted many readers. Louisa May Alcott's *Little Women* (1868–1869) related the daily lives of four girls in a New England family, and Anna Sewell's *Black Beauty* (1877) charmed readers with the story of an abused horse that found a happy home.

After the 1870s, however, talented authors began to reject romanticism and escapism, turning instead to realism. Determined to portray life as it was, they studied local dialects, wrote regional stories, and emphasized "true" relationships between people. This reflected broader social trends, such as industrialism; evolutionary theory, which emphasized the effect of the environment on humans; and pragmatism, which stressed the relativity of values.

Regionalist authors such as Joel Chandler Harris and George Washington Cable depicted life in the South. Hamlin Garland described the grimness of life on the Great Plains. Sarah Orne Jewett wrote about everyday life in rural New England. Another regionalist, Bret Harte, achieved fame with stories about the California mining camps, particularly in his popular tale "The Outcasts of Poker Flat."

Mark Twain became the country's most outstanding realist author. Growing up along the Mississippi River in Missouri, the young Samuel Langhorne Clemens observed life with a humorous and skeptical eye. Adopting a pen name from the river term "mark twain" (two fathoms), his works drew on his own experiences. In *The Adventures of Tom Sawyer* (1876) and *The Adventures of Huckleberry Finn* (1884), Twain used dialect and common speech instead of literary language, a technique that changed American prose style.

Other writers, the naturalists, became impatient even with realism. Pushing Darwinian theory to its limits, they wrote of a world in which a merciless environment determined human fate. Often focusing on economic hardship, naturalist writers studied the poor, the lower classes, and the criminal mind; they brought to their writing the social worker's passion for direct and honest experience.

Stephen Crane spent a night in a seven-cent lodging house on the Bowery in New York City and in "An Experiment in Misery" captured the smells and sounds of the poor. Crane depicted the carnage of war in *The Red Badge of Courage* (1895) and the impact of poverty in *Maggie: A Girl of the Streets* (1893). Jack London, another naturalist author, traced the power of nature over civilized society in *The Sea Wolf* (1904) and *The Call of the Wild* (1903), his classic tale of a sled dog that preferred the harsh wilderness to the world of human beings.

Theodore Dreiser, the foremost naturalist writer, portrayed human beings tossed about by forces beyond their understanding or control. In *Sister Carrie* (1901), he followed the moral decline of a young farm girl who takes an exhausting job in a Chicago shoe factory, is seduced by men, and embarks on a successful but morally bankrupt career.

Like other naturalists, Dreiser focused on environment and character. He thought writers should tell the truth about human affairs, not fabricate romance. *Sister Carrie*, he said, was "not intended as a piece of literary craftsmanship, but was a picture of conditions."

Quick Check

What were some of the major changes in literature during these years?

The Presidential Election of 1896

20.5 Why was the presidential election of 1896 so important?

The election of 1896 was known as the "battle of the standards" because it focused primarily on the gold versus silver standards of money. It was exciting and decisive. New voting patterns replaced old, a new majority party confirmed its dominance, and national policy shifted to suit new realities.

20.1
20.2
20.3
20.4
20.5
20.6

20.1

20.2

20.3

20.4

20.5

20.6

The Mystique of Silver

Support for free silver coinage grew swiftly after 1894, dominating the South and West, appearing even in the farming regions of New York and New England. Prosilver literature flooded the country. Pamphlets issued by the millions argued silver's virtues.

People wanted quick solutions to the economic crisis. During 1896, unemployment shot up, and farm income and prices fell to the lowest point in the decade. "I can remember back as far as 1858," an Iowa hardware dealer said in February 1896, "and I have never seen such hard times as these are." Prosilver people offered a solution, simple but compelling: the free and independent coinage of silver at the ratio of 16 ounces of silver to every ounce of gold. Free coinage meant that the U.S. mints would coin all the silver offered for sale to them. Independent coinage meant that the country would coin silver regardless of the policies of other nations, nearly all of which were on the gold standard.

It is difficult now to understand the faith the silverites placed in silver as a cure for the depression. But faith it was, and observers compared it to religious fervor. Underlying it all was a belief in a quantity theory of money: The silverites believed the amount of money in circulation determined the level of activity in the economy. If money was short, that meant there was a limit on economic activity and ultimately a depression. Coining silver and gold meant more money in circulation, more business for everyone, and thus prosperity. Farm prices would rise; laborers would find work.

By 1896, silver was also a symbol. It had moral and patriotic dimensions—by going to a silver standard, the United States could assert its independence in the world—and it stood for a wide range of popular grievances. For many, it reflected rural values rather than urban ones, would shift power away from the Northeast, and favored the downtrodden instead of the well-to-do.

Silver was more than just a political or economic issue. It was a social movement, one of the largest in American history, but its life span turned out to be brief. As a mass phenomenon, it flourished between 1894 and 1896, then succumbed to electoral defeat, the return of prosperity, and the onset of fresh concerns. But in its time, the silver movement bespoke a national mood and won millions of followers.

The Republicans and Gold

Scenting victory over the discredited Democrats, numerous Republicans fought for the party's presidential nomination, including a Republican favorite, William McKinley of Ohio.

Able, calm, and affable, McKinley had served in the Union army during the Civil War. In 1876, he won a seat in Congress, where he became the chief sponsor of the tariff act named for him. Marcus A. Hanna, his campaign manager and friend, built a powerful national organization that featured McKinley as "the advance agent of prosperity," an alluring slogan during a depression. When the Republican convention met in June, McKinley had the nomination in hand. He backed a platform that favored the gold standard against the free coinage of silver.

Republicans favoring silver proposed a prosilver platform, but the convention overwhelmingly defeated it. Twenty-three silverite Republicans, far fewer than prosilver forces had hoped, marched out of the convention hall. The remaining delegates waved handkerchiefs and flags and shouted "Good-bye" and "Put them out." Hanna stood on a chair screaming "Go! Go! Go!" William Jennings Bryan, who was there as a special correspondent for a Nebraska newspaper, climbed on a desk to get a better view.

The Democrats and Silver

Silver, meanwhile, had captured large segments of the Democratic party in the South and West. Despite President Cleveland's opposition, more than 20 Democratic state platforms called for free silver in 1894. Power in the party shifted to the South, where it remained for decades. The party's base narrowed; its outlook increasingly reflected

20.1

20.2

20.3

20.4

20.5

20.6

southern views on silver, race, and other issues. In effect, the Democrats became a sectional—no longer a national—party.

The anti-Cleveland Democrats had their issue, but they lacked a leader. Out in Nebraska, William Jennings Bryan, a young former congressman, saw the opportunity to take on that role. He was barely 36 years old and had relatively little political experience. But he had spent months wooing support, and he was a captivating public speaker—tall, slender, and handsome, with a resounding voice that, in an era without microphones, projected easily into every corner of an auditorium.

The silver Democrats were in charge of the 1896 Democratic convention. Their platform stunned the party's Cleveland wing. It demanded the free coinage of silver, attacked Cleveland's actions in the Pullman strike, and censured his sales of gold bonds. On July 9, as delegates debated the platform, Bryan's moment came. Striding to the stage, he raised a hand for silence, waiting for the applause to die down. He would not contend with the previous speakers, he began, for "this is not a contest between persons. The humblest citizen in all the land, when clad in the armor of a righteous cause, is stronger than all the hosts of error. I come to speak to you in defense of a cause as holy as the cause of liberty—the cause of humanity."

((• 📖 Read the Document   **William Jennings Bryan,** *Cross of Gold* **(1896)**

WILLIAM JENNINGS BRYAN William Jennings Bryan was well known for his dramatic speeches. During the Democratic Convention of 1896, Bryan delivered his best-known speech, which attacked the gold standard. His stirring rhetoric captivated his audience and won him the Democratic presidential nomination for the election of 1896.

20.1

20.2

20.3

20.4

20.5

20.6

Quick Check

What won William Jennings Bryan
the Democratic nomination in 1896?

The delegates were captivated. Like a trained choir, they rose, cheered each point, and sat back to listen for more. Easterners, Bryan said, liked to praise businessmen but forgot that plain people—laborers, miners, and farmers—were businessmen, too. Shouts rang through the hall, and delegates pounded on chairs. Savoring each cheer, Bryan defended silver. Then came the famous closing: "Having behind us the producing masses of this nation and the world . . . we will answer their demand for a gold standard by saying to them: 'You shall not press down upon the brow of labor this crown of thorns, you shall not crucify mankind upon a cross of gold.'"

Bryan moved his fingers down his temples, suggesting blood trickling from his wounds. He ended with his arms outstretched as on a cross. Letting the silence hang, he dropped his arms, stepped back, then started to his seat. Suddenly, there was pandemonium. Delegates shouted and cheered. When the tumult subsided, they adopted the anti-Cleveland platform, and the next day, Bryan won the presidential nomination.

Campaign and Election

The Democratic convention presented the Populists with a dilemma. The People's party had assumed that neither major party would endorse silver. Now it faced a painful choice: Nominate an independent ticket and split the silverite forces, or nominate Bryan and give up its separate identity as a party.

The choice shattered the People's party. Its convention nominated Bryan, but rather than accept the Democratic candidate for vice president, it named Tom Watson instead. The Populists' endorsement probably hurt Bryan as much as it helped. It won him relatively few votes, since many Populists would have voted for him anyway. It also identified him as a Populist, which he was not, allowing the Republicans to accuse him of heading a ragtag army of malcontents. The squabble over Watson seemed to prove that the Democratic–Populist alliance could never stay together long enough to govern.

In August 1896, Bryan set off on a campaign that became an American legend. Much of the conservative Democratic eastern press had deserted him. So he went directly to the voters, the first presidential candidate in history to do so in a systematic way. By his own count, Bryan traveled 18,009 miles, visited 27 states, and spoke 600 times to 3 million people. He built skillfully on a new "merchandising" style of campaign in which he worked to educate and persuade voters.

Bryan summoned voters to an older America, where farms were as important as factories, where the virtues of rural and religious life outweighed the lure of the city, where common people ruled, and opportunity existed for all. He drew on the Jeffersonian tradition of rural virtue, distrust of central authority, and faith in human reason.

Urged to take the stump against Bryan, McKinley replied, "I might just as well put up a trapeze on my front lawn and compete with some professional athlete as go out speaking against Bryan." The Republican candidate let voters come to him. Railroads brought them by the thousands into McKinley's hometown of Canton, Ohio, and he spoke to them from his front porch. Through the press, he reached as many people as Bryan's more strenuous effort. Appealing to labor, immigrants, well-to-do farmers, businessmen, and the middle class, McKinley defended economic nationalism and the advancing urban-industrial society.

On election day, voter turnout was extraordinarily high, a measure of the intense interest. By nightfall, the outcome was clear: McKinley won 50 percent of the vote to Bryan's 46 percent. He won the Northeast and Midwest and carried four border states. In the cities, McKinley crushed Bryan (see Map 20.3).

The election struck down the Populists, whose totals sagged nearly everywhere. Many Populist proposals were later adopted under different leadership. The graduated income tax, crop loans to farmers, the secret ballot, and direct election of U.S. senators all were early Populist ideas. But the People's party never could win a majority of the voters, and failing that, it declined rapidly after 1896.

Quick Check

What were the most important
results of the 1896 election?

20.1

20.2

20.3

20.4

20.5

20.6

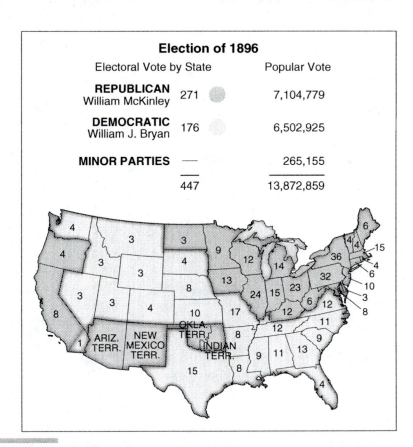

Election of 1896

	Electoral Vote by State		Popular Vote
REPUBLICAN William McKinley	271		7,104,779
DEMOCRATIC William J. Bryan	176		6,502,925
MINOR PARTIES	—		265,155
	447		13,872,859

MAP 20.3 ELECTION OF 1896 This map illustrates McKinley's victories over a large swatch of states in the North, Midwest and Pacific Coast. It also shows the greater reach of the Democratic party under William Jennings Bryan, though the states he carried in the West tended to have few electoral votes.

The McKinley Administration

20.6 What did McKinley accomplish that placed the results of the 1896 election on a solid basis?

The election of 1896 cemented the voter realignment of 1894 and initiated a generation of Republican rule. For more than three decades after 1896, with only a brief Democratic resurgence under Woodrow Wilson, the Republicans remained the country's majority party.

McKinley took office in 1897 under favorable circumstances. To everyone's relief, the economy had begun to revive. The stock market rose, factories again churned out goods, and farmers prospered. Farm prices climbed sharply during 1897 on bumper crops of wheat, cotton, and corn. Gold discoveries in Australia and Alaska—together with a new cyanide process for extracting gold from ore—enlarged the world's gold supply, decreased its price, and inflated the currency as the silverites had hoped. For the first time since 1890, the 1897 Treasury statements showed a comfortable gold reserve.

McKinley and the Republicans basked in the glow. They became the party of progress and prosperity, an image that helped them win victories until another depression hit in the 1930s. McKinley's popularity soared. An activist president, he set the policies of the administration. Conscious of the limits of power, he maintained close ties with Congress and worked to educate the public on national choices and priorities. McKinley established new relations with the press and traveled far more than previous presidents. In some ways, he began the modern presidency.

Shortly after taking office, he summoned Congress into special session to revise the tariff. In July 1897, the Dingley Tariff raised average tariff duties to a record level. As the

20.1

20.2

20.3

20.4

20.5

20.6

WILLIAM McKINLEY This Republican campaign poster of 1896 depicts candidate William McKinley as the champion of commerce and civilization. The sun rising behind the flag McKinley is holding suggests that a new day will dawn with a Republican administration.

final burst of nineteenth-century protectionism, it caused trouble for the Republican party. By the end of the 1890s, consumers, critics, and the Republicans themselves were questioning the tariff's usefulness in the maturing American economy.

From the 1860s to the 1890s, the Republicans had built their party on a pledge to *promote* economic growth through the use of state and national power. By 1900, with the industrial system firmly in place, the focus had shifted. The need to *regulate*, to control the effects of industrialism, became a central public concern. McKinley prodded the Republicans to meet that shift, but he died before his plans matured.

McKinley toyed with lowering the tariff, but one obstacle stood in the way: The government needed revenue, and tariff duties were one of the few taxes the public would support. The Spanish–American War of 1898 persuaded people to accept greater federal power and, with it, new forms of taxation. In 1899, McKinley spoke of lowering tariff barriers in a world that technology had made smaller. "God and man have linked

20.1

20.2

20.3

20.4

20.5

20.6

TABLE 20.3 THE ELECTION OF 1900

Candidate	Party	Popular Vote	Electoral Vote
McKinley	Republican	7,207,923	292
Bryan	Democrat	6,358,133	155
Woolley	Prohibition	209,004	0
Debs	Socialist	94,768	0

the nations together," he said in his last speech at Buffalo, New York, in 1901. "Isolation is no longer possible or desirable."

In 1898 and 1899, the McKinley administration focused on the war with Spain, the peace treaty that followed, and the dawning realization that the war had made the United States a world power. In March 1900, Congress passed the **Gold Standard Act**, which declared gold the standard of currency and ended the silver controversy that had dominated the 1890s.

The presidential campaign of 1900 replayed the McKinley–Bryan fight of 1896. McKinley's running mate was Theodore Roosevelt, hero of the Spanish–American War and governor of New York, who was nominated for vice president to capitalize on his popularity and, his enemies hoped, to sidetrack his political career into oblivion. Bryan stressed imperialism and the trusts; McKinley stressed his record at home and abroad. The result in 1900 was a landslide (see Table 20.3).

On September 6, 1901, six months after his second inauguration, McKinley stood in a receiving line at the Pan-American Exposition in Buffalo, New York. Leon Czolgosz, a 28-year-old unemployed laborer and anarchist, moved through the line and, reaching the president, shot him. Surgeons probed the wound but could find nothing. A recent discovery called the X ray was on display at the exposition, but it was not used. On September 14, McKinley died, and Vice President Theodore Roosevelt became president. A new century had begun.

Gold Standard Act Passed by Congress in 1900, this law made all currency redeemable in gold. The United States remained on the gold standard until 1933.

Conclusion: A Decade's Dramatic Changes

As the funeral train carried McKinley's body back to Ohio, Mark Hanna, McKinley's old friend and ally, sat slumped in his parlor car. "I told William McKinley it was a mistake to nominate that wild man at Philadelphia," he mourned. "I asked him if he realized what would happen if he should die. Now look, that damned cowboy is president of the United States!"

Hanna's world had changed, and so had the nation's—not so much because "that damned cowboy" was suddenly president, but because events in the 1890s had powerful effects. In the course of that decade, political patterns shifted, the presidency acquired fresh power, and massive unrest prompted social change. The war with Spain brought a new empire and worldwide responsibilities. Economic hardship posed difficult questions about industrialization, urbanization, and the quality of American life. Worried, people embraced new ideas and causes. Reform movements begun in the 1890s flowered in the Progressive Era after 1900.

Technology continued to alter how Americans lived. In 1896, Henry Ford produced a two-cylinder, four-horsepower car, the first of the famous line that bore his name. In 1899, the first automobile salesroom opened in New York, and some innovative thinkers were already imagining a network of service stations to keep the new cars running. At Kitty Hawk, North Carolina, Wilbur and Orville Wright, two bicycle manufacturers, neared the birth of powered flight.

The realignments that peaked in the 1890s seem distant, yet decisions in those years shaped nearly everything that followed them. In character and influence, the 1890s still have repercussions in the twenty-first century.

Chapter Review

Politics of Stalemate

20.1 Why was there a stalemate between Republicans and Democrats until the mid-1890s? p. 457

For more than two decades after Reconstruction, there was a stalemate, in which the Democrats and Republicans fought for votes and focused on a handful of "doubtful" states. In general, Democrats dominated the South, and Republicans controlled crucial sections of the North. Presidents reestablished the authority of their office.

The Rise of the Populist Movement

20.2 What factors led to the formation and growth of the Farmers' Alliance and People's party? p. 462

In the late 1880s and early 1890s, farmers in the South and West joined the Farmers' Alliance, and later the People's party. The People's party failed, as voters turned to the Democrats in the presidential election of 1892.

The Crisis of the Depression

20.3 What were the main political and labor effects of the panic and depression of the 1890s? p. 467

The depression encouraged people to rethink their views on the causes of poverty and unemployment. It discredited President Cleveland and crushed the Democrats in the midterm elections of 1894, giving the Republican party a long-term lease on power.

Changing Attitudes

20.4 What changes in outlook did the panic and depression of the 1890s bring about? p. 470

The depression led people to reconsider the roles of the government, the economy, and society. They had once thought that people lost their jobs because of their own failings; now they knew that economic forces were at fault. People joined organizations like women's clubs, church groups, and farm societies to discuss cures for the situation. More women and children worked. Realism and naturalism dominated American literature.

The Presidential Election of 1896

20.5 Why was the presidential election of 1896 so important? p. 471

The election of 1896 brought to a head the fight between supporters of silver and gold, established the Republicans as the majority party, and shaped the nation's politics until 1932.

The McKinley Administration

20.6 What did McKinley accomplish that placed the results of the 1896 election on a solid basis? p. 475

The McKinley administration profited from economic recovery. It enacted the gold standard, passed a new tariff, and defeated Spain. How to *regulate* big business instead of simply promoting it became a new challenge.

Timeline

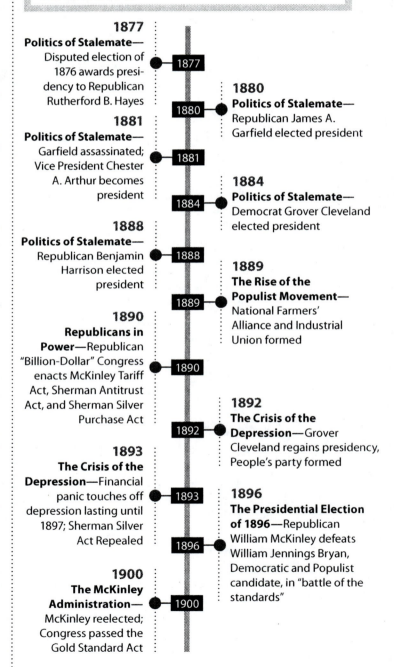

1877
Politics of Stalemate—Disputed election of 1876 awards presidency to Republican Rutherford B. Hayes

1880
Politics of Stalemate—Republican James A. Garfield elected president

1881
Politics of Stalemate—Garfield assassinated; Vice President Chester A. Arthur becomes president

1884
Politics of Stalemate—Democrat Grover Cleveland elected president

1888
Politics of Stalemate—Republican Benjamin Harrison elected president

1889
The Rise of the Populist Movement—National Farmers' Alliance and Industrial Union formed

1890
Republicans in Power—Republican "Billion-Dollar" Congress enacts McKinley Tariff Act, Sherman Antitrust Act, and Sherman Silver Purchase Act

1892
The Crisis of the Depression—Grover Cleveland regains presidency, People's party formed

1893
The Crisis of the Depression—Financial panic touches off depression lasting until 1897; Sherman Silver Act Repealed

1896
The Presidential Election of 1896—Republican William McKinley defeats William Jennings Bryan, Democratic and Populist candidate, in "battle of the standards"

1900
The McKinley Administration—McKinley reelected; Congress passed the Gold Standard Act

21 Toward Empire
1865–1902

Roosevelt and the Rough Riders

Many **Americans regretted** the start of the war with Spain that began in April 1898, but many others welcomed it. Many highly respected people believed that nations must fight every now and then to prove their power and test their spirit.

Theodore Roosevelt, 39 years old in 1898, was one of them. Nations needed to fight in order to survive, he thought. Roosevelt argued strenuously for war with Spain for three reasons: first, to free Cuba and expel Spain from the hemisphere; second, because of "the benefit done to our people by giving them something to think of which isn't material gain"; and third, because the army and navy needed the practice.

In 1898, Roosevelt was serving in the important post of assistant secretary of the navy. When war broke out, he resigned to join the army, rejecting the advice of Secretary of the Navy John Long, who warned he would only "ride a horse and brush mosquitoes from his neck in the Florida sands." Long was wrong—dead

LEARNING OBJECTIVES

21.1 ((•	21.2 ((•	21.3 ((•
Why did Americans look outward in the last half of the nineteenth century? p. 481	What were the causes and results of the war with Spain? p. 488	What were the various viewpoints about the acquisition of empire after the war with Spain? p. 496

TR AND THE ROUGH RIDERS IN ACTION A blend of Ivy League athletes and western frontiersmen, the Rough Riders became the most famous military unit in the war.

((• Listen to **Chapter 21** on **MyHistoryLab**

From Chapter 21 of *American Stories: A History of the United States*, Third Edition. H. W. Brands, R. Hal Williams, T. H. Breen and Ariela J. Gross Copyright © 2015 by Pearson Education, Inc. All rights reserved.

⊙ Watch the Video Series on MyHistoryLab

Learn about some key topics related to this chapter with the
MyHistoryLab Video Series: Key Topics in U.S. History.

1 The American Empire The United States is that rare exception in history where a former colony becomes a major imperial power. This video discusses America's territorial ambitions. It also profiles two U.S. secretaries of state responsible for achieving them—William H. Seward, who purchased Alaska from the Russian Empire, and James G. Blaine who promoted an expansive foreign policy that resulted in an overseas empire.

⊙ Watch on **MyHistoryLab**

Coup in Hawaii The McKinley Tariff Act had the unintended effect of leading to a coup that ended the reign of Queen Liliuokalani and an independent Hawaii. This video reveals how American sugar growers and other foreign interests deposed the queen, whose move toward more control over her country threatened the duty-free export of sugar to the mainland. **2**

Watch on **MyHistoryLab** ⊙

3 The Spanish-American War The Spanish-American War of 1898 is the stuff of colorful battles and personalities, such as Theodore Roosevelt's Rough Riders and Admiral Dewey's victory in Manila Bay. However, the war resulted from an intense determination to establish an overseas presence for the young nation—to establish and protect trade, provide ports and coal stations for its shipping, and the like. This video looks at how the proponents of U.S. imperialism and international power took advantage of the weakest colonial power, the kingdom of Spain, and won from it control of numerous island territories.

⊙ Watch on **MyHistoryLab**

War in the Philippines In winning the Spanish-American War, not only did the United States gain possession of the Philippines, but it also inherited a war of independence, as this video reveals. It discusses how U.S. administrators and soldiers quickly cast aside high-minded principles and morals to engage in a bloody guerilla war with Filipino freedom fighters. **4**

Watch on **MyHistoryLab** ⊙

wrong—and later had the grace to admit it: "Roosevelt was right. His going into the Army led straight to the Presidency."

Roosevelt chose to enlist his own regiment. After telephone calls to friends and telegrams to the governors of Arizona, New Mexico, and Oklahoma asking for "good shots and good riders," he had more than enough men. The First United States Volunteer Cavalry, an intriguing mixture of Ivy League athletes and western frontiersmen, was born.

Known as the Rough Riders, it included men from the Harvard, Yale, and Princeton clubs of New York City, the Somerset Club of Boston, and New York's exclusive Knickerbocker Club. Former college athletes—football players, tennis players, and track stars—enlisted. Woodbury Kane, a wealthy yachtsman, signed up and volunteered for kitchen duty.

Other volunteers came from the West—natural soldiers, Roosevelt called them, "tall and sinewy, with resolute, weather-beaten faces, and eyes that looked a man straight in the face without flinching." Among the cowboys, hunters, and prospectors were Bucky O'Neill, a legendary Arizona sheriff and Indian fighter; a half dozen other sheriffs and Texas Rangers; many Indians; a famous broncobuster; and an ex-marshal of Dodge City, Kansas.

Eager for war, the men trained hard, played harder, and rarely passed up a chance for an intellectual discussion—if Roosevelt's memoir of the war is to be believed. Once, he overheard Bucky O'Neill and a Princeton graduate "discussing Aryan word roots together, and then sliding off into a review of the novels of Balzac, and a discussion as to how far Balzac could be said to be the founder of the modern realistic school of fiction." Discipline was lax, and enlisted men got on easily with the officers.

The troops howled with joy when orders came to join the invasion army for Cuba. They set sail on June 14, 1898, and Lieutenant Colonel Roosevelt, who had performed a war dance for the troops the night before, caught their mood: "We knew not whither we were bound, nor what we were to do; but we believed that the nearing future held for us many chances of death and hardship, of honor and renown. If we failed, we would share the fate of all who fail; but we were sure that we would win, that we should score the first great triumph in a mighty world-movement."

That "world-movement," Roosevelt was sure, would establish the United States as a world power, whose commerce and influence would extend around the globe, particularly in Latin America and Asia. As he hoped, the nation in the 1890s underwent dramatic expansion, building on the foreign policy decisions of administrations from Lincoln to William McKinley. Policymakers fostered business interests abroad, strengthened the navy, and extended American influence into Latin America and the Pacific. Differences over Cuba resulted in a war with Spain that brought new colonies and colonial subjects, establishing for the first time an American overseas empire.

America Looks Outward

21.1 Why did Americans look outward in the last half of the nineteenth century?

The overseas expansion of the 1890s differed in several important respects from earlier expansion. From its beginning, the American republic had been expanding. After the first landings in Jamestown and Plymouth, settlers pushed westward: into the trans-Appalachian region, the Louisiana Territory, Florida, Texas, California, Arizona, and New Mexico. Most of these lands were contiguous with U.S. territory, and most were intended for settlement, usually agricultural.

The expansion of the 1890s was different. It involved island possessions, most of them already thickly populated. The new territories were intended less for settlement than for use as naval bases, trading outposts, or commercial centers on major trade routes. Most were viewed as colonies, not as states-in-the-making.

Historian Samuel F. Bemis described the overseas expansion of the 1890s as "the great aberration," a time when the country adopted expansionist policies that did not fit with its history. Other historians, pointing to expansionist tendencies in thought and foreign policy that surfaced during the last half of the nineteenth century, have found a developing pattern that led naturally to the overseas adventures of the 1890s. In the view of Walter LaFeber, "The United States did not set out on an expansionist path in the late 1890s in a sudden, spur-of-the-moment fashion. The overseas empire that Americans controlled in 1900 was not a break in their history, but a natural culmination."

Catching the Spirit of Empire

Throughout history, most people have tended to focus on domestic concerns, and after the Civil War, Americans were no exception. Among other things, they focused on Reconstruction, the movement westward, and simply making a living. Throughout the nineteenth century, Americans enjoyed "free security" without fully appreciating it. Sheltered by two oceans and the British navy, they could enunciate bold policies such as the Monroe Doctrine, which instructed European nations to stay out of the affairs of the Western Hemisphere, while remaining virtually impregnable to foreign attack.

isolationism A belief that the United States should avoid entanglements with other nations.

Imperialism The policy of extending a nation's power over other areas through military conquest, economic domination, or annexation.

Quick Check

Why did Americans resist for a long time involvement in events abroad?

In those circumstances a sense of **isolationism** spread, fostering a desire to avoid foreign entanglements. Some people even wanted to abolish the foreign service, considering it an unnecessary expenditure, a dangerous profession that might lead to involvement in the struggles of the world's great powers.

In the 1870s and after, however, Americans' interest in events abroad increased. There was a growing sense of internationalism, which stemmed in part from the telegraphs, telephones, and undersea cables that kept people better informed about political and economic developments in distant lands. Many Americans wanted to expand the country's borders, but relatively few were interested in **imperialism**. Expansion meant the kind of growth that had brought California and Oregon into the American system. Imperialism meant imposing control over other peoples through annexation, military conquest, or economic domination.

Reasons for Expansion

Several developments in these years shifted attention outward across the seas. The end of the frontier, announced officially in the census report of 1890, sparked fears about diminishing opportunities at home. Further growth, it seemed to some, must take place abroad. Factories and farms multiplied, producing more goods than the domestic market could consume. Both farmers and industrialists looked for new overseas markets, and the growing volume of exports—including more manufactured goods—changed American trade relations with the world. In 1898, the United States exported more than it imported, beginning a trend that lasted through the 1960s.

To some extent, Americans were also caught up in a worldwide scramble for empire. In the last third of the century, Britain, France, and Germany divided up Africa and looked covetously at Asia. The idea of imperialistic expansion was in the air, and the great powers measured their greatness by the colonies they acquired.

Adherents of expansion drew on Charles Darwin's theories of evolution. They pointed, for example, to *The Origin of Species*, whose subtitle was *The Preservation of Favoured Races in the Struggle for Life*. Applied to human and social development, biological concepts seemed to call for the triumph of the fit and the elimination of the unfit. "In this world," said Theodore Roosevelt, who considered himself one of the fit, "the nation that has trained itself to a career of unwarlike and isolated ease is bound, in the end, to go down before other nations which have not lost the manly and adventurous qualities."

John Fiske, a popular writer and lecturer, argued for Anglo-Saxon racial superiority, a result of the process of natural selection. The English and Americans, Fiske said, would occupy every land on the globe that was not already "civilized," bringing the advances of commerce and democratic institutions.

The career of Josiah Strong, a Congregational minister and fervent expansionist, suggested the strength of these developing ideas. A champion of overseas missionary work, Strong traveled through the West for the Home Missionary Society, and in 1885, drawing on his experiences, he published *Our Country: Its Possible Future and Its Present Crisis* and became a national celebrity. An immediate best-seller, *Our Country* argued for expanding American trade and dominion. Trade was important, Strong said, because the desire for material things was a hallmark of civilized people. So was the Christian religion. By exporting both trade and religion, Americans could civilize and Christianize "inferior" races around the world. As Anglo-Saxons, they were members of a God-favored race destined to lead the world.

Taken together, these currents in social, political, and economic thought prepared Americans for a larger role in the world. The change was gradual, and there was never a day when people woke up with a sudden interest in overseas expansion. But change there was, and by the 1890s, Americans were ready to reach out into the world in a more determined and deliberate fashion than ever before. For almost the first time, they felt the need for a foreign "policy."

Quick Check

What were the causes behind American expansion?

OUR COUNTRY:

ITS POSSIBLE FUTURE AND ITS PRESENT CRISIS.

BY

REV. JOSIAH STRONG, D. D.,
GENERAL SECRETARY OF THE EVANGELICAL ALLIANCE
FOR THE UNITED STATES, NEW YORK.

With an Introduction, by
PROF. AUSTIN PHELPS, D. D.

"We live in a new and exceptional age. America is another name for Opportunity. Our whole history appears like a last effort of the Divine Providence in behalf of the human race."—*Emerson.*

ONE HUNDREDTH THOUSAND.

PUBLISHED BY

THE BAKER & TAYLOR CO.,

740 AND 742 BROADWAY, NEW YORK.

FOR

THE AMERICAN HOME MISSIONARY SOCIETY.

OUR COUNTRY Josiah Strong (1847–1916) was a Protestant minister who advocated in his works and speeches the responsibility of the Anglo-Saxons to civilize and Christianize "inferior" races around the world. Strong's opinions influenced support among American Protestants, by the late 1890s, for the development of an expansionist and imperialist foreign policy.

Foreign Policy Approaches, 1867–1900

Rarely consistent, American foreign policy in the last half of the nineteenth century took different approaches to different areas of the world. In relation to Europe, seat of the dominant world powers, policymakers promoted trade and tried to avoid diplomatic entanglements. In North and South America, they based policy on the Monroe Doctrine, a recurrent dream of annexing Canada or Mexico, a hope for trade, and Pan-American unity against the nations of the Old World. In the Pacific, they coveted Hawaii and other outposts on the sea-lanes to China.

Secretary of State William Henry Seward, who served from 1861 to 1869, pushed an expansive foreign policy. "Give me . . . fifty, forty, thirty more years of life," he told a Boston audience in 1867, "and I will give you possession of the American continent and control of the world." Seward, it turned out, had only five more years of life, but he developed a vision of an American empire stretching south into Latin America and west to the shores of Asia. His vision included Canada and Mexico; Caribbean islands as bases to protect a canal across Central America; and Hawaii and other islands as stepping-stones to Asia, which Seward and others considered a bottomless market for farm and manufactured goods.

In 1867, he concluded a treaty with Russia to purchase Alaska (which was promptly labeled "Seward's Folly"), partly to sandwich western Canada between American territory and lead to its annexation. As the American empire spread, Seward thought, Mexico City would become its capital.

James G. Blaine served briefly as secretary of state under Presidents James Garfield and Chester Arthur in 1881 and laid plans to establish closer commercial relations with Latin America. His successor, Frederick T. Frelinghuysen, changed Blaine's approach but not his strategy. Like Blaine, Frelinghuysen wanted to find Caribbean markets for American goods; he negotiated separate reciprocity treaties with Mexico, Spanish-ruled Cuba and Puerto Rico, the British West Indies, Santo Domingo, and Colombia. Using these treaties, Frelinghuysen hoped not only to obtain markets for American goods but to bind these countries to American interests.

When Blaine returned to the State Department in 1889 under President Benjamin Harrison, he moved again to expand markets in Latin America. Drawing on earlier ideas, he envisaged a hemispheric system of peaceful intercourse, arbitration of disputes, and expanded trade. He also wanted to annex Hawaii.

Harrison and Blaine toyed with acquiring naval bases in the Caribbean and elsewhere, but in general they focused on Pan-Americanism and tariff reciprocity. Blaine presided over the first Inter-American Conference in Washington on October 2, 1889, where delegates from 19 American nations negotiated agreements to promote trade and created the International Bureau of the American Republics, later renamed the Pan-American Union, to exchange political, scientific, and cultural knowledge. The conference, a major step in hemispheric relations, led to later meetings promoting trade and other agreements.

Grover Cleveland, Harrison's successor, also pursued an aggressive policy toward Latin America. In 1895, he brought the United States precariously close to war with Britain over a boundary dispute between Venezuela and British Guiana. Cleveland sympathized with Venezuela, and he and Secretary of State Richard Olney urged Britain to arbitrate the dispute. When Britain failed to act, Olney drafted a stiff diplomatic note affirming the Monroe Doctrine, asserting U.S. predominance in the Western Hemisphere, and denying European nations the right to meddle in its affairs.

Four months passed before Lord Salisbury, the British prime minister and foreign secretary, replied. Rejecting Olney's arguments, he sent two letters. The first bluntly repudiated the Monroe Doctrine as international law. The second, carefully reasoned and sometimes sarcastic, rejected Olney's arguments for the Venezuelan boundary. Enraged, Cleveland defended the Monroe Doctrine and asked Congress for authority to appoint a commission to decide the boundary and enforce its decision.

Preoccupied with larger diplomatic problems in Africa and Europe, Britain changed its position. In November 1896, the two countries signed a treaty of arbitration, under which Britain and Venezuela divided the disputed territory. Though Cleveland's approach was clumsy—throughout the crisis, for example, he rarely consulted Venezuela—the incident demonstrated a growing determination to exert American power in the Western Hemisphere. Cleveland and Olney had persuaded Britain to recognize the U.S.'s dominance, and they had increased American influence in Latin America. The Monroe Doctrine assumed new importance. In averting war, an era of Anglo-American friendship was also begun.

Quick Check

What were the main characteristics of American foreign policy between 1867 and 1900?

The Lure of Hawaii

The Hawaiian Islands offered a tempting way station to Asian markets. (See Map 21.1). In the early 1800s, they were already called the "Crossroads of the Pacific," and ships of many nations stopped there. In 1820, the first American missionaries arrived to convert the islanders to Christianity. Like missionaries elsewhere, they advertised Hawaii's economic and other benefits and attracted new settlers. Their children later dominated Hawaiian political and economic life and played an important role in annexation.

After the Civil War, the United States tightened its connections with the islands. The reciprocity treaty of 1875 allowed Hawaiian sugar to enter the United States free of duty and bound the Hawaiian monarchy to make no territorial or economic concessions to other powers. The treaty made Hawaii economically dependent on the United States; its political clauses effectively made Hawaii an American protectorate. In 1887, a new treaty reaffirmed these arrangements and granted the United States exclusive use of Pearl Harbor, a magnificent harbor that had early caught the eye of naval strategists.

MAP 21.1 HAWAIIAN ISLANDS The Hawaiian Islands provided the United States with both a convenient stopping point on the way to Asian markets and a strategic naval station in the Pacific.

Following the 1875 treaty, white Americans in Hawaii became more and more influential in the islands' political life. The McKinley Tariff Act of 1890 ended the special status given Hawaiian sugar and awarded American producers a bounty of two cents a pound. Hawaiian sugar production dropped dramatically, unemployment rose, and property values fell. The following year, the weak King Kalakaua died. His successor Queen Liliuokalani was a strong-willed nationalist. Resentful of white minority rule, she decreed a new constitution that gave greater power to native Hawaiians.

In response, the American residents revolted in January 1893 and called on the United States for help. John L. Stevens, the American minister in Honolulu, sent 150 marines ashore from the cruiser *Boston* to help the rebels, and within three days, the bloodless revolution was over. Queen Liliuokalani surrendered "to the superior force of the United States," and the victorious rebels set up a provisional government. On February 14, 1893, President Harrison's secretary of state, John W. Foster, and delegates of the new government signed a treaty annexing Hawaii to the United States.

But only two weeks remained in Harrison's term, and the Senate refused to ratify the agreement. President Cleveland promptly withdrew the treaty; he then sent a representative to investigate the rebellion. The investigation revealed that the Americans' role in it had been improper, and Cleveland decided to restore the queen to her throne. He made the demand, but the provisional government in Hawaii refused and instead established the Republic of Hawaii, which the embarrassed Cleveland had to recognize.

The debate over Hawaiian annexation, continuing through the 1890s, foreshadowed the later debate over the treaty to end the Spanish-American War. People in favor of annexation pointed to Hawaii's strategic location, argued that Japan, Germany, or Britain might seize the islands if the United States did not, and suggested that Americans had a responsibility to civilize and Christianize the native Hawaiians. Opponents warned that annexation might lead to a colonial army and colonial problems, the inclusion of a "mongrel" population in the United States, and rule over an area not destined for statehood.

Annexation finally came in 1898 in the midst of excitement over victories in the Spanish-American War. The year before, President William McKinley had sent a treaty of annexation to the Senate, but opponents stalled it.

THE LAST HAWAIIAN QUEEN The first step toward American annexation of Hawaii came in 1893 when Queen Liliuokalani was overthrown. Hawaii was annexed to the United States as a possession in 1898 and became a U.S. territory in 1900.

Quick Check

For what three reasons were the Hawaiian Islands important to American policymakers?

In 1898, annexationists redoubled arguments about Hawaii's commercial and military importance. McKinley and congressional leaders switched strategies to seek a joint resolution, rather than a treaty, for annexation. A joint resolution required only a majority of both houses, while a treaty needed a two-thirds vote in the Senate. The annexation measure then moved quickly through Congress, and McKinley signed it on July 7, 1898. His signature, giving the United States a naval and commercial base in the mid-Pacific, achieved a goal policymakers had sought since the 1860s.

The New Navy

Navies were vital in the scramble for colonies, and in the 1870s, the United States had almost no naval power. One of the world's most powerful fleets during the Civil War, the American navy had fallen into rapid decline. By 1880, there were fewer than 2000 vessels, only 48 of which could fire a gun. Ships rotted, and many officers left the service.

Read the Document Alfred Thayer Mahan, "The Interest of America in Sea Power" (1897)

A TOP-HEAVY NAVY This 1881 cartoon depicted "our top-heavy navy," a decrepit vessel sinking with idle officers.

Conditions changed during the 1880s. A group of rising young officers, steeped in a new naval philosophy, argued for an expanded, fast, aggressive fleet capable of fighting battles across the seas. Big-navy proponents pointed to the growing fleets of Britain, France, and Germany, arguing that the United States needed to protect its economic and other interests in the Caribbean and Pacific.

In 1883, Congress authorized construction of four steel ships, marking the beginning of the new navy. Between 1885 and 1889, Congress budgeted funds for 30 more ships. The initial building program focused on lightly armored fast cruisers for raiding enemy merchant ships and protecting American shores, but after 1890, it shifted to constructing a seagoing offensive battleship navy capable of challenging the strongest fleets of Europe.

Alfred Thayer Mahan and Benjamin F. Tracy were two of the main advocates for the new navy. Austere and scholarly, Mahan was the era's most influential naval strategist. After graduating from the Naval Academy in 1859, he devoted a lifetime to studying the influence of sea power in history; for more than two decades, he headed the Newport Naval War College, where officers imbibed the latest strategic thinking. A clear, logical writer, Mahan summarized his beliefs in major books, including *The Influence of Sea Power upon History, 1660–1783* (1890) and *The Interest of America in Sea Power* (1897).

Mahan's reasoning was simple and, to that generation, persuasive. Industrialism, he argued, produced vast surpluses of agricultural and manufactured goods, for which markets must be found. Markets involved distant ports; reaching them required a large merchant marine and a powerful navy to protect it. Navies, in turn, needed coaling stations and repair yards. Coaling stations meant colonies, and colonies became strategic bases, the foundation of a nation's wealth and power. The bases might serve as markets themselves, but they were more important as stepping-stones to other objectives, such as the markets of Latin America and Asia.

Mahan called attention to the worldwide race for power, a race, he warned, the United States could not afford to lose. To compete in the struggle, Mahan argued, the United States must expand. It needed strategic bases, a powerful oceangoing navy, a canal across Central America to link the East Coast with the Pacific, and Hawaii as a way station on the route to Asia.

Mahan influenced a generation of policymakers in the United States and Europe; one of them, Benjamin F. Tracy, became Harrison's secretary of the navy in 1889. Tracy organized the Bureau of Construction and Repair to design and build new ships, established the Naval Reserve in 1891, and built the first American submarine in 1893. He also adopted the first heavy rapid-fire guns, smokeless powder, torpedoes, and heavy armor. Above all, Tracy joined with big-navy advocates in Congress to push for a far-ranging battleship fleet capable of attacking distant enemies. He wanted two fleets of battleships, eight ships in the Pacific and 12 in the Atlantic. He got four first-class battleships.

In 1889, when Tracy entered office, the United States ranked twelfth among world navies; in 1893, when he left, it ranked seventh and was climbing rapidly. "The sea," he predicted in 1891, "will be the future seat of empires. And we shall rule it as certainly as the sun doth rise." By the end of the 1890s, the navy had 17 steel battleships, six armored cruisers, and many smaller craft. It ranked third in the world.

Quick Check

What led the United States to build a new steel navy?

War With Spain

21.2   What were the causes and results of the war with Spain?

The war with Spain in 1898 bolstered national confidence, altered older, more insular patterns of thought, and reshaped how Americans saw themselves and the world. Its outcome pleased some people but troubled others, who raised questions about war itself, colonies, and subject peoples. The war left a lingering strain of isolationism and antiwar feeling that affected later policy. It also left an American empire, small by European standards, but new to the American experience because it was overseas. When the war ended, American possessions stretched into the Caribbean and deep into the Pacific. American influence went further still, and the United States was recognized as a "world power."

The Spanish-American War established the United States as a dominant force for the twentieth century. It brought America colonies, millions of colonial subjects, and the responsibilities of governing an empire and protecting it. For better or worse, it involved the country in other nations' arguments and affairs. The war strengthened the office of the presidency, swept up the nation in a tide of emotion, and confirmed Americans' long-standing belief in the superiority of the New World over the Old. When it was over, Americans looked outward as never before, touched, they were sure, with a special destiny.

A War for Principle

By the 1890s, Cuba and the nearby island of Puerto Rico comprised nearly all that remained of Spain's once vast empire in the New World. Cuban insurgents had repeatedly rebelled against Spanish rule, including a decade-long rebellion from 1868 to 1878 (the Ten Years' War) that failed to achieve independence. The depression of 1893 damaged the Cuban economy, and the Wilson-Gorman Tariff of 1894 prostrated it. The tariff raised duties on sugar, Cuba's lifeblood, 40 percent. With the island's sugar market in ruins, discontent with Spanish rule heightened. In February 1895, revolt again broke out.

Recognizing the importance of the nearby United States, Cuban insurgents established a junta in New York City to raise money, buy weapons, and wage a propaganda war to sway American opinion. Conditions in Cuba were grim.

In January 1896, Spain sent a new commander to Cuba, General Valeriano Weyler Nicolau. Relentless and brutal, Weyler gave the rebels ten days to lay down their arms. He then put into effect a "reconcentration" policy designed to move the native population into camps and destroy the rebellion's popular base. Herded into fortified areas, Cubans died by the thousands, victims of unsanitary conditions, overcrowding, and disease.

There was a wave of sympathy for the insurgents, stimulated by the newspapers; but so-called **yellow journalism**, sensationalist reporting practiced mainly by a handful of newspapers in New York City that were eager to increase sales, did not cause the war. The conflict stemmed from larger disputes in policies and perceptions between Spain and the United States. Grover Cleveland, under whose administration the rebellion began, preferred Spanish rule to the kind of turmoil that might invite foreign intervention. Opposed to the annexation of Cuba, he issued a proclamation of neutrality and tried to restrain public opinion.

Taking office in March 1897, President McKinley also urged neutrality but leaned slightly toward the insurgents. He sent an aide on a fact-finding mission to Cuba; the aide reported in mid-1897 that Weyler's policy had wrapped Cuba "in the stillness of death and the silence of desolation." McKinley then offered to mediate between Spain and the rebels, but, concerned over the suffering, he criticized Spain's "uncivilized and inhuman" conduct. The United States, he made clear, did not contest Spain's right to fight the rebellion but insisted it be done within humane limits.

Late in 1897, a new government in Madrid recalled Weyler and agreed to offer the Cubans autonomy. It also declared an amnesty for political prisoners and released Americans from Cuban jails. The new initiatives pleased McKinley, though he again warned Spain that it must find a humane end to the rebellion. In January 1898, however, Spanish army officers led riots in Havana against the new autonomy policy, shaking the president's confidence in Madrid's control over conditions in Cuba.

McKinley ordered the battleship *Maine* to Havana to demonstrate strength and protect American citizens if necessary. On February 9, 1898, the *New York Journal*, a leader of the yellow press, published a letter stolen from Enrique Dupuy de Lôme, the Spanish minister in Washington. In the letter, which was private correspondence to a friend, de Lôme called McKinley "weak," "a would-be politician," and "a bidder for the admiration of the crowd." The insult angered Americans; McKinley himself was more worried about sections of the letter that revealed Spanish insincerity in the negotiations. De Lôme immediately resigned and went home, but the damage was done.

A few days later, at 9:40 in the evening of February 15, an explosion tore through the hull of the *Maine*, riding at anchor in Havana harbor. The ship, a trim symbol of the new steel navy, sank quickly; 266 lives were lost. McKinley cautioned patience and promised an immediate investigation. Crowds gathered on Capitol Hill and outside the

yellow journalism To sell newspapers before and during the Spanish-American War, publishers William Randolph Hearst and Joseph Pulitzer engaged in blatant sensationalization of the news, which became known as "yellow journalism." Although it did not cause the war, it helped turn U.S. public opinion against Spain.

👁 Watch the Video   Burial of the *Maine* Victims

MAINE BURIAL This photo of the burial procession of victims of the *Maine* was taken at Key West, FL, on March 27, 1898. Two hundred sixty-six sailors and marines were killed in the explosion in Havana harbor.

White House, mourning the lost men. Soon there was a new slogan: "Remember the *Maine* and to Hell with Spain!"

The most recent study of the *Maine* incident blames the sinking on an accidental internal explosion, caused perhaps by spontaneous combustion in poorly ventilated coal bunkers. In 1898, Americans blamed it on Spain. Spaniards were hanged in effigy in many communities. Roosevelt, William Jennings Bryan, and others urged war, but McKinley hoped that Spain might yet agree to an armistice and perhaps Cuban independence.

In early March 1898, to be ready for war if it came, McKinley asked for $50 million in emergency defense appropriations, a request Congress promptly approved. The unanimous vote stunned Spain; allowing the president a latitude that was highly unusual for the era, Congress appropriated the money "for the National defense and for each and every purpose connected therewith to be expended at the discretion of the President." In late March, the report of the investigating board blamed the sinking of the *Maine* on an external (and thus presumably Spanish) explosion. Pressure for war increased.

On March 27, McKinley cabled Spain his final terms. He asked Spain to declare an armistice, end the reconcentration policy, and—implicitly—move toward Cuban independence. When the Spanish answer came, it conceded some things, but not, in McKinley's judgment, the important ones. Spain offered to suspend hostilities but left its commander in Cuba to set the length and terms of the suspension. It also revoked the reconcentration policy. But Spain made no mention of a true armistice, McKinley's offer to mediate, or Cuba's independence.

Reluctantly McKinley asked Congress on April 11, 1898, for authority to send American troops to Cuba. On April 19, Congress passed a joint resolution declaring Cuba independent and authorizing the president to use the army and navy to expel the Spanish from it. The **Teller Amendment**, offered by Colorado Senator Henry M. Teller, pledged that the United States had no intention of annexing Cuba.

On April 21, in response to an American ultimatum to grant Cuba independence, Spain severed diplomatic relations. The following day, McKinley proclaimed a blockade of Cuba and called for 125,000 volunteers. On Monday, April 25, Congress passed a declaration of war, and McKinley signed it.

Some historians have suggested that in leading the country toward war, McKinley was weak and indecisive, a victim of war hysteria in Congress and the country; others have called him a wily manipulator for war and imperial gains. In truth, he was neither. Throughout the crisis, McKinley pursued a moderate course that sought to end the suffering in Cuba, promote Cuba's independence, and allow Spain time to adjust to the loss of the remnant of its American empire. He wanted peace, as did Spain, but in the end, the conflicting national interests of the two countries brought them to war.

Teller Amendment In this amendment to the declaration of war on Spain in 1898, the United States pledged that it did not intend to annex Cuba and that it would recognize Cuban independence after the Spanish-American War.

Quick Check

What were the three main causes of the war with Spain in 1898?

The Spanish-American War

Ten weeks after the declaration of war, the fighting was over. For Americans, they were ten glorious, dizzying weeks, with victories to fill every headline and slogans to suit every taste. No war can be a happy occasion for those who fight it, but the Spanish-American War came closer than most. Declared in April, it ended in August. Relatively few Americans died in the fighting, and the quick victory seemed to verify burgeoning American power, though the author Sherwood Anderson suggested that fighting a weakened Spain was "like robbing an old gypsy woman in a vacant lot at night after a fair." John Hay, soon to be McKinley's secretary of state, called it "a splendid little war."

At the outset, the United States was militarily unprepared. The regular army consisted of only 28,000 officers and men, most of them more experienced in quelling Indian uprisings than fighting large-scale battles.

When McKinley called for 125,000 volunteers, as many as 1 million young Americans responded. Ohio alone had 100,000 volunteers. Keeping the regular army units intact, War Department officials enlisted the volunteers in National Guard units that were then integrated into the national army. Men clamored to join. William Jennings Bryan, a pacifist by temperament, took command of a regiment of Nebraska volunteers; Roosevelt chafed to get to the front. The secretary of war feared "there is going to be more trouble to satisfy those who are not going than to find those who are willing to go."

In an army inundated with men, problems of equipment and supply quickly appeared. The regulars had the new .30-caliber Krag-Jorgensen rifles, but National Guard units carried Civil War Springfield rifles that used old black-powder cartridges. The cartridges gave off a puff of smoke when fired, neatly marking the troops' position. Spanish troops had modern Mausers with smokeless powder, which they used to devastating effect. Food and sickness were also problems. Tropical disease felled many soldiers. Scores took ill after landing in Cuba and the Philippines, and half a regiment was sometimes unable to answer the bugle call.

Americans then believed that "a foreign war should be fought by the hometown military unit acting as an extension of their community." Soldiers identified with their hometowns, dressed in the local fashion, and thought of themselves as members of a town unit in a national army. The poet Carl Sandburg, 20 years old in 1898, rushed to join the army and called his unit a "living part" of his hometown of Galesburg, Illinois. And the citizens of Galesburg, for their part, took a special interest in Sandburg's unit, in a fashion repeated in countless towns across the country.

Not surprisingly, then, National Guard units mirrored the social patterns of their communities. Since everyone knew each other, there was an easygoing familiarity, tempered by the deference that went with hometown wealth, occupation, education, and length of residence. Enlisted men resented officers who grabbed too much authority, and they expected officers and men to call each other by their first names. Sandburg knew most of the privates in his unit, had worked for his corporal, and had gone to school with the first lieutenant.

Quick Check

What was the nature of this "Splendid Little War," as Mckinley's secretary of state described it?

Each community thought of the hometown unit as its own unit, an extension of itself. In later wars, the government censored news and dominated press relations. There was little censorship in the war with Spain, and the freshest news arrived in the latest letter home. Small-town newspapers printed news of the men, and townswomen knit special red or white bellybands of stitched flannel, thought to ward off tropical fevers. Towns sent food, clothing, and occasionally even local doctors to the front.

African American Soldiers in the War

When the invasion force sailed for Cuba, nearly one-fourth of it was African American. In 1898, the regular army included four African American regiments: the Twenty-fourth and Twenty-fifth Infantry and the Ninth and Tenth Cavalry. Black regiments had served with distinction against the Indians in the West, where most African American troops were posted. No eastern community would accept them. A troop of the Ninth Cavalry was stationed in Virginia in 1891, but it was ordered back to the West after whites complained.

When the war broke out, the War Department called for five black volunteer regiments. Military authorities were sure that blacks had a natural immunity to the climate and diseases of the tropics. But most state governors refused to accept black volunteers. African American leaders protested the discrimination. The McKinley administration intervened, and in the end, the volunteer army included more than 10,000 black troops.

The four black regiments in the West were ordered to camps in the South to prepare for the invasion of Cuba. Crowds and cheers followed the troop trains across the Plains, but as they crossed into Kentucky and Tennessee, the cheering stopped, and the troops were hustled onward. Station restaurants refused to serve them; waiting rooms were segregated.

Many black soldiers were not prepared to put up with this treatment. Those stationed near Chickamauga Park, Tennessee, shot "at some whites who insulted them" and forcibly desegregated the railroad cars on the line into Chattanooga. Troops training near Macon, Georgia, refused to ride in the segregated "trailers" attached to the trolleys, and fights broke out.

THE BATTLE OF SAN JUAN HILL *Charge of the 24th and 25th Colored Infantry and Rescue of the Rough Riders at San Juan Hill, July 2, 1898,* colored lithograph by Kurz and Allison, 1899 (above). The Twenty-fourth and Twenty-fifth Colored Infantry regiments served with exceptional gallantry in the Spanish-American War.

✳ Explore the Spanish-American War on MyHistoryLab

HOW DID THE UNITED STATES BUILD AN OVERSEAS EMPIRE IN THE 1890s?

By the end of the 1800s, American territorial expansion had reached across the continent. This territory was not "free land" but territory that formerly belonged to Native Americans. During the last decade of the century, the United States began to acquire an empire overseas. The country obtained many of its new possessions in 1899 through defeating Spain in a war the previous year. From the perspectives of the inhabitants of these territories, U.S. victory in the war meant trading one imperial master, Spain, for another as the territories of the United States spread from the Caribbean Sea across the Pacific Ocean.

SAN JUAN HILL One of the pivotal events in the Spanish-American War of 1898 and the conquest of Cuba was the capture of the blockhouse on San Juan Hill by American forces—including Col. Theodore Roosevelt's cavalry unit, the "Rough Riders"—on July 2, 1898.

UNITED STATES ACQUISITIONS, 1890s

Location	Year	From
Hawaii	1898	Annexation
Cuba	1899	Spain
Puerto Rico	1899	Spain
Guam	1899	Spain
Philippines	1899	Spain

SOURCE: Library of Congress

KEY QUESTIONS   Use *MyHistoryLab Explorer* to answer these questions:

Analysis ▶▶▶ *Where and how did the Spanish-American War unfold?*

Map the war's major battles.

Response ▶▶▶ *How did American territorial claims change between 1790 and 1900?*

Map the expansion of the United States, paying particular attention to the trends of the 1890s.

Comparison ▶▶▶ *What were domestic attitudes toward the new overseas empire?*

See how American expansion was represented at home.

Quick Check

What role did African American troops play in the Spanish-American war?

More than 4000 black troops training near Tampa and Lakeland, Florida, found segregated saloons, cafés, and drugstores. "Here the Negro is not allowed to purchase over the same counter in some stores as the white man purchases over," Chaplain George W. Prioleau charged. "Why sir, the Negro of this country is a freeman and yet a slave. Talk about fighting and freeing poor Cuba and of Spain's brutality; of Cuba's murdered thousands, and starving reconcentradoes. Is America any better than Spain?"

When the invasion force sailed, segregation continued on some of the troopships. Blacks were assigned to the lowest decks, or whites and blacks were placed on different sides of the ship. But the confusion of war often ended the problem, if only temporarily. Blacks took command as white officers died, and Spanish troops soon came to fear the "smoked Yankees," as they called them. Black soldiers played a major role in the Cuban campaign and probably staved off defeat for the Rough Riders at San Juan Hill. In Cuba, they won 26 Certificates of Merit and five Congressional Medals of Honor.

The Course of the War

Mahan's Naval War College had begun studying strategy for a war with Spain in 1895. By 1898, it had a detailed plan for operations in the Caribbean and Pacific. Naval strategy was simple: Destroy the Spanish fleet, damage Spain's merchant

AFRICAN AMERICANS IN THE WAR WITH SPAIN. Charles Young, an 1889 graduate of West Point, was the only African American officer in the army during the Spanish-American War except for a few chaplains.

marine, and harry the colonies or the coast of Spain. Planners were excited; two steam-powered armored fleets had yet to meet in battle anywhere in the world. The army's task was more difficult. It had to defend the United States, invade Cuba and probably Puerto Rico, and undertake possible action in far-flung places such as the Philippines or Spain itself.

Even before war was declared, the secretary of war arranged joint planning between the army and navy. Military intelligence was accurate, and planners knew the numbers and locations of the Spanish troops. Earlier they had rejected a proposal to send an officer in disguise to map Cuban harbors; such things, they said, were simply not done in peacetime. Still, the War Department's new Military Information Division, a sign of the increasing professionalization of the army, had detailed diagrams of Spanish fortifications in Havana and other points. On April 20, 1898, McKinley summoned the strategists to the White House. To the dismay of those who wanted a more aggressive policy, they decided on the limited strategy of blockading Cuba, arming the insurgents, and annoying the Spanish with small thrusts by the army.

Victories soon changed the strategy. In case of war, long-standing naval plans had called for a holding action against the Spanish base in the Philippines. On May 1, 1898, with the war barely a week old, Commodore George Dewey, commander of the Asiatic Squadron based at Hong Kong, destroyed the Spanish fleet in Manila Bay. Suddenly, Manila and the Philippines lay within American grasp. At home, Dewey portraits, songs, and poems blossomed everywhere, and his calm order to the flagship's captain—"You may fire when ready, Gridley"—hung on every tongue. Dewey had four modern cruisers, two gunboats, and a Civil War paddle steamer. He sank eight obsolete Spanish warships. Dewey had no troops to attack the Spanish army in Manila, but the War Department, stunned by the speed and size of the victory, quickly raised an expeditionary force. On August 13, 1898, the troops accepted the surrender of Manila, and with it, the Philippines. (See Map 21.2.)

McKinley and his aides were worried about Admiral Pascual Cervera's main Spanish fleet, thought to be headed across the Atlantic for an attack on Florida. On May 13, the navy found Cervera's ships near Martinique in the Caribbean but then lost them again. A few days later, Cervera slipped secretly into the harbor of Santiago de Cuba, a city on the island's southern coast. A spy in the Havana telegraph office alerted the Americans, and on May 28, a superior American force under Admiral William T. Sampson bottled Cervera up.

In early June, Marines seized Guantánamo Bay, the great harbor on the south of the island. They established depots for the navy to refuel and pinned down Spanish troops in the area. On June 21, an invasion force of about 17,000 landed at Daiquiri on Cuba's southeastern coast. All was confusion, but the Spanish offered no resistance. Helped by Cuban insurgents, the Americans pushed west toward Santiago, which they hoped to surround and capture.

The first battle broke out at Las Guasimas, a crossroads on the Santiago road. After a sharp fight, the Spanish fell back. On July 1, the Rough Riders, troops from the four black regiments, and the other regulars reached the fortifications at El Caney and San Juan Hill. Black soldiers of the Twenty-fifth Infantry charged the El Caney blockhouses, surprising the Spanish defenders with Comanche yells. For the better

MAP 21.2 SPANISH-AMERICAN WAR, PACIFIC THEATER Commodore Dewey, promoted to admiral immediately after the naval victory at Manila Bay, was the first hero of the war.

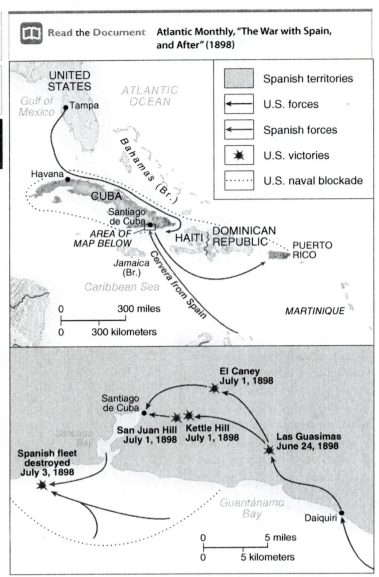

📖 **Read the Document** **Atlantic Monthly, "The War with Spain, and After" (1898)**

MAP 21.3 SPANISH-AMERICAN WAR, CARIBBEAN THEATER President McKinley set up a "war room" in the White House, following the action on giant maps with red and white marking pins.

Quick Check

What were the main events of the war itself?

part of a day, the defenders held back the army's elite corps. In the confusion of battle, Roosevelt rallied an assortment of infantry and cavalry to take Kettle Hill, adjacent to San Juan Hill.

They charged directly into the Spanish guns, Roosevelt at their head, mounted on a horse, a blue polka-dot handkerchief floating from the brim of his sombrero. "I waved my hat and we went up the hill with a rush," he recalled in his autobiography. Actually, it was less easy. Losses were heavy: 89 Rough Riders were killed or wounded in the attack. Dense foliage concealed the enemy and smokeless powder gave no clue to their position. At nightfall, the surviving Spanish defenders withdrew, and the Americans prepared for the counterattack.

American troops now occupied the ridges overlooking Santiago. They were weakened by sickness, a fact unknown to the Spanish, who decided the city was lost. The Spanish command in Havana ordered Cervera to run for the open sea, although he knew the attempt was hopeless. On the morning of July 3, Cervera's squadron steamed down the bay and out through the harbor's narrow channel, but the waiting American fleet closed in, and in a few hours every Spanish vessel was destroyed. Two weeks later, Santiago surrendered. (See Map 21.3).

Soon thereafter, troops, meeting little resistance, occupied Puerto Rico. Cervera had commanded Spain's only battle fleet, and when it sank, Spain was helpless against attacks on the colonies or even its own shores. The war was over. Lasting 113 days, it took relatively few lives, most of them the result of accident, yellow fever, malaria, and typhoid in Cuba. Of the 5500 Americans who died in the war, only 379 were killed in battle. The navy lost one man in the battle at Santiago Bay and only one to heatstroke in the stunning victory in Manila Bay.

Acquisition of Empire

21.3 What were the various viewpoints about the acquisition of empire after the war with Spain?

Late in the afternoon of August 12, 1898, representatives of Spain and the United States met in McKinley's White House office to sign the preliminary instrument of peace. Secretary of State William R. Day beckoned a presidential aide over to a large globe, remarking, "Let's see what we get by this."

What the United States got was more territory and even more responsibilities. According to the preliminary agreement, Spain granted independence to Cuba, ceded Puerto Rico and the Pacific island of Guam to the United States, and allowed Americans to occupy Manila until the two countries reached final agreement on the Philippines. To McKinley, the Philippines were the problem. Puerto Rico was close to the mainland, and even many opponents of expansion wanted to take it. Guam was too small and unknown to merit attention. The Philippines, on the other hand, were huge, sprawling, populous, and thousands of miles from America.

McKinley weighed a number of alternatives for the Philippines, but he liked none of them. He believed he could not give the islands back to Spain; public opinion would not allow it. He might turn them over to another nation, but then they would fall, as he later said, "a golden apple of discord, among the rival powers." Germany, Japan, Britain, and Russia had all expressed interest in acquiring them. Germany even sent a fleet to Manila and laid plans to take the Philippines if the United States let them go.

Rejecting those alternatives, McKinley considered independence for the islands but was soon talked out of it. People who had been there, reflecting the era's racism, told him the Filipinos were not ready for independence. He thought of establishing an American protectorate but discarded the idea, convinced it would bring American responsibilities without full American control. Finally, McKinley decided the only practical policy was to annex the Philippines, with an eye to future independence after a period of tutelage.

At first hesitant, American opinion was swinging to the same conclusion. Religious and missionary organizations appealed to McKinley to hold on to the Philippines in order to "Christianize" them, although most Filipinos were already Roman Catholics. Some merchants and industrialists saw the islands as the key to the China market and the wealth of Asia. Many Americans simply regarded them as the legitimate fruits of war. In October 1898, representatives of the United States and Spain met in Paris to discuss a peace treaty. Spain agreed to recognize Cuba's independence, assume the Cuban debt, and cede Puerto Rico and Guam to the United States.

On instructions from McKinley, the American representatives also demanded the cession of the Philippines: "Grave as are the responsibilities and unforeseen as are the difficulties which are before us, the President can see but one plain path of duty—the acceptance of the archipelago," the instructions said. In return, the United States offered to pay $20 million. Spain resisted but had little choice. On December 10, 1898, American and Spanish representatives signed the **Treaty of Paris**.

Treaty of Paris Treaty in December 1898 ending the Spanish-American War. Under its terms, Spain recognized Cuba's independence, assumed the Cuban debt, and ceded Puerto Rico, Guam, and the Philippines to the United States.

The Treaty of Paris Debate

Submitted to the Senate for ratification, the treaty set off a storm of debate. Industrialist Andrew Carnegie, reformer Jane Addams, labor leader Samuel Gompers, Mark Twain, and many others argued forcefully against annexing the Philippines. Annexation, the anti-imperialists protested, violated the very principles of independence and self-determination on which the United States was founded.

Some labor leaders feared cheap labor from new Pacific colonies. Gompers warned about the "half-breeds and semi-barbaric people" who might undercut wages and the union movement. Other anti-imperialists argued against assimilation of different races: "Spanish-Americans," as one said, "with all the mixture of Indian and negro blood, and Malays and other unspeakable Asiatics, by the tens of millions!" Such racist views were also common among those favoring expansion, and the anti-imperialists usually focused on different arguments. If the United States established a tyranny abroad, they were sure, there would soon be tyranny at home.

William Jennings Bryan scoffed at the argument that colonies were good for trade: "It is not necessary to own people to trade with them." Many thought the country's republican ideals could not be reconciled with subjugating people abroad. To Booker T. Washington, the country had more important things to think about at home, including its treatment of Indians and blacks. Carnegie was so upset that he offered to buy Filipino independence with a personal check for $20 million.

In November 1898, opponents of expansion formed the **Anti-Imperialist League** to fight the treaty. Membership centered in New England; the cause was less popular in the West and South. It enlisted more Democrats than Republicans, though never a majority of either. Their lack of a coherent program weakened the anti-imperialists. Some favored keeping naval bases in the conquered areas. Some wanted Hawaii and Puerto Rico but not the Philippines. Others wanted nothing at all to do with any colonies. Most simply wished that Dewey had sailed away after beating the Spanish at Manila Bay.

Anti-Imperialist League An organization formed in 1898 to fight the Treaty of Paris ending the Spanish-American War. Members opposed acquiring overseas colonies, believing it would subvert American ideals and institutions. Membership centered in New England; the cause was less popular in the South and West.

CARL SCHURZ

CARL SCHURZ Carl Schurz and the other anti-imperialists of the American Anti-Imperialist League lobbied President McKinley not to annex the Philippines after the Spanish-American War in 1898. These anti-imperialists argued that the annexation of the Philippines would violate republican principles.

The debate in the Senate lasted a month. Pressing for ratification, McKinley toured the South to rally support and consulted closely with senators. Though opposed to taking the Philippines, Bryan supported ratification in order to end the war; his support influenced some Democratic votes. Still, on the final weekend before the vote, the treaty was two votes short. That Saturday night, news reached Washington that fighting had broken out between American troops and Filipino insurgents who demanded immediate independence. The news increased pressure to ratify the treaty, which the Senate did on February 6, 1899, with two votes to spare. An amendment promising independence as soon as the Filipinos established a stable government lost by one vote. The United States had a colonial empire. (See Map 21.4).

Guerrilla Warfare in the Philippines

Historians rarely write of the **Philippine-American War**, a guerrilla war between American troops and the newly freed Filipinos, but it was an important event in American history. The war with Spain was over three months after it began, but war with the Filipinos lasted more than three years. Four times as many American soldiers fought in the Philippines as in Cuba. For the first time, Americans fought men of a different color in an Asian guerrilla war. The Philippine-American War of 1898–1902

Quick Check

What were the main arguments on each side in the debate over the treaty that ended the war?

Philippine-American War A war fought from 1899 to 1902 to quell Filipino resistance to U.S. control of the Philippine Islands.

498

took a heavy toll: 4300 American lives and thousands of Filipino lives (estimates range from 50,000 to 200,000).

Emilio Aguinaldo, the Filipino leader, was 29 years old in 1898. An early organizer of resistance to Spain, he had gone into exile in Hong Kong, from where he welcomed the outbreak of the Spanish-American War. Certain the United States would grant independence, he worked for an American victory. Filipino insurgents helped guide Dewey into Manila Bay, and Dewey sent a ship to Hong Kong to bring back Aguinaldo to lead an uprising against the Spanish. On June 12, 1898, the insurgents proclaimed their independence.

Cooperating with the Americans, they drove the Spanish out of many areas. In the liberated regions, Aguinaldo established local governments and appointed provincial governors. He waited for American recognition, but McKinley and others had concluded that the Filipinos were not ready. Soon, warfare broke out between the Filipinos and Americans over Filipino independence.

By late 1899, the American army had dispersed the organized Filipino army, but claims of victory proved premature. Aguinaldo shifted to guerrilla tactics, striking suddenly and then melting into the jungle or friendly native villages. In many areas, the Americans ruled the day, the guerrillas the night. Both sides committed atrocities. The Americans used brutal, Weyler-like tactics. After any attack on an American patrol, the Americans burned all the houses in the district. They tortured people and executed prisoners. They herded people into protected "zones." Seizing or destroying food outside the zones, they starved guerrillas into submission.

Bryan tried to turn the election of 1900 into a debate over imperialism, but the attempt failed. For one thing, he himself refused to give up the silver issue, which cost him support among anti-imperialists in the Northeast who were for gold (see Chapter 20). McKinley, moreover, took advantage of the surging economy and defended expansion as an accomplished fact. Riding a wave of patriotism and prosperity, McKinley won the election handily—by an even larger margin than he had in 1896.

In 1900, McKinley sent a special commission to the islands under William Howard Taft, a prominent Ohio judge. Directed to establish a civil government, the commission organized municipal administrations and, in stages, created a government for the

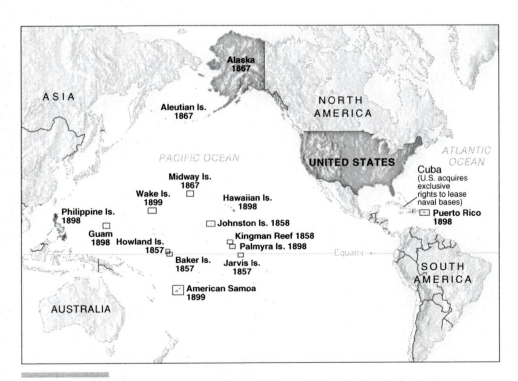

MAP 21.4 AMERICAN EMPIRE, 1900 With the Treaty of Paris, the United States gained an expanded colonial empire stretching from the Caribbean to the far Pacific. It embraced Puerto Rico, Alaska, Hawaii, part of Samoa, Guam, the Philippines, and a chain of Pacific islands. The dates on the map refer to the date of U.S. acquisition.

Quick Check

What were the causes and consequences of the Philippine-American War?

Philippines. In March 1901, five American soldiers tricked their way into Aguinaldo's camp deep in the mountains and took him prisoner. Back in Manila, he urged his people to end the fighting. Some guerrillas held out for another year, but to no avail. On July 4, 1901, authority was transferred from the army to Taft, who was named civilian governor of the islands, and his civilian commission. McKinley reaffirmed his purpose to grant the Filipinos self-government as soon as they were deemed ready for it.

Given broad powers, the Taft Commission introduced many changes. New schools provided education and vocational training for Filipinos of all social classes. The Americans built roads and bridges, reformed the judiciary, restructured the tax system, and introduced sanitation and vaccination programs. They established local governments built on Filipino traditions and hierarchies. Taft encouraged Filipino participation in government. Over the next 40 years, other measures broadened Filipino rights. Independence finally came on July 4, 1946, nearly 50 years after Aguinaldo proclaimed it.

The Open Door

Poised in the Philippines, the United States had become an Asian power on the doorstep of China. Weakened by years of warfare and rebellion, China in 1898 and 1899 was unable to resist foreign influence. Japan, Britain, France, Germany, and Russia eyed it covetously, dividing parts of the country into "spheres of influence." They forced China to grant "concessions" that allowed them exclusive rights to develop particular areas and threatened American hopes for trade.

McKinley first outlined a new China policy in 1898 when he said that Americans sought trade, "but we seek no advantages in the Orient which are not common to all. Asking only the open door for ourselves, we are ready to accord the open door to others." In September 1899, Secretary of State John Hay addressed identical diplomatic notes to Britain, Germany, and Russia, and later to France, Japan, and Italy, asking them to join the United States in establishing the **Open Door policy**. This policy urged three agreements: Nations possessing a sphere of influence would respect the rights and privileges of other nations in that sphere; the Chinese government would continue to collect tariff duties in all spheres; and nations would not discriminate against other nations in levying port dues and railroad rates within their respective spheres of influence.

Under the Open Door policy, the United States would retain many commercial advantages it might lose if China were partitioned into spheres of influence. McKinley and Hay also attempted to preserve for the Chinese some semblance of national authority. Britain most nearly accepted the principle of the Open Door. Russia declined to approve it. The other powers, sending evasive replies, stated they would agree only if all the other nations did. Hay tried to turn the situation to American advantage by boldly announcing in March 1900 that all the powers had accepted the Open Door policy.

The policy's first test came three months later with the outbreak of the Boxer Rebellion in Peking (now Beijing). In June 1900, a secret, intensely nationalistic Chinese society called the Boxers tried to oust all foreigners from their country. Overrunning Peking, they drove foreigners into their legations and penned them up for nearly two months. In the end, the United States, Britain, Germany, Japan, and other powers sent troops to lift the siege.

Fearing that the rebellion gave some nations, especially Germany and Russia, an excuse to expand their spheres of influence, Hay sent off another round of Open Door notes affirming U.S. commitment to equal commercial opportunity and respect for China's independence. While the first Open Door notes had implied recognition of China's continued independence, the second notes explicitly stated the need to preserve it. Together, the two notes comprised the Open Door policy, which became a central element in American diplomacy in the Far East.

The policy tried to help China, but it also led to further American meddling in Chinese affairs. Moreover, by committing itself to a policy that Americans were not prepared to defend militarily, the McKinley administration laid the basis for later controversy with Japan and other expansion-minded powers in the Pacific.

Open Door policy This policy established free trade between the United States and China in 1900 and attempted to induce European nations and Japan to recognize the territorial integrity of China. It marked a departure from the American tradition of isolationism and signaled the country's growing involvement in the world.

Quick Check

What was the "Open Door" policy toward China?

Conclusion: Outcome of the War with Spain

The war with Spain over, Roosevelt and the Rough Riders sailed for home in mid-August 1898. They sauntered through the streets of New York, the heroes of the city. A few weeks later, Roosevelt bade them farewell. They presented him with a reproduction of Frederick Remington's famed bronze *The Bronco-Buster*, and, close to tears, he told them, "I am proud of this regiment beyond measure." Roosevelt was soon governor of New York and on his way to the White House.

Other soldiers were also glad to be home, although they sometimes resented the reception they found. "The war is over now," said Winslow Hobson, a black trooper from the Ninth Ohio, "and Roosevelt . . . and others (white of course) have all there is to be gotten out of it." Bravery in Cuba and the Philippines won some recognition for black soldiers, but the war itself set back the cause of civil rights. It spurred talk about "inferior" races, at home and abroad, and united whites in the North and South. "The Negro might as well know it now as later," a black editor said, "the closer the North and South get together by this war, the harder he will have to fight to maintain a footing." A fresh outburst of segregation laws and lynching occurred during the decade after the war.

McKinley and the Republican party soared to new heights of popularity. Firmly established, the Republican majority dominated politics until 1932. Scandals arose about the food provided for the troops and the conduct of the War Department, but there was none of the sharp sense of deception and betrayal that was to mark the years after World War I. In a little more than a century, the United States had grown from 13 states stretched along a thin Atlantic coastline into a world power that reached from the Caribbean to the Pacific. As Seward and others had hoped, the nation now dominated its own hemisphere, dealt with European powers on more equal terms, and was a major power in Asia. (See Map 21.5).

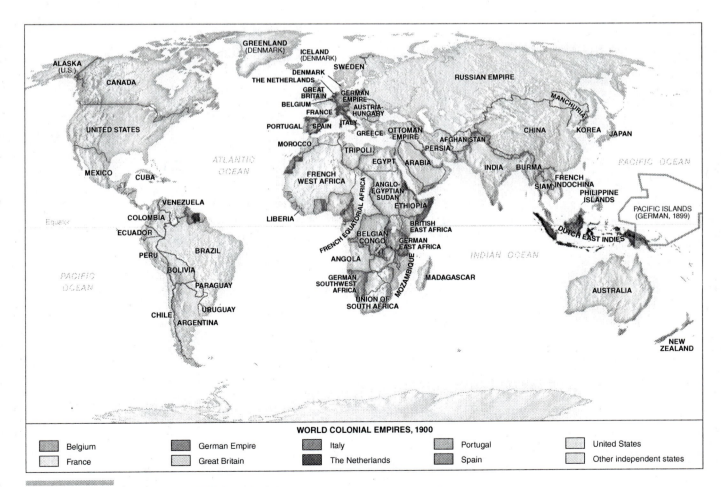

WORLD COLONIAL EMPIRES, 1900

Belgium	German Empire	Italy	Portugal	United States
France	Great Britain	The Netherlands	Spain	Other independent states

MAP 21.5 WORLD COLONIAL EMPIRES, 1900 Events of the nineteenth century increased European hegemony over the world. By 1900, most independent African nations had disappeared and the major European nations had divided the continent among themselves. In the East, the European powers and Japan took advantage of China's internal weakness to gain both trading ports and economic concessions.

Chapter Review

America Looks Outward

21.1 Why did Americans look outward in the last half of the nineteenth century? p. 481

In the late nineteenth century, Americans increasingly looked overseas, influenced by the example of other nations and confidence in what their country could offer other peoples, including Christianity, commerce, and American values. Policymakers were sure that the nation needed a navy, colonial outposts, foreign markets, and a new foreign policy.

War with Spain

21.2 What were the causes and results of the war with Spain? p. 488

In 1898, the United States fought a war with Spain, which resulted in a quick victory and enormous changes for American society, including a larger military, an increased role for the federal government in American life, the acquisition of colonies, and increased power for the presidency.

Acquisition of Empire

21.3 What were the various viewpoints about the acquisition of empire after the war with Spain? p. 496

In the peace treaty ending the war with Spain, the United States acquired a new empire, including Puerto Rico, Guam, and the Philippines. For the first time, the United States owned territories overseas, to which it did not intend to grant statehood. That, together with historical, racial, and other arguments, caused an angry debate between those in favor and those opposing the new colonies. Adding to the furor was the outbreak of warfare between American troops and Filipino insurgents in the Philippines.

Timeline

1867
America Looks Outward—The United States purchases Alaska from Russia

1867

1875
America Looks Outward—Reciprocity treaty binds Hawaii economically and politically to the United States

1875

1887
America Looks Outward—Treaty with Hawaii gives the United States exclusive use of Pearl Harbor

1887

1893
America Looks Outward—Americans in Hawaii overthrow Queen Liliuokalani; provisional government established

1893

1898
War with Spain—Congress declares war against Spain (April)
Acquisition of Empire—The United States annexes Hawaii (July); Treaty of Paris ends Spanish-American War (December); United States sends Open Door notes; Philippine-American War erupts

1898

1902
Acquisition of Empire—Philippine-American War ends with American victory

1902

22 The Progressive Era 1895–1917

Muckrakers Call for Reform

In 1902, Samuel S. McClure, the shrewd owner of *McClure's Magazine*, sensed something astir in the country that his reporters were not covering. Like *Life*, *Munsey's*, the *Ladies' Home Journal*, and *Cosmopolitan*, *McClure's* was reaching more and more people—more than 250,000 readers a month. Americans were snapping up the new popular magazines filled with eye-catching illustrations and up-to-date fiction. Advances in photoengraving during the 1890s reduced the cost of illustrations; income from advertisements also rose sharply. By 1900, some magazines earned $60,000 an issue from advertising alone, and publishers could price them as low as 10 cents a copy.

McClure was always chasing new ideas and readers, and in 1902, certain that something was happening in the public mood, he told one of his editors, 36-year-old Lincoln Steffens, a former

LEARNING OBJECTIVES

22.1	22.2	22.3	22.4
How did industrialism change after 1900? p. 505	How did mass production affect women, children, immigrants, and African Americans? p. 510	Why were there so many strikes in this period? p. 518	What happened to art and culture in these years so filled with change? p. 521

THE MUCKRAKERS At the beginning of the twentieth century, magazines enjoyed increasing popularity. *McClure's Magazine* pioneered investigative journalism. The November 1902 edition featured the first installment of Ida Tarbell's two-year series on Standard Oil that exposed the corrupt practices and deals that had helped create the company.

((· Listen to Chapter 22 on MyHistoryLab

Watch the Video Series on MyHistoryLab

Learn about some key topics related to this chapter with the *MyHistoryLab Video Series: Key Topics in U. S. History*.

 1 **The Evolution of Industrialism** By the late 1800s, the Industrial Revolution in the United States brought about deep economic divide in the population. The growth of steel, oil and railroad industries, fueled by cheap immigrant labor, were marked by the creation of huge corporations called trusts or monopolies. It was common for some companies to buy smaller competitors in an effort to control the market. As industry grew, laborers were often paid less and consumers paid more for products. Progressive era movements encouraged unionization—collective bargaining—to achieve improved working conditions and better wages.

 Watch on MyHistoryLab

The Other Side of Industry The quality of life experienced by the working class in the American Industrial Revolution of the early 1900s was inversely correlated the success of the business owners for whom they worked. As mechanization increased work became increasingly arduous and wages decreased. Workdays could last as many as sixteen hours. The unsafe conditions of factories were highlighted by the Triangle Shirtwaist Fire of 1911 in New York which killed hundreds of laborers in a cramped high-rise factory. Farmers, who made up about one third of the population, also faced hardship during this period. Land-holders lived comfortably while tenant farmers struggled. **2**

Watch on MyHistoryLab

3 **Unions Grow in Power** By the beginning of the 20th century Unions had become an increasing component of Industrial life. While they varied in approach, the central goal was collective negotiation for improved wages and working conditions on behalf of laborers. Unions such as American Federation of Labor (AFL), the Women's Trade Union League (WTL) and the International Workers of the World (IWW) used work stoppage as their most significant negotiation tactic. The backlash against the Unions was notable—middle class consumers blamed the growing union movement for episodes of violence that periodically came out of protests and higher prices for product.

 Watch on MyHistoryLab

A Changing Urban Culture The growing consumer prosperity of the early 20th century brought about a variety of cultural shifts in cities centers such as Boston, Chicago, Philadelphia, and New York. As the population grew, city-dwellers relied increasingly on mass-produced products such as food and clothing. The industrial economy grew in tandem with service sector jobs such as advertising, health care, and hospitality. A culture of leisure was born, as opportunities to enjoy the arts including theater, music, films, and sporting events became commonplace. **4**

Watch on MyHistoryLab

Wall Street reporter, to find out what it was: "Get out of here, travel, go—somewhere. Buy a railroad ticket, get on a train, and there, where it lands you, there you will learn to edit a magazine."

Steffens went west. In St. Louis, he came across a young district attorney, Joseph W. Folk, who had found a trail of corruption linking politics and some of the city's respected business leaders. Eager for help, Folk named names to the editor from New York. "It is good business men that are corrupting our bad politicians," he stressed. "It is the leading citizens that are battening on our city." Steffens's story, "Tweed Days in St. Louis," appeared in the October 1902 issue of *McClure's*.

The November *McClure's* carried the first installment of Ida Tarbell's scathing "History of the Standard Oil Company." In January 1903, Steffens was back with "The Shame of Minneapolis," another tale of corrupt partnership between business and politics. McClure had what he wanted, and in the January issue he printed an editorial, "Concerning Three Articles in This Number of

McClure's, and a Coincidence That May Set Us Thinking." Steffens on Minneapolis, Tarbell on Standard Oil, and an article on abuses in labor unions—all, McClure said, on different topics but actually on the same theme: corruption in American life: "Capitalists, workingmen, politicians, citizens—all breaking the law, or letting it be broken."

Readers were enthralled, and articles and books by other **muckrakers**—Theodore Roosevelt coined the term in 1906 to describe the writers who made a practice of exposing the corruption of public and prominent figures—spread swiftly. *Collier's* had articles on questionable stock market practices, patent medicines, and the beef trust. Novelist Upton Sinclair tackled the meatpackers in *The Jungle* (1906). In 1904, Steffens collected his *McClure's* articles in *The Shame of the Cities,* with an introduction expressing confidence that reform was possible, "that our shamelessness is superficial, that beneath it lies a pride which, being real, may save us yet."

Muckraking flourished from 1903 to 1909, and while it did, good writers and bad investigated almost every corner of American life: government, labor unions, big business, Wall Street, health care, the food industry, child labor, women's rights, prostitution, ghetto life, and life insurance.

The muckrakers were a journalistic voice of a larger movement in American society. Called **progressivism,** it lasted from the mid-1890s through World War I. Like muckraking itself, progressivism reflected worry about society, the effects of industrialization and urbanization, social disorder, political corruption, and many other issues. With concerns so large, progressivism often had a sense of crisis and urgency, although it was rooted in a spirit of hopefulness and confidence in human progress. For varying reasons, thousands of people became concerned about their society. Separately and together, they set out to cure the ills they saw around them. The efforts of the so-called progressives changed the nation and gave the era its name.

muckrakers Writers who made a practice between 1903 and 1909 of exposing the wrongdoings of public figures and corporations and highlighting social and political problems.

progressivism Movement for social change between the late 1890s and World War I. Its origins lay in a fear of big business and corrupt government and a desire to improve living conditions. Progressives set out to cure the social ills brought about by industrialization and urbanization, social disorder, and corruption.

The Changing Face of Industrialism

22.1 How did industrialism change after 1900?

As the new century turned, conditions in America were better than just a few years before. Farms and factories were prosperous again; in 1901, for the first time in years, the economy reached full capacity. Farm prices rose almost 50 percent between 1900 and 1910. Unemployment dropped. "In the United States of today," a Boston newspaper said in 1904, "everyone is middle class. The resort to force, the wild talk of the nineties are over. Everyone is busily, happily getting ahead."

Everyone, of course, was not middle class, nor was everyone getting ahead. "Wild talk" persisted. Many of the problems that had angered people in the 1890s continued into the new century, and millions of Americans still suffered from poverty and disease. Racism sat even more heavily on African Americans in both South and North, and hostility to immigrants from southern and eastern Europe, Mexico, and Asia was increasing. Yet economic conditions were better for many people, and as a result, prosperity became one of the keys to understanding the era and the nature of progressive reform.

The start of the new century was another key, for it influenced people to take a fresh look at themselves and their times. Excited about beginning the twentieth century, people believed technology and enterprise would shape a better life. Savoring the word *new,* they talked of the new poetry, new cinema, new history, new democracy, new woman, new art, new immigration, new morality, and new city. Presidents Theodore Roosevelt and Woodrow Wilson called their political programs the New Nationalism and the New Freedom, respectively.

The word *mass* also cropped up frequently. Victors in the recent war with Spain, Americans took pride in teeming cities, burgeoning corporations, and other marks of the mass society. They enjoyed the fruits of mass production, read mass circulation newspapers and magazines, and took mass transit from the growing spiral of suburbs into the central cities.

Behind mass production lay significant changes in the nation's industrial system. Businesses grew at a rapid rate. They were large in the three decades after the Civil War, but between 1895 and 1915, industries became mammoth, employing thousands

✳ Explore Cities and Factories on MyHistoryLab

HOW DID CITIES TRANSFORM THE UNITED STATES AT THE END OF THE 1800s?

During the course of the nineteenth century, the United States changed dramatically from a country of farming communities and few cities to a country that had fully industrialized, which broadened its economy and made it no longer just agrarian-based. Industrialization not only resulted in the increasing number of factories, it also benefited agriculture, especially after the Civil War, as it became less dependent on manual labor. Because these factories required more labor and less agriculture, the populations of cities and towns increased as Americans left the countryside for urban industrial work. Urban growth, too, resulted from the millions of immigrants flowing to the United States seeking new and better opportunities. The changes accelerated with the end of the 1800s and, by 1920, for the first time in U.S. history, more Americans lived in cities and towns than in rural communities.

NEW YORK CITY As increasing numbers of immigrant families settled in New York City's Lower East Side during the 1890s and 1900s, many were forced to live in crowded tenement apartments. Here, children gather on a firescape not only because it provided room to play and avoid the adults inside, but for sunlight and fresh air.

RURAL VS. URBAN AS A PERCENTAGE OF U.S. POPULATION

Year	Rural	Urban
1900	60.4%	39.6%
1910	54.4%	45.6%
1920	48.8%	51.2%

SOURCE: U.S. Census Bureau.

KEY QUESTIONS Use **MyHistoryLab Explorer** to **answer** these **questions:**

Analysis ▶▶▶ *Which regions became more urbanized?*

Map the location of major urban centers and manufacturing sites.

Response ▶▶▶ *Who worked in the factories?*

Explore demographic patterns of the labor force.

Cause ▶▶▶ *Where did the millions of newcomers to the United States reside?*

Chart patterns of immigrant settlement to consider the reasons behind them.

of workers and equipped with assembly lines to turn out huge quantities of the company's product. Inevitably, changes in management attitudes, business organization, and worker roles influenced the entire society. Inevitably, too, the growth of giant businesses gave rise to a widespread fear of "trusts" and a desire among many progressive reformers to break them up or regulate them.

The Innovative Model T

In the movement toward large-scale business and mass production, the automobile industry was one of those that led the way. In 1895, there were only four cars on the nation's roads; in 1917, there were nearly 5 million, and the automobile had already helped work a small revolution in industrial methods and social mores.

In 1903, Henry Ford and a few associates formed the Ford Motor Company, the firm that transformed the business. That year, Ford sold the first Ford car. The price was high, and in 1905, Ford raised prices still higher. Sales plummeted. In 1907, he lowered the price; sales and revenues rose. Ford learned an important lesson of the modern economy: A smaller unit profit on a large number of sales meant enormous revenues. In 1908, he introduced the Model T, a four-cylinder, 20-horsepower "Tin Lizzie," costing $850, and available only in black. The first year 11,000 were sold.

"I am going to democratize the automobile," Ford proclaimed. "When I'm through everybody will be able to afford one, and about everyone will have one." The key was mass production, and, after many experiments, Ford copied the techniques of meatpackers who moved carcasses along overhead trolleys from station to station. Adapting the process to automobile assembly, Ford in 1913 set up moving assembly lines in his plant in Highland Park, Michigan, that dramatically reduced the time and cost of producing cars. Emphasizing continuous movement, he strove for a nonstop flow from raw material to finished product. In 1914, he sold 248,000 Model Ts.

Quick Check

How did Henry Ford revolutionize the automobile industry?

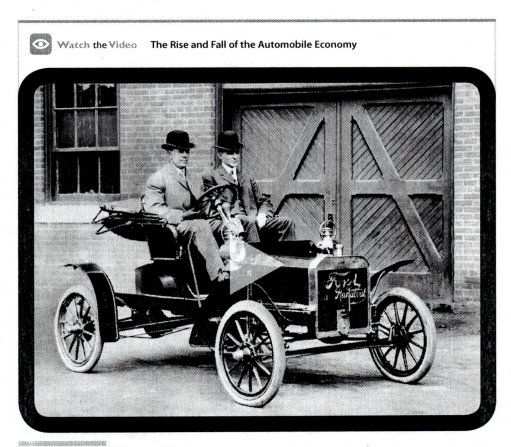

Watch the Video **The Rise and Fall of the Automobile Economy**

RISE OF MASS PRODUCTION Henry Ford built his first car in 1896, then produced improved models, each designated by a letter of the alphabet. Shown here are Henry Ford and a friend in a 1905 Model N, Ford's best-selling model before the Model T debuted in 1908. The "Tin Lizzie" was Ford's "motorcar for the multitudes," affordably priced so that every family could own one. The automobile changed American life and the American landscape as it spawned the development of paved roads, traffic lights, and numerous auto-related businesses.

That year, Ford workers assembled a car in 93 minutes, one-tenth the time it had taken just eight months before. On a single day in 1925, Ford set a record by turning out 9109 Model Ts, a new car every 10 seconds of the workday.

The Burgeoning Trusts

As businesses like Ford's grew, capital and organization became increasingly important, and the result was the formation of a growing number of trusts. Standard Oil started the trend in 1882, but the greatest momentum came two decades later. Between 1898 and 1903, a series of mergers and consolidations swept the economy. Many smaller firms disappeared, swallowed up in giant corporations. By 1904, large-scale combinations of one form or another controlled nearly two-fifths of the capital in manufacturing in the country. (See Figure 22.1).

The result was not monopoly but oligopoly—control of a commodity or service by a small number of large, powerful companies. Six great financial groups dominated the railroad industry; a handful of holding companies controlled utilities and steel. Rockefeller's Standard Oil owned about 85 percent of the oil business. After 1898, financiers and industrialists formed the Amalgamated Copper Company, Consolidated Tobacco, U.S. Rubber, and many others. By 1909, just 1 percent of the industrial firms were producing nearly half of all manufactured goods.

Though the trend has been overstated, finance capitalists such as J. P. Morgan tended to replace the industrial capitalists of an earlier era. Able to finance the mergers and reorganizations, investment bankers played a greater and greater role in the economy. A multibillion-dollar financial house, J. P. Morgan and Company operated a network of control that ran from New York City to every industrial and financial center in the nation. Like other investment firms, it held directorships in many corporations, creating "interlocking directorates" that allowed it to control many businesses.

Massive business growth set off a decade-long debate over what government should do about the trusts. Some critics who believed that the giant companies were responsible for stifling individual opportunity and raising prices wanted to break them

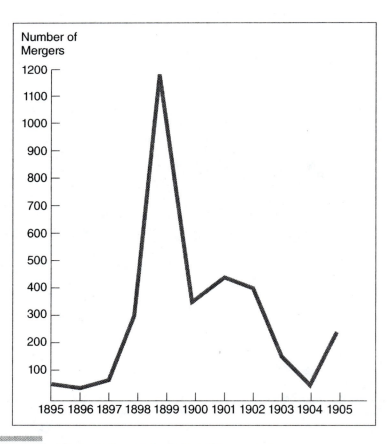

FIGURE 22.1 BUSINESS CONSOLIDATION (MERGERS), 1895–1905.

up into small competitive units. Others argued that large-scale business was a mark of the times and that it produced more goods and better lives.

The debate over the trusts was one of the issues that shaped the Progressive Era, but it was never a simple contest between high-minded reformers and greedy business titans. Some progressives favored big business; others wanted it broken up. Business leaders themselves were divided. Some welcomed reformers' assaults on giant competitors. As a rule, both progressives and business leaders drew on similar visions of the country: complex, expansive, hopeful, managerially minded, and oriented toward results and efficiency. They both believed in private property and the importance of economic progress. In fact, in working for reform, the progressives often drew on the managerial methods of a business world they sought to regulate.

Managing the Machines

Mass production changed the direction of American industry. Size, system, organization, and marketing became increasingly important. Management focused on speed and product, not on workers. Assembly-line technology changed tasks and, to some extent, values. The goal was no longer to make a unique product that would be better than the one before. "The way to make automobiles," Ford said as early as 1903, "is to make one automobile like another automobile, to make them all alike, to make them come through the factory just alike."

In a development that rivaled assembly lines in importance, businesses established industrial research laboratories where scientists and engineers developed new products. General Electric founded the first one in 1900, housed in a barn. It soon attracted experts who improved light bulbs, invented the cathode-ray tube, worked on early radio, and even tinkered with atomic theory. Du Pont opened its labs in 1911, Eastman Kodak in 1912, and Standard Oil in 1919. As the source of new ideas and technology, the labs altered life in the twentieth and twenty-first centuries.

Through all this, business became large-scale, mechanized, and managed. While many shops still employed fewer than a dozen workers, the proportion of such shops shrank. By 1920, close to one-half of all industrial workers toiled in factories employing more than 250 people. More than one-third worked in factories that were part of multiplant companies.

Industries that processed materials—iron and steel, paper, cement, and chemicals—were increasingly automated and operated continuously. Workers in those industries could not fall behind. Foremen still managed the laborers on the factory floor, but the rules increasingly came down from a central office where trained professional managers supervised production flow. Systematic record keeping, cost accounting, and inventory and production controls became widespread. Workers lost control of the work pace. "If you need to turn out a little more," a manager at Swift and Company said, "you speed up the conveyor a little and the men speed up to keep pace."

Folkways of the workplace—workers passing job-related knowledge to each other, performing their tasks with little supervision, setting their own pace, and in effect running the shop—began to give way to "scientific" labor management. More than anyone else, Frederick Winslow Taylor, an inventive mechanical engineer, strove to extract maximum efficiency from each worker: "In the past the man has been first; in the future the system must be first."

In *The Principles of Scientific Management* (1911), Taylor proposed two major reforms. First, management must take responsibility for job-related knowledge and classify it into "rules, laws, and formulae." Second, management should control the workplace "through *enforced* standardization of methods, *enforced* adoption of the best implements and working conditions, and *enforced* cooperation." Although few factories wholly adopted Taylor's principles, the doctrines of scientific management spread through American industry.

Workers caught up in the changing industrial system experienced the benefits of efficiency and productivity; in some industries, they earned more. But they also suffered important losses. Performing repetitive tasks, they seemed part of the machinery, moving to the pace and needs of their mechanical pacesetters. Bored, they might easily lose pride of workmanship, though many workers, it is clear, did not. Efficiency engineers experimented with tools and methods, a process many workers found unsettling.

Quick Check
What factors led to the rapid growth of trusts?

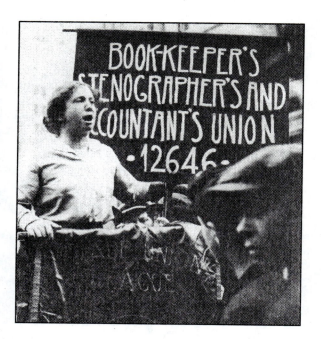

TRAGEDY AT THE TRIANGLE COMPANY Fire nets were of no avail to the workers at the Triangle Shirtwaist Company who jumped from the upper stories to escape the flames. Speaking to a mass meeting after the fire, labor organizer Rose Schneiderman inveighed against a system that treated human beings as expendable commodities.

Jobs became not only monotonous but dangerous. As machines and assembly lines sped up, boredom or miscalculation could bring disaster. In March 1911, a fire at the Triangle Shirtwaist Company in New York focused nationwide attention on unsafe working conditions. When the fire started, 500 men and women, mostly Italians and eastern European Jews, were just finishing their workday. Firefighters arrived within minutes, but they were already too late. Terrified seamstresses raced to the exits to escape the flames, but the company had locked most exit doors to prevent theft and to shut out union organizers. Many died in the stampede down the narrow stairways or the single fire escape. Others, trapped on the top stories far above the reach of the fire department's ladders, jumped to their deaths on the street below: 146 people died.

A few days later, 80,000 people marched silently in the rain in a funeral procession up Fifth Avenue. A quarter million people watched. At a mass meeting to protest factory working conditions, Rose Schneiderman, a 29-year-old organizer for the Women's Trade Union League, told New York City's civic and religious leaders that they had not done enough, they had not cared: "We have tried you good people of the public and we have found you wanting. . . . Every week I must learn of the untimely death of one of my sister workers. Every year thousands of us are maimed. The life of men and women is so cheap and property is so sacred."

The outcry impelled New York's governor to appoint a State Factory Investigating Commission that recommended laws to shorten the workweek and improve safety in factories and stores.

Quick Check

What methods emerged to help manage the workers and machinery on the factory floor?

Society's Masses

22.2 How did mass production affect women, children, immigrants, and African Americans?

Spreading consumer goods through society, mass production not only improved people's lives but sometimes cost lives, too. Tending the machines, as Rose Schneiderman pointed out, took hard, painful labor, often under dangerous conditions. As businesses expanded, the labor force increased tremendously to keep up with the demand for workers in the factories, mines, and forests. Women, African Americans, Asian Americans, and Mexican Americans played larger and larger roles. Immigration soared. Between 1901 and 1910, nearly 8.8 million immigrants entered the United States; between 1911 and 1920, another 5.7 million came.

For many of these people, life was harsh, spent in crowded slums and long hours on the job. Fortunately, the massive unemployment of the 1890s was over, and in many skilled trades, such as cigar making, there was plenty of work to go around. Though the economic recovery helped nearly everyone, the less skilled continued to be the less fortunate. Migrant workers, lumberjacks, ore shovelers, and others struggled to find decent-paying jobs.

Under such circumstances, many people fought to make a living, and many, too, fought to improve their lot. Their efforts, along with those of the reform-minded people who came to their aid, became another important hallmark of the Progressive Era.

Better Times on the Farm

While people continued to flee the farms—by 1920, fewer than one-third of all Americans lived on farms, and fewer than one-half lived in rural areas—farmers themselves prospered, the beneficiaries of greater production and expanding urban markets. Rural free delivery (RFD), begun in 1896, helped diminish the farmers' sense of isolation and changed farm life. The delivery of mail to the farm door opened that door to a wider world; it exposed farmers to urban thinking, national advertising, and political events. In 1911, more than one billion newspapers and magazines were delivered over RFD routes.

Parcel post (1913) permitted the sending of packages through the U.S. mail. Mail-order houses flourished; rural merchants suffered. Within a year, 300 million packages

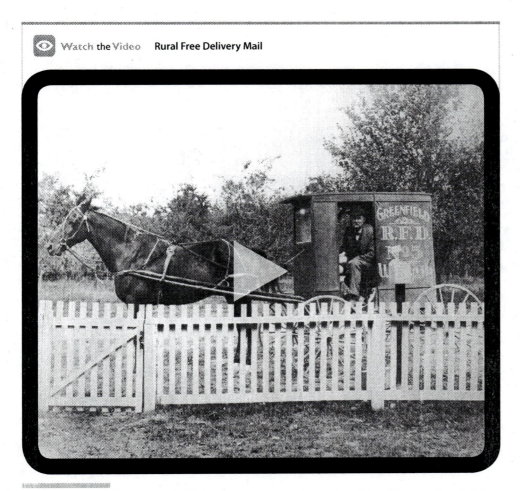

Watch the Video   **Rural Free Delivery Mail**

THE WEST VIRGINIA EXPERIMENT The West Virginia experiment with rural free delivery was launched in relative obscurity and in an atmosphere of hostility. Critics of the plan claimed it was impractical and too expensive to have a postal carrier trudge over rutted roads and through forests trying to deliver mail in all kinds of weather.

were being mailed annually. While telephones and electricity did not reach most rural areas for decades, better roads, mail-order catalogs, and other innovations knit farmers into the larger society. Early in the new century, Mary E. Lease—who in her Populist days had urged Kansas farmers to raise less corn and more hell—moved to Brooklyn.

Farmers still had problems. Land prices rose with crop prices, and farm tenancy increased, especially in the South. Tenancy grew from one-quarter of all farms in 1880 to more than one-third in 1910. Many southern tenant farmers were African Americans, and they suffered from farm-bred diseases. In one of the reforms of the Progressive Era, in 1909, the Rockefeller Sanitary Commission, acting on recent scientific discoveries, began a sanitation campaign that eventually wiped out the hookworm disease.

In the arid West, irrigation transformed the land as the federal government and private landholders joined to import water from mountain watersheds. The dry lands bloomed, and so did a rural class structure that sharply separated owners from workers. Under the Newlands Act of 1902, the secretary of the interior formed the U.S. Reclamation Service, which gathered a staff of thousands of engineers and technicians, "the largest bureaucracy ever assembled in irrigation history."

Dams and canals channeled water into places such as California's Imperial Valley. As the water streamed in, cotton, cantaloupes, oranges, tomatoes, lettuce, and other crops streamed out to national markets. By 1920, Idaho, Montana, Utah, Wyoming, Colorado, and Oregon had extensive irrigation systems, all drawing on scarce water supplies; California, the foremost importer of water, had 4.2 million acres under irrigation, many of them picked by migrant workers from Mexico, China, and Japan.

Quick Check

Why did conditions on the farm improve after 1900?

Women and Children at Work

More women worked. In 1900, more than 5 million worked—one-fifth of all adult women—and among those aged 14 to 24, the employment rate was almost one-third. Of those employed, single women outnumbered married women by seven to one, yet more than one-third of married women worked. Most women held service jobs. Only a few held higher-paying jobs as professionals or managers.

In the 1890s, women made up more than one-quarter of medical school graduates. Using a variety of techniques, men gradually squeezed them out, and by the 1920s, only about 5 percent of the graduates were women. Few women taught in colleges and universities, and those who did were expected to resign if they married.

More women than men graduated from high school. With professions like medicine and science largely closed to them, they often turned to the new "business schools" that offered training in stenography, typing, and bookkeeping. In 1920, more than one-quarter of all employed women held clerical jobs. Many others taught school.

Far more black women than white women had always worked. The reason was usually economic; an African American man or woman alone could rarely support a family. Unlike many white women, black women tended to remain in the labor force after marriage or the start of a family. They also had less opportunity for job advancement. In 1920, between one-third and one-half of all African American women who were working were restricted to personal and domestic service jobs.

Critics charged that women's employment endangered the home, threatened their reproductive functions, and even, as one man said, stripped them of "that modest demeanor that lends a charm to their kind." Adding to these fears, the birthrate continued to drop between 1900 and 1920, and the divorce rate soared, in part because more working-class men took advantage of the newer moral freedom and deserted their families. By 1916, there was one divorce for every nine marriages as compared to one for 21 in 1880.

Many children also worked. In 1900, about 3 million children—nearly 20 percent of those between ages 5 and 15—held full-time or almost full-time jobs. Twenty-five thousand boys under 16 worked in mining; 20,000 children under 12, mainly girls, worked in southern cotton mills. But as public indignation grew, the use of child labor shrank.

Determined to do something about the situation, the Women's Trade Union League lobbied the federal Bureau of Labor to investigate the conditions under which

((• [icon] Read the Document   John Spargo, from *The Bitter Cry of the Children* (1906)

BREAKER BOYS Breaker boys, who picked out pieces of slate from the coal as it rushed past, often became bent-backed and suffered respiratory diseases such as bronchitis and tuberculosis after years of working 14 hours a day in the coal mines. Accidents—and deaths—were common in the mines.

women and children worked. Begun in 1907, the investigation took four years and produced 19 volumes of data, some of it shocking, all of it factual. In 1911, spurred by the data, the Children's Bureau was formed within the U.S. Bureau of Labor, with Grace Abbott, a social worker, at its head.

Numerous middle-class women became involved in the fight for reform. Many others, reflecting the ongoing changes in the family, took increasing pride in homemaking and motherhood. Mother's Day, the national holiday, was formally established in 1913. Women who preferred fewer children turned increasingly to birth control, which became more acceptable. Margaret Sanger, a nurse and outspoken social reformer, led a campaign to give physicians broad discretion in prescribing contraceptives.

Quick Check

In what conditions did women and children work in the early twentieth century?

The Niagara Movement and the NAACP

In 1900, eight of every ten African Americans still lived in rural areas, mainly in the South. Most were poor sharecroppers. Jim Crow laws segregated many schools, railroad cars, hotels, and hospitals. Poll taxes and other devices disfranchised blacks and many poor whites. Violence was common; from 1900 to 1914, white mobs murdered more than 1000 black people.

Many African Americans labored on the cotton farms and in the railroad camps, sawmills, and mines of the South under conditions of peonage. Peons traded their lives and labor for food and shelter. Often illiterate, they were forced to sign contracts allowing the planter "to use such force as he or his agents may deem necessary to require me to remain on his farm and perform good and satisfactory services." Armed guards patrolled the camps and whipped those trying to escape.

Few blacks belonged to labor unions, and blacks almost always earned less than whites in the same job. In Atlanta, white electricians earned $5.00 a day, blacks $3.50. Black songs such as "I've Got a White Man Workin' for Me" (1901) voiced more hope than reality. Illiteracy among African Americans dropped from 45 percent in 1900 to 30 percent in 1910, but nowhere were they given equal school facilities, teachers' salaries, or educational materials. In 1910, scarcely 8000 African American youths attended high schools in all the states of the Southeast.

African American leaders grew increasingly impatient with this kind of treatment, and in 1905 a group of them, led by sociologist W. E. B. Du Bois, met near Niagara Falls, New York (they met on the Canadian side of the Falls, since no hotel on the American side would take them). There they pledged action on equal access to voting, economic opportunity, integration, and equality before the law. Rejecting Booker T. Washington's gradualist approach, the **Niagara Movement** claimed "every single right that belongs to a freeborn American, political, civil and social; and until we get these rights we will never cease to protest."

The Niagara Movement focused on equal rights and the education of African American youth: "They have a right to know, to think, to aspire." Keeping alive a program of militant action, it spawned later civil rights movements. Du Bois was its inspiration. In *The Souls of Black Folk* (1903) and other works, he called eloquently for justice and equality.

Still, race riots broke out in Atlanta, Georgia, in 1906 and Springfield, Illinois, in 1908, the latter the home of Abraham Lincoln. Unlike the riots of the 1960s, white mobs invaded black neighborhoods, burning, looting, and killing. They lynched two blacks—one 84 years old—in Springfield.

William E. Walling, a wealthy southerner and settlement house worker; Mary Ovington, a white anthropology student; and Oswald Garrison Villard, grandson of the famous abolitionist William Lloyd Garrison, were outraged. With other reformers, white and black (among them Jane Addams and John Dewey), they called for the conference that organized the **National Association for the Advancement of Colored People (NAACP)**, which swiftly became the most important civil rights organization in the country. Created in 1909, within five years the NAACP had 50 branches and more than 6000 members. Walling headed it, and Du Bois, the only African American among the top officers, directed publicity and edited its magazine, *The Crisis*.

Joined by the National Urban League, which was created in 1911, the NAACP pressured employers, labor unions, and the government on behalf of African Americans. It had some victories. In 1918, during World War I, the NAACP and the National Urban League persuaded the federal government to form a special Bureau of Negro Economics within the Labor Department to look after the interests of African American workers.

Despite these gains, African Americans continued to experience disfranchisement, poor job opportunities, and segregation. As Booker T. Washington said in 1913, "I have never seen the colored people so discouraged and so bitter as they are at the present time."

Immigrants in the Labor Force

While more women and African Americans were working, much of the huge increase in the labor force in these years came from outside the country, particularly from Europe and Mexico. Between 1901 and 1920, 14.5 million immigrants entered the country, more than in any previous 20-year period. Continuing the trend begun in the 1880s, many came from southern and eastern Europe. Still called the "new" immigrants, they met hostility from "older" immigrants of northern European stock who

Niagara Movement A movement, led by W. E. B. Du Bois, that focused on equal rights for and the education of African American youth. Rejecting the gradualist approach of Booker T. Washington, it favored militant action and claimed for African Americans all the rights afforded to other Americans.

NAACP Created in 1909, this organization became the most important civil rights organization in the country.

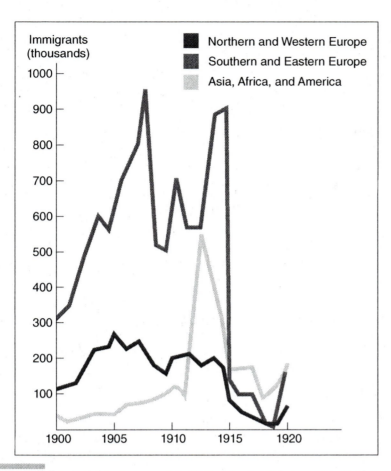

FIGURE 22.2 IMMIGRATION TO THE UNITED STATES, 1900–1920 (BY AREA OF ORIGIN).

Note: For purposes of classification, "Northern and Western Europe" includes Great Britain, Ireland, Scandinavia, the Netherlands, Belgium, Luxembourg, Switzerland, France, and Germany. "Southern and Eastern Europe" includes Poland, Austria-Hungary, Russia and the Baltic States, Romania, Bulgaria, European Turkey, Italy, Spain, Portugal, and Greece. "Asia, Africa, and America" includes Asian Turkey, China, Japan, India, Canada, the Caribbean, Latin America, and all of Africa.

SOURCE: U.S. Bureau of the Census, *Historical Statistics of the United States, Colonial Times to 1970*, Bicentennial Edition, Washington, DC, 1975.

questioned their values, religion (often Catholic or Jewish), traditions, and appearance (See Figure 22.2).

Immigrant patterns often departed from traditional stereotypes. Immigrants, for example, moved both to and from their homelands. Fifty percent or more of the members of some groups returned home, although the proportion varied. Jews and Czechs often brought their families to resettle in America; Serbs and Poles tended to come singly, intent on earning enough money to make a fresh start at home. Some migrants—Italian men, in particular—virtually commuted, returning home every slack season. These temporary migrants became known as **birds of passage**. The outbreak of World War I trapped thousands who had planned to return to Europe.

Older residents lumped the newcomers together, ignoring geographic, religious, and other differences. Preserving important regional distinctions, Italians, for example, tended to settle as Calabreses, Venetians, Abruzzis, and Sicilians. Yet to old-stock Americans, they were all simply Italians. Henry Ford and other employers tried to erase the differences through English classes and "Americanization" programs. The Ford Motor Company ran a school where immigrant employees were first taught to say, "I am a good American." At the graduation ceremony, the pupils acted out a gigantic pantomime in which, clad in their old-country dress, they filed into a large "melting pot." When they emerged, they were wearing identical American-made clothes, and each was waving an American flag.

Labor groups soon learned to counter these techniques. The Women's Trade Union League (WTUL) urged workers to ignore business-sponsored English lessons

birds of passage Immigrants who came to the United States to work and save money and then returned to their native countries during the slack season.

because they did not "tell the girl worker the things she really wants to know. They do not suggest that $5 a week is not a living wage. They tell her to be respectful to her employer."

In another significant development at the beginning of the twentieth century, for the first time, many Mexicans immigrated, especially after a revolution in Mexico in 1910 forced them to flee across the border into Texas, New Mexico, Arizona, and California. Their exact numbers were unknown. American officials did not count border crossings until 1907, and even then, many migrants avoided the official immigration stations. Almost all came from the Mexican lower class, eager to escape peonage and violence in their native land. Labor agents called *coyotes*—usually in the employ of large corporations or ranchers—recruited Mexican workers.

Between 1900 and 1910, the Mexican population of Texas and New Mexico nearly doubled; in Arizona, it more than doubled; in California, it quadrupled. In all four states, it doubled again between 1910 and 1920. After 1900, almost 10 percent of the population of Mexico moved to the American Southwest. (See Figure 22.3).

In time, these Mexican Americans and their children transformed the Southwest. They built most of the early highways in Texas, New Mexico, and Arizona; dug the irrigation ditches that watered crops; laid railroad track; and picked the cotton and vegetables that clothed and fed millions of Americans. Many lived in shacks and shanties along the railroad tracks, isolated in a separate Spanish-speaking world. Like other immigrant groups, they also formed enclaves in the cities; these *barrios* became cultural islands of family life, foods, church, and festivals.

Fewer people emigrated from China in these years, deterred in part by anti-Chinese laws and hostility. Like many other immigrants, most Chinese who came wanted to make money and return home. They mined, farmed, and worked as common laborers. In their willingness to work hard for low wages, their desire to preserve clan and family

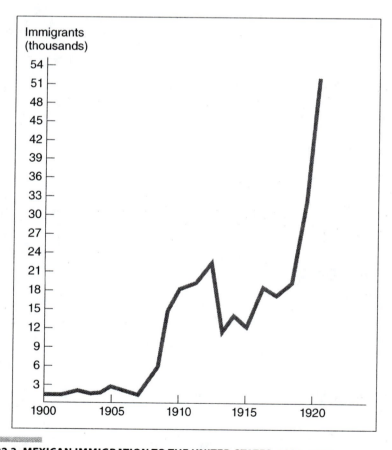

FIGURE 22.3 MEXICAN IMMIGRATION TO THE UNITED STATES, 1900–1920.

IMMIGRANTS FROM ASIA Japanese immigrants wait with a Methodist deaconess in the administration building of the immigration station at Angel Island, near San Francisco. Quota systems and exclusionary laws limited Asian immigration, while other laws placed restrictions on the immigrants, curtailing their right to own or even rent agricultural land. Some Asian immigrants, after months of detention at Angel Island, were refused permission to enter the United States and were forced to return to their homelands.

SOURCE: California Historical Society

associations from China, and their strong ties to their home villages, Chinese Americans resembled other immigrant groups, but they differed in two important respects. As late as 1920, men outnumbered women by ten to one in the Chinese American population, and with a male median age of 42, the elderly dominated their communities.

The Chinese-American population differed in another respect as well. Unlike other immigrant groups, whose numbers tended to grow, the number of Chinese Americans shrank in these years—from about 125,000 in the early 1880s to just over 60,000 in 1920. After 1910, the U.S. government set up a special immigration facility at Angel Island in San Francisco Bay, but unlike European immigrants who landed at Ellis Island in New York and were quickly sent on, Chinese immigrants were kept for weeks and months, examined and reexamined, before being allowed to cross the narrow band of water to San Francisco.

Many Japanese also arrived at Angel Island, and though at first fewer in numbers than the Chinese, they developed communities along the Pacific coast, where they settled mainly on farms. The number of Japanese Americans grew. In 1907, the heaviest year of immigration from Japan, nearly 31,000 Japanese entered the United States; by 1920, there were 111,000 Japanese in the country, nearly three-quarters of them in California.

As the newcomers arrived from Asia, Europe, and Mexico, nativist sentiment, which had criticized earlier waves of immigrants, intensified. Old-stock Americans sneered at their dress and language. Racial theories emphasized the superiority of northern Europeans, and the new "science" of eugenics suggested the need to control the population growth of "inferior" peoples. Hostility to Catholics and Jews was common but also touched other groups.

In 1902, Congress prohibited immigration from China. Presidents Taft and Wilson vetoed statutes requiring literacy tests designed to curtail immigration from southern and eastern Europe in 1913 and 1915. In 1917, another such measure passed despite Wilson's veto. Other measures tried to limit immigration from Mexico and Japan.

Quick Check

In what ways did immigrants adjust, or not adjust, to their new society?

Conflict in the Workplace

22.3 Why were there so many strikes in this period?

A ssembly lines, speedups, long hours, and low pay increased American industrial output (and profits) after 1900; they also gave rise to strikes and other labor unrest. Sometimes unions led strikes; sometimes workers just walked off the job. Whatever the cause, strikes were frequent. In one industry, in one city—the meatpacking industry in Chicago—there were 251 strikes in 1903 alone.

Strikes and absenteeism increased after 1910; labor productivity dropped 10 percent between 1915 and 1918, the first such decline in memory. In many industries, labor turnover became a serious problem; workers changed jobs in droves. Union membership grew. In 1900, only about a million workers—less than 4 percent of the workforce—belonged to unions. By 1920, 5 million workers belonged, 13 percent of the workforce. (See Figure 22.4).

As tensions grew between capital and labor, some middle-class people feared that, unless the workers' situation improved, there might be violence or even revolution. This fear motivated some of the labor-oriented reforms of the Progressive Era. While some reform supporters genuinely wanted to improve labor's lot, others embraced reform because they were afraid of violent upheaval.

Organizing Labor

Samuel Gompers's American Federation of Labor (AFL), by far the largest union organization, remained devoted to the interests of skilled craftspeople. While it sought better wages and working conditions, it also sought to limit entry into the crafts and protect worker prerogatives. Within limits, the AFL found acceptance among giant business corporations eager for conservative policies and labor stability.

Of the 8 million female workers in 1910, only 125,000 belonged to unions. Gompers continued to resist organizing them, saying they were too emotional and, as union organizers, "had a way of making serious mistakes." Margaret Dreier Robins, an organizer of proven skill, scoffed at that: "These men died twenty years ago and are just walking around dead!"

Robins helped found the **Women's Trade Union League** in 1903. The WTUL led the effort to organize women into trade unions, lobby for legislation protecting female workers, and educate the public on the problems and needs of working women. It accepted all working women who would join, regardless of skill (although not, at first, African American women), and it won crucial financial support from well-to-do women such as Anne Morgan, daughter of the feared financier J. P. Morgan. Robins's close friend Jane Addams belonged, as did Mary McDowell, the "Angel of the Stockyards," who worked with slaughterhouse workers in Chicago; Julia Lathrop, who tried

Women's Trade Union League (WTUL) Founded in 1903, this group worked to organize women into trade unions. It also lobbied for laws to safeguard female workers and backed strikes, especially in the garment industry. While it never attracted many members, its leaders were influential enough to give the union considerable power.

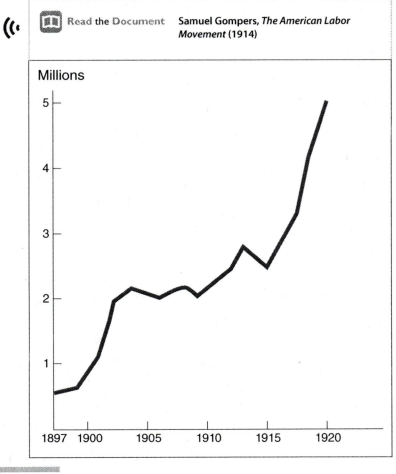

22.1

22.2

22.3

22.4

((•   **Read the Document**   **Samuel Gompers,** *The American Labor Movement* **(1914)**

Millions

FIGURE 22.4 LABOR UNION MEMBERSHIP, 1897–1920.

SOURCE: *U.S. Bureau of the Census, Statistical Abstract of the United States: 1982–1983*, 103rd ed., Washington, DC, 1982.

to improve the lot of wage-earning children; and Dr. Alice Hamilton, a pioneer in American research on the causes of industrial disease.

The WTUL never had more than a few thousand members, but its influence extended far beyond its membership. In 1909, it supported the "Uprising of the 20,000," a strike of shirtwaist workers in New York City. When female employees of the Triangle Shirtwaist Company tried to form a union, the company fired them, and they walked out; 20,000 men and women in 500 other shops followed. Strike meetings were conducted in three languages—English, Yiddish, and Italian—and before being forced to go back to work, the strikers won a shorter workweek and a few other gains. Sadly, the Triangle women lost out on another important demand—for unlocked shop doors and safe fire escapes. Their loss proved lethal in the famous Triangle Shirtwaist Company fire of 1911.

The WTUL also backed a strike in 1910 against Hart, Schaffner and Marx, Chicago's largest manufacturer of men's clothing. One day, Annie Shapiro, the 18-year-old daughter of Russian immigrants, was told her wages were being cut from $7 a week to $6.20. That was a large cut, and along with 16 other young women, Shapiro refused to accept it and walked out. "We had to be recognized as people," she said later. Other women joined them, and the revolt spread.

Within days, 40,000 garment workers were on strike, about half of them women. Manufacturers hurried to negotiate, and the result was the important Hart, Schaffner agreement, which created an arbitration committee composed of management and labor to handle grievances and settle disputes. The first successful experiment in

Industrial Workers of the World (IWW) Founded in 1905, this radical union, also known as the Wobblies, aimed to unite the American working class into one union. It organized unskilled and foreign-born laborers, advocated social revolution, and led strikes.

collective bargaining, it became the model for agreements that govern industrial relations today.

Another union, the **Industrial Workers of the World (IWW)**, attracted the most attention (and fears) in these years. Unlike the WTUL, it welcomed everyone regardless of gender or race. Unlike the AFL, it tried to organize the unskilled and foreign-born who worked in the mass production industries. Founded in Chicago in 1905, it aimed to unite the American working class into a mammoth union to promote labor's interests. Its motto—"An injury to one is an injury to all"—stressed labor solidarity, as had the earlier Knights of Labor. But unlike the Knights, the IWW, or Wobblies as they were known, urged social revolution.

"It is our purpose to overthrow the capitalist system by forcible means if necessary," William D. "Big Bill" Haywood, one of its founders, said; and he went on in his speeches to say he knew of nothing a worker could do that "will bring as much anguish to the boss as a little sabotage in the right place." IWW leaders included Mary Harris ("Mother") Jones, a famous veteran of battles in the Illinois coalfields; Elizabeth Gurley Flynn, a fiery young radical who joined as a teenager; and Haywood himself, the strapping one-eyed founder of the Western Federation of Miners.

The IWW led a number of major strikes. Strikes in Lawrence, Massachusetts (1912), and Paterson, New Jersey (1912), attracted national attention: in Lawrence, when the strikers sent their children, ill-clad and hungry, out of the city to stay with sympathetic families; in Paterson, when they rented New York's Madison Square Garden for a massive labor pageant. IWW leaders welcomed the revolutionary tumult sweeping Russia and other countries. In the United States, they thought, a series of local strikes would provoke capitalist repression, then a general strike, and eventually a workers' commonwealth.

The IWW fell short of these objectives, but during its lifetime—from 1905 to the mid-1920s—it made major gains among immigrant workers in the Northeast, migrant farm laborers on the Plains, and loggers and miners in the South and Far West. In factories like Ford's, it recruited workers resentful of the speedups on the assembly lines. Although IWW membership probably amounted to no more than 100,000 at any one time, workers came and left so often that its total membership may have reached 1 million.

Concerned about labor unrest, some business leaders used violence and police action to keep workers in line, but others turned to the new fields of applied psychology and personnel management. A school of industrial psychology emerged. As had Taylor, industrial psychologists studied workers' routines and showed that job satisfaction also affected output. As a result, some businesses established industrial relations departments, hired public relations firms to improve their corporate image, and linked productivity to job safety and worker happiness.

To please employees, companies printed newsletters and organized softball teams; they awarded prizes and celebrated retirements. Ford created a "sociology department" staffed by 150 experts who showed workers how to budget their incomes and care for their health. They even taught them how to shop for meat.

On January 5, 1914, Ford took another significant step. He announced the $5 day, "the greatest revolution," he said, "in the matter of rewards for workers ever known to the industrial world." With a stroke, he doubled the wage rate for common labor, reduced the work day from nine hours to eight, and established a personnel department to place workers in appropriate jobs. The next day, 10,000 applicants stood outside the gates.

As a result, Ford had the pick of the labor force. Turnover declined; absenteeism, previously as much as one-tenth of all Ford workers every day, fell to 0.3 percent. Output increased; the IWW at Ford collapsed. The plan increased wages, but it also gave the company greater control over a more stable labor force. Workers had to meet a behavior code to qualify for the $5 day. At first scornful of the "utopian" plan, business leaders across the country soon copied it, and on January 2, 1919, Ford announced the $6 day.

Quick Check

How did labor organize to protect its interests, and how did some businesses, like Ford, respond?

A New Urban Culture

22.4 What happened to art and culture in these years so filled with change?

For many Americans, the quality of life improved significantly between 1900 and 1920. Jobs were relatively plentiful, and, in a development of great importance, more and more people were entering the professions as doctors, lawyers, teachers, and engineers. With comfortable incomes, a growing middle class could take advantage of new lifestyles, inventions, and forms of entertainment. Mass production could not have worked without mass consumption, and Americans in these years increasingly became a nation of consumers.

Production and Consumption

In 1900, business firms spent about $95 million on advertising; 20 years later, they spent more than $500 million. Ads and billboards touted cigarettes, cars, perfumes, and cosmetics. Advertising agencies boomed. Using new sampling techniques, they developed modern concepts of market testing and research. Sampling customer preferences also made businesses more responsive to public opinion on social and political issues.

Mass production swept the clothing industry and dressed more Americans better than any people ever had been before. Using lessons learned in making uniforms during the Civil War, manufacturers for the first time developed standard clothing and shoe sizes that fit most bodies. Clothing prices dropped; the availability of inexpensive "off-the-rack" clothes lessened distinctions between the rich and poor. By 1900, nine of every ten men and boys wore the new "ready-to-wear" clothes.

In 1900, manufacturing workers earned on average $418 a year. In 1920, they earned $1342 a year, though inflation took much of the increase. While the middle class expanded, the rich also grew richer. In 1920, the new income tax showed the first accurate tabulation of income, and it confirmed what many had suspected all along. Five percent of the population received almost one-fourth of all income.

Quick Check

What were some of the characteristics of mass production?

Living and Dying in an Urban Nation

In 1920, the median age of the population was only 25. (It is now 35.) Immigration accounted for part of the population's youthfulness, since most immigrants were young. Thanks to medical advances and better living conditions, the death rate dropped and the average life span increased. Between 1900 and 1920, life expectancy rose from 49 to 56 years for white women and from 47 to 54 years for white men. It rose from 33 to 45 years for blacks and other racial minorities.

Despite the increase in life expectancy, infant mortality remained high; nearly 10 percent of white babies and 20 percent of minority babies died in the first year of life. In comparison to today, fewer babies on average survived to adolescence, and fewer people survived beyond middle age. In 1900, the death rate among people between 45 and 65 was more than twice the modern rate. As a result, there were relatively fewer older people—in 1900, only 4 percent of the population was older than 65, compared to nearly 13 percent today. Fewer children than today knew their grandparents. Still, improvements in health care helped people live longer, and as a result, the incidence of cancer and heart disease increased.

Cities grew and, by any earlier standards, they grew on a colossal scale. Downtowns became a central hive of skyscrapers, department stores, warehouses, and hotels. Strips of factories radiated from the center. As street railways spread, cities took on a systematic pattern of socioeconomic segregation, usually in rings. The innermost ring filled with immigrants, circled by a belt of working-class housing. The remaining rings marked areas of rising affluence outward toward wealthy suburbs, which themselves formed around shopping strips and grid patterns of streets that restricted social interaction.

The giants were New York, Chicago, and Philadelphia, industrial cities that turned out every kind of product from textiles to structural steel. Smaller cities such as Rochester, New York, or Cleveland, Ohio, specialized in manufacturing a specific line of goods or processing regional products for the national market. Railroads instead of highways tied things together; in 1916, the rail network, the largest in the world, reached its peak—254,000 miles of track that carried more than three-fourths of all intercity freight tonnage.

Step by step, cities adopted their twentieth-century forms. Between 1909 and 1915, Los Angeles, a city of 300,000 people, passed ordinances that gave rise to modern urban zoning. For the first time, the ordinances divided a city into three districts of specified use: a residential area, an industrial area, and an area open to residence and a limited list of industries. Other cities followed. Combining several features, the New York zoning law of 1916 became the model for the nation; within a decade, 591 cities copied it.

Zoning ordered city development, keeping skyscrapers out of factory districts, factories out of the suburbs. It also had social repercussions. In the South, zoning became a tool to extend racial segregation; in northern cities, it acted against ethnic minorities. Jews in New York, Italians in Boston, Poles in Detroit, and African Americans in Chicago—zoning laws held them all at arm's length. Like other migrants, African Americans often preferred to settle together, but zoning also helped put them there. By 1920, ten districts in Chicago were more than three-quarters black. In Los Angeles, Cleveland, Detroit, and Washington, D.C., most blacks lived in only two or three wards.

Quick Check

What were some of the characteristics of the new urban culture?

Popular Pastimes

Thanks to changing work rules and mechanization, many Americans enjoyed more leisure time. The average workweek for manufacturing laborers fell from 60 hours in 1890 to 51 in 1920. By the early 1900s, white-collar workers might spend only 8 to 10 hours a day at work and a half day on Saturday. Greater leisure time gave more people more opportunity for play, and people flocked to places of entertainment. Baseball entrenched itself as the national pastime. Automobiles and streetcars carried fans to ballparks; attendance at major league games doubled between 1903 and 1920. Football also drew fans, although critics attacked its violence and the use of "tramp athletes," nonstudents whom colleges paid to play. In 1905, the worst year, 18 players were killed and 150 seriously injured.

Alarmed, President Theodore Roosevelt—who had once said, "I am the father of three boys [and] if I thought any one of them would weigh a possible broken bone against the glory of being chosen to play on Harvard's football team I would disinherit him"—called a White House conference to clean up college sports. The conference founded the Intercollegiate Athletic Association, which in 1910 became the National Collegiate Athletic Association (NCAA).

Movie theaters opened everywhere. By 1910, there were 10,000 of them, drawing a weekly audience of 10 million people. Admission was usually 5 cents, and movies stressing laughter and pathos appealed to a mass market. In 1915, D. W. Griffith, a talented and creative director—as well as a racist—produced the first movie spectacular: *Birth of a Nation*. Griffith adopted new film techniques, including close-ups, fade-outs, and artistic camera angles.

Phonographs brought ready-made entertainment into the home. By 1901, phonograph and record companies included the Victor Talking Machine Company, the Edison Speaking Machine Company, and Columbia Records. Ornate mahogany

Watch the Video   **A Vaudeville Act**

VAUDEVILLE Consisting of a wide variety of acts, vaudeville was probably the most popular mass entertainment in the early 1900s. With the addition of jugglers, pantomimists, magicians, and others, the number of vaudeville theaters increased exponentially.

Victrolas became standard fixtures in middle-class parlors. Early records were usually of vaudeville skits; orchestral recordings began in 1906. In 1919, 2.25 million phonographs were produced; two years later, more than 100 million records were sold.

As record sales grew, families sang less and listened more. Music became a business. In 1909, a copyright law provided a 2-cent royalty on each piece of music on phonograph records or piano rolls. The royalty, small as it was, offered welcome income to composers and publishers, and in 1914, composer Victor Herbert and others formed the American Society of Composers, Authors, and Publishers (ASCAP) to protect musical rights and royalties.

Vaudeville, increasingly popular after 1900, matured around 1915. Drawing on the immigrant experience, it voiced the variety of city life and included skits, songs, comics, acrobats, and magicians. Dances and jokes showed an earthiness new to mass audiences. By 1914, stage runways extended into the crowd; women performers had bared their legs and were beginning to show glimpses of the midriff.

In songs like "St. Louis Blues" (1914), W. C. Handy took the black southern folk music of the blues to northern cities. Gertrude "Ma" Rainey, the daughter of minstrels, sang in black vaudeville for nearly 35 years. Performing in Chattanooga, Tennessee, about 1910, she came across a 12-year-old orphan, Bessie Smith, who became the "Empress of the Blues." Smith's voice was huge and sweeping. She made more than 80 records for the Race division of Columbia Records that together sold nearly ten million copies.

Another musical innovation came north from New Orleans. Charles (Buddy) Bolden, a cornetist; Ferdinand "Jelly Roll" Morton, a pianist; and a youngster named

Quick Check

How did people use their new leisure time?

Louis Armstrong played an improvisational music that had no formal name. Reaching Chicago, it became "jas," then "jass," and finally "jazz." Jazz jumped, and jazz musicians relied on feeling and mood.

Experimentation in the Arts

"There is a state of unrest all over the world in art as in all other things," the director of New York's Metropolitan Museum said in 1908. "It is the same in literature, as in music, in painting, and in sculpture."

Isadora Duncan and Ruth St. Denis transformed dance. Departing from traditional ballet steps, both women stressed improvisation, emotion, and the human form. The lofts and apartments of New York's Greenwich Village attracted artists, writers, and poets interested in experimentation and change. To these artists, the city was the focus of national life and the sign of a new culture. Robert Henri and the realist painters known to their critics as the **Ashcan School**—relished the city's excitement. They wanted, a friend said, "to paint truth and to paint it with strength and fearlessness and individuality."

Ashcan School Early twentieth-century realist painters who portrayed the slums and streets of the nation's cities and the lives of ordinary urban dwellers. They often advocated political and social reform.

To the realists, a painting carried into the future the look of life as it happened. Their paintings depicted street scenes, colorful crowds, and slum children swimming in the river. In paintings such as the *Cliff Dwellers*, George W. Bellows captured the color and excitement of the tenements; John Sloan, one of Henri's most talented students, painted the vitality of ordinary people and familiar scenes.

In 1913, a show at the New York Armory presented 1600 modernist paintings, prints, and sculptures. The work of Picasso, Cézanne, Matisse, Brancusi, Van Gogh, and Gauguin dazed and dazzled American observers. Critics attacked the show as worthless and depraved; a Chicago official wanted it banned because the "idea that people can gaze at this sort of thing without [it] hurting them is all bosh."

The postimpressionists changed the direction of twentieth-century art and influenced adventuresome American painters. John Marin, Max Weber, Georgia O'Keeffe, Arthur Dove, and other modernists experimented in ways foreign to Henri's realists. Defiantly avant-garde, they shook off convention and experimented with new forms. Using bold colors and abstract patterns, they worked to capture the energy of urban life.

There was also an extraordinary outburst of poetry. In 1912, Harriet Monroe started the magazine *Poetry* in Chicago, the hotbed of the new poetry; Ezra Pound and Vachel Lindsay, both daring experimenters with ideas and verse, published in the first issue. T. S. Eliot published the classic "Love Song of J. Alfred Prufrock" in *Poetry* in 1915. Others experimenting with new techniques in poetry included Robert Frost (*North of Boston*, 1914), Edgar Lee Masters (*Spoon River Anthology*, 1915), and Carl Sandburg (*Chicago Poems*, 1916). Sandburg's poem "Chicago" celebrated the vitality of the city.

Quick Check

What were some of the important changes in the arts in the period?

Conclusion: A Ferment of Discovery and Reform

Manners and morals change slowly, and many Americans overlooked the importance of the first two decades of the twentieth century. Yet sweeping change was under way; anyone who doubted it could visit a gallery, see a film, listen to music, or read one of the new literary magazines. Garrets and galleries were filled with a breathtaking sense of change. "There was life in all these new things," Marsden Hartley, a modernist painter, recalled. "There was excitement, there was healthy revolt, investigation, discovery, and an utterly new world out of it all."

The ferment of progressivism in city, state, and nation reshaped the country. In a burst of reform, people built playgrounds, restructured taxes, regulated business, won the vote for women, shortened working hours, altered political systems, opened kindergartens, and improved factory safety. They tried to fulfill the national promise of dignity and liberty.

Marsden Hartley, it turned out, had voiced a mood that went well beyond painters and poets. Across society, people in many walks of life were experiencing a similar sense of excitement and discovery. Racism, repression, and labor conflict were present, to be sure, but there was also talk of hope, progress, and change. In politics, science, journalism, education, and a host of other fields, people believed for a time that they could make a difference, and in trying to do so, they became part of the progressive generation.

Chapter Review

The Changing Face of Industrialism

22.1 How did industrialism change after 1900? p. 505

As prosperity returned after the late 1890s, the American industrial system underwent important changes. Mass production, spurred by the spread of the moving assembly line, turned out more and more products for American and foreign consumers. New management methods organized workers on the factory floor. Jobs became both routine and more dangerous. Trusts grew.

Society's Masses

22.2 How did mass production affect women, children, immigrants, and African Americans? p. 510

While life improved for many people in the post-1900 industrial society, many others faced challenges: women and children in the workforce, and laborers in their efforts to organize. Between 1901 and 1920, some 14.8 million immigrants entered the country and began the difficult process of adjusting to life in their new home. All of these people faced difficult challenges due to low wages, dangerous working conditions, and the steady demands of the factory system.

Conflict in the Workplace

22.3 Why were there so many strikes in this period? p. 518

Low wages, speeded-up assembly lines, and dangerous conditions in the workplace brought about numerous attempts to organize workers for their own defense. The Women's Trade Union League had many successes. The International Workers of the World, a radical union, wanted to place workers in control. In the end, Samuel Gompers and the American Federation of Labor won the allegiance of most workers.

A New Urban Culture

22.4 What happened to art and culture in these years so filled with change? p. 521

In the dozen years after 1900, American culture changed in important ways. Cities took on their modern form. Suburbs flourished. Sports became increasingly popular, reflecting people's increased leisure time. Experimentation occurred in literature, poetry, painting, and the arts.

Timeline

1903
The Changing Face of Industrialism—Ford Motor Company formed

Conflict in the Workplace—Women's Trade Union League (WTUL) formed

1903

1905
Conflict in the Workplace—Industrial Workers of the World (IWW) established

1905

Society's Masses—African American leaders inaugurate the Niagara Movement

1910
Society's Masses—NAACP founded

1910

1911
Conflict in the Workplace—Fire at the Triangle Shirtwaist Company kills 146 people

1911

1913
The Changing Face of Industrialism—Ford introduces the moving assembly line

1913

1915
The New Urban Culture—D. W. Griffith produces the first movie spectacular, *Birth of a Nation*

1915

1916
The New Urban Culture—New York sets the pattern for zoning laws across the nation

1916

1917
Society's Masses—Congress requires literacy test for immigrants

1917

23 From Roosevelt to Wilson in the Age of Progressivism 1900–1920

On a sunny spring morning in 1909, Theodore Roosevelt, wearing the greatcoat of a colonel of the Rough Riders, left New York for a safari in Africa. An ex-president at age 50, he had turned over the White House to his chosen successor, William Howard Taft, and was now off for "the joy of wandering through lonely lands, the joy of hunting the mighty and terrible lords" of Africa, "where death broods in the dark and silent depths."

Some of Roosevelt's enemies hoped he would not return. "I trust some lion will do its duty," Wall Street magnate J. P. Morgan said. Always prepared, Roosevelt took nine extra pairs of eyeglasses, and, just in case, brought expert hunters along with him. When the nearsighted Roosevelt took aim, three others aimed at the same animal. "Mr. Roosevelt had a fairly good idea of the general direction," the safari leader said, "but we couldn't take chances with the life of a former president."

LEARNING OBJECTIVES

23.1 ((•	23.2 ((•	23.3 ((•	23.4 ((•	23.5 ((•	23.6 ((•
What were the six major characteristics of progressivism? p. 530	What methods did progressive reformers use to attack problems in the cities and states? p. 537	How would you describe the personality and programs of Theodore Roosevelt? p. 539	What were the major measures of Theodore Roosevelt's term from 1905 to 1909? p. 542	Why was the presidency of William Howard Taft so difficult for him? p. 545	What were the central principles of Woodrow Wilson's New Freedom? p. 549

THE TROUBLES OF WILLIAM HOWARD TAFT A 1910 *Puck* cartoon shows Taft snarled in the intricacies of office.

From Chapter 23 of *American Stories: A History of the United States*, Third Edition. H. W. Brands, R. Hal Williams, T. H. Breen and Ariela J. Gross Copyright © 2015 by Pearson Education, Inc.

((• Listen to **Chapter 23** on MyHistoryLab

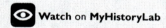 **Watch the Video Series on MyHistoryLab**

Learn about some key topics related to this chapter with the *MyHistoryLab Video Series: Key Topics in U.S. History.*

1 **The Progressive Era: 1900–1916** This video is an introduction to the Progressives and the Progressive Era of the early twentieth century. Ranging from politicians to educators, journalists, and even novelists, the Progressives were social reformers who believed that the problems of American society could be solved through the power of government.

◉ Watch on MyHistoryLab

Theodore Roosevelt This video profiles Theodore Roosevelt. The very model of the Progressive politician, Roosevelt championed many of the Progressive causes from his position as President. An avid outdoorsman, he established the national park system to advance conservation. As a trust buster, he tried to oversee the growth of businesses so big they had a harmful effect on the social and economic life of the nation.

Watch on MyHistoryLab **2** ◉

3 **Industrial Workers of the World** This video describes how the dangers of the late nineteenth-century industrial workplace, especially in mining, as well as other unfair labor practices inspired socialists and anarchists to found a universal worker organization known as the Industrial Workers of the World (IWW) Members of the IWW were dubbed "Wobblies" by their detractors for their radical ideas.

◉ Watch on MyHistoryLab

Nineteenth Amendment The successful passage of the Nineteenth amendment of the Constitution in 1920 achieved women's suffrage in the United States. This video explores the background of the movement to give women the right to vote, especially the work of two groups, the National American Woman Suffrage Association and the National Woman's Party.

Watch on MyHistoryLab **4** ◉

It was all good fun, and afterward Roosevelt set off on a tour of Europe. He attended the funeral in London of King Edward VII of Britain with the crowned heads of Europe, dined with the king and queen of Italy in Rome—an experience he likened to "a Jewish wedding on the East Side of New York"—and happily spent five hours reviewing troops of the German Empire in Berlin. Less happily, he followed events back home, where, many friends told him, Taft was not working out as president. Gifford Pinchot, Roosevelt's close companion in the conservation movement, came to Italy to complain personally about Taft, and at almost every stop, letters awaited him from other disappointed Republicans.

Taft was puzzled by it all. Honest and warmhearted, he had intended to continue Roosevelt's policies, even writing Roosevelt that he would "see to it that your judgment in selecting me as your successor and bringing about that succession shall be vindicated." But the conservative and progressive wings of the Republican Party split, and Taft often sided with the conservatives. Among progressive Republicans, Taft's troubles stirred talk of a Roosevelt "back from Elba" movement, akin to Napoleon's return from exile in 1815.

23.1
23.2
23.3
23.4
23.5
23.6

23.1

23.2

23.3

23.4

23.5

23.6

CONSERVATIONIST AS HUNTER An avid sportsman, President Teddy Roosevelt supported measures protecting wildlife in the United States, including designating Pelican Island, Florida, as the nation's first wildlife refuge.

Thousands gathered to greet Roosevelt on his return from Europe. He sailed into New York harbor on June 18, 1910, to the sound of naval guns and cheers. Characteristically, he had helped make the arrangements: "If there is to be a great crowd, do arrange it so that the whole crowd has a chance to see me and that there is as little disappointment as possible." Greeting Pinchot, one of Taft's leading opponents, with a hearty "Hello, Gifford," Roosevelt slipped away to his home in Oyster Bay, New York, where other friends awaited him.

He carried with him a touching letter from Taft, received just before he left Europe: "I have had a hard time—I do not know that I have had harder luck than other Presidents, but I do know that thus far I have succeeded far less than have others. I have been conscientiously trying to carry out your policies but my method of doing so has not worked smoothly." Taft invited Roosevelt to spend a night or two at the White House, but Roosevelt declined, saying that ex-presidents should not visit Washington. Relations between the two friends cooled.

A year later, there was no thought of friendship, only a desperate fight between Taft and Roosevelt for the Republican presidential nomination. Taft won, but, angry and ambitious, Roosevelt bolted and helped form the **Progressive (or "Bull Moose") party**, to unseat Taft and recapture the White House. With Taft, Roosevelt, Woodrow Wilson (the Democratic party's candidate), and Socialist party candidate Eugene V. Debs all in the race, the election of 1912 became one of the most exciting in American history.

It was also one of the most important. People were worried about the social and economic effects of urban-industrial growth. The election of 1912 provided a forum for those worries, and, to a degree unusual in American politics, it pitted deeply opposed candidates against one another and outlined differing views of the nation's future. In the battle between Roosevelt and Wilson, it also brought to the forefront some of the currents of progressive reform.

Those currents built on a number of important developments, including the rise of a new professional class, reform movements designed to cure problems in the cities and states, and the activist, achievement-oriented administrations of Roosevelt and Wilson. Together they produced the age of progressivism.

Progressive (or "Bull Moose") Party This political party was formed by Theodore Roosevelt to advance progressive ideas and unseat President William Howard Taft in 1912.

23.1

23.2

23.3

23.4

23.5

23.6

The Spirit of Progressivism

23.1 What were the six major characteristics of progressivism?

One way or another, progressivism touched all aspects of society. Politically, it fostered a reform movement that sought cures for the problems of city, state, and nation. Intellectually, it drew on the expertise of the new social sciences and reflected a shift from older absolutes such as religion to newer schools of thought that emphasized relativism and the role of the environment in human development. Culturally, it inspired fresh modes of expression in dance, film, painting, literature, and architecture. Touching individuals in different ways, progressivism became a set of attitudes as well as a definable movement.

Though it was broad and diverse, six characteristics defined progressivism as a whole. First, the progressives acted out of concern about the effects of industrialization and the conditions of industrial life. While their viewpoints varied, their goals were to humanize and regulate big business, not harm it.

In pursuing these objectives, the progressives displayed a second characteristic: a fundamental optimism about human nature, the possibilities of progress, and people's capacity to recognize problems and take action to solve them. Progressives believed they could "investigate, educate, and legislate"—learn about a problem, inform people about it, and, with the help of an informed public, find and enforce a solution.

Third, more than many earlier reformers, the progressives were confident that they had the right to intervene in people's lives. They knew best, some of them thought, and as a result, their ideas had an element of coercion. Fourth, while progressives preferred if possible to achieve reform through voluntary means, they tended to turn to the authority of the state and government at all levels to effect the reforms they wanted.

Fifth, many progressives drew on a combination of evangelical Protestantism (which gave them the desire—and, they thought, the duty—to purge the world of sins like prostitution and drunkenness) and the natural and social sciences (whose theories made them confident that they could understand and control the environment in which people lived). Progressives tended to view the environment as a key to reform, thinking—as some economists, sociologists, and other social scientists were suggesting—that if they could change the environment, they could change the individual.

Finally, progressivism was distinctive because it touched virtually the whole nation. Not everyone, of course, was a progressive, and there were many who opposed or ignored progressives' ideas. There were also those who were untouched by progressive reforms and those whom the movement overlooked. But in one way or another, a remarkable number of people were caught up in it, giving progressivism a national reach and a mass base.

That was one of the features, in fact, that set it off from populism, which had appealed mostly to the rural South and West. Progressivism drew support from across society. "The thing that constantly amazed me," said William Allen White, a leading progressive journalist, "was how many people were with us." Progressivism appealed to the expanding middle class, prosperous farmers, and skilled laborers; it also attracted significant support in the business community.

The progressives believed in progress and disliked waste. No single issue or concern united them all. Some wanted to clean up city governments, others to clean up city streets. Some wanted to purify politics or control corporate abuses, others to eradicate poverty or prostitution. Some demanded social justice in the form of women's rights, child labor laws, temperance, and factory safety. They were Democrats, Republicans, Socialists, and independents.

23.1

23.2

23.3

23.4

23.5

23.6

✳ Explore the Age of Progressivism on MyHistoryLab

WHAT MARKED THE PROGRESSIVE ERA IN THE UNITED STATES?

In the first couple decades of the 1900s, the Progressive movement played an important role in American politics. To define the movement is difficult because it was composed of numerous different reform movements, ranging from one calling for the establishment of safety regulations for food to another advocating the creation of new national parks. Its believers stretched across political party lines. The main unifying feature of the progressives was the belief in the power of government to improve society. Two progressive campaigns

THE SUFFRAGE MOVEMENT This storefront office in Cleveland, Ohio, as well as its signage, shows how well organized the woman suffrage movement had become by 1912. Here women show their support for an amendment to the state constitution to give them the right to vote. The right to vote in national elections would not come until 1920, with the ratification of the Nineteenth Amendment to the U.S. Constitution.

in particular—the movement for woman suffrage and another for the prohibition of spirituous liquors—marked the period. Both campaigns were successful, though Prohibition, which was extremely controversial, failed in the end. Most presidential candidates of the major parties during the period were progressives, although after his 1908 election, Taft came to be recognized as more a conservative than a progressive.

PROGRESSIVE CANDIDATES FOR PRESIDENT

Election	Republican Party	Democratic Party	Progressive Party	Socialist Party of America
1900	**William McKinley**	William Jennings Bryan*		
1904	**Theodore Roosevelt***	Alton B. Parker		Eugene V. Debs
1908	**William Howard Taft***	William Jennings Bryan*		Eugene V. Debs
1912	William Howard Taft	**Woodrow Wilson***	Theodore Roosevelt*	Eugene V. Debs
1916	Charles E Hughes*	**Woodrow Wilson***		
1920	**Warren G. Harding**	James M. Cox*		

Winner is in bold.

Asterisk indicates progressive candidate.

SOURCE: National Archives and Record Administration, http://www.archives.gov/federal-register/electoral-college/scores.html#1892.

KEY QUESTIONS Use **MyHistoryLab** *Explorer* to answer these questions:

Analysis ▶▶▶ *Along what lines did the regional vote for president fall during this period?*
Consider the role of Progressivism in national politics.

Response ▶▶▶ *Where were Prohibition laws more common?*
Map the popularity of the ban on alcohol.

Consequence ▶▶▶ *How did opinions on woman suffrage differ by region?*
Chart the development of legislation granting women's right to vote across states.

23.1

23.2

23.3

23.4

23.5

23.6

Progressives believed in a better world and in people's ability to achieve it. They paid people, as a friend said of social reformer Florence Kelley, "the high compliment of believing that, once they knew the truth, they would act upon it." Progress depended on knowledge. The progressives stressed individual morality and collective action, the scientific method, and the value of expert opinion. Like contemporary business leaders, they valued system, planning, management, and predictability. They wanted not only reform but efficiency.

The Rise of the Professions

Progressivism fed on an organizational impulse that encouraged people to join forces, share information, and solve problems. Between 1890 and 1920, a host of national societies and associations took shape—nearly four hundred of them in just three decades. Groups such as the National Child Labor Committee, which lobbied for legislation to regulate the employment and working conditions of children, were formed to attack specific issues. Other groups reflected one of the most significant developments in American society at the turn of the century—the rise of the professions.

Growing rapidly in these years, the professions—law, medicine, religion, business, teaching, and social work—provided the leadership of much of the progressive movement. The professions attracted young, educated men and women, who in turn were part of a larger trend: a dramatic increase in the number of people working in administrative and professional jobs. In businesses, these people were managers, architects, technicians, and accountants. In city governments, they were experts in everything from education to sanitation. They organized and ran the urban-industrial society.

These professionals formed part of a new middle class whose members did not derive their status from birth or inherited wealth, as had many members of the older middle class. Instead, they moved ahead through education and personal accomplishment and worked to become doctors, lawyers, ministers, and teachers. Proud of their skills, they were ambitious and self-confident, and they thought of themselves as experts who could use their knowledge to benefit society.

To assert their status, they formed professional societies to look after their interests and govern entry into their professions. Just a few years before, for example, a doctor had become a doctor simply by stocking up on patent medicines and hanging out a sign. Now doctors began to insist they were part of a medical profession, and they wanted to set educational requirements and minimum standards for practice. In 1901, they reorganized the American Medical Association (AMA) and made it into a modern, national, professional society.

Other groups and professions showed the same pattern. Lawyers formed bar associations, created examining boards, and lobbied for regulations restricting entry into the profession. Teachers organized the National Education Association (1905) and pressed for teacher certification and compulsory education laws. Social workers formed the National Federation of Settlements (1911); business leaders created the National Association of Manufacturers (1895) and the U.S. Chamber of Commerce (1912); and farmers joined the National Farm Bureau Federation to spread information about farming and improve their lot.

The Social-Justice Movement

Progressivism began in the cities during the 1890s. It first took form around settlement workers and others interested in freeing individuals from the crushing impact of cities and factories.

Ministers, intellectuals, social workers, and lawyers joined in a **social-justice movement** that focused national attention on the need for tenement house laws, more stringent child labor legislation, and better working conditions for women. They pressured municipal agencies for more and better parks, playgrounds, day nurseries,

Quick Check

What were the causes and results of the rise of the professions?

social-justice movement During the 1890s and after, this movement attracted followers who sought to free people from the often devastating impact of urban life. It focused on the need for housing reform, more stringent child labor regulations, and better working conditions for women.

23.1

23.2

23.3

23.4

23.5

23.6

PROGRESSIVISM IN ACTION An Infant Welfare Society nurse treats the baby of an immigrant family in Chicago. Medical discoveries and improvements in the quality of medical education fostered an interest in public health work among the social-justice reformers.

schools, and community services. Blending private and public action, settlement leaders turned increasingly to government aid.

Social-justice reformers were more interested in social cures than individual charity. Unlike earlier reformers, they saw problems as endless and interrelated; individuals became part of a city's larger patterns. With that insight, social-service casework shifted from a focus on an individual's well-being to a scientific analysis of neighborhoods, occupations, and classes.

Social-justice reformers, banding together to work for change, formed the National Conference of Charities and Corrections, which in 1915 became the National Conference of Social Work. Controlled by social workers, the conference reflected the growing professionalization of reform. Through it, social workers shared experiences and methodology and tried to establish themselves as a separate field within the social sciences. Once content with informal training sessions in a settlement house living room, they now founded professional schools at Chicago, Harvard, and other universities. After 1909, they had their own professional magazine, the *Survey*, and instead of piecemeal reforms, they aimed at a comprehensive program of minimum wages, maximum hours, workers' compensation, and widows' pensions.

Quick Check

What were the aims of the social-justice movement?

The Purity Crusade

Working in city neighborhoods, social-justice reformers were often struck by the degree to which alcohol affected those they were trying to help. Workers drank away their wages; some men spent more time in saloons than at home. Drunkenness caused violence and angered employers who did not want intoxicated workers on the job. In countless ways, alcohol wasted human resources, the reformers believed, and with business leaders, ministers, and others, they crusaded to remove the evils of drink from American life.

At the head of the crusade was the Women's Christian Temperance Union (WCTU). Founded in the 1870s, by 1911 the WCTU had nearly 250,000 members and was the largest organization of women in American history to that time. In 1893, it was joined by the Anti-Saloon League, and together the groups pressed to abolish

23.1

23.2

23.3

23.4

23.5

23.6

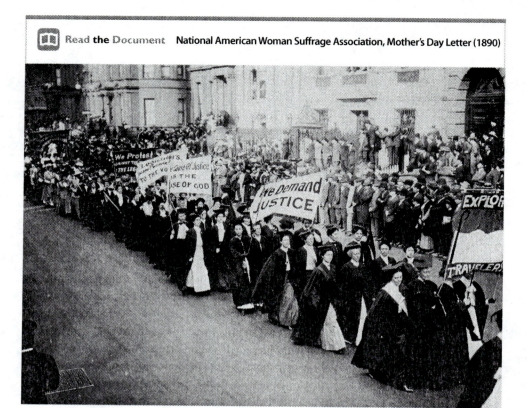

Read the Document   National American Woman Suffrage Association, Mother's Day Letter (1890)

VOTES FOR WOMEN Woman suffrage was a key element in the social-justice movement. Without the right to vote, women working for reform had little power to influence elected officials to support their endeavors.

alcohol and the places where it was consumed. By 1916, they had succeeded in 19 states, but as drinking continued elsewhere, they pushed for a nationwide law. In the moral fervor of World War I, they succeeded, and the Eighteenth Amendment, prohibiting the manufacture, sale, and transportation of intoxicating liquors, took effect in January 1920.

The amendment encountered troubles in the 1920s as the social atmosphere changed, but when it passed, progressives thought Prohibition was a major step toward eliminating social instability and moral wrong. In a similar fashion, some progressive reformers also worked to eliminate prostitution, convinced that poverty and ignorance drove women to the trade. By 1915, nearly every state had banned brothels, and in 1910, Congress passed the Mann Act, which prohibited the interstate transportation of women for immoral purposes. Like that against liquor, the campaign against prostitution reflected the era's desire to purify and elevate, often through the instrument of government action.

Woman Suffrage, Women's Rights

Women played a large role in the social-justice movement. Feminists were particularly active, especially in the political sphere, between 1890 and 1914—more active then, in fact, than at any other time until the 1960s. Some working-class women pushed for higher wages and better working conditions. College-educated women—5000 a year graduated after 1900—took up careers in the professions, from which some of them supported reform. From 1890 to 1910, the work of a number of national women's organizations, including the National Council of Jewish Women, the National Congress of Mothers, and the Women's Trade Union League, furthered the aims of the progressive movement.

Excluded from most of these organizations, African American women formed their own groups. The National Association of Colored Women was founded in 1895, 14 years before the better-known, male-oriented NAACP. The women's organization was the first African American social-service agency in the country.

23.1

23.2

23.3

23.4

23.5

23.6

From 200,000 members in 1900, the General Federation of Women's Clubs grew to more than 1 million by 1912. The clubs met, as they had before, for coffee and literary conversation, but they also began to look closely at conditions around them.

Forming an Industrial Section and a Committee on Legislation for Women and Children, the federation supported reforms to safeguard child and women workers, improve schools, ensure pure food, and beautify the community. Reluctantly at first, in 1914, the federation finally supported woman suffrage, a cause that dated back to the first women's rights convention in Seneca Falls, New York, in 1848. Divided over tactics since the Civil War, the suffrage movement suffered from disunity, male opposition, indecision over whether to act at the state or national level, resistance from the Catholic Church, and opposition from liquor interests, who linked the cause to Prohibition.

Because politics was an avenue for reform, growing numbers of women activists became involved in the suffrage movement. After years of disagreement, the two major suffrage organizations, the National Woman Suffrage Association and the American Woman Suffrage Association, merged in 1890 to form the **National American Woman Suffrage Association** under Susan B. Anthony. The merger opened a new phase of the suffrage movement, characterized by unity and a tightly controlled national organization.

In 1900, Carrie Chapman Catt, a superb organizer, became president of the National American Woman Suffrage Association. By 1920 it had nearly 2 million members. Catt and Anna Howard Shaw, who became the association's head in 1904, believed in organization and peaceful lobbying to win the vote. Alice Paul and Lucy Burns, founders of the Congressional Union, were more militant; they interrupted public meetings, focused on Congress rather than the states, and in 1917 picketed the White House.

Significantly, Catt, Paul, and others changed the argument for woman suffrage. Nineteenth-century suffragists had claimed the vote as a natural right, owed to women as much as men. Now, they stressed a pragmatic argument: Since women were more sensitive to moral issues than men, they would use their votes to help create a better society. They would support temperance, clean government, laws to protect workers, and other reforms. This argument attracted progressives who believed the women's vote would purify politics. In 1918, Congress passed a constitutional amendment stating simply that the right to vote shall not be denied "on account of sex." Enough states followed, and, after three generations of suffragist efforts, the Nineteenth Amendment took effect in 1920. (see Map 23.1).

National American Woman Suffrage Association Founded by Susan B. Anthony in 1890, this organization worked to secure women the right to vote. It stressed careful organization and peaceful lobbying.

Quick Check

How did women go about getting the vote?

A Ferment of Ideas: Challenging the Status Quo

A dramatic shift in ideas became one of the most important forces behind progressive reform. Most of the ideas focused on the role of the environment in shaping human behavior. Progressive reformers accepted society's growing complexity, called for factual treatment of piecemeal problems, allowed room for new theories, and, above all, rejected age-encrusted divine or natural "laws" in favor of thoughts and actions that worked.

A new doctrine called **pragmatism**, based on dealing with things practically to see if they worked, emerged in this ferment of ideas. It came from William James, a brilliant Harvard psychologist

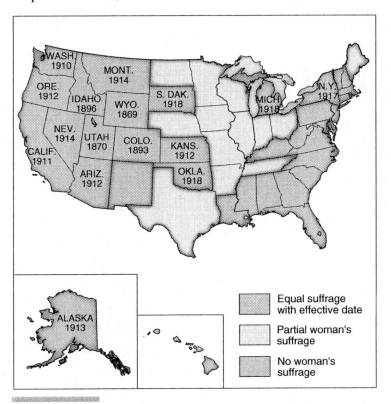

MAP 23.1 WOMAN SUFFRAGE BEFORE 1920 State-by-state gains in woman suffrage were mainly limited to the Far West and were agonizingly slow in the early twentieth century.

WASH. 1910
MONT. 1914
ORE. 1912
IDAHO 1896
WYO. 1869
S. DAK. 1918
MICH. 1918
N.Y. 1917
NEV. 1914
UTAH 1870
COLO. 1893
KANS. 1912
CALIF. 1911
ARIZ. 1912
OKLA. 1918
ALASKA 1913

Equal suffrage with effective date

Partial woman's suffrage

No woman's suffrage

23.1

23.2

23.3

23.4

23.5

23.6

pragmatism An early twentieth-century doctrine, based on the ideas of William James. Pragmatists were impatient with the concept of truth as an abstract reality. They believed that truth should work for the individual and that people were not only shaped by their environment but also helped to shape it. If an idea worked, it became truth.

who became the key figure in American thought from the 1890s to World War I. Warm and tolerant, James was impatient with theories that regarded truth as abstract. Truth, he believed, should work for the individual, and it worked best not in abstraction, but in action.

The environment, James thought, not only shaped people; they shaped it. In *Pragmatism* (1907), he praised "tough-minded" individuals who could live in a world with no easy answers. The tough-minded accepted change; they knew how to pick manageable problems, gather facts, discard ideas that did not work, and act on those that did. Ideas that worked became truth.

The most influential educator of the Progressive Era, John Dewey, applied pragmatism to educational reform. A friend and disciple of William James, he argued that thought evolves in relation to the environment and that education is directly related to experience. In 1896, Dewey founded a separate School of Pedagogy at the University of Chicago, with a laboratory in which educational theory based on the newer philosophical and psychological studies could be tested and practiced.

Dewey introduced an educational revolution that stressed children's needs and capabilities. He opposed memorization, rote learning, and dogmatic, authoritarian teaching methods; he emphasized personal growth, free inquiry, and creativity.

Rejecting the older view of the law as universal and unchanging, lawyers and legal theorists instead viewed it as a reflection of the environment—an instrument for social change. Law reflected the environment that shaped it. Judges began to favor "sociological jurisprudence" that related the law to social reform.

In Denver, Colorado, after Judge Ben Lindsey sentenced a boy to reform school for stealing coal, the boy's mother, grief-stricken, beat her head against the wall. Lindsey investigated the case and found that the father was a smelting worker dying of lead poisoning; the family needed coal for heat. From such experiences, Lindsey concluded that children were not born with a genetic tendency to crime; the environment in which they grew made them good or bad. Lindsey "sentenced" youthful offenders

Read the Document   Eugene V. Debs, from "The Outlook for Socialism in America" (1900)

EUGENE DEBS Presidential campaign poster for Eugene V. Debs on the Socialist Party of America ticket in 1904. The poster's imagery appeals to industrial workers, miners, and farmers, and its slogan "Workers of the world unite" was the party's key call to action to challenge the injustices of capitalism.

23.1

23.2

23.3

23.4

23.5

23.6

to education and good care. He worked for playgrounds, slum clearance, public baths, and technical schools. Known as the "Kids' Judge," he attracted visitors from as far away as Japan, who wanted to study and copy his methods.

Socialism, a reformist political philosophy, grew dramatically before World War I. Eugene V. Debs, president of the American Railway Union, in 1896 formed the Social Democratic party. Gentle and reflective, not at all the popular image of the wild-eyed radical, Debs was thrust into prominence by the Pullman strike (see Chapter 20). In 1901, he organized the Socialist Party of America. Neither Debs nor the party ever developed a cohesive platform, nor was Debs an effective organizer. But he was eloquent, passionate, and visionary.

Although torn by factions, the Socialist party doubled in membership between 1904 and 1908, then tripled by 1912. Running for president, Debs garnered 100,000 votes in 1900; 400,000 in 1904; and 900,000 in 1912, the party's peak year.

Quick Check

In what ways did ideas change in the years after 1900 and open up new avenues to reform?

Reform in the Cities and States

23.2 What methods did progressive reformers use to attack problems in the cities and states?

Progressive reformers realized government could be a crucial agent in accomplishing their goals. They wanted to curb the influence of "special interests" and, through political reforms such as the direct primary and the direct election of senators, make government follow the public will. Once it did, they welcomed government action at whatever level was appropriate.

As a result of this thinking, the use of federal power increased, as did the power and prestige of the presidency. Progressives not only lobbied for government-sponsored reform but also worked in their home neighborhoods, cities, and states; much of the significant change occurred in local settings, outside the national limelight. Most important, the progressives believed in experts' ability to solve problems. At every level—local, state, and federal—thousands of commissions and agencies took form. Staffed by trained experts, they oversaw a multitude of matters from railroad rates to public health.

Interest Groups and the Decline of Popular Politics

Placing government in the hands of experts was one way to get it out of the hands of politicians and political parties. The direct primary, which allowed voters rather than parties to choose candidates, was another way. These initiatives and others like them were part of a fundamental change in how Americans viewed their political system.

As one sign of the change, fewer and fewer people were going to the polls. Voter turnout dropped dramatically after 1900, when the intense partisanship of the decades after the Civil War gave way to media-oriented political campaigns based largely on the candidates' personalities. From 1876 to 1900, the average turnout in presidential elections was 77 percent. From 1900 to 1916, it was 65 percent. In the 1920s, it dropped to 52 percent, close to the average today. (see Figure 23.1). Turnout was lowest among young people, immigrants, the poor, and, ironically, newly enfranchised women.

The falloff had many causes, but among the most important was that people had found another way to achieve some of the objectives they had once assigned to political parties. The "interest group" became important in this era and a major feature of politics ever after. Professional societies, trade associations, labor organizations, farm lobbies, and other interest groups worked outside the party system to pressure government for things their members wanted. Social workers, women's clubs, reform groups, and others learned to apply similar pressure, and the result was much of the significant legislation of the Progressive Era.

Quick Check

What brought about the dramatic drop in voter turnout in these years?

23.1

23.2

23.3

23.4

23.5

23.6

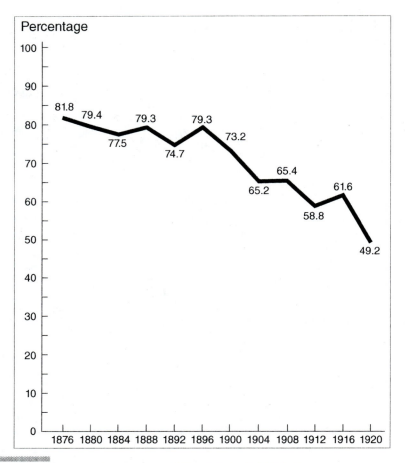

FIGURE 23.1 VOTER PARTICIPATION IN PRESIDENTIAL ELECTIONS, 1876–1920.

Reform in the Cities

During the early twentieth century, urban reform movements, many of them born in the depression of the 1890s, spread across the nation. In 1894, the National Municipal League was organized. It became the forum for debate over civic reform, changes in the tax laws, and municipal ownership of public utilities. Within a few years, nearly every city had a variety of clubs and organizations directed at improving the quality of city life.

In the 1880s, reformers would call a conference, pass resolutions, and go home; after 1900, they formed associations, adopted long-range policies, and hired a staff to achieve them. In the mid-1890s, only Chicago had an urban reform league with a full-time paid executive; within a decade, every major city had such leagues.

In city after city, reformers reordered municipal government. Tightening controls on corporate activities, they broadened the scope of utility regulation and restricted city franchises. They updated tax assessments, often skewed in favor of corporations, and tried to clean up the electoral machinery. Devoted to efficiency, they developed a trained civil service to oversee planning and operations. The generation of the 1880s also had believed in civil service, but the goal then was mostly negative: to get spoilsmen out and "good" people in. Now the goal was efficiency and, above all, results.

In constructing their model governments, urban reformers often turned to recent advances in business management and organization. They stressed continuity and expertise, a system in which professional experts staffed a government overseen by elected officials. At the top, the elected leader surveyed the breadth of city, state, or national affairs and defined directions. Below, a corps of experts—trained in the various disciplines of the new society—funneled those directions into specific, scientifically based policies.

Reformers created a growing number of regulatory commissions and municipal departments. They hired engineers to oversee utility and water systems, physicians and nurses to improve health, and city planners to develop parks and highways.

Quick Check

How did reformers try to improve life in the cities?

Action in the States

Reformers soon discovered, however, that many problems lay beyond a city's boundaries, and they turned to the state governments. From the 1890s to 1920, reformers worked to stiffen state laws regulating the labor of women and children, create and strengthen commissions to regulate railroads and utilities, impose corporate and inheritance taxes, improve mental and penal institutions, and allocate more funds for state universities, which were viewed as the training ground for the experts and educated citizenry the new society needed.

To regulate business, virtually every state created regulatory commissions to examine corporate books and hold public hearings. Building on earlier experience, state commissions after 1900 were given new power to initiate actions, rather than await complaints, and in some cases to set maximum prices and rates. Dictating company practices, they pioneered regulatory methods later adopted in federal legislation of 1906 and 1910.

Historians have long praised the regulation movement, but the commissions did not always act wisely or even in the public interest. Elected commissioners often knew little about corporate affairs. To win election, some promised specific rates or reforms, obligations that might bias the commission's investigative functions. Appointive commissions sometimes fared better, but they too had to oversee extraordinarily complex businesses such as the railroads.

To the progressives, commissions offered a way to end the corrupt alliance between business and politics. Another way to do that was to "democratize" government by reducing the power of politicians and increasing the influence of the electorate. To achieve that, progressives backed three measures: the initiative, which allowed voters to propose new laws; the referendum, which allowed them to accept or reject a law at the ballot box; and the recall, which enabled them to remove an elected official.

Oregon adopted the initiative and referendum in 1902; by 1912, 12 states had them. In 1913, the Seventeenth Amendment provided for the direct election of U.S. senators. By 1916, all but three states had direct primaries, which allowed the people, rather than nominating conventions, to choose candidates for office.

As governor of Wisconsin between 1901 and 1906, Robert M. La Follette developed the "Wisconsin Idea," one of the most important reform programs in the history of state government. He established an industrial commission, the first in the country, to regulate factory safety and sanitation. He improved education, workers' compensation, public utility controls, and resource conservation. He lowered railroad rates and raised railroad taxes. Under his prodding, Wisconsin became the first state to adopt a direct primary for all political nominations and a state income tax. Theodore Roosevelt called La Follette's Wisconsin "the laboratory of democracy," and the Wisconsin Idea soon spread to many other states.

After 1905, the progressives looked more and more to Washington. For one thing, Teddy Roosevelt was there, with his zest for publicity and his alluring grin. But progressives also sensed that many concerns—corporations and conservation, factory safety and child labor—crossed state lines. Federal action seemed desirable; specific reforms fit into a larger plan perhaps best seen from the nation's center. In 1906, La Follette became a U.S. senator, and the focus of progressivism shifted to Washington.

23.1

23.2

23.3

23.4

23.5

23.6

Quick Check

How did the states respond to the new industrial society?

The Republican Roosevelt

23.3 How would you describe the personality and programs of Theodore Roosevelt?

When President William McKinley died of gunshot wounds in September 1901, Vice President Theodore Roosevelt succeeded him in the White House. The new president initially vowed to carry on McKinley's policies. He continued some, developed others of his own, and brought to them all the exuberance of his own personality.

23.1

23.2

23.3

23.4

23.5

23.6

At age 42, Roosevelt was then the youngest president in American history. In contrast to the dignified McKinley, he was open, aggressive, and high-spirited. At his desk by 8:30 every morning, he worked through the day, usually with visitors for breakfast, lunch, and dinner. Politicians, labor leaders, industrialists, poets, artists, and writers paraded through the White House.

If McKinley reduced presidential isolation, Roosevelt virtually ended it. The presidency, he thought, was the "bully pulpit," a forum of ideas and leadership for the nation. The president was "a steward of the people bound actively and affirmatively to do all he could for the people." Self-confident, Roosevelt enlisted talented associates, including Elihu Root, secretary of war and later secretary of state; William Howard Taft, secretary of war; Gifford Pinchot, the nation's chief forester and leading conservationist; and Oliver Wendell Holmes, Jr., whom he named to the Supreme Court.

In 1901, Roosevelt invited Booker T. Washington to dinner at the White House. Many southerners protested—"a crime equal to treason," a newspaper said—and they protested again when Roosevelt appointed several African Americans to important federal offices in South Carolina and Mississippi. At first, Roosevelt considered building a biracial "black-and-tan" southern Republican party, thinking it would foster racial progress and his own renomination in 1904.

But Roosevelt soon retreated. In parts of the South, he supported "lily-white" Republican organizations, and his policies often reflected his own belief in African American inferiority. He said nothing when 12 people died in a race riot in Atlanta in 1906. He blamed African American soldiers stationed near Brownsville, Texas, after a night of violence there in August 1906. Acting on little evidence, he discharged "without honor" three companies of African American troops, six of whom held the Congressional Medal of Honor.

Busting the Trusts

"There is a widespread conviction in the minds of the American people that the great corporations known as trusts are in certain of their features and tendencies hurtful to the general welfare," Roosevelt reported to Congress in 1901. Like most people, however, the president wavered on the trusts. Large-scale production and industrial growth, he believed, were natural and beneficial; they needed only to be controlled. Still, he distrusted the trusts' impact on local enterprise and individual opportunity. Distinguishing between "good" and "bad" trusts, he pledged to protect the former while controlling the latter.

In 1903, Roosevelt asked Congress to create a Department of Commerce and Labor, with a Bureau of Corporations to investigate interstate commerce. Congress balked; Roosevelt called in reporters and, in an off-the-record interview, charged that John D. Rockefeller had organized the opposition to the measure. The press spread the word, and in the outcry that followed, the proposal passed easily. Roosevelt was delighted. With the new Bureau of Corporations publicizing its findings, he thought, the glare of publicity would eliminate most corporate abuses.

Roosevelt also undertook direct legal action. In 1902, he instructed the Justice Department to sue the Northern Securities Company for violating the Sherman Antitrust Act. It was a shrewd move. A mammoth holding company, Northern Securities controlled the massive rail networks of the Northern Pacific, Great Northern, and Chicago, Burlington & Quincy railroads.

In 1904, the Supreme Court ordered the company dissolved. Roosevelt was jubilant and he initiated several other antitrust suits. In 1902, he had also moved against the beef trust, an action western farmers and urban consumers both applauded. After a lull, he initiated suits in 1906 and 1907 against the American Tobacco Company, the Du Pont Corporation, the New Haven Railroad, and Standard Oil.

But Roosevelt's policies were not always clear, nor his actions consistent. He asked for (and received) business support in his bid for reelection in 1904. Industrial leaders

23.1
23.2
23.3
23.4
23.5
23.6

Read the Document Theodore Roosevelt, from *The Strenuous Life* (1900)

TRUST-BUSTER A cartoon illustrating Theodore Roosevelt's promise to break up only those "bad trusts" that were hurtful to the general welfare. Despite his reputation as a "trustbuster," Roosevelt dissolved relatively few trusts.

gave large donations. J. P. Morgan himself later testified that he gave $150,000 to Roosevelt's campaign. In 1907, acting in part to avert a threatened financial panic, the president permitted Morgan's U.S. Steel to absorb the Tennessee Coal and Iron Company, an important competitor.

Roosevelt, in truth, was not a trustbuster, although he was frequently called that. William Howard Taft, his successor in the White House, initiated 90 antitrust indictments in four years—nearly twice the 44 Roosevelt did in the seven years of his presidency. Instead, Roosevelt used antitrust threats to keep businesses within bounds. Regulation, he believed, was a better way to control large-scale enterprise.

Quick Check

What were Theodore Roosevelt's views on the trusts?

"Square Deal" in the Coalfields

A few months after announcing the Northern Securities suit, Roosevelt intervened in a major labor dispute involving the anthracite coal miners of northeastern Pennsylvania. Led by John Mitchell, a moderate, the United Mine Workers demanded wage increases, an eight-hour workday, and company recognition of the union. The coal companies refused, and in May 1902, 140,000 miners walked off the job. The mines closed.

As the months passed and the strike continued, coal prices rose. With winter coming on, schools, hospitals, and factories ran short of coal. Public opinion turned against the companies. Morgan and other industrial leaders privately urged them to settle, but the companies refused.

Roosevelt was furious. Complaining of the companies' arrogance, he invited both sides in the dispute to an October 1902 conference at the White House. There, Mitchell took a moderate tone and offered to submit the issues to arbitration, but the companies would not budge. Roosevelt ordered the army to prepare to seize the mines and then leaked word of his intent to Wall Street leaders.

Alarmed, Morgan and others again urged a settlement, and the companies finally agreed to accept the recommendations of an independent commission the president would appoint. In late October, the strikers returned to work. In March 1903, the commission awarded them a 10 percent wage increase and a cut in working hours. It recommended, however, against union recognition. The coal companies, in turn, were encouraged to raise prices to offset the wage increase.

More and more, Roosevelt saw the federal government as an honest and impartial "broker" between powerful elements in society. Rather than leaning toward labor, he pursued a middle way to curb corporate and labor abuses, abolish privilege, and enlarge individual opportunity. Conservative by temperament, he sometimes backed reforms in part to head off more radical measures.

During the 1904 campaign, Roosevelt called his actions in the coal miners' strike a "square deal" for both labor and capital, a term that stuck to his administration. Roosevelt was not the first president to take a stand for labor, but he was the first to bring opposing sides in a labor dispute to the White House to settle it. He was also the first to threaten to seize a major industry and to appoint an arbitration commission whose decision both sides agreed to accept.

Quick Check

In what ways did Theodore Roosevelt enlarge presidential power by intervening in the 1902 coal strike?

Roosevelt Progressivism at its Height

23.4 What were the major measures of Theodore Roosevelt's term from 1905 to 1909?

n the election of 1904, the popular Roosevelt crushed his Democratic opponent, Alton B. Parker of New York, and the Socialist Eugene V. Debs of Indiana. (see Table 23.1). On election night, overjoyed, he pledged that "under no circumstances will I be a candidate for or accept another nomination," a statement he later regretted.

Regulating the Railroads

After his election, Roosevelt laid out a reform program that included railroad regulation, employers' liability for federal employees, greater federal control over corporations, and laws regulating child labor, factory inspection, and slum clearance in the

TABLE 23.1 THE ELECTION OF 1904

Candidate	Party	Popular Vote	Electoral Vote
T. Roosevelt	Republican	7,623,486	336
Parker	Democrat	5,077,911	140
Debs	Socialist	402,400	0
Swallow	Prohibition	258,596	0

District of Columbia. He turned first to railroad regulation. In the Midwest and Far West, the issue was popular, and reform governors like La Follette urged federal action. Roosevelt maneuvered cannily. As the legislative battle opened, he revealed that Standard Oil had reaped $750,000 a year from railroad rebates. He also skillfully traded congressional support for a strong railroad measure in return for his promise to postpone reducing the tariff, a stratagem that came back to plague Taft.

Triumph came with passage of the **Hepburn Act** of 1906. A significant achievement, the act strengthened the rate-making power of the Interstate Commerce Commission (ICC), increased the number of commissioners from five to seven, empowered it to fix reasonable maximum railroad rates, and broadened its jurisdiction to include oil pipeline, express, and sleeping car companies. ICC orders were binding, pending court appeals, thus placing the burden of proof of injustice on the companies. Delighted, Roosevelt viewed the Hepburn Act as a major step in his plan for expert federal control over industry.

23.1
23.2
23.3
23.4
23.5
23.6

Hepburn Act A 1906 law that strengthened the power of the **Interstate Commerce Commission (ICC)** to regulate the railroads.

Quick Check
Why and how did Theodore Roosevelt want to regulate the railroads?

Cleaning Up Food and Drugs

Soon Roosevelt was dealing with two other important bills aimed at regulating the food and drug industries. Muckraking articles had cited filthy conditions in meatpacking houses, but Upton Sinclair's *The Jungle* (1906) set off a storm of indignation. Ironically, Sinclair had set out to write a novel about the packinghouse workers, the "wage slaves of the Beef Trust," hoping to do for wage slavery what Harriet Beecher Stowe had done for chattel slavery. But readers largely ignored his story of the workers and seized instead on his graphic descriptions of what went into their meat.

Sinclair was disappointed: "I aimed at the public's heart, and by accident I hit it in the stomach." He had, indeed. After reading *The Jungle*, Roosevelt ordered an investigation. The result, he said, was "hideous," and he threatened to publish the entire "sickening report" if Congress did not act. Meat sales plummeted in the United States and Europe. Demand for reform grew. Alarmed, the meat packers themselves supported a reform law, which they hoped would be just strong enough to still the clamor. The Meat Inspection Act of 1906, stronger than the packers wanted, set rules for sanitary meatpacking and government inspection of meat products.

A second measure, the Pure Food and Drug Act, passed more easily. Samuel Hopkins Adams, a muckraker, exposed the dangers of patent medicines in several sensational articles in Collier's. Patent medicines, Adams pointed out, contained mostly alcohol, drugs, and "undiluted fraud." Dr. Harvey W. Wiley, the chief chemist in the Department of Agriculture, led a "poison squad" of young assistants who experimented with the medicines. With evidence in hand, Wiley pushed for regulation; Roosevelt and the recently reorganized AMA joined the fight, and the act passed in 1906. Requiring manufacturers to list certain ingredients on labels, it was a pioneering effort to ban the manufacture and sale of adulterated, misbranded, or unsanitary food or drugs.

Quick Check
What laws regulated the food and drug industries?

Conserving the Land

An expert on birds, Roosevelt loved nature and the wilderness, and some of his most enduring accomplishments came in the field of **conservation**, an effort to preserve nature. Working closely with Gifford Pinchot, chief of the Forest Service, he established the first comprehensive national conservation policy. To Roosevelt, conservation meant the wise use of natural resources, not locking them away, so those who thought that wilderness should be preserved rather than developed generally opposed his policies. But when Roosevelt took office in 1901, there were 45 million acres in government preserves. By 1908, there were almost 195 million. (see Map 23.2).

conservation President Theodore Roosevelt made this principle one of his administration's top goals. Conservation in his view aimed at protecting the nation's natural resources, but called for the wise use of them rather than locking them away.

23.1

23.2

23.3

23.4

23.5

23.6

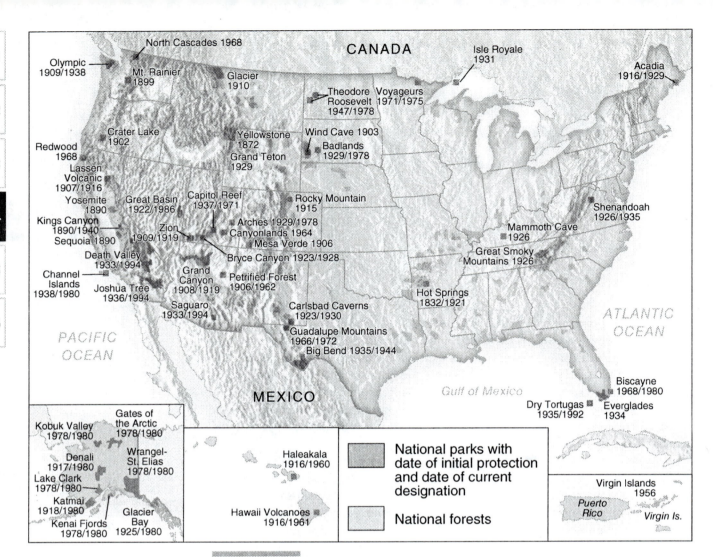

MAP 23.2 NATIONAL PARKS AND FORESTS During the presidency of Theodore Roosevelt, who considered conservation his most important domestic achievement, millions of acres of land were set aside for national parks and forests.

TABLE 23.2 THE ELECTION OF 1908

Candidate	Party	Popular Vote	Electoral Vote
Taft	Republican	7,678,908	321
Bryan	Democrat	6,409,104	162
Debs	Socialist	402,820	0
Chafin	Prohibition	252,821	0

As 1908 approached, Roosevelt became increasingly strident in his demand for reforms. He attacked "malefactors of great wealth," urged greater federal regulatory powers, criticized the federal courts' conservatism, and called for laws protecting factory workers. Many business leaders blamed him for a severe financial panic in 1907, and conservatives in Congress stiffened their opposition. Divisions between Republican conservatives and progressives grew.

Immensely popular, Roosevelt prepared in 1908 to turn over the White House to William Howard Taft, his close friend and colleague. As expected, Taft soundly defeated William Jennings Bryan, who was making his third try for the presidency (see Table 23.2). The Republicans retained control of Congress. Taft seemed ready and willing to carry on the Roosevelt legacy.

Quick Check

What did Theodore Roosevelt accomplish with regard to the environment?

The Ordeal of William Howard Taft

23.1

23.2

23.3

23.4

23.5

23.6

23.5 Why was the presidency of William Howard Taft so difficult for him?

Taking office in 1909, Taft felt "just a bit like a fish out of water." The son of a distinguished Ohio family and a graduate of Yale Law School, he became an Ohio judge, solicitor general of the United States, and a judge of the federal circuit court. In 1900, McKinley asked him to head the Philippine Commission (see Chapter 21), charged with the difficult and challenging task of forming a civil government in the Philippines. Later, Taft was named the first governor general of the Philippines. In 1904, Roosevelt appointed him secretary of war. In all these positions, Taft was a skillful administrator. He worked quietly behind the scenes, avoided controversy, and shared none of Roosevelt's zest for politics. A good-natured man, Taft had personal charm and infectious humor. He fled from fights rather than seeking them out, and he preferred quiet solitude to political maneuvering: "I don't like politics," he said. "I don't like the limelight."

Weighing close to 300 pounds, Taft enjoyed conversation, golf and bridge, good food, and plenty of rest. Compared to the hardworking Roosevelt and Woodrow Wilson, he was lazy. He was also honest, kindly, and amiable, and in his own way, he knew how to get things done.

Taft's years as president were not happy. As it turned out, he presided over a Republican party torn with tensions that Roosevelt had either brushed aside or concealed. The tariff, business regulation, and other issues split conservatives and progressives, and Taft often wavered or sided with the conservatives. Taft revered the past and distrusted change; although an ardent supporter of Roosevelt, he never had Roosevelt's faith in government's ability to impose reform and alter individual behavior. He named five corporation attorneys to his cabinet, leaned toward business over labor, and spoke of a desire to "clean out the unions."

Taft's reputation has suffered by comparison to the flair of Roosevelt and the moral majesty of Wilson. Taft was an honest and sincere president who—sometimes firm, sometimes befuddled—faced a series of important and troublesome problems.

Party Insurgency

Taft started his term with an attempt to curb the powerful Republican speaker of the House, Joseph "Uncle Joe" Cannon of Illinois. Using the powers of his position, Cannon had been setting House procedures, appointing committees, and virtually dictating legislation. Straightforward and crusty, he often opposed reform. In March 1909, 30 Republican congressmen joined Taft's effort to curb Cannon's power, and the president sensed success. But Cannon retaliated and, threatening to block all tariff bills, forced a compromise. Taft stopped the anti-Cannon campaign in return for Cannon's pledge to help with tariff cuts.

Opposition to high rates was growing among Republicans. The House passed a bill lowering rates, but in the Senate, Nelson W. Aldrich of Rhode Island added more than 800 amendments raising the rates the House had approved.

La Follette and other Republicans attacked the bill as the child of special interests. In speeches on the Senate floor they called themselves "progressives," invoked Roosevelt's name, and urged Taft to defeat the high-tariff proposal. Taft tried to compromise, but in the end, he backed Aldrich. The Payne–Aldrich Act, passed in November 1909, called for higher rates than the original House bill, though it lowered them from the Dingley Tariff of 1897. An unpopular law, Payne–Aldrich helped discredit Taft and revealed the tensions in the Republican Party.

Republican progressives and conservatives drifted apart. Taft resented the persistent pinpricks of the progressives, who criticized virtually everything he did. He tried to find middle ground but leaned more and more toward the conservatives. During a

23.1

23.2

23.3

23.4

23.5

23.6

Quick Check

What were the motives of the
Republicans in Congress who
opposed William Howard Taft?

nationwide speaking tour in 1909, he praised Aldrich, scolded the low-tariff insurgents, and called the Payne–Aldrich Act "the best bill that the Republican Party ever passed."

By early 1910, progressive Republicans in Congress no longer looked to Taft for leadership. They again challenged Cannon, and again Taft wavered. In an outcome embarrassing to the president, the progressives managed to curtail Cannon's authority to dictate committee assignments and schedule debate. In progressive circles, talk grew of a Roosevelt return to the White House.

The Ballinger–Pinchot Affair

The conservation issue further damaged relations between Roosevelt and Taft. In 1909, Richard A. Ballinger, Taft's secretary of the interior, put up for sale a million acres of public land that Pinchot, who had stayed on as Taft's chief forester, had withdrawn from sale. Pinchot, fearing that Ballinger would hurt conservation programs, protested. Seizing on a report that Ballinger had helped sell Alaskan coal lands to a syndicate that included J. P. Morgan, he asked Taft to intervene. After investigating, Taft supported Ballinger, although he asked Pinchot to remain in office.

Pinchot refused to drop the matter. He provided material for two anti-Ballinger magazine articles and wrote a critical public letter that Senator Dolliver of Iowa read to the Senate. Taft then fired the insubordinate Pinchot, which, though appropriate, lost the president more support. Newspapers followed the controversy for months, and muckrakers assailed the administration's "surrender" to Morgan and other "despoilers of the national heritage."

The controversy obscured Taft's contributions to conservation. He won from Congress the power to remove lands from sale and conserved more land than Roosevelt did. Still, the controversy tarred Taft and upset Roosevelt.

Quick Check

What was the Ballinger–Pinchot
Controversy?

Taft Alienates the Progressives

In 1910, Taft backed a bill to empower the ICC to fix maximum railroad rates. Progressive Republicans favored that plan but attacked Taft's proposal for a special Commerce Court to hear appeals from ICC decisions because most judges were conservative and rejected attempts to regulate railroad rates. Progressives also thought the railroads had been consulted too closely in drawing up the bill. Democratic and Republican progressives tried to strengthen the bill; Taft made support of it a test of party loyalty.

The Mann–Elkins Act of 1910 gave something to everyone. It gave the ICC power to set rates, stiffened long- and short-haul regulations, and placed telephone and telegraph companies under ICC jurisdiction. These provisions delighted progressives. In a trade-off, conservative Republican senators pledged to support statehood for Arizona and New Mexico, which were both predicted to be Democratic. In return, enough Democratic senators voted for the Commerce Court provision to pass the bill. While pleased with the act, Taft and the Republican Party lost further ground. In key votes, progressive Republicans defied Taft.

Taft attempted to defeat the progressive Republicans in the 1910 elections. He helped form anti-progressive organizations and campaigned against progressive Republican candidates for the Senate. Progressive Republicans organized a nationwide network of anti-Taft Progressive Republican Clubs.

The 1910 election results were a major setback for Taft and conservative Republicans. The high cost of living gave an edge to the progressive wings in both major parties, lending support to their attack on the tariff and the trusts. In party primaries, progressive Republicans overwhelmed most Taft candidates. In the general election, they fared better than the conservatives, which increased progressive influence in the Republican Party.

For Republicans of all persuasions, however, it was a difficult election. The Democrats swept the urban-industrial states. New York, New Jersey, Indiana, and even Taft's Ohio elected Democratic governors. For the first time since 1894, Republicans lost control of both the House and the Senate. Taft called it "not only a landslide, but a tidal wave and holocaust all rolled into one general cataclysm."

23.1
23.2
23.3
23.4
23.5
23.6

SHARING THE BURDEN According to this 1913 cartoon, the new income tax legislation distributed the tax burden more evenly, so that contributions from the wealthy eased some of the burden on the working class.

Despite the defeat, Taft pushed through important measures before his term ended. With Democratic help, he backed laws to regulate safety in mines and on railroads, create a Children's Bureau in the federal government, establish employers' liability for all work done on government contracts, and mandate an eight-hour day for government workers.

In 1909, Congress initiated the Sixteenth Amendment authorizing an income tax, which, along with woman suffrage, was one of the most significant legislative measures of the twentieth century. The amendment took effect in 1913.

An ardent supporter of competition, Taft relentlessly campaigned against trusts. The Sherman Antitrust Act, he said in 1911, "is a good law that ought to be enforced, and I propose to enforce it." That year, the Supreme Court in cases against Standard Oil and American Tobacco established the "rule of reason," which allowed the Court to determine whether a business presented "reasonable" restraint on trade. Taft thought the decisions gave the Court too much discretion and pushed ahead with the antitrust effort.

In October 1911, he sued U.S. Steel for acquiring the Tennessee Coal and Iron Company in 1907. Roosevelt had approved the acquisition, and the suit seemed designed to impugn his action. Enraged, he attacked Taft, who, for once, fought back. He accused Roosevelt of undermining the conservative tradition in the country and began to undercut progressive Republicans. Anti-Taft Republicans increasingly urged Roosevelt to run for president. In February 1912, he announced, "My hat is in the ring."

Quick Check

How did Taft lose the support of Republican progressives?

Differing Philosophies in the Election of 1912

Delighted Democrats looked on as Taft and Roosevelt fought for the Republican nomination. As the incumbent, Taft controlled the party machinery, and when the

23.1

23.2

23.3

23.4

23.5

23.6

Watch the Video Bull Moose Campaign Speech

THE BULL MOOSE CAMPAIGN "I'm feeling like a bull moose!" declared Teddy Roosevelt while campaigning in 1912 as a Progressive, inadvertently renaming the new political party. The patch depicts a strong, independent animal, much like Roosevelt himself. In 1904, Roosevelt had won re-election by promising to give Americans a "square deal."

Republican convention met in June 1912, he took the nomination. In July, the Democrats met in Baltimore and, confident of victory, struggled through 46 ballots before finally nominating Woodrow Wilson, the reform-minded governor of New Jersey.

A month later, anti-Taft and progressive Republicans—now calling themselves the Progressive party—whooped it up in Chicago. Naming Roosevelt for president at its convention, the Progressive party—soon known as the Bull Moose party—set the stage for the first important multi-party presidential contest since 1860.

Taft was out of the running before the campaign even began: "I think I might as well give up so far as being a candidate is concerned," he said in July. "There are so many people in the country who don't like me." He stayed home and made no speeches before the election. Roosevelt campaigned strenuously, even completing one speech after being shot in the chest by an anti–third-term fanatic. "I have a message to deliver," he said, "and will deliver it as long as there is life in my body."

Roosevelt called his program the **New Nationalism**. An important phase in the shaping of twentieth-century American political thought, it demanded a national approach to the country's affairs and a strong president to deal with them. The New Nationalism called for efficiency in government and society. It exalted the executive and the expert; urged social-justice reforms to protect workers, women, and children; and accepted "good" trusts. The New Nationalism encouraged large

New Nationalism President Theodore Roosevelt's program calling for a national approach to the country's affairs and a strong president to deal with them; efficiency in government and society; and protection of children, women, and workers. It accepted "good" trusts; and exalted the expert and the executive. It also encouraged large concentrations of capital and labor.

concentrations of labor and capital, serving the nation's interests under a forceful federal executive.

For the first time in history, a major political party enlisted women in its organization. Jane Addams, the well-known settlement worker (see Chapter 22), seconded Roosevelt's nomination at Chicago, and she and other women played a leading role in the Progressive campaign. Some labor leaders who saw potential for union growth and some business leaders who saw relief from destructive competition and labor strife supported the new party.

Wilson called his program the **New Freedom**. It emphasized business competition and small government. A states' rights Democrat, he wanted to rein in federal authority, using it only to sweep away special privilege, release individual energies, and restore competition. Drawing on the thinking of Louis D. Brandeis, the brilliant legal reformer, he echoed the Progressive party's social-justice objectives, while attacking Roosevelt's planned state. For Wilson, the vital issue was not a planned economy but a free one: "The history of liberty is the history of the limitation of governmental power. If America is not to have free enterprise, then she can have freedom of no sort whatever."

In the New Nationalism and New Freedom, the election of 1912 offered competing philosophies of government. Both Roosevelt and Wilson saw the central problem of the American nation as economic growth and its effect on individuals and society. Both focused on the government's relation to business, both believed in bureaucratic reform, and both wanted to use government to protect the ordinary citizen. But Roosevelt welcomed federal power, national planning, and business growth; Wilson distrusted them all.

On election day, Wilson won 6.3 million votes to 4.1 million for Roosevelt, and 900,000 for Eugene V. Debs, the Socialist party candidate. Taft finished third with 3.5 million votes. The Democrats also won control of both houses of Congress (see Map 23.3).

23.1

23.2

23.3

23.4

23.5

23.6

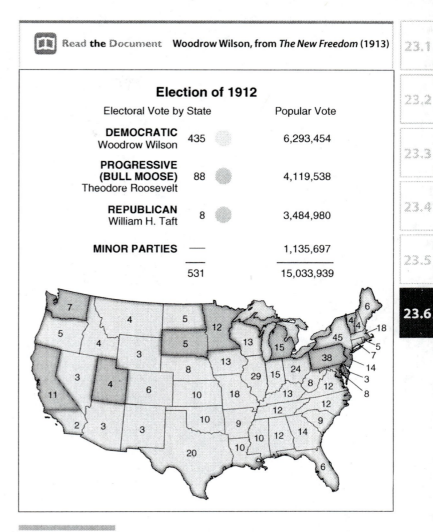

Read the Document Woodrow Wilson, from *The New Freedom* (1913)

Election of 1912

	Electoral Vote by State		Popular Vote
DEMOCRATIC Woodrow Wilson	435		6,293,454
PROGRESSIVE (BULL MOOSE) Theodore Roosevelt	88		4,119,538
REPUBLICAN William H. Taft	8		3,484,980
MINOR PARTIES	—		1,135,697
	531		15,033,939

MAP 23.3 THE ELECTION OF 1912 In the election of 1912, Woodrow Wilson managed to extend the appeal of the Democratic party well beyond its traditional roots in the South, carrying large portions of the Northeast, Midwest, and West. Note, however, that the combined popular vote for the two Republican candidates, Roosevelt and Taft, still exceeded the popular vote for Wilson, who won because of the Republican split.

New Freedom Woodrow Wilson's program, which emphasized business competition and small government. It sought to rein in federal authority, release individual energy, and restore competition. It achieved many of the progressive social-justice objectives while pushing for a free economy rather than a planned one.

Quick Check

What were the two opposing philosophies in the presidential election of 1912?

Woodrow Wilson's New Freedom

23.6 What were the central principles of Woodrow Wilson's New Freedom?

I f under Roosevelt social reform took on the excitement of a circus, "under Wilson it acquired the dedication of a sunrise service." Born in Virginia in 1856 and raised in the South, Wilson was the son of a Presbyterian minister. As a young man, he wanted a career in public service, and he trained himself carefully in history and oratory. A moralist, he reached judgments easily. Once reached, almost nothing shook them. Opponents called him stubborn and smug.

23.1

23.2

23.3

23.4

23.5

23.6

From 1890 to 1902 he served as professor of jurisprudence and political economy at Princeton. In 1902, he became president of the university. Eight years later, he was governor of New Jersey, where he campaigned to reform election procedures, abolish corrupt practices, and strengthen railroad regulation.

Wilson's rise was rapid, though he knew relatively little about national issues and personalities. But he learned fast, and in some ways, the lack of experience served him well. He had few political debts to repay and brought fresh perspectives to older issues. Ideas intrigued Wilson; details bored him. Although outgoing at times, he could also be cold and aloof, and aides soon learned that he preferred loyalty and flattery to candid criticism.

Prone to self-righteousness, Wilson often turned differences of opinion into bitter personal quarrels. Like Roosevelt, he believed in strong presidential leadership. A scholar of the party system, he cooperated closely with Democrats in Congress, and he was among the most effective presidents in terms of passing bills that he supported. Forbidding in individual conversation, Wilson could move crowds with graceful oratory. Unlike Taft, and to a greater degree than Roosevelt, he could inspire.

The New Freedom in Action

On the day of his inauguration, Wilson called Congress into special session to lower the tariff. When the session opened on April 8, 1913, Wilson himself was there, the first president since John Adams in 1801 to appear personally before Congress. In forceful language, he urged Congress to reduce tariff rates.

As the bill moved through Congress, Wilson showed exceptional skill. He worked closely with congressional leaders, and when lobbyists threatened the bill in the Senate, he appealed for popular support. The result was a triumph for Wilson and the Democratic Party. The **Underwood Tariff Act** lowered tariff rates about 15 percent and removed duties from sugar, wool, and other consumer goods.

Underwood Tariff Act This 1913 law reduced tariff rates and levied a graduated income tax to make up for the lost revenue.

To make up for lost revenue, the act also levied a modest graduated income tax, authorized under the new Sixteenth Amendment. Marking a significant shift in the American tax structure, it imposed a 1 percent tax on individuals and corporations earning more than $4000 annually and an additional 1 percent tax on incomes of more than $20,000. Above all, the act reflected a new unity within the Democratic Party, which had worked together to pass a difficult tariff law.

Encouraged by his success, Wilson decided to keep Congress in session through the hot Washington summer. Now he focused on banking reform, and the result in December 1913 was the **Federal Reserve Act**, the most important domestic law of his administration.

Federal Reserve Act This 1913 act created a central banking system, consisting of 12 regional banks governed by the Federal Reserve Board. It was an attempt to provide the United States with a sound yet flexible currency.

To provide the United States with a sound yet flexible currency, the act established the country's first efficient banking system since Andrew Jackson killed the second Bank of the United States in 1832. It created 12 regional banks, each to serve the banks of its district. A Federal Reserve Board, appointed by the president, governed the nationwide system.

A compromise law, the act blended public and private control of the banking system. Private bankers owned the federal reserve banks but answered to the presidentially appointed Federal Reserve Board. The reserve banks were authorized to issue currency, and through the discount rate—the interest rate at which they loaned money to member banks—they could raise or lower the amount of money in circulation. Monetary affairs no longer depended solely on the price of gold. Within a year, nearly half the nation's banking resources were in the Federal Reserve System.

Clayton Antitrust Act This law outlawed interlocking directorates (in which the same people served as directors for several competing companies), forbade policies that created monopolies, and made corporate officers responsible for antitrust violations. It also declared that unions were not conspiracies in restraint of trade and outlawed the use of injunctions in labor disputes unless they were necessary to protect property.

The **Clayton Antitrust Act** (1914) completed Wilson's initial legislative program. It prohibited unfair trade practices, forbade pricing policies that created monopoly, and made corporate officers personally responsible for antitrust violations. Delighting Samuel Gompers and the labor movement, the act declared that unions were not conspiracies in restraint of trade, outlawed the use of injunctions in labor disputes except to protect property, and approved lawful strikes and picketing.

In November 1914, Wilson proudly announced the completion of his New Freedom program. Tariff, banking, and antitrust laws promised a brighter future, he said, and it was now "a time of healing because a time of just dealing." Many progressives were aghast. That Wilson could think society's ills were so easily cured, the *New Republic* said, "casts suspicion either upon his own sincerity or upon his grasp of the realities of modern social and industrial life."

Quick Check

What characterized Woodrow Wilson's New Freedom program?

Wilson Moves Toward the New Nationalism

Distracted by the start of war in Europe, Wilson gave less attention to domestic issues for more than a year. When he took up reform again, he increasingly adopted Roosevelt's New Nationalism and blended it with the New Freedom to set it off from his earlier policies.

One of Wilson's problems was Congress. To his dismay, the Republicans gained substantially in the 1914 elections. Reducing the Democratic majority in the House, they swept key industrial and farm states. A recession also struck the economy, which had been hurt by the outbreak of the European war in August 1914. Some business leaders blamed the tariff and other New Freedom laws.

Preoccupied with such problems, Wilson blocked significant action in Congress through most of 1915. He refused to support minimum wages for women workers, sidetracked a child labor bill as unconstitutional, and opposed a bill to establish long-term credits for farmers. He also refused to endorse woman suffrage, arguing that it was a state matter, not a federal one.

Wilson's record on race disappointed African Americans and many progressives. He had appealed to African American voters in 1912, and a number of African American leaders campaigned for him. Soon after the inauguration, Oswald Garrison Villard, a leader of the NAACP, proposed a National Race Commission to study race relations. Initially sympathetic, Wilson rejected the idea because he feared losing southern Democratic votes in Congress. He appointed many southerners to high office, and for the first time since the Civil War, southern views on race dominated Washington.

At one of Wilson's first cabinet meetings, the postmaster general proposed segregating African American federal workers. No one dissented, including Wilson. Government bureaus began to segregate offices, shops, rest rooms, and restaurants. Employees who objected were fired. African American leaders, progressives, and clergymen protested. Wilson backed away from the policy, although he insisted that segregation benefited African Americans.

As 1916 began, Wilson again pushed for reforms. The result was a river of reform laws, which began the second, more national-minded phase of the New Freedom. With scarcely a backward glance, Wilson embraced parts of Roosevelt's New Nationalism campaign.

In part, he was motivated by the approaching presidential election. Wilson owed his victory in 1912 to the Republican split, but Roosevelt was moving back into Republican ranks, and he might use issues connected with the war in Europe against Wilson. Moreover, many progressives were disappointed with Wilson's failure to support reform legislation on farm credits, child labor, and woman suffrage.

But Wilson was popular within the labor movement. Where Roosevelt had sought a balance between business and labor, Wilson defended union recognition and collective bargaining. In 1913, he appointed William B. Wilson, a respected leader of the United Mine Workers, as the first head of the Labor Department and strengthened its Division of Conciliation.

23.1

23.2

23.3

23.4

23.5

23.6

In August 1916, a threatened railroad strike revealed Wilson's sympathies with labor. Like Roosevelt, he invited the two sides to the White House, where he urged the railroad companies to grant an eight-hour day and labor leaders to abandon the demand for overtime pay. Labor leaders accepted the proposal; railroad leaders did not. "I pray God to forgive you, I never can," Wilson said as he left the room. Ending the threat of a strike, the Adamson Act imposed the eight-hour day on interstate railways and established a federal commission to study the railroad problem. The act was a milestone in the expansion of the federal government's authority to regulate industry.

In September, Wilson signed the Tariff Commission Act, creating an expert commission to recommend tariff rates. The same month, the Revenue Act of 1916 boosted income taxes and furthered tax reform. Four thousand members of the National American Woman Suffrage Association cheered when Wilson finally supported woman suffrage. Two weeks later he endorsed the eight-hour day for all workers.

The 1916 presidential election was close, but Wilson won it on the issues of peace and progressivism. By the end of 1916, he and the Democratic Party had enacted most of the important parts of Roosevelt's Progressive party platform of 1912. To do it, Wilson accepted much of the activism of the New Nationalism, including greater federal power and commissions governing trade and tariffs, in place of much of the restraint of the New Freedom. In mixing the two programs, he blended some of the competing doctrines of the Progressive Era, established the primacy of the federal government, and foreshadowed Franklin D. Roosevelt's pragmatic New Deal of the 1930s.

Quick Check

In what five ways did Wilson move more closely to Theodore Roosevelt's ideas of New Nationalism?

Conclusion: The Fruits of Progressivism

The election of 1916 showed how deeply progressivism had reached into American society. "We have in four years," Wilson said that fall, "come very near to carrying out the platform of the Progressive party as well as our own; for we are also progressives."

In retrospect, however, 1916 also marked the beginning of progressivism's decline. At most, the years of progressive reform lasted from the 1890s to 1921, and they were largely compressed into a single decade between 1906 and American entry into World War I in 1917. Many problems the progressives addressed but did not solve; and some important ones, such as race, they did not even tackle. Yet their regulatory commissions, direct primaries, city improvements, and child labor laws marked an era of important and measured reform.

The institution of the presidency expanded. From the White House radiated executive departments that guided many activities. Independent commissions, operating within flexible laws, supplemented executive authority.

These developments owed much to both Roosevelt and Wilson. To manage a complex society, Roosevelt developed a simple formula: expert advice; growth-minded policies; a balancing of business, labor, and other interests; the use of publicity to gather support; and stern but often permissive oversight of the economy. Roosevelt strengthened the executive office, and he called on the newer group of professional, educated, public-minded citizens to help him: "I believe in a strong executive," he said, "I believe in power."

At first, Wilson had different ideas, wanting to dismantle much of Roosevelt's governing apparatus. But, driven by outside forces and changes in his own thinking, he soon moved in directions similar to those Roosevelt had championed. Starting out to disperse power, he eventually consolidated it.

Through such movements, government at all levels accepted responsibility for the welfare of various elements in the social order. A reform-minded and bureaucratic society took shape, in which men and women, labor and capital, political parties and social classes competed for shares in the expansive framework of twentieth-century life. But reform had limits. As both Roosevelt and Wilson found, the new government agencies, understaffed and underfinanced, depended on the responsiveness of those they sought to regulate.

Soon a far darker cloud appeared on the horizon. The spirit of progressivism rested on a belief in human potential, peace, and progress. After Napoleon's defeat in 1815, a century of peace began in western Europe. War seemed a dying phenomenon. "It looks as though this were going to be the age of treaties rather than the age of wars," an American said in 1912, "the century of reason rather than the century of force." It was not to be. Two years later, the most devastating of wars broke out in Europe, and in 1917, Americans were fighting on the battlefields of France.

23.1

23.2

23.3

23.4

23.5

23.6

Chapter Review

The Spirit of Progressivism

23.1 What were the six major characteristics of progressivism? p. 530

Progressivism sought cures for social and economic problems and was defined by six major characteristics: (1) a desire not to harm big business but to humanize and regulate it; (2) optimism about human nature; (3) a willingness to intervene in people's lives; (4) a tendency to stress the authority of the state and the government; (5) belief in the environment as a key to reform; and (6) a nationwide base.

Reform in the Cities and States

23.2 What methods did progressive reformers use to attack problems in the cities and states? p. 537

Progressive reformers turned increasingly to the government to carry out their measures. At the same time, ironically, fewer people tended to vote. Reformers focused on life in the growing cities. Robert M. La Follette of Wisconsin personified the movement. His focus was on improving factory safety, regulating the railroads, and adopting political reforms.

The Republican Roosevelt

23.3 How would you describe the personality and programs of Theodore Roosevelt? p. 539

Roosevelt attacked some trusts and, through the courts, broke up a railroad holding company. His intervention in the coal strike of 1902 reflected his active, energetic personality and represented an advance in presidential power.

Roosevelt Progressivism at Its Height

23.4 What were the major measures of Theodore Roosevelt's term from 1905 to 1909? p. 542

Winning easy election in 1904, Roosevelt persuaded Congress to improve railroad regulation, backed pure food and drug laws, and enlarged national parks. In all these actions, he reflected the values of the progressive generation: a reliance on experts, a faith in government power to initiate reform, and a desire to tame big business.

The Ordeal of William Howard Taft

23.5 Why was the presidency of William Howard Taft so difficult for him? p. 545

Roosevelt had left Taft a variety of difficult problems, including the tariff and a widening split between progressive and conservative Republicans. Taft increasingly alienated the progressives and Roosevelt. In the election of 1912, Taft finished third behind Woodrow Wilson and Roosevelt.

Woodrow Wilson's New Freedom

23.6 What were the central principles of Woodrow Wilson's New Freedom? p. 549

Victorious in 1912, Wilson set out to put into effect the central principles of his New Freedom program, including tariff reform, an antitrust law, and the Federal Reserve Act, a measure that still guides our economy today. By 1916, however, Wilson found greater value in Roosevelt's New Nationalism, which had emphasized government intervention and measures to protect women, labor, and other groups.

Timeline

1894
The Spirit of Progressivism— National Municipal League formed to work for reform in cities — 1894

1901
The Republican Roosevelt— Theodore Roosevelt becomes president — 1901

1904
The Republican Roosevelt—Roosevelt elected president — 1904

1908
The Ordeal of William Howard Taft—Taft elected president — 1908

1909
The Ordeal of William Howard Taft—Payne–Aldrich Tariff Act divides Republican Party — 1909

1912
Woodrow Wilson's New Freedom— Progressive party nominates Roosevelt for president; Woodrow Wilson elected president — 1912

1913
Woodrow Wilson's New Freedom—Federal Reserve Act reforms U.S. banking system
The Spirit of Progressivism— Sixteenth Amendment authorizes income tax; Seventeenth Amendment provides for direct election of senators. — 1913

1916
Woodrow Wilson's New Freedom— Wilson reelected president — 1916

1920
The Spirit of Progressivism— Nineteenth Amendment gives women the right to vote — 1920

24 The Nation at War 1901–1920

The Sinking of the *Lusitania*

On May 1, 1915, the **German** embassy took out the following advertisement in the *New York World* as a warning to Americans and other voyagers setting sail for England:

NOTICE—
Travellers intending to embark on the Atlantic voyage are reminded that a state of war exists between Germany and her allies and Great Britain and her allies; that the zone of war includes the waters adjacent to the British Isles; that, in accordance with formal notice given by the Imperial German Government, vessels flying the flag of Great Britain, or of any of her allies, are liable to destruction in those waters and that travelers sailing in the war zone on ships of Great Britain or her allies do so at their own risk.

At 12:30 that afternoon, the British luxury steamship *Lusitania* set sail from New York to Liverpool. Secretly, it carried a load of ammunition as well as passengers.

THE LUSITANIA IS SUNK; 1,000 PROBABLY ARE LOST

A FATEFUL TORPEDO With the sinking of the *Lusitania*, the American people learned firsthand of the horrors of total war. President Wilson's decision to protest the incident through diplomacy kept the United States out of the war—but only temporarily.

LEARNING OBJECTIVES

24.1	24.2	24.3	24.4	24.5	24.6
What were the main events that showed the United States was becoming a world power? p. 557	What did Woodrow Wilson mean by "moral diplomacy"? p. 560	What were the reasons behind and dangers of Wilson's neutrality policy? p. 561	How did the United States' entry affect the course of World War I? p. 567	What programs and changes did World War I bring at home? p. 571	What mistakes did Wilson make in negotiating the Treaty of Versailles? p. 575

From Chapter 24 of *American Stories: A History of the United States*, Third Edition. H. W. Brands, R. Hal Williams, T. H. Breen and Ariela J. Gross Copyright © 2015 by Pearson Education, Inc. All rights reserved.

Listen to Chapter 24 on MyHistoryLab

24.1
24.2
24.3
24.4
24.5
24.6

👁 Watch the Video Series on MyHistoryLab

Learn about some key topics related to this chapter with the *MyHistoryLab Video Series: Key Topics in U.S. History.*

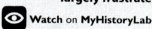 **World War I: 1914–1920** How did the United States get involved in a global conflict far away in Western Europe? This video answers this question by exploring the roots of World War I and how European imperialism threatened vital American interests. Although President Woodrow Wilson embraced American participation in the war as a way to positively affect the eventual peace, his goal was largely frustrated.

👁 Watch on **MyHistoryLab**

A World and a Nation in Upheaval This video examines the controversial issue of American neutrality in World War I, which favored Great Britain and forced a German response that almost guaranteed U.S. entry into the war on the side of Great Britain and her allies. The discussion also highlights such contributory factors as submarine warfare and the sinking of the *Lusitania* as well as the discovery of the Zimmerman Telegram.

Watch on **MyHistoryLab** 👁

 The United States at War When the United States entered World War I, it faced a tremendous challenge in getting its military and society onto a war footing. This video covers such topics as the formation of the American Expeditionary Force, "war socialism" in industry, the military draft, and the suppression of the language and culture of German Americans to achieve national unity.

👁 Watch on **MyHistoryLab**

Winning a Hard-Fought Peace In brokering the peace between the victorious Allies and the defeated Central Powers Woodrow Wilson faced many challenges abroad and at home. The U.S. Senate voted to join the new League of Nations, and Wilson's primary war objective failed tragically.

Watch on **MyHistoryLab** 👁

The steamer left two hours late, but it held several speed records and could easily make up the time. The passenger list of 1257 was the largest since the outbreak of war in Europe in August 1914. It took six days for it to reach the coast of Ireland. German U-boats (submarines) were known to patrol the dangerous waters there. When the war began, Britain imposed a naval blockade of Germany. In return, Germany in February 1915 declared the area around the British Isles a war zone; all enemy vessels, armed or unarmed, were at risk. Germany had only a handful of U-boats, but they were a new and frightening weapon. On February 10, President Woodrow Wilson warned Germany of its "strict accountability" for American losses from U-boat attacks.

Off Ireland, the passengers lounged on the deck of the *Lusitania*. As if it were peacetime, the ship sailed straight ahead, with no zigzag maneuvers to throw off pursuit. But the U-20 was there, and its commander, seeing a large ship, fired a single torpedo. Seconds after it hit, a boiler exploded and blew a hole in the *Lusitania*'s side. The ship listed immediately, hindering the launching of lifeboats, and in 18 minutes it sank. Nearly 1200 people died, including 128 Americans. As the ship's bow lifted and went under, the U-20 commander for the first time read the name: *Lusitania*.

The sinking, the worst marine disaster since the *Titanic* went down with 1500 people in 1912, horrified Americans. Theodore Roosevelt called it "an act of piracy" and demanded war. Most Americans, however, wanted to stay out of war; like Wilson, they hoped negotiations could solve the problem. "There is such a thing," Wilson said a few days after the sinking, "as a man being too proud to fight. There is such a thing as a nation being so right that it does not need to convince others by force."

In a series of diplomatic notes, Wilson demanded a change in German policy. The first *Lusitania* note (May 13, 1915) called on Germany to abandon unrestricted submarine warfare, disavow the sinking, and compensate for lost American lives. Germany sent an evasive reply, and Wilson drafted a second note (June 9) insisting on specific pledges. Fearful the demand would lead to war, Secretary of State William Jennings Bryan resigned. Wilson sent it anyway and followed with a third note (July 21)—almost an ultimatum—warning Germany that the United States would view similar sinkings as "deliberately unfriendly."

Unbeknownst to Wilson, Germany had already ordered U-boat commanders not to sink passenger liners without warning. In August 1915, a U-boat mistakenly torpedoed the British liner *Arabic*, killing two Americans. Wilson protested, and Germany, eager to keep the United States out of the war, backed down. The *Arabic* pledge (September 1) promised that U-boats would stop and warn liners, unless they tried to resist or escape. Germany also apologized for American deaths on the *Arabic*, and for the rest of 1915, U-boats hunted freighters, not passenger liners.

Although Wilson had achieved his immediate goal, the *Lusitania* and *Arabic* crises contained the elements that led to war. Trade and travel tied the world together, and Americans no longer hid behind safe ocean barriers. New weapons, such as the submarine, strained old rules of international law. But while Americans sifted the conflicting claims of Britain and Germany, they hoped for peace. A generation of progressives, confident of human progress, did not easily accept war.

Wilson also hated war, but he found himself caught up in a worldwide crisis that demanded the best in American will and diplomacy. In the end, diplomacy failed, and in April 1917, the United States entered a war that changed the nation's history. Building on several major trends in American foreign policy since the 1890s, the years around World War I established the United States as a world power, confirmed its dominance in Latin America, and ended with a war with Germany and its allies that had far-reaching results.

A New World Power

24.1 What were the main events that showed the United States was becoming a world power?

A s they had in the late nineteenth century, Americans after 1900 paid relatively little attention to foreign affairs. Newspapers and magazines ran stories every day about events abroad, but people were more concerned with what was going on at home.

For Americans at the time, foreign policy was something to be left to the president, an attitude the presidents themselves favored. Foreign affairs became an arena in which they could exert a free hand, largely unchallenged by Congress or the courts, and Roosevelt, Taft, and Wilson all did so.

The foreign policy they pursued from 1901 to 1920 was aggressive and nationalistic. During these years, the United States intervened in Europe, the Far East, and Latin America. It dominated the Caribbean.

In 1898, the United States left the peace table after the war with Spain possessing the Philippines, Puerto Rico, and Guam. Holding distant possessions required a colonial policy; it also required a change in foreign policy, reflecting an outward approach. From the Caribbean to the Pacific, policymakers paid attention to issues and countries they had earlier ignored. Like other nations in these years, the United States built a large navy, protected its colonial empire, and became increasingly involved in economic ventures abroad.

Building the Panama Canal

Convinced the United States should take a more active international role, Theodore Roosevelt spent his presidency preparing the nation for world power. Working with Secretary of War Elihu Root, he modernized the army, using lessons learned from the

24.1

24.2

24.3

24.4

24.5

24.6

24.1

24.2

24.3

24.4

24.5

24.6

war with Spain. Roosevelt and Root established the Army War College, imposed stiff tests for promotion, and in 1903 created a general staff to oversee military planning and mobilization. Determined to end dependence on the British fleet, Roosevelt doubled the strength of the navy during his term in office.

Stretching his authority to the limits, Roosevelt took steps to consolidate the country's new position in the Caribbean and Central America. European powers, which had long resisted American initiatives there, now accepted American supremacy. Preoccupied with problems in Europe, Asia, and Africa, Britain agreed to U.S. plans for an isthmian canal in Central America and withdrew much of its forces from the area.

Roosevelt wanted a canal to link the Atlantic and Pacific oceans across the isthmus connecting North and South America. Secretary of State John Hay negotiated with Britain the Hay–Pauncefote Treaty of 1901, which permitted the United States to construct and control an isthmian canal, provided it would be open to ships of all nations.

Delighted, Roosevelt began selecting the route. One route, 50 miles long, traversed the rough, swampy Panama region of Colombia. A French company had tried and failed to dig a canal there. To the northwest, another route ran through mountainous Nicaragua. Although 200 miles long, it followed natural waterways, which would make construction easier.

In 1899, an Isthmian Canal Commission recommended the shorter route through Panama. Roosevelt agreed and authorized Hay to negotiate an agreement with the Colombian representative in Washington, Thomas Herrán. The Hay–Herrán Convention, 1903, gave the United States a 99-year lease, with option for renewal, on a canal zone 6 miles wide. In exchange, the United States would pay Colombia a one-time fee of $10 million and an annual rental of $250,000.

To Roosevelt's dismay, the Colombian Senate rejected the treaty because it infringed on Colombian sovereignty and because the Colombians wanted more money. Calling them "jack rabbits" and "contemptible little creatures," Roosevelt considered seizing Panama, then hinted he would welcome a Panamanian revolt. In November 1903, the Panamanians took the hint, and Roosevelt quickly supported them. Sending the cruiser *Nashville* to prevent Colombian troops from putting down the revolt, he recognized the new Republic of Panama.

Two weeks later, the **Hay–Bunau–Varilla Treaty** with Panama granted the United States control of a canal zone 10 miles wide across the Isthmus of Panama. In return, the United States guaranteed the independence of Panama and agreed to pay the same fees offered Colombia. On August 15, 1914, the first ocean steamer sailed through the canal, which had cost $375 million to build (see Map 24.1).

Roosevelt took great pride in the canal, calling it "by far the most important action in foreign affairs." Defending his methods, he said in 1911, "If I had followed traditional conservative methods, I would have submitted a dignified state paper of 200 pages to Congress and the debate on it would have been going on yet; but I took the Canal Zone and let Congress debate; and while the debate goes on the Canal does also."

From 1903 to 1920, the United States intervened often in Latin America to protect the canal, promote regional stability, and exclude foreign influence. One problem was Latin American debts to European powers. Many countries in the Western Hemisphere owed money to European governments and banks, and often these nations were poor, unstable, and unable to pay. The situation invited European intervention. In 1902, Venezuela defaulted on debts; Britain, Germany, and Italy sent Venezuela an ultimatum and blockaded its ports. American pressure forced a settlement, but foreign debts remained a problem.

Hay–Bunau–Varilla Treaty This 1903 treaty with Colombia granted the United States control over a canal zone 10 miles wide across the Isthmus of Panama.

MAP 24.1 THE PANAMA CANAL ZONE Construction of the canal began in 1904, and despite landslides, steamy weather, and yellow fever, work was completed in 1914.

In 1904, when the Dominican Republic defaulted on its debts, Roosevelt made a major announcement. Known as the **Roosevelt Corollary** to the Monroe Doctrine, the new policy warned Latin American nations to keep their affairs in order or face American intervention.

Applying his corollary immediately, Roosevelt in 1905 took charge of the Dominican Republic's revenue system. American officials collected customs and used them to pay the country's debts. Within two years, Roosevelt also established protectorates in Cuba and Panama. In 1912, the Senate added the Lodge Corollary, which warned foreign corporations not to purchase harbors and other sites of military significance in Latin America. The Roosevelt Corollary guided American policy in Latin America until the 1930s, when Franklin D. Roosevelt's Good Neighbor policy replaced it.

Roosevelt Corollary A corollary to the Monroe Doctrine, which asserted that the United States would intervene in Latin American affairs if those countries could not keep their affairs in order.

Quick Check
What did Theodore Roosevelt do to build the Panama Canal?

Ventures in the Far East

The Open Door policy toward China and possession of the Philippines shaped American actions in the Far East. Congress refused to fortify the Philippines, and the islands were vulnerable to Japanese attack. Roosevelt wanted to balance Russian and Japanese power, and he was not unhappy when war broke out between them in 1904. As Japan won victory after victory, however, Roosevelt grew worried. Acting on a request from Japan, he offered to mediate the conflict. Both Russia and Japan accepted: Russia because it was losing, Japan because it was financially drained.

In August 1905, Roosevelt convened a peace conference at Portsmouth, New Hampshire. The conference ended the war, but Japan emerged as the dominant force in the Far East. Roosevelt then sent Secretary of War Taft to Tokyo to negotiate the Taft–Katsura Agreement, 1905, which recognized Japan's dominance over Korea in return for its promise not to invade the Philippines. Giving Japan a free hand in Korea violated the Open Door policy, but Roosevelt argued that he had little choice.

To show Japan his determination, Roosevelt sent 16 battleships of the new American fleet around the world, including a stop in Tokyo in October 1908. European naval experts felt certain Japan would attack the fleet, but the Japanese welcomed it. In 1908, the two nations reached the Root–Takahira Agreement, in which they promised to maintain the status quo in the Pacific, uphold the Open Door, and support Chinese independence.

Quick Check
What were Theodore Roosevelt's policies toward China and Japan?

Taft and Dollar Diplomacy

In foreign as well as domestic affairs, President Taft tried to continue Roosevelt's policies. For secretary of state he chose Philander C. Knox, Roosevelt's attorney general, and together they pursued a policy of "**dollar diplomacy**" to promote American financial and business interests abroad. The policy had profit-seeking motives, but it also aimed to substitute economic ties for military alliances.

Intent, like Roosevelt, on supremacy in the Caribbean, Taft worked to replace European loans with American ones, thereby reducing the danger of outside meddling. In the Far East, Knox worked closely with Willard Straight, an agent of American bankers, who argued that dollar diplomacy was the financial arm of the Open Door. Straight had close ties to Edward H. Harriman, the railroad magnate, who wanted to build railroads in Manchuria in northern China. Knox approached Britain, Japan, and Russia to organize an international syndicate to loan China money to purchase the Manchurian railroads, but in January 1910, all three turned him down.

This was a blow to American policy and prestige in Asia. Russia and Japan cooperated with each other and staked out spheres of influence in violation of the Open Door. Japan resented Taft's initiatives in Manchuria, and China's distrust of the United States deepened. Instead of cultivating friendship, as Roosevelt had envisioned, Taft had started an intense rivalry with Japan for commercial advantage in China.

dollar diplomacy The Taft administration's policy in the early 1900s to promote U.S. financial and business interests abroad, especially in Latin America.

Quick Check
What was the essential idea behind Taft's "dollar diplomacy"?

24.1

24.2

24.3

24.4

24.5

24.6

Foreign Policy Under Wilson

24.2 What did Woodrow Wilson mean by "moral diplomacy"?

When he took office in 1913, Woodrow Wilson knew little about foreign policy. During the 1912 campaign, he mentioned foreign policy only when it affected domestic concerns. "It would be the irony of fate if my administration had to deal chiefly with foreign affairs," he said to a friend before becoming president. And so it was. During his two terms, Wilson faced crisis after crisis in foreign affairs, including the outbreak of World War I.

The idealistic Wilson believed in an ethical world in which militarism, colonialism, and war were brought under control. He stressed morality over material interests and said during one crisis, "The force of America is the force of moral principle." Rejecting dollar diplomacy, Wilson initially chose **moral diplomacy** to bring right to the world, preserve peace, and extend the blessings of democracy.

moral diplomacy Policy of President Woodrow Wilson that rejected "dollar diplomacy." Rather than focusing mainly on economic ties with other nations, Wilson sought to practice morality in international relations, preserve peace, and extend to other peoples the blessings of democracy.

Troubles Across the Border

William Jennings Bryan, whom Wilson appointed secretary of state, was also an amateur in foreign relations and a fervent pacifist. Like Wilson, he believed in the American duty to "help" less favored nations.

Wilson and Bryan promised a dramatic new approach in Latin America, concerned not with the "pursuit of material interest" but with "human rights" and "national integrity." Yet in the end, Wilson, distracted by other problems and impatient with the results of his idealistic approach, continued the Roosevelt–Taft policies. He defended the

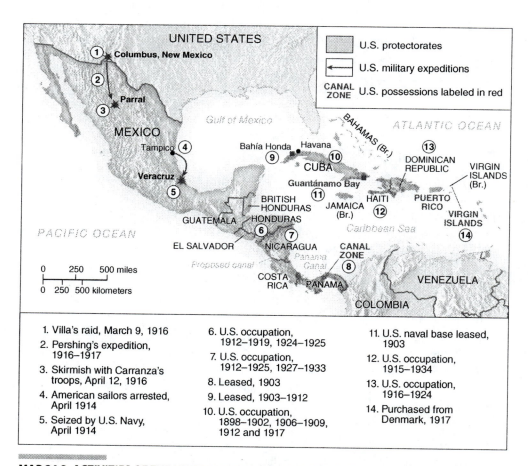

1. Villa's raid, March 9, 1916
2. Pershing's expedition, 1916–1917
3. Skirmish with Carranza's troops, April 12, 1916
4. American sailors arrested, April 1914
5. Seized by U.S. Navy, April 1914

6. U.S. occupation, 1912–1919, 1924–1925
7. U.S. occupation, 1912–1925, 1927–1933
8. Leased, 1903
9. Leased, 1903–1912
10. U.S. occupation, 1898–1902, 1906–1909, 1912 and 1917

11. U.S. naval base leased, 1903
12. U.S. occupation, 1915–1934
13. U.S. occupation, 1916–1924
14. Purchased from Denmark, 1917

MAP 24.2 ACTIVITIES OF THE UNITED STATES IN THE CARIBBEAN, 1898–1930 During the first three decades of the twentieth century, the United States policed the Caribbean, claiming the right to take action when it judged Latin American countries were doing a bad job of running their affairs.

24.1

24.2

24.3

24.4

24.5

24.6

Monroe Doctrine, gave unspoken support to the Roosevelt Corollary, and intervened in Latin America more than had either Roosevelt or Taft (see Map 24.2).

Wilson's moral diplomacy encountered one of its greatest challenges across the border in Mexico. Porfirio Díaz, president of Mexico for 37 years, was overthrown in 1911, and a liberal reformer, Francisco I. Madero, became president. But Madero could not keep order. With support from wealthy landowners, the army, and the Catholic Church, General Victoriano Huerta ousted Madero in 1913 and arranged his murder. Most European nations recognized Huerta, but Wilson, calling him a "butcher," refused. Instead, he announced a new policy: To win American recognition, revolutionary regimes in Latin America must not only exercise power but be "a just government based upon law, not upon arbitrary or irregular force."

On that basis, Wilson maneuvered to oust Huerta. In 1914, he stationed warships off Mexico's ports to cut off arms shipments to the Huerta regime. Trouble followed. On April 9, 1914, several American sailors, who had gone ashore in Tampico to purchase supplies, were arrested. They were promptly released, but the American admiral demanded an apology and a 21-gun salute to the American flag. Huerta agreed—if the Americans also saluted the Mexican flag.

Wilson asked Congress for authority to use military force if needed; then, just as Congress acted, he learned that a German ship was landing arms at Veracruz on Mexico's eastern coast. With Wilson's approval, American warships shelled the harbor, and marines took the city against heavy resistance. Outraged, Mexicans of all factions denounced the invasion, and the two countries hovered on the edge of war.

Retreating, Wilson explained that he desired only to help Mexico. Argentina, Brazil, and Chile offered to mediate, and tensions eased. In July 1914, weakened by an armed rebellion, Huerta resigned. Wilson recognized the new government, headed by Venustiano Carranza, an associate of Madero. But in 1916, Francisco ("Pancho") Villa, one of Carranza's generals, revolted. Hoping to goad the United States into doing something that would help him seize power, Villa raided border towns, killing 18 American civilians.

In response, Wilson ordered General John J. Pershing to seize Villa. Pershing led 6000 troops on a punitive expedition deep into Mexico. At first, Carranza agreed to the invasion, but as the Americans pushed farther and farther into his country, he changed his mind. As the wily Villa eluded Pershing, Carranza protested bitterly, and Wilson, worried about events in Europe, ordered Pershing home.

Wilson had laudable goals; he wanted to help the Mexicans achieve political and agrarian reform. But his tone and methods were condescending. Wilson tried to impose progressive reform on a society sharply divided along class and other lines. With little forethought, he interfered in the affairs of another country, and in doing so he revealed the themes—moralism, combined with pragmatic self-interest and a desire for peace—that also shaped his policies in Europe.

Quick Check

How and why did Wilson get Involved in Mexico, and how did his involvement reflect his "moral diplomacy"?

Toward War

24.3 What were the reasons behind and dangers of Wilson's neutrality policy?

In May 1914, Colonel Edward M. House, Wilson's close friend and adviser, sailed to Europe on a fact-finding mission. Tensions there were rising. "The situation is extraordinary," he reported to Wilson. "There is too much hatred, too many jealousies."

In Germany, the ambitious Kaiser Wilhelm II coveted a world empire to match those of Britain and France. Germany had military treaties with Turkey and Austria-Hungary, a sprawling, multinational central European empire. In another alliance, Britain, France, and Russia agreed to aid each other in case of attack.

On June 28, 1914, an assassin linked to Serbia murdered Archduke Franz Ferdinand, heir to the Austro-Hungarian throne. Within weeks, Germany, Turkey, and Austria-Hungary (the Central Powers) were at war with Britain, France, and Russia (the Allied

24.1

24.2

24.3

24.4

24.5

24.6

Powers). Americans were shocked at the events. Wilson immediately proclaimed neutrality and asked Americans to remain "impartial in thought as well as in action." The war, he said, was one "with which we have nothing to do, whose causes cannot touch us."

In private, Wilson was stunned. A man who loved peace, he had long admired the British parliamentary system, and he respected the leaders of the British Liberal party, who supported social programs akin to his own. "Everything I love most in the world," he said, "is at stake."

The Neutrality Policy

In general, Americans accepted neutrality. They saw no need to enter the conflict, especially after the Allies in September 1914 halted the first German drive toward Paris. America resisted involvement in other countries' problems, except for Latin America, and had a tradition of avoiding foreign entanglements.

Many of the nation's large number of progressives saw additional reasons to resist. They thought war violated the very spirit of progressive reform. Why demand safer factories in which people could work and then kill them by the millions in war? To many progressives, moreover, Britain represented international finance, which they detested. Germany, on the other hand, had pioneered some of their favorite social reforms, including health insurance, universal education, and old age pensions. Above all, progressives were sure that war would end reform. It consumed money and attention; it inflamed emotions.

Watch **the** Video The Outbreak of World War I

HIS ROYAL HIGHNESS
THE GRAND DUKE FERDINAND OF AUSTRIA.

A CAUSE FOR WAR Franz Ferdinand (1863–1914) was born in Graz, Austria. As the heir to the Austro-Hungarian empire, his assassination on June 29, 1914 sparked the First World War, setting off one by one a series of entangling alliances.

As a result, Jane Addams, Florence Kelley, and other progressives fought to keep the United States out of war. In late 1915, they formed the American Union Against Militarism, to throw, they said, "a monkey wrench into the machinery" of war. In 1915, Addams helped organize the League to Limit Armament, and she and Carrie Chapman Catt formed the Woman's Peace Party to organize women against the war.

The war's outbreak also tugged at the emotions of millions of Americans. At the deepest level, most, bound by common language and institutions, sympathized with the Allies and blamed Germany for the war. Like Wilson, many Americans admired English literature, customs, and law; they remembered Lafayette and France's help during the American Revolution. Germany seemed arrogant and militaristic. When the war began, it invaded Belgium to strike at France and violated a treaty that the German chancellor called "just a scrap of paper."

Both sides tried to sway American opinion. German propaganda tended to stress strength and will; Allied propaganda called on historical ties and publicized German atrocities, real and alleged. In the end, the propaganda probably made little difference. Ties of heritage and the course of the war, not propaganda, decided the American position. At the outset, no matter which side they cheered for, Americans preferred simply to remain at peace.

24.1
24.2
24.3
24.4
24.5
24.6

Quick Check

What were the factors behind Wilson's neutrality policy?

Freedom of the Seas

The demands of trade tested American neutrality and confronted Wilson with difficult choices. Under international law, neutral countries could trade in nonmilitary goods with all belligerent countries. But Britain controlled the seas, and it intended to cut off shipments of war materials to the Central Powers.

As soon as war broke out, Britain blockaded German ports and limited what Americans could sell to Germany. American ships had to carry cargoes to neutral ports from which, after examination, they could be carried to Germany. As time passed, Britain forbade the shipment to Germany of all foodstuffs and most raw materials, seized and censored mail, and "blacklisted" American firms that dealt directly with the Central Powers.

Again and again, Wilson protested against such infringements on neutral rights. Sometimes Britain complied, sometimes not, and Wilson often grew angry. But, needing American support and supplies, Britain was careful to disrupt German-American trade without disrupting Anglo-American relations. When necessary, it also promised to reimburse American businesses after the war.

Other than the German U-boats, there were no constraints on trade with the Allies, and a flood of Allied war orders fueled the American economy. To finance the purchases, the Allies borrowed from American bankers. By 1917, loans to Allied governments exceeded $2 billion; loans to Germany came to only $27 million.

In a development that influenced Wilson's policy, the war produced the greatest economic boom in the nation's history. Loans and trade drew the United States ever closer to the Allied cause. And although Wilson often protested British maritime policy, the protests involved American goods and money; U-boats threatened American lives.

Quick Check

In what ways did the demands of trade test American neutrality?

The U-Boat Threat

A relatively new weapon—the *Unterseeboot*, or submarine—strained international law. Legally, a submarine had to surface, warn a ship to stop, send a boarding party to check papers and cargo, then allow passengers and crew to board lifeboats before sinking the vessel. Flimsy and slow, however, submarines could ill afford to surface while the prey radioed for help.

When Germany announced its submarine campaign in February 1915, Wilson protested sharply, calling the sinking of merchant ships without checking cargo "a wanton act." The Germans promised not to sink American ships—an agreement that lasted until 1917—and thereafter the issue became Americans' right to sail on the ships of belligerent nations. In March 1915, an American citizen aboard the British liner *Falaba* perished when the ship was torpedoed off the Irish coast. Bryan urged Wilson

24.1

24.2

24.3

24.4

24.5

24.6

THE U-BOAT A new and terrifying weapon of the war was the German U-boat, which attacked silently and without warning.

to forbid Americans to travel in the war zones, but the president, determined to stand by the principles of international law, refused.

Wilson reacted more harshly in May and August of 1915 when U-boats sank the *Lusitania* and the *Arabic*. He demanded that the Germans protect passenger vessels and pay for American losses. At odds with Wilson's understanding of neutrality, Bryan resigned as secretary of state in June 1915. Robert Lansing, a lawyer and counselor in the State Department, replaced him. Lansing brought a very different spirit to the job. He favored the Allies and believed that a German-dominated world would threaten democracy. He urged strong stands against German violations of American neutrality.

In February 1916, Germany declared unrestricted submarine warfare against all armed ships. Lansing told Germany it would be held strictly accountable for American losses. A month later, a U-boat torpedoed the unarmed French steamer *Sussex* without warning, drowning several Americans. Arguing that the sinking violated the *Arabic* pledge, Lansing urged Wilson to break relations with Germany. Wilson refused, but on April 18, he sent an ultimatum to Germany, stating that unless the Germans immediately ceased attacking cargo and passenger ships, the United States would sever relations.

The German government yielded. In the *Sussex* pledge of May 4, 1916, it promised to shoot on sight only enemy warships.

A short period of friendly relations between Germany and the United States ensued. The pledge applied not only to passenger liners but to all merchant ships, belligerent or not. There was one problem: Wilson had taken such a strong position that if Germany renewed submarine warfare on merchant shipping, war was likely. Most Americans, however, viewed the agreement as a diplomatic stroke for peace by Wilson, and the issues of peace and preparedness dominated the presidential election of 1916.

The Election of 1916

The "preparedness" issue pitted antiwar groups against those who wanted to prepare for war. Bellicose as always, Teddy Roosevelt led the preparedness campaign. He called Wilson "yellow" for not pressing Germany harder after the *Lusitania* sinking, but Wilson refused to be browbeaten.

Both sides attacked his position. Preparedness advocates charged cowardice; pacifists denounced any attempt at military readiness. The difficulty of his situation, plus

> **Quick Check**
>
> How did German submarines threaten to involve the United States in the war?

24.1

24.2

24.3

24.4

24.5

24.6

the growing U-boat crisis, soon changed Wilson's mind. In mid-1915, he asked the War Department to increase military planning, and later that year, approved large increases in the army and navy, which upset peace-minded progressives.

For their standard-bearer in 1916, the Republicans nominated Charles Evans Hughes, a moderate justice of the Supreme Court. Hughes seemed to have all the qualifications for victory. A former reform governor of New York, he could lure back the Roosevelt progressives and appeal to Republican conservatives. To woo the Roosevelt wing, Hughes called for a tougher line against Germany, thus allowing the Democrats to label him the "war" candidate. Even so, Roosevelt and others considered Hughes a "bearded iceberg," a dull campaigner who wavered on important issues.

The Democrats renominated Wilson in a convention marked by spontaneous demonstrations for peace. Picking up the theme, Wilson said in October, "I am not expecting this country to get into war." The campaign slogan "He kept us out of war" was repeated endlessly, and just before the election, the Democrats took full-page ads in leading newspapers:

> You Are Working—Not Fighting!
> Alive and Happy—Not Cannon Fodder!
> Wilson and Peace with Honor?
>
> or
>
> Hughes with Roosevelt and War?

On election night, Hughes swept most of the East, and Wilson retired at 10 p.m. thinking he had lost. During the night, the results came in from California, New Mexico, and North Dakota; all supported Wilson—California by just 3773 votes. Holding the Democratic South, he carried key states in the Midwest and West and took much of the labor and progressive vote. Women—who were then allowed to vote in presidential elections in 12 states—also voted heavily for Wilson (see Map 24.3).

Quick Check

What were the two key issues and the main results of the 1916 presidential election?

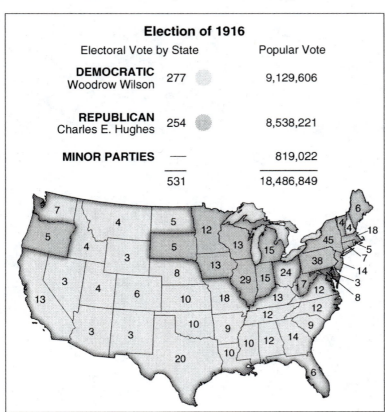

MAP 24.3 ELECTION OF 1916 Involving issues of war and peace, the election of 1916 was a crucial contest, dividing the electorate as this electoral map shows. Republican Hughes carried many of the populist states of the East, only to lose as Wilson carried much of the South and West. Concealed in the returns was the increasing role of women in American elections.

24.1

24.2

24.3

24.4

24.5

24.6

The Final Months of Peace

Just before election day, Britain further limited neutral trade, and there were reports Germany was going to renew unrestricted submarine warfare. Fresh from his victory, Wilson redoubled his efforts for peace. Aware that time was running out, he hoped to start negotiations to end the bloodshed and create a peaceful postwar world.

In December 1916, he asked both sides to state their war aims. Should they do so, he pledged the "whole force" of the United States to end the war. The Allies refused, although they promised privately to negotiate if the German terms were reasonable. The Germans replied evasively and in January 1917 revealed their real objectives. Close to forcing Russia out of the war, Germany sensed victory and wanted territory in eastern Europe and Africa.

On January 22, in an eloquent speech before the Senate, Wilson called for a "peace without victory." Outlining his own ambitious aims, he urged respect for all nations, freedom of the seas, arms limitations, and a League of Nations to keep the peace: "Only a peace between equals can last, only a peace the very principle of which is equality and a common participation in a common benefit." Many Europeans were impressed, but it was too late. The Germans had already decided to unleash the submarines and gamble on a quick end to the war. Even as Wilson spoke, U-boats were in the Atlantic west of Ireland, preparing to attack.

On January 31, the German ambassador in Washington informed Lansing that beginning February 1, U-boats would sink on sight all ships—passenger or merchant, neutral or belligerent, armed or unarmed—in the waters around Britain and France. Staking everything on a last effort, the Germans calculated that if they could sink

Watch **the** Video American Entry into WWI

WILSON'S RE-ELECTION Wilson's re-election in 1916 owed a great deal to the campaign slogan, "He kept us out of war." But the resumption of unrestricted submarine warfare by Germany in 1917 significantly changed the international situation. Several U.S. merchant ships were sunk in March by German U-boats. That April, Wilson called Congress into extraordinary session to ask for a declaration of war against Germany.

600,000 tons of shipping a month, they could defeat Britain in six months. As he had pledged in 1916, Wilson severed relations with Germany, although he still hoped for peace.

On February 25, the British government privately gave Wilson a telegram intercepted from Arthur Zimmermann, the German foreign minister, to the German ambassador in Mexico. A day later, Wilson asked Congress for authority to arm merchant ships to deter U-boat attacks. When La Follette and a handful of others threatened to filibuster, Wilson published the Zimmermann telegram. It proposed an alliance with Mexico in case of war with the United States, offering financial support and recovery of Mexico's "lost territory" in New Mexico, Texas, and Arizona.

Spurred by a wave of public indignation toward the Germans, the House passed Wilson's measure, but La Follette and others still blocked action in the Senate. On March 9, 1917, Wilson ordered merchant ships armed on his own authority. On March 13, the navy instructed all vessels to fire on submarines. Between March 12 and March 21, U-boats sank five American ships, and Wilson decided on war.

He called Congress into special session and on April 2, 1917, asked for a declaration of war. Pacifists in Congress managed to postpone a vote for four days. Finally, on April 6, the declaration of war passed, with 50 members of the House and six senators voting against it. Even then, the country was divided over entry into the war.

24.1

24.2

24.3

24.4

24.5

24.6

Quick Check
How did the United States finally get involved in the war?

Over There

| 24.4 | How did the United States' entry affect the course of World War I? |

With a burst of patriotism, the United States entered a war its new allies were in danger of losing. In April, the Germans sank 881,000 tons of Allied shipping, the greatest amount for any one month during the war. There were mutinies in the French army and a costly British failure in Flanders. In November, the Bolsheviks seized power in Russia, and, led by V. I. Lenin, they signed a separate peace treaty with Germany in March 1918, freeing German troops to fight in the West. German and Austrian forces routed the Italian army in the Alps, and the Allies braced for a spring 1918 offensive (see Map 24.4).

Mobilization

The United States was not prepared for war. Some Americans hoped the declaration of war itself might daunt the Germans; others thought that naval escorts of Allied shipping or supplying money and arms to the Allies would produce victory without sending troops.

Bypassing older generals, Wilson named John J. ("Black Jack") Pershing, leader of the Mexican campaign, to head the American Expeditionary Force (AEF). Pershing inherited an army unready for war. In April 1917, it had 200,000 officers and men, equipped with 300,000 old rifles, 1500 machine guns, 55 obsolete airplanes, and two field radio sets. Its most recent battle experience had been chasing Pancho Villa around northern Mexico. It had not caught him.

Although some in Congress preferred a voluntary army of the kind that had fought in the Spanish-American War, Wilson turned to conscription, which he considered both efficient and democratic. In May 1917, the **Selective Service Act** required all men between the ages of 21 and 30 (later changed to 18 and 45) to register. In June,

Selective Service Act This 1917 law required all American men between the ages of 21 and 30 to register for a military draft. The age limits were later changed to 18 and 45.

Read the Document The Zimmermann Telegram (1917)

MAP 24.4 EUROPEAN ALLIANCES AND BATTLEFRONTS, 1914–1917 Allied forces suffered early defeats on the eastern front (Tannenberg) and in the Dardanelles (Gallipoli). In 1917, the Allies were routed in the Alps (Caporetto); the western front then became the critical theater of the war.

9.5 million men registered for the draft. By the end of the war, 24.2 million men had registered, and about 2.8 million were inducted into the army.

The draft included black men as well as white, and four African American regiments were among the first sent into action in France. Despite their contributions, however, American commanders allowed no black soldiers to march in the victory celebrations that eventually took place in Paris.

Quick Check

How did the United States mobilize for war?

War in the Trenches

World War I may have been the most terrible war of all time, more terrible even than World War II and its vast devastation. After the early offensives, the European armies dug themselves into trenches only hundreds of yards apart in places. Artillery, poison gas, hand grenades, flame throwers, and a new weapon—rapid-fire machine guns—kept them pinned down.

Even in moments of respite, the mud, rats, cold, fear, and disease took a heavy toll. Deafening bombardments shook the earth, and shell shock—now called post-traumatic stress disorder or PTSD—was common. From time to time, troops went "over the top" of the trenches to attack the enemy's lines, but the costs were enormous. The German offensive at Verdun in 1916 killed 600,000 men; the British lost 20,000 on the first day of an offensive on the Somme.

The first American soldiers reached France in June 1917. By March 1918, 300,000 Americans were there. By war's end, 2 million men had crossed the Atlantic.

As expected, on March 21, 1918, the Germans launched a massive assault in western Europe. With help from troops from the Russian front, by May the Germans were just 50 miles from Paris. In their first action, the Americans blocked the Germans at Château-Thierry and four weeks later forced them out of Belleau Wood, a crucial stronghold. On July 15, the Germans threw everything into a last

24.1

24.2

24.3

24.4

24.5

24.6

drive for Paris, but they were halted at the Marne River, and in three days of battle they were finished. "On the 18th," the German chancellor said, "even the most optimistic among us knew that all was lost. The history of the world was played out in three days."

With the German drive stalled, the Allies counterattacked along the entire front. On September 12, 500,000 Americans and a smaller contingent of French drove the Germans from the St. Mihiel salient. Two weeks later, 896,000 Americans attacked between the Meuse River and the Argonne Forest. Focusing on a main railroad supply line for the German army, American troops broke through in early November, cut the line, and drove the Germans back along the whole front (see Map 24.5).

The German high command knew that the war was lost. On October 6, 1918, Germany appealed to Wilson for an armistice. By the end of the month, Turkey, Bulgaria, and Austria-Hungary were out of the war. At 4 a.m. on November 11, Germany signed the armistice. The Americans had lost 48,909 dead and 230,000 wounded; losses to disease brought the total of dead to more than 112,000.

The American contribution, although small compared to the enormous costs to European nations, was vital. Fresh, enthusiastic American troops raised Allied morale; they helped turn the tide at a crucial point in the war.

Quick Check

Why might World War I have been
the most terrible war of all time?

MAP 24.5 THE WESTERN FRONT: U.S. PARTICIPATION, 1918 The turning point of the war came in July, when the German advance was halted at the Marne. The "Yanks," now a fighting force, were thrown into the breach. They helped stem the tide and mount the counteroffensives that ended the war.

24.1
24.2
24.3
24.4
24.5
24.6

✳ Explore World War I on MyHistoryLab

HOW DID THE SO-CALLED "WAR TO END ALL WARS" PLAY OUT?

In the first years of the twentieth century, the powers of Europe were entangled in a system of alliances that, in theory, created a balance of power. In practice, the alliance created tensions as nations grew increasingly industrialized and armed. The Balkans provided the spark for this "powder keg," setting in motion the alliance system that caused the initial declarations of war in 1914 between the Central Powers—Germany, Austria-Hungary, the Ottoman Empire, and Bulgaria—and the Allies—France, Great Britain, and Russia. Other countries eventually joined the Allies, including Italy and Japan. Having preferred an isolationist stance on world affairs, the United States was a latecomer to the conflict, joining the Allies in 1917. The war, which introduced new weapons such as poison gas, tanks, and increasingly modern aircraft,

THE COST OF WAR The United States entered World War I in 1917 after it declared war against Germany. This photograph shows an Allied soldier escorting a captured German combatant.

brought incredible devastation for the European powers. The United States was spared much of the toll and emerged out of the war as a new global power.

HUMAN TOLL OF WORLD WAR I (in millions)

	Dead	Wounded
Central Powers	3.38	3.6
Allies	5.1	12.8
Civilians	13.0	–

SOURCE: Ellis, John and Cox, Michael. *The World War I Databook: The Essential Facts and Figures for all the Combatants.* London: Aurum Press, 2001; Urlanis, Boris, *Wars and Population.* Moscow: Progress Publishers, 1971.

KEY QUESTIONS Use **MyHistoryLab** *Explorer* to answer these **questions:**

Cause ▶▶▶ *How did the European international system set the stage for war?*

Chart the alliances that helped create World War I.

Consequence ▶▶▶ *How did the battle lines slow the war's course between 1915 and 1917?*

Map the trenches that were key in the failure of both sides to secure easy victory.

Analysis ▶▶▶ *What were the war's demographic and geopolitcal after effects?*

Trace the changes in boundaries in the war's aftermath and the death tolls for the involved countries.

Over Here

24.1

24.2

24.3

24.4

24.5

24.6

24.5 What programs and changes did World War I bring at home?

V ictory at the front depended on economic and emotional mobilization at home. Consolidating federal authority, Wilson moved quickly in 1917 and 1918 to organize war production and distribution. An idealist who knew how to sway public opinion, he also recognized the need to enlist American emotions. To him, the war for people's minds, the "conquest of their convictions," was as vital as conquest on the battlefield.

The Conquest of Convictions

A week after war was declared, Wilson formed the **Committee on Public Information (CPI)** to mobilize support for the war, and asked George Creel, an outspoken progressive journalist, to head it. Creel hired progressives such as Ida Tarbell and Ray Stannard Baker and recruited thousands of people in the arts, advertising, and film industries to publicize the war. He worked out a system of voluntary censorship with the press, plastered walls with colorful posters, and issued more than 75 million pamphlets.

Stoked by the propaganda campaign, anti-German sentiment spread. Many schools stopped teaching the German language—California's state education board called it a language "of autocracy, brutality, and hatred." Sauerkraut became "liberty cabbage"; saloonkeepers removed pretzels from the bar. Orchestral works by Bach, Beethoven, and Brahms vanished from concert halls.

Committee on Public Information (CPI) Created in 1917 by President Wilson and headed by progressive journalist George Creel, this organization rallied support for American involvement in World War I through art, advertising, and film. Creel worked out a system of voluntary censorship with the press and distributed posters and pamphlets.

Read **the** Document Espionage Act (1917)

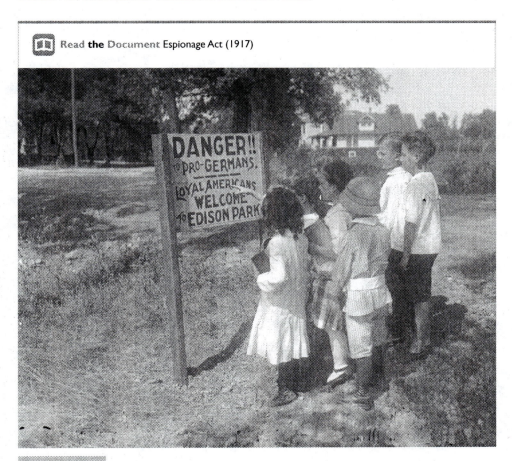

WARTIME HATRED Anti-German sentiment escalated dramatically after the United States entered the war in April 1917. A wave of verbal and physical attacks on German Americans was accompanied by a campaign to repress German culture. In this photograph from 1917, children stand in front of an anti-German sign posted in the Edison Park community of Chicago, Illinois. As the sign suggests, some Americans questioned the loyalty of their German American neighbors.

24.1

24.2

24.3

24.4

24.5

24.6

Espionage Act of 1917 This law, passed after the United States entered World War I, imposed sentences of up to 20 years on anyone found guilty of aiding the enemy, obstructing recruitment of soldiers, or encouraging disloyalty. It allowed the postmaster general to remove from the mail any materials that incited treason or insurrection.

Sedition Act A World War I law that imposed harsh penalties on anyone using "disloyal, profane, scurrilous, or abusive language about the U.S. government, flag, or armed forces."

Quick Check

What measures did Wilson pass to sway American opinions?

Wilson encouraged anti-German sentiment. "Woe be to the man or group of men that seeks to stand in our way," he told peace advocates soon after the war began. The **Espionage Act of 1917** imposed sentences of up to 20 years for persons found guilty of aiding the enemy, obstructing military recruitment, or encouraging disloyalty. It allowed the postmaster general to remove from the mails materials that incited treason or insurrection. The Trading-with-the-Enemy Act of 1917 authorized the government to censor the foreign language press.

In 1918, the **Sedition Act** imposed harsh penalties on anyone using "disloyal, profane, scurrilous, or abusive language" about the government, flag, or armed forces uniforms. In all, more than 1500 persons were arrested under the new laws.

The sedition laws clearly went beyond any clear or present danger. There were, to be sure, German spies in the country, and Germans who wanted to encourage strikes in American arms factories. Moreover, the government and national leaders were painfully aware of how divided Americans had been about entering the war. They set out to promote unity—by force, if necessary—to convince Germany that the nation was united.

But none of this warranted a nationwide program of repression. Conservatives took advantage of wartime feelings to try to stamp out American socialists, who were vulnerable because, unlike European socialists, they continued to oppose the war even after their country had entered it. Using the sedition laws, conservatives harried the Socialist party and the Industrial Workers of the World.

Wilson's postmaster general banned from the mails more than a dozen socialist publications, including the *Appeal to Reason*, which went to more than 500,000 people weekly. In 1918, Eugene V. Debs, the Socialist party leader, delivered a speech denouncing capitalism and the war. He was convicted of violating the Espionage Act and spent the war in a penitentiary. Nominated as the Socialist party candidate for president in 1920, Debs—prisoner 9653—won nearly a million votes, but the Socialist movement never fully recovered from the repression of the war.

OPPOSITION TO THE WAR Eugene V. Debs, serving time in an Atlanta penitentiary for speaking against the war, is shown here after receiving word of his nomination for the presidency. Debs campaigned in 1920 from behind bars.

24.1
24.2
24.3
24.4
24.5
24.6

A Bureaucratic War

Quick, effective action was needed to win the war. To meet the need, Wilson and Congress set up nearly 5000 new federal agencies. Staffed largely by businessmen, the agencies had unprecedented funds and powers.

By the time the war ended, it had cost $32 billion in direct war expenses—in an era when the entire federal budget rarely exceeded $1 billion. To raise the money, the administration sold about $23 billion in "Liberty Bonds" and, using the new Sixteenth Amendment, boosted taxes on corporations and personal incomes.

At first, Wilson tried to organize the wartime economy along decentralized lines like his early New Freedom thinking. But that proved unworkable, and he moved instead to a series of highly centralized planning boards, each with broad authority over a specific area of the economy. Boards controlled virtually every aspect of transportation, agriculture, and manufacturing. Though only a few of them were as effective as Wilson had hoped, they did coordinate the war effort to some degree.

The **War Industries Board (WIB)**, one of the most powerful of the new agencies, oversaw the production of all American factories. Headed by millionaire Bernard M. Baruch, a Wall Street broker and speculator, it determined priorities, allocated raw materials, and fixed prices. It told manufacturers what they could and could not make. The WIB set the output of steel and regulated the number of stops on elevators. Working closely with business, Baruch for a time acted as the dictator of the American economy.

Herbert Hoover, the hero of a campaign to feed starving Belgians after Germany invaded Belgium in 1914 and cut it off from most of its supplies of imported food, headed a new **Food Administration Board**. He set out with customary energy to supply food to the armies overseas. Appealing to the "spirit of self-sacrifice," Hoover convinced people to observe "meatless" and "wheatless" days. He fixed prices to boost production, bought and distributed wheat, and encouraged people to plant "victory gardens" behind homes, churches, and schools.

At another new agency, the Fuel Administration, Harry A. Garfield, the president of Williams College, introduced daylight saving time, rationed coal and oil, and imposed gasless days when motorists could not drive. The Railroad Administration dictated traffic over nearly 400,000 miles of track—standardizing rates, limiting passenger travel, and speeding arms shipments. The War Shipping Board coordinated shipping, the Emergency Fleet Corporation supervised shipbuilding, and the War Trade Board oversaw foreign trade.

As never before, the government intervened in American life. Businessmen flocked to Washington to run the new agencies, and the partnership between government and business grew closer. As government expanded, so did business. Industries such as steel, aluminum, and cigarettes boomed, and wartime contracts increased corporate profits threefold between 1914 and 1919.

War Industries Board (WIB) This government agency oversaw the production of American factories during World War I.

Food Administration Board A government agency that encouraged Americans to save food during World War I.

Quick Check

What were the main bureaucratic measures that shaped American war policy in World War I?

Labor in the War

Labor also entered into a partnership with government, although the results were more limited than in the business–government alliance. Samuel Gompers, president of the AFL, served on Wilson's Council of National Defense, an advisory group formed to unify business, labor, and government. Gompers hoped to trade labor peace for labor advances, and he formed a War Committee on Labor to enlist workers' support for the war. With the blessing of the Wilson administration, membership in the AFL and other unions grew from about 2.7 million in 1916 to more than 4 million in 1919.

Hoping to encourage production and avoid strikes, Wilson adopted many of the objectives of the social-justice reformers. He supported an eight-hour day in war-related industries and improved wages and working conditions. In May 1918, he named Felix Frankfurter, a brilliant young law professor, to head a new War Labor Board (WLB). The agency standardized wages and hours, and it protected the right of labor to organize and bargain collectively.

24.1
24.2
24.3
24.4
24.5
24.6

WOMEN AT WORK Housewives did not leave home for the factory en masse in 1917 as they did during World War II, but many women already employed outside the home found new, well-paying opportunities in jobs previously held by men.

The WLB also ordered equal pay for equal work for women in war industries. In 1914, the war stopped the flow of European immigrants, and in 1917, the draft began to take many American men. Women, African Americans, and Mexican Americans filled the resulting labor shortage. One million women worked in war industries. Some took jobs men had held, but most moved from one set of "women's jobs" into another.

Still, there were new opportunities and in some cases higher pay. In food, airplane, and electrical plants, women made up one-fifth or more of the workforce. As their wages increased, so did their expectations; some became more militant and clashed with male co-workers.

Looking for more people to fill wartime jobs, corporations recruited southern blacks. Beginning in 1916, northern labor agents traveled across the South, promising jobs, high wages, and free transportation. Soon the movement northward became a flood. Between 1916 and 1918, more than 450,000 African Americans left the Old South for the booming industrial cities of St. Louis, Chicago, Detroit, and Cleveland. In the decade before 1920, Detroit's black population grew by more than 600 percent, Cleveland's by more than 300 percent, and Chicago's by 150 percent. (see Map 24.6).

Most of the newcomers were young, unmarried, and skilled or semiskilled. The men found jobs in factories, railroad yards, steel mills, packinghouses, and coal mines; black women worked in textile factories, department stores, and restaurants. In their new homes, African Americans found greater racial freedom but also different living conditions. If the South was often hostile, the North could be impersonal and lonely. Accustomed to the pace of the farm—ruled by the seasons and the sun—blacks who entered the industrial sector now worked for hourly wages in mass production industries, where time clocks and line supervisors dictated the daily routine.

Growing competition for housing and jobs increased racial tensions. In mid-1917, a race war in East St. Louis, Illinois, killed nine whites and about 40 blacks. Chicago, New York City, Omaha, and other cities had race riots. Lynch mobs killed 48 blacks in 1917, 63 in 1918, and 78 in 1919. Ten of the victims in 1919 were war veterans, several still in uniform.

Blacks were increasingly inclined to fight back. Two hundred thousand blacks served in France—42,000 as combat troops. Returning home, they expected better treatment. "I'm glad I went," a black veteran said. "I done my part and I'm going to fight right here till Uncle Sam does his."

"Lift Ev'ry Voice and Sing," composed in 1900, became known as the "Negro National Anthem." Parents bought black dolls for their children, and W. E. B. Du Bois spoke of a "New Negro," proud and more militant: "We return. We return from fighting. We return fighting."

24.1

24.2

24.3

24.4

24.5

24.6

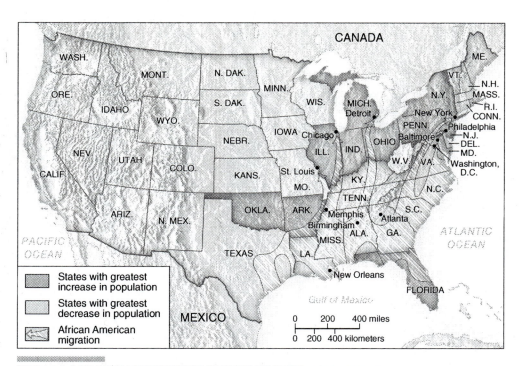

CANADA

MAP 24.6 AFRICAN AMERICAN MIGRATION NORTHWARD, 1910–1920 The massive migration of African Americans from the South to the North during World War I changed the dynamics of race relations in the United States.

Eager for cheap labor, farmers and ranchers in the Southwest persuaded the federal government to relax immigration restrictions. Between 1917 and 1920, more than 100,000 Mexicans migrated into Texas, Arizona, New Mexico, and California. The Mexican American population grew from 385,000 in 1910 to 740,000 in 1920. Tens of thousands of Mexican Americans moved to Chicago, St. Louis, Omaha, and other northern cities to take wartime jobs. Often scorned and insecure, they created urban barrios similar to the Chinatowns and Little Italys around them.

Like most wars, World War I affected patterns at home as much as abroad. Business profits grew, factories expanded, and industries turned out huge amounts of war goods. Government authority swelled, and people came to expect different things of their government. Labor, women, and blacks made gains. Society assimilated some of the shifts, but social and economic tensions grew, and when the war ended, they spilled over in the strikes and violence of the Red Scare (see Chapter 25).

The United States emerged from the war the strongest economic power in the world. In 1914, it was a debtor nation. Americans owed foreign investors about $3 billion. Five years later, the United States had become a creditor nation. Foreign governments owed more than $10 billion, and foreign citizens owed American investors nearly $3 billion. The war marked a shift in economic power rarely equaled in history.

Quick Check

What were four effects the war had on labor?

The Treaty of Versailles

24.6 What mistakes did Wilson make in negotiating the Treaty of Versailles?

Long before the fighting ended, Wilson began to plan for the peace. Like many others, he was disconcerted when the Bolsheviks in Russia began revealing the secret agreements among Britain, France, Italy, and czarist Russia to divide up Turkey and Germany's colonies. To place the war on a higher plane, he outlined a far-reaching, nonpunitive settlement before Congress on January 8, 1918. Wilson's **Fourteen Points** were generous and far-sighted, but they failed to satisfy wartime emotions for vindication. (see Table 24.1).

Fourteen Points In January 1918, President Woodrow Wilson presented these terms for a far-reaching, nonpunitive settlement of World War I and the establishment of a League of Nations. While generous and optimistic, the Points did not satisfy wartime hunger for revenge and were largely rejected by European nations.

24.1

24.2

24.3

24.4

24.5

24.6

TABLE 24.1 WOODROW WILSON'S FOURTEEN POINTS, 1918: SUCCESS AND FAILURE IN IMPLEMENTATION

1. Open covenants of peace openly arrived at	Not fulfilled
2. Absolute freedom of navigation on the seas in peace and war	Not fulfilled
3. Removal of all economic barriers to the equality of trade among nations	Not fulfilled
4. Reduction of armaments to the level needed only for domestic safety	Not fulfilled
5. Impartial adjustments of colonial claims	Not fulfilled
6. Evacuation of all Russian territory; Russia to be welcomed into the society of free nations	Not fulfilled
7. Evacuation and restoration of Belgium	Fulfilled
8. Evacuation and restoration of all French lands; return of Alsace-Lorraine to France	Fulfilled
9. Readjustment of Italy's frontiers along lines of Italian nationality	Compromised
10. Self-determination for the former subjects of the Austro-Hungarian Empire	Compromised
11. Evacuation of Rumania, Serbia, and Montenegro; free access to the sea for Serbia	Compromised
12. Self-determination for the former subjects of the Ottoman Empire; secure sovereignty for Turkish portion	Compromised
13. Establishment of an independent Poland, with free and secure access to the sea	Fulfilled
14. Establishment of a League of Nations, which would include the U.S., affording mutual guarantees of independence and territorial integrity	Not fulfilled

Sources: Data from G. M. Gathorne-Hardy, *The Fourteen Points and the Treaty of Versailles* (Oxford Pamphlets on World Affairs, no. 6, 1939), pp. 8–34; Thomas G. Paterson et al., *American Foreign Policy: A History Since 1900,* 2nd ed., vol. 2, pp. 282–293.

Britain and France distrusted Wilsonian idealism as a basis for peace. They had lost huge amounts of blood and treasure during the war. They wanted Germany disarmed and crippled; they wanted its colonies; and they were skeptical of the principle of self-determination. As the war ended, the Allies, who had in fact made secret commitments with one another, balked at making the Fourteen Points the basis of peace. When Wilson threatened to negotiate a separate treaty with Germany, however, they appeared to give in.

Wilson had won an important victory, but difficulties lay ahead. As Georges Clemenceau, the 78-year-old French premier, said, "God gave us the Ten Commandments, and we broke them. Wilson gives us the Fourteen Points. We shall see."

A Peace at Paris

Unfortunately, Wilson made a grave error just before the peace conference began. He appealed to voters to elect a Democratic Congress in November 1918, saying that any other result would be "interpreted on the other side of the water as a repudiation of my leadership." Republicans were furious, especially those who had supported the Fourteen Points; Wilson's problems deepened when the Democrats lost both the House and Senate.

Two weeks after the elections, Wilson announced he would attend the peace conference. This was a dramatic break from tradition, and Republicans attacked his personal involvement.

They renewed criticism when he named the rest of the delegation: Secretary of State Lansing; Colonel House; General Tasker H. Bliss, a military expert; and Henry White, a career diplomat. Wilson named no senator; the only Republican was White.

In selecting the delegation, Wilson passed over Henry Cabot Lodge, the powerful Republican senator from Massachusetts who opposed the Fourteen Points and would soon head the Senate Foreign Relations Committee. He also decided not to appoint Elihu Root or ex-President Taft, both of them enthusiastic internationalists. Never good at accepting criticism or delegating authority, Wilson wanted a delegation he could control—an advantage at the peace table but not in a battle over the treaty at home. Wilson received a tumultuous welcome in London, Paris, and Rome. Never before had

24.1
24.2
24.3
24.4
24.5
24.6

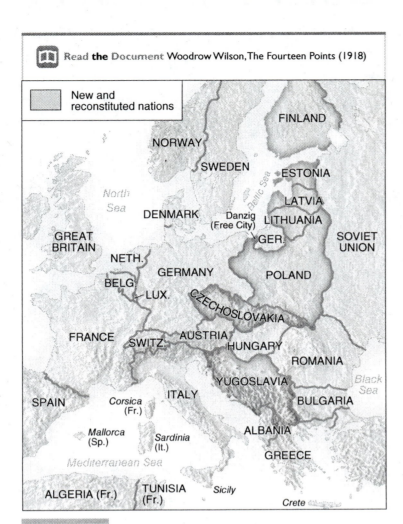

📖 Read the Document Woodrow Wilson, The Fourteen Points (1918)

MAP 24.7 EUROPE AFTER THE TREATY OF VERSAILLES, 1919 The treaty changed the map of Europe, creating new and reconstituted nations. (Note the boundary changes from the map on p. 570.)

such crowds acclaimed a democratic political figure. In Paris, two million people lined the Champs-Elysees, threw flowers, and shouted, "Wilson le Juste [the just]" as his carriage drove by. Overwhelmed, Wilson was sure that Europeans shared his goals and would force their leaders to accept his peace. He was wrong. Like their leaders, many people on the Allied side hated Germany and wanted revenge and a peace that reflected victory.

Opening in January 1919, the Peace Conference at Paris continued until May. Although 27 nations were represented, the "Big Four" dominated it: Wilson; Clemenceau of France, tired and stubborn, determined to end the German threat forever; David Lloyd George, the crafty British prime minister who had pledged to squeeze Germany "until the pips squeak"; and the Italian prime minister, Vittorio Orlando. A clever negotiator, Wilson traded various "small" concessions for his major goals—national self-determination, a reduction in tensions, and a League of Nations to enforce the peace.

Wilson still had to surrender some important principles. Violating the principle of self-determination, the treaty created two new nations—Poland and Czechoslovakia—with large German-speaking populations. It divided up the German colonies in Asia and Africa. Instead of a peace without victory, it made Germany accept responsibility for the war and demanded enormous reparations—which eventually totaled $33 billion. It made no mention of disarmament, free trade, or freedom of the seas. Instead of an open covenant openly arrived at, the treaty was drafted behind closed doors (see Map 24.7).

But Wilson deflected some of the most extreme Allied demands, and he won his coveted League of Nations, "to achieve international peace and security." The League included a general assembly; a nine-member council composed of the United States, Britain, France, Italy, Japan, and four nations elected by the assembly; and a court of international justice. League members pledged to submit to arbitration every dispute threatening peace and to

Quick Check

What were the main considerations in the negotiations over the peace treaty to end the war?

24.1

24.2

24.3

24.4

24.5

24.6

THE TREATY OF VERSAILLES Sir William Orpen, The Signing of Peace in the Hall of Mirrors, Versailles, May 28, 1919. Although the United States played a major role in drafting the treaty, the Senate never ratified the document. Instead, the United States made a separate peace with Germany in 1921.

impose military and economic sanctions against nations resorting to war. Article X, for Wilson the heart of the League, obliged members to protect one another's independence and territorial integrity.

Wilson returned home in February 1919 to discuss the draft treaty with Congress and the people. Most Americans, the polls showed, favored the League; 33 governors endorsed it. But over dinner with the Senate and House Foreign Relations Committees, Wilson learned of the strength of congressional opposition. On March 3, Senator Lodge produced a "round robin" signed by 37 senators declaring they would not vote for the treaty without amendment. Should the numbers hold, Lodge had enough votes to defeat it.

Returning to Paris, Wilson attacked his critics, while he worked for changes to improve the chances of Senate approval. In return for major concessions, the Allies agreed that domestic affairs remained outside League jurisdiction (exempting the Monroe Doctrine) and allowed nations to withdraw after two years' notice. On June 28, 1919, they signed the treaty in the Hall of Mirrors at Versailles, and Wilson went home for his most difficult fight.

Rejection in the Senate

There were 96 senators in 1919, 49 of them Republicans. William E. Borah of Idaho led 14 Republican "irreconcilables" who opposed the League on any grounds. Twelve "mild reservationists" led by Frank B. Kellogg of Minnesota accepted the treaty but wanted amendments that would not greatly weaken the treaty. Finally, 23 Lodge-led "strong reservationists" wanted major changes that the Allies would have to approve.

Only four Democratic senators opposed the treaty. Democrats and Republicans willing to compromise had enough votes to ratify it, once a few reservations were inserted. Biding for time to allow public opposition to grow, Lodge scheduled lengthy hearings and spent two weeks reading the 268-page treaty aloud. Democrats urged Wilson to appeal to the Republican "mild reservationists," but he refused: "Anyone who opposes me in that I'll crush!"

In September, Wilson took his case directly to the people. In the Midwest, his speeches aroused little emotion, but on the Pacific Coast he won ovations, which heartened him. In Pueblo, Colorado, he delivered one of the most eloquent speeches of his career. People wept as he talked of Americans who had died in battle and the hope that they would never fight again in foreign lands. But that night Wilson fell ill.

24.1

24.2

24.3

24.4

24.5

24.6

TABLE 24.2 THE ELECTION OF 1920

Candidate	Party	Popular Vote	Electoral Vote
Harding	Republican	16,152,200	404
Cox	Democrat	9,147,353	127
Debs	Socialist	917,799	0

On October 2, Mrs. Wilson found him unconscious on the White House floor. A stroke had paralyzed his left side.

After the stroke, Wilson could not work more than an hour or two at a time. Only family members, his secretary, and his physician could see him. For more than seven months, he did not meet with the cabinet. Focusing his remaining energy on the fight over the treaty, Wilson lost touch with other issues, and critics charged that his wife, Edith Bolling Wilson, ran the government.

On November 6, 1919, while Wilson convalesced, Lodge finally reported the treaty out of committee, along with "Fourteen Reservations," one for each of Wilson's points. The most important reservation stipulated that implementation of Article X, Wilson's key article, required congressional approval before any American intervention abroad.

On November 19, the treaty—with the Lodge reservations—failed, 39 to 55. Following Wilson's instructions, the Democrats voted against it. A motion to approve without the reservations lost 38 to 53, with only one Republican voting in favor. The defeat brought pleas for compromise, but neither Wilson nor Lodge would back down. When the treaty with reservations again came up for a vote on March 19, 1920, Wilson ordered the Democrats to oppose it. Although 21 of them defied him, enough obeyed his orders to defeat it, 49 to 35, seven votes short of the necessary two-thirds majority.

To Wilson, walking now with a cane, one chance remained: the presidential election of 1920. He thought of running for a third term, but his party shunted him aside. The Democrats nominated Governor James M. Cox of Ohio, with the young and popular Franklin D. Roosevelt, assistant secretary of the navy, for vice president. Wilson called for "a great and solemn referendum" on the treaty. The Democratic platform endorsed the treaty but agreed to accept reservations that clarified the American role in the League.

Senator Warren G. Harding of Ohio, who had nominated Taft in 1912, won the Republican nomination. Harding waffled on the treaty, but that made little difference. Voters wanted a change. Harding took 61 percent of the vote and beat Cox by seven million votes. (see Table 24.2). Without a peace treaty, the United States remained technically at war. In July 1921, almost three years after the last shot was fired, Congress finally passed a joint resolution ending the war.

Quick Check

Why was the treaty defeated in the Senate?

Conclusion: Postwar Disillusionment

After 1919, disillusionment set in. World War I was feared before it started, popular while it lasted, and hated when it ended. To a whole generation that followed, it appeared futile, killing without cause, sacrificing without benefit. Books, plays, and movies depicted it as waste, horror, and death.

The war and its aftermath damaged the humanitarian, progressive spirit of the early years of the century. It killed "something precious and perhaps irretrievable in the hearts of thinking men and women." Progressivism survived into the 1920s and the New Deal, but the old conviction and popular support were gone. Fights over the war and the League drained people's energy and enthusiasm.

Confined to bed, Woodrow Wilson died in Washington in 1924, three years after Harding, the new president, promised "not heroics but healing; not nostrums but normalcy; not revolution but restoration." Nonetheless, the "war to end all wars" and the spirit of Woodrow Wilson left an indelible imprint on the country.

Chapter Review

A New World Power

24.1 What were the main events that showed the United States was becoming a world power? p. 557

After winning the Spanish-American War, American presidents began to exert more influence in the world. Roosevelt took extraordinary steps to build the Panama Canal. He enlarged the country's role in the Western Hemisphere and tried to deal with the growing power of Japan. Taft focused on protecting American economic interests abroad.

Foreign Policy Under Wilson

24.2 What did Woodrow Wilson mean by "moral diplomacy"? p. 560

Wilson hoped to focus on domestic affairs but was soon involved in crises abroad. He first tried what he called "moral diplomacy," asking the United States and other countries to treat each other in a moral manner, especially in Europe and Mexico. In Mexico, he had praiseworthy aims but misjudged the country.

Toward War

24.3 What were the reasons behind and dangers of Wilson's neutrality policy? p. 561

With the outbreak of war in Europe in 1914, Wilson proclaimed neutrality, which was difficult to maintain. Neutrality, he hoped, would favor neither side and keep the United States out of war. Progressives knew that war would distract attention from reform. Submarine warfare offered new threats, which Wilson tried to control but could not. On April 6, 1917, the United States joined the war.

Over There

24.4 How did the United States' entry affect the course of World War I? p. 567

The United States entered the war at a crucial time for the Allies. American troops helped stop the last German offensive in 1918. Entry into the war gave the United States a stake in the peace treaty.

Over Here

24.5 What programs and changes did World War I bring at home? p. 571

American participation in World War I drew on many of the techniques of progressive reformers, including using people with expertise and exploiting bureaucracy. The War Industries Board oversaw the production of all American factories; the Food Administration Board looked after food for the armies overseas. The government played a larger role in American life than ever before.

The Treaty of Versailles

24.6 What mistakes did Wilson make in negotiating the Treaty of Versailles? p. 575

Wilson's Fourteen Points sought to reduce armaments, lower trade barriers, provide for self-determination, and establish a League of Nations to prevent further wars. He was forced to compromise at Versailles, but the Senate refused to ratify the peace treaty when he would not compromise on issues such as the League of Nations.

Timeline

1901
A New World Power—
Hay–Pauncefote Treaty with Britain empowers United States to build isthmian canal

1901

1904
A New World Power—
Theodore Roosevelt's corollary to Monroe Doctrine

1904

1914
Toward War—World War I begins

A New World Power—Panama Canal completed;

Wilson wins reelection

1914

1917
Toward War—Wilson calls for "peace without victory" (January);

Germany resumes unrestricted U-boat warfare (February);

United States enters World War I (April)

1917

1918
The Treaty of Versailles—Wilson outlines Fourteen Points (January); Armistice ends the war (November)

1918

1919
The Treaty of Versailles—Peace negotiations in Paris (January); Senate defeats Treaty of Versailles

1919

1920
The Treaty of Versailles—Warren G. Harding elected president

1920

25 Transition to Modern America 1919–1928

Wheels For The Millions

The **moving assembly line that** Henry Ford opened at Highland Park, Michigan, in 1913 to manufacture the Model T cars marked only the first step toward full mass production and the beginning of America's worldwide industrial supremacy. A year later, Ford began buying large plots of land along the Rouge River southeast of Detroit. He envisioned a vast industrial tract where machines, moving through a sequence of carefully arranged operations, would transform raw materials into finished cars, trucks, and tractors. The key would be control over the flow of goods at each step along the way—from lake steamers and railroad cars bringing in the coal and iron ore, to overhead conveyor belts and huge turning tables carrying the moving parts past the stationary workers on the assembly line. "Everything must move," Ford commanded, and by the mid-1920s at River Rouge, as the plant became known, it did.

Ford began fulfilling his industrial dream in 1919 when he built a blast furnace and foundry to make engine blocks for both the Model T and his tractors. By 1924, more than 40,000 workers were turning out

ASSEMBLY LINE On the assembly line at a Ford plant in Dearborn, Michigan, workers performed repetitive tasks on the car chassis that moved by at a rate of 6 feet per minute. (Source: Hulton Collection/Hulton Archive/Getty Images)

LEARNING OBJECTIVES

25.1 ((	25.2 ((	25.3 ((	25.4 ((
What was new about the American economy in the 1920s? p. 583	How did life in the cities change after World War I? p. 585	How did conservatives resist the changes of the decade? p. 589	How did the politics of the 1920s reflect changes in the economy and in American society? p. 596

 Listen to Chapter 25 on MyHistoryLab

From Chapter 25 of *American Stories: A History of the United States*, Third Edition. H. W. Brands, R. Hal Williams, T. H. Breen and Ariela J. Gross Copyright © 2015 by Pearson Education, Inc.

Watch the Video Series on MyHistoryLab

Learn about some key topics related to this chapter with the *MyHistoryLab Video Series: Key Topics in U.S. History*

1 **The Twenties: 1920–1928** The Roaring Twenties were a decade of great contrasts. Some Americans celebrated an era of new affluence and freedom, especially for women, and experienced the new writing of the Lost Generation and the Harlem Renaissance. Others dealt with the effects of Prohibition and a backlash against immigrants, liberals, and anyone perceived as un-American.

 Watch on **MyHistoryLab**

Women's Rights Following the Nineteenth Amendment, women continued to make advances and contributions to American society. This video profiles women in culture, medicine, politics, and especially in the workplace. Equal rights, however, continued to elude women in this decade. Many faced continued resistance and hostility, even on the part of other women who saw progress as having gone too far.

Watch on **MyHistoryLab**

2

3 **The Scopes Trial** With former presidential candidate William Jennings Bryan arguing for the prosecution and famous defense attorney Clarence Darrow for the school teacher–defendant, the Scopes trial pitted fundamentalists and modernists in a contest between the Bible and the science of evolution. This video examines the background, verdict, and aftermath of the court case that riveted the nation's attention during the summer of 1925.

 Watch on **MyHistoryLab**

The New Power of Advertising Much of the consumer culture we have today can be traced back to the revolution in advertising that took place during the Roaring Twenties. This video profiles the increasing power of advertising as businesses took advantage of new technologies such as radio, to reach consumers. It also covers the shift toward focusing on the self-image of the person buying the product rather than on the merits of the product itself.

Watch on **MyHistoryLab**

4

nearly all the metal parts used to make Ford vehicles. One tractor factory took just over 28 hours to convert raw ore into a new farm implement.

Visitors from all over the world marveled at River Rouge. Some were disturbed by the jumble of machines (by 1926, there were 43,000 in operation) and the apparent congestion on the plant floor, but industrial experts recognized that the arrangement led to incredible productivity because "the work moves and the men stand still." A trained engineer summed it up best when he wrote that a visitor to the plant "sees each unit as a carefully designed gear which meshes with other gears and operates in synchronism with them, the whole forming one huge, perfectly-timed, smoothly-operating industrial machine of almost unbelievable efficiency."

In May 1927, after producing more than 15 million Model Ts, Ford closed the assembly line at Highland Park. For the next six months, his engineers worked on a more compact and efficient assembly line at River Rouge for the Model A, which went into production in November. By then, River Rouge had more than justified Ford's vision. "Ford had brought together everything at a single site and on a scale no one else had ever attempted," concluded historian Geoffrey Perrett. "The Rouge plant became to a generation of engineers far more than a factory. It was a monument."

Mass production, born in Highland Park in 1913 and perfected at River Rouge in the 1920s, became the hallmark of American industry. Other carmakers copied Ford's methods, and soon his emphasis on the flow of parts moving past stationary workers became the standard in nearly every American factory. The moving assembly line—with its emphasis on uniformity, speed, precision, and coordination—took away the last vestiges of craftsmanship and turned workers into near robots. It led to amazing efficiency that produced both high profits for manufacturers and low prices for buyers. By the mid-1920s, the price of the Model T had dropped from $950 to $290.

Most important, mass production contributed to a consumer goods revolution. American factories turned out a flood of automobiles, electrical appliances, and other items that made life easier and more pleasant for most Americans. The result was the creation of a distinctively modern America, one marked by the material abundance that has characterized American society ever since.

But the abundance came at a price. The 1920s have been portrayed as a decade of escape and frivolity, and for many Americans they were just that. But those years also were an era of transition: a time when the old America of traditional rural values gave way to a new America of sometimes unsettling urban values. The transition was often wrenching, and many Americans clung desperately to the old ways. Modernity won, but not without a struggle.

The Second Industrial Revolution

25.1 What was new about the American economy in the 1920s?

The first Industrial Revolution in the late nineteenth century had catapulted the United States to the forefront among the world's richest and most developed nations. With the advent of the new consumer goods industries, the American people by the 1920s enjoyed the highest standard of living on earth. After a brief postwar depression, a great boom began in 1922, peaked in 1927, and lasted until 1929. In this brief period, American industrial output nearly doubled, and the gross national product rose by 40 percent. Most of this explosive growth took place in industries producing consumer goods—automobiles, appliances, furniture, and clothing. Equally important, the national per capita income increased by 30 percent to $681 in 1929. American workers became the highest paid in history. Combined with the expansion of installment credit that allowed customers to buy now and pay later, this income growth sparked a purchasing spree like nothing the nation had ever experienced.

The key to the new affluence lay in technology. The moving assembly line Ford pioneered became a standard feature in American plants. Electric motors replaced steam engines as the basic source of energy in factories; by 1929, electricity supplied 70 percent of industrial power. Efficiency experts used time and motion studies to break down the industrial process into minute parts, and then showed managers and workers how to maximize the output of their labor. Production per worker-hour increased an amazing 75 percent: In 1929, a workforce no larger than that of 1919 was producing almost twice as many goods.

The Automobile Industry

The automobile industry, which became the nation's largest in the 1920s, exemplifies the nature of the consumer goods revolution. Rapid growth was its hallmark. In 1920, the nation had 10 million cars; by 1929, 26 million were on the road. Production jumped from fewer than 2 million units a year to more than 5 million.

The automobile boom, at its peak from 1922 to 1927, depended on Americans' apparently insatiable appetite for cars. But the market became saturated as more and more of those who could afford the new luxury became car owners. Marketing became as crucial as production. Automobile makers began to rely heavily on advertising and annual model changes, seeking to make customers dissatisfied with their old vehicles and eager to order new ones. Despite these efforts, sales slumped in 1927 when Ford stopped making the Model T, picked up the next year with the new Model A, but began to slide again in 1929. The new industry revealed a basic weakness in the consumer goods economy; once people had bought an item with a long life—what economists call a durable good—they would not buy another one for a few years. The consumer revolution also bypassed much of rural America, where farmers struggled against falling prices.

Amid the urban affluence, few noticed the underlying problems. Instead, contemporary observers focused on how the automobile stimulated the rest of the economy. The mass production of cars required huge quantities of steel; new rolling mills had to be built to supply sheet steel for car bodies. Rubber factories boomed with the demand for tires, and paint and glass suppliers had more business than ever before. The auto changed the pattern of city life, leading to a suburban explosion. Real estate developers, no longer dependent on streetcars and railway lines, could now build houses in ever wider concentric circles around the central cities.

The automobile affected all aspects of American life in the 1920s. Filling stations replaced smithies and stables on the main streets. In Kansas City, Missouri, Jess D. Nichols built the first shopping center, Country Club Plaza, and set an example other suburban developers quickly followed.

Even in smaller communities, the car ruled. In Muncie, Indiana, site of a famous sociological survey in the 1920s, one elder replied when asked what was taking place, "I can tell you what's happening in just four letters: A-U-T-O!" A nation that had always revered symbols of movement, from the *Mayflower* to the covered wagon, now had a new icon to worship.

Quick Check

How did the auto industry drive the rest of the economy?

Patterns of Economic Growth

Automobiles were the most conspicuous of the consumer products that flourished in the 1920s, but certainly not the only ones. The electrical industry grew almost as quickly. Central power stations, where massive steam generators converted coal into electricity, brought current into the homes of city and town dwellers. Two-thirds of all American families enjoyed electricity by 1929, and they spent vast sums on washing machines, vacuum cleaners, refrigerators, and ranges. The new appliances made housework easier and ushered in an age of leisure.

NEW YORK CITY Howard Thain's painting, *The Great White Way—Times Square*, captures the bright lights and excitement of New York's entertainment center in the Roaring Twenties. (Source: Collection of The New York Historical Society, accession number 1963.150)

Radio broadcasting and motion picture production also boomed. The early success of KDKA in Pittsburgh stimulated the growth of more than 800 independent radio stations, and by 1929, NBC had formed the first successful radio network. Five nights a week, *Amos 'n' Andy*, a comic serial featuring two "blackface" white vaudevillians, held the attention of millions of Americans. The film industry thrived in Hollywood, reaching its maturity in the mid-1920s when every large city had huge theaters seating as many as 4,000 people. With the advent of the "talkies" by 1929, average weekly movie attendance climbed to nearly 100 million.

Other industries also prospered. Production of light metals such as aluminum and magnesium became a major business. Chemical engineering came of age with the invention of synthetics, ranging from rayon for clothing to cellophane for packaging. Americans found a new spectrum of products to buy—cigarette lighters, wristwatches, heat-resistant glass cooking dishes, and rayon stockings, to name a few.

The most distinctive feature of the new consumer-oriented economy was the emphasis on marketing. Advertising earnings rose from $1.3 billion in 1915 to $3.4 billion in 1926. Skillful practitioners such as Edward Bernays and Bruce Barton sought to control public taste and consumer spending by identifying the good life with the possession of the latest product of American industry, whether it was a car, a refrigerator, or a brand of cigarettes. Chain stores advanced rapidly at the expense of small retail shops. A&P dominated the retail food industry, growing from 400 stores in 1912 to 15,500 by 1932. Woolworth's "five-and-tens" spread almost as rapidly, while such drugstore chains as Rexall and Liggetts—both owned by one huge holding company—opened outlets in nearly every town and city.

Uniformity and standardization, the characteristics of mass production, now prevailed. The farmer in Kansas bought the same kind of car, the same groceries, and the same pills as the factory worker in Pennsylvania. Sectional differences in dress, food, and furniture began to disappear. Even regional accents were threatened with extinction by the advent of radio and films, which promoted a standard national dialect devoid of local flavor.

Despite all these changes, the New Era, as business leaders labeled the decade, was less prosperous than it appeared. The revolution in consumer goods disguised the decline of many traditional industries in the 1920s. Hardest hit of all was agriculture. By 1921, farm exports had fallen by more than $2 billion. In addition, during the decade, factory wages rose only a modest 11 percent; in 1929, nearly half of American families earned less than $1,500 a year. Organized labor proved unable to advance the interests of workers, and union membership fell. In fact, middle- and upper-class Americans were the only groups who thrived in the 1920s. The rewards of this second Industrial Revolution went to the managers—the engineers, bankers, and executives—who directed it. All these factors contributed to economic instability. The boom of the 1920s would end in a great crash.

Quick Check

What other industries contributed to the boom of the 1920s?

City Life in the Roaring Twenties

25.2   How did life in the cities change after World War I?

The city replaced the countryside as the focal point of American life in the 1920s. The 1920 census revealed that for the first time, slightly more than half of the population lived in cities (defined broadly to include all places of more than 2,500 people). During the decade, the metropolitan areas grew rapidly as both rural whites and blacks migrated to find jobs in the new consumer industries. Between 1920 and 1930, cities with populations of 250,000 or more added some 8 million people to their ranks. New York City grew by nearly 25 percent, while Detroit's population more than doubled.

In the cities, life was different. The old community ties of home, church, and school were absent, but important gains replaced them—new ideas, new creativity, new perspectives. Some city dwellers became lost and lonely without the old institutions; others thrived.

Women and the Family

The urban culture of the 1920s witnessed important changes in the American family. This vital institution began to break down under the impact of economic and social change. A new freedom for women and children seemed to be emerging in its wake.

Although World War I accelerated the process by which women left the home for work, the postwar decade witnessed a return to the slower pace of the prewar years. During the 1920s the percentage of working women barely changed. Two million more women were employed in 1930 than in 1920, but this represented an increase of only 1 percent. Most women workers, moreover, had low-paying jobs, ranging from stenographers to maids. The number of women doctors actually decreased, and even though women earned nearly one-third of all graduate degrees, only 4 percent of full professors were female. For the most part, men monopolized the professions, with women relegated to such fields as teaching and nursing.

Women had won the right to vote in 1920, but the Nineteenth Amendment had less impact than its proponents had hoped. Adoption of the amendment robbed women of a unifying cause, and the exercise of the franchise itself did little to change sex roles. Men remained the principal breadwinners in the family; women cooked, cleaned, and reared the children. "The creation and fulfillment of a successful home," a *Ladies Home Journal* writer advised women, "is a bit of craftsmanship that compares favorably with building a beautiful cathedral."

The feminist movement, however, still showed signs of vitality. Social feminists pushing for humanitarian reform won enactment of the Sheppard–Towner Act of 1921, which provided for federal aid to establish state programs for maternal and infant health care. Although the failure to enact the child labor amendment in 1925 marked the beginning of a decline in humanitarian reform, for the rest of the decade, women's groups worked for good-government measures, the inclusion of women on juries, and consumer legislation.

Other women looked beyond politics to express themselves. In the larger cities, some quickly adopted what critic H. L. Mencken called the flapper image, portrayed most strikingly by artist John Held, Jr. Cutting their hair short, raising their skirts above the knee, and binding their breasts, "flappers" set out to compete on equal terms with men on the golf course and in the speakeasy. Young women delighted in shocking their elders—they rouged their cheeks and danced the Charleston. Women smoked cigarettes and drank alcohol in public more freely than before. The flappers assaulted the traditional double standard, demanding that equality with men should include sexual fulfillment before and during marriage. New and more liberal laws doubled the divorce rate; by 1928, there were 166 divorces for every 1,000 marriages, compared to only 81 in 1900.

The family also changed in other ways. The average family became smaller as easier access to effective birth control methods enabled couples to limit the number of their offspring. More married women took jobs outside the home, bringing in income and gaining a measure of independence (although their pay was always lower than men's). Young people, who had once joined the labor force in their teens, now discovered adolescence as a stage of life. A high school education was no longer uncommon, and college attendance increased.

Prolonged adolescence led to new strains on the family in the form of youthful revolt. Freed of the burden of earning a living at an early age, youths went on a spree. Heavy drinking, casual sex, and a constant search for excitement became the hallmarks of the upper-class youth F. Scott Fitzgerald immortalized. "I have been kissed

Read the Document   Margaret Sanger, Family Planning (1926)

NATIONAL WOMAN'S PARTY After passage of the Nineteenth Amendment, activist Alice Paul and the National Woman's Party continued to fight for women's equality. Here, as women stand and cheer, Paul stands on a balcony at the National Woman's Party headquarters and unfurls a banner in celebration of the state of Tennessee's ratification of the Nineteenth Amendment.

by dozens of men," one of his characters commented. "I suppose I'll kiss dozens more." The theme of rebellion against parental authority, which ran through all aspects of the 1920s, was at the heart of the youth movement.

Quick Check

How did women's lives change during the 1920s?

Popular Culture in the Jazz Age

Excitement ran high in the cities as both crime waves and highly publicized sports events flourished. Prohibition ushered in such distinctive features of the decade as speakeasies, bootleggers, and bathtub gin. Crime rose sharply as middle- and upper-class Americans broke the law to gain access to alcoholic beverages. City streets became the scene of violent shootouts between rival bootleggers; by 1929, Chicago had witnessed more than 500 gangland murders. Underworld czars controlled illicit empires; Al Capone's empire produced revenue of $60 million a year.

Sports became a national mania as people found more leisure time. Golf boomed, with some 2 million men and women playing on nearly 5,000 courses. Spectator sports attracted even more attention. Boxing drew huge crowds to see fighters such as Jack Dempsey and Gene Tunney. Baseball attendance soared. More than 20 million fans attended games in 1927, the year Babe Ruth became a national idol by hitting 60 home runs. On college campuses, football became more popular than ever. Universities vied to build massive stadiums, seating upward of 70,000 people.

The arts also flourished. Authors Ernest Hemingway, F. Scott Fitzgerald, John Dos Passos, and Sinclair Lewis chronicled the experience of the post–World War I

Read the Document Eleanor Rowland Wembridge, "Petting and the Campus" (1925)

THE JAZZ AGE New dances were introduced on the dance floors of ballrooms and clubs in the 1920s jazz era. One of the most popular new dances was the Charleston—a dance associated with the rebellious image of the flapper. Here, two daring flappers dance the Charleston on the roof of Chicago's Hotel Sherman in 1926.

Harlem Renaissance An African American cultural, literary, and artistic movement centered in Harlem, in New York City, in the 1920s. Harlem, the largest black community in the world outside of Africa, was considered the cultural capital of African Americans.

generation. In New York City, the **Harlem Renaissance**—an outpouring of African American literature, theater, visual arts, and music, especially jazz—made Manhattan seem the most exciting place on earth.

In what Frederick Lewis Allen called "the ballyhoo years," the popular yearning for release led people to seek vicarious thrills in all kinds of ways—applauding Charles Lindbergh's solo flight across the Atlantic, cheering Gertrude Ederle's swim across the English Channel, and flocking to such bizarre events as six-day bicycle races, dance marathons, and flagpole sittings. It was a time of pure pleasure-seeking, when people sought to escape from the increasingly drab world of the assembly line by worshiping heroes.

Sex became a popular topic as Victorian standards crumbled. Sophisticated city dwellers seemed to be intent on exploring a new freedom in sexual expression. Plays and novels focused on adultery, and the new urban tabloids—led by the *New York Daily News*—delighted in telling their readers about love nests and kept women. The popular songs of the decade, such as "Hot Lips" and "Burning Kisses," were less romantic and more explicit than those of years before. Hollywood exploited the obsession with sex by producing movies with such provocative titles as *Up in Mabel's Room*, *A Shocking Night*, and *Women and Lovers*. Theda Bara and Clara Bow, the "vamp" and the "It" girl, set the model for feminine seductiveness, while the actor Rudolph Valentino became the heartthrob of millions of American women. Young people embraced the new permissiveness, with the automobile giving couples an easy way to escape parental supervision.

25.1

25.2

25.3

25.4

Quick Check

What did people do with their spare time during the decade?

The Conservative Counterattack

25.3 How did conservatives resist the changes of the decade?

The shift of population from the countryside to the city heightened social tensions. Intent on preserving traditional values, rural Americans saw in the city all that was evil in contemporary life. Saloons, whorehouses, little Italys and little Polands, communist cells, free love, and atheism—all were identified with the city. Accordingly, the countryside struck back, aiming to restore the primacy of the Anglo-Saxon and predominantly Protestant culture it revered. This counterattack won considerable support in the cities from those who were recently uprooted from their rural backgrounds.

Other factors intensified the counterattack. The war had unleashed a nationalistic spirit that craved unity and conformity. In a nation where one-third of the people were foreign born, the attack on immigrants and the call for 100-percent Americanism took

HARLEM RENAISSANCE Archibald Motley, *Barbecue*. Motley, one of the artists of the Harlem Renaissance, combined the traditions of his native New Orleans with the energy and rhythms of 1920s Harlem.

on a frightening zeal. When the war was over, groups such as the American Legion tried to root out "un-American" behavior and insisted on cultural and political conformity. The prewar progressive reform spirit added to the social tension. Stripped of much of its idealism, progressivism focused on such social problems as drinking and illiteracy to justify repressive measures such as prohibition and immigration restriction. The result was tragic. Amid the emergence of a new urban culture, the movements that aimed to preserve the values of an earlier America only complicated an already difficult period of cultural transition.

The Fear of Radicalism

Red Scare A wave of anticommunist, antiforeign, and antilabor hysteria that swept over America in 1919. It resulted in the deportation of many alien residents and violated the civil liberties of many of its victims.

The first and most intense outbreak of national alarm, an anti-radical hysteria known as the **Red Scare**, came in 1919. The heightened nationalism of World War I, which aimed to achieve unity at the expense of ethnic diversity, found a new target in communism. The Russian Revolution of 1917 and the triumph of Marxism frightened many Americans. A growing turn to communism among American radicals (especially the foreign born) heightened these fears. Although their numbers were tiny—at most there were 60,000 communists in the United States in 1919—some communists were highly visible in the cities. Labor unrest seemed to magnify their influence.

A general strike in Seattle, a police strike in Boston, and a violent strike in the iron and steel industry alarmed Americans in the spring and summer of 1919. A series of bombings led to panic. First the mayor of strikebound Seattle received a small brown package containing a homemade bomb; then an alert New York postal employee detected 16 bombs addressed to famous citizens (including John D. Rockefeller); and finally, on June 2, a bomb shattered the front of Attorney General A. Mitchell Palmer's home. Although the man who delivered it was blown to pieces, authorities quickly identified him as an Italian anarchist from Philadelphia.

In the ensuing outcry, Palmer led the attack on the alien threat. A Quaker and a progressive, Palmer abandoned his earlier liberalism to launch a massive roundup of foreign-born radicals. In raids that began on November 7, federal agents seized suspected anarchists and communists and held them for deportation with no regard for due process of law. In December, 249 aliens—including such well-known radical leaders as Emma Goldman and Alexander Berkman—were sent to Russia aboard the *Buford*, dubbed the "Soviet Ark" by the press. Nearly all were innocent of the charges against them. A month later, Palmer rounded up nearly 4,000 suspected communists in one evening. Federal agents broke into homes, meeting halls, and union offices without search warrants. Many native-born Americans were caught in the dragnet and spent days in jail before being released; aliens were deported without hearings or trials.

For a time, the Red Scare seemed to reflect the views of the American people. Instead of condemning their government's action, citizens voiced their approval and urged more drastic steps. One patriot said his solution to the alien problem was simple: "S.O.S.—ship or shoot." General Leonard Wood, the former army chief of staff, favored placing Bolsheviks on "ships of stone with sails of lead," while evangelist Billy Sunday preferred to take "these ornery, wild-eyed Socialists" and "stand them up before a firing squad and save space on our ships." Inflamed by such public statements, legionnaires in Centralia, Washington, dragged a radical from the town jail, castrated him, and hanged him from a railway bridge. The coroner's report blandly stated that the victim "jumped off with a rope around his neck and then shot himself full of holes."

The very extremism of the Red Scare led to its rapid demise. In early 1920, courageous officials from the Department of Labor insisted on due process and full hearings before anyone else was deported. Prominent leaders spoke out against the acts of terror. Charles Evans Hughes, the defeated GOP candidate for president in 1916, offered

((• 📖 Read the Document   A. Mitchell Palmer, The Menace of Communism (1920)

A. MITCHELL PALMER United States Attorney General A. Mitchell Palmer organized and implemented law enforcement raids against suspected communists and other radicals in 1919 and 1920. The Palmer raids, part of a nationwide Red Scare, involved the arrest of over 3,000 persons and the deportation of nearly 500 resident aliens.

to defend six socialists expelled from the New York legislature; Ohio Senator Warren G. Harding, the embodiment of middle-class values, declared that "too much has been said about bolshevism in America." Finally, Palmer himself, with evident presidential ambition, went too far. In April 1920, he warned of a revolution to occur on May 1; the entire New York City police force, 11,000 strong, was placed on duty to prepare for imminent disaster. When no bombings or violence took place on May Day, the public began to react against Palmer's hysteria. Despite an explosion on Wall Street in September that killed 33 people, the Red Scare died out by the end of 1920. Palmer passed into obscurity, factionalism splintered the tiny Communist party, and the American people tried to forget their loss of balance.

Yet the Red Scare exerted a continuing influence on American society in the 1920s. The foreign born knew that they were viewed with hostility and suspicion. Two Italian aliens in Massachusetts, Nicola Sacco and Bartolomeo Vanzetti, were arrested in May 1920 for a payroll robbery and murder. The prosecutor and jury condemned them more for their radical ideas than for any evidence of criminal conduct, and the judge referred to them as "those anarchist bastards." Despite a worldwide effort that became the chief liberal cause of the 1920s, the courts rejected all appeals. Sacco, a shoemaker,

Quick Check

What was the "Red Scare"?

prohibition The ban on the manufacture, sale, and transportation of alcoholic beverages in the United States. The Eighteenth Amendment, adopted in 1919, established prohibition. It was repealed by the Twenty-First Amendment in 1933.

and Vanzetti, a fish peddler, were electrocuted on August 23, 1927. Their fate symbolized the bigotry and intolerance that made the 1920s one of the least attractive decades in American history.

Prohibition

In December 1917, Congress passed the Eighteenth Amendment, prohibiting the manufacture and sale of alcoholic beverages, and then sent the amendment to the states for ratification. In January 1919, Nebraska became the necessary thirty-sixth state to ratify it, and **prohibition** became the law of the land.

Effective January 16, 1920, the Volstead Act, which implemented prohibition, banned most commercial production and distribution of beverages containing more than one-half of 1 percent of alcohol by volume. (Exceptions were made for medicinal and religious uses of wine and spirits. Production for one's private use was also allowed.) Prohibition was the result of both a rural effort of the Anti-Saloon League, backed by Methodist and Baptist clergymen, and the urban progressive concern over the social disease of drunkenness, especially among industrial workers. The moral issue had already led to the enactment of prohibition laws in 26 states by 1920; the effort to extend this "noble experiment" to the cities, where ethnic groups such as the Germans and Irish resented it and the well-to-do and sophisticated almost totally ignored it, was a tragedy.

Drinking did decline under prohibition. Americans consumed much less alcohol in the 1920s than in the prewar years. Rural areas became almost totally dry, and in the cities, the consumption of alcoholic beverages dropped sharply among the lower classes, who could not afford the high prices for bootleg liquor. Among the middle class and the wealthy, however, drinking became fashionable. Bootleggers supplied whiskey, which quickly replaced lighter drinks such as wine and beer. The alcohol was either smuggled from abroad (a $40-million-a-year business by 1924) or illicitly manufactured in America. Exotic products such as Jackass Brandy, Soda Pop Moon, and Yack Yack Bourbon were common—and could be fatal. Despite the risk of illness or death from extraordinarily high alcohol content or poor distillation, Americans consumed some 150 million quarts of liquor a year in the 1920s. Bootleggers took in nearly $2 billion annually, about 2 percent of the gross national product.

Urban resistance to prohibition finally led to its repeal in 1933. But in the intervening years, it bred a profound disrespect for the law. The flamboyant excesses of bootleggers were only the more obvious evils prohibition spawned. In city after city, police openly tolerated the traffic in liquor, and judges and prosecutors let bootleggers pay merely token fines, creating almost a system of licenses. Prohibition satisfied the countryside's desire for vindication, yet rural and urban America alike suffered from this overzealous attempt to legislate morals.

The Ku Klux Klan

The most ominous expression of protest against the new urban culture was the rebirth of the Ku Klux Klan. On Thanksgiving night in 1915, on Stone Mountain in Georgia, Colonel William J. Simmons and 34 followers founded the modern Klan. Only "native born, white, gentile Americans" could join "the Invisible Empire, Knights of the Ku Klux Klan." Membership grew slowly during World War I, but after 1920, fueled by postwar fears and shrewd promotional techniques, the Klan mushroomed. In villages, towns, and small cities across the nation, Anglo-Saxon Protestant men flocked into the Klan's new chapters, seeking to relieve their anxiety over a changing society by embracing the Klan's rituals and demonstrating their hatred of blacks, aliens, Jews, and Catholics.

The Klan of the 1920s, unlike the night riders of the post–Civil War era, was not just anti-black; the threat to American culture, as Klansmen perceived it, also came

Quick Check

How effective was prohibition?

THE KU KLUX KLAN A 1925 Ku Klux Klan demonstration in Cincinnati, Ohio, attended by nearly 30,000 robed members and marked by the induction of 8,000 young boys in the Junior Order. The original Klan, formed during the Reconstruction era to terrorize former slaves, disbanded in 1869. The Klan that formed in 1915 declined after the mid-1920s but did not officially disband until 1944.

from aliens—Italians and Russians, Jews and Catholics. They attributed much of the tension and conflict in society to the prewar flood of immigrants, foreigners who spoke different languages, worshiped in strange churches, and lived in distant, threatening cities. The Klansmen struck back by coming together and enforcing their own values. They punished blacks who did not know their place, women who practiced the new morality, and aliens who refused to conform. Beating, flogging, burning with acid— even murder—were condoned. They also tried more peaceful coercion, formulating codes of behavior and seeking communitywide support.

The Klan entered politics, at first hesitantly, then with growing confidence. The KKK gained control of the legislatures in Texas, Oklahoma, Oregon, and Indiana; in 1924, it blocked a resolution of censure at the Democratic national convention. With an estimated 5 million members by the mid-1920s, the Klan seemed to be fully established.

Its appeal lay in the sanctuary it offered to insecure and anxious people. Protestant to the core, the members found in the local Klavern a reassurance missing in their churches. The poor and ignorant became enchanted with the titles, ranging from Imperial Wizard to Grand Dragon, and gloried in the ritual that centered around the letter K: Each Klan had its own "Klalendar," held its weekly "Klonklave" in the local "Klavern," and followed the rules set forth in the Kloran. Members found a sense of identity in the group activities, whether they were peaceful picnics, ominous parades in white robes, or fiery cross burnings at night.

Although it was a men's organization, the Klan did not neglect the family. There was a Women's Order, a Junior Order for boys, and a Tri-K Klub for girls. Members had to be born in America, but foreign-born Protestants could join a special Krusaders

✳ Explore Racial Violence in the United States, 1880–1930, on MyHistoryLab

WHAT WAS THE RELATIONSHIP BETWEEN RACIAL INEQUALITY AND VIOLENCE IN THE SOUTH DURING THE EARLY 1900s?

Though slaves were freed by the Thirteenth Amendment, the promises of equality offered to African Americans during Reconstruction under the Fourteenth and Fifteenth Amendments did not last long or went unfulfilled. White southerners worked to ensure that African Americans remained subordinate in the South. This system of discrimination used in part legal loopholes to disenfranchise African Americans, though outright violence was also employed to maintain white control. Some white southerners used lynching against African Americans who threatened the status quo. Victims were generally accused of some—often exaggerated—crime and subsequently hanged without a

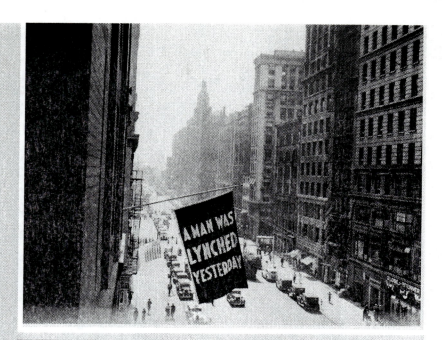

A GRIM REMINDER This flag was flown from the New York City headquarters of the NAACP whenever an African American had been lynched—summary execution without trial—in the South.

SOURCE: Everett Collection Inc./Alamy

trial. Lynching became a tool to maintain the social, political, and economic dominance of white southerners over African-American communities.

TOTAL LYNCHINGS IN SELECTED STATES, 1900–1931

State	Total
Alabama	132
Arkansas	127
Florida	170
Georgia	302
Louisiana	172
Mississippi	285
Texas	201

SOURCE: Lynchings by States and Counties in the United States 1900 to 1931, Research Department, Tuskegee Institute, http://memory.loc.gov/.

KEY QUESTIONS Use **MyHistoryLab** *Explorer* to **answer** these **questions:**

Analysis ▶▶▶ *In what regions of the South were lynchings most common?*

Consider the reasons behind such patterns.

Consequence ▶▶▶ *How did white literacy rates correspond to the frequency of lynchings in particular areas?*

Explore the relationship between these two elements.

Response ▶▶▶ *How did local economic patterns affect the prevalence of lynchings?*

Consider connections between land ownership and violence against African Americans.

affiliate. Only blacks, Catholics, Jews, and prostitutes were beyond redemption to these lonely and anxious men who chanted:

United we stick
Divided we're stuck.
The better we stick
The better we Klux!

The Klan fell even more quickly than it rose. Its more violent activities—which included kidnapping, lynching, burning synagogues and Catholic churches, and murdering a priest—began to offend the nation's conscience. Misuse of funds and sexual scandals among Klan leaders, notably in Indiana, repelled many of the rank and file; counterattacks by traditional politicians ousted the KKK from control in Texas and Oklahoma. Membership declined sharply after 1925; by 1929, the Klan had virtually disappeared. But its spirit lived on, testimony to the recurring demons of nativism and hatred that have surfaced periodically throughout the American experience.

Quick Check
What groups did the Ku Klux Klan persecute during the 1920s?

Immigration Restriction

The **nativism**, or hostility to things foreign, that permeated the Klan found its most successful outlet in the immigration legislation of the 1920s. The sharp increase in immigration in the late nineteenth century had led to a broad-based movement, spearheaded by organized labor and New England aristocrats such as Henry Cabot Lodge, to restrict the flow of people from Europe. In 1917, over President Wilson's veto, Congress enacted a literacy test that reduced the number of immigrants allowed into the country. The war caused a much more drastic decline—from an average of 1 million a year between 1900 and 1914 to only 110,000 in 1918.

After the armistice, however, rumors spread of a flood of people seeking to escape war-ravaged Europe. Kenneth Roberts, a popular historical novelist, warned that all Europe was on the move, with only the limits of steamship space likely to stem the flow. Worried congressmen spoke of a "barbarian horde" and a "foreign tide" that would inundate the United States with "dangerous and deadly enemies of the country." Even though the actual number of immigrants, 810,000 in 1920 (fewer than the prewar yearly average), did not match these projections, Congress in 1921 passed an emergency immigration act, which restricted immigration from Europe to 3 percent of the number of nationals from each country living in the United States in 1910.

The nativists were not satisfied. The quotas still permitted more than 500,000 Europeans to come to the United States in 1923, nearly half of them from southern and eastern Europe. The declining percentage of Nordic immigrants alarmed writers such as Madison Grant, who warned the American people that lesser breeds with inferior genes were about to overwhelm the Anglo-Saxon stock that had founded the nation: "These immigrants adopt the language of the native American, they wear his clothes and are beginning to take his women, but they seldom adopt his religion or understand his ideals."

Psychologists, relying on primitive IQ tests the army had used in World War I, confirmed this judgment. One senator claimed that all the nation's ills were due to an "intermingled and mongrelized people" as he demanded that racial purity replace the older reliance on the melting pot. In 1924, the **National Origins Quota Act** limited immigration from Europe to 150,000 a year; allocated most of the available slots to Great Britain, Ireland, Germany, and Scandinavia; and banned Asian immigrants. The measure passed Congress with overwhelming rural support.

The new restrictive legislation marked the most enduring achievement of the rural counterattack. Unlike the Red Scare, prohibition, and the Klan, the quota system would survive until the 1960s, enforcing a racist bias that excluded Asians and limited the

nativism Hostility to things foreign.

National Origins Quota Act
This 1924 law established a quota system that restricted immigration from Asia and southern and Eastern Europe and reduced the annual total of immigrants.

Quick Check

What was the National Origins Quota Act?

immigration of Italians, Greeks, and Poles to a few thousand a year while permitting a steady stream of Irish, English, and Scandinavian immigrants. Large corporations, no longer dependent on armies of unskilled immigrant workers, did not object to the 1924 law; the machine had replaced the immigrant on the assembly line. Yet the victory was incomplete. A growing tide of Mexican laborers, exempt from the quota act, flowed across the Rio Grande to fill the continuing need for unskilled workers on farms and in the service trades. Mexican immigrants, as many as 100,000 a year, strengthened an element in the national ethnic mosaic that would grow until it became a major force in American society.

The Fundamentalist Challenge

Another significant—and the longest-lasting—challenge to the new urban culture was rooted in the traditional religious beliefs of millions of Americans who felt alienated from city life, science, and much of what modernization entailed. Sometimes this challenge was direct, as when Christian fundamentalists campaigned against teaching evolution in the public schools. Their success in Tennessee touched off a court battle, the **Scopes trial**, that drew the attention of the entire country to the small town of Dayton in the summer of 1925, when a high school biology teacher was prosecuted for teaching evolution. The trial court convicted John Scopes, affirming the fundamentalist view, but the spectacle drew the derision of many Americans who saw nothing threatening about Darwin's theory.

Scopes Trial Also called the "monkey trial," the 1924 Scopes trial was a contest between modern liberalism and religious fundamentalism. John T. Scopes was prosecuted for teaching Darwinian evolution in defiance of Tennessee state law. He was found guilty and fined $100. Scopes's conviction was later set aside on a technicality.

Other aspects of the fundamentalist challenge were more subtle but no less important in countering the modernizing trend. As middle- and upper-class Americans drifted into a genteel Christianity that stressed good works and respectability, the Baptist and Methodist churches clung to the old faith. Aggressive fundamentalist sects such as the Churches of Christ, the Pentecostals, and Jehovah's Witnesses grew rapidly. While church membership increased from 41.9 million in 1916 to 54.5 million in 1926, the number of churches actually declined during the decade. More and more rural dwellers drove their cars into town on Sundays instead of attending the local crossroads chapel.

Many of those who came to the city in the 1920s brought their religious beliefs with them and found new outlets for them. Thus, evangelist Aimee Semple McPherson enjoyed amazing success in Los Angeles with her Church of the Four-Square Gospel, building the Angelus Temple to seat more than 5,000 worshipers. And in Fort Worth, the Reverend J. Frank Norris erected a 6,000-seat sanctuary for the First Baptist Church, bathing it in spotlights so it could be seen for 39 miles across the North Texas prairie.

Far from dying out, as divinity professor Thomas G. Oden noted, biblical fundamentalism retained "remarkable grassroots strength among the organization men and the industrialized mass society of the 20th century." The rural counterattack, while challenged by the city, enabled older American values to survive amidst the new mass production culture.

Quick Check

How did the Scopes trial reflect the strength of conservative religious thought?

Republican Politics

25.4 How did the politics of the 1920s reflect changes in the economy and in American society?

The tensions between city and countryside also shaped politics in the 1920s. On the whole, it was a Republican decade. The GOP ("Grand Old Party") controlled the White House from 1921 to 1933 and had majorities in both houses of Congress from 1919 to 1931. The Republicans used their return to power after World War I to halt further reform legislation and establish a friendly relationship between government and business.

Harding, Coolidge, and Hoover

The Republicans regained the White House in 1920 with the election of Warren G. Harding of Ohio. Harding won the nomination when he became the compromise choice after the convention deadlocked. Handsome and dignified, Harding reflected both the virtues and the blemishes of small-town America. Originally a newspaper publisher in Marion, he had made many friends and few enemies throughout his career as a legislator, lieutenant governor, and finally, after 1914, U.S. senator. Conventional in outlook, Harding was a genial man who lacked the capacity to govern and who, as president, broadly delegated power.

He made some good cabinet choices, notably Charles Evans Hughes as secretary of state and Herbert C. Hoover as secretary of commerce, but two corrupt officials—Attorney General Harry Daugherty and Secretary of the Interior Albert Fall—sabotaged his administration. Daugherty became involved in questionable deals that led to his forced resignation; Fall was the chief figure in the **Teapot Dome scandal**. In return for nearly $400,000 in loans and bribes, Fall helped two oil promoters secure leases on naval oil reserves in Elk Hills, California, and Teapot Dome, Wyoming. The scandal came to light after Harding's death from a heart attack in

Teapot Dome scandal A 1924 scandal in which Secretary of the Interior Albert Fall was convicted of accepting bribes in exchange for leasing government-owned oil lands in Wyoming (Teapot Dome) and California (Elks Hill) to private businessmen.

Read the Document Executive Orders and Senate Resolutions on Teapot Dome (1920)

SCANDAL During the administration of William H. Taft, the U.S. government had set aside tracts of oil-rich land to be held in reserve for the U.S. Navy, to be used in case of national emergency. The land was under the control and discretion of the secretary of the Navy.

1923. Fall served a year in jail, and the reputation of the Harding administration never recovered.

Vice President Calvin Coolidge assumed the presidency upon Harding's death, and his honesty and integrity reassured the nation. Coolidge, born in Vermont of old Yankee stock, had gained national attention in 1919 as governor of Massachusetts when he had dealt firmly with a Boston police strike by declaring, "There is no right to strike against the public safety by anybody, anywhere, any time." A reserved, reticent man, Coolidge became famous for his epigrams, which contemporaries mistook for wisdom. "The business of America is business," he proclaimed. "The man who builds a factory builds a temple; the man who works there worships there." He believed his duty was to preside benignly over, not govern, the nation. "Four-fifths of all our troubles in this life would disappear," he said, "if we would just sit down and be still." Calvin Coolidge, one observer noted, "aspired to become the least President the country ever had; he attained his desire." Satisfied with the prosperity of the mid-1920s, the people reelected Coolidge to a full term by a wide margin in 1924.

When Coolidge announced in 1927 that he did not "choose to run" again, Herbert Hoover became the Republican choice to succeed him. The ablest GOP leader of the decade, Hoover epitomized the American myth of the self-made man. Orphaned as a boy, he had worked his way through Stanford University and had gained wealth and fame as a mining engineer. During World War I, he had displayed administrative skills in directing Wilson's food program at home and relief activities abroad. Sober, intelligent, and hardworking, Hoover embodied the nation's faith in individualism and free enterprise.

As secretary of commerce under Harding and Coolidge, Hoover had sought cooperation between government and business. He helped American manufacturers and exporters expand their overseas trade and supported a trade association movement to encourage cooperation rather than cutthroat competition among smaller American companies. He saw business and government not as antagonists, but as partners, working together to achieve efficiency and affluence for all Americans. His optimistic view of the future led him to declare in his speech accepting the Republican presidential nomination in 1928 that "we in America today are nearer to the final triumph over poverty than ever before in the history of any land."

Quick Check

Who were the Republican presidents of the 1920s?

A New Kind of Conservatism

During the 1920 campaign, Harding urged a return to "not heroism, but healing, not nostrums, but normalcy." Misreading his speechwriter's "normality," he coined a new word that became the theme for the Republican administrations of the 1920s. Aware that the public was tired of zealous, reform-minded presidents such as Teddy Roosevelt and Woodrow Wilson, Harding and his successors sought a return to traditional Republican policies. In some areas they were successful, but in others the Republican leaders had to adjust to the new realities of a mass production society. The result was a mixture of traditional and innovative measures that was neither wholly reactionary nor entirely progressive.

The most obvious attempt to go back to the Republicanism of William McKinley came in tariff and tax policy. Fearful of a flood of postwar European imports, Congress passed an emergency tariff act in 1921 and followed it a year later with the protectionist Fordney–McCumber Tariff Act. The net effect was to raise the basic rates substantially over the moderate Underwood Tariff schedules of the Wilson period.

Secretary of the Treasury Andrew Mellon, a wealthy Pittsburgh banker and industrialist, worked hard to achieve a similar return to normalcy in taxation. Condemning the high wartime tax rates on businesses and wealthy individuals, Mellon pressed for repealing an excess profits tax on corporations and slashing personal rates on the rich. Using the new budget system Congress adopted in 1921, he reduced government spending from its World War I peak of $18 billion to just over $3 billion by 1925, creating a slight surplus. Congress responded in 1926 by cutting the highest income tax bracket to a modest 20 percent.

The revenue acts of the 1920s greatly reduced the burden of taxation; by 1929, the government was collecting one-third less than it had in 1921, and the number of people paying income taxes dropped from more than 6.5 million to 4 million. Yet the greatest relief went to the wealthy. The public was shocked to learn in the 1930s that J. P. Morgan, Jr. and his 19 partners had paid no income tax at all during the depths of the Great Depression.

The growing crisis in American farming during the decade forced the Republican administrations to seek new solutions. The end of the European war led to a sharp decline in farm prices and a return to overproduction. Southern and western lawmakers formed a farm bloc in Congress to press for special legislation for American agriculture. The farm bloc supported the higher tariffs, which included protection for constituents' crops, and helped pass legislation to create federal supervision over stockyards, packinghouses, and grain trading.

This special-interest legislation failed to get at the root of overproduction, however. Farmers then supported more controversial measures to raise domestic crop prices by having the government sell the surplus overseas at low world prices. Coolidge vetoed the legislation on the grounds that it involved unwarranted government interference in the economy.

Yet the government's role in the economy increased in the 1920s. Republicans widened the scope of federal activity and nearly doubled the ranks of government employees. Hoover led the way in the Commerce Department, establishing new bureaus to help make American industry more efficient in housing, transportation, and mining. Under his leadership, the government encouraged corporations to develop welfare programs that undercut trade unions, and he tried to minimize labor disturbances by devising new federal machinery to mediate disputes. Instead of going back to the laissez-faire tradition of the nineteenth century, the Republican administrations of the 1920s were pioneering a close relationship between government and private business.

Quick Check

What was new about the Republican approach to government?

The Election of 1928

To challenge Hoover in 1928, the Democrats selected Al Smith of New York. Born on the Lower East Side of Manhattan of mixed Irish-German ancestry, Smith was the prototype of the urban Democrat. He was Catholic; he was associated with a big-city machine; he was a "wet" who wanted to end prohibition. Starting out working in the Fulton Fish Market as a boy, he had joined Tammany Hall (the Democratic party in New York City) and climbed the political ladder, rising from subpoena server to state legislator to governor, a post he held with distinction for nearly a decade. But as the embodiment of the big-city East, Smith had to struggle to gain the support of the West and South. His lack of education, poor grammar, and distinctive New York accent all hurt him, as did his eastern provincialism. When reporters asked him about his appeal in the states west of the Mississippi, he replied, "What states are west of the Mississippi?"

The choice facing the American voter in 1928 seemed unusually clear-cut. Hoover was a Protestant, a dry, and an old-stock American who stood for efficiency and individualism; Smith was a Catholic, a wet, a descendant of immigrants, and was associated with big-city politics. Just as Smith appealed to new voters in the cities, so Hoover won

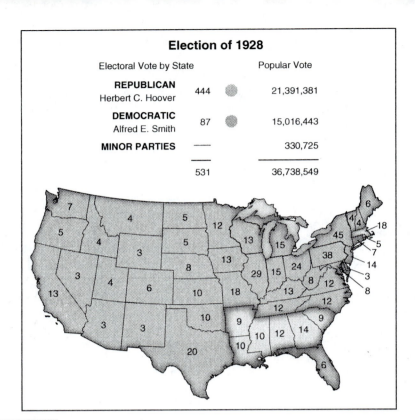

Election of 1928

	Electoral Vote by State	Popular Vote
REPUBLICAN Herbert C. Hoover	444	21,391,381
DEMOCRATIC Alfred E. Smith	87	15,016,443
MINOR PARTIES	—	330,725
	531	36,738,549

MAP 25.1   ELECTION OF 1928

the support of many old-line Democrats who feared the city, Tammany Hall, and the pope.

Yet beneath the surface, as Allan J. Lichtman pointed out, there were "striking similarities between Smith and Hoover." Both were self-made men who embodied the American belief in freedom of opportunity and upward mobility. Neither advocated significant economic change or redistribution of national wealth or power. Though religion proved to be the most important issue for the voters, hurting Smith far more than prohibition or his identification with the city, the Democratic candidate's failure to spotlight the growing cracks in prosperity or offer alternative economic policies ensured his defeat.

The 1928 election was a dubious victory for the Republicans. Hoover won easily, defeating Smith by more than 6 million votes and carrying such Democratic states as Oklahoma, Texas, and Florida (see Map 25.1). But Smith for the first time won a majority for the Democrats in the nation's 12 largest cities. A new Democratic electorate was emerging, consisting of Catholics and Jews, Irish and Italians, Poles and Greeks. The task was to unite the traditional Democrats of the South and West with the urban voters of the Northeast and Midwest.

Quick Check

How did the election of 1928 summarize the divisions of the period?

Conclusion: The Old and The New

Prohibition and the president-elect's natural reserve muted election night celebrations at Hoover's campaign headquarters. Had Hoover known what lay ahead for the country and his presidency, no doubt the party would have been even more somber.

During the 1920s, America struggled to enter the modern era. The economics of mass production and the politics of urbanization drove the country forward, but the persistent appeal of individualism and rural-based values held it back. Americans achieved greater prosperity than ever before, but it was unevenly distributed. Further, as the outbursts of nativism, bigotry, and intolerance revealed, prosperity hardly guaranteed generosity or unity. Nor did it guarantee continued prosperity, even for those who benefited initially. As much as America changed during the 1920s, in one crucial respect the country remained as before. The American economy, for all its remarkable productive capacity, was astonishingly fragile. This was the lesson Hoover was soon to learn.

Chapter Review

The Second Industrial Revolution

25.1 What was new about the American economy in the 1920s? p. 583

The American economy in the 1920s underwent a second industrial revolution. Powered by electricity and featuring the mass production of automobiles and other consumer goods, the second industrial revolution lifted the American standard of living to new heights.

City Life in the Roaring Twenties

25.2 How did life in the cities change after World War I? p. 585

During the 1920s, the focus of American life shifted to the cities, which for the first time contained most of the American population. Women found new opportunities to express themselves, and sports, music, literature, and the arts flourished as never before.

The Conservative Counterattack

25.3 How did conservatives resist the changes of the decade? p. 589

The changes of the 1920s alarmed many conservatives, who tried to resist them. The police and courts cracked down on radicals; prohibition outlawed liquor; the Ku Klux Klan attacked immigrants and minorities; Congress restricted immigration; and fundamentalist Christians decried the changing code of morality and the teaching of evolution in the schools.

Republican Politics

25.4 How did the politics of the 1920s reflect changes in the economy and in American society? p. 596

The 1920s were a decade of Republican politics. Presidents Harding, Coolidge, and Hoover favored business and the wealthy. In the election of 1928, voters had a clear choice between Hoover, the candidate of the countryside and conservatism, and Al Smith, the candidate of the cities and change. Hoover won in a landslide.

Timeline

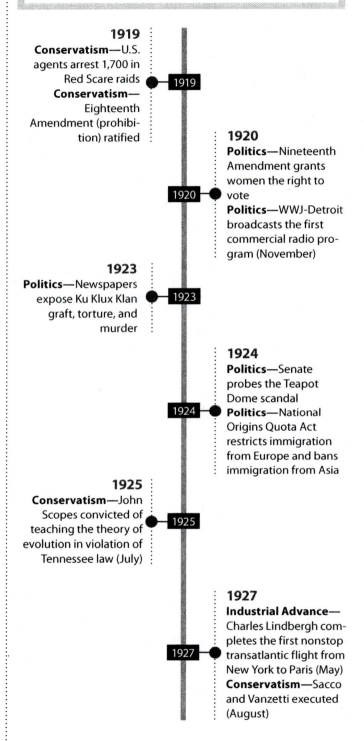

1919
Conservatism—U.S. agents arrest 1,700 in Red Scare raids
Conservatism—Eighteenth Amendment (prohibition) ratified

1920
Politics—Nineteenth Amendment grants women the right to vote
Politics—WWJ-Detroit broadcasts the first commercial radio program (November)

1923
Politics—Newspapers expose Ku Klux Klan graft, torture, and murder

1924
Politics—Senate probes the Teapot Dome scandal
Politics—National Origins Quota Act restricts immigration from Europe and bans immigration from Asia

1925
Conservatism—John Scopes convicted of teaching the theory of evolution in violation of Tennessee law (July)

1927
Industrial Advance—Charles Lindbergh completes the first nonstop transatlantic flight from New York to Paris (May)
Conservatism—Sacco and Vanzetti executed (August)

26 Franklin D. Roosevelt and the New Deal 1929–1939

The Struggle Against Despair

Oscar Heline never forgot the **terrible** waste of the Great Depression. "Grain was being burned," he told interviewer Studs Terkel. "It was cheaper than coal." Heline lived in Iowa, in the heart of the farm belt. "A county just east of here, they burned corn in their courthouse all winter.... You couldn't hardly buy groceries for corn." Farmers, desperate for higher prices, resorted to destruction. "People were determined to withhold produce from the market—livestock, cream, butter, eggs, what not. If they would dump the produce, they would force the market to a higher level. The farmers would man the highways, and cream cans were emptied in ditches and eggs dumped out. They burned the trestle bridge, so the trains wouldn't be able to haul grain."

Film critic Pauline Kael recounted a different memory of the 1930s. Kael, a college student in California during the Great Depression, was struck by how many students were missing fathers: "They had wandered off in disgrace because they couldn't support their families. Other

LEARNING OBJECTIVES

26.1	26.2	26.3	26.4	26.5
What were the causes and effects of the Great Depression? p. 605	How did Franklin Roosevelt fight the depression? p. 609	How did the New Deal reform American life? p. 613	What was the lasting impact of the New Deal? p. 617	How and why did the New Deal end? p. 621

THE GREAT DEPRESSION During the Great Depression, market prices for produces were so low that farmers could scarcely afford to harvest their crops. Many resorted to destroying produce in an attempt to limit supplies and force prices higher, among them were these striking dairy farmers in Illinois dumping cans of milk on to the street.

From Chapter 26 of *American Stories: A History of the United States*, Third Edition. H. W. Brands, R. Hal Williams, T. H. Breen and Ariela J. Gross Copyright © 2015 by Pearson Education, Inc.

 Listen to **Chapter 26** on MyHistoryLab

Watch the Video Series on MyHistoryLab

Learn about some key topics related to this chapter with the
MyHistoryLab Video Series: Key Topics in U.S. History

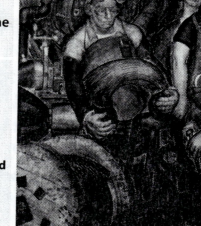

1 The Great Depression & The New Deal: 1929 – 1940 This
introductory video provides an overview of key events
of the Great Depression of the 1930s, which was the
most severe economic challenge that the United States
has ever endured. On the heels of the 1929 stock market
crash, a three-year spate of bank failures further weakened
the nation's financial system while the Dust Bowl plunged
the middle of the country into an agricultural crisis.

Watch on **MyHistoryLab**

The Great Depression This video probes deeper into the hardships facing the nation during the
1930s. In the 1920s, the United States avoided the general malaise that had afflicted the international
economy following the conclusion of World War I. However, with the Stock Market Crash of 1929, the
"Roaring 20s" gave way to an economic depression that quickly spread across the United States and led
to widespread unemployment. **2**

Watch on **MyHistoryLab**

3 Presidential Responses to the Depression This video explains how President Herbert Hoover's response
to the nation's economic woes differed from Franklin Delano Roosevelt's promise of a "New Deal" for
America. When elected President in 1932, FDR brought renewed hope to a country that sorely needed it.

Watch on **MyHistoryLab**

The New Deal President Roosevelt set out immediately to address an ailing nation. This video
chronicles FDR's presidency from its first 100 days and the rise of New Deal programs, such as the
Civilian Conservation Corps (CCC) and Tennessee Valley Authority (TVA), to a successful bid for
re-election in 1936 and the second wave of New Deal initiatives that followed. **4**

Watch on **MyHistoryLab**

fathers had killed themselves, so the family could have the insurance. Families had totally broken
down." Kael and many of her classmates struggled to stay in school: "There were kids who didn't
have a place to sleep, huddling under bridges on the campus. I had a scholarship, but there were
times when I didn't have any food. The meals were often three candy bars."

Howard Worthington resorted to trickery after losing his job in Chicago. One Easter Sunday
during the depression, when his son was four years old, Worthington couldn't afford enough
eggs for a proper egg hunt. So he devised a plan: "I hid a couple in the piano and all around.
Tommy got his little Easter basket, and as he would find the eggs, I'd steal 'em out of the basket
and re-hide them…. He hunted Easter eggs for three hours and he never knew the difference."

No American who lived through the Great Depression ever forgot it. As the stories of Heline,
Kael, and Worthington show, the memories were of hard times, but also of determination, adaptation, and survival.

The depression decade had an equally profound effect on American institutions. To cope
with poverty and dislocation, Americans looked to government as never before, and in doing so
transformed American politics and public life. The agent of the transformation—the man America
turned to in its moment of trial—was Franklin D. Roosevelt (FDR). His answer to the country's
demands for action was an ambitious program called the **New Deal**.

New Deal President Franklin
Delano Roosevelt's program to
combat the Great Depression.

604

The Great Depression

| 26.1 | What were the causes and effects of the Great Depression? |

The depression of the 1930s shocked Americans who had grown used to prosperity. The consumer revolution of the 1920s had fostered confidence that the American way of life would continue to improve. But following the collapse of the stock market in late 1929, factories closed, machines fell silent, and millions of Americans looked for jobs that didn't exist.

The Great Crash

The consumer goods revolution contained the seeds of its own demise. The productive capacity of the automobile and appliance industries grew faster than the effective demand for the products they produced. Each year after 1924, fewer cars, refrigerators, and ranges were sold, a natural consequence as more and more people already owned these durable goods. Production faltered, and in 1927, a mild recession occurred. The sale of durable goods declined, and construction of houses and buildings fell slightly.

Even so, individuals with ready cash invested heavily in the stock market. The market had advanced in spurts during the 1920s; the value of all stocks listed on the New York Stock Exchange rose from $27 billion in 1925 to $67 billion in early 1929. The strongest surge began in the spring of 1928, when investors believed they could make a killing in the market despite the declining production figures. People bet their savings on speculative stocks. Corporations used their cash reserves to lend money to brokers who in turn lent it to investors on margin; in 1929, for example, the Standard Oil Company of New Jersey loaned out $69 million a day in this fashion.

Investors could now play the market on credit, buying stock listed at $100 a share with $10 down and $90 on margin, using the broker's loan for the balance. If the stock advanced to $150, the investor could sell and reap a 500-percent gain on the $10 investment. And in the bull market climate of the 1920s, everyone was sure the market would go up.

By 1929, it seemed the whole nation was engaged in speculation. In city after city, brokers opened branches, each complete with a stock ticker and a huge board showing the latest Wall Street quotations. People filled the seats in the customers' rooms in these offices, cheering the advances of their favorite stocks. Newspapers printed the stock averages on their front pages.

In reality, though, more people were spectators than speculators; fewer than three million Americans owned stocks in 1929, and only about 500,000 were active buyers and sellers. But the bull market became a national obsession, assuring everyone that the economy was healthy and preventing serious analysis of its flaws. When the market soared to more than $80 billion in total value by mid-summer, the Wall Street Journal proclaimed: "The outlook for the fall months seems brighter than at any time."

And then things changed, almost overnight. On October 24—later known as Black Thursday—the rise in stock prices faltered, and investors nervously began to sell. Such leading stocks as RCA and Westinghouse lost nearly half their value in a single day. Speculators panicked as their creditors demanded new collateral, and the panic caused prices to plummet still further. Within weeks the gains of the previous two years had vanished.

The great stock market crash soon spilled over into the larger economy. Banks and other financial institutions suffered heavy losses in the market and curtailed lending for consumer purchases. As consumers stopped buying, factories cut back production, laying off workers and reducing hours. The layoffs and cutbacks lowered purchasing power even further, so fewer people bought cars and appliances. More factory layoffs resulted, and some plants closed entirely, making even less money available to purchase consumer goods.

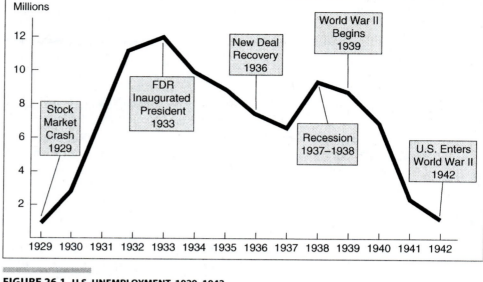

FIGURE 26.1 U.S. UNEMPLOYMENT, 1929–1942

This downward economic spiral continued for four years. By 1932, 25 percent of the workforce was unemployed. (See Figure 26.1.) Steel production was down to 12 percent of capacity. The vast assembly lines in Detroit produced only a trickle of cars each day. The gross national product fell to 67 percent of the 1929 level. The bright dream of mass production had become a nightmare.

The basic explanation for the Great Depression is overproduction: U.S. factories produced more goods than the American people could consume. The problem was not that the market for such products was fully saturated. In 1929, millions of Americans still did not own cars, radios, or refrigerators. But many of them could not afford the new products. There were other contributing causes—unstable economic conditions in Europe, the agricultural decline since 1919, corporate mismanagement, and excessive speculation—but it all came down to the fact that people did not have enough money to buy the consumer products coming off the assembly lines.

Quick Check

Why were speculative stocks problematic?

The Effect of the Depression

It is difficult to measure the human cost of the Great Depression. The material hardships were bad enough. Men and women lived in lean-tos made of scrap wood and metal. Families went without meat and fresh vegetables for months, existing on soup and beans. The psychological burden was even greater: Americans suffered through year after year of grinding poverty with no letup. The unemployed stood in line for hours waiting for relief checks; veterans sold apples or pencils on street corners, their manhood—once prized so highly by the nation—in question. People left the city for the countryside but found no refuge on the farm. Crops rotted in the fields because prices were too low to make harvesting worthwhile; sheriffs fended off angry crowds as banks foreclosed long-overdue mortgages on once prosperous farms.

Few escaped the suffering. African Americans who had left the poverty of the rural South for factory jobs in the North were among the first to be laid off. Mexican immigrants, who had replaced European immigrants, competed with angry citizens now willing to do stoop labor in the fields and lay tracks on the railroads. Immigration officials used technicalities to halt and even reverse the flow across the Rio Grande; nearly 500,000 Mexicans were deported in the 1930s, including families with children born in the United States.

The poor—black, brown, and white—survived because they knew better than most Americans how to exist in poverty. They stayed in bed in cold weather to keep warm and avoid burning calories; they patched their shoes with rubber from discarded tires, heated only the kitchens of their homes, and ate scraps that others would reject.

📖 Read the Document   **Women on the Breadlines (1932)**

26.1

26.2

26.3

26.4

26.5

LINING UP FOR FOOD The Great Depression devastated millions who lost their jobs and often the means to provide food and shelter for themselves and their families. Local and private charities could not keep up with the demands for assistance, and many looked to the federal government. Breadlines stretched as far as the eye could see.

The middle class, which had always lived with high expectations, was hit hard. Professionals and white-collar workers refused to ask for charity even while their families went hungry. One New York dentist and his wife committed suicide and left a note saying, "We want to get out of the way before we are forced to accept relief money." People who fell behind in their mortgage payments lost their homes and faced eviction when they could not pay the rent. Health care declined. Middle-class people stopped going to doctors and dentists regularly, unable to pay in advance for services rendered.

Even the well-to-do were affected, giving up many of their former luxuries and weighed down with guilt as they watched former friends and business associates become impoverished. "My father lost everything in the depression" became an all-too-familiar refrain among young people who dropped out of college.

Many Americans sought escape in movement. Men, boys, and women rode the rails in search of jobs, hopping freights to move south in the winter or west in the summer. On the Missouri Pacific alone, vagrants increased from just over 13,000 in 1929 to nearly 200,000 in 1931. One town in the Southwest hired special police to keep vagrants from leaving the boxcars. Tramps had to keep on the move, but they did find a sense of community in the hobo jungles that sprang up along the major railroad routes. Here they could find a place to eat and sleep and people with whom to share their misery. Louis Banks, a black veteran, told interviewer Studs Terkel what these informal camps were like:

Black and white, it didn't make any difference who you were, 'cause everybody was poor. All friendly, sleep in a jungle. We used to take a big pot and cook food, cabbage, meat and beans all together. We all set together, we made a tent. Twenty-five or thirty would be out on the side of the rail, white and colored: They didn't have no mothers or sisters, they didn't have no home, they were dirty, they had overalls on, they didn't have no food, they didn't have anything.

Quick Check

How did the Great Depression affect individual lives?

✳ Explore the Great Depression on MyHistoryLab

HOW BAD WAS THE GREAT DEPRESSION?

Although alternating boom and bust cycles have proven an integral part of modern capitalism, the economic hard times that prevailed throughout the 1930s stand out as an exceptional case. Never before, and never since, have environmental, political, and economic factors combined to create so deep and so prolonged an economic catastrophe as that which Americans experienced during the era of the Great Depression. In the accompanying graph, notice the extremely high rates of unemployment that American workers endured during the 1930s compared to other, more moderate, spikes in unemployment that have occurred during other periods of economic distress.

WAITING FOR AID A famous quote from the depression: "Serious depression seems improbable; recovery of business next spring, with further improvement in the fall." —*HES, November 10, 1929*

UNEMPLOYED PERONS AS A PRECENTAGE OF THE CIVILIAN LABOR FORCE

SOURCE: U.S. Census Bureau

KEY QUESTIONS Use **MyHistoryLab** *Explorer* to answer these **questions:**

Cause ▶▶▶ *How did financial sector instability contribute to the Great Depression?*

Map the spread of bank failures in the United States from 1928–1933.

Consequence ▶▶▶ *Where did the depression hit the hardest?*

Map the differences in regional economic impacts over time.

Choices ▶▶▶ *How did geographic mobility help Americans facing economic hardship?*

Map the migration of Americans into and out of areas during the depression.

Fighting the Depression

26.2 How did Franklin Roosevelt fight the depression?

T he Great Depression presented an enormous challenge for American political
leadership. The Republicans' inability to overcome the economic catastrophe
enabled the Democrats to regain power. Although they failed to achieve full
recovery before the outbreak of World War II, the Democrats did alleviate
some of the suffering and establish political dominance.

The Emergence of Roosevelt

The Great Depression took Herbert Hoover by surprise. At first the Republican
president relied on the natural working of the economy to restore prosperity. When
this failed, he called for voluntary cooperation among businesses to maintain wages
and employment. To relieve the suffering of the unemployed, he looked to local
governments and private charities. Eventually, and reluctantly, Hoover agreed to
federal assistance to business, but by then the depression had become overwhelming. His mishandling of the **Bonus Army**—jobless World War I veterans who
traveled to Washington seeking federal help and were forcibly dispersed by General
Douglas MacArthur and the regular army—made Hoover the most unpopular man
in America by 1932.

His successor as president was Franklin D. Roosevelt. Born into the old Dutch
aristocracy of New York, FDR was a distant cousin of the Republican Teddy Roosevelt.
He grew up with all the advantages of wealth: private tutors, his own sailboat and pony,
trips to Europe, and education at elite private schools. His strong-willed mother gave
him a priceless sense of self-confidence. After graduation from Harvard, he attended
law school but left to plunge into politics. He served in the New York legislature and
then went to Washington as assistant secretary of the navy under Wilson, a post he
filled capably during World War I. Defeated as the Democratic vice presidential candidate in 1920, Roosevelt had just begun a banking career when polio struck in 1921. He
fought back bravely, and though he never again walked unaided, he reentered politics
and was elected governor of New York in 1928.

Roosevelt's dominant trait was his ability to persuade and motivate other people.
He possessed a deep, rich voice; a winning smile; and a buoyant confidence he transmitted to others. Some believed he was too vain and superficial as a young man, but
his bout with polio gave him both an understanding of human suffering and a broad
political appeal as a man who had overcome heavy odds. He understood the give-
and-take of politics, knew how to use flattery to win over doubters, and was especially
effective in exploiting the media, whether bantering with reporters or reaching out
to the American people on the radio. Although his mind was quick and agile, he had
little patience with philosophical nuances; he dealt with perceptions of issues, not their
deeper substance, and displayed a flexibility toward political principles that often dis-
mayed even his warmest admirers.

Roosevelt took advantage of the opportunity the Great Depression offered.
With the Republicans discredited, he cultivated the two wings of the divided
Democrats, appealing to both the traditionalists from the South and West and the
new urban elements in the North. After winning the party's nomination in 1932,
he broke with tradition by flying to Chicago and accepting in person, telling the
cheering delegates, "I pledge you—I pledge myself to a new deal for the American
people."

In the fall, he defeated Herbert Hoover by a landslide. (See Map 26.1.) Farmers and
workers, Protestants and Catholics, immigrants and native born rallied behind the new
leader who promised to restore prosperity.

Bonus Army In June 1932, a
group of 20,000 World War I
veterans marched on Washington,
D.C., to demand immediate
payment of their "adjusted
compensation" bonuses voted
by Congress in 1924. Congress
rejected their demands, and
President Herbert Hoover had the
Bonus Army forcibly dispersed.

Quick Check

How did Franklin Roosevelt's
background prepare him to deal
with the Great Depression?

Watch the Video   Franklin D. Roosevelt, First Inaugural Address (1932)

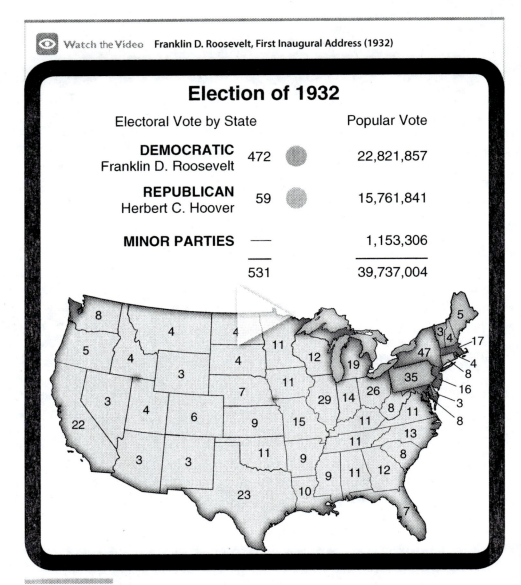

Election of 1932

	Electoral Vote by State		Popular Vote
DEMOCRATIC Franklin D. Roosevelt	472		22,821,857
REPUBLICAN Herbert C. Hoover	59		15,761,841
MINOR PARTIES	—		1,153,306
	531		39,737,004

MAP 26.1 ELECTION OF 1932 In the 1932 presidential election, Franklin Roosevelt trounced Herbert Hoover in both the popular and electoral votes.

The Hundred Days

When Franklin Roosevelt took office on March 4, 1933, the nation's economy was on the brink of collapse. Unemployment stood at nearly 13 million, one-fourth of the labor force; banks were closed in thirty-eight states. On inauguration morning, the governors of New York and Illinois closed the banks in the nation's two largest cities, thus bringing the country's financial transactions to a halt. Speaking from the steps of the Capitol, FDR declared boldly, "First of all, let me assert my firm belief that the only thing we have to fear is fear itself—nameless, unreasoning, unjustified terror." Then he announced he would call Congress into special session and request "broad executive power to wage a war against the emergency, as great as the power that would be given to me if we were in fact invaded by a foreign foe."

Within the next ten days, Roosevelt won his first great New Deal victory by saving the nation's banks. On March 5, he issued a decree closing the banks and called Congress back into session. His aides presented new banking legislation to Congress on March 9; both houses passed it within hours, and FDR signed it that evening. The measure provided for government supervision and aid to the banks. Strong ones would be reopened with federal support, weak ones closed. Government loans would bolster those in difficulty.

On March 12, FDR addressed the nation by radio in the first of his **fireside chats**. In conversational tones, he told the public what he had done. Some banks would

Fireside chats Radio addresses by President Franklin D. Roosevelt from 1933 to 1944, in which he spoke to the American people about such issues as the banking crisis, Social Security, and World War II. The chats enhanced Roosevelt's popularity among ordinary Americans.

reopen the next day, with the government standing behind them. Other banks, once they became solvent, would open later, and the American people could safely put their money back into these institutions. The next day, March 13, the nation's largest and strongest banks reopened their doors; at the end of the day, customers had deposited more cash than they withdrew. The crisis was over; gradually, other banks opened, and the bank runs and failures ceased.

"Capitalism was saved in eight days," boasted one of Roosevelt's advisers. Most surprising was the conservative nature of FDR's action. Instead of nationalizing the banks, he had simply thrown the government's resources behind them and preserved private ownership. Though other New Deal measures would be more radical, Roosevelt set a tone in the banking crisis. He was out to reform and restore the American economic system, not change it drastically. He drew on the progressive tradition and his experience with World War I mobilization to fashion a moderate program of government action.

For the next three months, until it adjourned in June, Congress responded to presidential initiatives. During these "Hundred Days," Roosevelt sent fifteen major requests to Congress and received back fifteen pieces of legislation. A few created agencies have become part of American life. The **Tennessee Valley Authority (TVA)** was one of the most ambitious of Roosevelt's New Deal measures. This innovative effort at regional planning built dams in seven states to control floods, ease navigation, and produce electricity. (See Map 26.2.) The **Civilian Conservation Corps (CCC)** put jobless young men from cities to work in the forests planting trees, fighting fires, and building roads and trails. Though not part of the Hundred Days, the final commitment to the idea of work relief came in 1935 when Roosevelt established the **Works Progress Administration (WPA)** to spend nearly $5 billion authorized by Congress for emergency relief. The WPA put the unemployed on the federal payroll, so they could earn enough to meet their basic needs and stimulate the stagnant economy.

Other New Deal agencies were temporary measures to meet specific economic problems of the depression. None were completely successful; the depression would continue for another six years, immune even to Roosevelt's magic. But psychologically,

Tennessee Valley Authority (TVA) A New Deal effort created in 1933 to build dams and power plants on the Tennessee River. Its programs helped raise the standard of living for millions in the Tennessee River valley.

Civilian Conservation Corps (CCC) One of the most popular New Deal programs, the CCC provided 300,000 young men between the ages of 18 and 25 with government jobs in reforestation and other conservation projects.

Works Progress Administration (WPA) New Deal agency to provide work relief for the unemployed.

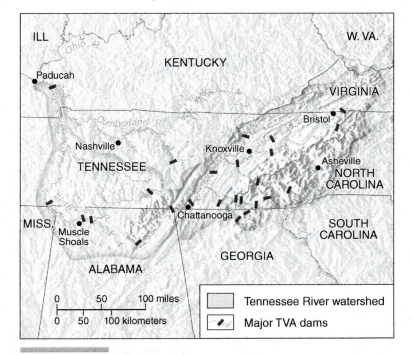

MAP 26.2 THE TENNESSEE VALLEY AUTHORITY The Tennessee Valley Authority (TVA) served a seven-state region in the Southeast.

Quick Check

What were the principal accomplishments of the hundred days?

National Recovery Administration (NRA) This New Deal agency was created in 1933 to promote economic recovery and revive industry during the Great Depression. It permitted manufacturers to establish industrywide codes of "fair business practices" setting prices and production levels. It also provided for minimum wages and maximum working hours for labor and guaranteed labor the right to organize and bargain collectively (Section 7a). The Supreme Court declared it unconstitutional in 1935.

the nation turned the corner in the spring of 1933. Under FDR, the government seemed to be responding to the economic crisis, enabling people for the first time since 1929 to look to the future with hope.

Steps Toward Recovery

Two major New Deal programs launched during the Hundred Days were aimed at industrial and agricultural recovery. One was the **National Recovery Administration (NRA)**, FDR's attempt to achieve economic advance through planning and cooperation among government, business, and labor. In the midst of the depression, business owners were intent on stabilizing production and raising prices. Labor leaders were equally determined to spread work through maximum hours and to put a floor under workers' income with minimum wages.

The NRA hoped to achieve both goals by permitting companies in each major industry to cooperate in writing codes of fair competition that would set realistic limits on production, allocate percentages to individual producers, and set firm guidelines for prices. Section 7a of the enabling act mandated protection for labor in all the codes by establishing maximum hours, minimum wages, and the guarantee of

THE NRA The National Recovery Administration blue eagle signaled a firm's participation in the National Recovery Act. Roosevelt's innovative program met resistance, and signs modeled on this original example attempted to make participation patriotic and respectable.

collective bargaining by unions. No company could be compelled to join, but the New Deal sought complete participation by appealing to patriotism. Each firm that took part could display a blue eagle and stamp the symbol on its products. Under Hugh Johnson, the NRA quickly enrolled the nation's leading companies and unions. By the summer of 1933, more than 500 industries had adopted codes that covered 2.5 million workers.

But the NRA bogged down in a huge bureaucratic morass. The codes were too detailed to enforce easily. Written by the largest companies, the rules favored big business over smaller competitors. Labor became disenchanted with Section 7a. The minimum wages were often near starvation level, while business avoided collective bargaining by creating company unions that did not represent workers' real needs. After a brief upsurge in early 1933, industrial production began to sag as disillusionment with the NRA grew. By 1934, more and more business owners were complaining, calling the agency the "National Run Around." Few mourned when the Supreme Court invalidated the NRA in 1935 on constitutional grounds. Self-interest and greed had defeated the idea of trying to overcome the depression by relying on voluntary cooperation between competing businesses and labor leaders.

Farm recovery fared better. Henry A. Wallace, FDR's secretary of agriculture, came up with an answer to the farmers' old dilemma of overproduction. The government would set production limits for wheat, cotton, corn, and other leading crops. The **Agricultural Adjustment Administration (AAA)**, created by Congress in May 1933, allocated acreage among individual farmers, paying them subsidies (raised by a tax on food production) to take land out of production. Unfortunately, Wallace preferred not to wait until the 1934 planting season to implement this program. So farmers were paid in 1933 to plow under crops they had already planted and kill livestock they were raising. Faced with the problem of hunger in the midst of plenty, the New Deal seemed to respond by destroying the plenty.

The AAA program worked better in 1934 and 1935 as land removed from production led to smaller harvests and rising prices for crops. Farm income rose for the first time since World War I, increasing from $2 billion in 1933 to $5 billion by 1935. Severe weather, especially Dust Bowl conditions on the Great Plains, contributed to the crop-limitation program, but most of the gain in farm income came from the subsidy payments themselves rather than from higher market prices. Though the Supreme Court in 1936 ruled the AAA unconstitutional, Congress reenacted its essential features in acceptable form.

On the whole, large farmers benefited most from the New Deal's agricultural program. Possessing the capital to buy machinery and fertilizer, they could farm more efficiently than before on fewer acres of land. Small farmers, tenants, and sharecroppers fared less well, receiving little of the government payments and often being driven off the land as owners took the acreage previously cultivated by tenants and sharecroppers out of production. Some three million people left the land in the 1930s, crowding into the cities where they swelled the relief rolls. In the long run, the New Deal reforms improved the efficiency of American agriculture, but at a human cost.

Agricultural Adjustment Administration (AAA) Created by Congress in 1933 as part of the New Deal, this agency attempted to restrict agricultural production by paying farmers subsidies to take land out of production. The object was to raise farm prices, and it did, but the act did nothing for tenant farmers and sharecroppers. The Supreme Court declared it unconstitutional in 1936.

Quick Check

How did the new deal try to promote recovery of industry and agriculture?

Reforming American Life

| 26.3 | How did the New Deal reform American life? |

During his first two years in office, FDR had concentrated on fighting the Great Depression by shoring up the sagging American economy. Only a few new agencies, notably TVA, sought to make permanent changes in national life. Roosevelt was developing a "broker-state" concept of government, responding to pressures from organized elements such as corporations, labor unions, and farm groups while ignoring the needs and wants of the dispossessed, who had no clear political voice. The early New Deal tried to assist bankers and industrialists, large farmers, and union members, but it did little to help the elderly and the poor.

The continuing depression and high unemployment began to create pressure for more sweeping changes. Roosevelt either had to provide more radical programs to end historical inequities in American life, or defer to others' solutions to the nation's ills.

Challenges to FDR

Discontent was widespread by 1935. In the upper Midwest, progressives and agrarian radicals, led by Minnesota governor Floyd Olson, were calling for government action to raise farm and labor income. "I am a radical in the sense that I want a definite change in the system," Olson declared. "I am not satisfied with patching." Upton Sinclair, the muckraking novelist, was nearly elected governor of California in 1934 on the slogan "End poverty in California." A violent strike shut down textile plants in twenty states. The most serious challenge to Roosevelt's leadership, however, came from three demagogues who captured national attention in the mid-1930s.

The first was Father Charles Coughlin, a Roman Catholic priest from Detroit, who had originally supported FDR. In his rich, melodious voice, Coughlin appealed to the discontented with a mixture of crank monetary schemes and anti-Semitism. He denounced the New Deal in late 1934 as the "Pagan Deal" and founded his own

((• 📖 Read the Document **Mrs. Henry Weddington, Letter to President Roosevelt (1938)**

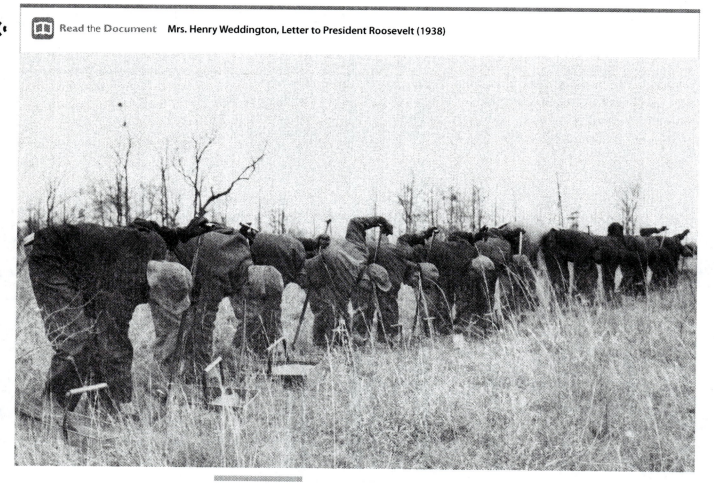

WORK RELIEF Federal work relief programs helped millions maintain their self-respect. Workers in the CCC received $30 a month for planting trees and building parks and trails.

National Union for Social Justice. Increasingly vitriolic, he called for monetary inflation and nationalizing the banking system in his weekly radio sermons to a rapt audience of more than thirty million.

A more benign but equally influential figure appeared in California. Francis Townsend, a 67-year-old physician, developed a scheme in 1934 to assist the elderly, who were suffering greatly during the depression. The Townsend Plan proposed giving everyone over age 60 a monthly pension of $200 with the proviso that it must be spent within thirty days. Although the plan was designed less as an old-age pension than as a way to stimulate the economy, the elderly embraced the proposal as a holy cause, joining Townsend Clubs across the country. Despite the criticism from economists that the plan would transfer more than half the national income to less than 10 percent of the population, more than ten million people signed petitions endorsing the Townsend Plan. Few politicians dared oppose it.

Huey Long, the flamboyant senator from Louisiana, was the third new voice of protest. Like Coughlin, an original supporter of the New Deal, Long had become a major political threat to the president by 1935. A shrewd, ruthless, yet witty man, Long mocked those in power. The Kingfish (a nickname he borrowed from a character on the Amos 'n' Andy radio show) announced a nationwide "Share the Wealth" movement in 1934. He spoke grandly of taking from the rich to make "every man a king," guaranteeing each American a home worth $5,000 and an annual income of $2,500. To finance the plan, Long advocated seizing all fortunes of more than $5 million and taxing incomes greater than $1 million at 100 percent. By 1935, Long claimed to have 27,000 Share the Wealth clubs and a mailing list of more than seven million people, including workers, farmers, college professors, and even bank presidents. Democratic leaders feared that if Long ran as a third-party candidate in 1936 he might attract three to four million votes, possibly enough to swing the election to the Republicans. Although an assassin killed Huey Long in Louisiana in September 1935, his popularity showed that the New Deal needed to do more to help those in distress.

Quick Check

Who were Charles Coughlin, Francis Townsend, and Huey Long, and what did they want?

Social Security

When the new Congress met in January 1935, Roosevelt was ready to support reform measures to take the edge off national dissent. In the midterm elections, the Republicans had lost thirteen seats in the House and retained less than one-third of the Senate. Many of the Democrats were to the left of Roosevelt, favoring increased spending and more sweeping federal programs. "Boys—this is our hour," exulted FDR's assistant Harry Hopkins. "We've got to get everything we want ... now or never." Congress quickly appropriated $4.8 billion for the WPA and was prepared to enact virtually any proposal that Roosevelt offered.

The most significant reform enacted in 1935, and the most important reform of the entire New Deal, was the **Social Security Act**. The Townsend movement had reminded Americans that the United States, alone among modern industrial nations, had never developed a welfare system to aid the aged, disabled, and unemployed. A cabinet committee began studying the problem in 1934. Roosevelt sent its recommendations to Congress the following January.

The proposed legislation had three major parts. First, it provided for old-age pensions financed equally by a tax on employers and workers. It also gave states federal matching funds to provide modest pensions for the destitute elderly. Second, it set up a system of unemployment compensation on a federal–state basis, with employers paying a payroll tax and each state setting benefit levels and administering the program locally. Finally, it provided for direct federal grants to the states, on a matching basis, for welfare payments to the blind, handicapped, needy elderly, and dependent children.

Social Security Act The 1935 Social Security Act established a system of old age, unemployment, and survivors' insurance funded by wage and payroll taxes.

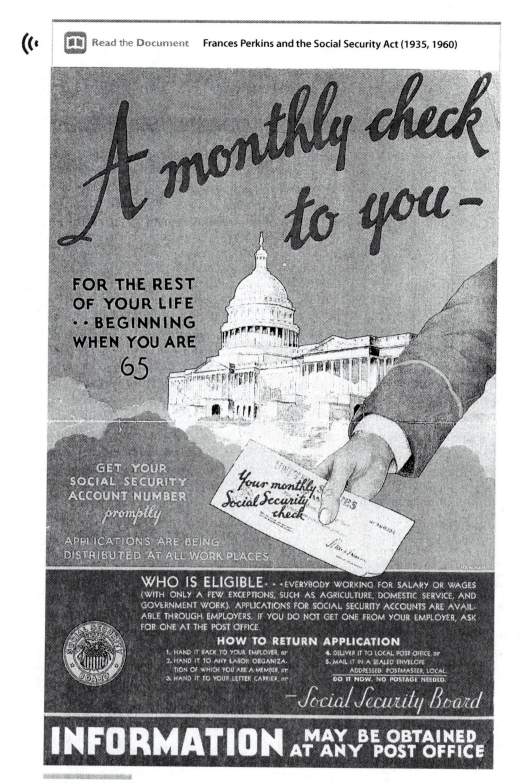

((• 📖 Read the Document Frances Perkins and the Social Security Act (1935, 1960)

SOCIAL SECURITY Despite the administration's boosterism, many believed that Social Security could not fulfill its promises.

Although conservatives mourned the passing of traditional American reliance on self-help and individualism, others argued that the measure did not go far enough. Democratic leaders, however, defeated efforts to incorporate Townsend's proposal for $200 monthly pensions and increases in unemployment benefits. Congress then passed the Social Security Act by overwhelming margins.

Critics pointed out its shortcomings. The old-age pensions were paltry. Designed to begin in 1942, they ranged from $10 to $85 a month. Many of those who most needed protection in their old age, such as farmers and domestic servants, were excluded. And all participants, regardless of income or economic status, paid in at the same rate, with no supplement from the general revenue. The trust fund also took out of circulation money that was desperately needed to stimulate the economy in the 1930s.

Other portions of the act were equally questionable. The cumbersome unemployment system offered no aid to those currently out of work, only to people who would lose their jobs in the future, and the benefits (depending on the state) ranged from barely adequate to substandard. The outright grants to the handicapped and dependent children were minute; in New York City, for example, a blind person received only $5 a week in 1937.

The conservative nature of the legislation reflected not only Roosevelt's fiscal orthodoxy, but his political realism. Despite the severity of the depression, he realized that establishing a system of federal welfare went against deep American convictions. A tax on participants gave those involved in the pension plan a vested interest in Social Security. He wanted them to feel they had earned their pensions and that no one would dare take them away. "With those taxes in there," he explained privately, "no damned politician can ever scrap my social security program." Above all, FDR had established the principle of government responsibility for the aged, the handicapped, and the unemployed. Whatever its defects, Social Security was a landmark of the New Deal, creating a system to provide for the welfare of individuals in a complex industrial society.

Quick Check

What motivated the Social Security Act, and what did it accomplish?

The Impact of the New Deal

26.4 What was the lasting impact of the New Deal?

The New Deal influenced the quality of life in the United States in the 1930s. Government programs reached into areas hitherto untouched. Many of them brought about long-overdue improvements, but others failed to reduce historic inequities. The most important advances came with the growth of labor unions; conditions for working women and minorities in non-unionized industries showed no comparable advance.

The Rise of Organized Labor

At the onset of the Great Depression, trade unions had fewer than three million workers. Most were in the American Federation of Labor (AFL), composed of craft unions for skilled workers. Basic industries, such as steel and automobiles, were unorganized; wages and working conditions for the great mass of unskilled workers were poor. Section 7a of the NRA had increased the AFL's ranks, but the union's conservative leaders, eager to cooperate with business, failed to organize the mass-production industries.

John L. Lewis took the lead in forming mass unions. The son of a Welsh coal miner, Lewis was dynamic and ruthless. He had led the United Mine Workers since 1919 and was determined to spread the benefits of unions throughout industry. Lewis first battled with the leadership of the AFL. After being expelled, he renamed his group the Congress of Industrial Organizations (CIO) and announced that he would use the **Wagner Act**, which provided federal support for efforts to unionize workers, to extend collective bargaining to the auto and steel industries.

Within five years, Lewis had scored remarkable victories. Some came easily. The big steel companies, led by U.S. Steel, surrendered without a fight in 1937; management realized that federal support put the unions in a strong position. The automobile industry was less obliging. When General Motors (GM), the first target, resisted, the new United Automobile Workers (UAW) developed an effective strike technique. In

Wagner Act The 1935 Wagner Act, formally known as the National Labor Relations Act, created the National Labor Relations Board to supervise union elections and designate winning unions as official bargaining agents. The board could also issue cease-and-desist orders to employers who dealt unfairly with their workers.

December 1936, GM workers in Flint, Michigan, simply sat down in the factory, refusing to leave until the company recognized their union, and threatening to destroy the tools and machines if they were removed forcibly. When the governor refused to call out the National Guard to break the strike, GM conceded and signed a contract with the UAW. So did Chrysler. But Henry Ford chose to fight, hiring strikebreakers and beating up organizers. Ford did not recognize the UAW until 1941. Smaller steel companies, led by Republic Steel, also resisted even more violently; in 1937, police shot ten strikers. The companies eventually reached a settlement with the steelworkers' union in 1941.

By the end of the 1930s, the CIO had some five million members, slightly more than the AFL. In addition to the automaking and steel unions, the CIO and the AFL had organized the textile, rubber, electrical, and metal industries. For the first time, unskilled as well as skilled workers were unionized. Women and African Americans benefited from the creation of the CIO, not because the union followed enlightened policies, but because they were a large part of the unskilled workforce that the CIO organized.

Yet despite these impressive gains, only 28 percent of all Americans (excluding farmworkers) belonged to unions by 1940. Millions in the restaurant, retail, and service trades remained unorganized, working long hours for low wages. Employer resistance and traditional hostility to unions blocked progress, as did the aloof attitude of FDR, who pronounced, "A plague on both your houses," for labor and management, during the steel strike. The Wagner Act in 1935 had helped open the way, but labor leaders such as Lewis, Philip Murray of the Steel Workers Organizing Committee, and Walter Reuther of the UAW deserved most of the credit for union achievements.

The New Deal Record on Help to Minorities

The Roosevelt administration's attempts to aid the downtrodden were least effective with racial minorities. The Great Depression had hit blacks hard. Sharecroppers and tenant farmers had seen the price of cotton drop from 18 to 6 cents a pound, far below the level needed to sustain a family on the land. In the cities, the saying "Last hired, first fired" proved all too true; by 1933, more than 50 percent of urban blacks were unemployed. Hard times sharpened racial prejudice. "No jobs for niggers until every white man has a job" became a rallying cry for whites in Atlanta.

The New Deal helped African Americans survive the depression, but it never tried to confront racial injustice in the federal relief programs. Although New Deal programs served blacks and whites, southern blacks received much smaller weekly payments. In the early days, NRA codes permitted lower wage scales for blacks, while the AAA led to the eviction of thousands of black tenants and sharecroppers. African American leaders referred to the NRA as standing for "Negro Robbed Again" and dismissed the AAA as "a continuation of the same old raw deal." Nor did later reform measures help much. Neither the minimum wage nor Social Security covered farmers or domestic servants, who comprised 65 percent of all African American workers. An NAACP official said that Social Security "looks like a sieve with the holes just large enough for the majority of Negroes to fall through."

Yet African Americans still rallied behind Roosevelt's leadership, abandoning their historic ties to the Republican party. In 1936, more than 75 percent of those African Americans who voted supported FDR. In part, this switch came in response to Roosevelt's appointment of prominent African Americans to high-ranking positions, such as William H. Hastie in the Interior Department and Mary McLeod Bethune (founder and president of Bethune-Cookman College) in the National Youth Administration. Eleanor Roosevelt denounced racial discrimination throughout the decade, most notably in 1939 when the Daughters of the American Revolution refused to let African American contralto Marian Anderson sing in Constitution Hall. The first lady and Interior Secretary Harold Ickes arranged for Anderson to perform at the Lincoln Memorial, where 75,000 people heard her on Easter Sunday.

Quick Check

How did the New Deal benefit organized labor?

MINORITIES AND THE NEW DEAL With the statue of Abraham Lincoln as a backdrop, African American contralto Marian Anderson sang on the steps of the Lincoln Memorial in a concert on April 9, 1939.

26.1

26.2

26.3

26.4

26.5

Perhaps the most influential factor in African Americans' political switch was the color-blind policy of Harry Hopkins. He had more than one million blacks working for the WPA by 1939, many of them as teachers and artists. The New Deal provided assistance to 40 percent of the nation's blacks during the depression. Uneven as his record was, Roosevelt had still done more to aid this oppressed minority than any president since Lincoln. One African American newspaper commented that while "relief and WPA are not ideal, they are better than the Hoover bread lines and they'll have to do until the real thing comes along."

The New Deal did far less for Mexican Americans. Most of them were agricultural laborers, and their wages in California fields dropped from 35 to 14 cents an hour by 1933. The pool of unemployed migrant labor expanded rapidly with Dust Bowl conditions in the Great Plains and the flight of "Okies" and "Arkies" to the cotton fields of Arizona and the truck farms of California. The Roosevelt administration cut off any further influx from Mexico by barring any immigrant "likely to become a public charge"; local authorities shipped migrants back to Mexico to reduce the welfare rolls.

The New Deal relief program did aid thousands of Mexican Americans in the Southwest in the 1930s, although migrant workers had difficulty meeting state requirements. The WPA hired Mexican Americans for construction and cultural programs,

👁 Watch the Video **Dorothea Lange and Migrant Mother**

MIGRANT MOTHER Dorothea Lange's photograph of a migrant mother with children became an iconic image of the Great Depression and a spur to public support for the poor.

but after 1937, such employment was denied to aliens. Overall, Mexican Americans suffered economic hardship and got little federal assistance.

Native Americans, after decades of neglect, fared slightly better under the New Deal. Roosevelt appointed John Collier, a social worker who championed Indian rights, as commissioner of Indian affairs. In 1934, the Indian Reorganization Act stressed tribal unity and autonomy instead of attempting (as previous policy had) to transform Indians into self-sufficient farmers by granting them small plots of land. Collier employed more Native Americans in the Indian Bureau, supported education on the reservations, and encouraged tribes to produce native handiwork such as blankets and jewelry. Despite modest gains, however, Indians—who numbered about a third of a million—remained the most impoverished citizens in America.

Quick Check

What did the New Deal accomplish, and not accomplish, for minorities?

The New Deal's End

26.5 How and why did the New Deal end?

The New Deal reached its high point in 1936, when Roosevelt was overwhelmingly reelected and the Democrats strengthened their hold on Congress. This triumph was deceptive. In the next two years, Roosevelt met with defeats in Congress. Yet he remained a popular political leader who had restored American self-confidence as he strove to meet the challenges of the Great Depression.

The Supreme Court Fight

Roosevelt's resounding reelection went to his head. In 1937, he attempted to remove the one obstacle remaining in his path—the Supreme Court. During his first term, the Court had ruled several New Deal programs unconstitutional, most notably the NRA and the AAA. Only three of the nine justices were sympathetic to the need for emergency measures in the midst of the depression. Two others were unpredictable. Four justices were bent on using the Constitution to block Roosevelt's proposals. All were elderly men. Justice Willis Van Devanter had planned to retire in 1932 but remained on the Court because he believed Roosevelt to be "unfitted and unsafe for the Presidency."

When Congress convened in 1937, the president offered a startling proposal to overcome the Court's threat to the New Deal. Instead of seeking a constitutional amendment either to limit the Court's power or to clarify the constitutional issues, FDR chose an oblique attack. Declaring the Court was falling behind schedule because of the age of its members, he asked Congress to appoint a new justice for each member of the Court over the age of 70, up to a maximum of six.

COURT PACKING FDR's battle with the Supreme Court provoked both sympathy and contempt among political cartoonists of the day. In the cartoon on the right, the NRA blue eagle lies dead, nailed to the wall by the Supreme Court. The cartoon on the left, titled "Do We Want a Ventriloquist Act in the Supreme Court?" satirizes FDR's "court-packing" scheme.

"Court-packing" scheme
Concerned that the conservative Supreme Court might declare all his New Deal programs unconstitutional, President Franklin D. Roosevelt asked Congress to allow him to appoint additional justices to the Court. Both Congress and the public rejected this "court-packing" scheme.

Quick Check

What prompted Roosevelt to try to "Pack" the Supreme Court, and how did the effort turn out?

Although this **"court-packing" scheme**, as critics dubbed it, was perfectly legal, it outraged conservatives and liberals, who realized it could set a dangerous precedent. Republicans let prominent Democrats such as Senator Burton Wheeler of Montana lead the fight against Roosevelt's plan. Despite pressure from the White House, the Senate blocked early action on the proposal.

The Court defended itself well. Chief Justice Charles Evans Hughes pointed out to the Senate Judiciary Committee that in fact the Court was not behind schedule as Roosevelt charged. The Court then surprised observers by approving such controversial measures as the Wagner Act and Social Security. In the midst of the struggle, Justice Van Devanter resigned, enabling FDR to make his first appointment to the Court since taking office in 1933. Believing he had proved his point, the president allowed his court-packing plan to die in the Senate.

By 1939, four more vacancies occurred, and Roosevelt was able to appoint such distinguished jurists as Hugo Black, William O. Douglas, and Felix Frankfurter to the Supreme Court. Yet the price was high. The Court fight had weakened the president's relations with Congress, opening deep rifts among Democrats. Senators and representatives who had voted reluctantly for Roosevelt's measures during the depths of the Great Depression now felt free to oppose further New Deal reforms.

The New Deal in Decline

The legislative record during Roosevelt's second term was meager. Aside from laws on minimum wages and maximum hours, Congress did not extend the New Deal into any new areas. Attempts to institute national health insurance and pass anti-lynching legislation failed. Disturbed by the congressional resistance, Roosevelt set out in 1938 to defeat conservative Democratic congressmen and senators, primarily in the South. His targets gleefully charged the president with interference in local politics; only one of them lost in the primaries. The failure of this attempted purge further strained Roosevelt's relations with Congress.

The worst blow came in the economic sector. The slow but steady improvement in the economy suddenly gave way to a sharp recession in late summer 1937. In the following ten months, industrial production fell by one-third, and nearly four million workers lost their jobs. Critics of the New Deal labeled the downturn "the Roosevelt recession," and business executives claimed that it reflected a lack of confidence in FDR's leadership.

The criticism was overblown but not without basis. To reduce budget deficits, Roosevelt had cut back on WPA and other government programs after the election. Federal contributions to consumer purchasing power fell from $4.1 billion in 1936 to less than $1 billion in 1937. For months, Roosevelt refused to restore government spending. Finally, in April 1938, he asked Congress for a $3.75 billion relief appropriation, and the economy began to revive. But FDR's premature attempt to balance the budget had meant two more years of hard times and had marred his reputation as the energetic foe of the depression.

The political result of the attempted purge and the recession was a Republican upsurge. In 1938, the GOP gained 81 seats in the House, eight in the Senate, and 13 governorships. The party many thought dead suddenly had new life. The Democrats still held a sizable majority in Congress, but their margin in the House was deceptive. There were 262 Democratic representatives to 169 Republicans, but 93 southern Democrats held the balance of power. Increasingly after 1938, anti–New Deal southerners voted with Republican conservatives to block social and economic reforms. Thus, not only was the New Deal over by the end of 1938, but a new bipartisan conservative coalition that would prevail for a quarter century had formed in Congress.

Conclusion: The New Deal and American Life

The New Deal lasted just five years, and most of its measures came in two legislative bursts in the spring of 1933 and summer of 1935. Yet nearly every aspect of economic, social, and political development in the decades that followed bore the imprint of Roosevelt's leadership.

Quick Check

How did Roosevelt's relationship with Congress change?

The least impressive achievement of the New Deal came in the economic realm. Whatever credit Roosevelt is given for relieving human suffering during the Great Depression must be balanced against his failure to restore prosperity in the 1930s. The moderate nature of his programs, especially the unwieldy NRA, led to slow and halting industrial recovery. Although government spending was responsible for much of the improvement that was made, FDR never embraced the concept of planned deficits, striving instead for a balanced budget. As a result, by 1939, the nation had barely reached the 1929 level of production, and nearly ten million men and women were still unemployed.

Roosevelt also refused to make sweeping changes in the American economic system. Aside from the TVA, there were no broad experiments in regional planning and no attempts to alter free enterprise beyond imposing limited forms of government regulation. The New Deal did nothing to alter the basic distribution of wealth and power in the nation. The outcome preserved the traditional capitalist system under a thin overlay of federal control.

More significant change occurred in American society. With Social Security, the government acknowledged its responsibility to provide for those unable to care for themselves in an industrial society. The Wagner Act stimulated the growth of labor unions to balance corporate power, and the minimum wage law provided a needed floor for many workers.

Yet the New Deal tended to help only more vocal and organized groups, such as union members and commercial farmers. Those without effective voices or political clout—African Americans, Mexican Americans, women, sharecroppers, restaurant and laundry workers—received little help. For all the appealing rhetoric about the "forgotten man," Roosevelt did little more than Hoover for the long-term needs of the dispossessed.

The most lasting impact of the Roosevelt leadership came in politics. Taking advantage of the emerging power of ethnic voters and capitalizing on the frustration growing out of the depression, FDR was a genius at forging a new coalition. Overcoming the friction between rural and urban Democrats that had prolonged Republican supremacy in the 1920s, he attracted new groups to the Democratic party, principally African Americans and organized labor. His political success led to a major realignment that lasted long after he left the scene.

His political achievement also revealed the true nature of Roosevelt's success. He was a brilliant politician who recognized the essence of leadership in a democracy— appealing directly to the people and giving them a sense of purpose. He infused them with the same indomitable courage and jaunty optimism that had marked his own battle with polio. Thus, despite his limitations as a reformer, Roosevelt was the leader the American people needed in the 1930s—a president who provided the psychological lift that helped them endure and survive the Great Depression.

Chapter Review

The Great Depression

26.1 What were the causes and effects of the Great Depression? p. 605

The Great Depression resulted from imbalances in the American economy that developed during the 1920s. Wealth was unequally distributed, depriving millions of the purchasing power necessary to keep America's factories and farms operating at full capacity. The depression threw millions out of work, out of their homes, and into despair.

Fighting the Depression

26.2 How did Franklin Roosevelt fight the depression? p. 609

Roosevelt persuaded Congress to pass relief, recovery, and reform measures known collectively as the New Deal. Begun during the Hundred Days, the New Deal stabilized the banks, reorganized American industry, assisted American agriculture, and put Americans to work conserving and restoring the nation's resources.

Reforming American Life

26.3 How did the New Deal reform American life? p. 613

In responses to the challenges of Charles Coughlin, Francis Townsend, and Huey Long, Roosevelt persuaded Congress to approve sweeping measures to reform American life. The Social Security Act established old-age and disability pensions to alleviate poverty among the elderly and those unable to work.

The Impact of the New Deal

26.4 What was the lasting impact of the New Deal? p. 617

The New Deal encouraged the emergence of organized labor as a major force in American economic life. It modestly improved the lot of African Americans, although it failed to tackle the racial prejudice that was at the heart of much black poverty. It did little for Mexican Americans, and only a bit more for Native Americans.

The New Deal's End

26.5 How and why did the New Deal end? p. 621

After a high point in 1936, the New Deal declined as a result of Roosevelt's overreaching in the court-packing effort, growing resistance from conservatives, and a recession in 1937 that reminded the country that the New Deal had not ended the Great Depression.

Timeline

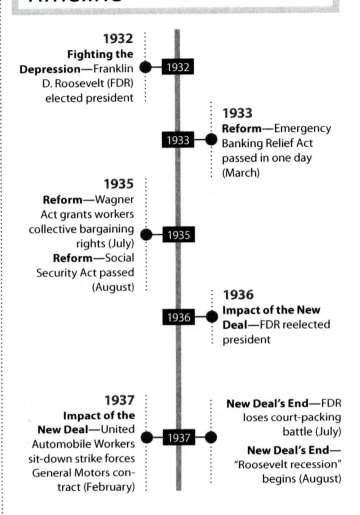

1932
Fighting the Depression—Franklin D. Roosevelt (FDR) elected president

1932

1933

1933
Reform—Emergency Banking Relief Act passed in one day (March)

1935
Reform—Wagner Act grants workers collective bargaining rights (July)
Reform—Social Security Act passed (August)

1935

1936

1936
Impact of the New Deal—FDR reelected president

1937
Impact of the New Deal—United Automobile Workers sit-down strike forces General Motors contract (February)

1937

New Deal's End—FDR loses court-packing battle (July)

New Deal's End— "Roosevelt recession" begins (August)

27 America and the World 1921–1945

A Pact without Power

On August 27, 1928, U.S. **Secretary of State** Frank B. Kellogg, French Premier Aristide Briand, and representatives of 12 other nations met in Paris to sign a treaty outlawing war. Hundreds of spectators crowded into the ornate clock room of the French Foreign Ministry to watch the ceremony. Six huge klieg lights enabled photographers to record the moment for a world eager for peace. Briand declared, "Peace is proclaimed." Then Kellogg signed the document with a foot-long gold pen given to him by French citizens as a token of Franco-American friendship. In the United States, a senator called the **Kellogg–Briand Pact** "the most telling action ever taken in human history to abolish war."

In reality, the pact was the result of American determination to avoid involvement in the European alliance system. In June 1927, Briand had invited the United States to sign a treaty outlawing war between the two nations. The invitation struck a sympathetic response, especially among pacifists who had

KELLOG-BRIAND PACT Diplomats at the signing of the Kellogg-Briand Pact, a sincere but fruitless effort to banish war from international affairs.

LEARNING OBJECTIVES

27.1	27.2	27.3	27.4	27.5
What was isolationism, and why was it so appealing to Americans in the 1920s and 1930s? p. 627	How did the United States go from neutrality in the 1930s to war in 1941? p. 630	How did America and its allies halt the advances of Germany and Japan? p. 634	How did American domestic life change during World War II? p. 640	How did the war end, and what were its consequences? p. 644

 Listen to Chapter 27 on MyHistoryLab

From Chapter 27 of *American Stories: A History of the United States*, Third Edition. H. W. Brands, R. Hal Williams, T. H. Breen and Ariela J. Gross Copyright © 2015 by Pearson Education, Inc. All rights reserved.

Watch the Video Series on MyHistoryLab

Learn about some key topics related to this chapter with the *MyHistoryLab Video Series: Key Topics in U.S. History.*

1 World War II: 1939–1945 This introductory video examines why the United States fought in World War II. During the war, under the leadership of Franklin Delano Roosevelt and Harry Truman, the United States defeated fascism and became a true superpower. At the end of the war it helped to establish the United Nations.

 Watch on MyHistoryLab

Origins of World War II This video looks at the causes of World War II, especially its roots in the previous world war and the Great Depression. Although technically neutral after the conflict broke out in 1939, the United States favored Great Britain against Germany and opposed Japanese expansion in Asia. This led Japan to attack the United States at Pearl Harbor in December 1941 and prompted Germany to declare war on the United States shortly thereafter. **2**

Watch on MyHistoryLab

3 Japanese American Internment The attack on Pearl Harbor and the declaration of war led political leaders on the West Coast to call for interment of persons of Japanese ancestry, including some Japanese-American U.S. citizens (Nisei). These groups were seen as security risks and potential spies or traitors. This video discusses how the federal government rounded up over 100,000 individuals and placed them in internment camps for the duration of the war.

 Watch on MyHistoryLab

The End of the War This video describes the last phase of World War II, which saw the final defeat of Germany, the liberation of the Nazi concentration camps, and the first use of atomic weapons against Japan at Hiroshima and Nagasaki. The background to the postwar peace is also examined, for the ideological differences of the United States and its ally, the Soviet Union, resulted in the Cold War that followed the Allied victory. **4**

 Watch on MyHistoryLab

Kellogg–Briand Pact Also called the Pact of Paris, this 1928 agreement was the brainchild of U.S. Secretary of State Frank B. Kellogg and French Premier Aristide Briand. Its signatories, eventually including nearly all nations, pledged to shun war as an instrument of policy. It had little effect on the conduct of world affairs.

advocated outlawing war throughout the 1920s, but the State Department feared correctly that Briand's true intention was to strengthen ties between France and the United States. The French had already created a network of alliances with the smaller countries of eastern Europe; an antiwar treaty with the United States would at least ensure American sympathy, if not involvement, in case another war broke out in Europe. Kellogg outmaneuvered Briand by proposing to extend the pledge against war to all nations. Briand, who had wanted a bilateral treaty with the United States, had to agree, and the diplomatic charade culminated in the elaborate signing ceremony in Paris.

Eventually nearly every nation in the world signed the Kellogg–Briand Pact, but the effect was negligible. All promised to renounce war as an instrument of national policy, except of course, as the British made clear, in self-defense. Enforcement of the treaty relied solely on the moral force of world opinion. The pact was, as one senator shrewdly commented, only "an international kiss."

Unfortunately, the pact was also symbolic of American foreign policy immediately following World War I. Instead of asserting the role of world leadership its resources and power commanded, the United States went its own way, extending its trade and economic dominance but refusing to take the lead in maintaining world order. This retreat from responsibility seemed unimportant in the 1920s, when exhaustion from World War I ensured relative peace and tranquility. But in the 1930s, when aggressive powers threatened world order in Europe and Asia, the American people retreated even deeper, searching for an isolationist policy that would spare them the agony of another great war.

There was no place to hide in the modern world, however. The Nazi onslaught in Europe and Japanese expansion in Asia finally convinced America to reverse its isolationism and enter World War II in December 1941, when the chances for an Allied victory seemed most remote. With incredible swiftness, the nation mobilized its military and industrial strength. American armies were soon fighting on three continents, the U.S. Navy controlled the world's oceans, and American factories were sending war supplies to more than 20 Allied countries.

When victory came in 1945, the United States was the most powerful nation in the world. But the end of the war brought a new era of tension and rivalry. This time the United States could not retreat from responsibility. World War II was a coming of age for American foreign policy.

Isolationism

27.1 What was isolationism, and why was it so appealing to Americans in the 1920s and 1930s?

American disillusionment with international affairs became evident soon after World War I. The Senate's rejection of the Treaty of Versailles left the United States outside the League of Nations, where it remained for the life of that ill-fated organization. American financial connections to Europe grew during the 1920s, but the United States kept its distance politically. The retreat from an active world policy in the 1920s turned into a headlong flight back to isolationism in the 1930s. Two factors were responsible. First, the depression made foreign policy seem remote and unimportant. As unemployment increased and the economic crisis intensified after 1929, many people grew apathetic about events abroad. Second, when the danger of war abroad did finally penetrate the American consciousness, it only strengthened the desire to stay out of it.

Three powerful and discontented nations were on the march in the 1930s—Germany, Italy, and Japan. In Germany, Adolf Hitler came to power in 1933 as the head of the National Socialist, or Nazi, movement. A shrewd and charismatic leader, Hitler capitalized on both domestic discontent and bitterness over World War I. Blaming the Jews for Germany's ills and asserting the supremacy of the "Aryan" race of blond, blue-eyed Germans, he quickly imposed a totalitarian dictatorship in which the Nazi party ruled, and he, the Leader or *Führer*, was supreme. At first, his foreign policy seemed harmless, but as he consolidated his power, the threat he represented to world peace became clear. Hitler took Germany out of the League of Nations, reoccupied the Rhineland, and formally denounced the Treaty of Versailles. His massive rearmament and boasts of uniting all Germans into a Greater Third Reich that would last 1,000 years terrified his European opponents, blocking any effective challenge to his regime.

In Italy, another dictator, Benito Mussolini, had come to power in 1922. Emboldened by Hitler's success, he embarked on an aggressive foreign policy in 1935. His invasion of the independent African nation of Ethiopia led its emperor, Haile Selassie, to call on the League of Nations for support. With Britain and France far more concerned about Hitler than events in East Africa, the League's halfhearted measures failed to halt Mussolini's conquest of all of Ethiopia. "Fifty-two nations had combined to resist aggression," commented historian A. J. P. Taylor; "all they accomplished was that Haile Selassie lost all his country instead of only half." Collective security had failed its most important test.

Japan was the third threat to world peace. Militarists began to dominate the government in Tokyo by the mid-1930s, intimidating and even assassinating their liberal opponents. By 1936, Japan had also left the League of Nations. A year later, its armies invaded China, marking the beginning of the Pacific phase of World War II.

The resurgence of militarism in Germany, Italy, and Japan undermined the Versailles settlement and destroyed the balance of power. Britain and France in Europe proved as powerless as China in Asia to stop the tide of aggression. In 1937, the three totalitarian nations signed a pact forming a Berlin–Rome–Tokyo axis. This alliance of the **Axis Powers** ostensibly was aimed at communism and the Soviet Union, but it threatened the entire world. Only a determined American response could unite the other nations against the Axis threat. Unfortunately, the United States deliberately avoided this leadership until it was nearly too late.

Axis Powers During World War II, the alliance between Italy, Germany, and Japan was known as the "Rome–Berlin–Tokyo axis," and the three members were called the Axis Powers. They fought against the Allied Powers, led by the United States, Britain, and the Soviet Union.

The Lure of Pacifism and Neutrality

The danger of war abroad increased American desire for peace and noninvolvement. Memories of World War I were vivid. Erich Maria Remarque's novel *All Quiet on the Western Front*, and the movie based on it, reminded people of the brutality of war. Historians began to treat the Great War as a mistake, criticizing Wilson for not preserving American neutrality and claiming the British had duped the United States

 Read the Document   Franklin D. Roosevelt, "The Four Freedoms" (1941)

ANTI-WAR PROTESTS The pacifism that swept college campuses in the 1930s touched students at the University of Chicago. These undergraduates hold placards bearing antiwar slogans as they wait to join a parade as part of a nationwide demonstration against war.

into entering the war. Walter Millis's *America's Road to War, 1914–1917*, published in 1935, was hailed for exposing how "a peace-loving democracy, muddled but excited, misinformed and whipped to a frenzy, embarked upon its greatest foreign war."

American youth were determined not to repeat their elders' mistakes. Pacifism swept college campuses. At Brown University, 72 percent of the students opposed military service in wartime. At Princeton, undergraduates formed the Veterans of Future Wars, a parody on veterans' groups, to demand a bonus of $1000 apiece before they marched off to a foreign war. In April 1934, students and professors walked out of class to attend massive antiwar rallies, which became an annual rite of spring in the 1930s. Demonstrators carried signs reading "Abolish the R.O.T.C." and "Build Schools—Not Battleships." Pacifist orators urged students to pledge not to support their country "in any war it might conduct."

The pacifist movement found a scapegoat in the munitions industry. Books exposing the unsavory tactics of large arms dealers such as Krupp in Germany and Vickers in Britain led to a demand to curb these "merchants of death." Senator Gerald Nye of North Dakota headed a Senate committee that spent two years investigating American munitions dealers. The committee revealed the enormous profits firms such as Du Pont reaped from World War I, but Nye also charged that bankers and munitions makers were responsible for American intervention in 1917. No proof was forthcoming, but the public—prepared to believe the worst of businessmen during the Great Depression—accepted the "merchants of death" thesis.

The Nye Committee's revelations culminated in legislation. Congress passed three **neutrality acts** to keep the United States out of war. A 1935 law banned the sale of arms to nations at war and warned Americans not to sail on belligerent ships. In 1936, a second act banned loans to countries at war. A third neutrality act in 1937 made these prohibitions permanent and required, on a two-year trial basis, that all trade, other than in munitions, between the United States and belligerent powers be conducted on a cash-and-carry basis. American ships were forbidden to carry any goods or passengers to the ports of any nation at war or fighting a civil war.

neutrality acts Laws in the 1930s that forbade selling munitions or lending money to belligerents. The 1937 act required that all other trade with countries at war be conducted on a cash-and-carry basis.

Quick Check
What was the purpose of the neutrality acts?

War in Europe

The neutrality legislation played directly into Hitler's hands. Bent on conquering Europe, he could now proceed without worrying about American interference. In March 1938, he seized Austria in a bloodless coup. Six months later, he demanded the Sudetenland, a province of Czechoslovakia with a largely German population. When the British and French leaders agreed to meet with Hitler at Munich to resolve the crisis, FDR approved. Roosevelt kept the United States aloof from the decision to appease Hitler by surrendering the Sudetenland. But he gave his tacit approval of appeasement by telling the British prime minister that he shared his "hope and belief that there exists today the greatest opportunity in years for the establishment of a new order based on justice and on law."

Six months after the meeting at Munich, Hitler violated his promises by seizing nearly all of what remained of Czechoslovakia. In the United States, Roosevelt permitted the State Department to press for revising the neutrality acts. The administration's proposal to repeal the arms embargo and place all trade with belligerents, including munitions, on a cash-and-carry basis met stubborn resistance from isolationists. They argued that cash-and-carry would favor Britain and France, who controlled the sea. The House rejected the measure by a narrow margin, and the Senate's Foreign Relations Committee voted 12 to 11 to postpone neutrality revision.

In July 1939, Roosevelt finally abandoned his aloof position and pleaded with Senate leaders to reconsider. The president's and secretary of state's warnings that war in Europe was imminent failed to impress the isolationists. Senator William Borah, who had led the fight against the League of Nations in 1919, responded that he believed the chances for war in Europe were remote. Vice President John Nance Garner told FDR that neutrality revision was dead: "You haven't got the votes, and that's all there is to it."

Quick Check

What was the American response to the outbreak of war in Europe?

On September 1, 1939, Hitler began World War II by invading Poland. Two days later, Britain and France declared war, although they could not prevent the German conquest of Poland. Russia had refused Western overtures for a common front against Germany and signed a nonaggression treaty with Hitler in late August. This Nazi–Soviet Pact enabled Germany to avoid a two-front war; the Russians' reward was half of Poland.

Roosevelt proclaimed American neutrality, but the successful aggression by Nazi Germany brought into question the isolationist assumption that American well-being did not depend on the European balance of power. Strategic and ideological considerations undermined the belief that the United States could safely pursue a policy of neutrality and noninvolvement. The long retreat from responsibility was about to end as Americans came to realize that their own democracy and security were at stake in the European war.

The Road to War

27.2 How did the United States go from neutrality in the 1930s to war in 1941?

For two years, the United States tried to remain at peace while war raged in Europe and Asia. In contrast to the mood in 1914–1917, when Wilson attempted to be impartial during World War I, the American people this time displayed overwhelming sympathy for the Allies and distaste for Germany and Japan. Roosevelt openly favored an Allied victory, but fear of isolationist criticism compelled him to move slowly, and often deviously, in helping Britain and France.

From Neutrality to Undeclared War

Two weeks after the outbreak of war in Europe, Roosevelt called Congress into special session to revise the neutrality legislation. He wanted to supply weapons to Britain and France, but he refused to state this openly. Instead, he again asked Congress to replace the arms embargo with cash-and-carry regulations. Belligerents could purchase war supplies in the United States, but they would have to pay cash and transport the goods in their own ships. Public opinion supported the president, and Congress passed the legislation in November 1939.

Dramatic German victories profoundly affected American opinion. Quiet during the winter of 1939–1940, the Germans struck in the spring. In April, they seized Denmark and Norway. On May 10, they unleashed the *blitzkrieg* (lightning war) on the western front. Using tanks, infantry, and dive-bombers in close coordination, the German army overran the Netherlands, Belgium, and Luxembourg en route to France. It split the British and French forces, driving the British off the continent at Dunkirk. In June, France fell to Hitler's war machine.

Americans were stunned. Hitler had taken only six weeks to achieve what Germany had failed to do in four years in World War I. Suddenly they realized they had a stake in the outcome; if Britain fell, Hitler might gain control of the British navy. Instead of a barrier, the Atlantic would be a highway for German penetration of the New World.

Roosevelt responded with a policy of all-out aid to the Allies, short of war. In a speech at Charlottesville, Virginia, in June (just after Italy invaded France), he denounced Germany and Italy as representing "the gods of force and hate. . . . The whole of our sympathies lies with those nations that are giving their life blood in combat against these forces." It was too late to help France, but in September, FDR transferred 50 old destroyers to Britain in exchange for rights to build air and naval bases in the British West Indies. Giving warships to a belligerent nation was a breach of neutrality, but Roosevelt stressed the importance of guarding the Atlantic approaches, calling the destroyers-for-bases deal "the most important action in the reinforcement of our national defense that has been taken since the Louisiana Purchase."

Read the Document   Charles Lindbergh, Radio Address (1941)

CHARLES LINDBERGH The famous American aviator-hero Charles Lindbergh was one of several prominent isolationist Americans who joined a public campaign in 1939 and between 1940–1941 to preserve American neutrality as the military conflict in Europe began to rage.

Isolationists attacked this departure from neutrality. The *St. Louis Post-Dispatch* proclaimed, "Dictator Roosevelt Commits Act of War." The America First Committee protested the drift toward war. Such diverse individuals as aviator-hero Charles Lindbergh, conservative Senator Robert A. Taft of Ohio, socialist leader Norman Thomas, and liberal educator Robert M. Hutchins condemned FDR for involving the United States in a foreign conflict. Voicing belief in a "Fortress America," they denied that Hitler threatened American security and claimed that the nation could defend itself regardless of what happened in Europe.

Opponents of the isolationists organized the Committee to Defend America by Aiding the Allies. Eastern Anglophiles, moderate New Dealers, and liberal Republicans made up the bulk of the membership. Kansas newspaper editor William Allen White was chairman. The White Committee, as it became known, advocated unlimited assistance to Britain short of war, although some of its members favored entering the conflict. Above all, the interventionists challenged the isolationist premise that events in Europe did not affect American security. "The future of western civilization is being decided upon the battlefield of Europe," White declared.

In the ensuing debate, the American people gradually sided with the interventionists. The Battle of Britain—Germany's air assault on Britain—helped. "Every time

TABLE 27.1 THE ELECTION OF 1940

Candidate	Party	Popular Vote	Electoral Vote
Roosevelt	Democratic	27,244,160	449
Willkie	Republican	22,305,198	82

Hitler bombed London, we got a couple of votes," noted one interventionist. In 1940, Congress increased the defense budget from $2 billion to $10 billion and approved the first peacetime draft in American history.

The sense of crisis affected domestic politics. Roosevelt ran for an unprecedented third term in 1940 because of the European war; the Republicans nominated Wendell Willkie, a former Democratic businessman who shared FDR's commitment to aid Britain. Both candidates appealed to peace sentiment during the campaign, but Roosevelt's decisive victory made it clear that the nation supported his departure from neutrality (see Table 27.1).

After the election, FDR took his boldest step. Responding to Prime Minister Winston Churchill's warning that Britain was running out of money, the president asked Congress to approve a new program to provide goods and weapons to countries fighting aggressors. Roosevelt's call for America to become "the great arsenal of democracy" seemed straightforward enough, but he acted deviously by calling it **Lend-Lease** and comparing it to loaning a neighbor a garden hose to put out a fire.

Isolationists denounced Lend-Lease as unnecessary and untruthful. "Lending war equipment is a good deal like lending chewing gum," commented Senator Taft. "You don't want it back." In March 1941, however, Congress authorized the president to "sell, transfer title to, exchange, lease, lend, or otherwise dispose of" war supplies to "any country the President deems vital to the defense of the United States." A $7-billion appropriation ended the "cash" part of cash-and-carry and assured Britain full access to American war supplies.

The "carry" problem remained. German submarines were sinking more than 500,000 tons of shipping a month. Britain desperately needed the help of the American navy in escorting convoys across the U-boat–infested North Atlantic. Roosevelt, fearful of isolationist reaction, responded with naval patrols in the western half of the ocean. Hitler placed his submarine commanders under strict restraints to avoid drawing America into the European war. Nevertheless, incidents occurred. In September 1941, after a U-boat narrowly missed torpedoing an American destroyer tracking it, Roosevelt denounced the German submarines as the "rattlesnakes of the Atlantic" and ordered the navy to convey British ships halfway across the ocean.

Undeclared naval war followed. On October 17, 1941, a German submarine damaged the U.S. destroyer *Kearney*; ten days later, another U-boat sank the *Reuben James*, killing more than 100 American sailors. FDR ordered the destroyers to shoot U-boats on sight. He also asked Congress to repeal the "carry" section of the neutrality laws and permit American ships to deliver supplies to Britain. In mid-November, Congress approved these moves by slim margins. Now American merchant ships would also become targets. By December, it seemed that repeated sinkings would soon lead to a formal declaration of war against Germany.

In leading the nation to the brink of war in Europe, Roosevelt opened himself to criticism from both sides in the domestic debate. Interventionists believed he had been too cautious in dealing with the danger Nazi Germany posed. Isolationists claimed he had misled the American people by professing peace while plotting war. Roosevelt was certainly less than candid, relying on executive discretion to engage in provocative acts in the North Atlantic. He agreed with the interventionists that a German victory would threaten American security. But he also was aware that a poll in September 1941 showed nearly 80 percent of the American people wanted to stay out of World War II. Realizing that leading a divided nation into war would be disastrous, FDR played for time, inching the country toward war while waiting for the Axis nations to make the ultimate move. Japan finally obliged at Pearl Harbor.

Lend-Lease In 1941, Congress gave President Franklin D. Roosevelt the authority to sell, lend, lease, or transfer war materials to any country whose defense he declared vital to that of the United States.

Quick Check

How did FDR overcome the opposition to war?

Showdown in the Pacific

Japan had taken advantage of the war in Europe to expand in Asia. Although they had conquered the populous coastal areas of China, the Japanese had been unable to overcome Chiang Kai-shek, whose Nationalist forces retreated into the vast interior of the country. The German defeat of France and the Netherlands in 1940, however, left their colonies in the East Indies and Indochina defenseless. Japan now set out to incorporate these territories—rich in oil, tin, and rubber—into what it called a Greater East Asia Co-Prosperity Sphere.

The Roosevelt administration countered with economic pressure. Japan depended heavily on the United States for petroleum and scrap metal. In July 1940, Roosevelt set up a licensing and quota system for exporting these crucial materials to Japan and banned the sale of aviation gasoline altogether. With Britain fighting for survival and France and the Netherlands occupied by Germany, the United States was now employing economic sanctions to defend Southeast Asia against Japanese expansion.

Tokyo appeared unimpressed. In September, Japanese troops occupied bases in northern French Indochina, and Japan signed the Tripartite Pact with Germany and Italy, a defensive treaty that confronted the United States with a possible two-ocean war. The new Axis pact confirmed American suspicions that Japan was part of a worldwide totalitarian threat. Roosevelt and his advisers, however, saw Germany as the primary danger; thus they pursued a policy of all-out aid to Britain while hoping that economic measures alone would deter Japan.

The embargo on aviation gasoline, extended to include scrap iron and steel in late September 1940, was a burden Japan could bear, but banning all oil shipments was different. Japan was entirely dependent on petroleum imports from the United States and the Dutch East Indies. To ease the economic pressure through negotiation, Japan sent a new envoy to Washington in spring 1941. But the talks broke down. Tokyo wanted a free hand in China and an end to American sanctions; the United States insisted that Japan evacuate all of China.

In July 1941, Japan occupied all of Indochina, beginning the chain of events that led to war. Washington knew of this aggression before it occurred. Naval intelligence had broken the Japanese diplomatic code and was reading all messages between Tokyo and its embassy in Washington. On July 25, 1941, Roosevelt froze all Japanese assets in the United States. This step, intended only as a temporary warning, became a permanent embargo due to positive public reaction and State Department zeal. Trade with Japan, including the vital oil shipments, stopped. When the Dutch government-in-exile took similar action, Japan faced a dilemma: To get oil shipments resumed, Tokyo would have to end its aggression; the alternative would be to seize the needed petroleum supplies in the Dutch East Indies, which would mean war.

After a final diplomatic effort failed, General Hideki Tojo, an army militant, became the new premier of Japan. To mask its war preparations, Tokyo sent yet another envoy to Washington with new proposals. Code breaking enabled American diplomats to learn that the Japanese terms were unacceptable even before they were presented. Military leaders urged President Roosevelt to reach at least a temporary settlement with Japan to give them time to prepare American defenses in the Pacific. Secretary of State Cordell Hull, however, refused any concession; on November 26, he again demanded Japan withdraw from China.

The Japanese response came two weeks later. On the evening of December 6, 1941, the first 13 parts of the reply to Hull's note arrived at the Japanese embassy in Washington, with the fourteenth part to follow the next morning. Naval intelligence decoded the message faster than the embassy clerks. Roosevelt read it that night and commented, "This means war." The next day, December 7, the fourteenth part revealed that Japan rejected the American position.

Officials in Washington immediately sent warnings to American bases in the Pacific, but they arrived too late. At 7:55 in the morning, just before 1 P.M. in Washington, Japanese carrier-based planes caught the American fleet at Pearl Harbor by surprise. In little more than an hour, they crippled the Pacific fleet and its major base, sinking four battleships, damaging four more, and killing more than 2,400 American sailors.

PEARL HARBOR Four American battleships were destroyed in the surprise attack on Pearl Harbor, December 7, 1941. Caught completely off guard, U.S. forces still managed to shoot down 29 enemy planes.

Pearl Harbor On December 7, 1941, Japanese warplanes attacked the U.S. fleet at Pearl Harbor, Hawaii. The attack marked America's entrance into World War II.

Quick Check

What led Japan to attack Pearl Harbor?

In Washington, the Japanese envoys had requested a meeting with Secretary Hull at 1 P.M. Just before the meeting, news arrived of the attack on **Pearl Harbor**. Hull read the note the Japanese handed him and then, unable to restrain himself any longer, burst out, "In all my fifty years of public service, I have never seen a document that was more crowded with infamous falsehoods and distortions—on a scale so huge that I never imagined until today that any government was capable of uttering them."

Speaking before Congress the next day, President Roosevelt termed December 7 "a date which will live in infamy" and asked for a declaration of war on Japan. With only one dissenting vote, both branches passed the measure. On December 11, Germany and Italy declared war against the United States; the nation was now fully involved in World War II.

Turning the Tide Against the Axis

27.3 How did America and its allies halt the advances of Germany and Japan?

The outlook for victory was bleak. Hitler's armies controlled Europe, from Norway in the north to Greece in the south. Despite their nonaggression pact, Germany had invaded Russia in June 1941. Although they had failed to capture either Moscow or Leningrad, the Nazi forces had conquered Ukraine and by 1942 were threatening to cross the Volga River and seize vital oil fields in the Caucasus. In North Africa, General Erwin Rommel's Afrika Korps had pushed the British back into Egypt and threatened the Suez Canal (see Map 27.1).

The situation was no better in Asia. Within three months after Pearl Harbor, the Japanese had conquered British Malaya and Burma and the Dutch East Indies, with its valuable oil fields, and were pressing the British back in New Guinea. American forces under General Douglas MacArthur had been overwhelmed in the Philippines. With

MAP 27.1 WORLD WAR II IN EUROPE AND NORTH AFRICA The tide of battle shifted in this theater during the winter of 1942–1943. At Stalingrad the Russians turned back a massive German assault on the eastern front, and the Allied forces recaptured North Africa.

the American navy still recovering from Pearl Harbor, Japan controlled the Pacific as far as Hawaii (see Map 27.2).

Over the next two years, the United States and its allies would halt the German and Japanese offensives in Europe and Asia. But then they faced the challenge of driving back the enemy, freeing the conquered areas, and defeating the Axis powers on their home territory. The struggle would require sacrifice and heavy losses; World War II would test American will and resourcefulness to the utmost.

Wartime Partnerships

The greatest single advantage that the United States and its partners possessed was their willingness to form a genuine coalition to defeat the Axis powers. Although the wartime alliance was often strained, it still permitted considerable coordination. In contrast, Germany and Japan each fought a separate war without any attempt at cooperation.

The United States and Britain achieved a complete partnership. A Combined Chiefs of Staff, headquartered in Washington, directed Anglo-American military operations. The close cooperation between Roosevelt and Churchill ensured a common

MAP 27.2 WORLD WAR II IN THE PACIFIC The tide of battle turned in the Pacific the same year as in Europe. The balance of sea power shifted back to the United States from Japan after the naval victories of 1942.

strategy. The leaders decided that a German victory was the greater danger and thus gave priority to the war in Europe. In December 1941, Roosevelt and Churchill signed a Declaration of the United Nations, to which 26 countries eventually subscribed, that pledged them to defeat the Axis powers.

Relations with the other members of the United Nations coalition in World War II were less harmonious. The decision to defeat Germany first displeased the Chinese, who had been fighting Japan since 1937. Roosevelt tried to appease Chiang Kai-shek with a trickle of supplies, flown in at great risk by Americans over the Himalayas from India. France posed a more delicate problem. FDR virtually ignored the Free French government-in-exile under General Charles de Gaulle. Roosevelt preferred to deal with the pro-German regime at Vichy in France, because it controlled the French fleet and most of France's overseas territories.

The greatest strain within the wartime coalition was with the Soviet Union. Although Roosevelt had recognized the Soviet regime in 1933, ties were not close. The Russian refusal to pay prerevolutionary debts and Soviet support of communists in the United States in the 1930s intensified American distaste for Stalin's regime. The great Russian purge trials and the Nazi–Soviet alliance from 1939 to 1941, along with deep-seated cultural and ideological differences, made wartime cooperation difficult.

Ever the pragmatist, Roosevelt tried to establish a more cordial relationship with Russia during the war. Even before Pearl Harbor, he extended Lend-Lease aid to Russia, and after American entry into the war, only the difficulty of delivering the supplies limited this economic assistance. Eager to keep Russia in the war, the president promised in May 1942 that the United States would create a second front in Europe by the end of that year—a pledge he could not fulfill. But in January 1943, Roosevelt and Churchill met in Casablanca, Morocco, where they demanded unconditional surrender, vowing that the Allies would fight until the Axis nations were completely defeated.

Despite these promises, the Soviet Union bore the brunt of battle against Hitler, fighting alone against two-thirds of the German army. The United States and Britain, grateful for the respite to build up their forces, could only promise future help and send supplies. The result was a rift that never healed—one that did not prevent the defeat of Germany but did ensure future tensions between the Soviet Union and the West.

27.1

27.2

Quick Check | **27.3**

What countries were America's principal allies during the war?

27.4

27.5

Halting the German Blitz

From the outset, the United States favored an invasion across the English Channel. Army planners, led by Chief of Staff George C. Marshall and his protégé, Dwight D. Eisenhower, were convinced such a frontal assault would be the quickest way to win the war. Roosevelt concurred, in part because it fulfilled his second-front commitment to the Soviets.

Eisenhower's initial plan called for a full-scale invasion of Europe in the spring of 1943 and a temporary beachhead in France in the fall of 1942 if necessary to keep Russia in the war. But the British, remembering the heavy casualties of trench warfare in World War I, and hoping to protect the route to India, their most important colony, preferred a perimeter approach. Air and naval attacks around the edge of the continent, especially in the Mediterranean, would be a prelude to an invasion of Germany. British strategists wanted to invade North Africa first. Roosevelt also wanted American troops

Watch the Video   **Hitler and Roosevelt**

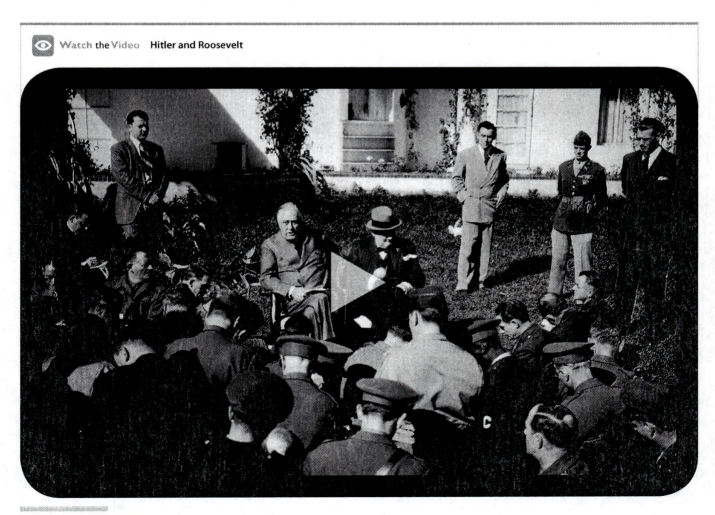

CHURCHILL AND ROOSEVELT At their meeting at Casablanca, Morocco, in January 1943, President Roosevelt and British Prime Minister Winston Churchill announced that the unconditional surrender of the Axis powers would be the only acceptable basis for ending the war.

fighting Germans before the end of 1942 to offset pressure at home to concentrate on the Pacific; hence, he overruled objections from his military advisers, and American and British troops landed in Morocco and Algeria in November 1942.

The British also attacked Rommel at El Alamein in Egypt and soon forced the Afrika Korps to retreat to Tunisia. Eisenhower, delayed by poor roads and bad weather, was slow in bringing up his forces from the west, and in their first encounter with Rommel at the Kasserine Pass south of Tunis, inexperienced American troops suffered a humiliating defeat. General George Patton rallied the demoralized soldiers, and by May 1943, Germany had been driven from Africa, leaving behind nearly 300,000 prisoners.

During these same months, the Soviets had broken the back of German military power in the Battle of Stalingrad. Turned back at the critical bend in the Volga, Hitler had poured in division after division in what was ultimately a lost cause.

At Churchill's insistence, FDR agreed to follow up the North African campaign by invading Sicily and then Italy in the summer of 1943. Italy dropped out of the war when Mussolini fled to Germany, but the Italian campaign was a strategic dead end. Germany sent in enough divisions to establish a strong defense, and Allied troops had to fight their way slowly up the peninsula, suffering heavy casualties.

Moreover, these Mediterranean operations delayed the second front until June 1944. Meanwhile, the Soviets began to push the Germans out of Russia and looked forward to the conquest of eastern Europe, where they could establish "friendly" communist regimes. Having borne the brunt of the fighting against Nazi Germany, Russia was ready to claim its reward—the postwar domination of eastern Europe.

Quick Check

Where did the Allies achieve early victories over Germany?

Checking Japan in the Pacific

Both the decision to defeat Germany first and the vast expanses of the Pacific dictated the nature of the war against Japan. The United States conducted amphibious island-hopping campaigns rather than attempt to reconquer Southeast Asia and China. There would be two separate American offensives. One, led by Douglas MacArthur, would move from New Guinea back to the Philippines, while the other, commanded by Admiral Chester Nimitz, was directed at key Japanese islands in the Central Pacific. The original plan called for the two offensives to come together for the final invasion of the Japanese home islands.

Success in the Pacific depended on control of the sea. The devastation at Pearl Harbor gave Japan the edge, but fortunately, the United States had not lost any of its four aircraft carriers. In the Battle of the Coral Sea in May 1942, American naval forces blocked a Japanese thrust to outflank Australia. The turning point came one month later at Midway. A Japanese task force threatened this remote American outpost more than 1,000 miles west of Pearl Harbor; Japan's real objective was to destroy what remained of the American Pacific fleet. Superior air power enabled Nimitz's forces to engage the enemy at long range. Japanese fighters shot down 35 of 41 attacking torpedo bombers, but a second wave of dive-bombers sank three Japanese carriers. In all, Japan lost four carriers at Midway compared to the loss of just one American carrier. It was the first defeat the modern Japanese navy had ever suffered, and it left the United States in control of the Central Pacific.

American forces then launched their first Pacific offensive in the Solomon Islands, east of New Guinea, in August 1942. Both sides suffered heavy losses, but six months later, the Japanese were driven from the key island of Guadalcanal. MacArthur also began the long, slow, bloody job of driving the Japanese back along the north coast of New Guinea.

By early 1943, Japan was on the defensive, and the United States was preparing to penetrate the Gilbert, Marshall, and Caroline Islands and recapture the Philippines. Just as Russia had broken German power in Europe, so the United States, fighting alone except for Australia and New Zealand, had halted the Japanese. And, like the USSR in eastern Europe, America expected to reap the rewards of victory by dominating the Pacific in the future.

Quick Check

How did the United States break Japan's momentum in the Pacific?

✳ Explore World War II in the Pacific on MyHistoryLab

WHAT WERE U.S. INTERESTS IN THE PACIFIC THEATER OF WORLD WAR II?

As the United States built its overseas colonies in the Pacific during the decades prior to World War II, Japanese leaders, who were trying to build a colonial empire for their own country, felt threatened. Industrialization and a growing population in Japan meant that the country needed more resources than the home islands could provide. Following the example of European colonial powers, Japan began its own course of expansion during the late 1800s. Soon the empire of Japan acquired Korea, China, and islands in the Pacific as tributary colonies. Imperial competition with the United States prompted a surprise attack on the American naval base at Pearl Harbor on December 7, 1941, bringing the United States into World War II. Initially the Japanese enjoyed military success across the Pacific, but soon the United States began to push the Japanese forces back toward the home islands. Both before and during the course of the war, the Japanese committed a number of atrocities, both against military foes and civilians. In the United States, the American government removed over 100,000 Japanese-Americans and Japanese resident aliens to relocation centers in the West. Japan finally surrendered in August 1945 after the cites of Hiroshima and Nagasaki were nearly destroyed by the first atomic bombs used in combat and dropped by U.S. warplanes.

THE ATOMIC BOMB This aerial photograph shows the mushroom cloud over the Japanese city of Nagasaki on August 9, 1945, following the detonation of the second atomic bomb that, with the bombing of Hiroshima, led to Japan's surrender and the end of World War II

SELECTED MAJOR U.S. PACIFIC THEATER EVENTS

Year	Event	Victor
1941	Attack on Pearl Harbor	Japan
1942	Battle of Bataan	Japan
1942	Battle of Midway	U.S.
1942	Battle of Guadalcanal	U.S./Allied
1944	Battle of Leyte	U.S./Allied
1945	Battle of Iwo Jima	U.S.
1945	Battle of Okinawa	U.S./Allied
1945	Hiroshima: First Atomic Bombing	
1945	Nagasaki: Second Atomic Bombing	

KEY QUESTIONS Use **MyHistoryLab** *Explorer* to answer these **questions:**

Analysis ▶▶▶ *How did the Japanese military initially succeed across the Pacific in the war?*

Map the progress of early Japanese victories.

Response ▶▶▶ *What atrocities did Japanese armed forces commit to various groups?*

Understand these offenses.

Consequence ▶▶▶ *How did the U.S. government violate the civil rights of its own people during the war?*

See the unfolding of the Japanese Evacuation Program.

The Home Front

World War II affected American life more than the Great Depression had. While American soldiers and sailors fought overseas, the nation underwent sweeping social and economic changes. American industry worked to capacity to meet the need for war materials. Increased production in industry and agriculture benefited workers and farmers. The expansion of war-related industries encouraged people to move to where new jobs had sprung up. Women entered the paid workforce; rural dwellers relocated to urban areas; and northerners and easterners sought new opportunities and homes in the South and West. FDR also benefited from the return to prosperity the war brought on. The economic recovery helped him win a fourth term in 1944.

The Arsenal of Democracy

American industry made the nation's most important contribution to victory. Although more than 15 million Americans served in the armed forces, it was the nearly 60 million who worked on farms and factories who achieved the miracle of production that ensured the defeat of Germany and Japan. Manufacturing plants that had run at half capacity through the 1930s now hummed with activity. In Detroit, automobile assembly lines were converted to produce tanks and airplanes. At Henry Ford's giant Willow Run factory, covering 67 acres, 42,000 workers turned out a B-24 bomber every hour. Henry J. Kaiser, a California industrialist who constructed huge West Coast shipyards to meet the demand for cargo vessels and landing craft, operated on an equally large scale. His plant in Richmond, California, reduced the time to build a merchant ship from 105 to 14 days. In part, America won the battle of the Atlantic by building ships faster than German U-boats could sink them.

This vast industrial expansion, however, created problems. In 1942, President Roosevelt appointed Donald Nelson, a Sears, Roebuck executive, to head a War Production Board (WPB). A jovial, easygoing man, Nelson soon was outmaneuvered by the army and navy, which preferred to negotiate directly with large corporations. The WPB allowed business to claim rapid depreciation, and thus huge tax credits, for new plants and awarded lucrative cost-plus contracts for urgently needed goods. Shortages of critical materials such as steel, aluminum, and copper led to an allocation system based on military priorities. Rubber, cut off by the Japanese conquest of Southeast Asia, was particularly scarce; the administration finally began gasoline rationing in 1943 to curb pleasure driving and prolong tire life. The government built 51 synthetic-rubber plants, which by 1944 were producing nearly a million tons a year for the tires of American airplanes and military vehicles. All in all, the nation's factories turned out twice as many goods as did German and Japanese industry combined.

Roosevelt revealed the same tendency toward compromise in directing the economic mobilization as he did in shaping the New Deal. When the Office of Price Administration—which tried to curb inflation by controlling prices and rationing scarce goods such as sugar, canned food, and shoes—clashed with the WPB, FDR appointed James Byrnes to head an Office of Economic Stabilization. Byrnes, a former South Carolina senator and Supreme Court justice, used political judgment to settle disputes between agencies and keep all groups happy. The president also compromised with Congress, which pared down the administration's requests for large tax increases. Borrowing financed half the cost of the war, although taxes did rise. A $7-billion tax increase in 1942 included so many new taxpayers that in 1943 the Treasury Department instituted a new practice—withholding income taxes from workers' wages.

Quick Check

How was industry reorganized during the war?

A Nation on the Move

The war led to a vast migration of the American population. Young men left home for training camps and service overseas. Defense workers and their families, 9 million people in all, moved to work in the booming war industries. Norfolk, Virginia; San Diego, California; Mobile, Alabama; and other centers of defense production grew by more than 50 percent in just a year or two. Rural areas lost population while coastal regions, especially along the Pacific and the Gulf of Mexico, drew millions of people. Putting army camps, aircraft factories, and shipyards in the South and West created boom conditions in the future Sunbelt. California's population increased by nearly 2 million in less than five years.

This massive relocation caused severe social problems. Housing was in short supply. Migrating workers crowded into house trailers and boardinghouses, bringing unexpected windfalls to landlords. In one boomtown, a reporter described an old Victorian house that had five bedrooms on the second floor: "Three of them held two cots apiece, the two others held three cots." But the owner revealed that "the third floor is where we pick up the velvet. . . . We rent to workers in different shifts . . . three shifts a day . . . seven bucks a week apiece."

Family life suffered under these conditions. The number of marriages increased, as young people searched for something to hang on to amidst wartime turmoil, but so did the divorce rate. The baby boom that would peak in the 1950s began during the war and brought its own problems. Few publicly funded day-care centers were available, and working mothers worried about their "latchkey children." Schools in boom areas could not cope with the influx of new students; teacher shortages, intensified by the lure of higher wages in war industries, compounded the education crisis.

Despite these problems, women found the war a time of economic opportunity. Women's employment outside the home rose from 14 million in 1940 to 19 million

Watch the Video **Rosie the Riveter**

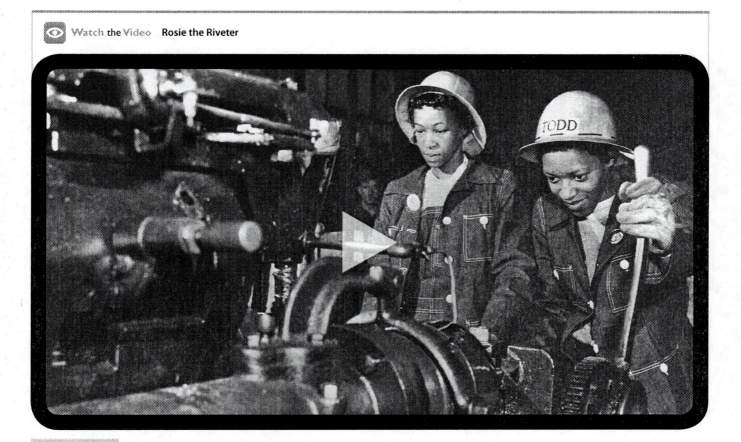

WOMEN AID WAR EFFORT As men left for military service in World War II and U.S. industry expanded to keep up with the defense needs, millions of women joined the paid labor force. The women shown here are operating a bolt-cutting machine at a factory in Erie, Pennsylvania.

by 1945. Most of the new women workers were married, and many were middle-aged, thus broadening the composition of the female workforce, which in the past had been composed primarily of young single women. Women entered industries once viewed as exclusively male; by the end of the war, they tended blast furnaces in steel mills and welded hulls in shipyards alongside men. Few challenged the traditional view of gender roles, yet the wartime experience temporarily undermined the concept that woman's proper place was in the home. Women enjoyed the hefty weekly paychecks, which rose by 50 percent from 1941 to 1943, and they took pride in their contributions to the war effort. "To hell with the life I have had," commented a former fashion designer. "This war is too damn serious, and it is too damn important to win it."

African Americans shared in the wartime migration, but racial prejudice limited their social and economic gains. Nearly one million served in the armed forces, but relatively few saw combat. The army placed black soldiers in segregated units, usually led by white officers, and used them for service and construction tasks. The navy relegated them to menial jobs until late in the war. African Americans were denied the chance to become petty officers, Secretary of the Navy Frank Knox explained, because "men of the colored race . . . cannot maintain discipline among men of the white race."

A. PHILIP RANDOLPH A. Philip Randolph (1889–1979) was a prominent African American labor leader and civil rights leader. In 1941, FDR and Randolph reached a political compromise that averted a threatened march on Washington, D.C., demanding integration of the military and an end to racial discrimination in defense industries and government employment.

African American civilians fared better. In 1941, black labor leader A. Philip Randolph threatened a massive march on Washington to force President Roosevelt to end racial discrimination in defense industries and government employment and to integrate the armed forces. FDR persuaded Randolph to call off the march and drop his integration demand in return for an executive order creating a Fair Employment Practices Committee (FEPC) to ban racial discrimination in war industries. As a result, African American employment by the federal government rose from 60,000 in 1941 to 200,000 by 1945. The FEPC was less successful in the private sector. Underfunded and understaffed, it could act on only one-third of the 8000 complaints it received. The nationwide shortage of labor did more than the FEPC to raise black employment during wartime. African Americans moved from the rural South to northern and western cities, finding jobs in the automobile, aircraft, and shipbuilding industries.

The movement of an estimated 700,000 people helped transform black–white relations from a regional issue into a national concern that could no longer be ignored. The limited housing and recreational facilities for both black and white war workers created tensions that led to urban race riots. On a hot Sunday evening in June 1943, blacks and whites began exchanging insults and then blows near Belle Isle recreation park in Detroit. The next day, a full-scale riot broke out in which 23 blacks and 9 whites died. The fighting raged for 24 hours until national guard troops restored order. Later that summer, only personal intervention by New York Mayor Fiorello LaGuardia quelled a Harlem riot in which six blacks died.

These outbursts of racial violence fueled the resentments that would grow into the postwar civil rights movement. For most African Americans, despite economic gains, World War II was a reminder of the inequality of American life. "Just carve on my tombstone," remarked one black soldier in the Pacific, "'Here lies a black man killed fighting a yellow man for the protection of a white man.'"

More than 300,000 Mexican Americans served in the armed forces and shared some of the same experiences as African Americans. Although they were not as segregated, many served in the 88th Division, made up largely of Mexican American officers and troops, which earned the nickname "Blue Devils" in the Italian campaign. At home, Spanish-speaking people left rural Texas, New Mexico, and California for jobs in the cities, especially in aircraft plants and petroleum refineries. Despite low wages and union resistance, they improved their economic position substantially. But they still faced discrimination based on skin color and language, most notably in the Los Angeles "zoot suit" riots in 1943 when white sailors attacked Mexican American youths dressed in their distinctive outfits—long jackets worn with pants tightly pegged at the ankles. The racial prejudice heightened feelings of ethnic identity and led returning Mexican American veterans to form organizations such as the American G.I. Forum to press for equal rights.

Native Americans joined the military in large numbers relative to their share of the population. Citing their warrior heritage, many enlisted without waiting for the draft to select them. "Since when has it been necessary for Blackfeet to draw lots to fight?" one member of that tribe asked scornfully. Native Americans fought in various theaters; among the most celebrated were the Navajo "code talkers," radiomen of the U.S. Marine Corps who employed their tribal language to frustrate Japanese eavesdropping.

A tragic counterpoint to the voluntary movement of American workers in search of jobs was the forced relocation of 120,000 Japanese Americans from the West Coast. Responding to racial fears in California after Pearl Harbor, President Roosevelt approved an army order in February 1942 to move all Japanese Americans on the West Coast to concentration camps in the interior. More than two-thirds of those detained were Nisei, native-born Americans whose only "crime" was their Japanese ancestry. Forced to sell their farms and businesses at distress prices, the Japanese Americans lost their worldly goods and their liberty. Herded into ten hastily built detention centers in seven western and southern states, they became prisoners in flimsy barracks behind barbed wire, guarded by armed troops.

Quick Check

How did the war affect women and minorities?

Appeals to the Supreme Court proved fruitless; in 1944, six justices upheld relocation on grounds of national security in wartime. Beginning in 1943, individual Nisei could win release by pledging their loyalty and finding a job away from the West Coast. Some 35,000 left the camps during the next two years, including more than 13,000 who joined the armed forces. The all-Nisei 442nd Combat Team served gallantly in Europe, losing more than 500 men in battle and winning more than 1000 citations for bravery. One World War II veteran remembers that when his unit was in trouble, the commander would issue a familiar appeal: "Call in the Japs."

For other Nisei, the experience was bitter. More than 5000 renounced their American citizenship and chose to live in Japan after the war. The government did not close down the last detention center until March 1946. Japanese Americans never experienced the torture and mass death of the German concentration camps, but their treatment was a disgrace to a nation fighting for freedom and democracy. Finally, in 1988, Congress voted an indemnity of $1.2 billion for the estimated 60,000 surviving Japanese Americans detained during World War II. Susumi Emori, who had been moved with his wife and four children from his farm in Stockton, California, to a camp in Arkansas, felt vindicated. "It was terrible," he said, with tears in his eyes, "but it was a time of war. Anything can happen. I didn't blame the United States for that."

Victory

27.5 How did the war end, and what were its consequences?

World War II ended with surprising swiftness. By 1943, the Axis tide had been turned in Europe and Asia, and Russia, the United States, and Britain mounted the offensives that began to drive Germany and Japan back across the vast areas they had conquered to their final defeat.

The long-awaited second front finally came in June 1944. For two years, the United States and Britain built up a force of nearly three million troops and an armada of ships and landing craft to carry them across the English Channel. Hoping to catch Hitler by surprise, Eisenhower chose the Normandy peninsula, where the lack of good harbors had led to lighter German fortifications. Allied aircraft bombed northern France for six weeks preceding the assault to block German reinforcements once the invasion began.

D-Day, when the invasion would begin, was set for June 5, but bad weather forced a delay. Relying on a forecasted break in the storm, Eisenhower gambled on going ahead on June 6. During the night, three divisions parachuted behind the German defenses; at dawn, American, British, and Canadian troops fought their way ashore at five points along a 60-mile stretch of beach, encountering stiff resistance. By the end of the day, however, Eisenhower had won his beachhead; a week later, more than 300,000 men were pushing back the Germans through the hedgerows of Normandy. The breakthrough came on July 25 when General Omar Bradley decimated the enemy with a massive artillery and aerial bombardment at Saint-Lô, opening a gap for George Patton's Third Army. American tanks raced across the French countryside, trapping thousands of Germans and liberating Paris by August 25. Allied troops reached the Rhine River by September, but a shortage of supplies, especially gasoline, forced a three-month halt.

Hitler took advantage of this breathing spell to counterattack in what became known as the Battle of the Bulge. In mid-December, the remaining German armored divisions burst through a weak point in the Allied lines in the Ardennes Forest, hoping to reach the coast and cut off nearly one-third of Eisenhower's forces. Tactical surprise and bad weather, which prevented Allied air support, led to a huge bulge in the American lines. But an airborne division at the key crossroads of Bastogne, in Belgium, held off a much larger German force. Allied reinforcements and air power then broke the attack. By committing nearly all his reserves to this offensive, Hitler had delayed

D-Day June 6, 1944, the day Allied troops crossed the English Channel and opened a second front in western Europe during World War II. The "D" stands for "disembarkation": to leave a ship and go ashore.

Eisenhower's advance into Germany by a few months, but he also had fatally weakened German resistance.

The end came quickly. American and British bombers had been pounding German cities for many months. Hamburg had been leveled in 1943; Dresden joined the list in early 1945. The destruction included tens of thousands of civilian lives and provoked controversy then and later, but it also hindered the German war effort during the critical final phase. A massive Russian offensive in mid-January swept toward Berlin. Bradley's troops, finding a bridge the Germans had left intact, crossed the Rhine on March 7. Although the British favored a concentrated drive on Berlin, the Allied forces advanced on a broad front, capturing the industrial Ruhr basin and breaking the Nazi death grip on prisoner populations, including the tragic remnant of the **Nazi Holocaust**, the slaughter of six million Jews and other persons whom Hitler's regime despised. The Americans and British met the Russians at the Elbe River in late April. With the Red Army already in the streets of Berlin, Hitler committed suicide on April 30. A week later, on May 7, 1945, Eisenhower accepted the unconditional surrender of all German forces. Just 11 months and a day after the landings in Normandy, the Allies had brought the war in Europe to a successful conclusion.

Nazi Holocaust The slaughter of six million Jews and other persons by Hitler's regime.

War Aims and Wartime Diplomacy

The American contribution to Hitler's defeat was relatively minor compared to the damage the Soviet Union inflicted. At the height of the German invasion of Russia, more than 300 Soviet divisions had battled 250 German ones. The United States and Britain used only 58 divisions in the Normandy invasion. As his armies overran Poland and the Balkans, Stalin was determined to control this region, which had been the historic pathway for Western invasions of Russia. Delay in opening the second front and an innate distrust of the West convinced the Soviets that they should maximize their gains by imposing communist regimes on eastern Europe.

American postwar goals were different. Now believing the failure to join the League of Nations in 1919 had led to the coming of World War II, the American people and their leaders vowed to put their faith in a new attempt at collective security. At Moscow in 1943, Secretary of State Cordell Hull had won Russian agreement to participate in a world organization at the war's end. The first wartime Big Three conference brought together Roosevelt, Churchill, and Stalin at Tehran, Iran, in late 1943. Stalin reaffirmed this commitment and promised to enter the war against Japan once Germany was defeated.

By the time the Big Three met again in February 1945 at the **Yalta Conference**, the military situation favored the Russians. While British and American forces were still recovering from the Battle of the Bulge, the Red Army was within 50 miles of Berlin. Stalin drove hard bargains. He refused to give up communist domination of Poland and the Balkans, although he did agree to Roosevelt's request for a Declaration of Liberated Europe, which called for free elections without providing for enforcement or supervision. Stalin also promised to enter the Pacific war three months after Germany surrendered. In return, Roosevelt offered concessions in Asia, including Russian control over Manchuria. While neither a sellout nor a betrayal, as some critics have charged, Yalta was a diplomatic triumph for the Soviets—one that reflected Russia's major contribution to victory in Europe.

Yalta Conference A wartime conference in February 1945 in which the Allies agreed to final plans for the defeat of Germany and the terms of its occupation. The Soviets agreed to allow free elections in Poland, but these were never held.

For the president, the long journey to Yalta proved too much. His health continued to fail after his return to Washington. In April, FDR left for Warm Springs, Georgia, where he had always been able to relax. He was sitting for his portrait at midday on April 12, 1945, when he complained of a "terrific headache," slumped forward, and died.

The nation mourned a man who had gallantly met the challenges of the Depression and global war. Unfortunately, FDR had not prepared his successor for the problems that lay ahead. The defeat of Nazi Germany dissolved the strongest bond between the United States and the Soviet Union. With different histories, cultures, and ideologies, the two nations were bound to drift apart. The inexperienced Harry Truman had to manage the rivalry that was destined to develop into the future Cold War.

Quick Check

How did the objectives of the United States and the Soviet Union conflict?

Triumph and Destruction in the Pacific

The total defeat of Germany in May 1945 turned eyes toward Japan. Although the combined chiefs of staff had estimated it would take 18 months after Germany's surrender to conquer Japan, American forces moved faster. Admiral Nimitz swept through the Gilbert, Marshall, and Caroline Islands in 1944, securing bases and building airfields for American B-29s to bombard the Japanese home islands. MacArthur cleared New Guinea of the last Japanese defender in early 1944, and American troops landed in the Philippines on October 20. Manila fell in early February 1945. The Japanese navy, in a Pacific version of the Battle of the Bulge, launched a daring three-pronged attack on the American invasion fleet in Leyte Gulf. The U.S. Navy blunted all three thrusts, sinking four carriers and ending any further Japanese naval threat.

Japan's defeat was now inevitable. The United States had three possible ways to proceed. The military favored a full-scale invasion, beginning on the southernmost island of Kyushu in November 1945 and culminating with a climactic battle for Tokyo in 1946; hundreds of thousands of casualties were expected. Diplomats, in contrast, urged the United States to modify the unconditional surrender formula to permit Japan to retain its emperor.

((• 🕮 Read the Document   John A. Siemes, An Eyewitness to Hiroshima (1945)

BOMBING OF NAGASAKI The atomic bomb dropped on Nagasaki, a provincial capital and naval base in southern Japan, on August 9, 1945, virtually obliterated the city and killed more than 60,000 people. Only buildings made with reinforced concrete remained standing after the blast.

The third option involved the **Manhattan Project**, the top-secret program that developed the atom bomb. Scientists, many of them refugees from Europe, had worked since 1939 to perfect this deadly new weapon. In the New Mexico desert on July 16, 1945, they successfully tested the first atomic bomb, creating a fireball brighter than several suns and a telltale mushroom cloud that rose some 40,000 feet above an enormous crater in the desert floor.

Truman had been unaware of the Manhattan Project before he became president. Now he simply followed the recommendation of a committee headed by Secretary of War Henry L. Stimson to drop the bomb on a Japanese city. The committee rejected inviting the Japanese to observe a demonstration shot at a remote Pacific site or giving advance notice of the bomb's destructive power. Neither Truman nor Stimson had qualms about dropping the bomb without warning. They viewed it as a legitimate wartime measure to save the lives of hundreds of thousands of Americans—and Japanese—that would be lost in a full-scale invasion.

Weather conditions on August 6 dictated the choice of Hiroshima as the bomb's target. The explosion incinerated four square miles of the city, killing more than 60,000. Two days later, Russia entered the war against Japan. On August 9, the United States dropped a second bomb on Nagasaki. No more atomic bombs were available, but no more were needed. The emperor personally commanded his ministers to surrender unconditionally on August 14, 1945. Three weeks later, Japan signed a formal capitulation on the decks of the battleship *Missouri* in Tokyo Bay. World War II was over.

Years later, scholars charged that Truman had more in mind than defeating Japan when he decided to use the atomic bomb. Citing air force and naval officers who claimed a blockade or conventional air attacks could defeat Japan, these revisionists suggested the bomb was really dropped to impress the Soviet Union with the United States' exclusive possession of the ultimate weapon. The evidence indicates that while Truman and his associates were aware of the possible effect on the Soviet Union, their primary motive was to end World War II as quickly and effortlessly as possible. Saving American lives, along with a desire for revenge for Pearl Harbor, was uppermost in the decision to bomb Hiroshima and Nagasaki. Yet in using the atomic bomb to defeat Japan, the United States virtually guaranteed a postwar arms race with the Soviet Union.

Conclusion: The Transforming Power of War

The second great war of the twentieth century changed American life. For the first time, the nation had achieved its military potential. In 1945, the United States was unquestionably the strongest country on earth, with 12 million men and women in uniform; a vast array of shipyards, aircraft plants, and munitions factories in full production; and a monopoly over the atomic bomb. For better or worse, it was now launched on a global career. In the future, the United States would be involved in all parts of the world, from Western Europe to remote jungles in Asia, from the nearby Caribbean to the distant Persian Gulf. And despite its enormous strength in 1945, the nation's new world role would encompass failure and frustration as well as power and dominion.

The war's legacy was equally strong at home. Four years of fighting brought about industrial recovery and unparalleled prosperity. The old pattern of unregulated free enterprise was as much a victim of the war as of the New Deal; big government and huge deficits had now become the norm. Economic control passed from New York and Wall Street to Washington and Pennsylvania Avenue. Far-reaching changes in American society would become apparent only decades later. Such distinctive patterns of recent American life as the baby boom and the growth of the Sunbelt began during wartime. World War II was a watershed in twentieth-century America, ushering in a new age of global concerns and domestic upheaval.

Manhattan Project The top-secret World War II program that produced the first atomic weapons.

27.1

27.2

27.3

27.4

27.5

Manhattan Project The top-secret World War II program that produced the first atomic weapons.

Quick Check

What was the role of the atomic bomb in ending the war against Japan?

Chapter Review

Isolationism

27.1 What was isolationism, and why was it so appealing to Americans in the 1920s and 1930s? p. 627

Disillusionment with the outcome of World War I led to a policy of isolationism, by which Americans hoped to avoid responsibility for the peace of Europe and Asia, and to spare themselves the agony of war if peace failed. Isolationism had traditionally served Americans well, and many Americans expected that it would continue to do so.

The Road to War

27.2 How did the United States go from neutrality in the 1930s to war in 1941? p. 630

FDR gradually led the United States from neutrality in the 1930s to war in 1941, responding to German and Japanese aggression with careful political and diplomatic steps, including aid to Britain, an undeclared naval war against Germany, and economic pressure on Japan, which lashed out by attacking Pearl Harbor.

Turning the Tide Against the Axis

27.3 How did America and its allies halt the advances of Germany and Japan? p. 634

The United States formed an alliance with Britain and the Soviet Union against Germany and Japan. American and British forces fought the Germans in North Africa and Italy, while Soviet forces beat back the Germans in Russia. American ships and planes defeated Japanese forces at the Coral Sea and Midway.

The Home Front

27.4 How did American domestic life change during World War II? p. 640

During the war, American industry churned out equipment at a rate unimagined before 1941. Record numbers of women and minorities entered the workforce. But 120,000 Japanese Americans were forced into concentration camps.

Victory

27.5 How did the war end, and what were its consequences? p. 644

The war in Europe ended in May 1945 after Allied and Soviet forces overran Germany. The war in the Pacific ended after the atomic bombing of Hiroshima and Nagasaki, and left the United States in undisputed control of Japan.

Timeline

1936
Road to War—Hitler's troops reoccupy Rhineland

1936

1937

1937
Isolationism—FDR signs permanent Neutrality Act (May)

1938
Road to War—Munich Conference appeases Hitler (September)

1938

1939

1939
Road to War—Germany invades Poland; World War II begins

1941
Road to War—Japan attacks Pearl Harbor; United States enters World War II

1941

1942
Turning the Tide—United States defeats Japanese at Battle of Midway (June); Allies land in North Africa (November)

1942

1944
Turning the Tide—Allies land on Normandy beachheads

1944

1945

1945
Victory—Germany surrenders unconditionally (May); United States drops atomic bombs on Hiroshima and Nagasaki; Japan surrenders (August)

28 The Onset of the Cold War 1945–1960

The Potsdam Summit

"I **am getting ready to go see** Stalin and Churchill," President Truman wrote to his mother in July 1945, "and it is a chore." On board the cruiser Augusta, the new president complained in his diary about the upcoming **Potsdam Conference**: "How I hate this trip! But I have to make it—win, lose, or draw—and we must win. I am giving nothing away except to save starving people and even then I hope we can only help them to help themselves."

Halfway around the world, Joseph Stalin left Moscow a day late because of a slight heart attack. The Soviet leader hated to fly, so he traveled by rail. Moreover, he ordered the heavily guarded train to detour around Poland for fear of an ambush, further delaying his arrival. When he arrived in Potsdam, a suburb of Berlin miraculously spared the total destruction that the Allies had wrought in the German capital, he was ready to claim the spoils of war.

POTSDAM CONFERENCE Churchill, Truman, and Stalin during the Potsdam Conference in July 1945.

LEARNING OBJECTIVES

28.1 ((•	28.2 ((•	28.3 ((•	28.4 ((•
How did the Cold War begin? p. 651	What was containment, and why was it adopted? p. 654	How did the Cold War expand from Europe to Asia? p. 659	How did the Cold War affect life in America? p. 664

Watch the Video Series on MyHistoryLab

Learn about some key topics related to this chapter with the
MyHistoryLab Video Series: Key Topics in U.S. History.

1 **The Cold War: 1945–1953** Although the United States
and the Soviet Union were allies during the World War II,
a mutual mistrust still lurked in the background. With
the end of the war and the Soviet Union's development
of an atomic bomb, the two superpowers, one capitalist
and one communist, vied for economic, political, and
military influence around the globe. This video provides an introduction to the Cold
War, a unique conflict that saw two nations face off without ever meeting on the
battlefield.

Watch on MyHistoryLab

Origins of the Cold War This video explores the tensions that existed between the Soviet Union and
the United States before and after World War II. Of special significance is the Yalta Conference, where
arrangements were made for keeping the peace after the war. The video also looks at the formation of
the United Nations, an organization designed prevent World War III.

2

Watch on MyHistoryLab

3 **Truman Doctrine and the Marshall Plan** This video examines the Truman Doctrine and the Marshall
Plan, two initiatives that expanded the global influence of the United States . The Truman Doctrine
declared that the United States would use its resources to support free nations against communist
attack or rebellion. The Marshall Plan provided funds to rebuild Western Europe and keep its people
from electing communist governments.

Watch on MyHistoryLab

The Korean War This video explores the Korean War, in which the United States and the United Nations
attempted to halt communist North Korea's invasion of South Korea. Called a "police action," the Korean
War legitimized the UN's role as a peacekeeper. For the United States, it proved that America would go
to war to contain communism—establishing a precedent for the Vietnam War.

4

Watch on MyHistoryLab

Potsdam Conference The final wartime meeting of the leaders of the United States, Britain, and the Soviet Union was held at Potsdam, outside Berlin, in July 1945. Their failure to agree about the future of Europe led to the Cold War.

These two men, one the veteran revolutionary who had been in power for two decades, the other an untested leader in office for barely three months, symbolized the enormous differences that now separated the wartime allies. Stalin was above all a realist. Brutal in securing total control at home, he was more flexible in his foreign policy, bent on exploiting Russia's victory in World War II rather than aiming at world domination. Cunning and caution were the hallmarks of his diplomatic style. Short and ungainly, he waited, catlike, behind his unassuming facade, ready to pounce on an opponent with his "brilliant, terrifying tactical mastery." Truman, in contrast, personified traditional Wilsonian idealism. Lacking Roosevelt's guile, the new president placed his faith in international cooperation. Like many Americans, he took his country's innate goodness for granted. Self-assured to the point of cockiness, he came to Potsdam clothed in the armor of self-righteousness.

Truman and Stalin met for the first time on July 17, 1945. "I told Stalin that I am no diplomat," the president recorded in his diary, "but usually said yes and no to questions after hearing all the argument." The Russian dictator's reaction to Truman remains a mystery, but Truman believed the first encounter went well: "I can deal with Stalin. He is honest—but smart as hell."

Together with Winston Churchill and his replacement as prime minister, Clement Attlee, whose Labour party had just triumphed in British elections, Truman and Stalin clashed for the next ten days over such difficult issues as reparations, the Polish borders, and Eastern Europe. Truman presented the ideas and proposals formulated by his advisers; he saw his task as essentially procedural, and when he presided, he moved the agenda along briskly. After he had "banged through" three items one day, he commented, "I am not going to stay around this terrible place all summer, just to listen to speeches. I'll go home to the Senate for that." In an indirect, roundabout way, he informed Stalin of the existence of the atomic bomb, tested successfully in the New Mexico desert just before the conference began. Truman offered no details, and the impassive Stalin asked for none, commenting only that he hoped the United States would make "good use of it against the Japanese."

Reparations were the crucial issue at Potsdam. The Russians wanted to rebuild their war-ravaged economy with German industry; the United States feared it would be saddled with the entire cost of caring for the defeated Germans. A compromise was finally reached. Each side would take reparations primarily from its own occupation zone, a solution that foreshadowed the division of Germany. "Because they could not agree on how to govern Europe," wrote historian Daniel Yergin, "Truman and Stalin began to divide it." The other issues were referred to a Council of Foreign Ministers, which would meet in the fall in London.

The Potsdam Conference thus ended on a note of harmony; beneath the surface, however, the bitter antagonism of the Cold War was festering. A dozen years later, Truman described himself as "an innocent idealist" surrounded by wolves. He claimed that all the agreements reached at Potsdam were "broken as soon as the unconscionable Russian Dictator returned to Moscow!" He added ruefully, "And I liked the little son of a bitch."

Potsdam marked the end of the wartime alliance. America and Russia, each distrusting the other, began a long, bitter confrontation. For the next decade, the two superpowers would vie to control postwar Europe, and later clash over the spread of communism to Asia. When Truman's and Stalin's successors met for the next summit conference, at Geneva in 1955, the Cold War was at its height.

The Cold War Begins

28.1 How did the Cold War begin?

The conflict between the United States and the Soviet Union began gradually. For two years, the nations tried to negotiate their differences over the division of Europe and the atomic bomb. The Council of Foreign Ministers provided the forum. Beginning in London in 1945 and meeting with their Russian counterparts in Paris, New York, and Moscow, American diplomats searched for a way to live in peace with a suspicious Soviet Union.

The Division of Europe

The fundamental disagreement was over control of postwar Europe. In the east, the Red Army had swept over Poland and most of the Balkans, laying the basis for Soviet domination there. American and British forces had liberated Western Europe from Scandinavia to Italy. The Russians, mindful of past invasions from the west across the plains of Poland, were intent on imposing communist governments loyal to Moscow in the Soviet sphere. The United States, on the other hand, upheld the principle of national self-determination, insisting the people in each country should freely elect their postwar rulers. The Soviets saw this demand as subversive, since they knew that popularly chosen regimes would be unfriendly to Russia. Suspecting American duplicity, Stalin brought down an **Iron Curtain** (Churchill's phrase for the suppression of individual rights in Eastern Europe) and created satellite governments (see Map 28.1).

Germany was the key. The temporary zones of occupation hardened into permanent divisions. Ignoring the Potsdam agreement that the country be treated as an economic unit, the United States, Britain, and France were by 1946 refusing to permit

Iron Curtain Winston Churchill coined the phrase "Iron Curtain" to refer to the boundary in Europe that divided Soviet-dominated Eastern and Central Europe from Western Europe.

((• 📖 Read the Document **Churchill's Iron Curtain Speech (March 5, 1946)**

MAP 28.1 EUROPE AFTER WORLD WAR II The heavy red line splitting Germany shows in graphic form the division of Europe between the Western and Soviet spheres of influence. "From Stettin in the Bapholtic to Trieste in the Adriatic," said Winston Churchill in a speech at Fulton, Missouri, in 1946, "an iron curtain has descended across the Continent."

the Russians to take reparations from the industrial western zones. The initial harsh occupation policy gave way to more humane treatment of the German people and a slow but steady economic recovery. The United States, Britain, and France merged their zones and championed the unification of all Germany. Russia, fearing a resurgence of German military power, responded by intensifying the communization of its zone, which included the jointly occupied city of Berlin. By 1947, Britain, France, and the United States were planning to transfer their authority to an independent West Germany.

The Soviet Union also consolidated its grip on Eastern Europe in 1946 and 1947. One by one, communist regimes replaced coalition governments in Poland, Hungary, Romania, and Bulgaria. Moving cautiously to avoid provoking the West, Stalin used communism to dominate half of Europe, both to protect the Soviet state and to advance its power. The climax came in March 1948 when a communist coup in Czechoslovakia overthrew a democratic government and gave the Soviets a strategic foothold in central Europe.

The division of Europe was an inevitable aftereffect of World War II. Both sides were intent on imposing their values in the areas their troops liberated. The Russians were no more likely to withdraw from Eastern Europe than the United States and Britain were from Germany, France, and Italy. A frank recognition of competing spheres of influence might have avoided escalating tension. But the Western nations, remembering Hitler's aggression in the 1930s, began to see Stalin as an equally dangerous threat to their well-being. Instead of accepting him as a cautious leader bent on protecting Russian security, they perceived him as an aggressive dictator leading a communist drive for world domination.

Quick Check

What caused the division of Europe after World War II?

The Atomic Dilemma

Overshadowing all else was the atomic bomb. Used by the United States with deadly success at Hiroshima and Nagasaki, the new weapon raised problems that would have been difficult for even friendly nations to resolve. Given Soviet–American tensions, the effect was disastrous.

The wartime policy followed by Roosevelt and Churchill ensured a postwar nuclear arms race. Instead of informing their major ally of the developing atomic bomb, they kept it secret. Stalin learned of the Manhattan Project through espionage and started a Soviet atomic program in 1943. By the time Truman informed Stalin of the weapon's existence at Potsdam, the Russians, aided by information from spies in the United States, were on the way to making their own bomb.

After the war, the United States developed a disarmament plan that would turn control of fissionable material, then the processing plants, and ultimately the American stockpile of bombs over to an international agency. When President Truman appointed financier Bernard Baruch to present this proposal to the United Nations, Baruch added sanctions against violators and exempted the international agency from the UN veto. Ignoring scientists who pleaded for a more cooperative position, Baruch followed instead the advice of Army Chief of Staff Dwight D. Eisenhower, who cited the rapid demobilization of the American armed forces (from nearly 12 million personnel in 1945 to fewer than 2 million in 1947) to argue that "we cannot at this time limit our capability to produce or use this weapon." In effect, the **Baruch Plan**, with its multiple stages and emphasis on inspection, would preserve the American atomic monopoly indefinitely.

The Soviets responded predictably. Ambassador Andrei Gromyko presented a simple plan calling for a total ban on producing and using the new weapon and destroying all existing bombs. The Russian proposal reflected the same perception of national self-interest as the Baruch Plan. Russia still had nearly 3 million men under arms in 1947 and wanted to maximize its conventional strength by outlawing the atomic bomb.

No agreement was possible. Neither the United States nor the Soviet Union could abandon its position without surrendering a vital interest. To preserve its monopoly, America stressed inspection and control; to neutralize the U.S. advantage, Russia advocated immediate disarmament. The nuclear dilemma, inherent in the Soviet–American rivalry, blocked any negotiated settlement. Instead, the two superpowers agreed to disagree, and each concentrated on taking maximum advantage of its wartime gains. Thus the Russians exploited the territory they had conquered in Europe while the United States retained its economic and strategic advantages over the Soviet Union. The result was the Cold War.

Baruch Plan In 1946, Bernard Baruch presented an American plan to control and eventually outlaw nuclear weapons. The plan called for UN control of nuclear weapons in three stages before the United States gave up its stockpile. Soviet insistence on immediate nuclear disarmament without inspection doomed the Baruch Plan and led to a nuclear arms race between the United States and the Soviet Union.

Quick Check

How did the atomic bomb influence international relations?

Containment

28.2 What was containment, and why was it adopted?

A major departure in American foreign policy occurred in January 1947, when General George C. Marshall, the wartime army chief of staff, became secretary of state. Calm, mature, and orderly, Marshall had the capability—honed in World War II—to think in broad strategic terms. An extraordinarily good judge of ability, he relied on gifted subordinates to implement his policies, and on two men in particular: Dean Acheson and George Kennan.

Acheson, an experienced Washington lawyer and bureaucrat, was appointed undersecretary of state and given free rein by Marshall to conduct American diplomacy. Acheson seemed more British than American, with his patrician manners, impeccable Ivy League clothes, and bushy mustache. Keenly intelligent, he had a carefully cultivated reputation for arrogance and a low tolerance for mediocrity. An ardent Anglophile, he wanted the United States to take over a faltering Britain's role as the arbiter of world affairs. Recalling the lessons of Munich, he opposed appeasement and advocated negotiating only from strength.

George Kennan, Marshall's other mainstay, headed the new Policy Planning Staff. A career diplomat, Kennan had become a Soviet expert, mastering Russian language, history, and culture. He had served in Moscow in the 1930s and during World War II and distrusted the Soviet regime. In a crucial telegram in 1946, he warned that the Kremlin believed "that there can be no compromise with rival power," arguing that only sustained resistance could halt the expansion of Russian power. As self-assured as Acheson, Kennan believed that neither Congress nor public opinion should interfere with the experts' conduct of foreign policy.

In the spring of 1947, a sense of crisis impelled Marshall, Acheson, and Kennan to set a new course in American diplomacy. Dubbed **containment**, after an article by Kennan in *Foreign Affairs*, the new policy both consolidated the evolving postwar anticommunism and established guidelines that would shape America's role in the world for more than two decades. Kennan proposed "a long-term, patient but firm, and vigilant containment of Russian expansive tendencies." Such a policy would not lead to immediate victory, Kennan warned. In the long run, however, he believed that the United States could force the Soviet Union to adopt more reasonable policies and live in peace with the West.

containment First proposed by George Kennan in 1947, containment became the basic strategy of the United States throughout the Cold War. Kennan argued that firm American resistance would eventually compel Moscow to adopt more peaceful policies.

The Truman Doctrine

The initial step toward containment came in response to an urgent appeal. Since March 1946, Britain had been supporting the Greek government in a bitter civil war against communist guerrillas. On February 21, 1947, the British informed the United States that they could no longer afford to aid Greece or Turkey, the latter under Soviet pressure for access to the Mediterranean. Believing the Russians responsible for the strife in Greece (in fact, they were not), Marshall, Acheson, and Kennan decided the United States would have to assume Britain's traditional role as the dominant power in the eastern Mediterranean.

Worried about congressional support, especially since the Republicans had gained control of Congress in 1946, Marshall met with the legislative leadership in February. He outlined the problem; then Acheson warned that "a highly possible Soviet breakthrough might open three continents to Soviet penetration." Comparing the situation in Greece to one rotten apple spoiling an entire barrel, Acheson warned that "the corruption of Greece would infect Iran and all to the east. It would also carry infection to Africa through Asia Minor and Egypt, and to Europe through Italy and France." Claiming that the Soviets were "playing one of the greatest gambles in history," Acheson concluded that "we and we alone were in a position to break up the play."

GEORGE F. KENNAN George F. Kennan (1904–2005) was an American political advisor, diplomat, political scientist, and historian. Kennan was instrumental in developing the policy of containment concerning the Soviet Union that dominated the immediate post–World War II era.

The bipartisan group of congressional leaders was impressed. Finally, Republican Senator Arthur H. Vandenberg said he would support the president, but added that to ensure public backing, Truman would have to "scare hell" out of the American people.

The president followed that advice. On March 12, 1947, he asked Congress for $400 million for military and economic assistance to Greece and Turkey. In what became known as the **Truman Doctrine**, he made clear that the stakes were far higher than just these two countries: "It must be the policy of the United States to support free peoples who are resisting attempted subjugation by armed minorities or by outside pressure." Both the House and the Senate approved the program by margins of better than three to one.

The Truman Doctrine was an informal declaration of cold war against the Soviet Union. Truman used the crisis to secure congressional approval and build a national consensus for the policy of containment. The Greek civil war ended in 1949, but the American commitment to oppose communist expansion, whether by internal subversion or external aggression, placed the United States on a collision course with the Soviet Union around the globe.

Truman Doctrine In 1947, President Truman asked Congress for money to aid the Greek and Turkish governments that were then threatened by communist rebels. Truman asserted that the United States was committed to support free people everywhere against communist attack or rebellion.

Quick Check

What was the significance of the Truman Doctrine?

The Marshall Plan

Western Europe, however, was far more vital to U.S. interests than was the eastern Mediterranean. Yet by 1947, many Americans believed that Western Europe was open to Soviet penetration. The problem was economic. Despite $9 billion in piece-meal American loans, the European countries had difficulty recovering from World War II. Food was scarce, with millions existing on less than 1500 calories a day; industrial machinery was broken down and obsolete; years of depression and war had demoralized workers. The cruel winter of 1947, the worst in 50 years, compounded the problem. Resentment and discontent led to votes for communist parties, especially in Italy and France. It seemed as though all Europe might drift into the communist orbit.

In the weeks following the proclamation of the Truman Doctrine, American officials dealt with this problem. Secretary of State Marshall, returning from a frustrating meeting in Moscow, warned that "the patient is sinking while the doctors deliberate." Acheson believed that it was time to extend American "economic power" in Europe, "to call an effective halt to the Soviet Union's expansionism," and "to create a basis for political stability and economic well-being." The experts drew up a plan for the massive infusion of American capital to finance the recovery of Europe. Speaking at Harvard on June 5, 1947, Marshall offered economic aid to all the nations of Europe if they could agree on ways to achieve "the revival of a working economy in the world so as to permit the emergence of political and social conditions in which free institutions can exist."

The fate of the **Marshall Plan**, as the aid program was called, depended on the reaction of the Soviet Union and Congress. Marshall had taken, as one American diplomat said, "a hell of a gamble" by including Russia in his offer of aid. At a meeting in Paris in July 1947, the Soviet foreign minister ended the suspense. Neither the Soviet Union nor its satellites would take part, apparently because Moscow saw the Marshall Plan as an American attempt to weaken its control over Eastern Europe. The other European countries then formally requested $17 billion in assistance over the next four years.

Congress appointed a special joint committee to investigate the proposal. The administration pointed out that the Marshall Plan would help the United States by stimulating trade with Europe and check Soviet expansion. The latter argument proved decisive. When the Czech coup touched off a war scare in March 1948, Congress approved the Marshall Plan by heavy majorities. Over the next four years, the huge American investment generated an industrial revival in Western Europe that became self-sustaining by the 1950s. The communist threat faded, and a prosperous Europe became a bonanza for American farmers, miners, and manufacturers.

Marshall Plan A massive aid program begun in 1947 to rebuild the war-torn economies of Western Europe. The plan was motivated by both humanitarian concerns and fear of communism.

Quick Check

What was the purpose of the Marshall Plan?

The Western Military Alliance

The third and final phase of containment came in 1949 with the **North Atlantic Treaty Organization (NATO)**. NATO grew out of European fears of Russian military aggression.

Recalling Hitler's tactics in the 1930s, Western Europeans wanted assurance that the United States would protect them from attack as they began to achieve economic recovery. American diplomats were sympathetic. "People could not go ahead and make investments for the future," commented Averell Harriman, the American ambassador in Moscow, "without some sense of security."

Britain, France, Belgium, the Netherlands, and Luxembourg began the process in March 1948 with the Brussels Treaty, providing for collective self-defense. In January 1949, President Truman called for a broader defense pact; ten European nations, from Norway to Italy, joined the United States and Canada in signing the North Atlantic Treaty in Washington on April 4, 1949. This departure from the traditional policy of isolation—the United States had not signed such a treaty since the French alliance in the eighteenth century—caused debate, but the Senate ratified it in July by a vote of 82 to 13.

North Atlantic Treaty Organization (NATO) In 1949, the United States, Canada, and ten European nations formed this military mutual-defense pact.

NATO had two main features. First, the United States committed itself to defend Europe. The key clause stated: "An armed attack against one or more shall be considered an attack against them all." In effect, the United States was extending its atomic shield over Europe. The second feature was designed to reassure Europeans that the United States would honor this commitment. In late 1950, Truman appointed Dwight D. Eisenhower NATO supreme commander and stationed four American divisions in Europe as the nucleus of the NATO army. It was believed the threat of American troop involvement in any Russian assault would deter the Soviet Union from attacking.

The NATO alliance escalated the Cold War. Whatever its advantage in building a sense of security among Europeans, it represented an overreaction to the Soviet danger. Americans and Europeans alike were attempting to apply the lessons of Munich—that appeasement of aggressors led to more aggression—to the Cold War. But Stalin was not Hitler, and the Soviets were not the Nazis. There was no evidence of any Russian plan to invade Western Europe, and given the American atomic bomb, none was likely. NATO intensified Russian fears of the West and thus increased international tension.

Quick Check

What were the important features of NATO?

The Berlin Blockade

The main Russian response to containment came in 1948 at the West's most vulnerable point. American, British, French, and Soviet troops each occupied a sector of

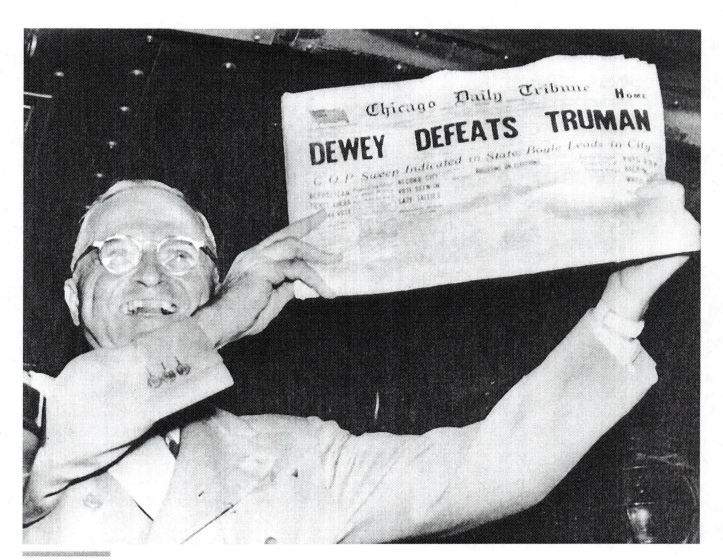

ELECTION NIGHT DRAMA A jubilant Harry Truman, on the morning after his 1948 election win, displays the headline blazoned on the front page of the *Chicago Daily Tribune*—a newspaper that believed the pollsters.

BERLIN AIRLIFT The Berlin airlift of 1948–1949 broke the Soviet blockade. Called "Operation Vittles," it provided food and fuel for West Berliners. Here, children atop a pile of rubble wave to an American cargo plane flying overhead.

Berlin airlift In 1948, in response to a Soviet land blockade of Berlin, the United States carried out a massive effort to supply the 2 million Berlin citizens by air. The airlift forced the Soviets to end the blockade in 1949.

Berlin, but the city was more than 100 miles within the Russian zone of Germany (see Map 28.1). Stalin decided to test his opponents' resolve by cutting off rail and road traffic to Berlin on June 20, 1948.

The Berlin blockade caught Truman unprepared. He had his hands full resisting efforts to force him off the Democratic ticket and faced a difficult reelection against Republican Governor Thomas E. Dewey of New York. The alternatives were unappealing. The United States could withdraw its forces and lose not just a city but the confidence of all Europe; it could try to send in reinforcements and fight for Berlin; or it could attempt to find a diplomatic solution. Characteristically, Truman told the military that there would be no pulling out. "We were going to stay, period," an aide reported him saying.

The president and his advisers then implemented the decision. Rejecting proposals to send an armored column down the main highway, the administration adopted a two-phase policy. The first part was a massive airlift of food, fuel, and supplies for the 10,000 troops and the 2 million civilians in Berlin. Fifty-two C-54s and 80 C-47s carried 2500 tons to Berlin every 24 hours. To guard against Soviet interruption of the **Berlin airlift**, Truman transferred 60 American B-29s, capable of delivering atomic bombs, to bases in Britain. The president was bluffing; the B-29s were not equipped with atomic bombs, but the threat was effective.

The world teetered on the edge of war. Stalin did not disrupt the flights to Berlin, but he rejected American diplomatic initiatives. Although the Russians could have halted it by jamming radar or shooting down the defenseless cargo planes, the airlift increased to more than 4000 tons a day. Dewey supported the president, thus removing foreign policy from the campaign. Yet the tension was fierce. In September, Truman asked his advisers to brief him "on bases, bombs, Moscow, Leningrad, etc." "I have a terrible feeling afterward that we are very close to war," he confided in his diary. "I hope not."

Slowly, the tension eased. The Russians did not shoot down any planes, and the daily airlift climbed to nearly 7000 tons. Truman, a decided underdog, won a surprising second term in November over a complacent Dewey, in part because the Berlin crisis had rallied the nation behind his leadership. In early 1949, the Soviets ended the blockade in return for another meeting of the Council of Foreign Ministers on Germany—a conclave that was as unproductive as all the earlier ones.

The Berlin crisis marked the end of the initial phase of the Cold War. The airlift had shown the world the triumph of American ingenuity over Russian stubbornness. Yet the Cold War had still cut Europe in two. Behind the Iron Curtain, the Russians had consolidated control over the areas their troops won in the war, while the United States had used the Marshall Plan to revitalize Western Europe. But a divided continent was a far cry from the wartime hopes for a peaceful world. And the rivalry that began in Europe would spread into a worldwide contest between the superpowers.

Quick Check

How did the United States respond to the Berlin blockade?

The Cold War Expands

28.3   How did the Cold War expand from Europe to Asia?

The rivalry between the United States and the Soviet Union grew in the late 1940s and early 1950s. Both sides rebuilt their military forces with new methods and weapons. The diplomatic competition spread as each of the superpowers sought to enhance its influence in East Asia. By the time Truman left office in 1953, the Cold War had become global.

The Military Dimension

After World War II, American leaders were intent on reforming the nation's military system. Two goals were uppermost. First, nearly everyone agreed in the aftermath of Pearl Harbor that the U.S. armed services should be unified into an integrated system. The Cold War reinforced this decision. Without unification, declared George Marshall in 1945, "there can be little hope that we will be able to maintain through the years a military posture that will secure for us a lasting peace." Planners also realized the need for new institutions to coordinate military and diplomatic strategy, so the nation could counter threats to its security.

In 1947, the **National Security Act** established a Department of Defense, headed by a civilian secretary of cabinet rank presiding over three separate services—the army, the navy, and the new air force. The act also created the Central Intelligence Agency (CIA) to coordinate the intelligence-gathering activities of government agencies and a National Security Council (NSC)—composed of the service secretaries, the secretary of defense, and the secretary of state—to advise the president regarding the nation's security.

Despite the appearance of equality among the services, the air force became the dominant power in the atomic age, based on its capability both to deter an enemy from attacking and to wage war if deterrence failed. President Truman, intent on reducing defense expenditures, allotted the air force more than one-half the total of his 1949 military budget. After the Czech coup and the resulting war scare, Congress granted an additional $3 billion to the military. The appropriation included funds for a new B-36 to replace the B-29 as the nation's primary strategic bomber.

American military planners received even greater support in 1949 after the Soviet Union exploded its first atomic bomb. Truman appointed a committee to explore an all-out effort to build a hydrogen bomb to maintain American nuclear supremacy.

National Security Act Congress passed the National Security Act in 1947 in response to perceived threats from the Soviet Union after World War II. It established the Department of Defense and created the Central Intelligence Agency (CIA) and National Security Council.

NSC-68 National Security Council planning paper No. 68 redefined America's national defense policy. Adopted in 1950, it committed the United States to a massive military buildup to meet the challenge posed by the Soviet Union.

Quick Check

What changes did the Cold War prompt in American military institutions and policies?

Some scientists had technical objections to the H-bomb. Others opposed it on moral grounds, claiming that its enormous destructive power (intended to be 1000 times greater than the atomic bomb) made it unthinkable. George Kennan suggested a new effort at international arms control with the Soviets, but Dean Acheson—who succeeded Marshall as secretary of state in 1949—believed the United States had to develop the hydrogen bomb before the Soviet Union. When Acheson presented the committee's favorable report to the president in January 1950, Truman took only seven minutes to decide to go ahead.

Acheson also ordered the Policy Planning Staff (headed by Paul Nitze after Kennan resigned in protest) to draw up a new national defense policy. **NSC-68**, as the document became known, was based on the premise that the Soviet Union sought "to impose its absolute authority over the rest of the world" and thus "mortally challenged" the United States. Rejecting appeasement or a return to isolation, Nitze advocated massive expansion of American military power to overcome the Soviet threat. Contending the nation could afford to spend "upward of 50 percent of its gross national product" for security, NSC-68 proposed increasing defense spending from $13 to $45 billion annually. Approved in principle by the National Security Council in April 1950, NSC-68 symbolized the Truman administration's determination to win the Cold War regardless of cost.

THE H-BOMB The explosion of a U.S. test bomb over an uninhabited island in the Pacific on November 1, 1952, demonstrated to the world the fearsome power of the hydrogen bomb. This early H-bomb could destroy a city the size of Washington, D.C.

The Cold War in Asia

The Soviet–American conflict developed more slowly in Asia. At Yalta, the two superpowers had agreed to a Far Eastern balance of power, with the Russians dominating northeast Asia and the Americans controlling the Pacific, including Japan and its former island empire.

The United States quickly consolidated its sphere of influence. General Douglas MacArthur denied the Soviet Union any role in reconstructing Japan. Instead, he supervised the transition of the Japanese government into a constitutional democracy along Western lines, in which communists were barred from government. The Japanese renounced war in their new constitution, relying on American forces to protect their security. American policy was equally nationalistic in the Pacific. A trusteeship arrangement with the United Nations disguised the United States' control over the Marshall, Mariana, and Caroline Islands. American scientists conducted atomic bomb tests at the Bikini Atoll in 1946, and by 1949, MacArthur declared that the Pacific "had become an Anglo-Saxon lake and our line of defense runs through the chain of islands fringing the coast of Asia."

China lay between the Soviet and American spheres. When World War II ended, the country was torn between Chiang Kai-shek's Nationalists in the south and Mao Zedong's communists in the north. Chiang had American political and economic backing and official Soviet recognition. But corruption was widespread among the Nationalist leaders, and inflation that soon reached 100 percent a year devastated the Chinese middle classes and eroded Chiang's support. Mao used discipline and patriotic appeals to strengthen his hold on the peasantry and extend his influence. When the Soviets vacated Manchuria in 1946, after stripping it of the industrial machinery Japan had installed there, Mao obtained control of this rich northern province. Ignoring American advice, Chiang occupied Manchurian cities, overextending his supply lines and exposing his forces to communist counterattack.

American policy sought to prevent a Chinese civil war. Before he became secretary of state, George Marshall tried to form a coalition government between Chiang and Mao. For a few months in 1946, Marshall appeared to have succeeded, but in reality, compromise was impossible. Chiang insisted he "was going to liquidate communists," while Mao tried to play the United States against Russia. By 1947, as China plunged into full-scale civil war, the Truman administration had given up trying to influence the outcome. Political mediation had failed, military intervention was out of the question so soon after World War II, and continued American economic aid served only to appease domestic supporters of Chiang; 80 percent of the military supplies ended up in communist hands.

In late 1948, Mao drove the Nationalists out of Manchuria. By mid-1949, the communists had crossed the Yangtze River. Acheson reported that the civil war "was beyond the control of the government of the United States." An American military adviser told Congress that the Nationalist defeat was due to "the world's worst leadership" and "a complete loss of will to fight." Republican senators, however, blamed American diplomats for sabotaging the Nationalists and termed Acheson's report "a 1,054-page white-wash of a wishful, do-nothing policy." While the debate raged over responsibility for the "loss" of China, Chiang's forces fled the mainland for sanctuary on Formosa (Taiwan) in December 1949. Two months later, Mao and Stalin signed a treaty that seemed to place China in the Russian orbit.

The American response was twofold. First, the State Department refused to recognize the new regime in Beijing, maintaining instead formal diplomatic relations with the Nationalists on Formosa. Citing the Sino-Soviet alliance, Assistant Secretary of State Dean Rusk called the Beijing regime "a colonial Russian government" and declared, "It is not the Government of China. It does not pass the first test. It is not Chinese." Second, to compensate for the loss of China, the United States focused on Japan as its main ally in Asia. The State Department encouraged the buildup of Japanese industry. The Pentagon expanded bases on the Japanese home islands and Okinawa. A Japanese–American security pact led to the end of American occupation by 1952. The Cold War had now split East Asia in two.

Quick Check

What was the role of the United States in China's civil war?

The Korean War

The showdown between the United States and the Soviet Union in Asia came in Korea. Traditionally the cockpit of international rivalry in northeast Asia, Korea had been divided at the 38th parallel in 1945. The Russians installed a communist government under Kim Il-Sung in the industrial north. In the agrarian south, Syngman Rhee, a conservative nationalist, became the American-sponsored ruler. Neither regime heeded a UN call for elections to unify the country. The two superpowers pulled out most of their forces by 1949. The Russians, however, helped train a well-equipped army in the north, while the United States—fearful Rhee would seek unification through war—gave only limited military assistance to South Korea.

On June 25, 1950, the North Korean army suddenly crossed the 38th parallel in strength. Stalin had approved this aggression. In January 1950, he had told Mao Zedong that he was ready to overthrow the Yalta settlement in the Far East ("and to hell with it," he exclaimed to Mao). In April, when Kim Il-Sung came to Moscow, Stalin backed the assault, apparently thinking that the United States would abandon Syngman Rhee. But Stalin warned Kim not to count on Soviet assistance: "If you should get kicked in the teeth, I shall not lift a finger. You have to ask Mao for all the help." In May, despite reservations, Mao also approved the North Korean aggression.

Both Stalin and Mao had miscalculated the American response. Truman saw the invasion as a clear-cut case of Soviet aggression reminiscent of the 1930s: "Communism was acting in Korea just as Hitler, Mussolini, and the Japanese had acted ten, fifteen, and twenty years earlier." Following Acheson's advice, the president convened the UN Security Council and, taking advantage of a Soviet boycott, secured a resolution condemning North Korea as an aggressor and calling on the member nations to engage in a collective security action. Within days, American troops from Japan were in combat in South Korea. The conflict, which would last for more than three years, was technically a police action fought under UN auspices; in reality, the United States was at war with a Soviet satellite in Asia (see Map 28.2).

At first the North Koreans drove down the peninsula. But by August, American forces had halted them near Pusan. In September, General MacArthur launched an amphibious assault at Inchon, on the waist of Korea, cutting off and destroying most of the North Korean army in the south. Truman then began to shift from his original goal of restoring the 38th parallel to unifying Korea by military force.

The administration ignored Beijing's repeated warnings not to invade North Korea. "I should think it would be sheer madness for the Chinese to intervene," commented Acheson. Despite CIA reports of a massive Chinese force assembling in Manchuria, Truman and his advisers believed that the Soviet Union, not ready for all-out war, would restrain China. MacArthur was equally certain that China would not attack his troops in Korea. "We are no longer fearful of their intervention," he told Truman in October, adding that if they crossed the Yalu River into Korea, "there would be the greatest slaughter."

Rarely has an American president received worse advice. China was not a Soviet puppet. When UN forces crossed the 38th parallel and moved toward the

MAP 28.2 THE KOREAN WAR, 1950–1953 After a year of rapid movement up and down the Korean peninsula, the fighting stalled just north of the 38th parallel.

✳ Explore the Korean War on MyHistoryLab

WHY DID CONFLICT COME TO THE KOREAN PENINSULA?

After the defeat of Germany and Japan in World War II, many Americans feared a new foe: communism and its spread. The Korean Peninsula, which had been controlled by the Japanese Empire, was divided in two occupation areas after the war, with the Soviet Union controlling the north and the United States in the south. Though allies in World War II, relations between the United States and the Soviet Union chilled as Americans worried that the Soviets were trying to spread communism across the globe. The Soviet Union set up a communist government in its zone of Korea while the United States worked for a market-friendly administration in the south. Soon hostilities broke out on the peninsula in June 1950 as the North launched a surprise attack on the South. What followed was a war over ideology that ended in a stalemate three years later.

FIGHTING IN THE SKY U.S. F-86 Sabre fighter jets like this one saw much action against the comparable MiG 15s used by China during the Korean War.

CIVILIAN DEATHS IN THE KOREAN WAR

TOTAL DEATHS: 2.8 MILLION

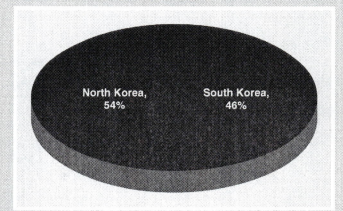

North Korea, 54%   South Korea, 46%

KEY QUESTIONS Use **MyHistoryLab** *Explorer* to answer these **questions:**

Response ▶▶▶ *How was communism portrayed in the United States during this time?*

Consider the public response to this ideology and to the Korean War.

Analysis ▶▶▶ *How did the two sides fare in the war as it unfolded?*

Map troop movements and advancements on the Korean Peninsula.

Cause ▶▶▶ *Why did the warring parties get involved in the conflict?*

Understand the rationale for the involvement of various players.

Yalu, a Chinese counterattack in late November caught MacArthur by surprise and drove his armies out of North Korea by the end of the year. MacArthur finally stabilized the fighting near the 38th parallel, but when Truman decided to give up his attempt to unify Korea, the general protested to Congress, calling for a renewed offensive and proclaiming, "There is no substitute for victory."

Truman then relieved the popular hero of the Pacific of his command on April 11, 1951. At first, MacArthur seemed likely to force the president to back down. Huge crowds welcomed him home and heard him call for victory over the communists in Asia. At a congressional hearing, the administration warned that MacArthur's strategy would expose all Europe to Soviet attack. General Omar Bradley, Truman's chief military adviser, pointed out that a "showdown" with communism in Asia would be "the wrong war, at the wrong place, at the wrong time, and with the wrong enemy."

Congress and the American people accepted MacArthur's recall. The Korean War became a stalemate near the 38th parallel as truce talks bogged down. The president had achieved his primary goal, defense of South Korea and the principle of collective security. Yet by taking the gamble to unify Korea by force, he had confused the American people and humiliated the United States in the eyes of the world.

The most significant result of the Korean conflict was massive American rearmament. The war led to the implementation of NSC-68—the army expanded to 3.5 million troops, the defense budget increased to $50 billion a year by 1952, and the United States acquired military bases from Saudi Arabia to Morocco. America was now committed to waging a global contest against the Soviet Union with arms as well as words.

Quick Check

How did the Korean war begin? How did it end?

The Cold War at Home

28.4 How did the Cold War affect life in America?

The Cold War cast a long shadow over American life in the late 1940s and early 1950s. Truman tried to carry on the New Deal reform tradition he had inherited from FDR, but the American people were more concerned about events abroad. The Republicans used dissatisfaction with postwar economic adjustment and fears of communist penetration of the United States to regain control of the White House in 1952 for the first time in 20 years.

Truman's Troubles

Matching his foreign policy successes with equal achievements at home was not easy for Harry S. Truman. As a loyal supporter of Franklin D. Roosevelt's New Deal during his Senate career, Truman had a reputation for being hardworking, reliable, and intensely partisan. But he was relatively unknown to the general public, and his background as a Missouri county official associated with Kansas City machine politics did not inspire confidence in his ability to lead the nation. Surprisingly well-read—especially in history and biography—Truman possessed sound judgment, the ability to reach decisions quickly, and a fierce and uncompromising sense of right and wrong.

Two weaknesses marred his performance in the White House. One was a fondness for old friends, which resulted in the appointment of Missouri and Senate cronies to high office. Attorney General Tom Clark, Secretary of the Treasury Charles Snyder, and White House military aide Harry Vaughn brought little credit to the administration, while the loss of such effective public servants as Secretary of the Interior Harold Ickes and Labor Secretary Frances Perkins hurt it. The president also lacked political vision. Failing to pursue a coherent legislative program of his own, he tried to perpetuate FDR's New Deal and fought a running battle with Congress.

The postwar mood was not conducive to extending New Deal reforms. Americans were weary of shortages and sacrifices; they wanted the consumer goods denied them under wartime conditions. But in the rush to convert industry from producing planes and tanks to cars and appliances, problems emerged. Prices and wages rose quickly as Congress ended wartime controls. With prices going up 25 percent in two years, workers demanded higher wages to offset the loss of overtime pay. Labor unrest swept the country in the spring of 1946, culminating in a walkout by coal miners that threatened to close down much of American industry and a paralyzing strike by railroad workers.

Truman was caught in the middle. Sensitive to union demands, he let businesses negotiate large pay increases for their workers and then pass on the cost to consumers as higher prices. He criticized Congress for weakening wartime price controls, but failed to offer anything else to curb inflation. Homemakers blamed him for the rising price of food. Organized labor called him the country's "No. 1 Strikebreaker" when he asked Congress for power to draft striking railway workers into the army.

Given this discontent, Truman's efforts to extend the New Deal met with little success. Congress ignored his September 1945 call for measures to ensure economic security and enacted only the Employment Act of 1946. This legislation created the Council of Economic Advisers to assist the president and asserted government responsibility for the state of the economy, but it failed to address Truman's original goal of mandatory federal planning to achieve full employment.

The Republicans took advantage of postwar economic woes to attack the Democrats. "To err is Truman," the GOP proclaimed and then adopted a two-word slogan for the 1946 congressional elections: "Had enough?" The American people, weary of inflation and labor unrest, elected Republican majorities in both the House and Senate for the first time since 1930.

Quick Check
What troubles did the country encounter on converting from war to peace?

Truman Vindicated

The president's relations with Congress became even stormier after the 1946 elections. Truman vetoed two GOP measures to give large tax cuts to the wealthy, but Congress overrode his veto of the **Taft–Hartley Act** in 1947, which outlawed specific union activities—including the closed shop and secondary boycotts. It also permitted the president to invoke an 80-day cooling-off period to delay strikes that might endanger national health or safety. Despite Truman's claim that it was a "slave-labor" bill, unions survived.

Truman's political fortunes reached their nadir in early 1948. Former vice president Henry A. Wallace, claiming to represent the New Deal, announced his third-party (Progressive) candidacy in the coming presidential contest. Worried Democrats sought to persuade Truman to step aside and allow General Dwight D. Eisenhower to become the Democratic candidate. When Eisenhower turned down bids from both parties, the Democrats reluctantly nominated Truman. His prospects for victory in the fall, however, looked dim—especially after disgruntled southerners bolted the Democratic party to protest a progressive civil rights platform. The Dixiecrats, as they became known, nominated Governor Strom Thurmond of South Carolina on a states' rights party ticket.

The defection of the Dixiecrats in the South and of Wallace's liberal followers in the North led experts to predict a Republican victory. Governor Thomas E. Dewey of New York, the GOP candidate, was so sure of winning that he waged a cautious and bland campaign designed to give him a free hand once he was in the White House. With nothing to lose, Truman barnstormed around the country denouncing the "do-nothing" Republican Eightieth Congress. The president's "give 'em hell" tactics reminded voters of how much they owed the Democrats for helping them survive the Great Depression. To the amazement of the pollsters, Truman won in November. The old Roosevelt coalition—farmers, organized labor, urban ethnic groups, and blacks—had held together, enabling Truman to remain in the White House and the Democrats to regain control of Congress (see Map 28.3).

Taft–Hartley Act This 1947 anti-union legislation outlawed the closed shop and secondary boycotts. It also authorized the president to seek injunctions to prevent strikes that threatened national security.

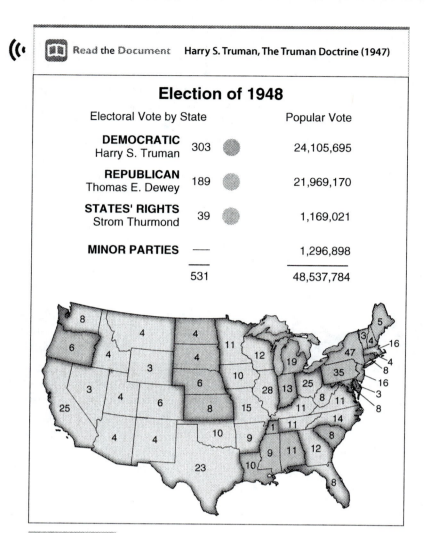

((• 📖 Read the Document   **Harry S. Truman, The Truman Doctrine (1947)**

Election of 1948

	Electoral Vote by State		Popular Vote
DEMOCRATIC Harry S. Truman	303	⬤	24,105,695
REPUBLICAN Thomas E. Dewey	189	⬤	21,969,170
STATES' RIGHTS Strom Thurmond	39	⬤	1,169,021
MINOR PARTIES	—		1,296,898
	531		48,537,784

MAP 28.3 THE ELECTION OF 1948.

There was one more reason for Truman's victory. During this election, held at the height of the Berlin crisis, the GOP failed to challenge Truman's conduct of the Cold War. Locked in a tense rivalry with the Soviet Union, the American people saw no reason to reject a president who had countered aggression overseas with the Truman Doctrine and the Marshall Plan. The Republicans, committed to support the bipartisan policy of containment, had allowed the Democrats to preempt the foreign policy issue. Until they found a way to challenge Truman's Cold War policies, GOP leaders had little chance to regain the White House.

The Loyalty Issue

Despite Truman's surprising victory, the Democrats were vulnerable in one area. Fear of communism abroad that had led to the bipartisan containment policy could be used against them at home by politicians who were more willing to exploit the public's anxiety.

Fear of radicalism had been a recurrent feature of American life since the early republic. Federalists had tried to suppress dissent with the Alien and Sedition Acts in the 1790s; the Know-Nothings had campaigned against foreigners and Catholics in the 1850s; and the Red Scare after World War I had targeted both aliens and radicals. The Cold War heightened traditional fears that subversion from abroad endangered the republic. The Truman administration's portrayal of the men in the Kremlin as revolutionaries bent on world conquest frightened Americans. They viewed the Soviet Union as a successor to Nazi Germany—a totalitarian police state that threatened the liberties of a free people.

Quick Check

What were the key issues in the 1948 presidential election?

Revelations of communist espionage stoked these fears, sparking a second Red Scare. Canadian officials uncovered a Soviet spy ring in 1946, and the House Un-American Activities Committee (HUAC) held hearings indicating that communist agents had flourished in the Agriculture and Treasury Departments in the 1930s.

Truman tried to dismiss the loyalty issue as a "red herring," but felt compelled to take protective measures, thus lending substance to the charges of subversion. In March 1947, he had initiated a loyalty program, ordering security checks of government employees to root out communists. Intended to remove subversives for whom "reasonable grounds exist for belief that the person involved is disloyal," within four years the Loyalty Review Board was dismissing workers as security risks if there was "reasonable doubt" of their loyalty. Thousands of government workers lost their jobs, charged with guilt by association with radicals or with membership in left-wing organizations. Often they had no opportunity to face their accusers.

The most famous disclosure came in August 1948, when Whittaker Chambers, a repentant communist, accused Alger Hiss of having been a Soviet spy in the 1930s. When Hiss, who had been a prominent diplomat, denied the charges, Chambers led investigators to a hollowed-out pumpkin on his Maryland farm. Inside were microfilms of confidential government documents. Chambers claimed that Hiss had passed these materials to him in the late 1930s. Although the statute of limitations prevented a charge of treason against Hiss, he was convicted of perjury in January 1950 and sentenced to a five-year prison term.

In 1948, the Justice Department charged 11 officials of the Communist party with advocating the violent overthrow of the government. After a long trial, the jury found them guilty, and they received prison sentences and heavy fines; in 1951, the Supreme Court upheld the convictions as constitutional.

Such repression failed, however, to reassure the nation. Events abroad intensified the sense of danger. The communist triumph in China in 1949 came as a shock; there were charges that "fellow travelers" in the State Department were responsible for "the loss of China." In September 1949, after the Russians had detonated their first atomic bomb, the end of America's nuclear monopoly was blamed on Soviet espionage. In early 1950, Klaus Fuchs—a British scientist who had worked on the Manhattan Project—admitted giving the Russians vital information about the A-bomb.

A few months later, the government charged American communists Ethel and Julius Rosenberg with conspiracy to transmit atomic secrets to the Soviet Union. In 1951, a jury found the Rosenbergs guilty of espionage, and Judge Irving Kaufman sentenced them to die for their "loathsome offense." Despite their claims of innocence and worldwide appeals on their behalf, the Rosenbergs were electrocuted on June 19, 1953. Thus by the early 1950s, nearly all the ingredients were at hand for a new outburst of hysteria—fear of Russia, evidence of espionage, and a belief in a vast conspiracy. Only a leader to release the intolerance was missing.

Quick Check

How did the fear of communism permeate American domestic life?

McCarthyism in Action

On February 12, 1950, Senator Joseph R. McCarthy of Wisconsin delivered a routine Lincoln's Birthday speech in Wheeling, West Virginia. This little-known Republican attracted national attention when he declared, "I have here in my hand a list of 205—a list of names that were made known to the secretary of state as being members of the Communist party and who nevertheless are still working and shaping policy in the State Department." The charge of communists in the State Department—repeated on different occasions with the number changed to 57, then 81—was never substantiated. But McCarthy's speech triggered a four-and-a-half-year crusade to hunt down alleged communists in government. The stridency and sensationalism of the senator's accusations soon won the name **McCarthyism**.

McCarthy's basic technique was the multiple untruth. He made charges of treasonable activities in government. While officials were refuting his initial accusations, he made new ones, so the corrections never caught up with the latest blast. He failed to

McCarthyism A sensationalist campaign by Senator Joseph McCarthy against supposed communists in government that began in 1950 and ended when the Senate censured him in 1954.

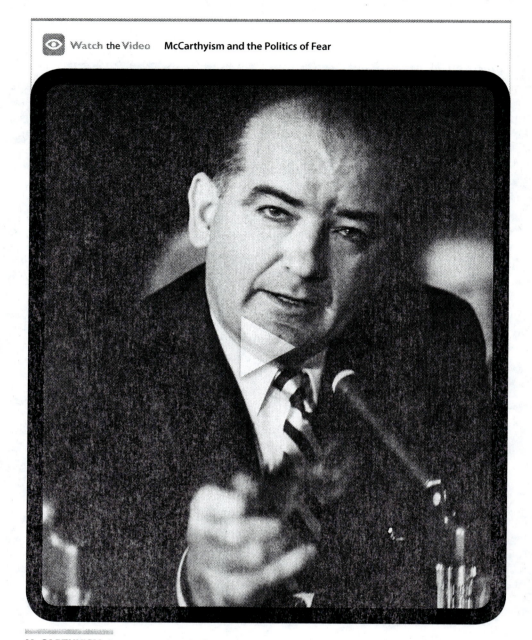

👁 Watch the Video   **McCarthyism and the Politics of Fear**

McCARTHYISM Senator Joseph McCarthy maintained a stream of unsubstantiated charges, always ready to make new accusations of communist infiltration before the preceding ones could be proven untrue.

unearth a single confirmed communist in government, but he kept the Truman administration in turmoil. Drawing on an army of informers, primarily disgruntled federal workers with grievances against their colleagues and superiors, McCarthy charged government agencies with harboring and protecting communist agents and accused the State Department of deliberately losing the Cold War. His briefcase bulged with documents, but he did little actual research, relying instead on reports (often outdated) from earlier congressional investigations. He exploited the press, combining current accusations with promises of future disclosures to guarantee headlines.

The secret of McCarthy's power was the fear he engendered in his Senate colleagues. In 1950, Maryland Senator Millard Tydings, who headed a committee critical of McCarthy's activities, lost reelection when McCarthy opposed him; other senators then ran scared. McCarthy delighted in making sweeping, startling charges of communist sympathies against prominent figures. A favorite target was patrician Secretary of State Dean Acheson, whom McCarthy ridiculed as the "Red Dean," with his "cane, spats, and tea-sipping little finger"; he even claimed that General George Marshall was an agent of the communist conspiracy. Nor were fellow Republicans immune. He called one GOP senator "a living miracle in that he is without question the only man who has lived so long with neither brains nor guts."

The attacks on the wealthy, famous, and privileged won McCarthy a devoted following, though at the height of his influence in early 1954, only 50 percent of the respondents in a Gallup poll approved of him. McCarthy drew disproportionate backing from working-class Catholics and ethnic groups, especially the Irish, Poles, and Italians, who normally voted Democratic. He offered a simple solution to the complicated Cold War: Defeat the enemy at home rather than continue to engage in costly foreign aid programs and entangling alliances abroad. Above all, McCarthy appealed to conservative Republicans in the Midwest who shared his right-wing views and felt cheated by Truman's upset victory in 1948. Even GOP leaders who viewed McCarthy with distaste, such as Robert A. Taft of Ohio, encouraged him to attack the vulnerable Democrats.

Quick Check

What was McCarthyism?

28.1

28.2

28.3

28.4

The Republicans in Power

In 1952, the GOP capitalized on national frustration to capture the presidency. The stalemate in Korea and the second Red Scare created a desire for political change; revelations of scandals involving individuals close to Truman intensified the feeling that someone needed to clean up "the mess in Washington." In Dwight D. Eisenhower, the Republican party found the perfect candidate to explore what one senator called K1C2—Korea, communism, and corruption.

Popular because of his amiable manner, winning smile, and heroic stature, Eisenhower alone appeared to have the ability to unite a divided nation. In the 1952 campaign, Ike displayed hidden gifts as a politician in running against Adlai Stevenson, the eloquent Illinois governor, whose appeal was limited to diehard Democrats and liberal intellectuals. Eisenhower allowed his young running mate, Senator Richard M. Nixon of California, to hammer away at the Democrats on the communist and corruption issues, but he himself delivered the most telling blow of all on the Korean War. Speaking in Detroit in late October, just after the fighting had intensified again in Korea, Ike promised to go personally to the battlefield "to bring the Korean War to an early and honorable end."

"That does it—Ike is in," reporters exclaimed after they heard this pledge. The hero of World War II had clinched his election by committing himself to end an unpopular

⊙ Watch the Video   Ike for President Campaign Ad

EISENHOWER ELECTED Eisenhower's landslide victories in 1952 and 1956 seemed to prove his slogan that Americans did, indeed, "like Ike," as expressed on this campaign button.

TABLE 28.1 THE ELECTION OF 1952

Candidate	Party	Popular Vote	Electoral Vote
Eisenhower	Republican	33,778,963	442
Stevenson	Democratic	27,314,992	89

war. Ten days later, he won the presidency handily, carrying 39 states, including four in the formerly solid Democratic South (see Table 28.1). The Republicans, however, fared less well in Congress; they gained just a slight edge in the House and controlled the Senate by only one seat.

Eisenhower fulfilled his campaign pledge. He spent three days in early December touring the battlefront in Korea, ruling out the new offensive the military favored: "Small attacks on small hills would not end the war." Instead he turned to diplomacy, relying on hints to China on the use of nuclear weapons to break the stalemated peace talks. These tactics, together with Stalin's death in March, finally led to an armistice on July 27, 1953, which ended the fighting but left Korea divided—as it had been before the war—near the 38th parallel.

The new president was less effective in dealing with McCarthy's continuing witch-hunt. Instead of toning down his anticommunist crusade after the Republican victory in 1952, McCarthy used his new position as chairman of the Senate Committee on Government Operations to ferret out communists on the federal payroll. He made charges against the foreign affairs agencies and demanded that books be purged from American information libraries overseas. Eisenhower's advisers urged the president to use his prestige to stop McCarthy. But Ike refused: "I will not get into a pissing contest with a skunk." Instead he played for time, hoping the American people would come to their senses.

The Wisconsin senator finally overreached himself. In early 1954, he uncovered an army dentist suspected of disloyalty and attacked the upper echelons of the army, telling one much-decorated general that he was "not fit to wear the uniform." The controversy culminated in the televised Army–McCarthy hearings. For six weeks, the senator exhibited his crude bullying to the American people. Viewers were repelled by his frequent outbursts that began with the insistent cry, "Point of order, Mr. Chairman, point of order," and by his attempt to smear the reputation of a young lawyer associated with army counsel Joseph Welch. Welch condemned McCarthy for his "reckless cruelty" and asked rhetorically, as millions watched, "Have you no sense of decency, sir?"

Courageous Republicans, led by Senators Ralph Flanders of Vermont and Margaret Chase Smith of Maine, joined Democrats to censure McCarthy in December 1954, by a vote of 67 to 22. McCarthy fell quickly from prominence. He died three years later virtually unnoticed and unmourned.

Yet his influence was profound. He paralyzed national life with what a Senate subcommittee described as "the most nefarious campaign of half-truth and untruth in the history of the Republic." He also helped impose a political and cultural conformity that froze dissent for the rest of the 1950s. Long after his passing, the nation tolerated loyalty oaths for teachers, banning left-wing books from public libraries, and blacklisting entertainers in radio, television, and films. Freedom of expression was inhibited, and new ideas and approaches stifled. The United States settled into a sterile Cold War consensus.

While Eisenhower could claim that his policy of giving McCarthy enough rope to hang himself had worked, a bolder and more forthright presidential attack on the senator might have spared the nation some of the excesses of the second Red Scare.

Quick Check

What foreign and domestic issues influenced the election of Eisenhower in 1952?

Conclusion: The Continuing Cold War

Eisenhower's election calmed things at home but did not end the Cold War abroad. During Ike's presidency, the United States extended its policy of containment and expanded its nuclear arsenal. Eisenhower himself wondered where it all would lead. In his second term, he tried to defuse tensions with the Soviet Union, and he warned about the danger of massive military spending in his farewell address to the American people: "In the councils of government, we must guard against the acquisition of unwarranted influence, whether sought or unsought, by the military-industrial complex. The potential for the disastrous rise of misplaced power exists and will persist."

Rarely has an American president been more prophetic. Defense spending would skyrocket as the Cold War escalated. Eisenhower had kept the peace, but he had failed to halt the momentum of the Cold War he had inherited from Truman.

Chapter Review

The Cold War Begins

28.1 How did the Cold War begin? p. 651

The Cold War began as the United States and the Soviet Union discovered that their interests in Europe conflicted. Each feared the other and, acting on its fears, took steps that heightened the other's fears. Atomic weapons made the mistakes of miscalculation far greater than in the past and everyone more fearful.

Containment

28.2 What was containment, and why was it adopted? p. 654

Containment was the American policy of preventing Soviet power and influence from expanding. It was adopted to preserve American interests without excessively risking war.

The Cold War Expands

28.3 How did the Cold War expand from Europe to Asia? p. 659

The United States and the Soviet Union took opposite sides in the Chinese civil war. Shortly after the communist victory in China, communist North Korea battled anticommunist South Korea. The United States sided with South Korea. The Soviet Union and Communist China backed North Korea.

The Cold War at Home

28.4 How did the Cold War affect life in America? p. 664

The Cold War spawned fears of communist subversion. It led to a campaign to ensure loyalty, and fostered McCarthyism, an exaggerated effort to find communists in every corner of American life. Although McCarthyism eventually burned itself out, it contributed to Eisenhower's election in 1952, which ended 20 years of Democratic control of the White House.

Timeline

1945
Cold War Begins—
Truman meets Stalin at Potsdam Conference (July)
— 1945

1947
Containment—
Truman Doctrine announced (March)
Cold War at Home—
Truman orders loyalty program for government employees (March)
Containment—
George Marshall outlines Marshall Plan (June)
— 1947

1948
Containment—Soviets begin blockade of Berlin (June)
Cold War at Home—
Truman elected president
— 1948

1949
Cold War Expands—
NATO treaty signed in Washington (April); Soviet Union tests its first atomic bomb (August)
— 1949

1950
Cold War Expands—
Truman authorizes developing hydrogen bomb (January)
Cold War at Home—
Senator Joseph McCarthy claims communists in government (February)
Cold War Expands—
North Korea invades South Korea (June)
— 1950

1951
Cold War Expands—
Truman recalls MacArthur from Korea
— 1951

1952
Cold War at Home—
Dwight D. Eisenhower elected president
— 1952

29 Affluence and Anxiety 1945–1960

Levittown: The Flight to the Suburbs

On May 7, 1947, William Levitt announced plans to build thousands of rental houses in a former potato field on Long Island, 30 miles from Midtown Manhattan. Using mass production techniques he had learned while erecting navy housing during the war, Levitt quickly built 4000 homes and rented them to young veterans and their wives eager to leave crowded city apartments or their parents' homes to begin raising families. A change in government financing regulations led him to offer his houses for sale in 1948 for a small amount down and a low monthly payment. Young couples, many of them the original renters, quickly bought the first 4000. By the time **Levittown**—as he called the new community—was completed in 1951, it contained more than 17,000 houses. So many babies were born there that it was called "Fertility Valley" and "the Rabbit Hutch."

LEARNING OBJECTIVES

29.1 ((	29.2 ((	29.3 ((
How did the American economy evolve after World War II? p. 675	How did American culture change after the war? p. 678	How did the civil rights movement develop in the 1940s and 1950s? p. 681

LEVITTOWN The houses of Levittown spread over 1200 acres of former potato fields on Long Island, New York.

From Chapter 29 of *American Stories: A History of the United States*, Third Edition. H. W. Brands, R. Hal Williams, T. H. Breen and Ariela J. Gross Copyright © 2015 by Pearson Education, Inc. All rights reserved.

((**Listen to Chapter 29 on MyHistoryLab**

Watch the Video Series on MyHistoryLab

Learn about some key topics related to this chapter with the *MyHistoryLab Video Series: Key Topics in U.S. History*

1 **The Affluent Society: 1953–1960** Following the end of the Korean War, Americans faced a changing society, workplace, economy, and popular culture, underlined by the ever present threat of nuclear annihilation. This video surveys many issues and groups—from labor unions to women in the rapidly growing American suburbs— who were seen by advertisers as key purchasers of the goods and services that made for the so-called "Affluent Society."

 Watch on MyHistoryLab

The Suburban Ideal This video profiles the young veterans of World War II and the Korean War whose desire to start families and own homes led to the "baby boom" of the 1950s and the explosive growth of American suburbs. However, not all Americans saw consumerism, careerism, and conformity as positive developments. The skeptics produced the defiant literature of the Beat Generation and the rebellious music of rock-and-roll .

Watch on MyHistoryLab

2

3 **The Age of Ike** The administration of President Dwight Eisenhower adopted a confrontational position in relation to communism around the globe, as this video demonstrates. The departments of State and Defense, as well as the Central Intelligence Agency, carried out the policy of "containment" on a global scale. Yet Eisenhower eventually came to fear that the "military–industrial complex",—the interlocking network of the U.S. military and American industry—could endanger the very nature of the American republic.

 Watch on MyHistoryLab

The Civil Rights Movement The Supreme Court decision of *Brown v. Board of Education* (1954) was an early key event in the civil rights movement. This video looks at the impact and enforcement of that decision. It also depicts the efforts of Martin Luther King, Jr. and many others to overturn the Jim Crow laws of the South, using legal and nonviolent strategies—such as the Montgomery (Alabama) bus boycott— to pave the way for the Civil Rights Act of 1964.

Watch on MyHistoryLab

4

Levittown In 1947, William Levitt used mass production techniques to build inexpensive houses in suburban New York to help relieve the postwar housing shortage. Levittown became a symbol of the postwar move to the suburbs.

Levitt built two more Levittowns, in Pennsylvania and New Jersey; each contained the same curving streets, neighborhood parks and playgrounds, and community swimming pools characteristic of his first development. The secret of Levittown's appeal was the basic house, a 720-square-foot Cape Cod design built on a concrete slab. It had a kitchen, two bedrooms, a bath, a living room with a fireplace and 16-foot picture window, and an expansion attic with room for two more bedrooms. Each house had the same interior, but four different exterior facades broke the monotony. The original house sold for $6,990 in 1948; even the improved ranch-style model sold for less than $10,000 in 1951.

Levitt's houses were ideal for young people starting out in life. They were cheap, comfortable, and efficient, and each house came with a refrigerator, stove, and washing machine. Despite the houses' conformity, the three Levittowns became surprisingly diverse communities; residents had a wide variety of religious, ethnic, and occupational backgrounds. African Americans, however, were rigidly excluded. In time, as the more successful families moved on to larger homes in more expensive neighborhoods, the Levittowns became enclaves for lower-middle-class families.

Levittown symbolized the most significant social trend of the postwar era in the United States—the flight to the suburbs. The residential areas surrounding cities such as New York and Chicago nearly doubled in the 1950s. While the population of central cities remained relatively stagnant, suburbs grew by 46 percent; by 1960, 60 million people, one-third of the nation, lived in suburban rings around the cities. A **baby boom** that started during World War II accompanied the massive shift in population from the central cities. Young married couples began to have three, four, or even five children (compared with only one or two children in American families during the 1930s). As a result, the nation's population grew by 19 percent between 1950 and 1960, the highest growth rate since 1910. (See Figure 29.1.)

The economy also boomed as residential construction soared. By 1960, one-fourth of all existing houses were less than ten years old, and factories were turning out large quantities of appliances and television sets for the new households. New consumer products—ranging from frozen foods to filter cigarettes, from high-fidelity phonographs to cars with automatic transmissions and tubeless tires—appeared. In the suburbs, the corner grocery gave way to the supermarket carrying a vast array of items that provided families with a more varied diet.

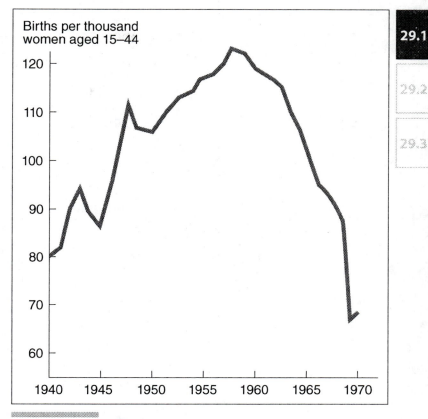

FIGURE 29.1 BIRTHRATE, 1940–1970

SOURCE: Compiled from U.S. Bureau of the Census, *Historical Statistics of the United States, Colonial Times to 1970*, Bicentennial Edition, Washington, DC, 1975.

Affluence replaced the poverty and hunger of the Great Depression for most Americans, but memories of the 1930s still haunted many. The obsession with material goods became almost desperate, as if houses, cars, and appliances could guarantee that the nightmare of depression would never return. Critics condemned the conformity of suburban life, charging the newly affluent with forsaking traditional American individualism to live in identical houses, drive look-alike cars, and accumulate the same material possessions.

Events abroad added to postwar anxiety. Nuclear war became a frightening possibility. The rivalry with the Soviet Union had led to the second Red Scare and charges of treason and disloyalty being leveled at loyal Americans. Many Americans joined Senator Joseph McCarthy in searching for the communist enemy at home rather than abroad. Loyalty oaths and book burnings revealed how insecure Americans had become in the Cold War. The 1950s also witnessed a growing demand by African Americans for equal opportunity in an age of abundance. The civil rights movement, and strident criticism of the consumer culture, revealed that forces for change were at work beneath the bland surface of suburban affluence.

baby boom The rise in births following World War II. Children born to this generation are referred to as "baby boomers."

The Postwar Boom

29.1 How did the American economy evolve after World War II?

For 15 years following World War II, the nation experienced unparalleled economic growth. Pent-up demand for consumer goods fueled industrial expansion. Government spending during the Cold War also stimulated the economy, offsetting brief recessions in 1949 and 1953 and moderating a steeper one during 1957–1958. By 1960, the American people had achieved an affluence that finally erased the lingering fears of the Great Depression.

Postwar Prosperity

Two long-term factors accounted for the economy's upward surge. First, American consumers—after being held in check by depression and wartime scarcities—finally were able to indulge their appetites for material goods. At the war's end, personal savings in the United States stood at more than $37 billion, providing a powerful stimulus to consumption. American factories could not turn out enough automobiles and appliances to satisfy the horde of buyers until 1950. In that year, the gross national product (GNP) reached $318 billion (50 percent higher than in 1940).

The Cold War provided the additional stimulus the economy needed when postwar expansion slowed. The Marshall Plan and other foreign aid programs financed a heavy export trade. The Korean War helped reverse a brief recession and ensured continued prosperity as the government spent massively on weapons and munitions. In 1952, the nation spent $44 billion, two-thirds of the federal budget, on national defense. Although Eisenhower managed to effect modest reductions, defense spending continued at a level of $40 billion throughout the decade.

The affluence of the 1950s made the fear of another Great Depression seem irrational. The baby boom and the spectacular growth of suburbia were great stimulants to the consumer goods industries. Manufacturers turned out an ever-increasing number of refrigerators, washing machines, and dishwashers to equip the kitchens of Levittown and its many imitators. The automobile industry thrived as two-car suburban families became common. In 1955, when oil was abundant and gasoline sold for less than 30 cents a gallon, Detroit sold a record eight million cars. The electronics industry also boomed. Consumers were eager to acquire the latest marvel of home entertainment—the television set.

Businesses snapped up office machines and the first generation of computers; industry installed electronic sensors and processors as automation grew, and the military appetite for electronic devices for its planes and ships was insatiable. As a result, American industry averaged more than $10 billion a year in capital investment, and the number of persons employed rose above the long-sought goal of 60 million nationwide.

Yet the economic abundance of the 1950s was not without its problems. While some sections of the nation (notably the Pacific Northwest and the emerging Sunbelt areas of the South and West) benefited enormously from the growth of the aircraft and electronics industries, older manufacturing regions, such as New England, fared less well. The steel industry increased its capacity during the decade, but fell behind the rate of national growth. Agriculture experienced bumper crops and low prices, so rural regions, like the vast Plains states, failed to share in the general affluence. Despite the boom, unemployment rose to more than 7 percent in a sharp recession that began in late 1957 and lasted through the summer of 1958. Economic growth slowed after 1955, causing concern about the continuing vitality of the economy.

None of these flaws, however, could disguise a prosperity that no one had dreamed possible in the 1930s. The GNP grew to $440 billion by 1960, more than double the 1940 level. More important, workers now labored fewer than 40 hours a week; they rarely worked on Saturdays, and nearly all enjoyed an annual two-week paid vacation. By the mid-1950s, the average American family had twice as much real income to spend as its counterpart had possessed in the boom years of the 1920s. From 1945 to 1960, per capita disposable income rose by $500—to $1845—for every man, woman, and child in the country. The American people, in one generation, had moved from poverty and depression to the highest standard of living the world had ever known.

Quick Check

Why was the economy able to prosper during the postwar decades?

Life in the Suburbs

Sociologists had difficulty describing the nature of suburban society in the 1950s. Some saw it as classless, while others noted the absence of both the very rich and the very poor and labeled it "middle class." Rather than forming a homogeneous social group, though, the suburbs contained a surprising variety of people, whether classified as "upper lower," "lower middle," and "upper middle," or simply as blue collar, white collar, and professional. Doctors and lawyers often lived in the same developments as salesclerks and master plumbers. The traditional distinctions of ancestry, education, and size of residence no longer differentiated people as easily as they once had.

Yet suburbs could vary widely, from working-class communities clustered near factories built in the countryside to old, elitist areas such as Scarsdale, New York, and Shaker Heights, Ohio. Most were almost exclusively white and Christian, but suburbs such as Great Neck on Long Island and Richmond Heights outside Miami enabled Jews and blacks to take part in the flight from the inner city.

Suburban life depended on the automobile. Highways and expressways allowed fathers to commute to jobs in the cities, often an hour or more away. Children might ride buses to and from school, but mothers had to drive them to piano lessons and Little League games. Two cars became a necessity for almost every suburban family, spurring the boom in automobile production. In 1948, only 59 percent of American families owned a car; a few years later, nearly every suburban family had at least one vehicle, and many had several.

In the new drive-in culture, people shopped at the stores that grew up first in "miracle miles" along the highways and later at the shopping centers that spread across the countryside in the 1950s. In 1946, the entire country had only eight shopping centers; hundreds appeared over the next 15 years, including Poplar Plaza in Memphis, with one large department store, 30 retail shops, and parking for more than 500 cars. In 1956, the first enclosed air-conditioned mall, the Southdale Shopping Center, opened outside Minneapolis.

Despite the increased mobility the car provided, the home became the focus for activities and aspirations. The postwar housing shortage that often forced young couples to live with their parents created an intense demand for new houses in the suburbs. Prospective buyers expressed a desire for "more space," "comfort and roominess," and "privacy and freedom of action" in their new residences. Men and women who moved to the suburbs prized the new kitchens with their built-in dishwashers, electric ovens, and gleaming counters; the extra bedrooms that ensured privacy from and for the children; the large garages that could be converted into recreation rooms; and the small, neat lawns that gave them an area for outdoor activities and a new way to compete with their neighbors. "Togetherness" became the code word of the 1950s. Families did things together, whether gathering around the TV sets that dominated living rooms, attending community activities, or taking vacations in huge station wagons.

But the new suburban lifestyle also had less attractive consequences. The extended family, in which several generations had lived in close proximity, was a casualty of the boom in small detached homes. As historian Kenneth Jackson noted, suburban life "ordained that most children would grow up in intimate contact only with their parents and siblings." For many families, grandparents, aunts and uncles, cousins, and more distant relatives would become remote figures, seen only on special occasions.

The nuclear family, typical of the suburb, did little to encourage feminism. After the war, many women who had entered the workforce returned to the home, where the role of wife and mother remained the ideal for women in the 1950s. Trends toward getting married earlier and having larger families reinforced the pattern of women devoting their efforts to housework and child raising rather than acquiring professional skills and pursuing careers outside the home. Adlai Stevenson, the Democratic presidential candidate in 1952 and 1956, extolling "the humble role of housewife," told Smith College graduates that there was much they could do "in the living room with a baby in your lap or in the kitchen with a can opener in your hand." Dr. Benjamin Spock's 1946 bestseller, *Baby and Child Care*, became a fixture in millions of homes, while the traditional women's magazines such as *McCall's* and *Good Housekeeping* thrived with articles on natural childbirth and inspirational pieces such as "Homemaking Is My Vocation."

Quick Check

How did the growth of suburbs
change the way Americans lived?

Nonetheless, the number of working wives doubled between 1940 and 1960. By 1960, 40 percent of American women, and nearly one-third of married women, had jobs outside the home. The expense of rearing and educating children led wives and mothers to seek to augment the family income, inadvertently preparing the way for a new demand for equality in the 1960s.

The Good Life?

29.2 How did American culture change after the war?

Consumerism became the dominant social theme of the 1950s. Yet even with an abundance of creature comforts and more leisure time, many Americans remained anxious and dissatisfied.

Areas of Greatest Growth

Organized religion flourished in the 1950s. Ministers, priests, and rabbis noted the rise in church and synagogue attendance in the new communities. Sociologist Will Herberg claimed that religious affiliation had become the primary identifying feature of modern American life, dividing the nation into three segments—Protestant, Catholic, and Jewish.

Observers condemned the bland, secular nature of suburban churches, which seemed to be part of the consumer society. "On weekdays one shops for food," wrote one critic, "on Saturdays one shops for recreation, and on Sundays one shops for the Holy Ghost." But the popularity of the Rev. Norman Vincent Peale, who urged people to "start thinking faith, enthusiasm and joy," suggested that the new churches filled a

I LOVE LUCY One of the most popular television programs of the 1950s was *I Love Lucy,* a situation comedy featuring the real-life husband-and-wife team of Lucille Ball and Desi Arnaz portraying the fictional couple Lucy and Ricky Ricardo.

genuine if shallow human need. But the emergence of neo-orthodoxy in Protestant seminaries, notably through the ideas of Reinhold Niebuhr, who sought to accommodate Christian teaching to the atomic age, and the spread of radical fundamentalism such as the Assemblies of God, indicated that millions of Americans still were searching for a more personal religious faith.

Schools were a problem for the growing new suburban communities. The increase in the number of school-age children, from 20 to 30 million in the first eight grades, overwhelmed many local districts, leading to demands for federal aid. Congress granted limited help for areas affected by defense plants and military bases, but Eisenhower's reluctance to unbalance the budget—along with traditional adherence to state control over public education—blocked further federal assistance before 1957, when the government reacted to *Sputnik*, the Soviet satellite that ushered in the space age, by sharply increasing federal support for science education.

A controversy also arose over education in the 1950s. Critics of "progressive" education called for sweeping educational reforms and a new stress on traditional academic subjects. Suburban communities had bitter fights; affluent parents demanded kindergarten enrichment programs and grade school foreign language instruction, while working-class people resisted such costly innovations. The one thing all seemed to agree on was the desirability of a college education. College enrollment increased from 1.5 million in 1940 to 3.6 million in 1960.

The largest advances were made in the exciting new medium of television. From a shaky start just after the war, TV boomed in the 1950s, pushing radio aside and undermining magazines. By 1957, three networks controlled the airwaves, reaching 40 million sets over nearly 500 stations. Advertisers soon took charge of the new medium, using techniques first pioneered in radio—including taped commercials, quiz shows, and soap operas.

At first, the insatiable demand for programs encouraged creativity. Playwrights such as Reginald Rose, Rod Serling, and Paddy Chayefsky wrote notable dramas for *Playhouse 90*, *Studio One*, and the *Goodyear Television Playhouse*. Broadcast live from cramped studios, these productions thrived on tight dramatic structures, movable scenery, and frequent close-ups of the actors.

Advertisers, however, quickly became disillusioned with the live dramatic programs, which usually dealt with controversial subjects or focused on ordinary people and events. Sponsors wanted shows that featured excitement, glamour, and instant success. Aware that contestants with unusual expertise (a shoemaker answering tough questions on operas, a grandmother stumping experts on baseball) fascinated audiences, producers began giving away huge cash prizes on *The $64,000 Question* and *Twenty-One*. In 1959, Charles Van Doren, a Columbia University professor, confessed he had been given the answers in advance to win $129,000 on *Twenty-One*. The three networks quickly replaced the big-prize quiz programs with comedy, action, and adventure shows such as *The Untouchables* and *Bonanza*. Despite its early artistic promise, television became a technologically sophisticated but safe conveyor of the consumer culture.

Quick Check

What was the effect of television on American life?

Critics of the Consumer Society

One striking feature of the 1950s was the disenchantment many authors and artists expressed. This disenchantment reached its most eloquent expression with the beats, literary groups that rebelled against the era's materialism. Jack Kerouac's novel *On the Road*, published in 1957, and Allen Ginsburg's poem *Howl* set the tone for the new movement. The name "beats" came from the quest for beatitude, a state of inner grace sought in Zen Buddhism. Flouting the respectability of suburbia, the "beatniks"—as middle America termed them—were easily identified by their long hair and bizarre clothing; they also had a penchant for sexual promiscuity and drugs. They were conspicuous dropouts from a society they found senseless. Poet Lawrence Ferlinghetti,

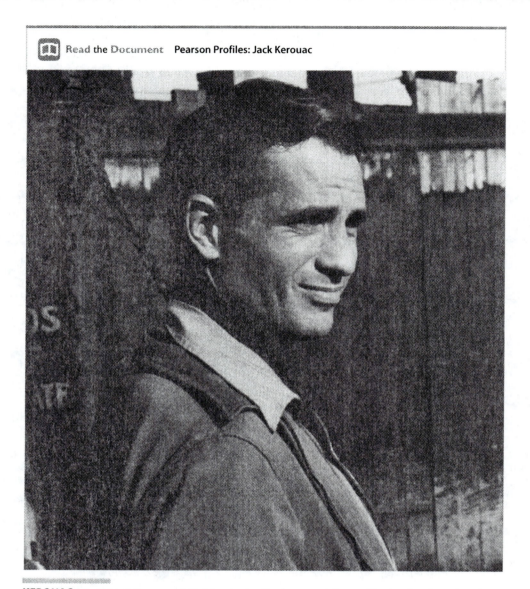

KEROUAC Novelist Jack Kerouac and his fellow beat writers bemoaned the moral bankruptcy of popular culture. They sought not to improve conditions but to find release from the moral and social confines constricting their lives and literary conventions circumscribing their writing. This photograph of Jack Kerouac was taken by beat poet Allen Ginsberg.

who held forth in the City Lights Bookshop in San Francisco (a favorite beats' resort), summed it up: "I was a wind-up toy someone had dropped wound up into a world already running down."

The social protest inherent in the books and poems of the beats found its counterpart in the rise of abstract expressionism. Abstract expressionists emphasized individuality and freedom from the constraints of representational, realistic art. Painters Jackson Pollock and Mark Rothko, among others, challenged mainstream America's notions about the form and function of art. For Pollock, the act of creating a painting was as important as the painting itself. Rothko pioneered a style known as color field painting; his works in this style are monumental pieces in which enormous areas of color lacking any distinct structure or central focus create a mood.

Despite the disapproval of mainstream Americans, the beat generation had compassion for their detractors. "We love everything," Kerouac proclaimed, "Billy Graham, the Big Ten, Rock and Roll, Zen, apple pie, Eisenhower—we dig it all." Yet, as highly visible nonconformists in an era of stifling conformity, the beats demonstrated a style of social protest that would flower into the counterculture of the 1960s.

Quick Check

What did critics find lacking in American postwar culture?

The Struggle Over Civil Rights

29.3 How did the civil rights movement develop in the 1940s and 1950s?

The questioning of American life was most evident in race relations, where the white majority continued to deny basic rights to the black minority. The contradiction between denouncing the Soviet Union for its human rights violations and the second-class status of African Americans began to arouse the national conscience. Fighting for freedom against communist tyranny abroad, Americans had to acknowledge the denial of freedom to a submerged minority at home.

African Americans had benefited economically from World War II, but they were still seriously disadvantaged. Those who had left the South for northern and western cities were concentrated in blighted and segregated neighborhoods, working at low-paying jobs, suffering discrimination, and not sharing fully in the postwar prosperity. African Americans' rising expectations in the postwar years led them to challenge racial segregation and inequality.

In the South, conditions were worse. State laws forced blacks to live almost totally segregated from white society. Not only did African Americans attend separate (and inferior) schools, but they also were rigidly segregated in all public facilities. They were forced to use separate waiting rooms in train stations, separate seats on all forms of transportation, separate drinking fountains, and even separate telephone booths and cemeteries. "Segregation was enforced at all places of public entertainment, including libraries, auditoriums, and circuses," Chief Justice Earl Warren noted. "There was segregation in the hospitals, prisons, mental institutions, and nursing homes. Even ambulance service was segregated."

Civil Rights as a Political Issue

Truman was the first president to attempt to alter the pattern of racial discrimination in the United States. In 1946, he appointed a presidential commission on civil rights. In 1947, in a report titled "To Secure These Rights," the commission recommended reinstating the wartime Fair Employment Practices Committee (FEPC), establishing a permanent civil rights commission, and denying federal aid to any state that segregated schools and public facilities. The president's ten-point legislative program proposed in 1948 included some of these measures, notably the establishment of a permanent FEPC and a civil rights commission. But southern resistance blocked action by Congress, and the inclusion of a strong civil rights plank in the 1948 Democratic platform led to the walkout of southern delegations and a separate States' Rights (Dixiecrat) ticket that fall.

African American voters in the North overwhelmingly backed Truman over Dewey in 1948. The African American vote in Los Angeles, Cleveland, and Chicago ensured the Democratic victory in California, Ohio, and Illinois. Truman responded by including civil rights legislation in his Fair Deal program in 1949. Again, however, southerners blocked congressional action on both a permanent FEPC and an anti-lynching measure.

Even though Truman was unable to secure significant legislation, he made civil rights an integral part of the Democratic reform program. Truman also used his executive power to assist African Americans. He strengthened the civil rights division of the Justice Department, which helped black groups challenge school segregation and restrictive housing covenants in the courts. Most important, in 1948 Truman ordered the desegregation of the armed forces. The navy and the air force quickly complied, but the army resisted until the personnel needs of the Korean War finally overcame its objections. By 1960, the armed forces were far more integrated than American society at large.

Quick Check

How did civil rights shape the politics of the postwar years?

❋ Explore the Civil Rights Movement on MyHistoryLab

HOW DID CONDITIONS FOR AFRICAN AMERICANS BEGIN TO CHANGE IN THE MID-1900s?

Laws in the South known as "Jim Crow laws"—regulations that banned African Americans and whites from, for example, marrying, dining, going to school, or socializing together—ensured racial discrimination. In the North, informal segregation undergirded the social structure. However, African American leaders started to make advancements in their fight for equality in the 1950s and 1960s. Civil rights activists protested across the South, attracting national attention. In the industrial cities of the North and West, large numbers of African Americans arrived in the Second Great Migration between 1940 and 1970 as they sought better opportunities than the South afforded them. From these cities, many also began to speak out for an end to racism.

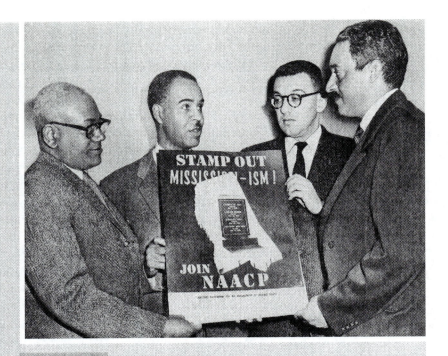

THE NAACP Holding a poster against racial bias in Mississippi are four NAACP leaders (l. to r.), Henry L. Moon, Roy Wilkins, Herbert Hill, and Thurgood Marshall.

SOURCE: *Library of Congress*

SHIFTS IN AFRICAN AMERICAN POPULATION IN SELECTED COUNTIES, 1940–1950

County	Change in Persons	Percent Change
Columbia County, Georgia	−1,108	−20
Cook County, Illinois	+226,822	+60
Los Angeles County, California	+142,672	+94
Quitman County, Mississippi	−2,416	−9
Wayne County, Michigan	+172,122	+70

SOURCE: *1950 Census, Historic GIS Data: Slavery, Citizenship, & Civil Rights,* Teaching American History Project, *www.upa.pdx.edu/IMS/currentprojects/TAHv3/Slave_Citizen_GIS.html.*

KEY QUESTIONS Use **MyHistoryLab** *Explorer* to **answer** these **questions:**

Cause ▶▶▶ *What challenges did African Americans face during the era of segregation?*

Use socioeconomic patterns to consider discrimination.

Comparison ▶▶▶ *In what parts of southern cities did African Americans live?*

Map segregation in selected urban centers.

Consequence ▶▶▶ *What was the demographic impact of the Second Great Migration?*

Consider the results of this move to the urban North and West.

BUS BOMBING The firebombing of a Greyhound bus carrying white and black civil rights activists challenging illegal segregation on interstate bus routes in the South during 1961 was undertaken by a mob outside of Anniston, Alabama. These civil rights activists barely escaped with their lives from this violent attack on their passive resistance efforts.

Desegregating the Schools

Schools soon became the primary target of civil rights advocates. The NAACP concentrated first on universities, winning admission for qualified African Americans to state graduate and professional schools. Led by Thurgood Marshall, NAACP lawyers then attacked segregation in the public schools. Challenging *Plessy v. Ferguson*, the 1896 Supreme Court decision that upheld the constitutionality of separate but equal public facilities (see Chapter 19), Marshall argued that even substantially equal but separate schools did profound psychological damage to African American children and thus violated the Fourteenth Amendment.

In 1954, in the case of **Brown v. Board of Education of Topeka**, the Supreme Court unanimously agreed. Chief Justice Earl Warren, recently appointed by President Eisenhower, flatly declared that "separate educational facilities are inherently unequal." To divide grade school children "solely because of their race," he argued, "generates a feeling of inferiority as to their status in the community that may affect their hearts and minds in a way unlikely ever to be undone." Despite this sweeping language, Warren realized that changing historic patterns of segregation would be difficult. Accordingly, in 1955 the Court ruled that school desegregation should proceed "with all deliberate speed" and left the details to the lower federal courts.

"All deliberate speed" proved to be agonizingly slow. The border states quickly complied with the Court's ruling, but the Deep South responded with massive resistance. White citizens' councils organized to retain racial separation; 101 representatives

Brown v. Board of Education of Topeka In 1954, the Supreme Court reversed the *Plessy v. Ferguson* decision (1896), which established the "separate but equal" doctrine. The *Brown* decision found segregation in schools inherently unequal and initiated a long and difficult effort to integrate the nation's public schools.

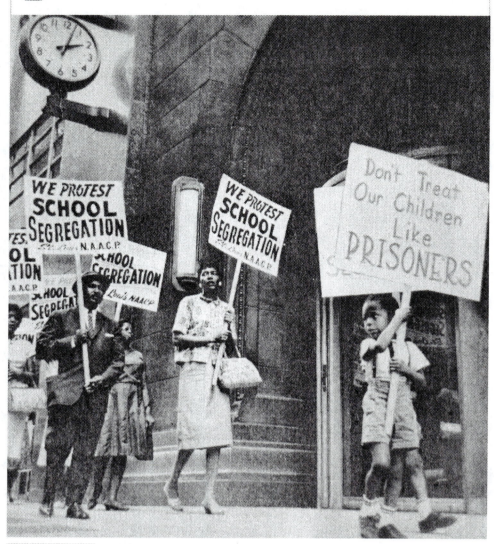

Read the Document *Brown v. Board of Education of Topeka, Kansas* (1954)

BROWN V. BOARD OF EDUCATION Demonstrators supporting the Supreme Court's 1954 *Brown v. Board of Education* ruling to desegregate the nation's schools. The ruling also sparked protests, many of them violent and destructive, by opponents of integration.

and senators signed a Southern Manifesto in 1956 denouncing the *Brown* decision as "a clear abuse of judicial power." School boards found ways to evade the Court's ruling. Pupil placement laws enabled officials to assign individual students to schools on the basis of scholastic aptitude, ability to adjust, and "morals, conduct, health and personal standards." These tactics led to long disputes in the federal courts; by 1960, less than 1 percent of the black children in the Deep South attended school with whites.

A conspicuous lack of presidential support further weakened the desegregation effort. Eisenhower believed that "cold law making" could not alter people's attitudes. Change could only come "by appealing to reason, by prayer, and by constantly working at it through our own efforts." Quietly, he worked to desegregate federal facilities, particularly in veterans' hospitals, navy yards, and the District of Columbia school system. Yet he refrained from endorsing *Brown*, which he believed had "set back progress in the South at least fifteen years."

Southern leaders mistook Ike's silence for support of segregation. In 1957, Governor Orval Faubus of Arkansas called out the National Guard to prevent the integration of Little Rock's Central High School on grounds of a threat to public order.

After 270 troops turned back nine African American students, a federal judge ordered the guardsmen removed; but when the black students entered the school, a mob of 500 jeering whites surrounded the building. Eisenhower, who had told Faubus that "the Federal Constitution will be upheld by me by every legal means at my command," sent in 1000 paratroopers to ensure the rights of the Little Rock Nine to attend Central High. The students finished the school year under armed guard. Then Little Rock authorities closed the school for two years; when it reopened, only three African Americans were in attendance.

Despite the snail's pace of school desegregation, the *Brown* decision led to other advances. In 1957, the Eisenhower administration proposed the first general civil rights legislation since Reconstruction. Senate Majority Leader Lyndon B. Johnson overcame strong southern resistance to avoid a filibuster, but at the expense of weakening the measure. The act, however, did create a permanent Commission for Civil Rights, one of Truman's original goals. It also provided for federal efforts aimed at "securing and protecting the right to vote." A second civil rights act in 1960 slightly strengthened the voting rights section.

Like the desegregation effort, the attempt to ensure African American voting rights in the South was still largely symbolic. Southern registrars used devices, ranging from intimidation to unfair tests, to deny African Americans suffrage. Yet the actions of

Watch the Video   How Did the Civil Rights Movement Change American Schools?

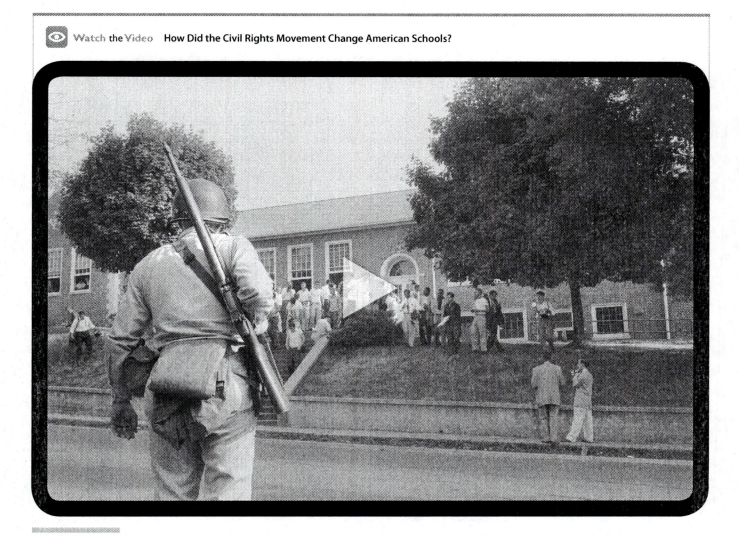

DESEGREGATING THE SCHOOLS Clinton High School, located in a small town of 5000 in eastern Tennessee, was the first public high school to desegregate. Clinton was also one of the first towns to witness the anger and hatred associated with school integration. On September 1, 1956, the National Guard and state troopers were called in to help control the violent crowds of protestors.

Quick Check

What was the importance of the case of Brown v. Board of Education of Topeka?

Congress and the Supreme Court marked a turning point in national policy toward racial justice.

The Beginnings of Black Activism

African Americans themselves were the most dynamic force for change. The shift from legal struggles in the courts to protest in the streets began in Montgomery, Alabama. On December 1, 1955, Rosa Parks—a black seamstress who had been active in the local NAACP—violated a city ordinance by refusing to give up her seat to a white man on a city bus. Her action, often viewed as spontaneous, grew out of a long tradition of black protest against rigid segregation in the South. Rosa Parks herself had been ejected from a bus a decade earlier for refusing to obey the driver's command, "Niggers move back." In 1953, black ministers in Baton Rouge, Louisiana, had mounted a weeklong boycott of that city's bus system and succeeded in modifying the segregated seating rules.

In Montgomery, Parks's arrest sparked a massive protest. Black women were particularly important in the movement, printing and handing out 50,000 leaflets to rally the African American community behind Parks. The protest also led to Martin Luther King, Jr.'s emergence as an eloquent spokesman for African Americans.

King agreed to lead a bus boycott. The son of a famous Atlanta preacher, he had recently taken his first church in Montgomery after earning a Ph.D. in theology at Boston University. Now he combined his wide learning with charismatic appeal to achieve a practical goal—fair treatment for the African Americans who made up the bulk of the riders on the city's buses.

The **Montgomery bus boycott** began with a modest goal. Instead of challenging the legality of segregated seating, King simply asked that seats be taken on a first-come, first-served basis, with African Americans being seated from the back and whites from the front of each bus. As the protest continued, however, and as protesters endured harassment and violence, the protesters became more assertive. Car pools enabled them to avoid using the buses. Soon protesters were insisting on an end to segregated seating as they sang their new song of protest:

> *Ain't gonna ride them buses no more*
> *Ain't gonna ride no more*
> *Why in the hell don't the white folk know*
> *That I ain't gonna ride no more.*

The boycott ended in victory when the Supreme Court ruled in November 1956 that the Alabama segregated seating law was unconstitutional. The protest movement had dented the wall of southern segregation, and Martin Luther King, Jr., had emerged as the leader of a new civil rights movement—to worldwide acclaim. In 1957, King founded the **Southern Christian Leadership Conference (SCLC)** to direct the crusade against segregation. He visited Third World leaders in Africa and Asia and paid homage to India's Mahatma Gandhi, who had influenced his reliance on nonviolent civil disobedience. He led a triumphant Prayer Pilgrimage to Washington on the third anniversary of the *Brown* decision, stirring the crowd of 30,000 with his demand for the right to vote. His cry "Give us the ballot" boomed in salvos that historian Taylor Branch likened to "cannon bursts in a diplomatic salute." King's remarkable voice became familiar to the entire nation. Unlike many African American preachers, King never shouted, yet his passion and a compelling cadence captured his audiences. "Though still a boy to many of his older listeners," Branch noted, "he had the commanding air of a burning sage."

Even more important, King's strategy and message fitted perfectly with the plight of his followers. Drawing on sources as diverse as Gandhi and Henry David Thoreau, King came out of the bus boycott with the concept of passive resistance. "If cursed," he had told protesters in Montgomery, "do not curse back. If struck, do not strike

Montgomery bus boycott In late 1955, African Americans led by Martin Luther King, Jr., boycotted the buses in Montgomery, Alabama, after seamstress Rosa Parks was arrested for refusing to move to the back of a bus. The boycott, which ended when the Supreme Court ruled in favor of the protesters, marked the beginning of a new, activist phase of the civil rights movement.

Southern Christian Leadership Conference An organization founded by Martin Luther King, Jr., to fight segregation through passive resistance, nonviolence, and peaceful confrontation.

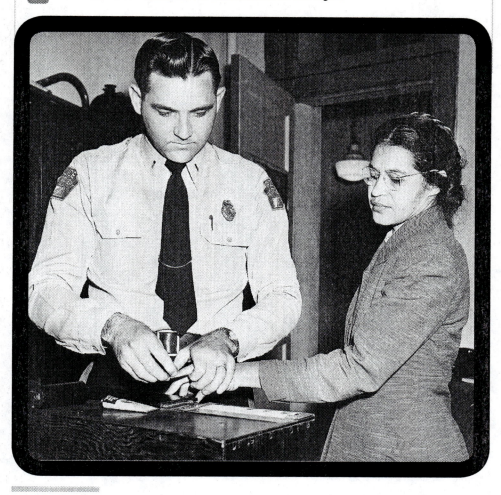

ROSA PARKS Rosa Parks's refusal to surrender her seat to a white man on a Montgomery, Alabama, bus led to a citywide bus boycott that brought Rev. Martin Luther King, Jr., to prominence as a leader of the civil rights movement. Parks is shown here being fingerprinted in February 1956 after her arrest for violating an anti-boycott law.

back, but evidence love and goodwill at all times." The essence of his strategy was to turn the apparent weakness of southern blacks—their lack of power—into a conquering weapon. His message to southern whites was unmistakable: "We will match your capacity to inflict suffering with our capacity to endure suffering. We will meet your physical force with soul force. We will not hate you, but we will not obey your evil laws. We will soon wear you down by pure capacity to suffer."

King's goal was to unite the broken community through bonds of Christian love. He hoped to use nonviolence to appeal to middle-class white America, "to the conscience of the great decent majority who through blindness, fear, pride or irrationality have allowed their consciences to sleep." The result, King prophesied, would enable future historians to say of the effort, "There lived a great people—a black people—who injected new meaning and dignity into the veins of civilization."

King was not alone in championing civil rights. Jo Ann Robinson helped pave the way in Montgomery with the Women's Political Caucus, and leaders as diverse as Bayard Rustin and Ella Baker advanced the cause at the grassroots level.

In February 1960, another spontaneous event sparked a further advance for passive resistance. Four African American students from North Carolina Agricultural and Technical College sat down at a lunch counter in Greensboro, North Carolina, and refused to move after being denied service. Other students, whites and blacks, joined in similar "sit-ins" across the South, as well as "kneel-ins" at churches and "wade-ins" at swimming pools. By 1961, 50,000 young people had desegregated public facilities in more than 100 southern cities. Thousands of the demonstrators were arrested and jailed, but the movement led to the formation of the **Student Nonviolent Coordinating Committee (SNCC)** in April 1960. The SCLC and SNCC, with their tactic of direct, though peaceful, confrontation, replaced the NAACP and its reliance on court action in the forefront of the civil rights movement. The change would eventually lead to success for the movement, but it also heightened social turmoil in the 1960s.

Conclusion: Restoring National Confidence

In 1959, President Eisenhower appointed a Commission on National Goals "to develop a broad outline of national objectives for the next decade and longer." Ten prominent citizens, led by Henry W. Wriston of Brown University, issued a report that called for increased military spending abroad, greater economic growth at home, broader educational opportunities, and more government support for scientific research and the arts. The consensus seemed to be that rather than a change of direction, all the United States needed was a renewed commitment to the pursuit of excellence.

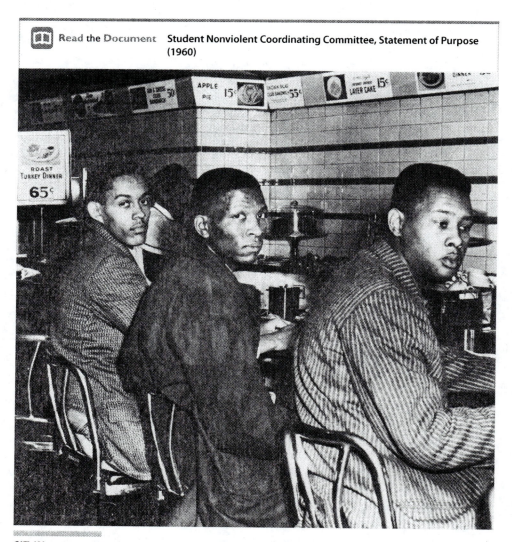

📖 Read the Document   **Student Nonviolent Coordinating Committee, Statement of Purpose (1960)**

SIT-IN In February 1960, black students from North Carolina A&T College staged a sit-in at a "whites only" lunch counter in Greensboro, North Carolina. Their nonviolent protest spurred similar demonstrations in public spaces across the South.

Quick Check

By what means did African American individuals and groups challenge segregation?

Student Nonviolent Coordinating Committee (SNCC) A group organized by students to work for equal rights for African Americans. It spearheaded peaceful sit-ins and marches in the early 1960s, but later grew more radical and changed its name to the Student National Coordinating Committee.

The 1950s ended with the national mood less troubled than when the decade began amid the turmoil of the second Red Scare and the Korean War, yet less tranquil or confident than Eisenhower had hoped it would be. The American people felt reassured about the economy, no longer fearing a return of the Great Depression. However, they were also aware that abundance did not guarantee the quality of everyday life and realized that there was still a huge gap between American ideals and the reality of race relations, in the North and the South.

Chapter Review

The Postwar Boom

29.1 How did the American economy evolve after World War II? p. 675

The American economy boomed after World War II, as the nation recovered from the Great Depression and the war. The GNP doubled between 1940 and 1960. Individuals spent heavily on housing, automobiles, and consumer goods, and the government on defense. New communities emerged in the suburbs and the Sunbelt states of the West and South.

The Good Life?

29.2 How did American culture change after the war? p. 678

American culture reflected both the promise of material prosperity and the failure of material goods to yield true happiness. More people went to church than ever; more young people went to college. Television provided endless information and entertainment. But suburban life exhibited a shallow sameness that prompted critics to question if it was worthwhile.

The Struggle over Civil Rights

29.3 How did the civil rights movement develop in the 1940s and 1950s? p. 681

Civil rights became a major issue after World War II. Truman desegregated the military, and federal courts ordered the desegregation of schools. Black activists such as Rosa Parks and Martin Luther King, Jr., led protests against segregation on buses and other public facilities. Students organized sit-ins.

Timeline

1947
Postwar Boom?—William Levitt announces first Levittown
— 1947

1948
1948 — **Civil Rights**—Truman desegregates the armed forces

1954
Civil Rights—Supreme Court orders schools desegregated in *Brown v. Board of Education of Topeka.*
— 1954

1955
1955 — **Civil Rights**—African Americans begin boycott of Montgomery, Alabama, buses (December)

1957
Civil Rights—Congress passes first Civil Rights Act since Reconstruction
— 1957

30 The Turbulent Sixties 1960–1968

Kennedy Versus Nixon: The First Televised Presidential Candidate Debate

O n Monday evening, September 26, 1960, John F. Kennedy and Richard M. Nixon faced each other in the nation's first televised debate between two presidential candidates. Kennedy, the relatively unknown Democratic challenger, had proposed the debates; Nixon, confident of his mastery of television, had accepted even though, as Eisenhower's vice president and the front-runner in the election, he had more to lose and less to gain.

Nixon arrived an hour early at the CBS studio in Chicago, looking tired and ill at ease. He was still recovering from a knee injury that had slowed his campaign and left him pale and weak. Makeup experts offered to hide Nixon's heavy beard and soften his prominent jowls, but instead he let an aide apply a light coat of "Lazy Shave," a pancake cosmetic. Kennedy, tanned from

NIXON DEBATES KENNEDY Richard Nixon (left) and John Kennedy debate during the 1960 presidential campaign.

LEARNING OBJECTIVES

30.1 ((•	30.2 ((•	30.3 ((•	30.4 ((•	30.5 ((•	30.6 ((•
How did the Cold War intensify under Kennedy? p. 693	What was the "New Frontier," and what did it accomplish? p. 698	What were Johnson's domestic priorities and what were his achievements? p. 701	How did Johnson's Vietnam policy evolve? p. 705	Why were there protests during the 1960s? p. 710	How did the Vietnam War influence American politics? p. 714

((• Listen to Chapter 30 on MyHistoryLab

30.1
30.2
30.3
30.4
30.5
30.6

Watch the Video Series on MyHistoryLab

Learn about some key topics related to this chapter with the *MyHistoryLab Video Series: Key Topics in U.S. History.*

1 The Sixties: 1960–1968 The 1960s, which opened with the promise of John F. Kennedy's presidency, saw much of that promise realized but it was cut short, by his assassination in 1963 and the escalation of the war in Vietnam. Perhaps no single decade in American history, as this introductory video presents, experienced so much change in everything from popular music to civil rights to social welfare legislation. Although the 1960s was marked by a new liberality in American society, the decade gave rise to conservative movement that dominated American life in coming decades.

 Watch on MyHistoryLab

2 Lyndon Johnson This video surveys the presidency of Lyndon B. Johnson, who attempted to continue the New Deal with his Great Society and War on Poverty reforms. These reforms gave rise to programs that improved the lives of many Americans but strained the federal budget. Together with the costly and disappointing Vietnam War, they helped drive Johnson from office.

Watch on MyHistoryLab

3 Vietnam The Vietnam War was intended to contain communism in Southeast Asia. However, it unleashed powerful forces in the United States for political, social, and even cultural change during the 1960s. In addition to revealing the background of the war, this video examines how it was fought, the increase in U.S. involvement after the Gulf of Tonkin Incident, and how American society dealt with the war, the peace movement, and the political realignments and social change that arose with the war.

 Watch on MyHistoryLab

4 For Everything There Is a Movement The 1960s was actually a decade of many movements. This video not only discusses the movement to achieve civil rights for African Americans. It also looks at the other groups that wanted similar rights. In addition, it portrays movements to end the war in Vietnam, encourage the Sexual Revolution, and protect the environment. These movements in turn, inspired counter-movements that sought to restore a "golden age" that existed before this restive decade of marchers, activists, and radicals.

Watch on MyHistoryLab

campaigning in California and well rested, wore light makeup. He also wore a dark blue suit better adapted to the intense television lighting.

At 8:30 P.M. central time, moderator Howard K. Smith welcomed an estimated 77 million viewers. Kennedy, echoing Abraham Lincoln, said that the nation faced the question of "whether the world will exist half-slave and half-free." Although the rules limited the first debate to domestic issues, Kennedy argued that foreign and domestic policy were inseparable. He accused the Republicans of letting the country drift at home and abroad: "I think it's time America started moving again." Nixon, caught off guard, seemed to agree with Kennedy's assessment of the nation's problems, but he contended that he had better solutions: "Our disagreement is not about the goals for America but only about the means to reach those goals."

For the rest of the hour, the two candidates answered questions from journalists. Radiating self-assurance, Kennedy used statistics and details to create the image of a man deeply knowledgeable about government. Nixon defended the Eisenhower record but seemed unsure of himself. The reaction shots of each candidate listening to the other's remarks showed Kennedy calm and serene, Nixon tense and uncomfortable.

Polls revealed a sharp swing to Kennedy. His performance impressed Democrats and independents who had thought him too young or inexperienced. Nixon suffered more from his unattractive image than from what he said; radio listeners thought the Republican candidate more than held his own. In three additional debates, Nixon improved his performance, wearing makeup to soften his appearance and taking the offensive. But the damage had been done. A post-election poll revealed that of 4 million voters whom the debates influenced, 3 million voted for Kennedy.

The televised debates were only one of many factors influencing the 1960 election. In essence, Kennedy won because he took advantage of all his opportunities. Lightly regarded by Democratic leaders, he won the nomination by appealing to the rank and file in the primaries. Then he astutely chose Lyndon Johnson of Texas as his running mate to blunt Nixon's southern strategy.

During the fall campaign, Kennedy promised to stimulate the economy and reform education, health care, and civil rights under the banner of the **New Frontier**. Abroad, he vowed he would lead the nation to victory over the Soviet Union in the Cold War. He met the issue of his Catholicism head on, telling Protestant ministers in Houston that as president he would always place country above religion. In his shrewdest move, he won over African American voters by helping to secure the release of Martin Luther King, Jr., from a Georgia jail where the civil rights leader was being held on a trumped-up charge.

The Democratic victory in 1960 was paper-thin. Kennedy's edge in the popular vote was only .02 percent, and voting irregularities in several states—notably Illinois and Texas—which went Democratic by slender majorities, tainted his wide margin in the electoral college (303 to 219) (see Map 30.1). Yet Kennedy's triumph marked a sharp political shift. In contrast to the aging Eisenhower, Kennedy symbolized youth, energy, and ambition. His mastery of the new medium of television reflected his sensitivity to the changes taking place in American life in the 1960s. He promised reform at home and advances abroad. Over the next eight years, he and Lyndon Johnson achieved many of their goals. Yet angry protests, violent demonstrations, and sweeping social change made the 1960s one of the stormiest decades in American history.

30.1
30.2
30.3
30.4
30.5
30.6

Read the Document John F. Kennedy, Inaugural Address (1961)

Election of 1960

	Electoral Vote by State		Popular Vote
DEMOCRATIC John F. Kennedy	303		34,227,096
Harry F. Byrd	15		—
REPUBLICAN Richard M. Nixon	219		34,108,546
MINOR PARTIES	—		502,363
	537		68,838,005

MAP 30.1 ELECTION OF 1960

New Frontier President John F. Kennedy's program to revitalize the stagnant economy and enact reform legislation in education, health care, and civil rights.

Kennedy Intensifies the Cold War

30.1 How did the Cold War intensify under Kennedy?

John F. Kennedy was determined to succeed where he believed Eisenhower had failed. Critical of his predecessor for holding down defense spending and apparently allowing the Soviet Union to open up a dangerous lead in nuclear missiles (in fact, it had not), Kennedy sought to warn the nation of its peril and lead it to victory in the Cold War.

30.1

30.2

30.3

30.4

30.5

30.6

In his inaugural address, the young president sounded the alarm. Ignoring the domestic issues aired during the campaign, he dealt primarily with the world: "Let every nation know, whether it wishes us well or ill, that we shall pay any price, bear any burden, meet any hardship, support any friend, oppose any foe to assure the survival and success of liberty. We will do all this and more."

From the start, Kennedy gave foreign policy top priority. In part, the decision reflected the perilous world situation, the immediate dangers ranging from troubles over Berlin to the emergence of Fidel Castro as a Soviet ally in Cuba. But it also corresponded to Kennedy's personal priorities. As a congressman and senator, he had been an intense cold warrior. Bored by committee work and legislative details, he had focused on foreign policy, gaining a seat on the Senate Foreign Relations Committee and publishing a book of speeches, *The Strategy of Peace*, in 1960.

His appointments reflected his determination to win the Cold War. His choice of Dean Rusk, an experienced but unassertive diplomat, to head the State Department indicated that Kennedy planned to be his own secretary of state. He surrounded himself with young, pragmatic advisers who prided themselves on toughness. These New Frontiersmen, later dubbed "the best and the brightest" by journalist David Halberstam, took a hard line on the Soviet Union and they believed that American security depended on superior force and the willingness to use it.

Containment in Southeast Asia

Two weeks before Kennedy's inauguration, Soviet Premier Nikita Khrushchev declared his support for "wars of national liberation." His words were actually aimed more at China than the United States; the two communist nations were rivals for influence in the Third World. But Kennedy, ignoring the Sino-Soviet split, concluded the United States and Russia were locked in a struggle for the hearts and minds of the uncommitted in Asia, Africa, and Latin America.

Calling for a new policy of nation building, Kennedy advocated financial and technical assistance to help Third World nations modernize and achieve stable pro-Western governments. Measures ranging from the idealistic Peace Corps to the ambitious Alliance for Progress—a massive economic aid program for Latin America—were part of this effort. Unfortunately, Kennedy relied even more on counterinsurgency to beat back the communist challenge in the Third World.

Southeast Asia offered the gravest test. After Vietnam gained independence from France in the mid-1950s, an anticommunist government emerged in the south, under Ngo Dinh Diem. A communist regime, headed by Ho Chi Minh, controlled the north. The United States supported Diem and South Vietnam and opposed Ho and North Vietnam.

When Kennedy entered the White House, North Vietnam was directing the insurgency of Vietcong rebels in the south. As the guerrilla war intensified in 1961, the president sent two trusted advisers, Walt Rostow and General Maxwell Taylor, to South Vietnam. They favored dispatching 8000 American combat troops. "As an area for the operation of U.S. troops," Taylor reported, "SVN [South Vietnam] is not an excessively difficult or unpleasant place to operate.... The risks of backing into a major Asian war by way of SVN are present but are not impressive."

The president decided against sending in combat troops, but he increased economic aid to Diem and the size of the U.S. military mission in Saigon. American advisers in Vietnam grew from fewer than 1000 in 1961 to more than 16,000 by late 1963. The flow of supplies and the creation of "strategic hamlets," fortified villages to protect the peasantry from the Vietcong, slowed the communist momentum. But by 1963, the situation had again become critical. Diem, a Christian aristocrat, had lost the support of his own people; Buddhist monks set themselves aflame in protests against him, and his own generals plotted his overthrow.

Kennedy was in a quandary. He realized that only the Vietnamese could determine the fate of South Vietnam: "In the final analysis, it is their war. They are the ones who have to win it or lose it." But Kennedy was not prepared to accept the possible loss of all Southeast Asia. It would be "a great mistake" to withdraw from South Vietnam, he told reporters: "Strongly on our mind is what happened in the case of China at the end of World War II, where China was lost. We don't want that." Although aides later claimed he planned to pull out after the 1964 election, Kennedy tacitly approved a coup that led to Diem's overthrow and murder on November 1, 1963. The resulting power vacuum in Saigon made further American involvement in Vietnam almost certain.

Quick Check
What was Kennedy's dilemma in Vietnam?

Containing Castro: The Bay of Pigs Fiasco

Kennedy's determination to check global communist expansion peaked in Cuba. In the 1960 campaign, pointing to the ties between the Soviet Union and Fidel Castro's regime, he had accused the Republicans of permitting a "communist satellite" on "our very doorstep." Kennedy had even backed "anti-Castro exile forces," calling them "fighters for freedom" who could overthrow Castro.

In fact, the Eisenhower administration had been training Cuban exiles in Guatemala since March 1960 as part of a CIA plan to topple Castro. Eisenhower had employed the CIA to oust unfriendly regimes in Iran in 1953 and Guatemala in 1954. Those successes caused Eisenhower and then Kennedy to dismiss skeptics who thought Castro would be harder to overthrow, and who contended that, in any case, covert operations damaged America's reputation. Senator J. William Fulbright of Arkansas, chairman of the Foreign Relations Committee, was especially critical, saying, "The Castro regime is a thorn in the flesh, but it is not a dagger in the heart." Kennedy, however, decided to proceed.

On April 17, 1961, 1400 Cuban exiles landed at the Bay of Pigs in southern Cuba. Even though the United States had masterminded the operation, Kennedy insisted on covert action, even canceling an American air strike on the beachhead. Castro's forces easily quashed the invasion. They killed nearly 500 exiles and captured the rest, in what became known as the **Bay of Pigs**.

Kennedy took personal responsibility for the defeat. In his address to the American people, however, he showed no remorse for violating a neighboring country's sovereignty, only regret at the outcome, and he warned the Soviets that "our restraint is not inexhaustible." He asserted that the United States would resist "communist penetration" in the Western Hemisphere, terming it part of the "primary obligations . . . to the security of our nation." For the remainder of his presidency, Kennedy harassed the Castro regime, imposing an economic blockade on Cuba, supporting raids by exiles from Florida, and failing to stop the CIA from launching bizarre plots to assassinate Castro.

Bay of Pigs In April 1961, a group of Cuban exiles organized and supported by the CIA landed on the southern coast of Cuba in an effort to overthrow Fidel Castro. When the invasion ended in disaster, President Kennedy took full responsibility for it.

Quick Check
What was the Bay of Pigs affair?

Containing Castro: The Cuban Missile Crisis

The climax of Kennedy's crusade came in October 1962 with the **Cuban missile crisis**. The Soviets had engaged in a massive arms buildup in Cuba, ostensibly to protect Castro from an American invasion. Republican candidates in the 1962 congressional elections called for a firm response; Kennedy contented himself with warning against introducing offensive weapons, believing their presence would threaten American security. Khrushchev denied any such intent, but secretly built sites for 24 medium-range (1000-mile) and 18 intermediate-range (2000-mile) missiles in Cuba. Later he claimed his purpose was purely defensive, but he was probably responding to pressures from his own military to close the enormous strategic gap in nuclear striking power that Kennedy's arms buildup had opened up.

Unfortunately, the Kennedy administration had stopped overflights of Cuba by U-2 spy planes in August. Fearful that Soviet surface-to-air missiles could bring down the American spy plane and create an international incident, the White House, over the objections of the CIA, limited U-2 flights to the air space bordering the island. When direct overflights resumed on October 14, they showed indisputable photographic evidence of the missile sites, which were nearing completion.

Cuban missile crisis In October 1962, the United States and the Soviet Union came close to nuclear war when President John F. Kennedy insisted that Nikita Khrushchev remove the 42 missiles he had secretly deployed in Cuba. The Soviets eventually did so, and the crisis ended.

30.1

30.2

30.3

30.4

30.5

30.6

Kennedy decided to keep this development secret while he consulted with close advisers about how to respond. Their initial preference for an immediate air strike gave way to discussion of either a full-scale invasion or naval blockade of Cuba. The president and his advisers rejected a proposal to withdraw obsolete American Jupiter missiles from Turkey in return for a similar Russian pullout in Cuba. Kennedy finally agreed to a two-step procedure. He would proclaim a quarantine of Cuba to prevent new missiles from arriving and threaten a nuclear confrontation to force the removal of those already there. If the Russians did not cooperate, the United States would invade Cuba and dismantle the missiles.

On October 22, the president told the nation about the Soviet missiles and his plans to remove them. He blamed Khrushchev for "this clandestine, reckless, and provocative threat to world peace" and made it clear that a missile attack from Cuba would lead to "a full retaliatory response upon the Soviet Union."

For the next six days, the world hovered on the brink of nuclear catastrophe. Khrushchev replied defiantly, accusing Kennedy of pushing mankind "to the abyss of a world nuclear-missile war." Sixteen Soviet ships continued toward Cuba, while the American navy deployed to intercept them 500 miles from the island. In Florida, nearly 250,000 men were being concentrated in the largest invasion force ever assembled in the continental United States.

The first break came at midweek when the Soviet ships halted to avert a confrontation at sea. "We're eyeball to eyeball," commented Secretary of State Dean Rusk, "and I think the other fellow just blinked." On Friday, Khrushchev sent Kennedy a long, rambling letter offering a face-saving way out: Russia would remove the missiles in return for an American promise never to invade Cuba. The president was ready to accept when a second Russian message insisted that the Jupiter missiles be withdrawn from Turkey. Heeding the advice of his brother, Attorney General Robert Kennedy, the

((• 📖 Read the Document   Executive Discussions on the Cuban Missile Crisis (1962)

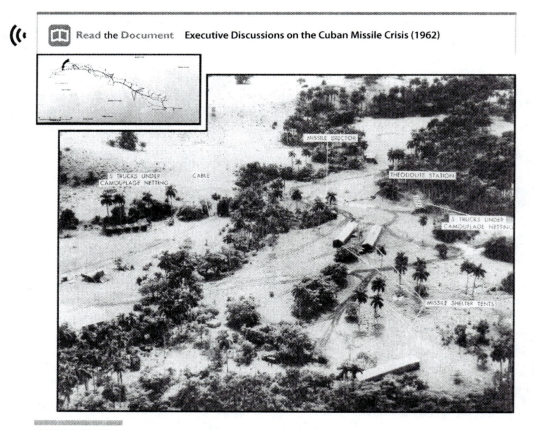

MISSILE SITES Aerial photographs taken by a U-2 reconnaissance plane flying over Cuba revealed the presence of Russian missile sites under construction on the island. Recently released information about the type and number of Soviet nuclear warheads in Cuba reveals just how imminent was the threat of nuclear war had the Soviets not capitulated to U.S. demands for removal of the missiles.

30.1

30.2

30.3

30.4

30.5

30.6

president refused to bargain; Khrushchev had endangered world peace by putting the missiles in Cuba secretly, and he must take them out immediately. Nevertheless, while the military went ahead with plans to invade Cuba, the president, again heeding his brother's advice, made one last appeal for peace. Ignoring the second Russian message, he cabled Khrushchev accepting his original offer.

On Saturday, October 27, Robert Kennedy told Soviet Ambassador Anatoly Dobrynin it was the last chance to avert nuclear confrontation: "We had to have a commitment by tomorrow that those bases would be removed. He should understand that if they did not remove those bases, we would remove them." If Khrushchev did not back down, "there would be not only dead Americans but dead Russians as well."

In reality, Kennedy was not ready to risk nuclear war. His brother assured Dobrynin that the Jupiter missiles would soon be removed from Turkey. The president preferred that the missile swap be done privately, but 25 years later, Dean Rusk revealed that JFK had instructed him to arrange a deal through the United Nations involving "the removal of both the Jupiters and the missiles in Cuba." In recently released transcripts of his meetings with his advisers, the president reaffirmed his intention to make a missile trade with Khrushchev publicly as a last resort to avoid nuclear war: "We can't very well invade Cuba with all the toil and blood when we could have gotten them out by making a deal on the same missiles in Turkey."

Kennedy never had to make this concession. At nine the next morning, Khrushchev agreed to remove the missiles in return only for Kennedy's promise not to invade Cuba. The crisis was over.

The world, however, had come close to a nuclear conflict. We now know the Soviets had nuclear warheads in Cuba, not only for 20 of the medium-range missiles, but also for short-range tactical launchers for use against an American invasion. If Kennedy had approved the military's recommendations to invade Cuba, the consequences might have been disastrous.

The peaceful resolution of the crisis became a triumph for Kennedy. His party overcame the Republican challenge in the November elections, and his popularity soared. The American people, on the defensive since *Sputnik*, felt that they had proved their superiority over the Russians. Arthur Schlesinger, Jr., Kennedy's confidant and biographer, claimed that the Cuban crisis showed the "the ripening of an American leadership unsurpassed in the responsible management of power. . . . It was this combination of toughness and restraint, of will, nerve and wisdom, so brilliantly controlled, so matchlessly calibrated, that dazzled the world."

The Cuban missile crisis also had more substantial results. Shaken by their close call, Kennedy and Khrushchev installed a "hot line" for direct communication between Washington and Moscow in an emergency. Stalled negotiations over reducing nuclear testing resumed, leading to the limited test ban treaty of 1963, which outlawed tests in the atmosphere while still permitting them underground. Above all, Kennedy displayed a new maturity. In a speech in June 1963, he shifted from the rhetoric of confrontation to that of conciliation. Speaking of the Russians, he said, "Our most basic common link is the fact that we all inhabit this planet. We all breathe the same air. We all cherish our children's future. And we are all mortal."

But the missile crisis also had an unfortunate consequence. Those who believed that the Russians understood only the language of force were confirmed in their penchant for a hard line. Hawks who had backed Kennedy's military buildup believed events had justified a policy of nuclear superiority. The Russians drew similar conclusions. Aware the United States had a four-to-one advantage in nuclear striking power during the Cuban crisis, one Soviet official told his American counterpart, "Never will we be caught like this again." The Soviets embarked on a crash program to build up their navy and overtake the American lead in nuclear missiles. Within five years, they had the nucleus of a modern navy and more ICBMs than the United States. Kennedy's fleeting triumph thus escalated the arms race. His legacy was bittersweet: short-term success and long-term anxiety.

Quick Check

What were the causes and consequences of the Cuban missile crisis?

The New Frontier at Home

Kennedy hoped to change history at home and abroad. His election marked the arrival of a new generation of leaders. For the first time, people born in the twentieth century who had entered political life after World War II were in charge of national affairs. Kennedy's inaugural call to get the nation moving again was particularly attractive to young people, who had shunned political involvement under Eisenhower.

The new administration reflected Kennedy's aura of youth and energy. Major cabinet appointments went to activists—notably Connecticut governor Abraham Ribicoff as secretary of health, education, and welfare; labor lawyer Arthur J. Goldberg as secretary of labor; Arizona congressman Stuart Udall as secretary of the interior; and Robert McNamara as secretary of defense. The most controversial choice was Robert Kennedy for attorney general. Critics scoffed at his lack of legal experience, leading JFK to joke that he wanted to give Bobby "a little experience before he goes out to practice law." In fact, the president prized his brother's loyalty and advice.

Equally important were the members of the White House staff who handled domestic affairs. Like their counterparts in foreign policy, these New Frontiersmen—Kenneth O'Donnell, Theodore Sorensen, Richard Goodwin, and Walter Heller—prided themselves on being tough and pragmatic. In contrast to Eisenhower, Kennedy relied heavily on academics and intellectuals to help him infuse the nation with energy and direction.

Kennedy's greatest asset was his own personality. A cool, attractive, and intelligent man, his sense of style endeared him to the American public. Encouraged by his wife, Jacqueline, the president invited artists and musicians to White House functions and sprinkled his speeches with references to Emerson and Shakespeare. He seemed to be a new Lancelot, bent on calling forth the best in national life; admirers likened his inner circle to King Arthur's Camelot. Reporters loved him, both for his fact-filled and candid press conferences and for his wit. After an embarrassing foreign policy failure, when his standing in the polls actually went up, he remarked, "It's just like Eisenhower. The worse I do, the more popular I get."

Moving Slowly on Civil Rights

Kennedy faced a dilemma over civil rights. Despite his lack of a strong record in the Senate, he had portrayed himself during the 1960 campaign as a crusader for African American rights. He promised to attack segregation in the Deep South, but his fear of alienating southern Democrats forced him to downplay civil rights legislation.

The president's solution was to defer congressional action in favor of executive leadership. Robert Kennedy expanded the Eisenhower administration's efforts to achieve voting rights for southern blacks. To register disfranchised citizens, the Justice Department worked with the civil rights movement—notably the Student Nonviolent Coordinating Committee (SNCC)—in the Deep South. In two years, the Kennedy administration increased the number of voting rights suits fivefold. Yet the attorney general could not force the FBI to protect the civil rights volunteers who risked their lives by encouraging African Americans to register. "SNCC's only contact with federal authority," noted one observer, "consisted of the FBI agents who stood by taking notes while local policemen beat up SNCC members."

Other efforts had equally mixed results. Vice President Lyndon Johnson headed a presidential Commission on Equal Employment Opportunities that worked with defense industries and other government contractors to increase jobs for African Americans. But a limited budget and a reliance on voluntary cooperation prevented dramatic gains; African American employment improved only in direct proportion to economic growth in the early 1960s.

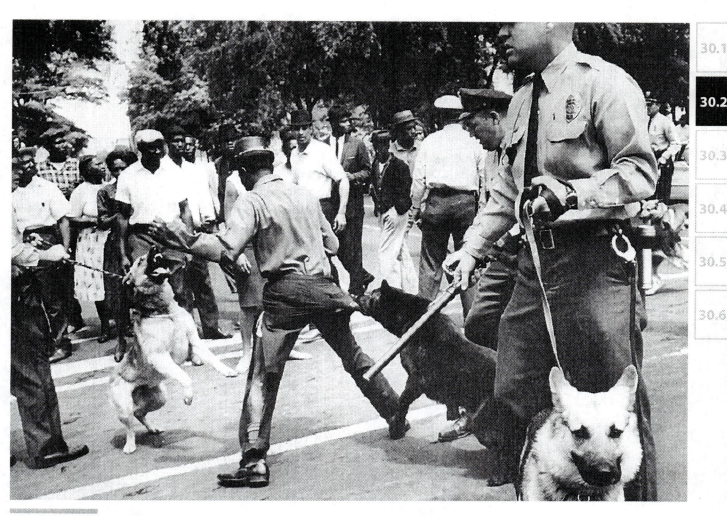

30.1

30.2

30.3

30.4

30.5

30.6

POLICE TURN BACK DEMONSTRATORS The attempts of African Americans to end discrimination and secure their civil rights met with violent resistance in Birmingham, Alabama, where police used snarling dogs, fire hoses, clubs, and electric cattle prods to turn back the unarmed demonstrators.

Kennedy did appoint African Americans to high positions: Robert Weaver became chief of the federal housing agency. Thurgood Marshall, who pleaded the *Brown* school desegregation case before the Supreme Court, was named to the U.S. Court of Appeals. On the other hand, Kennedy also appointed as federal judge a Mississippi jurist who referred to African Americans in court as "niggers" and once compared them to "a bunch of chimpanzees."

The civil rights movement rejected Kennedy's indirect approach. In May 1961, the Congress of Racial Equality (CORE) sponsored a **freedom ride** in which a biracial group tested a Supreme Court decision outlawing segregation in all bus and train stations used in interstate commerce. In Birmingham, Alabama, a mob of angry whites attacked the freedom riders. The attorney general dispatched hundreds of federal marshals to protect them, but the president was more upset at the distraction the protesters created. Kennedy directed one of his aides to call the leaders of CORE: "Tell them to call it off. Stop them."

In September, after the attorney general convinced the Interstate Commerce Commission to ban segregation in interstate terminals and buses, the **freedom rides** ended. The Kennedy administration then sought to prevent further confrontations by involving civil rights activists in its voting drive.

A pattern of belated reaction to southern racism marked Kennedys' basic approach. When James Meredith sought admission to the all-white University of Mississippi in 1962, the president and the attorney general worked with Mississippi Governor Ross Barnett to avoid violence. However, the night before Meredith enrolled at the university, a mob attacked the federal marshals and National Guard troops sent to protect him. The violence left two dead and 375 injured, including 166 marshals and 12 guardsmen, but Meredith attended the university and graduated.

freedom ride Sponsored by the Congress of Racial Equality (CORE), freedom rides on buses by civil rights advocates in 1961 in the South were designed to test the enforcement of federal regulations that prohibited segregation in interstate public transportation.

30.1

30.2

30.3

30.4

30.5

30.6

Quick Check

What was Kennedy's response to the civil rights movement?

In 1963, Kennedy sent the deputy attorney general to face down Governor George C. Wallace, a segregationist who had promised "to stand in the schoolhouse door" to prevent the integration of the University of Alabama. After a brief confrontation, Wallace yielded, and two African American students desegregated the university.

"I Have a Dream"

Martin Luther King, Jr., finally forced Kennedy to openly support racial justice. In the spring of 1963, King began a massive protest in Birmingham, one of the South's most segregated cities. Marches and demonstrations aimed at integrating public facilities and opening up jobs for African Americans led to police harassment and arrests, including that of King himself. Police Commissioner Eugene "Bull" Connor was determined to crush the civil rights movement; King was equally determined to prevail. Writing from his cell in Birmingham, he vowed to bring the issue of racial injustice to national attention.

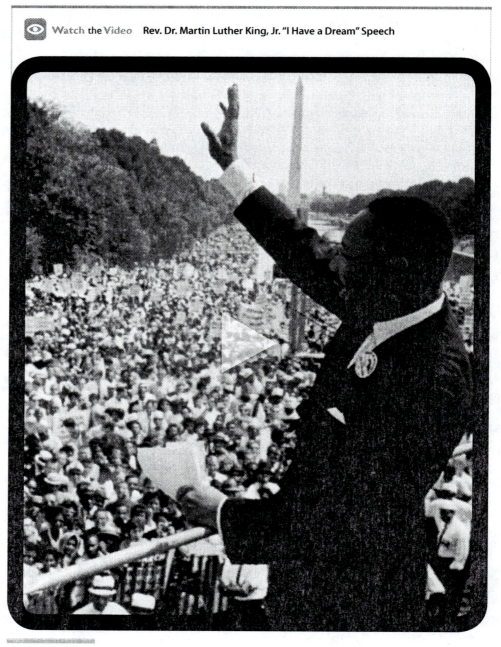

Watch the Video   **Rev. Dr. Martin Luther King, Jr. "I Have a Dream" Speech**

"I HAVE A DREAM" Rev. Martin Luther King, Jr., addresses the crowd at the March on Washington in August 1963. In his speech, King recounted the difficulties of blacks' struggle for freedom, then stirred the crowd with the description of his dream for America: "I have a dream that one day this nation will rise up and live out the true meaning of its creed—we hold these truths to be self-evident, that all men are created equal."

Connor played directly into King's hands. On May 3, as 6000 children marched in place of the jailed protesters, authorities responded with clubs, police dogs, and high-pressure water hoses strong enough to take the bark off a tree. With a horrified nation watching this brutality on television, the Kennedy administration arranged a settlement that ended the violence and granted most of the protesters' demands.

More important, Kennedy finally called for action. "We are confronted primarily with a moral issue," he told the nation on June 11. "It is as old as the Scriptures and is as clear as the American Constitution." Eight days later, the administration sponsored civil rights legislation providing equal access to all public accommodations and an extension of voting rights for African Americans.

Despite pleas from the government to stop demonstrations and protests, civil rights leaders kept pressure on the administration. On August 28, more than 200,000 marchers gathered in a **March on Washington** for a day-long rally in front of the Lincoln Memorial. The climax was Martin Luther King, Jr.'s eloquent description of his dream for America:

> When we let freedom ring, when we let it ring from every village and every hamlet, from every state and every city, we will be able to speed up that day when all God's children, black men and white men, Jews and Gentiles, Protestants and Catholics, will be able to join hands and sing, in the words of that old Negro spiritual, "Free at last! Free at last! Thank God almighty, we are free at last!"

30.1

30.2

30.3

30.4

30.5

30.6

March on Washington In August 1963, civil rights leaders organized a massive rally in Washington to urge passage of President John F. Kennedy's civil rights bill. The high point was Martin Luther King, Jr.'s "I Have a Dream" speech.

Quick Check

How did King's role evolve during the Kennedy years?

LBJ's Great Society

30.3 What were Johnson's domestic priorities and what were his achievements?

The New Frontier came to a violent end on November 22, 1963, when Lee Harvey Oswald assassinated Kennedy as the president rode in a motorcade in Dallas. The shock stunned the world. The American people were bewildered by the rapid sequence of events: the brutal killing of their young president; the televised slaying of Oswald by Jack Ruby in the basement of the Dallas police headquarters; Jacqueline Kennedy's composure and dignity at the state funeral; and the hurried Warren Commission report, which identified Oswald as the lone assassin. Critics would later charge that Oswald had been part of a vast conspiracy, but at the time, the prevailing national reaction was a numbing sense of loss.

Lyndon B. Johnson quickly filled the vacuum left by Kennedy's death. Sworn in aboard Air Force One as he returned to Washington, Johnson reassured world leaders of American political stability. Five days after the tragedy in Dallas, Johnson spoke eloquently to a joint session of Congress: "Today in the moment of new resolve, I would say to all my fellow Americans, 'Let us continue.'" Asking Congress to enact Kennedy's tax and civil rights bills as a tribute to the fallen leader, LBJ concluded, "Let us here highly resolve that John Fitzgerald Kennedy did not live or die in vain."

Johnson in Action

Johnson suffered from the inevitable comparison with his young and stylish predecessor. LBJ was aware of his own lack of polish; he surrounded himself with Kennedy advisers and insiders, hoping their air of sophistication would rub off on him. Johnson's assets were real—he possessed an intimate knowledge of Congress, incredible energy and determination to succeed, and a fierce ego. When a young marine officer tried to direct him to the proper helicopter, saying, "This one is yours," Johnson replied, "Son, they are all my helicopters."

LBJ's height and intensity gave him a powerful presence; he dominated any room he entered and delighted in using his physical power of persuasion. One Texas politician explained why he had given in to Johnson: "Lyndon got me by the lapels and put

LYNDON B. JOHNSON President Johnson applies the "Johnson treatment" to Senator Margaret Chase Smith. A shrewd politician and master of the legislative process, Johnson always knew which votes he could count on, those he couldn't, and where and how to apply pressure to swing votes his way.

his face on top of mine and he talked and talked and talked. I figured it was either getting drowned or joining."

Yet LBJ could not project his intelligence and vitality to large audiences. Unlike Kennedy, his televised speeches were stilted and awkward. Trying to belie his reputation as a riverboat gambler, he came across like a foxy grandpa, clever, calculating, and not to be trusted. He lacked Kennedy's wit and charm. Reporters delighted in describing how he berated his aides or shocked the nation by showing the scar from an operation.

Whatever his shortcomings in style, however, Johnson's ability to deal with Congress was far greater than Kennedy's. He had more than 30 years of experience in Washington as a legislative aide, congressman, and senator. His encyclopedic knowledge of the legislative process and his shrewd manipulation of senators had made him the most influential Senate leader in history. Famed for "the Johnson treatment," a legendary ability to use personal persuasion to reach his goals, Johnson in fact relied more on his ties with the Senate's power brokers—or "whales," as he called them—than on his exploitation of the "minnows."

Above all, Johnson sought consensus. Indifferent to ideology, he had moved easily from New Deal liberalism to oil-and-gas conservatism as his career advanced. He had cultivated Richard Russell of Georgia, leader of the Dixie bloc, but he also had taken Hubert Humphrey, a Minnesota liberal, under his wing. He had performed a balancing act on civil rights, working with the Eisenhower administration to pass the 1957 Voting Rights Act, yet weakening it to avoid alienating southern Democrats. When Kennedy dashed Johnson's own presidential ambitions in 1960, LBJ had gracefully agreed to be his running mate and had endured the disappointment of the vice presidency loyally and silently. Thrust into power, Johnson used his gifts wisely. Citing his favorite scriptural passage from Isaiah, "Come now, and let us reason together, saith the Lord," he concentrated on passing Kennedy's tax and civil rights bills in 1964.

The tax cut came first. Aware of the power Senate Finance Committee Chairman Harry Byrd, a Virginia conservative, wielded, Johnson astutely lowered Kennedy's projected $101.5 billion budget for 1965 to $97.9 billion. Although Byrd voted against the tax cut, he let the measure out of his committee, telling Johnson, "I'll be working for you behind the scenes." In February, Congress reduced personal income taxes by more than $10 billion, touching off an economic boom. Consumer spending increased by $43 billion during the next 18 months, and new jobs opened up at the rate of one million a year.

Johnson was even more influential in passing the Kennedy civil rights measure. Staying in the background, he encouraged liberal amendments that strengthened the bill in the House. With Hubert Humphrey leading the floor fight in the Senate, Johnson refused all efforts at compromise, counting on public pressure to force northern Republicans to abandon their traditional alliance with southern Democrats. Everett M. Dirksen of Illinois, the GOP leader in the Senate, finally led a Republican vote to end a 57-day filibuster.

The 1964 Civil Rights Act, signed on July 2, outlawed segregation in public facilities, established an Equal Employment Opportunity Commission to lessen racial discrimination in employment, and protected African American voting rights. An amendment sponsored by segregationists to obstruct the bill added gender to the prohibition of discrimination in Title VII of the act; women's groups would use the clause to secure government support for greater equality in employment and education.

Quick Check

How did Johnson's personality influence his politics?

The Election of 1964

Johnson now wanted to win the presidency in his own right—and to win by a landslide.

Searching for a cause of his own, LBJ found one in poverty. Economists had been warning since the late 1950s that the prevailing affluence disguised persistent and deep-seated poverty. Johnson made proposals that Kennedy had been developing his own. In his January 1964 State of the Union address, LBJ announced, "This administration, today, here and now, declares unconditional war on poverty in America." During the next eight months, Johnson fashioned a comprehensive poverty program under the direction of R. Sargent Shriver, Kennedy's brother-in-law. The president added $500 million to existing programs to come up with a $1 billion effort that Congress passed in August 1964.

The new Office of Economic Opportunity (OEO) set up programs ranging from Head Start for preschoolers to the Job Corps to give high school dropouts vocational training. The emphasis was on self-help, with the government providing money and know-how so the poor could benefit from day care centers, consumer education classes, legal aid services, and adult remedial reading programs. The level of funding was never high enough to meet the OEO's ambitious goals, and an attempt to include representatives of the poor in the Community Action Program led to bitter feuding with city and state officials. Nonetheless, the **war on poverty**, along with the economic growth the tax cut provided, helped reduce the ranks of the poor by nearly 10 million between 1964 and 1967.

The new programs established Johnson's reputation as a reformer in an election year, but he still faced two challenges. The first came from Robert Kennedy, who remained attorney general but who wanted to become vice president and Johnson's successor in the White House. Desperate to succeed without Kennedy's help, LBJ commented, "I don't need that little runt to win" and chose Hubert Humphrey as his running mate. Kennedy then left the cabinet and was elected U.S. senator from New York.

The second challenge was posed by the Republican candidate, Senator Barry Goldwater, an outspoken conservative from Arizona. An attractive and articulate man, Goldwater advocated a rejection of the welfare state and a return to unregulated free enterprise. To Johnson's delight, Goldwater placed ideology ahead of political expediency. The senator attacked the Tennessee Valley Authority, denounced Social Security, and favored a hawkish foreign policy. "In Your Heart, You Know He's Right," read the Republican slogan, to which Democrats replied, "Yes, Far Right." In reference to a careless Goldwater comment about using nuclear weapons, Johnson backers also punned, "In Your Heart, You Know He Might."

war on poverty Lyndon Johnson declared war on poverty in his 1964 State of the Union address. A new Office of Economic Opportunity (OEO) oversaw programs to help the poor.

TABLE 30.1 THE ELECTION OF 1964

Candidate	Party	Popular Vote	Electoral Vote
Johnson	Democratic	43,126,506	486
Goldwater	Republican	27,176,799	52

Great Society President Lyndon Johnson's name for his version of the Democratic reform program. In 1965, Congress passed many Great Society measures, including Medicare, civil rights legislation, and federal aid to education.

Quick Check

What were the key issues in the election of 1964?

Johnson stuck to the middle of the road, embracing the liberal reform program—which he now called the **Great Society**—while stressing balanced budgets and fiscal orthodoxy. The more Goldwater sagged in the polls, the harder Johnson campaigned, determined to achieve his landslide. On election day, LBJ received 61.1 percent of the popular vote and an overwhelming majority in the electoral college; Goldwater carried only Arizona and five Deep South states (see Table 30.1). The Democrats also won huge gains in Congress, controlling the House by 295 to 140 and the Senate by 68 to 32. Kennedy's legacy and Goldwater's candor had enabled Johnson to break the conservative grip on Congress for the first time in a quarter century.

The Triumph of Reform

LBJ moved quickly to secure his legislative goals. Despite solid majorities in both houses, including 70 first-term Democrats who had ridden into office on his coattails, Johnson knew he would have to enact the Great Society as swiftly as possible: "Doesn't matter what kind of majority you come in with. You've got just one year when they treat you right, and before they start worrying about themselves."

Johnson gave two traditional Democratic reforms—health care and education—top priority. Aware of strong opposition to a comprehensive medical program, LBJ settled for **Medicare**, which mandated health insurance under the Social Security program for Americans over age 65 and for the disabled, and a supplementary Medicaid program for the poor. To symbolize the end of a long struggle, Johnson flew to Independence, Missouri, so Harry Truman could witness the ceremonial signing of the Medicare law, which had its origins in Truman's 1949 health insurance proposal.

Medicare The 1965 Medicare Act provided Social Security funding for hospitalization insurance for people over age 65 and the disabled and a voluntary plan to cover doctor bills paid in part by the federal government.

LBJ overcame the religious hurdle on education by supporting a child-benefit approach, allocating federal money for the education of students in parochial and public schools. The Elementary and Secondary Education Act of 1965 provided more than $1 billion in federal aid, the largest share going to school districts with the most impoverished pupils.

Civil rights was the most difficult test of Johnson's leadership. Martin Luther King, Jr., concerned that 3 million southern blacks were still denied the right to vote, in early 1965 chose Selma, Alabama, as a test case. The white authorities in Selma, led by Sheriff James Clark, broke up the demonstrations with cattle prods and bullwhips. More than 2000 African Americans were jailed. In March, after TV cameras showed deputies brutally halting a march from Selma to Montgomery, the president ordered the Alabama National Guard to federal duty to protect the demonstrators, had the Justice Department draw up a new voting rights bill, and addressed Congress on civil rights: "I speak tonight for the dignity of man and the destiny of democracy." Calling the denial of the right to vote "deadly wrong," LBJ vowed, "Their cause must be our cause, too. Because it is not just Negroes, but really it is all of us who must overcome the crippling legacy of bigotry and injustice."

Five months later, Congress passed the **Voting Rights Act of 1965**. Again Johnson had worked with Senate Republicans to break a southern filibuster and assure its passage. The act banned literacy tests in states and counties in which less than half the population had voted in 1964 and provided for federal registrars in these areas to assure African Americans the franchise.

Voting Rights Act of 1965 The 1965 Voting Rights Act banned literacy tests for voting rights and provided for federal registrars to assure the franchise to minority voters.

The results were dramatic. In less than a year, 166,000 African Americans were added to the voting rolls in Alabama; African American registration went up 400

30.1

30.2

30.3

30.4

30.5

30.6

percent in Mississippi. By 1970, the percentage of eligible African American voters who had registered had risen from 40 to 65 percent. For the first time since Reconstruction, African Americans had become active participants in southern politics.

Before the 89th Congress ended its first session in 1965, it had passed 89 bills. These included measures to create two new cabinet departments (Transportation and Housing and Urban Development); acts to provide for highway safety and clean air and water; large appropriations for higher education, public housing, and the war on poverty; and sweeping immigration reform. In nine months, Johnson had enacted the entire Democratic reform agenda.

The man responsible for this great leap forward, however, had not won the public adulation he craved. His legislative skills had made the most of the 1964 Democratic landslide, but the people denied Johnson the warmth and praise they had showered on Kennedy. Reporters continued to portray him as a crude wheeler-dealer; as a maniac who drove around Texas back roads at 90 miles an hour, one hand on the wheel and the other holding a beer; or as a bully who picked up his dog by the ears. No one was more aware of this lack of affection than LBJ himself. His public support, he told an aide, is "like a Western river, broad but not deep."

Johnson's realization of the fragility of his popularity was accurate. The Cold War began to divert his attention from domestic concerns and eventually, in the case of Vietnam, would overwhelm him. Yet his legislative achievements were remarkable. In one brief outburst of reform, he had accomplished more than any president since FDR.

Difficulties abroad would dim the luster of the Johnson presidency, but they could not diminish the impact of the Great Society on American life. Federal aid to education, Medicare and Medicaid, and the civil rights acts of 1964 and 1965 changed the nation irrevocably. The aged and the poor were guaranteed medical care; federal funds improved education; and African Americans could attend integrated schools, enjoy public facilities, and gain political power by exercising the right to vote. But even at this moment of triumph for liberal reform, dissent and rebellion were brewing.

Quick Check

What were the major reforms of Johnson's great society?

Johnson Escalates the Vietnam War

30.4   How did Johnson's Vietnam policy evolve?

Johnson stressed continuity in foreign policy just as he had in enacting Kennedy's domestic reforms. He shared his fallen predecessor's Cold War convictions. And, feeling less confident about dealing with international issues, he relied heavily on Kennedy's advisers—notably Secretary of State Rusk, Secretary of Defense McNamara, and McGeorge Bundy (the national security adviser until the even more hawkish Walt Rostow replaced him in 1966).

Johnson had broad exposure to national security affairs. He had served on the Naval Affairs Committee in the House before and during World War II, and as Senate majority leader he had been consulted on the crises of the 1950s. A confirmed cold warrior, he had seen in the 1940s how the communist triumph in China had damaged the Democratic party. "I am not going to lose Vietnam," he told the American ambassador to Saigon in 1963. "I am not going to be the president who saw Southeast Asia go the way China went."

Aware of the problems Castro had caused Kennedy, LBJ moved to contain communism in the Western Hemisphere. When a military junta overthrew a leftist regime in Brazil, Johnson offered covert aid and open encouragement. He also forced Panama to restrain rioting aimed at the American presence in the Canal Zone.

In 1965, to block the possible emergence of a Castro-type government, LBJ sent 20,000 troops to the Dominican Republic. Johnson's flimsy justifications—ranging from the need to protect American tourists to a dubious list of suspected communists

30.1

30.2

30.3

30.4

30.5

30.6

among the rebel leaders—alienated liberal critics in the United States, particularly Senator Fulbright, a former Johnson favorite. The intervention ended in 1966 with the election of a conservative government. Fulbright, however, attacked Johnson's foreign policy in *The Arrogance of Power*, a biting analysis of the fallacies of containment. Fulbright's defection symbolized a growing gap between the president and liberal intellectuals; the more LBJ struggled to uphold Kennedy's Cold War policies, the more Congress, the media, and the universities attacked him.

The Vietnam Dilemma

But Vietnam, not Latin America, became Johnson's obsession and led ultimately to his downfall. Inheriting a commitment that dated back to Eisenhower to support South Vietnam, the new president believed he had to continue Kennedy's policy there. Diem's overthrow only three weeks before Kennedy's assassination led to a power struggle in Saigon that prevented Johnson from thoroughly reassessing the strategic alternatives in Southeast Asia. In 1964, seven different governments ruled South Vietnam; power changed hands three times within one month. According to an American officer, Saigon "fairly smelled of discontent," with "workers on strike, students demonstrating, [and] the local press pursuing a persistent campaign of criticism of the new government."

Resisting pressure for direct military involvement, LBJ continued Kennedy's policy of economic and technical assistance. He sent 7000 more military advisers and an additional $50 million in aid. While he insisted the Vietnamese themselves had to win the war, he expanded American support for covert operations, including amphibious raids on the North.

These undercover activities led to the Gulf of Tonkin affair. On August 2, 1964, North Vietnamese torpedo boats attacked the *Maddox*, an American destroyer engaged in intelligence gathering in the Gulf of Tonkin. The North Vietnamese believed the American ship had been involved in a South Vietnamese raid nearby. The *Maddox* escaped unscathed, but the navy sent in another destroyer, the *C. Turner Joy*. On August 4, the two destroyers, responding to sonar and radar contacts, opened fire on North Vietnamese gunboats. Johnson ordered retaliatory air strikes on North Vietnamese naval bases. Later investigation indicated that the North Vietnamese gunboats had not launched a second attack on the American ships.

The next day, the president asked Congress to authorize "all necessary measures to repel any armed attack against the forces of the United States and to prevent further aggression." He did not need this authority; he had already ordered the retaliatory air strike. Later, critics charged that LBJ wanted a blank check from Congress to escalate the Vietnam War, but such a motive is unlikely. He had already rejected immediate intervention. In part, he wanted the **Gulf of Tonkin Resolution** to demonstrate to North Vietnam the American determination to defend South Vietnam. "The challenge we face in Southeast Asia today," he told Congress, "is the same challenge that we have faced with courage and that we have met with strength in Greece and Turkey, in Berlin and Korea." He also wanted to preempt the issue from Barry Goldwater, who had been advocating a tougher policy. By taking a firm stand on the Gulf of Tonkin incident, Johnson could both impress the North Vietnamese and outmaneuver a rival at home.

Congress responded with alacrity. The House acted unanimously, while only two senators voted against the resolution. Johnson's standing in the Gallup poll shot up from 42 to 72 percent, and he had blocked Goldwater from exploiting Vietnam as a campaign issue.

In the long run, however, this easy victory proved costly. Having used force once against North Vietnam, LBJ was more likely to do so in the future. And although he apparently had no intention of widening the conflict in August 1964, the congressional resolution was broad enough to enable him to use whatever level of force he wanted—including unlimited military intervention. Above all, when he did wage war in Vietnam, he left himself open to the charge of deliberately misleading Congress.

Gulf of Tonkin Resolution After a North Vietnamese attack on an American destroyer in the Gulf of Tonkin in 1964, Congress gave President Lyndon Johnson authority in this resolution to use force in Vietnam.

Quick Check

What happened in the Gulf of Tonkin, and how did it reflect Johnson's Vietnam problem?

30.1
30.2
30.3
30.4
30.5
30.6

✳ Explore the Vietnam War on MyHistoryLab

WHAT DID THE WAR IN VIETNAM MEAN FOR THE UNITED STATES?

Between 1955 and 1975, a civil war raged across Vietnam between a communist government in the north and an anticommunist government in the south. In the context of the Cold War, the United States supported the South Vietnamese government, hoping to stop the spread of communism. In the early 1960s, the American government began increasing its troop presence in Vietnam and in 1965 sent its first combat units. American military intervention expanded across South Vietnam in Vietnam and into the neighboring countries of Southeast Asia. As casualties with little in the way of military progress, the intervention became increasingly unpopular at home and anti-war protests proliferated. Some 58,000 American servicemen and women died before the United States withdrew in 1975. Soon after, the South Vietnamese government fell and the country was united under a single communist government.

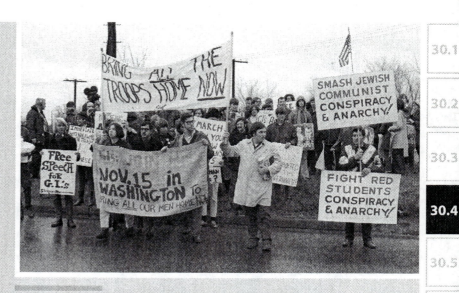

PROTESTING THE WAR This antiwar march against U.S. involvement in Southeast Asia is met by a lone counter-protester at Fort Devens in Ayer, Massachusetts, in 1970.

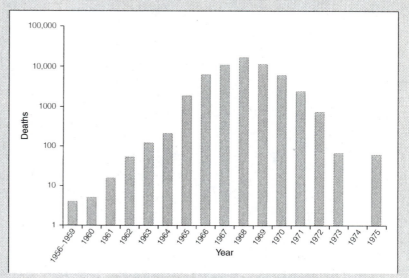

SOURCE: "Statistical Information about Fatal Casualties of the Vietnam War National Archives", National Archives, http://www.archives.gov/research/military/vietnam-war/casualty-statistics.html#home.

KEY QUESTIONS — Use **MyHistoryLab** *Explorer* to **answer** these **questions:**

Cause ▶▶▶ *What geographic challenges did American forces face in Vietnam?*

Map features that hindered the U.S. military effort.

Response ▶▶▶ *What was the significance of various U.S. military operations in Vietnam, especially the Tet Offensive?*

Explore the unfolding of the war.

Consequence ▶▶▶ *What relationships may have existed between war deaths and other socio-economic factors in an area?*

Chart potential correlations and consider underlying reasons.

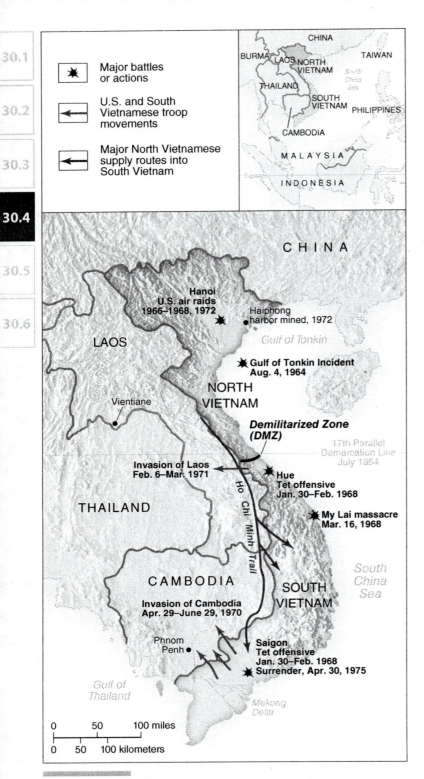

30.1
30.2
30.3
30.4
30.5
30.6

Major battles or actions

U.S. and South Vietnamese troop movements

Major North Vietnamese supply routes into South Vietnam

CHINA

BURMA LAOS NORTH VIETNAM TAIWAN
THAILAND SOUTH VIETNAM PHILIPPINES
CAMBODIA
MALAYSIA
INDONESIA

CHINA

Hanoi
U.S. air raids
1966–1968, 1972

Haiphong
harbor mined, 1972

LAOS

Gulf of Tonkin

Gulf of Tonkin Incident
Aug. 4, 1964

Vientiane

NORTH
VIETNAM

Demilitarized Zone
(DMZ)

17th Parallel
Demarcation Line
July 1954

Invasion of Laos
Feb. 6–Mar. 1971

Hue
Tet offensive
Jan. 30–Feb. 1968

THAILAND

My Lai massacre
Mar. 16, 1968

CAMBODIA

South
China
Sea

SOUTH
VIETNAM

Invasion of Cambodia
Apr. 29–June 29, 1970

Phnom
Penh

Saigon
Tet offensive
Jan. 30–Feb. 1968
Surrender, Apr. 30, 1975

Gulf of
Thailand

Mekong
Delta

0   50   100 miles
0   50   100 kilometers

MAP 30.2 SOUTHEAST ASIA AND THE VIETNAM WAR American combat forces in South Vietnam rose from 16,000 in 1963 to 500,000 in 1968, but a successful conclusion to the conflict was no closer.

Presidential credibility became Johnson's Achilles' heel; his downfall began with the Gulf of Tonkin Resolution.

Escalation

Full-scale American involvement in Vietnam began in 1965 in a series of steps designed primarily to prevent a North Vietnamese victory (see Map 30.2). With the political situation in Saigon growing more hopeless every day, the president's advisers urged the bombing of the north. American air attacks would block North Vietnamese infiltration routes, make Hanoi pay a heavy price, and encourage the South Vietnamese. But most important, as McGeorge Bundy reported after a visit to Pleiku (site of a Vietcong attack on an American base), "Without new U.S. action defeat appears inevitable—probably not in a matter of weeks or perhaps even months, but within the next year or so." In February 1965, Johnson cited the Pleiku attack in ordering a long-planned aerial bombardment of North Vietnamese targets.

The air strikes proved ineffective. In April, Johnson authorized using American combat troops in South Vietnam to protect American air bases. The Joint Chiefs then pressed the president for both unlimited bombing of the north and the aggressive use of American ground forces in the south. In mid-July, Secretary of Defense McNamara recommended sending 100,000 combat troops to Vietnam. He believed this escalation would lead to a "favorable outcome," but he also warned that an additional 100,000 soldiers might be needed in 1966 and that American battle deaths could be 500 a month (by 1968, they were 500 a week).

Other advisers, most notably Undersecretary of State George Ball, advocated a political settlement. Warning that the United States was likely to suffer "national humiliation," Ball told the president that he had "serious doubt that an army of westerners can successfully fight Orientals in an Asian jungle."

Johnson was torn: "Are we starting something that in two to three years we simply can't finish?" But he decided he had to persevere in Vietnam. Although he pared down McNamara's troop request, LBJ settled on a steady military escalation to compel Hanoi to accept a diplomatic solution. In July, the president increased the bombing of North Vietnam and allowed American commanders to conduct offensive operations in the south. He also approved the dispatch of 50,000 troops and the future commitment of 50,000 more.

These decisions formed "an open-ended commitment to employ American military forces as the situation demanded," wrote historian George Herring. They were "the closest thing to a formal decision for war in Vietnam." Convinced that withdrawal would destroy American credibility and that an invasion of the north would lead to World War III, Johnson opted for large-scale but limited military intervention. He also

30.1

30.2

30.3

30.4

30.5

30.6

feared the domestic consequences of either extreme. A pullout could cause a political backlash at home, as conservatives condemned him for betraying South Vietnam to communism. All-out war, however, would mean the end of his social programs. Once Congress focused on the conflict, he explained to biographer Doris Kearns Goodwin, "that bitch of a war" destroyed "the woman I really loved—the Great Society." So he settled for a limited war, committing 500,000 American troops to battle in Southeast Asia, while pretending it was a minor engagement and refusing to ask the American people for the support and sacrifice victory required.

Johnson was not solely responsible for the Vietnam War. He inherited both a policy that assumed Vietnam was a vital national interest and a deteriorating situation in Saigon that demanded a more active American role. Truman, Eisenhower, and Kennedy had taken the United States deep into the Vietnam maze; Johnson's fate was to find a way out. But LBJ bears full responsibility for how he tried to resolve his dilemma. The failure to confront the people with the stark choices the nation faced in Vietnam, the insistence on secrecy and deceit, the refusal to acknowledge that he had committed the United States to a dangerous military involvement—these were Johnson's sins in Vietnam. His lack of self-confidence in foreign policy and fear of domestic reaction led to his undoing.

Quick Check

Why did Johnson escalate American involvement in Vietnam?

Stalemate

For the next three years, Americans waged an intensive war in Vietnam and succeeded only in preventing a communist victory. Bombing proved ineffective. The rural, undeveloped nature of the North Vietnamese economy meant there were few industrial

((• 📖 Read the Document   James B. Stockdale, excerpt from *A Vietnam Experience: Ten Years of Reflection*, (1982)

VIETNAM U.S. troops wade through marshland during an operation on South Vietnam's Mekong Delta. Although the United States conducted thousands of air strikes over North Vietnam and committed a half million troops to the South, it failed to win the advantage.

30.1

30.2

30.3

30.4

30.5

30.6

targets; a refusal to bomb the main port of Haiphong allowed Soviet and Chinese arms to flow freely into the country. The efforts to destroy supply lines were equally unsuccessful. American planes pounded the Ho Chi Minh Trail that ran down through Laos and Cambodia, but the jungle canopy hid North Vietnamese shipments and their massive efforts to repair roads and bridges. In fact, the American air attacks, with their inadvertent civilian casualties, gave North Vietnam a propaganda weapon to rouse world opinion against the United States.

The war in the south went no better. American ground forces increased from 184,000 in late 1965 to more than 500,000 by early 1968, but the Vietcong still controlled much of the countryside. The search-and-destroy tactics the American commander, General William Westmoreland, employed proved ineffective. The Vietcong, aided by North Vietnamese regulars, were waging an insurgent war, ambushing and avoiding fixed positions. Westmoreland used superior American firepower wantonly, devastating the countryside and driving the peasantry into the arms of the guerrillas. Inevitably, these tactics led to the slaughter of innocent civilians, most notably at the hamlet of My Lai. In March 1968, an American company led by Lieutenant William Calley, Jr., massacred more than 200 unarmed villagers.

Westmoreland tried to wage a war of attrition that would finally reach a "crossover point" when communist losses each month would be greater than the number of new troops they could recruit. He hoped to lure the enemy into pitched battles in which American firepower would inflict heavy casualties. But the communists decided where and when the fighting would take place, provoking American attacks in remote areas of South Vietnam that favored the defenders and made Westmoreland pay heavily in American lives. By the end of 1967, the nearly 500,000 troops Johnson had sent to Vietnam had only achieved a bloody stalemate that was gradually turning the American people against a war they had once eagerly embraced.

Quick Check

What was the result of the escalation?

Years of Turmoil

30.5 Why were there protests during the 1960s?

The Vietnam War became the focal point for youthful protests that made the 1960s the most turbulent decade of the twentieth century. Disenchantment with middle-class values, an increase in college enrollments as a result of the baby boom, a reaction against the crass materialism of the affluent society—with its endless suburbs and shopping malls—led American youth to embrace an alternative lifestyle based on the belief that people are "sensitive, searching, poetic, and capable of love." They were ready to create a counterculture.

The agitation of the 1960s was at its height between 1965 and 1968, during the escalation of the Vietnam War. Disturbances on college campuses reflected discontent in other parts of society, from the urban ghettos to the lettuce fields of the Southwest. All who felt disadvantaged and dissatisfied—students, African Americans, Hispanics, Native Americans, women, hippies—took to the streets.

Protesting the Vietnam War

The most dramatic aspect of the youthful rebellion came in opposing the Vietnam War. The first student "teach-ins"—organized but informal discussions and debates—began at the University of Michigan in March 1965 and spread across the nation. More than 20,000 protesters, under the auspices of the **Students for a Democratic Society (SDS)**,

Students for a Democratic Society Founded in 1962, the SDS was a popular college student organization that protested shortcomings in American life, notably racial injustice and the Vietnam War. It led thousands of protests before it split apart in the late 1960s.

30.1

30.2

30.3

30.4

30.5

30.6

a radical student organization, gathered in Washington in April to hear Joan Baez and Judy Collins sing antiwar songs. "End the War in Vietnam Now, Stop the Killing" read the signs.

One of the ironies of the Vietnam War was the system of draft deferments, which enabled most college students to avoid military service. As a result, the children of the well-to-do, who were more likely to attend college, were able to escape the draft. One survey revealed that men from disadvantaged families, including a disproportionately large number of black and Hispanic Americans, were twice as likely to be drafted and fight in Vietnam as those from more privileged backgrounds. Consequently, a sense of guilt led many college activists whose student status saved them from Vietnam to take the lead in denouncing an unjust war.

As the fighting in Southeast Asia intensified in 1966 and 1967, the protests grew larger and the slogans more extreme. "Hey, hey, LBJ, how many kids did you kill today?" chanted students as they proclaimed, "Hell, no, we won't go!" At the Pentagon in October 1967, more than 100,000 demonstrators—mainly male students but also housewives, teachers, and young professionals—confronted military policemen guarding the heart of the nation's war machine.

The climax came in the spring of 1968. Driven by opposition to the war and concern for social justice, the SDS and African American radicals at Columbia University joined forces in April. They seized five buildings, paralyzing one of the country's leading colleges. After eight tense days, the New York City police regained control. The brutal repression inflamed protest elsewhere. Students held sit-ins and marches at more than 100 colleges.

The students failed to stop the war, but they did gain a voice in their education. Administrations allowed undergraduates to sit on faculty curriculum-planning committees and gave up their rigid control of dormitory and social life. But the students' greatest impact lay outside politics and the campus. They spawned a cultural uprising that transformed the manners and morals of America.

Quick Check
What forms did opposition to the war in Vietnam take?

The Cultural Revolution

In contrast to the elitist political revolt of the SDS, the cultural rebellion by youth in the 1960s was pervasive. Led by college students, young people challenged the prevailing adult values in clothing, hairstyles, sexual conduct, work, and music. Blue jeans and love beads replaced business suits and wristwatches; long hair and unkempt beards for men, bare feet and bralessness for women became a uniform of protest. "Flower children" communes emerged.

Music became the touchstone of the new departure. Folksingers such as Joan Baez and Bob Dylan, popular for their social protest songs in the mid-1960s, gave way first to rock groups such as the Beatles, whose lyrics were often suggestive of drug use, and then to "acid rock" as symbolized by the Grateful Dead. The climactic event of the decade was the Woodstock concert in upstate New York, when 400,000 young people indulged in a three-day festival of rock music, drugs, and public sex.

Former Harvard psychology professor Timothy Leary encouraged youth to join him in trying out the drug scene. Millions accepted his invitation to "tune in, turn on, drop out" literally, as they experimented with marijuana and LSD, a chemical hallucinogen. The ultimate expression of insurgency was the Yippie movement, led by Jerry Rubin and Abbie Hoffman. Shrewd buffoons who mocked the consumer culture, they capitalized on the mood of social protest to win attention. When testifying before a congressional committee investigating internal subversion, Rubin dressed as a Revolutionary War soldier; Hoffman appeared in the gallery of the New York Stock Exchange in 1967, raining money down on the cheering brokers.

Quick Check
How did young people challenge adult culture during the 1960s?

30.1

30.2

30.3

30.4

30.5

30.6

"Black Power"

The civil rights movement, which had spawned the mood of protest in the 1960s, fell on hard times later in the decade. The legislative triumphs of 1964 and 1965 were relatively easy victories over southern bigotry; now the movement faced the more complex problem of achieving economic equality in the cities of the North, where more than half of the nation's African Americans lived in poverty. The civil rights movement had raised the expectations of urban African Americans; frustration mounted as they failed to experience significant economic gain.

The first sign of trouble came in the summer of 1964, when African American teenagers in Harlem and Rochester, New York, rioted. The next summer, an outburst of rage and destruction swept over the Watts area of Los Angeles as the inhabitants burned buildings and looted stores. Riots in the summer of 1966 were less destructive, but in 1967, the worst ones yet took place in Newark and Detroit, where 43 were killed and thousands injured. The mobs attacked shops and stores, expressing a burning grievance against a consumer society from which their poverty excluded them.

The civil rights coalition fell apart, a victim of both its legislative success and economic failure. Black militants took over SNCC; they disdained white help and even reversed Martin Luther King's insistence on nonviolence. Their new leader, Stokely Carmichael, told blacks they should seize power in those parts of the South where they outnumbered whites: "I am not going to beg the white man for anything I deserve. I'm going to take it." His calls for "black power" became a rallying cry for more militant blacks who advocated the need for African Americans to form "our own institutions, credit unions, co-ops, political parties" and even write "our own history."

Others went further. H. Rap Brown, who replaced Carmichael as the leader of SNCC in 1967, told African Americans in Cambridge, Maryland, to "get your guns" and "burn this town down"; Huey Newton, a founder of the militant Black Panther party, proclaimed, "We make the statement, quoting from Chairman Mao, that Political Power comes through the Barrel of a Gun."

King suffered the most from this extremism. His denunciation of the Vietnam War cost him the support of the Johnson administration and alienated him from the more conservative civil rights groups such as the NAACP and the Urban League. He finally seized on poverty as the enemy to attack, but before he could lead his Poor People's March on Washington in 1968, he was assassinated in Memphis in April.

Blacks and whites realized the nation had lost its most eloquent voice for racial harmony. His tragic death made King a martyr, but it also led to one last outbreak of urban violence. African Americans exploded in riots in 125 cities; in Washington, D.C., buildings were set on fire within a few blocks of the White House. "It was as if the city were being abandoned to an invading army," wrote a British journalist. "Clouds of smoke hung over the Potomac, evoking memories of the London blitz."

Yet the emotions black nationalism engendered had a positive side. Leaders urged African Americans to take pride in their ethnic heritage, to embrace their blackness. African Americans began to wear Afros and dress in dashikis, stressing their African roots. Students demanded black studies programs in colleges; the word *Negro*—identified with white supremacy—disappeared from usage overnight, replaced by *Afro-American* or *black*. Singer James Brown expressed the sense of racial identity: "Say It Loud—I'm Black and I'm Proud."

Quick Check

What was "Black Power," and what did it represent?

Ethnic Nationalism

Other groups emulated the African American phenomenon. Native Americans decried the callous use of their identity as football mascots; in response, universities such as Stanford changed their symbols. Puerto Ricans demanded their

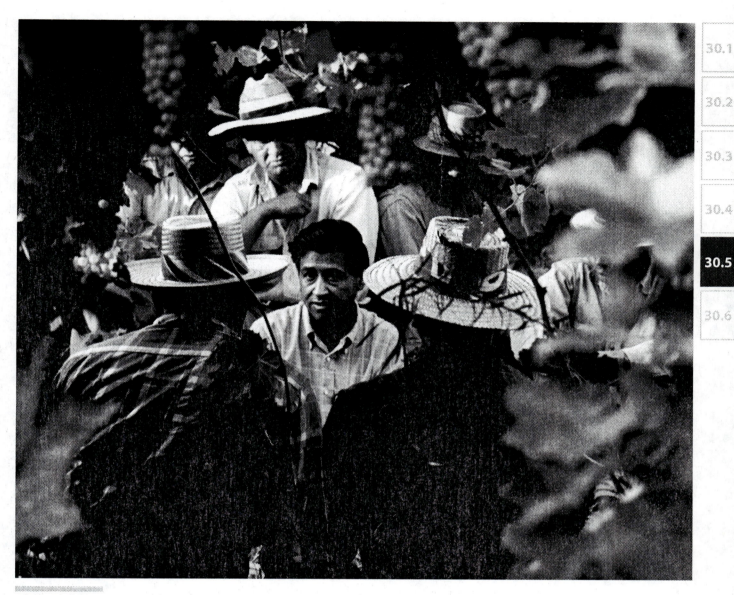

30.1
30.2
30.3
30.4
30.5
30.6

CÉSAR CHÁVEZ In March 1966, César Chávez, shown here talking with workers, led striking grape pickers on a 250-mile march from Delano, California, to the state capital at Sacramento to dramatize the plight of the migrant farmworkers.

history be included in textbooks. Polish, Italian, and Czech groups insisted on respect for their nationalities. Congress acknowledged these demands with the Ethnic Heritage Studies Act of 1972. Instead of trying to melt all groups down into a standard American type, Congress now gave what one sponsor of the measure called "official recognition to ethnicity as a positive constructive force in our society today."

Mexican Americans were in the forefront of the ethnic groups that became active in the 1960s. The primary impulse came from the efforts of César Chávez to organize the poorly paid grape and lettuce pickers in California into the National Farm Workers Association (NFWA). Chávez appealed to ethnic nationalism in mobilizing Mexican American field hands to strike against grape growers in the San Joaquin Valley in 1965. A national boycott of grapes by Mexican Americans and their sympathizers led to hard-fought victories over the growers. The five-year struggle resulted in a union victory in 1970, but at an enormous cost—95 percent of the farmworkers involved had lost their homes and cars. Nevertheless, the hourly wage of farmworkers in California rose from $1.20 in 1965 to $3.53 by 1977.

Chávez's efforts helped spark an ethnic consciousness among Mexican Americans that swept through the urban barrios of the Southwest. Mexican American leaders

30.1

30.2

30.3

30.4

30.5

30.6

campaigned for bilingual programs and improved educational opportunities. Young activists began to call themselves Chicanos, which had previously been a derogatory term, and take pride in their heritage; in 1968, they established the first Mexican American studies program at California State College at Los Angeles. Campus leaders called for reform, urging high school students to insist on improvements. Heeding such appeals, nearly 10,000 students at East Los Angeles high schools walked out of class in March 1968. Similar movements in San Antonio and Phoenix led to bilingual programs in grade schools and the hiring of more Chicano teachers.

Women's Liberation

Active as they were in the civil rights and antiwar movements, women soon learned that the male leaders of these causes were like corporate executives—they expected women to cook and type the communiqués while the men made the decisions. Women realized that they could only achieve respect and equality by mounting their own protest.

In some ways, the position of women in American society was worse in the 1960s than it had been in the 1920s. After 40 years, a lower percentage of women were enrolled in the nation's colleges and professional schools. Women were still relegated to stereotyped occupations such as nursing and teaching; there were few female lawyers and even fewer doctors. And gender roles, as portrayed in television commercials, assumed the husband was the breadwinner and the wife the homemaker.

Betty Friedan was one of the first to seize on the sense of grievance and discrimination that white middle-class women felt in the 1960s. In her 1963 book *The Feminine Mystique,* she called the American home "a comfortable concentration camp" and attacked the prevailing view that women were completely contented with housekeeping and child-rearing, claiming that housewives had no self-esteem or sense of identity. "I'm a server of food and putter on of pants and a bedmaker," a mother of four told Friedan, "somebody who can be called on when you want something. But who am I?"

The 1964 Civil Rights Act made it illegal to discriminate in employment on the basis of gender. Women filed suit for equal wages, demanded that companies provide day care for their infants and preschool children, and entered politics to lobby against laws that—in the guise of protecting a weaker gender—were unfair to women. As the women's liberation movement grew, its advocates began to attack laws banning abortion and fought to toughen the enforcement of rape laws.

The women's movement met many of the same obstacles as other protest groups in the 1960s. Women with more extreme views soon challenged the moderate leadership of the **National Organization for Women (NOW)**, founded by Friedan in 1966. Ti-Grace Atkinson and Susan Brownmiller attacked revered institutions—the family and the home—and called sexual intercourse with men a method of male domination. Many women were repelled by the harsh rhetoric of the extremists and expressed satisfaction with their lives. But despite these disagreements, most women supported the effort to achieve equal status with men.

Quick Check

What did Cesar Chavez want, and what did he get?

National Organization for Women (NOW) Founded in 1966, NOW called for equal employment opportunity and equal pay for women. It also championed the legalization of abortion and an equal rights amendment to the Constitution.

Quick Check

What were the aims of the women's rights movement?

The Return of Richard Nixon

30.6 How did the Vietnam War influence American politics?

The turmoil of the 1960s reached a crescendo in 1968 as the American people responded to the two dominant events of the decade—the war in Vietnam and the cultural insurgency at home. In an election marked by riots and the assassination of Robert Kennedy, Richard Nixon won the post denied to him in 1960.

Vietnam Undermines Lyndon Johnson

A Vietcong offensive in 1968 broke the stalemate in Vietnam and drove Lyndon Johnson from office. The North Vietnamese began a prolonged siege of an American marine base at Khe Sanh, deep in the northern interior. Fearing a decisive defeat, Westmoreland sent more than 40 percent of all American infantry and armored battalions into the two northernmost provinces of South Vietnam.

The Vietcong then used the traditional lull in the fighting at Tet, the Buddhist lunar New Year, to attack the cities. Beginning on January 30, 1968, the Vietcong struck at 36 of the 44 provincial capitals. The most daring raid came at the American embassy in Saigon. Although the guerrillas were unable to penetrate the embassy proper, for six hours television cameras caught the fighting in the courtyard before troops finally overcame the attackers.

Although caught off guard, American and South Vietnamese forces repulsed the **Tet offensive** everywhere except in Hue, the old capital, which was retaken only after three weeks of heavy fighting that left this beautiful city, in the words of one observer, "a shattered, stinking hulk, its streets choked with rubble and rotting bodies."

Tet was the turning point of the Vietnam War. Although the communists suffered heavy losses, they had scored a political victory. For months, Johnson had been telling the American people victory was in sight; suddenly the war appeared to be nearly lost. CBS-TV newscaster Walter Cronkite went to Saigon to find out what had happened. Horrified at what he saw, he exclaimed to his guides, "What the hell is going on? I thought we were winning the war." He returned to tell the American people, "It seems now more certain than ever that the bloody experience of Vietnam is to end in a stalemate."

Johnson reluctantly came to the same conclusion after the Joint Chiefs of Staff requested an additional 205,000 troops after the Tet offensive. He began to listen to his new secretary of defense, Clark Clifford, who had replaced McNamara in January 1968. In mid-March, after receiving advice from the "wise men," experienced cold warriors who included such illustrious figures as Dean Acheson and Omar Bradley, the president decided to limit the bombing of North Vietnam and negotiate with Hanoi. In a speech on March 31, 1968, Johnson outlined his plans for a new effort to end the war peacefully and then said, as proof of his sincerity, "I shall not seek, and I will not accept, the nomination of my party for another term as your president."

Three years of inconclusive fighting and mounting losses had disillusioned the American people and cost Lyndon Johnson the presidency. And the full price the nation would have to pay for its folly in Southeast Asia was still unknown—the Vietnam experience would cast a shadow over American life for years to come.

Tet offensive In February 1968, the Vietcong launched a major offensive in the cities of South Vietnam. Although caught by surprise, American and South Vietnam forces quashed this attack. But the Tet offensive was a blow to American public opinion and led President Lyndon Johnson to seek a negotiated peace.

Quick Check

How did Vietnam bring Johnson down?

The Republican Resurgence

The primary beneficiary of Johnson's Vietnam troubles was Richard Nixon. Written off as politically dead after his defeat for governor of California in 1962, Nixon had rebuilt his place within the party by working for Barry Goldwater in 1964 and for GOP congressional candidates two years later. Positioning himself squarely in the middle, he became the front-runner for the Republican nomination. At the GOP convention in Miami Beach, Nixon won an easy first-ballot nomination and chose Maryland governor Spiro Agnew as his running mate. Agnew, little known on the national scene, had won conservative support by taking a strong stand against African American rioters.

In the campaign, Nixon opened up a wide lead by avoiding controversy and capitalizing on discontent with the Vietnam War. He appeared to advocate an end to the conflict without taking a definite stand, hinting he had a secret formula for peace but never revealing what it was. Above all, he chose the role of reconciler for a nation torn by emotion, a leader who promised to reunite a divided country.

30.1
30.2
30.3
30.4
30.5
30.6

30.1

30.2

30.3

30.4

30.5

30.6

Vice President Hubert Humphrey, in contrast, seemed the symbol of division. Humphrey won the Democratic nomination after a bruising primary season that turned tragic when a deranged gunman assassinated Robert Kennedy in Los Angeles, and a bitter party convention that convulsed Chicago in antiwar protests and riots. Humphrey had Johnson's lukewarm support but was handicapped by LBJ's refusal to halt the bombing of North Vietnam. Only when Humphrey broke with Johnson in September by announcing that if elected he would "stop the bombing of North Vietnam as an acceptable risk for peace" did his campaign gain momentum.

Unfortunately for Humphrey, a third-party candidate cut deeply into the normal Democratic majority. George C. Wallace had gained national attention as the racist governor of Alabama whose motto was "Segregation now . . . segregation tomorrow . . . segregation forever." In 1964, he had shown surprising strength in northern Democratic primaries. By attacking black leaders and their liberal white allies, Wallace appealed to the sense of powerlessness among the urban working classes: "Liberals, intellectuals, and longhairs have run the country for too long. When I get to Washington, I'll throw all these phonies and their briefcases into the Potomac."

Running on the ticket of the American Independent Party, Wallace had support from more than 20 percent of the electorate in the September polls. But as the election neared, his following declined. Humphrey continued to gain, especially after Johnson agreed in late October to stop bombing North Vietnam. By November, the outcome was too close to call.

Nixon won with the smallest share of the popular vote of any winning candidate since 1916. But he swept a broad band of states from Virginia and the Carolinas to the Pacific for a clear-cut victory in the electoral college. Humphrey held on to the urban Northeast; Wallace took just five states in the Deep South, but his inroads into blue-collar districts in the North shattered the New Deal coalition (see Map 30.3).

Quick Check

How did Nixon capitalize on Johnson's troubles?

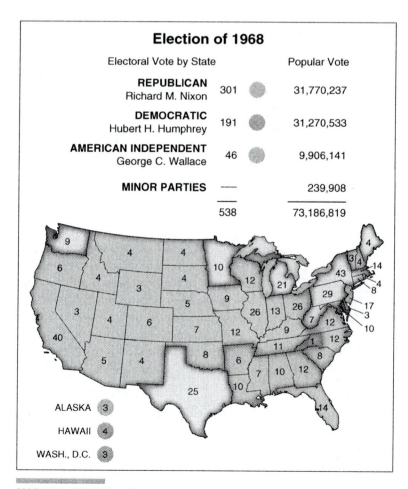

MAP 30.3 ELECTION OF 1968

Conclusion: The End of an Era

The election of 1968 repudiated the politics of protest and the cultural insurgency of the mid-1960s. The combined popular vote for Nixon and Wallace, 56.5 percent of the electorate, signified that a silent majority was fed up with violence and confrontation. Concern over psychedelic drugs, rock music, long hair, and sexual permissiveness had offset the usual Democratic advantage on economic issues and led to the election of a Republican president.

Nixon's victory marked the passing of two concepts that had guided American life since the 1930s. First, the liberal reform impulse, which reached its zenith with the Great Society legislation in 1965, had run its course. Civil rights, Medicare, and federal aid to education would remain, but Nixon's election signaled a reaction against the growth of federal power. The Vietnam debacle also spelled the end of an activist foreign policy that had begun with American entry into World War II. Containment, so successful in protecting Western Europe against the Soviet threat, had proved a disastrous failure when applied on a global scale. The last three decades of the twentieth century would witness a struggle to replace outmoded liberal internationalism with new policies at home and abroad.

30.1
30.2
30.3
30.4
30.5
30.6

Chapter Review

Kennedy Intensifies the Cold War

30.1 How did the Cold War intensify under Kennedy? p. 693

Kennedy increased American support to South Vietnam and pressured the Cuban government of Fidel Castro. Kennedy raised troop levels in Vietnam and authorized the overthrow of Diem. He ordered a covert operation against Castro at the Bay of Pigs (which failed) and delivered an ultimatum to the Soviets to pull their missiles out of Cuba (which succeeded).

The New Frontier at Home

30.2 What was the "New Frontier," and what did it accomplish? p. 698

The "New Frontier" was Kennedy's domestic program, and on its most important issue, civil rights, it achieved mixed results. Kennedy supported civil rights, but hesitantly. Black activists, especially Martin Luther King, Jr., pushed the cause of racial equality farther than Kennedy was prepared to take it.

LBJ's Great Society

30.3 What were Johnson's domestic priorities and what were his achievements? p. 701

Johnson's "Great Society" included the 1964 Civil Rights Act and the 1965 Voting Rights Act; Medicare, which provided health insurance for the elderly; and federal aid to education.

Johnson Escalates the Vietnam War

30.4 How did Johnson's Vietnam policy evolve? p. 705

Johnson seized upon an ambiguous incident in the Gulf of Tonkin to persuade Congress to grant him authority to escalate American involvement in Vietnam. He initiated a major troop buildup and air attacks against North Vietnam. The escalation produced only a bloody stalemate.

Years of Turmoil

30.5 Why were there protests during the 1960s? p. 710

During the 1960s, students protested the war in Vietnam. Many young people also rebelled against the values of their parents, experimenting with new kinds of music, clothing styles, and drugs. Black militants demanded faster progress toward racial equality, and sometimes employed violence to achieve it. César Chávez improved the lot of Mexican American farmworkers. Feminists sought greater equality for women.

The Return of Richard Nixon

30.6 How did the Vietnam War influence American politics? p. 714

Johnson's failure in Vietnam discredited his administration and produced desire for change. He abandoned plans to run for reelection in 1968, opening the door to Richard Nixon.

Timeline

1961
Cold War Intensifies— Cubans crush U.S.-backed Bay of Pigs invasion (April); Cold War Intensifies

1961

1962
Cold War Intensifies— Cuban missile crisis takes world to brink of nuclear war (October); Cold War Intensifies

1962

1963
Great Society—JFK assassinated; Lyndon B. Johnson sworn in as president (November)

1963

1964
Great Society—Civil Rights Act (July). Great Society
Escalation in Vietnam— Congress passes Gulf of Tonkin Resolution (August); Escalation in Vietnam

1964

1965
Escalation in Vietnam—LBJ commits 50,000 American troops to combat in Vietnam (July)
Great Society— Congress enacts Medicare and Medicaid (July). Great Society
Great Society—Voting Rights Act (August); Great Society

1965

1967
Years of Turmoil—Riots in Detroit kill 43, injure 2,000, leave 5,000 homeless (July); Years of Turmoil

1967

1968
Return of Nixon— Vietcong launch Tet offensive (January); Return of Nixon
Years of Turmoil— Martin Luther King, Jr., assassinated (April). Years of Turmoil

1968

31 To a New Conservatism 1969–1988

Reagan and America's Shift to the Right

In October 1964, the **Republican National Committee** sponsored a televised address by Ronald Reagan on behalf of Barry Goldwater's presidential candidacy. Reagan's speech had originally been aired on a Los Angeles station; the resulting outpouring of praise and campaign contributions led to its national rebroadcast.

In contrast to Goldwater's strident rhetoric, Reagan put the case for a return to individual freedom in relaxed, confident, and persuasive terms. Instead of the usual choice between increased government activity and less government involvement, often couched in terms of the left and the right, Reagan presented the options of either going up or down—"up to the maximum of human freedom consistent with law and order, or down to the ant heap of totalitarianism." Then, borrowing a phrase from FDR, he told his

RONALD REAGAN Ronald Reagan and his wife Nancy wave to the crowd during the 1980 Republican convention in Detroit.

LEARNING OBJECTIVES

31.1	31.2	31.3	31.4	31.5	31.6
What were the major accomplishments and failures of the Nixon presidency? p. 722	How were oil and inflation linked during the 1970s? p. 726	How did private life change during this period? p. 729	Why did the presidencies of Ford and Carter largely fail? p. 734	What was the "Reagan revolution"? p. 737	How did Reagan reshape American foreign relations? p. 740

From Chapter 31 of *American Stories: A History of the United States*, Third Edition. H. W. Brands, R. Hal Williams, T. H. Breen and Ariela J. Gross Copyright © 2015 by Pearson Education, Inc. All rights reserved.

 Listen to **Chapter 31** on **MyHistoryLab**

Watch the Video Series on MyHistoryLab

Learn about some key topics related to this chapter with the *MyHistoryLab Video Series: Key Topics in U.S. History.*

 From a Great Society to a Conservative One: 1969–1988
The liberalism of the 1960s gave way to the more conservative politics of the 1970s and 1980s. This video assesses the election of Richard M. Nixon in 1968, which signaled a political shift away from the Great Society programs of the 1960s to a more conservative social agenda. Foreign policy, especially under President Ronald Reagan in the 1980s, moved away from the détente of the 1970s to a more confrontational agenda with the Soviet Union. The movement politics of the 1960s made strides, especially for women's rights (*Roe v. Wade*) and supporters of gay rights enjoyed increased awareness (the Stonewall uprising), but also engendered further resistance to their issues.

Watch on MyHistoryLab

Watergate The Watergate scandal resulted in the resignation of President Richard M. Nixon and led to a growing distrust of the federal government. This video examines Watergate from its origins in the presidential election of 1972 (the burglary of Democratic National Committee headquarters) through the Nixon administration's cover-up of the crime, and the congressional hearings that finally forced Nixon to step aside or face impeachment in 1974.

Watch on MyHistoryLab

 The Women's Movement This video surveys the Women's movement during the 1970s and 1980s, when the right for a woman to have an abortion was ensured by the Supreme Court decision of *Roe v. Wade* and the Equal Rights Amendment was nearly added to the U. S. Constitution. While women continued to make gains in the workforce and in higher education (Title 9), the Stop ERA movement as well as a strong anti-feminist backlash strengthened the hand of conservative Republicans in the 1980s.

Watch on MyHistoryLab

Jimmy Carter Taking advantage of the post-Watergate mood of the nation in 1976, Jimmy Carter positioned himself as an outsider to beat Gerald Ford. This video profiles Carter and describes his early success as the first Democrat to hold the presidency since Lyndon Johnson. It also discusses the stagnant economy and the foreign policy disaster of the Iranian hostage crisis both of which contributed to his loss to Ronald Reagan in 1980.

Watch on MyHistoryLab

audience: "You and I have a rendezvous with destiny. We can preserve for our children this the last best hope of man on earth, or we can sentence them to take the first step into a thousand years of darkness."

Although the speech did not rescue Goldwater's candidacy, it marked the beginning of Ronald Reagan's political career. A popular actor whose movie career had begun to fade in the 1950s, Reagan had become a television performer as host of *The General Electric Theater*. His political views, once liberal, moved steadily to the right as he became a spokesperson for a major American corporation. In 1965, wealthy friends persuaded him to run for the California governorship.

Reagan was an attractive candidate. His approachable manner and mastery of television enabled him to present his strongly conservative message without appearing to be a rigid right-wing ideologue. He won handily by appealing to middle-class suburban resentment over taxes, welfare programs, and bureaucratic regulation.

In two terms as governor, Reagan displayed natural ability as a political leader. Instead of trying to implement all of his conservative beliefs, he proved flexible. Faced with a Democratic legislature, he yielded on raising taxes and increasing state spending while trimming the welfare rolls. Symbolic victories were his specialty. For example, he confronted campus radicals and fired Clark Kerr, chancellor of the University of California, while generously funding higher education.

When Reagan left the governor's office in 1974, signs pointed to a growing conservative mood across the nation. In a popular rebellion in 1978, California's voters passed Proposition 13, which slashed property taxes in half and resulted in a reduction in social services. The 1962 Supreme Court ruling in *Engel v. Vitale* outlawing school prayer on the grounds that it was "no part of the business of government to compose official prayers" outraged religious leaders. In the South, where prayers were the customary way to begin the school day, the reaction was intense. One Alabama congressman denounced the Supreme Court justices: "They put the Negroes in the schools and now they're driving God out."

Concern over school prayer, along with rising abortion and divorce rates, impelled religious groups to engage in political activity to defend what they viewed as traditional family values. Jerry Falwell, a Virginia radio and television evangelist, founded the **Moral Majority**, a fundamentalist group dedicated to preserving the "American way of life."

The population shift of the 1970s, especially the rapid growth of the Sunbelt region in the South and West, added momentum to the conservative upsurge. Those moving to the Sunbelt tended to be white, middle- and upper-class suburbanites—skilled workers, young professionals, and business executives attracted by both economic opportunity and a political climate stressing low taxes, less government regulation, and more reliance on the marketplace. The political impact of population shifts from East to West and North to South during the 1970s was reflected in the congressional gains (17 seats) by Sunbelt and Far West states after the 1980 census.

Conservatives also, for the first time since World War II, made their cause intellectually respectable. Scholars and academics on the right flourished in new "think tanks"; William Buckley and economist Milton Friedman became effective advocates of conservative causes in print and on television. **Neoconservatism**, led by Norman Podhoretz's magazine *Commentary*, became fashionable among intellectuals who were former liberal stalwarts. They denounced liberals for being too soft on the communist threat abroad and too willing to compromise high standards at home in the face of demands for equality from African Americans, women, and the disadvantaged. Neoconservatives called for reaffirming capitalism and emphasizing what was right about America rather than an obsessive concern with social ills.

By the end of the 1970s, a decade marked by military defeat in Vietnam, political scandal that destroyed the administration of Richard Nixon, economic ills that vexed the country under Gerald Ford and Jimmy Carter, and unprecedented strains on families and traditional institutions, millions of Americans had come to believe that Cold War liberalism had run its course. Ronald Reagan, as the acknowledged leader of the conservative resurgence, was ideally placed to capitalize on this discontent. His charm softened the hard edges of his right-wing call to arms, and his conviction that America could regain its self-confidence by reaffirming basic ideals had a broad appeal to a nation facing new challenges at home and abroad. In 1976, Reagan had barely lost to President Ford at the Republican convention; four years later, he won the Grand Old Party (GOP) nomination handily.

In his acceptance speech at the Republican convention in Detroit, Reagan set forth the themes that endeared him to conservatives: less government, a balanced budget, family values, and peace through greater military spending. Unlike Barry Goldwater, whose rigid ideology frightened people, Reagan offered reassurance and hope for the future. He spoke of restoring to the federal government "the capacity to do the people's work without dominating their lives." As historian Robert Dallek pointed out, Reagan "assured his listeners that he was no radical idealist courting defeat, but a sensible, thoroughly likable American with a surefire formula for success that would please everyone." In Ronald Reagan, the Republicans had found the perfect figure to lead Americans into a new conservative era.

Moral Majority In 1979, the Reverend Jerry Falwell founded the Moral Majority to combat "amoral liberals," drug abuse, "coddling" of criminals, homosexuality, communism, and abortion. The Moral Majority represented the rise of political activism among organized religion's radical right wing.

Neoconservatism Former liberals who advocated a strong stand against communism abroad and free market capitalism at home. These intellectuals stressed the positive values of American society in contrast to those liberals who emphasized social problems.

31.1

31.2

31.3

31.4

31.5

31.6

31.1

31.2

31.3

31.4

31.5

31.6

The Tempting of Richard Nixon

31.1 What were the major accomplishments and failures of the Nixon presidency?

F
ollowing the divisive campaign of 1968, Nixon's presidency proved to be one of the most controversial in American history. Though he broke new ground in relations with China and the Soviet Union and ended American fighting in Vietnam, the Watergate scandal forced him to resign the presidency.

Détente

Foreign policy was Nixon's pride and joy. He had thought long about the state of the world and was determined to improve it. To assist him, he appointed Henry Kissinger to be national security adviser. A refugee from Nazi Germany, Kissinger had become a professor of government at Harvard, the author of influential books, and an authority on international affairs. Nixon and Kissinger approached foreign policy from a practical, realistic perspective. They saw the Cold War not as an ideological struggle for survival with communism but as a traditional great-power rivalry, to be managed rather than won.

Nixon and Kissinger had a grand design. Realizing that recent events, especially the Vietnam War and the rapid Soviet arms buildup of the 1960s, had eroded America's primacy in the world, they planned a strategic retreat. Russia had military strength, but its economy was weak and it had a rival in China. Nixon planned to use American trade—notably grain and technology—to induce Soviet cooperation, while improving U.S. relations with China.

Nixon and Kissinger shrewdly played the China card as their first step toward achieving **détente**—a relaxation of tension—with the Soviets. In February 1972, accompanied by a planeload of reporters and camera crews, Nixon visited China, meeting with the communist leaders and ending more than two decades of Sino-American hostility. He established an American liaison mission in Beijing as a step toward diplomatic recognition.

The Soviets, who viewed China as a dangerous adversary, responded by agreeing to an arms control pact with the United States. The **Strategic Arms Limitation Talks (SALT)** had been under way since 1969. During a visit to Moscow in May 1972, Nixon signed two vital documents with Soviet leader Leonid Brezhnev. The first limited the two superpowers to 200 antiballistic missiles (ABMs) apiece; the second froze the number of offensive ballistic missiles for five years. These SALT I agreements recognized the existing Soviet lead in missiles, but the American deployment of multiple independently targeted reentry vehicles (MIRVs) ensured a strategic advantage for the United States.

The SALT I agreements were most important as a symbolic first step toward control of the nuclear arms race. They signified that the United States and the Soviet Union were trying to settle their differences peacefully.

détente President Richard Nixon and Henry Kissinger pursued a policy of détente, a French word meaning a relaxation of tension, with the Soviet Union to lessen the possibility of nuclear war in the 1970s.

Strategic Arms Limitation Talks (SALT) In 1972, the United States and the Soviet Union culminated four years of SALT by signing a treaty limiting the deployment of antiballistic missiles (ABM) and an agreement to freeze the number of offensive missiles for five years.

Quick Check

What was Détente and why did it appeal to Nixon?

Ending the Vietnam War

Vietnam remained the one foreign policy challenge that Nixon could not overcome. He had a three-part plan to end the conflict—gradual withdrawal of American troops, accompanied by training South Vietnamese forces to take over the combat role; renewed bombing; and a hard line in negotiations with Hanoi. The number of American soldiers in Vietnam fell from 540,000 in early 1969 to fewer than 30,000 by 1972; domestic opposition to the war declined sharply with the accompanying drop in casualties and reductions in the draft call.

Renewed bombing was the most controversial part of the plan. As early as the spring of 1969, Nixon secretly ordered raids on communist supply lines in neutral

31.1
31.2
31.3
31.4
31.5
31.6

KENT STATE UNIVERSITY The renewed bombing of North Vietnam and the invasion of Cambodia ordered by Nixon precipitated student protests at many campuses. At Kent State University in Ohio, national guardsmen killed four students.

Cambodia. Then in April 1970, he launched both air and ground strikes into Cambodia, causing an outburst of antiwar protests at home. Students demonstrated on campuses across the nation. Tragedy struck at Kent State University in Ohio in May. After rioters had firebombed an ROTC building, the governor sent in National Guard troops, who were taunted and harassed. The guardsmen then opened fire, killing four students and wounding 11 more. The victims were innocent bystanders; two were young women caught in the fusillade between classes. A week later, two African American student demonstrators were killed at Jackson State College in Mississippi; soon riots and protests raged on more than 400 campuses.

Nixon had no sympathy for the demonstrators, calling the students "bums" intent on "blowing up the campuses." The "silent majority" to whom he appealed seemed to agree; one poll showed that most Americans blamed the students, not the National Guard, for the deaths at Kent State. An "Honor America Day" program in Washington, D.C., on July 4, attracted 250,000 people, who heard Billy Graham and Bob Hope endorse the president's policies. Nixon's Cambodian invasion did little to shorten the Vietnam War, but the public reaction reinforced his resolve not to surrender.

The third tactic, negotiation with Hanoi, finally proved successful. Beginning in the summer of 1969, Kissinger held secret meetings with North Vietnam's foreign minister. In 1972, the two sides neared agreement, but South Vietnam blocked a settlement before the 1972 election. When the North Vietnamese tried to make last-minute changes, Nixon ordered heavy B-52 raids on Hanoi that finally led to the signing of a truce on January 27, 1973. In return for the release of all American prisoners of war, the United States agreed to remove its troops from South Vietnam within 60 days. The North Vietnamese, however, could keep their troops in the South, thus virtually guaranteeing future communist control of all Vietnam.

31.1

31.2

31.3

31.4

31.5

31.6

Quick Check

How did the Vietnam war end?

For two years after the accords, the communists waited. The Watergate scandal (see below) weakened Nixon's grip on foreign policy. By the time he was forced from office in August 1974, most Americans wanted to forget Vietnam. The following spring the communists mounted a major offensive and in just weeks took over all of Vietnam. Ten years after the American escalation of the war, and after the loss of 60,000 American lives, the effort to preserve South Vietnam from communism had proved a tragic failure.

The Watergate Scandal

Nixon's Vietnam problems and especially his formulation of détente made him sensitive to the unauthorized release of information about American foreign policy. Leaks might tip the administration's hand in sensitive negotiations with the communists. When leaks did occur, Nixon demanded that they be stopped. The White House established an informal office of covert surveillance—the so-called "plumbers"—which began by investigating national security breaches but, during the presidential campaign of 1972, branched out into spying on Nixon's Democratic opponents and engaging in political dirty tricks.

Five of the "plumbers" were arrested in June 1972 during a break-in at the headquarters of the Democratic National Committee at the Watergate office complex in Washington. The White House took pains to conceal its connection to what its spokesman dismissed as a "third-rate burglary attempt." Nixon personally ordered the cover-up. "I want you to stonewall it, let them plead the Fifth Amendment, cover up, or anything else," Nixon told John Mitchell, his campaign director and former attorney general.

The cover-up succeeded long enough to ensure Nixon's landslide reelection victory over Democrat George S. McGovern of South Dakota (see Map 31.1), but then began to unravel. James McCord, one of the Watergate burglars, broke the silence. Sentenced to a long jail term by Judge John Sirica, McCord asked for leniency, informing

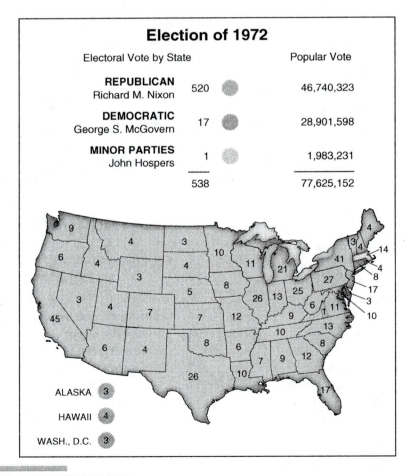

MAP 31.1 ELECTION OF 1972

Sirica that he had received money from the White House and had been promised a presidential pardon in return for his silence. By April 1973, Nixon was compelled to fire aide John Dean, who had directed the cover-up but refused to become a scapegoat. Two other aides, H. R. Haldeman and John Ehrlichman, resigned.

The Senate then appointed a special committee to investigate the **Watergate scandal**. In a dramatic testimony, Dean revealed the president's personal involvement in the cover-up. Still, it was basically a matter of whose word to believe—the president's or a discredited aide's—and Nixon hoped to weather the storm.

The committee's discovery of tape recordings of conversations in the Oval Office, made regularly since 1970, doomed Nixon. At first, the president invoked executive privilege to withhold the tapes. When Archibald Cox, the Watergate special prosecutor, demanded their release, Nixon fired him. Yet the new prosecutor, Leon Jaworski, continued to press for the tapes. Nixon tried to release only a few of the less damaging ones, but the Supreme Court ruled unanimously in July 1974 that the tapes had to be turned over to Jaworski.

By this time, the House Judiciary Committee had voted three articles of impeachment, charging Nixon with obstruction of justice, abuse of power, and contempt of

Watergate Scandal A break-in at the Democratic National Committee offices in the Watergate complex in Washington was carried out under the direction of White House employees. Disclosure of the White House involvement in the break-in and subsequent cover-up forced President Richard Nixon to resign in 1974.

31.1

31.2

31.3

31.4

31.5

31.6

((• 📖 Read the Document   House Judiciary Committee's Conclusion on Impeachment (1974)

'I HAVE DISCOVERED THAT ACCORDING TO A SECRET TAPE OF JUNE 23, 1972, I AM A CROOK.'

WATERGATE This Watergate cartoon by.Milwaukee Journal.cartoonist Bill Sanders, "I Have Discovered That According to a Secret Tape of June 23, 1972, I AM a crook," was published on August 6, 1974. The title is a play on Nixon's infamous "I am not a crook" speech given in November of 1973 during the height of the infamous scandal. The Watergate scandal revolved around Nixon's participation in the planning and cover-up of a break-in at the Democratic National Committee headquarters.

31.1

31.2

31.3

31.4

31.5

31.6

Congress. Faced with the release of tapes that directly implicated him in the cover-up, the president resigned on August 9, 1974.

Nixon's resignation proved to be the culmination of the Watergate scandal. The episode revealed the weaknesses and strengths of the American political system. Most regrettable was the abuse of presidential authority—a reflection both of the power of the modern presidency and of fatal flaws in Nixon's character. Unlike previous executive branch scandals, Watergate involved a lust for power rather than money. Having become president, Nixon did everything possible to retain his hold on the office. He used the plumbers to maintain executive secrecy and directed the Internal Revenue Service and the Justice Department to punish his enemies and reward his friends.

But Watergate also demonstrated the vitality of a democratic society. The press showed how investigative reporting could unlock even the most closely guarded executive secrets. Judge Sirica proved that an independent judiciary was still the best bulwark for individual freedom. And Congress rose to the occasion, both by investigating executive misconduct and by following a scrupulous and nonpartisan impeachment process that left Nixon with no chance to escape his fate.

The nation survived Watergate with its institutions intact. John Mitchell and 25 presidential aides went to jail. Congress, in decline since Lyndon Johnson's exercise of executive dominance, was rejuvenated, with its members now intent on extending congressional authority into other areas of American life.

Quick Check

Why was Nixon forced to resign?

Oil and Inflation

31.2 How were oil and inflation linked during the 1970s?

I n the midst of Watergate, war in the Middle East threatened a vital national interest: the unimpeded and inexpensive flow of oil to the United States. The resulting energy crisis helped spark raging inflation that profoundly affected the economy and American society.

War and Oil

On October 6, 1973, Egypt and Syria attacked Israel. The fighting followed decades of conflict between Israel and its Arab neighbors, which had only grown worse after the Israeli victory in the Six Day War of 1967. In that conflict, the Israelis seized the Golan Heights from Syria, the Sinai Peninsula from Egypt, and Jerusalem and the West Bank from Jordan. The Arabs ached for revenge, and in 1973, the Egyptians and Syrians caught Israel off guard. They won early battles but lost the initiative and were forced to give up the ground they had recovered. The Israelis would have won another victory if not for the diplomatic intervention of Nixon and Kissinger, who, despite America's support for Israel, believed a decisive Israeli victory would further destabilize the Middle East.

Organization of the Petroleum Exporting Countries (OPEC)
A cartel of oil-exporting nations.

An unforeseen consequence of the October War (also called the Yom Kippur War because it started on that Jewish holy day) offset the American diplomatic triumph, however. On October 17, the Arab members of the **Organization of the Petroleum Exporting Countries (OPEC)** announced a 5 percent cut in oil production, and vowed additional cuts of 5 percent each month until Israel surrendered the lands it had taken in 1967. Three days later, following Nixon's announcement of an emergency aid package for Israel, Saudi Arabia cut off oil shipments to the United States.

The Arab oil embargo had a disastrous impact on the American economy. With Arab producers cutting oil production by 25 percent from the September 1973 level, world supplies fell by 10 percent. For the United States, which imported one-third of its daily consumption, this meant a loss of nearly 2 million barrels a day. Long lines formed at gas stations as motorists who feared running out of fuel kept filling their tanks.

31.1
31.2
31.3
31.4
31.5
31.6

✳ Explore Energy and Conservation in the 1970s on MyHistoryLab

HOW DID AN ENERGY CRISIS EMBROIL AMERICA?

The 1970s brought domestic turmoil to the United States. Recession struck the economy during the first half of the decade and was followed by stagflation, a combination of high unemployment and inflation. These problems were fueled by rising energy prices, in particular the cost of oil. The OPEC tightened the world supply of oil to increase the profits of member countries, a move that drove up the cost of gasoline and electricity. Amid these problems, many Americans began calling for conservation of energy and more concern about the natural environment, helping to usher in the modern environmental movement.

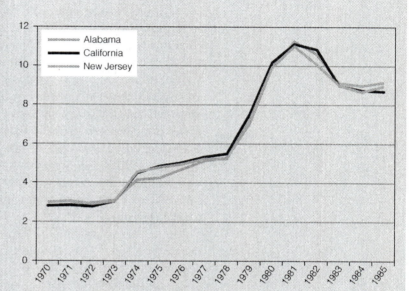

GASOLINE PRICES IN SELECTED STATES, 1970–1985

State	1970	1971	1972	1973	1974	1975	1976	1977	1978	1979	1980	1981	1982	1983	1984	1985
Alabama	2.82	2.85	2.95	3.08	4.14	4.26	4.7	5.12	5.27	7.04	9.89	11.24	10.61	9.07	8.98	9.15
California	2.8	2.84	2.79	3.08	4.47	4.84	5.04	5.33	5.48	7.47	10.19	11.13	10.82	8.96	8.74	8.68
New Jersey	2.99	3.04	2.9	3.08	4.55	4.79	4.95	5.23	5.21	7.16	9.94	10.99	10.06	9.01	8.67	8.95

*In dollars per million BTUs.
Source: U.S. Energy Information Administration, State Energy Data Systems, 1960–2010.

KEY QUESTIONS Use **MyHistoryLab** *Explorer* to answer these **questions:**

Response ▶▶▶ *What was the economic landscape of the United States in 1970?*

Explore population and the distribution of industries to consider the energy crisis's potential effects.

Comparison ▶▶▶ *How did rising energy prices affect different parts of the country?*

Map local effects of the crisis of the 1970s.

Consequence ▶▶▶ *How extensive were efforts at gasoline conservation?*

Chart per capita gasoline consumption in the United States.

31.1

31.2

31.3

31.4

31.5

31.6

Oil prices also rose dramatically. After the Arab embargo began, OPEC, led by the shah of Iran, raised crude oil prices fourfold. In the United States, gasoline prices at the pumps nearly doubled, while home heating fuel rose even more.

Nixon responded with temporary measures, including pleas to Americans to turn down their thermostats and avoid driving for pleasure. When the Arab oil embargo ended in March, after Kissinger negotiated an Israeli pullback in the Sinai, the American public relaxed. Gasoline became plentiful, thermostats were raised, and people resumed their love affair with the automobile.

The energy crisis, however, did not end with the lifting of the embargo. The Arab action marked the beginning of a new era in American history. The United States, with only 6 percent of the world's population, had been responsible for nearly 40 percent of the world's energy consumption. In 1970, domestic oil production began to decline; the embargo only highlighted the nation's dependence on other countries, notably those in the Persian Gulf, for its economic well-being. A nation that based its way of life on abundance and expansion suddenly was faced with the reality of limited resources and economic stagnation.

Quick Check

Why did oil prices quadruple in the 1970s?

The Great Inflation

The price spike from the October War was merely the first of the "oil shocks" of the 1970s. Cheap energy had been a primary contributor to the relentless growth of the American economy after World War II. The GNP had more than doubled between 1950 and 1973; the American people had come to base their standard of living on oil prices that yielded gas at about 35 cents a gallon. Large cars, sprawling suburbs, detached houses heated by fuel oil and natural gas and cooled by central air-conditioning produced a dependence on inexpensive energy that Americans took for granted.

The quadrupling of oil prices in 1973–1974 suddenly put all this at risk. Because oil or its equivalent in energy is required to produce and transport manufactured goods, the rising oil prices increased the prices of nearly everything else, including most services. (See Figure 31.1).

Other factors added to the trend of rising prices. The Vietnam War and the Great Society produced federal budget deficits that grew from $63 billion for the entire decade of the 1960s to $420 billion for the 1970s. Rapid population increases and poor harvests around the globe in the mid-1970s triggered a 20 percent rise in American food prices in 1973 alone. But the primary source of the great inflation of the 1970s was the increase in petroleum prices.

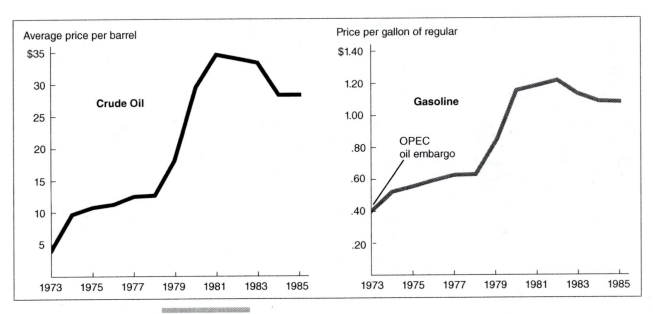

FIGURE 31.1 THE OIL SHOCKS Price Increases for Crude Oil and Gasoline, 1973–1985

31.1

31.2

31.3

31.4

31.5

31.6

The impact on consumers was staggering. The price of an automobile jumped 72 percent between 1973 and 1978. During the 1970s, the price of a hamburger doubled, milk went from 28 to 59 cents a quart, and a loaf of bread—the proverbial staff of life—rose from 24 to 89 cents. Wage increases failed to keep pace with inflation; in 1980, the real income of the average American family fell by 5.5 percent.

Often inflation signals economic exuberance, and rising prices indicate rapid growth. But the inflation of the 1970s reflected economic weakness. The great inflation contributed to a severe recession. American GNP dropped by 6 percent in 1974, and unemployment rose to more than 9 percent, the highest level since the Great Depression of the 1930s.

President Gerald R. Ford, who followed Richard Nixon into the White House (see below), responded belatedly to the economic crisis by proposing a tax cut to stimulate consumer spending. Congress passed a $23 billion reduction in taxes in early 1975, which led to a gradual recovery by 1976. The resulting budget deficits, however, helped keep inflation above 5 percent and prevented a return to full economic health.

Jimmy Carter of Georgia, who succeeded Ford, had little more success in reviving the economy. Federal deficits and relatively high interest rates kept the economy sluggish throughout 1977 and 1978. Then in 1979, the Iranian Revolution and the overthrow of the shah touched off another oil shock. OPEC took advantage of the situation to double prices over the next 18 months. A barrel of crude oil now cost more than $30. Gasoline prices climbed to more than $1 a gallon at American service stations, leading to even greater inflation than in 1973.

Finally, in late 1979, the Federal Reserve Board, led by Carter appointee Paul Volcker, began an effort to halt inflation by mandating increased bank reserves to curtail the supply of money in circulation. The new tight-money policy only heightened inflation in the short run by driving interest rates up to record levels. By the spring of 1980, the prime interest rate reached 20 percent.

Quick Check

How did rising oil prices help trigger the inflation of the 1970s?

Private Lives, Public Issues

31.3   How did private life change during this period?

S weeping changes in the private lives of Americans began in the 1970s and continued for the rest of the century. The traditional American family, with wage-earner husband and homemaker wife, gave way to much more diverse living arrangements. The number of working women, including wives and mothers, increased sharply; the wage gap between the sexes narrowed, but women still earned less than men. Then, after 1970, an active gay rights movement emerged as gay, lesbian, and bisexual Americans began to disclose their sexual identities and demand an end to discrimination.

The Changing American Family

Family life underwent significant shifts after 1970. The most notable was a decline in the number of families with two parents and one or more children under 18. By 1990, in only one two-parent family out of five was the mother solely engaged in child rearing. A few fathers stayed at home with the children, but in most of these families, both parents worked outside the home.

The traditional nuclear family of the 1950s no longer prevailed in America. The number of married couple households with children dropped from 30 percent in the 1970s to 23 percent by 2000. The number of unmarried couples doubled in the 1990s, while adults living alone surpassed the number of married couples with children for the first time in American history. "Being married is great," commented demographer William H. Frey, "but being married with kids is tougher in today's society with spouses in different jobs and expensive day care and schools."

31.1

31.2

31.3

31.4

31.5

31.6

The divorce rate, which doubled between the mid-1960s and the late 1970s, leveled off for the rest of the century. Nevertheless, half of all first marriages still ended in divorce. After a sharp fall in the 1970s, the birthrate climbed again as the baby boom generation matured. The number of births to women over age 30 increased, and single mothers comprised 7 percent of all households by 2000, a 25 percent increase since 1990. Conservatives, alarmed by the decline of the nuclear family, called for change. "We need to discourage people from living together outside of marriage," observed Bridget Maher of the Family Research Council, "and encourage them to have children within marriage."

For better or worse, the American family structure changed significantly in the last three decades of the twentieth century, with many people either never marrying or postponing marriage until late in the childbearing period. The traditional family unit, with the working father and the mother rearing the children at home, declined. Most mothers worked outside the home, and many were the sole support for their children. The proportion of children living with only one parent doubled in 20 years. Women without partners headed more than one-third of all impoverished families, and children made up 40 percent of the nation's poor. Although politicians, especially Republicans, would hail family values during campaigns, those values underwent great stress due to social changes in the last third of the twentieth century, and children suffered disproportionately.

Gains and Setbacks for Women

American women experienced significant changes in their way of life and their place in society in the last quarter of the twentieth century. There was a rapid movement of women into the labor force in the 1970s; six million more married women held jobs by 1980 as two incomes became increasingly necessary to keep up with inflation. The trend continued through the 1980s. Women filled 61 percent of the nearly 19 million new jobs created during that decade; many of these new jobs, however, were entry-level or low-paying service positions.

Women scored some impressive breakthroughs. They began to enter corporate boardrooms, became presidents of major universities, and were admitted to the nation's military academies. Women entered blue-collar, professional, and small-business fields traditionally dominated by men. Ronald Reagan's appointment of Sandra Day O'Connor to the Supreme Court in 1981 marked a historic first.

Yet women also encountered resistance. Most women continued to work in female-dominated fields—as nurses, secretaries, teachers, and waitresses. Those who entered such "male" areas as management and administration soon hit the so-called glass ceiling, which kept them from advancing beyond mid-level executive status. In 1990, only 4.3 percent of corporate officers were women. Most women in business worked at the middle and lower rungs of management in personnel and public relations, not key operational positions in sales and marketing that would lead to the boardroom; women held fewer than 3 percent of the top jobs in *Fortune* 500 companies. The economic boom of the 1990s, however, increased the number of women executives by 514,000 in 1998.

Even with these gains, however, by 2009 women's wages still averaged only 80 percent of men's earnings. Younger women did best; those between 16 and 24 earned 92 cents for every dollar paid to a male in the same age group, and in certain large cities young women earned more than young men. But the overall gap remained, and experts predicted that it would take years to close.

The most encouraging development for women came in business ownership, as more women went into business for themselves. The number of female business owners increased 40 percent between 1987 and 1992, twice the national rate of business growth. A women's trade group estimated that in 1996 women owned almost eight million businesses, employing more than 18 million workers—one out of four American workers. A speaker at the first National Women's Economic Summit in 1996 exaggerated only slightly in crediting her group with restoring prosperity, claiming that "the American economy has been revitalized in good measure because of the participation of and contributions of women business owners."

31.1

31.2

31.3

31.4

31.5

31.6

FEMALE ELECTRICIAN During the 1970s and 1980s, employment opportunities expanded for women, including jobs in fields traditionally dominated by men. This photograph from 1980 shows a woman working as a union electrician in Harlem.

Equal Rights Amendment (ERA) A proposed constitutional amendment passed by Congress in 1972 to guarantee women equal treatment under the law. The amendment failed to be ratified in 1982.

Roe v. Wade The 1973 Supreme Court decision that women have a constitutional right to abortion during the early stages of pregnancy.

Beyond economic opportunity, the women's movement had two goals. The first was ratification of the **Equal Rights Amendment (ERA)**. Approved by Congress in 1972, the ERA stated simply, "Equality of rights under the law shall not be denied or abridged by the United States or any state on account of sex." Within a year, 22 states had approved the amendment, but the effort gradually stalled. Opposition came in part from working-class women who feared, as one union leader explained, that "maids, laundry workers, hospital cleaners, or dishwashers" would lose the protection of state laws that regulated wages and hours of work for women. Right-wing activist Phyllis Schlafly led an effort to defeat the ERA, claiming the amendment would lead to unisex toilets, homosexual marriages, and the drafting of women. The National Organization for Women (NOW) persuaded Congress to extend the time for ratification by three years, but the deadline for ratification passed on June 30, 1982, with the ERA forces still three states short (see Map 31.2.). NOW leader Eleanor Smeal vowed to fight on: "The crusade is not over. We know that we are the wave of the future."

The women's movement devoted even more of its energies to protecting *Roe v. Wade*, the 1973 Supreme Court decision that guaranteed women's right to abortion. Right-to-life groups, consisting mainly of orthodox Catholics, fundamentalist Protestants, and conservatives, fought back. In 1978, with support from President Carter, Congress passed the Hyde amendment, which denied the use of federal funds

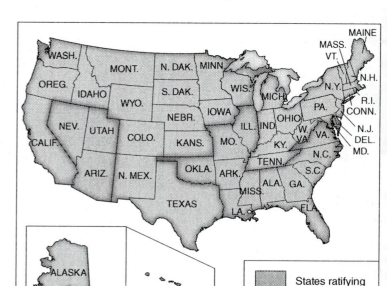

MAP 31.2 VOTING ON THE EQUAL RIGHTS AMENDMENT By the end of 1974, 34 states had ratified the ERA; Indiana finally approved the amendment in 1977, but the remaining 15 states held out, leaving ratification three states short of the required three-fourths majority.

31.1

31.2

31.3

31.4

31.5

31.6

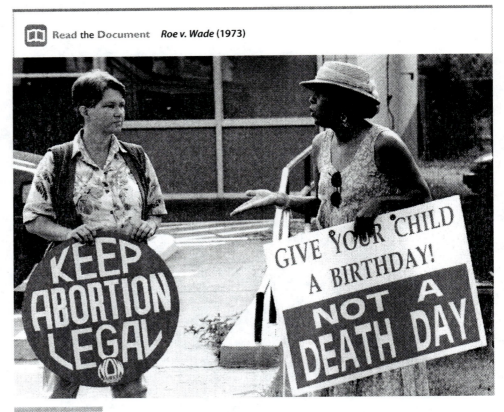

Read the Document *Roe v. Wade* (1973)

THE ABORTION DEBATE *Roe v. Wade* exerted a tremendous impact throughout the country, as only four states had enacted laws guaranteeing a woman widespread access to an abortion at the time of the ruling. The abortion issue continues to be a major source of controversy within U.S. politics and society.

to pay for abortions for poor women. Nevertheless, pro-choice groups organized privately funded family planning agencies and abortion clinics to give more women a chance to exercise their constitutional right to abortion.

As Presidents Reagan and Bush appointed more conservative judges to the Court, however, pro-choice groups began to fear the overturn of *Roe v. Wade*. The Court avoided a direct challenge, contenting itself with upholding the rights of states to regulate abortion clinics, imposing a 24-hour waiting period, and requiring the approval of a parent or judge before a minor could have an abortion. Abortion became an issue in presidential contests, with the Republicans upholding a pro-life position and the Democrats taking a pro-choice stand. Bill Clinton's election and appointment of Ruth Bader Ginsburg to the Court appeared to end the challenge to *Roe v. Wade*, but in 2000, the Court margin in rejecting a Nebraska law forbidding certain late-term abortions fell to a bare majority, 5–4. And the often violent protests of pro-life groups outside abortion clinics made getting an abortion difficult and dangerous. For many women, abortion was a hard-won right they had to struggle to protect.

Quick Check

What new challenges and opportunities faced women during the decade?

The Gay Liberation Movement

On the night of June 27, 1969, New York police raided the Stonewall Inn, a Greenwich Village bar frequented by "drag queens" and lesbians. As the patrons were being herded into vans, gay onlookers began to jeer and taunt the police. A riot broke out. "Beer cans and bottles were heaved at the windows and a rain of coins descended on the cops," reported the *Village Voice*. "Almost by signal the crowd erupted into cobblestone and bottle heaving." The next night, more than 400 police officers battled 2000 gay demonstrators in Greenwich Village. The two-day Stonewall Riots marked the beginning of the modern gay liberation movement. Refusing to be victims any longer, gays and lesbians affirmed their sexual orientation and demanded an end to discrimination against homosexuals.

Within days, two new organizations were formed in New York, the Gay Liberation Front and the Gay Activist Alliance, with branches and offshoots in cities across the country.

The basic theme of gay liberation was to urge all homosexuals to "come out of the closet" and affirm their sexual identity with pride not shame. The very act of coming out would bring freedom and self-respect. "Come out for freedom! Come out now!" proclaimed the Gay Liberation Front's newspaper. "Come out of the closet before the door is nailed shut!"

During the 1970s, hundreds of thousands of gays and lesbians responded to this call. They formed more than 1000 local clubs and organizations and won notable victories. In 1974, the American Psychiatric Association stopped classifying homosexuality as a mental disorder, and by 1980, half the states had repealed their sodomy statutes. The 2003 Supreme Court decision in *Lawrence v. Texas* struck down a Texas sodomy law and declared private consensual sex a matter of personal liberty. Gays fought hard for laws forbidding discrimination against homosexuals in housing and employment, and in 1980, the Democratic National Platform included a gay rights plank.

In the 1980s, however, AIDS put the gay liberation movement on the defensive. A disease caused by the HIV retrovirus that destroyed the human immune system, AIDS was almost always fatal until the introduction of new drugs in the mid-1990s. And because it was first diagnosed among male homosexuals, the gay community faced new condemnation at a time when its members were trying desperately to care for the many victims of the disease within their ranks. The gay organizations formed in the 1970s to win new rights now channeled their energies into caring for the ill, promoting safer sex practices, and fighting for more public funding to help conquer AIDS. In 1986, ACT UP (AIDS Coalition to Unleash Power) began violent demonstrations to shock the nation into doing more about AIDS. Its members disrupted public meetings, chained themselves to a New York Stock Exchange balcony, and spray-painted outlines of corpses on the streets of San Francisco to call attention to those who had died of AIDS.

The movement also continued to stimulate gay consciousness in the 1980s. In 1987, an estimated 600,000 gays and lesbians took part in a march on Washington on behalf of gay rights. Every year afterward, gay groups held a National Coming Out Day in October to encourage homosexuals to proclaim proudly their sexual identity. In a more controversial move, some gay leaders encouraged "outing"—releasing the names of prominent homosexuals, primarily politicians and movie stars—to make the nation aware of how many Americans were gay or lesbian. Gay leaders claimed there were more than 20 million gays and lesbians in the nation, basing this estimate on a Kinsey report that had stated in the late 1940s that one in ten American males had engaged in homosexual behavior. On the other hand, a sociological survey released in 1993 contradicted those numbers, finding only 1.1 percent of American males exclusively homosexual. Whatever the actual number, it was clear by the 1990s that gays and lesbians formed a significant minority that had forced the nation, however grudgingly, to respect its rights.

However, one victory eluded the gay liberation movement. In the 1992 election, gays and lesbians strongly backed Democratic candidate Bill Clinton, who promised, if elected, to end the ban on homosexuals in the military. In his first days in office, however, President Clinton stirred up resistance in the Pentagon and Congress when he tried to issue an executive order forbidding such discrimination. The Joint Chiefs of Staff and many Democrats, led by Georgia Senator Sam Nunn, claimed accepting gays and lesbians would destroy morale and weaken the armed forces. Clinton finally settled for the Pentagon's compromise "Don't ask, don't tell" policy that would permit homosexuals to serve in the military as they had in the past as long as they did not reveal their sexual preference and refrained from homosexual conduct. However disappointed gays and lesbians were in Clinton's retreat, their leaders understood that the real problem was the resistance of mainstream America to full acceptance of homosexuality.

Public attitudes toward gays and lesbians changed in the 1990s, but the growing tolerance had limits. In a 1996 poll, 85 percent of those questioned believed that gays should be treated equally in the workplace, up from 76 percent in 1992. Violence against gays, however, continued, most notably in the 1998 fatal beating of Matthew Shepard, a 21-year-old gay college student, in Wyoming. That attack spurred calls for hate-crime legislation, and the judge in the case, banning a so-called gay-panic defense, sentenced Shepard's assailants to two consecutive terms of life imprisonment.

31.1

31.2

31.3

31.4

31.5

31.6

The issue of same-sex marriage came to a head at the end of the century. In 1996, President Clinton signed the Defense of Marriage Act, which decreed that states did not have to recognize same-sex marriages performed elsewhere. But in 2000, following a state supreme court ruling, the Vermont legislature legalized civil unions between individuals of the same sex, enabling gays and lesbians to receive all the legal benefits available to married couples. Whether sanctioned by law or not, the number of gay and lesbian households steadily increased; the 2000 census revealed that there were nearly 600,000 homes in America headed by same-sex couples. While nearly one-quarter were in California and New York, there was at least one gay or lesbian couple living in 99 percent of the nation's counties.

Quick Check

What was "Gay Liberation," and how did the movement develop?

Politics and Diplomacy After Watergate

31.4 Why did the presidencies of Ford and Carter largely fail?

The era's economic and social disruptions contributed to problems of governance left over from Watergate. Even as many Americans worried about shrinking paychecks and disintegrating families, Congress challenged the prerogatives of the presidency. This made life in the White House difficult for Richard Nixon's immediate successors—and it made solving America's problems nearly impossible.

The Ford Administration

Gerald R. Ford was the first president who had never been elected to national office. Nixon had appointed him to the vice presidency to succeed Spiro Agnew, who had been forced to resign to avoid prosecution for accepting bribes while he was governor of Maryland. Ford, an amiable and unpretentious Michigan congressman who was House minority leader, seemed ready to restore confidence in the presidency when he replaced Nixon in August 1974.

But his honeymoon lasted only a month. On September 8, 1974, he shocked the nation by granting Richard Nixon a full and unconditional pardon for all federal crimes he may have committed. Some critics charged that Nixon and Ford had made a secret bargain; others pointed out how unfair it was for Nixon's aides to go to prison while the chief criminal went free. Ford apparently wanted to end the bitterness over Watergate, but his attempt backfired, eroding confidence in his leadership and linking him indelibly with the scandal.

Ford soon found himself fighting an equally difficult battle on behalf of the CIA. The Watergate scandal and the Vietnam fiasco had eroded confidence in the government and lent credibility to startling disclosures about covert actions. The president allowed the CIA to confirm some of the charges but then made things worse by blurting out to the press the juiciest item of all: The CIA had been involved in plots to assassinate foreign leaders.

Senate and House committees investigating the CIA now focused on the assassination issue, eventually charging that the agency had been involved in no fewer than eight separate attempts to kill Fidel Castro. The chairman of the Senate committee, Frank Church of Idaho, worried that the revelations would damage the reputations of Presidents Kennedy and Johnson; he likened the CIA to "a rogue elephant on the rampage."

In late 1975, Ford appointed George H. W. Bush, then a respected former Republican congressman, as the CIA's new director and gave him the authority to reform the agency and strengthen its role in shaping national security policy. Ford also issued an executive order outlawing assassination as an instrument of American foreign policy. To prevent future abuses, Congress created permanent House and Senate intelligence committees to exercise general oversight for covert CIA operations.

Ford proved less successful in his dealings with Congress on other issues. Although he prided himself on his good relations with members of both houses, he opposed Democratic measures such as federal aid to education and control over strip mining, and vetoed 39 separate bills. In fact, Ford, who as a congressman had opposed virtually every Great Society measure, proved far more conservative than Nixon in the White House.

Quick Check
What ended Ford's honeymoon with the American people?

Carter and American Malaise

Ford's lackluster record and the legacy of Watergate made the Democratic nomination a prize in 1976. Many candidates entered the contest, but a virtual unknown, former Georgia Governor James Earl Carter, became the front-runner. Aware of the voters' disgust with politicians of both parties, Carter ran as an outsider who could give the nation fresh and untainted leadership. On television, the basic Carter commercial showed him at his Georgia peanut farm, dressed in blue jeans, looking directly into the camera and saying, "I'll never tell a lie."

Voters took Carter at his word and elected him over Ford in a close contest (see Table 31.1). Unfortunately, Carter's outsider status, while attractive in a campaign, made governing as president difficult. He had no discernible political philosophy, no clear sense of direction. He called himself a populist, but that label meant little more than an appeal to the common man, an ironic appeal, given Carter's wealth. "The idea of a millionaire populist has always amused me," commented his attorney general, fellow Georgian Griffin Bell.

The Carter administration had little chance to succeed. The president strove for a balanced budget but had to accept mounting deficits. Federal agencies fought to save the environment and help consumers but only angered industry.

Joseph Califano, secretary of health, education, and welfare (HEW), failed repeatedly to effect long-overdue reforms. His attempts to overhaul the nation's welfare program, which had become a $30 billion annual operation serving 30 million Americans, won little support from the White House. Carter's unwillingness to take the risks involved in revamping the overburdened Social Security system by reducing benefits and raising the retirement age blocked Califano's efforts. And the HEW secretary finally gave up his attempt to draw up a national health insurance plan.

Informed by his pollsters in 1979 that he was losing the nation's confidence, Carter sought to redeem himself. After consulting advisers, he gave a speech in which he seemed to accuse the American people of creating "a crisis of confidence . . . that strikes at the very heart and soul and spirit of our national will." Then, a week after what his critics termed the "national malaise" speech, he requested the resignation of Califano and the secretary of the treasury. But neither the attempt to pin responsibility on the American people nor firing cabinet members could hide Carter's failure, despite good intentions and hard work, to provide the leadership the nation needed.

Quick Check
What mood did Carter detect in American society?

Troubles Abroad

After the Vietnam War, most Americans wanted to have little to do with the world. Military intervention had failed in Southeast Asia, and, with the economy in trouble, the country's economic leverage appeared minimal. Moreover, the point of détente was to diminish the need for American intervention abroad by directing the superpower contest with the Soviet Union into political channels.

Yet groups in the Third World didn't get the message of détente. In Central America, for example, there were uprisings against entrenched authoritarian regimes. In mid-1979,

TABLE 31.1 THE ELECTION OF 1976

Candidate	Party	Popular Vote	Electoral Vote
Jimmy Carter	Democratic	40,828,587	297
Gerald Ford	Republican	39,147,613	241

31.1

31.2

31.3

31.4

31.5

31.6

👁 Watch the Video **Jimmy Carter and the Crisis of Confidence**

JIMMY CARTER As national polls in the summer of 1979 reflected a profound loss of Americans' confidence in the leadership of President Jimmy Carter, the president attempted to rally the nation and redeem his presidency with his nationally televised "Crisis of Confidence" speech.

the Sandinistas in Nicaragua overthrew dictator Antonio Somoza. Despite American attempts to moderate the Sandinista revolution, the new regime moved steadily to the left, developing close ties with Cuba. In El Salvador, a leftist insurgency against a repressive regime put the United States in an awkward position. Unable to find an alternative between the extremes of reactionary dictatorship and radical revolution in Central America, Carter tried to encourage the military junta in El Salvador to carry out democratic reforms. But after the guerrillas launched a major offensive in January 1981, he authorized large-scale military assistance to the government, setting a precedent for the future.

Carter initially had better luck in the Middle East. In 1978, he invited Egyptian President Anwar Sadat and Israeli Prime Minister Menachem Begin to negotiate a peace treaty under his guidance at Camp David. For 13 days, Carter met with them, finally emerging with the **Camp David accords**. A framework for negotiations rather than an actual peace settlement, the accords nonetheless paved the way for a 1979 treaty between these antagonists. The treaty provided for the return of the Sinai to Egypt but left the fate of the Palestinians, the Arab inhabitants of the West Bank and the Gaza Strip, unsettled.

The Iranian Revolution in 1979 offset any sense of progress in the Middle East. Under Nixon and Kissinger, the United States had depended heavily on the shah for defense of the Persian Gulf. Carter continued this close relationship, despite growing

Camp David Accords In 1978, President Jimmy Carter mediated a peace agreement between the leaders of Egypt and Israel at Camp David. In 1979, Israel and Egypt signed a peace treaty based on the accords.

31.1
31.2
31.3
31.4
31.5
31.6

AMERICAN HOSTAGES Blindfolded American hostages stand among their Iranian captors after militants captured the American embassy in Tehran on November 4, 1979. The Iranians' capture of 53 American hostages and their violent attacks on the embassy shocked U.S. citizens.

domestic discontent with the shah's leadership. By 1978, Iran was in chaos as the exiled Ayatollah Ruholla Khomeini led a fundamentalist Muslim revolt that forced the shah to flee the country in January 1979.

In October 1979, Carter let the shah enter the United States for medical treatment. Mobs in Iran denounced the United States, and, on November 4, militants seized the U.S. embassy in Tehran and took 53 Americans prisoner. The ensuing **Iranian hostage crisis** revealed the decline of American power in the 1970s. Carter relied first on diplomacy and economic reprisals in a vain attempt to free the hostages. In April 1980, he authorized a desperate rescue mission that failed when helicopters broke down in the Iranian desert and an accident killed eight crewmen. The hostage crisis dragged on through 1980, a symbol of American weakness and a handicap to Carter in the presidential election.

Iranian hostage crisis In 1979, Iranian fundamentalists seized the American embassy in Tehran and held 53 Americans hostage for over a year. The hostages were released on January 20, 1981, the day Ronald Reagan became president.

Quick Check

What happened at Camp David, and why were Americans taken hostage in Iran?

The Reagan Revolution

31.5   What was the "Reagan revolution"?

After the turmoil of the 1960s, the economic and political troubles of the 1970s made Americans' turn to conservatism almost inevitable. The Watergate scandal won the Democrats a reprieve, but with Ronald Reagan, a decisive Republican victory was essentially assured.

The Election of 1980

In 1980, Jimmy Carter, who had used the Watergate trauma to win the presidency, found himself in trouble. Inflation, touched off by the second oil shock of the 1970s,

31.1

31.2

31.3

31.4

31.5

31.6

reached double-digit figures. The Federal Reserve Board's tighter money supply had led to a recession, with unemployment climbing to nearly 8 percent by July 1980. What Ronald Reagan dubbed the "misery index," the combined rate of inflation and unemployment, hit 28 percent early in 1980 and stayed above 20 percent throughout the year.

Foreign policy proved almost as damaging to Carter. The Soviet invasion of Afghanistan in 1979 had exploded hopes for continued détente and made Carter appear naive. The hostage crisis in Iran underlined the administration's helplessness.

Reagan and his running mate, George H. W. Bush, hammered away at the state of the economy and the world. Reagan scored heavily among traditionally Democratic blue-collar groups by blaming Carter for inflation, which robbed workers of any gain in real wages. Reagan also accused Carter of allowing the Soviets to outstrip the United States militarily and promised a massive buildup of American forces if he was elected. The independent candidacy of liberal Republican John Anderson, who appealed to voters disenchanted with Carter but not yet ready to embrace Reagan, further hurt Carter.

The president claimed that Reagan was too reckless to conduct American foreign policy in the nuclear age. Charging that the election would decide "whether we have peace or war," Carter tried to portray his Republican challenger as a warmonger. Reagan summarized the case against the administration by asking voters a simple question: "Are you better off now than you were four years ago?"

The answer was "no." Reagan carried 44 states and gained 51 percent of the popular vote. Carter won only six states and 41 percent of the popular vote. Anderson received the remaining 8 percent but failed to carry a single state. (See Map 31.3). The growing political

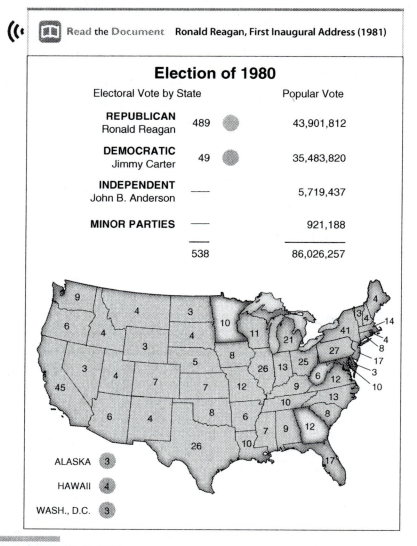

MAP 31.3 ELECTION OF 1980

power of the Sunbelt helped Reagan; he carried every state west of the Mississippi except Minnesota, the home state of Carter's running mate, Walter Mondale. In the South, Reagan lost only Georgia, Carter's home state. Even more impressive were Reagan's inroads into the old New Deal coalition. He received 50.5 percent of the blue-collar vote and 46 percent of the Jewish vote, the best showing by a Republican since 1928. Only one group remained loyal to Carter: African American voters gave him 85 percent of their ballots.

Republican gains in Congress were even more surprising. For the first time since 1954, the GOP gained control of the Senate, 53 to 46, and the party picked up 33 seats in the House.

Though the full implications of the 1980 election remained to be seen, the outcome suggested that the Democratic coalition that had dominated American politics since FDR was falling apart. In the eight presidential elections from 1952 to 1980, Republican candidates received 52.3 percent of the popular vote, compared with 47.7 percent for the Democrats. Reagan's victory thus marked the culmination of a Republican presidential realignment that ended a half-century of Democratic dominance.

Quick Check

Why did Americans find Reagan so attractive?

Cutting Taxes and Spending

When Ronald Reagan took office in January 1981, inflation had devastated the economy. Interest rates hovered near 20 percent, while the value of the dollar, compared to 1960, had dropped to just 36 cents. The new president blamed what he termed "the worst economic mess since the Great Depression" on high federal spending and excessive taxation. "Government is not the solution to our problems," Reagan announced in his inaugural address. "Government is the problem."

The president embraced the concept of **supply-side economics** as the remedy for the nation's economic ills. Supply-side economists believed that the private sector, if encouraged by tax cuts, would shift its resources from tax shelters to productive investment, leading to an economic boom that would provide enough new income to offset the lost revenue. Although many economists worried that the 30 percent cut in income taxes that Reagan favored would lead to large deficits, the president was confident that his program would both stimulate the economy and reduce the role of government.

The president made federal spending his first target. Quickly deciding not to attack such popular middle-class entitlement programs as Social Security and Medicare, and sparing critical social services for the "truly deserving needy," the so-called safety net, the Republicans slashed $41 billion from the budget by cutting other social services such as food stamps and reducing public service jobs, student loans, and support for urban mass transit. Reagan used his charm and powers of persuasion to woo conservative Democrats from the West and South. Appearing before a joint session of Congress only weeks after an attempt on his life, Reagan won a commanding 253 to 176 margin of victory for his budget in the House, and an even more lopsided vote of 78 to 20 in the Senate. A jubilant Reagan said he had achieved "the greatest reduction in government spending that has ever been attempted."

The president proved equally successful in trimming taxes. He initially advocated annual cuts of 10 percent in personal income taxes for three consecutive years. When the Democrats countered with a two-year plan that would reduce taxes by only 15 percent, Reagan compromised with a proposal to cut taxes by 5 percent the first year but insisted on the full 10 percent reduction for the second and third years. In July, both houses passed the tax cut.

The president's economic program yielded mixed results. A sharp recession during 1981–1982 (engineered partly by the Federal Reserve to reduce inflation) drove unemployment to its highest level since World War II, and the tax cuts contributed to record federal budget deficits. But the overall performance of the economy in the 1980s was decidedly better than in the 1970s, with inflation down and jobs up. And in getting the policies he wanted, Reagan demonstrated his ability to wield presidential power. As *Time* magazine commented, no president since FDR had "done so much of such magnitude so quickly to change the economic direction of the country."

supply-side economics The theory that tax cuts would stimulate the economy by giving individuals more incentive to earn more money, which would lead to greater investment and eventually larger tax revenues at a lower rate.

Quick Check

What was Reagan's philosophy on taxes?

31.1
31.2
31.3
31.4
31.5
31.6

31.1

31.2

31.3

31.4

31.5

31.6

Reagan and the World

31.6 How did Reagan reshape American foreign relations?

Reagan was determined to reverse American policy abroad no less than at home. He believed that under Carter, American prestige and standing in the world had dropped to an all-time low. Intent on restoring American pride and influence, Reagan devoted himself to strengthening America's defenses and recapturing world supremacy from the Soviet Union.

Challenging the "Evil Empire"

The president scored his first foreign policy victory on the day he took office, thanks to diplomatic efforts begun under Carter. On January 20, 1981, Iran released the American hostages and enabled Reagan to begin his presidency on a positive note.

He built upon this accomplishment by embarking on a major military expansion. Here again he continued efforts begun by Carter, who after the Soviet invasion of Afghanistan had persuaded Congress to fund a 5 percent increase in defense spending. But the Reagan expansion went beyond Carter's. Secretary of Defense Caspar Weinberger proposed more than doubling defense spending. The emphasis was on new weapons, ranging from the B-1 bomber and the controversial MX nuclear missile to the expansion of the navy from 456 to 600 ships. Despite opposition in Congress, Reagan and Weinberger got most of what they wanted, and by 1985 the defense budget exceeded $300 billion.

The justification for this spending was Reagan's belief that the Soviet Union threatened the well-being and security of the United States. Reagan saw the Russians as bent on world revolution, ready "to commit any crime, to lie, to cheat" to advance their cause. Citing what he called a "record of tyranny," Reagan denounced the Russians before the UN in 1982, claiming that "Soviet-sponsored guerrillas and terrorists are at work in Central and South America, in Africa, the Middle East, in the Caribbean and in Europe, violating human rights and unnerving the world with violence."

Given his view of Russia as "the evil empire," it is not surprising that Reagan continued the hard line that Carter had adopted after the invasion of Afghanistan. Abandoning détente, Reagan implemented a 1979 decision to place 572 Pershing II and cruise missiles in Western Europe within range of Moscow and other Russian cities to match Soviet deployment of medium-range missiles aimed at NATO countries. Despite Soviet protests, uneasiness in Europe, and a vocal opposition at home, the United States began putting the weapons in Britain and Germany in 1983. The Soviets, claiming the move gave them only ten minutes of warning time if America attacked, broke off disarmament negotiations in Geneva.

The nuclear arms race was now more dangerous than ever. The United States stepped up research and development of the **Strategic Defense Initiative (SDI)**, an antimissile system based on the use of lasers and particle beams to destroy incoming missiles in outer space. The media dubbed it "star wars." Critics doubted that SDI could be perfected, but they warned that even if it were, it would escalate the arms race by forcing the Russians to build more offensive missiles to overcome the American defense system. The Reagan administration, however, defended SDI as a legitimate attempt to free the United States from the deadly trap of deterrence, with its reliance on the threat of nuclear retaliation to keep the peace. Meanwhile, the Soviet Union kept deploying larger and more accurate land-based ICBMs. Although both sides observed the unratified SALT II agreements, the two superpowers had nearly 50,000 nuclear warheads between them.

Confrontation in Central America

Reagan saw the Soviet challenge as global. In Central America, an area of extremes of wealth, with a small landowning elite and masses of poor peasants, the United States had

Strategic Defense Initiative (SDI) Popularly known as "Star Wars," President Ronald Reagan's SDI proposed to construct an elaborate computer-controlled antimissile defense system capable of destroying enemy missiles in outer space.

Quick Check

Why did Reagan think the Soviet Union was evil, and what did he intend to do about it?

traditionally looked for moderate, middle-class regimes to support. But these were hard to find, and Washington often ended up backing right-wing dictatorships rather than the leftist groups that advocated land reform and redistribution of wealth. Yet oppression by U.S.-supported regimes often drove reformers to embrace revolution. (See Map 31.4).

This was what happened in Nicaragua. To strengthen the middle-class elements in the Sandinista government and avoid forcing Nicaragua into the Cuban and Soviet orbit, Carter had extended American economic aid.

The Reagan administration reversed this policy. Secretary of State Alexander Haig cut off aid to Nicaragua in 1981, accusing the Sandinistas of driving out the moderates, welcoming Cuban advisers and Soviet military assistance, and supporting leftist guerrillas in El Salvador. The criticism became a self-fulfilling prophecy as Nicaragua grew even more dependent on Cuba and the Soviet Union.

The United States and Nicaragua were soon on a collision course. In April 1983, declaring that "the national security of all the Americas is at stake in Central America," Reagan asked Congress for the money and authority to oust the Sandinistas. When Congress, fearful of repeating the Vietnam fiasco, refused, Reagan opted for covert action. The CIA began supplying the Contras, exiles fighting the Sandinistas from bases in Honduras and Costa Rica. The U.S.-backed rebels tried to disrupt the Nicaraguan economy, raiding villages, blowing up oil tanks, and mining harbors. Then, in 1984, Congress passed the Boland Amendment, prohibiting any U.S. agency from spending money in Central America. The withdrawal of U.S. financial backing left the Contras in a precarious position.

31.1
31.2
31.3
31.4
31.5
31.6

Quick Check

How did Reagan deal with leftists in Central America?

Guatemala. Military coup against President Cerezo fails, May 1989; free elections held, 1993.

Haiti. Duvalier forced out of office, Feb. 1986; military coup against elected government, 1991.

Jamaica. Former socialist Michael Manley elected prime minister, Feb. 1989.

Nicaragua. Sandinista rebels come to power, 1979; Sandinista government defeated by opposition candidate Violetta Barrios de Chamorro, Feb. 1990.

El Salvador. Civil war, 1980–1990; opposing sides hold peace talks, 1990; peace treaty signed, 1992.

Grenada. U.S. and regional forces land after military coup, Oct. 1983; elections held, Dec. 1984.

Panama. U.S. forces invade and capture drug trafficker General Manuel Noriega, Dec. 1989; Noriega is flown to federal prison in United States, Jan. 1990.

Panama Canal. Canal Zone comes under Panamanian control, 1979; Canal comes under Panamanian control in 2000.

MAP 31.4 TROUBLE SPOTS IN CENTRAL AMERICA AND THE CARIBBEAN U.S. involvement in Central American trouble spots intensified in the 1980s and early 1990s.

Trading Arms for Hostages

Reagan was reelected easily in 1984. Voters gave him credit for reviving the economy and challenging communism. Democratic candidate Walter Mondale provided a jolt to the campaign by choosing Representative Geraldine Ferraro of New York as his running mate. But even the presence of the first woman on the national ticket of a major American party couldn't dent Reagan's popularity. He won 59 percent of the popular vote and every state but Mondale's home, Minnesota (see Table 31.2).

Iran-Contra affair The Iran-Contra affair involved officials in the Reagan administration secretly and illegally selling arms to Iran and using the proceeds to finance the Contra rebels in Nicaragua.

Yet the troubles abroad persisted. Not long after Reagan's second inauguration, his policies in the Middle East and Central America converged in the **Iran-Contra affair**. In mid-1985, Robert McFarlane, the national security adviser, began a new initiative to restore American influence in the Middle East. Concerned over the fate of six Americans held hostage in Lebanon by groups thought to be loyal to Iran, McFarlane proposed trading American antitank missiles to Iran in return for their release. The Iranians, desperate for weapons in the war they had been waging against Iraq since 1980, seemed willing to comply.

McFarlane was soon in over his head. He relied heavily on a young marine lieutenant colonel assigned to the National Security Council (NSC), Oliver North. North in turn sought the assistance of CIA director William Casey, who saw the Iran initiative as an opportunity to use the NSC to mount the kind of covert operation denied the CIA under the post-1975 congressional oversight policy. In 1986, when John Poindexter, a naval officer with little political experience, replaced McFarlane as national security adviser, Casey persuaded the president to ship TOW antitank missiles and HAWK anti-aircraft missiles to Iran.

The arms deal with Iran was bad policy, but what came next was criminal. Ever since the Boland Amendment had cut off congressional funding, the Reagan administration had been searching for ways to supply the Contras in Nicaragua. North was put in charge of soliciting donations from wealthy right-wing Americans. In early 1986, North had what he later described as a "neat idea" (apparently shared by Casey)—he could use profits from selling weapons to Iran (charging as much as $10,000 for a TOW that cost the United States only $3,500) to finance the Contras. North's ploy was both illegal and unconstitutional, since it meant usurping the congressional power of the purse.

Ultimately the secret got out. Officials tried to shield Reagan, and it was unclear whether the president had approved the Contra diversion. Reagan's reputation was tarnished. Subordinates, including North and Poindexter, were prosecuted. Casey died of a brain tumor.

Reagan the Peacemaker

Americans' tolerance of Reagan's mistakes in the Iran-Contra affair resulted in part from the progress he was making in U.S.-Soviet relations. Elected as an anticommunist hardliner, Reagan advocated cooperation with Moscow during his second term.

A change in leadership in the Soviet Union had much to do with the change in Reagan's approach. The death of Leonid Brezhnev in 1982, followed in rapid succession by the deaths of his aged successors, Yuri Andropov and Konstantin Chernenko, led to the selection of Mikhail Gorbachev, a younger and more dynamic Soviet leader, in 1985. Gorbachev was intent on improving relations with the United States as part of his policy of *perestroika* (restructuring the Soviet economy) and *glasnost* (political openness). Soviet economic performance was deteriorating, and the war in Afghanistan had become a running sore. Gorbachev needed a breathing spell in the arms race and a reduction in Cold War tensions to carry out his domestic reforms.

TABLE 31.2 THE ELECTION OF 1984

Candidate	Party	Popular Vote	Electoral Vote
Reagan	Republican	54,455,075	525
Mondale	Democratic	37,577,185	13

31.1

31.2

31.3

31.4

31.5

31.6

Watch the Video Ronald Reagan at the Berlin Wall

REAGAN AND GORBACHEV IN RED SQUARE During the summits between the two leaders, the American public grew to admire the Soviet premier for his policies of *perestroika* (restructuring) and *glasnost* (openness).

Summit meetings between Reagan and Gorbachev broke the chill in superpower relations and led in December 1987 to an **Intermediate Nuclear Forces Treaty (INF)**, by which the two sides agreed to remove and destroy all intermediate-range missiles in Europe. The most important arms-control agreement since SALT I in 1972, the INF treaty raised hopes that an end to the Cold War was in sight.

During the president's last year in office, the Soviets cooperated with the United States in pressuring Iran and Iraq to end their long war. Gorbachev also pulled the last Soviet troops out of Afghanistan in 1989. By the time Reagan left office, his foreign policy triumphs had offset the Iran-Contra fiasco and helped redeem his presidency.

Conclusion: Challenging the New Deal

Though trouble dogged the final years of his presidency, Reagan's two terms reshaped American politics. The Democratic coalition forged by FDR during the New Deal finally broke down as the Republicans captured the South and made inroads into organized labor.

More significantly, Reagan challenged the liberal premises of the New Deal by asserting that the private sector, rather than the federal government, ought to be the source of remedies to most of America's ills. Reagan left intact the centerpieces of the welfare state—Social Security and Medicare—but trimmed other programs and made any comparable expansion of federal authority nearly impossible for 20 years. By the time he left office, small-government conservatism seemed the undeniable wave of the American future.

Intermediate Nuclear Forces Treaty (INF) Signed by President Ronald Reagan and Soviet President Mikhail Gorbachev in late 1987, this agreement provided for the destruction of all intermediate-range nuclear missiles and permitted on-site inspection for the first time during the Cold War.

Quick Check

What did the INF Treaty do?

Chapter Review

The Tempting of Richard Nixon

31.1 What were the major accomplishments and failures of the Nixon presidency? p. 722

Nixon opened diplomatic relations with China and initiated détente with the Soviet Union. He withdrew American troops from Vietnam, terminating a quarter-century of American involvement. But his role in the Watergate scandal led to a constitutional crisis that forced him from office in disgrace.

Oil and Inflation

31.2 How were oil and inflation linked during the 1970s? p. 726

Oil prices jumped dramatically in the 1970s, as a result of growing demand for oil and turmoil in the Middle East. Rising oil prices contributed to the worst inflation in modern American history.

Private Lives, Public Issues

31.3 How did private life change during this period? p. 729

The divorce rate rose significantly, and the number of married couples with children declined. More women entered the professions, and *Roe v. Wade* guaranteed their right to an abortion. Gay men and lesbians achieved greater freedom than before, though they still lacked rights accorded to heterosexuals.

Politics and Diplomacy after Watergate

31.4 Why did the presidencies of Ford and Carter largely fail? p. 734

Ford and Carter had to deal with the aftermath of Vietnam and Watergate and the economic disruptions that followed the oil price increases of the 1970s. Ford alienated many Americans by pardoning Nixon, and Carter fumbled the hostage crisis in Iran.

The Reagan Revolution

31.5 What was the "Reagan revolution"? p. 737

The Reagan revolution was the return to conservatism in American politics and diplomacy upon Reagan's 1980 election as president. Reagan pledged to reduce the role of government in American life and restore American honor and confidence abroad.

Reagan and the World

31.6 How did Reagan reshape American foreign relations? p. 740

Reagan rejected détente and challenged the Soviet Union more directly than any American president in decades. He called for the creation of the SDI missile system, and he waged covert war against leftists in Central America. The Iran-Contra affair, in which Reagan traded arms for hostages, tarnished his reputation, but he also negotiated the INF treaty with the Soviet Union.

Timeline

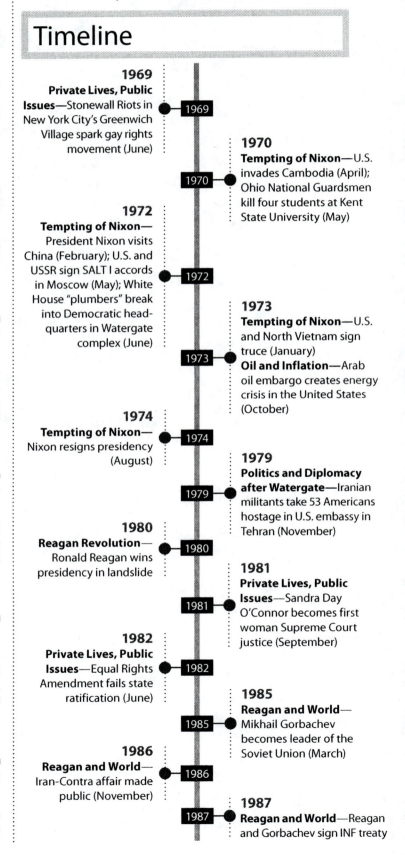

1969
Private Lives, Public Issues—Stonewall Riots in New York City's Greenwich Village spark gay rights movement (June)

1970
Tempting of Nixon—U.S. invades Cambodia (April); Ohio National Guardsmen kill four students at Kent State University (May)

1972
Tempting of Nixon—President Nixon visits China (February); U.S. and USSR sign SALT I accords in Moscow (May); White House "plumbers" break into Democratic headquarters in Watergate complex (June)

1973
Tempting of Nixon—U.S. and North Vietnam sign truce (January)
Oil and Inflation—Arab oil embargo creates energy crisis in the United States (October)

1974
Tempting of Nixon—Nixon resigns presidency (August)

1979
Politics and Diplomacy after Watergate—Iranian militants take 53 Americans hostage in U.S. embassy in Tehran (November)

1980
Reagan Revolution—Ronald Reagan wins presidency in landslide

1981
Private Lives, Public Issues—Sandra Day O'Connor becomes first woman Supreme Court justice (September)

1982
Private Lives, Public Issues—Equal Rights Amendment fails state ratification (June)

1985
Reagan and World—Mikhail Gorbachev becomes leader of the Soviet Union (March)

1986
Reagan and World—Iran-Contra affair made public (November)

1987
Reagan and World—Reagan and Gorbachev sign INF treaty

32 Into The Twenty-First Century 1989–2013

"This will not Stand": Foreign Policy in the Post–Cold War Era

O n the evening of **August 1, 1990, George H. W. Bush** sat in a T-shirt in the medical office in the basement of the White House. Bush was an avid golfer, but his duties as president kept him from playing as much as he would have liked, and when he did find time to squeeze in a round or some practice, he tended to overdo things. This summer day he had strained a shoulder muscle hitting practice balls, and now he rested on the exam table while a therapist applied deep heat. He planned a quiet evening and hoped the soreness would be gone by morning.

Two unexpected visitors altered his plans. Brent Scowcroft, Bush's national security adviser, and

GEORGE H.W. BUSH President George Bush confers with National Security Advisor Brent Scowcroft (left), White House Chief of Staff John Sununu (center), and Vice President Dan Quayle (right) at the Oval Office on August 1, 1990, following the Iraqi invasion of Kuwait.

LEARNING OBJECTIVES

32.1	32.2	32.3	32.3	32.3
What were the important issues in George H. W. Bush's presidency, and how were they handled? p. 748	How did the American population shift and grow between 1990 and 2013? p. 751	What were the accomplishments and failures of the Clinton administration? p. 756	How did George W. Bush become president, and what did he do in the White House? p. 760	What challenges faced Barack Obama and the American people during the first decade of the twenty-first century? p. 767

Listen to Chapter 32 on MyHistoryLab

From Chapter 32 of *American Stories: A History of the United States*, Third Edition. H. W. Brands, R. Hal Williams, T. H. Breen and Ariela J. Gross Copyright © 2015 by Pearson Education, Inc.

Watch the Video Series on MyHistoryLab

Learn about some key topics related to this chapter with the *MyHistoryLab Video Series: Key Topics in U.S. History*

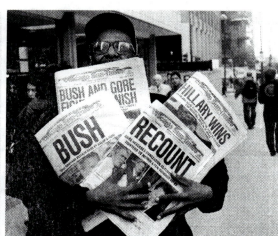

1 **Post–Cold War America: 1991–2000** The 1990s proved to be a pivotal decade for the contending forces of progressive politics and social and fiscal conservatism. This video provides an introduction to the decade as well as an overview of the presidency of George H. W. Bush, who continued the policies of Reagan era conservatism. It also touches on Bill Clinton's attempt to bring about a "Third Way" between the extremes of liberalism and conservatism.

 Watch on **MyHistoryLab**

The Los Angeles Riots In the summer of 1991, after a group of Los Angeles police officers were acquitted of all charges related to the beating of Rodney King, an African American, simmering racial tensions burst to the surface. This video describes how a simple traffic citation led to nearly a week of violence, and destruction that ultimately required military intervention. **2**

Watch on **MyHistoryLab**

3 **The Clinton Years** The election of President Bill Clinton in 1992 seemed improbable given that the incumbent George H.W. Bush had won the Gulf War and overseen the collapse of communism in Europe. However, aided by a strong showing by third-party candidate Ross Perot, Clinton won a surprise victory and took the Democratic Party in a more centrist direction while at the same time championing legislation meant to improve the lives of women and families. This video covers Clinton's election and a series of other highlights, including Clinton's sexual misconduct while in office, which led to his impeachment by the House of Representatives.

 Watch on **MyHistoryLab**

The Election of 2000 The highly controversial 2000 presidential election saw the Supreme Court intervene in the electoral process as it never had before. This video relates how the court halted a recount in Florida and thereby handed the election to George W. Bush despite Al Gore's victory in the popular vote. **4**

Watch on **MyHistoryLab**

Richard Haass, the Middle East expert of the National Security Council, appeared at the door of the exam room. Bush had known Scowcroft for years, and the look on his face told him something was amiss. Scowcroft's words confirmed the impression: "Mr. President, it looks very bad. Iraq may be about to invade Kuwait."

For months the Bush administration had been monitoring a territorial and financial dispute between Iraq and Kuwait. Iraqi dictator Saddam Hussein was rattling the saber against much smaller Kuwait, but he had rattled sabers before without actually using them. The previous week Saddam had met with the American ambassador in Iraq, April Glaspie, who came away with the belief that his bellicose talk was chiefly for political effect. The United States had indicated its displeasure with Saddam's threats, and Glaspie judged that he had gotten the message. "He does not want to further antagonize us," she wrote to Washington.

Saddam's decision to invade Kuwait at the beginning of August therefore caught the Bush administration by surprise. American intelligence agencies detected Iraq's mobilization; this was what brought Scowcroft and Haass to the White House on August 1. Haass suggested that the president call Saddam and warn him not to attack. But even as Bush considered this suggestion, Scowcroft received a message that the American embassy in Kuwait had reported shooting in Kuwait City. "So much for calling Saddam," Bush said. Within hours the Iraqi forces crushed Kuwaiti resistance.

Bush, Scowcroft, and other American officials recognized that the Iraqi takeover of Kuwait constituted the first crisis of the post–Cold War era. As Lawrence Eagleburger, the deputy secretary of state, asserted in an emergency meeting of the National Security Council, "This is the first test of the postwar system. As the bipolar world is relaxed, it permits this, giving people more flexibility because they are not worried about the involvement of the superpowers." During the Cold War, a de facto division of labor had developed, with the United States and the Soviet Union each generally keeping its clients and allies in line, typically by threatening to withhold weapons or other assistance. Had the Soviet Union still been a superpower, Saddam, a longtime recipient of Soviet aid, likely would have heeded Moscow's warnings to settle his dispute with Kuwait peacefully. But in 1990, the Soviet system was disintegrating, and the Kremlin's clients were on their own. "Saddam Hussein now has greater flexibility because the Soviets are tangled up in domestic issues," Eagleburger explained. The world was watching. "If he succeeds, others may try the same thing."

This belief shaped the Bush administration's response to the crisis. The president and his advisers understood that they were entering uncharted territory after the Cold War. As the sole remaining superpower, the United States could employ its military and economic resources more freely than at any time in history. But with that freedom came unprecedented responsibility. During the Cold War the United States could cite the threat of Soviet retaliation as reason to avoid intervening in the affairs of other countries; with that threat gone, American leaders would have to weigh each prospective intervention on its own merits. If one country attacked another, should the United States defend the victim? If the government of a country oppressed its own people, should the United States move to stop the oppression? These questions—and the answers American presidents gave to them—would define American foreign policy in the era after the Cold War.

Bush sensed the importance of the United States' responses, and he acted accordingly. He convened his principal deputies for a series of White House meetings. The particular stakes with Iraq and in the sounding Persian Gulf were discussed at length. "The rest of the world badly needs oil," Defense Secretary Dick Cheney observed, stating the obvious. Saddam's seizure of Kuwait gave him control of much of the world's oil supply, but the real prize was Saudi Arabia. "Saudi Arabia and others will cut and run if we are weak," Cheney predicted.

Bush consulted America's oldest allies. Britain's Margaret Thatcher urged the president to oppose Saddam most vigorously: "If Iraq wins, no small state is safe. We must win this. . . . We cannot give in to dictators."

Bush asked his generals what his military options were. "Iraq is not ten feet tall, but it is formidable," Norman Schwarzkopf, the U.S. commander for the Middle East, replied. American air power could punish Saddam and perhaps soften him up, but ground forces—in large numbers—would be required to guarantee victory.

By August 5, Bush had made up his mind. As he exited the helicopter that brought him back to the White House from another high-level meeting, reporters crowded the South Lawn. They asked what he was planning to do.

"I'm not going to discuss what we're doing in terms of moving forces, anything of that nature," Bush answered. "But I view it very seriously, not just that but any threat to any other countries." Bush was no orator, and these remarks were unscripted. But one sentence summarized the policy that soon began to unfold: "This will not stand, this aggression against Kuwait."

The First President Bush

What were the important issues in George H. W. Bush's presidency, and how were they handled?

Elected on the strength of his association with Ronald Reagan, George H. W. Bush appeared poised to confirm the ascendancy of the conservative values Reagan forced to the center stage of American life. But events, especially abroad, distracted Bush, whose principal contribution proved to be in foreign affairs. Bush brought the Cold War to a peaceful and triumphant conclusion, and he launched America toward the twenty-first century, an era when the United States faced new opportunities and new challenges.

Republicans at Home

Democrats approached the 1988 presidential election with high hopes, having regained control of the Senate in 1986 and not having to face the popular Reagan. But Vice President George H. W. Bush proved a stronger candidate than almost anyone had expected, and in a contest that confirmed the Republicans' hold on the Sunbelt, he defeated Massachusetts Governor Michael Dukakis. (see Table 32.1).

Many people expected the policies of the Bush administration to reflect the reputation of the new president—bland and cautious, lacking in vision but safely predictable. At home, he lived up (or down) to his reputation, sponsoring few initiatives in education, health care, or environmental protection, while continuing the Reagan theme of limiting federal interference in the everyday lives of Americans. He vetoed family leave legislation, declined to endorse meaningful health care reform, and watered down civil rights proposals in Congress. The one exception was the **Americans with Disabilities Act (ADA)**, passed in 1990, which prohibited discrimination against the disabled in hiring, transportation, and public accommodations. Beginning in July 1992, ADA called for all public buildings, restaurants, and stores to be made accessible to those with physical handicaps and required that businesses with 25 or more workers hire new employees without regard to disability.

The soaring federal budget deficit took up much of Bush's time on domestic affairs. The deficits Bush inherited from Reagan topped $150 billion per year, and conventional financial wisdom dictated that something be done to bring them down. In campaigning for president, Bush had promised "no new taxes," but in 1990, he broke the pledge. In a deal negotiated with the Congress, he agreed to a budget that included new taxes and substantial spending cuts, especially on the military. The resulting agreement projected a savings of $500 billion over five years, half from reduced spending and half from new revenue generated mainly by increasing the top tax rate from 28 percent to 31 percent and raising the gasoline tax by 5.1 cents a gallon.

Unfortunately for the president, the budget deal coincided with the beginning of a slow but painful recession that ended the Republican prosperity of the 1980s. Not only did Bush face recriminations from voters for breaking a campaign pledge not to raise taxes, but the economic decline led to greatly reduced government revenues. As a result, the deficit continued to soar, rising from $150 billion in fiscal year 1989 to just under $300 billion in 1992. Despite the 1990 budget agreement, the national debt increased by more than $1 trillion during Bush's presidency.

Americans with Disabilities Act Passed by Congress in 1991, this act banned discrimination against the disabled in employment and mandated easy access to all public and commercial buildings.

TABLE 32.1 THE ELECTION OF 1988

Candidate	Party	Popular Vote	Electoral Vote
Bush	Republican	48,886,097	426
Dukakis	Democratic	41,809,074	111

Ending the Cold War

Bush might have accomplished more in domestic affairs had not the international developments begun during the Reagan years accelerated dramatically. Bush had been in office only months when the communist system of the Cold War began falling apart. In country after country in eastern Europe, communism gave way to democracy as the old order collapsed more quickly than anyone had expected.

An early attempt at anticommunist liberation failed. In May 1989, Chinese students began a month-long demonstration for democracy in Beijing's Tiananmen Square that attracted worldwide attention. Watching American television coverage of Gorbachev's visit to China in mid-May, Americans were fascinated to see the Chinese students call for democracy with a hunger strike and a replica of the Statue of Liberty. But on June 4, the Chinese leaders sent tanks and troops to Tiananmen Square to crush the demonstration. By the next day, full-scale repression swept over China; hundreds of protesters were killed, and thousands injured. Martial law quelled the dissent and shattered hopes for a democratic China.

Bush responded cautiously. He wanted to preserve American influence with the Chinese government. Hence, despite denouncing the crackdown, Bush sent National Security Adviser Brent Scowcroft to Beijing to maintain a working relationship with the Chinese leaders.

A far more promising trend toward freedom began in Europe in mid-1989. In June, Lech Walesa and his Solidarity movement won free elections in Poland. Soon the winds of change were sweeping over the former Iron Curtain countries. Hungary opened its borders to the West in September, allowing thousands of East Germans to flee to freedom. One by one, the repressive governments of East Germany, Czechoslovakia, Bulgaria, and Romania fell. The most heartening scene took place in East Germany in early November when new communist leaders suddenly announced the opening of the Berlin Wall. Workers quickly demolished a 12-foot-high section of this despised symbol of the Cold War, joyously singing a German version of "For He's a Jolly Good Fellow."

Most people realized that Mikhail Gorbachev was responsible for the liberation of eastern Europe. In late 1988, the Soviet leader signaled the spread of his reforms to the Soviet satellites by announcing that the Brezhnev doctrine, which called for Soviet control of eastern Europe, was now replaced with "the Sinatra doctrine," which meant that the people of this region could do things "their way." Gorbachev's refusal to use armed force to keep repressive regimes in power permitted the long-delayed liberation of the captive peoples of eastern Europe.

Yet by the end of 1991, both Gorbachev and the Soviet Union had become victims of the demise of communism. On August 19, 1991, hard-line communists placed Gorbachev under arrest. Boris Yeltsin, the newly elected president of the Russian Republic, broke up the coup by mounting a tank in Moscow and demanding Gorbachev's release. The Red Army rallied to Yeltsin's side. The coup failed, and Gorbachev was released, only to resign in December 1991 after the 15 republics in the old USSR dissolved the Soviet Union. Russia, by far the largest and most powerful of these republics, joined with ten others to form a loose alignment called the Commonwealth of Independent States (CIS). Yeltsin then disbanded the Communist party and continued Gorbachev's reforms to establish democracy and a free market system in Russia.

The Bush administration, although criticized for its caution, welcomed the demise of communism. Bush facilitated the reunification of Germany and offered economic assistance to Russia and the other members of the CIS. On the critical issue of nuclear weapons, Bush and Gorbachev in 1991 signed START I, agreeing to reduce nuclear warheads to fewer than 10,000 apiece. In 1992, Bush and Yeltsin agreed on the terms of START II, which would eliminate land missiles with multiple warheads and reduce the number of nuclear weapons on each side to just over 3000, a level not seen since the mid-1960s.

((• 🏛 Read the Document   George H.W. Bush, Gulf War Address (1991)

FIGHTING IN IRAQ Anti-aircraft fire lights up the sky over Baghdad, Iraq, during the Persian Gulf War. A month of strikes on Iraqi targets was followed by a ground offensive that lasted only 100 hours before Iraqi troops began to surrender and President Bush ordered a ceasefire.

The Gulf War

Amid the disintegration of the Soviet system, Iraq in August 1990 invaded Kuwait. Although Bush quickly concluded that Saddam Hussein's aggression must be reversed, removing Iraq from Kuwait took time and effort. The president started by persuading Saudi Arabia to accept a huge American troop buildup, dubbed Desert Shield. This would prevent Saddam from advancing into Saudi Arabia and allow the United States to launch a ground attack against Iraqi forces.

While the American buildup mounted, Bush arranged an international coalition to condemn the Iraqi invasion and endorse economic sanctions against Iraq. Not every member of the coalition subscribed to the "new world order" that Bush said the liberation of Kuwait would help establish, but all concurred in the general principle of deterring international aggression. Essential to the success of Bush's diplomatic offensive was the support of the Soviet Union, which during the Cold War had regularly blocked American initiatives in the United Nations. Soviet leaders may have wished to see Saddam punished, but they also hoped to receive American aid in restructuring their economy.

Congress required more convincing. Many Democrats supported economic sanctions against Iraq but opposed using force. Yet as the troop buildup in the Persian Gulf proceeded—as Operation Desert Shield evolved into **Operation Desert Storm**—and as the sanctions failed to dislodge Iraq from Kuwait, some skeptics came around. After securing UN support for military action, Bush persuaded Congress (with just five votes to spare in the Senate) to approve using force to liberate Kuwait.

On January 17, 1991, the president unleashed a devastating aerial assault on Iraq. After knocking out the Iraqi air defense network in a few hours, F-117A stealth fighters and Tomahawk cruise missiles hit key targets in Baghdad. The air attack wiped out command and control centers and enabled the bombers of the United States and its coalition partners (chiefly Britain) to demoralize the enemy troops.

After five weeks of this, Bush gave the order for the ground assault. Led by General Schwarzkopf, American and allied armored units swept across the desert in a great

Operation Desert Storm The American and coalition military offensive against Iraq in 1991, which liberated Kuwait and dealt a serious but not fatal blow to Saddam Hussein's regime.

Quick Check

How did Bush respond to international crises during his presidency?

flanking operation while U.S. marines and Saudi troops drove directly into Kuwait City. In just 100 hours, the American-led offensive liberated Kuwait and sent Saddam Hussein's vaunted Republican Guard fleeing back into Iraq.

President Bush, acting on the advice of General Colin Powell, chairman of the Joint Chiefs of Staff, then halted the advance and agreed to an armistice with Iraq. Critics claimed that with just a few more days of fighting, perhaps even just a few more hours, American forces could have ended Saddam's cruel regime. But the president, fearful of disrupting the allied coalition and of becoming mired down in a guerrilla war, stopped when he had achieved his announced goal of liberating Kuwait. Moreover, he hoped that a chastened Saddam would help balance the threat of Iran in the volatile Persian Gulf region.

The Changing Faces of America

32.2   How did the American population shift and grow between 1990 and 2013?

From the *Mayflower* to the covered wagon and beyond, movement has always characterized the American people. The late twentieth and early twenty-first centuries witnessed two significant shifts in the American population: continued movement internally to the Sunbelt region of the South and West, and an influx of immigrants from developing nations. These changes led to increased urbanization, greater ethnic diversity, and growing social unrest.

A People on the Move

By the 1990s, a majority of Americans lived in the **Sunbelt** of the South and West. Best defined as a broad band running across the country below the 37th parallel from the Carolinas to Southern California, the Sunbelt had begun to flourish with the buildup of military bases and defense plants during World War II. Rapid population growth continued with the stimulus of heavy Cold War defense spending and accelerated in the 1970s when lower labor costs and the favorable climate of the Sunbelt states attracted both high-technology firms and more established industries. Florida, Texas, and California led the way, each gaining more than 2 million new residents in the 1970s.

The flow continued over the next two decades. The Northeast and the Middle West continued losing people to the South and West, and in 1994, Texas surpassed New York as the nation's second most populous state. The 2000 census revealed that while all regions had gained population in the 1990s, the South and West had expanded by nearly 20 percent, compared to around 6 percent for the Northeast and Middle West. Phoenix, Arizona, was typical of the phenomenal growth of Sunbelt cities, adding a million residents in the 1990s to grow at a 45 percent rate. "Phoenix is flat and it's easy," explained a geographer who saw no end in sight. "You stick a shovel in the ground and pour a slab and you have a house."

The increasing urbanization of America had positive and negative aspects. People living in the large metropolitan areas were both more affluent and better educated than their rural counterparts. Family income among people living in the bigger cities and their suburbs was $9,000 a year higher, and three-fourths of the urban population had graduated from high school, compared to two-thirds of other Americans. A metropolitan American was twice as likely to be a college graduate as a rural resident. Yet higher urban crime rates, longer commutes in heavy traffic, and higher living costs offset these advantages. Nevertheless, the big cities and their suburbs continued to thrive, accounting for 80 percent of all Americans by 2000.

Another striking population trend was the rise in the number of the elderly. In 1900, only 4.1 percent of the population was aged 65 or older; by 2010, those over 65 made up more than 13 percent of the population. Census Bureau projections suggest that by 2030, one out of every five Americans will be over age 65.

Sunbelt A broad band of states running across the South from Florida to Texas, extending west and north to include California and the Pacific Northwest. Beginning in the 1970s, it experienced rapid economic and population growth.

IMMIGRANTS BECOME CITIZENS Newly sworn-in citizens of the United States wave U.S. flags during a naturalization ceremony in Miami on April 28, 2006. Days later, more than a million immigrants participated in a nationwide boycott called "A Day Without Immigrants" to protest the proposed tightening of U.S. immigration laws.

The Revival of Immigration

The flow of immigrants into the United States grew dramatically between 1990 and 2010. By 2010, a record high of 38 million foreign-born persons lived in the United States, constituting 12 percent of the population.

The new immigrants came mainly from Latin America and Asia. By 2010, over half the foreign-born population of the United States came from Latin America, about one-quarter from Asia, and about one out of seven from Europe. The new immigrants tended to settle in urban areas in six states—California, Texas, New York, Florida, Illinois, and New Jersey. In California especially, the influx of immigrants from Asia and Mexico created growing pressure on public services.

The arrival of so many immigrants was bound to lead to controversy over whether immigrants were a benefit or a liability to American society. A study by the National Academy of Sciences in 1997 reported that while government services used by immigrants—schools, welfare, health clinics—cost more initially than was collected from them in taxes, in the long run, immigrants and their families more than paid their way. Immigrants tended to help consumers and employers by working for relatively low wages in restaurants, the textile industry, and farming, but they hurt low-skilled U.S. workers, notably high school dropouts and many African Americans, by keeping wages low. Economist George J. Borjas, a refugee from Cuba, claimed that immigrants from developing countries lacked the education and skills to achieve the prosperity previous newcomers attained; instead of entering mainstream American life, they were likely to remain a permanent underclass.

Emerging Hispanics

Hispanics became the nation's largest ethnic group in 2002, surpassing African Americans for the first time. The Hispanic population climbed to over 49 million by 2010, accounting for 16 percent of the nation's population. "It doesn't surprise me," commented the leader of the League of Latin American Citizens. "Anybody that travels around . . . can see Latinos everywhere, working everywhere, trying to reach the American dream."

The Census Bureau identified four major Hispanic groups: Mexican Americans, Puerto Ricans, Cuban Americans, and other Hispanics, including many from Central America. Even though most of the Hispanic population was concentrated in cities such as New York, Los Angeles, San Antonio, and Miami, recent data showed a surprising geographical spread. Hispanics made up 20 percent of the population in individual counties in states such as Georgia, Iowa, and Minnesota. "The Latinization of the country is not just happening in New York, Miami, or L.A.," observed a Puerto Rican leader. "Its greatest impact is in the heartland in places like Reading, Pennsylvania; Lorain, Ohio; and Lowell, Massachusetts."

The Hispanic groups had several features in common. All were relatively youthful, with a median age of 27 (compared to 37 for the nation as a whole) and a high fertility rate. They tended to be relatively poor, with one-fourth falling below the poverty line, and to be employed in low-paying positions as manual laborers, domestic servants, and migrant workers. Although their position had improved considerably in the boom years of the 1980s and 1990s, Hispanics still lagged behind mainstream America. The poverty rate among Hispanics was twice the national average, and family median income in 2009 was $38,000 (against $50,000 for the country as a whole).

Lack of education was a key factor in preventing economic progress. Fewer Hispanics graduated from high school than other minorities, and their school dropout rate was the nation's highest at more than 50 percent. Hispanic leaders warned that these figures boded ill not just for their own group, but for society as a whole. "You either educate us," claimed a San Antonio activist, "or you pay for building more jails or for more welfare."

The entry of millions of illegal immigrants from Mexico, once derisively called "wetbacks" and now known as **undocumented aliens**, created a social problem for the nation and especially for the Southwest. Critics charged that the flagrant violation of the nation's border with Mexico had led to a subculture beyond the boundaries of law and ordinary custom. They argued that the aliens took jobs from U.S. citizens, kept wages artificially low, and received welfare and medical benefits that strained budgets in states such as Texas and California.

Defenders of the undocumented aliens contended that the nation gained from the abundant supply of workers who were willing to work in fields and factories at backbreaking jobs most Americans shunned. Moreover, defenders stated, illegal entrants usually paid sales and withholding taxes but rarely used government services for fear of being deported. Whichever view was correct, an exploited class of illegal aliens was living on the edge of poverty. As the *Wall Street Journal* observed, "The people who benefit the most from this situation are certainly the employers, who have access to an underground market of cheap, productive labor, unencumbered by minimum wage laws, union restrictions, or pension requirements."

Concern over economic competition from Mexican "illegals" had led Congress in 1986 to penalize employers who hired undocumented workers. Congress permitted those aliens who could show that they were living in the United States before 1982 to become legal residents; nearly 3 million accepted this offer of amnesty to become legal residents. Nevertheless, undocumented workers continued to flow north from Mexico in the 1990s and early 2000s—more than 500,000 in some years. The most widely accepted estimates indicated that about 11 million foreigners, mainly from Mexico and Central America, were living illegally in the United States in 2010.

Despite stepped-up border enforcement after the September 11, 2001, terrorist attacks, illegal immigrants continued to move north from Mexico and Central America. The trip could be dangerous, even lethal. Border Patrol agents counted as many as 500 deaths per year among migrants attempting to enter the United States illegally

Quick Check

What are some of the issues at the core of the immigration debate?

undocumented aliens Illegal immigrants, mainly from Mexico and Central America.

during the first decade of the twenty-first century. In Pima County, Arizona, alone, authorities discovered 40 bodies during two weeks in the summer of 2010. Yet the movement continued. As one Mexican official said, "There are great problems in the countryside. And that famous American dream keeps calling."

Advance and Retreat for African Americans

African Americans formed the second largest ethnic minority. In 2010, the United States had 39 million blacks, 12.5 percent of the population. Although the heaviest concentration of African Americans was in northern cities, notably New York and Chicago, there was a significant movement back to the South. This shift, which began in the 1970s and accelerated during the 1990s, meant that by 2010 more than half of those identifying themselves as black for the census lived in the 16 states of the Sunbelt. Family ties and ancestral roots explained much of this movement, but it also reflected the same economic incentives that drew so many other Americans to the Sunbelt.

African Americans made gains in certain areas of life. In 2010, more than 80 percent of blacks aged 25 and older had earned a high school diploma, a substantial increase during the previous generation. Nearly one in five African Americans possessed a college degree. The number of black-owned businesses grew significantly.

Yet in other respects African Americans did less well. The black poverty rate was nearly 25 percent, and the median income for black families was less than two-thirds of that for whites. Blacks remained clustered in entry-level jobs, where they faced

KATRINA In August 2005, catastrophic Hurricane Katrina devastated much of the Louisiana and Mississippi Gulf Coast. In the wake of the storm, the levee system of New Orleans failed and flooded nearly 80 percent of the city. Particularly hard hit were low-lying areas such as the Lower Ninth Ward, where police rescue boats are shown here rescuing residents.

competition from immigrants. The African American incarceration rate was much higher than the national average; in 2010, more than 10 percent of black males aged 25 to 29 were in prison, and, at current rates, one out of three black men could expect to spend time in a state or federal prison during his life. Blacks were also more likely to be victims of crime, especially violent crime. Homicide was the leading cause of death among black males between the ages of 15 and 34.

Two events, one from 1991 and the other from 2005, summarized the frustration African Americans felt. In March 1991, a bystander videotaped four Los Angeles policemen beating Rodney King, an African American who had been stopped for a traffic violation. The pictures of the rain of blows on King shocked the nation. Nearly a year later, when an all-white jury acquitted the four officers of charges of police brutality, rioting erupted in South Central Los Angeles that threatened the entire city when the police failed to respond promptly. In the aftermath of the riot, which took 53 lives (compared to 34 deaths in the 1965 riot in nearby Watts) and did more than $1 billion in damage, government and state agencies promised new help for inner-city dwellers. But the efforts produced little, and life for many urban blacks remained difficult and dangerous.

A tragedy of a different sort occurred 14 years later. In August 2005, Hurricane Katrina ravaged the Gulf Coast and broke levees in New Orleans. The high winds and water killed more than 1000 persons, destroyed hundreds of thousands of homes, and forced millions of men, women, and children to evacuate. Television cameras captured the plight of the thousands who took refuge in the New Orleans Superdome, only to be stranded when state and federal relief efforts failed. Most of those suffering the worst in New Orleans were black. Their neighborhoods were the lowest-lying in the city, and hence the worst flooded. Many lacked transportation to flee the city in advance of the hurricane; others lacked the means to pay for hotels or apartments had they been able to get out. Though the relief efforts were largely color-blind (despite allegations to the contrary), the experience demonstrated that poverty in America was not.

Americans from Asia and the Middle East

Asian Americans were the fastest-growing minority in 2000. As of 2010, there were more than 15 million Americans of Asian or Pacific Island descent. Although only 5 percent of the total population, they were increasing at seven times the national rate, and projections indicated that by 2050 one in ten Americans would be of Asian ancestry.

The Chinese formed the largest single group of Asian Americans, followed by Filipinos, Japanese, Indians, Koreans, and Vietnamese. Immigration was the primary reason for the rapid growth of all these groups except the Japanese; during the 1980s, Asia had provided nearly half of all immigrants to the United States. Though the influx slowed, the immigrants' children added to the Asian numbers.

Compared to other minorities, Asian Americans were well educated and affluent. Three out of four Asian youths graduated from high school, compared to fewer than one out of two blacks and Hispanics. Asian Americans also had the highest percentage of college graduates and doctoral degrees of any minority group; in fact, they were better represented in colleges and universities than the white majority. Many Asians entered professions, and the median income for Asian American families in 2010 was nearly 30 percent higher than the national average.

Not all fared so well, however. Refugees from Southeast Asia experienced hardship and persecution. The median family income for Vietnamese Americans was below the national average. Nearly half the Laotian refugees in Minnesota were unemployed because of difficulty learning to read and write English. Vietnamese fishermen on the Gulf Coast of Texas and Louisiana experienced repeated attacks on their livelihood and their homes. In the Los Angeles riots in 1992, Korean stores and shops were looted and firebombed.

But the overall experience of Asian Americans was positive. They came to America seeking economic opportunity, "to climb the mountain of gold." "People are looking for a better life," a Chinese spokeswoman explained. "It's as simple as that, and we will continue to come here, especially if the situations over there [in Asia] stay tight, or get worse."

The number of Americans from the Middle East grew almost as fast as those from Asia. By 2010, some 2 million Americans claimed Middle Eastern ancestry, 200,000 more than a generation earlier. Most came from Arab countries, Israel, and Iran. Concentrated in California, New York, and Michigan, Middle Eastern Americans were well educated; nearly half had college degrees. Many Arab Americans felt nervous after the terrorist attacks of September 11, 2001, committed by Arab extremists; some were assaulted by persons who blamed anyone of Arab descent for the mass murders. Yet most Arab Americans carried on as before, pursuing their interpretation of the American dream.

The New Democrats

| **32.3** | What were the accomplishments and failures of the Clinton administration? |

The Democrats, political victims of the runaway inflation of the 1970s, became the beneficiaries of the lingering recession of the early 1990s. Moving away from its traditional liberal reliance on big government, the party regained strength by choosing moderate candidates and tailoring its programs to appeal to the hard-pressed middle class. These tactics enabled the Democrats to regain

Watch the Video **Bill Clinton Sells Himself to America**

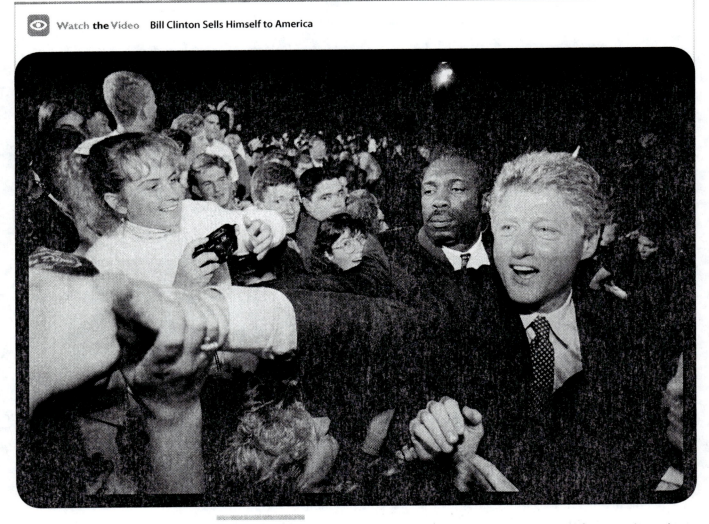

BILL CLINTON Twelve years of Republican administrations and economic turmoil left voters ready to make a change. Enter Bill Clinton, Democratic governor of Arkansas, who would best George Bush in the election of 1992 and go on to serve two full terms.

the White House in 1992 and retain it in 1996, despite a Republican sweep of Congress in 1994. The key figure in this political shift was Bill Clinton, who overcame early setbacks to reap the rewards of a sustained economic boom.

Clinton and Congress

A recession that began in 1990 soured voters on George H. W. Bush, allowing Clinton to defeat him in a three-way race that included eccentric Texas billionaire H. Ross Perot. Clinton proved to be the most adept politician since Franklin Roosevelt. Born in Hope, Arkansas, in 1946, Clinton weathered a difficult childhood with an alcoholic stepfather by developing skills at dealing with people and using personal charm to achieve his goals. Intelligent and ambitious, he completed his undergraduate work at Georgetown University, studied law at Yale, and spent two years as a Rhodes scholar at Oxford University in England. Entering politics, he was elected Arkansas attorney general and then governor. Defeated after his first term in 1980, Clinton won the nickname "Comeback Kid" by regaining the governor's office in 1982. He was elected three more times, earning a reputation as one of the nation's most successful young political leaders.

In keeping with the theme of his 1992 campaign, Clinton concentrated at first on the economy. In February 1993, he called for tax increases and spending cuts to achieve a balanced budget. Congress was skeptical of such unpopular measures, but Clinton cajoled, shamed, and threatened sufficient members to win approval of $241 billion in new taxes and $255 billion in spending cuts, for a total deficit reduction of $496 billion over four years. This earned Clinton the confidence of financial markets and helped fuel the economic boom of the 1990s.

Clinton scored another victory when Congress approved the **North American Free Trade Agreement (NAFTA)** in 1993. NAFTA, initiated and nearly completed by Bush, was a free trade plan that united the United States, Mexico, and Canada into a common market without tariff barriers. Clinton endorsed the treaty to secure American prosperity and spread American values. Critics complained that free trade would cost American workers their jobs as American companies moved production overseas; Ross Perot, the defeated 1992 third-party candidate, predicted a "giant sucking sound" as American jobs went south to Mexico. But Clinton won a bruising fight in the House and an easier contest in the Senate.

Although Clinton's NAFTA coalition included many congressional Republicans, on other issues the GOP opposed the president. Republicans said his budget entailed "the biggest tax increase in the history of the world," and they scuttled an ambitious attempt to revamp the nation's health care system. Leading the opposition was a young congressman from Georgia, Newton Leroy "Newt" Gingrich, who asked all GOP candidates in the 1994 congressional races to sign a ten-point **Contract with America**. The contract consisted of familiar conservative goals, including a balanced budget amendment to the Constitution, term limits for members of Congress, a line-item veto for the president, and a middle-class tax cut. For the first time in recent political history, a party sought to win Congress on ideological issues rather than relying on individual personalities.

Embarrassing disclosures involving Clinton's character made this tactic particularly effective. During the 1992 campaign, the *New York Times* had raised questions about a bankrupt Arkansas land development called Whitewater in which the Clintons had lost a modest investment. Other alleged scandals cropped up over activities that had taken place after Clinton was elected president. Travelgate was the name given to the firing, apparently at the urging of First Lady Hillary Clinton, of White House employees who arranged travel for the press covering the president. Then in early 1994, Paula Jones, a former Arkansas state employee, filed a sexual harassment suit, charging that in 1991 then-Governor Clinton had made sexual advances to her.

The outcome of the November 1994 vote stunned political observers. The Republicans gained nine seats in the Senate and 53 in the House to take control of both houses. Newt Gingrich became speaker of the House. The GOP also captured 32 governorships, including those of New York, California, and Texas, where George W. Bush, the son of the man Clinton beat in 1992, won handily.

North American Free Trade Agreement (NAFTA) A free trade plan among the United States, Canada, and Mexico enacted by Congress in 1993.

Quick Check

How did Clinton's relationship with Congress evolve throughout his administration

Contract with America In the 1994 congressional elections, Congressman Newt Gingrich had Republican candidates sign a document in which they pledged support for such things as a balanced budget amendment, term limits for members of Congress, and a middle-class tax cut.

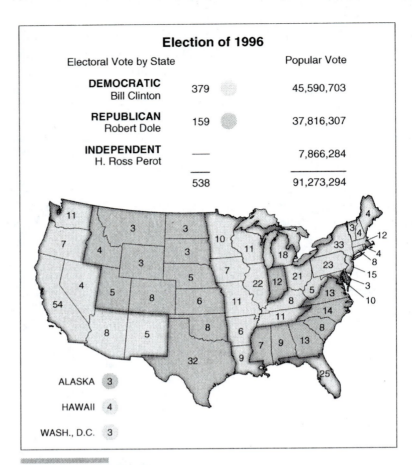

MAP 32.1 ELECTION OF 1996

The Republicans claimed a mandate to resume the Reagan revolution: to cut taxes, diminish the scope of government, and empower the private sector. Clinton and the Democrats managed to check the Republicans on matters of substance, but the Republicans in turn contrived to hobble Clinton. The administration and the Republicans collaborated on welfare reform and a modest increase in the minimum wage, but otherwise deadlock descended on Washington.

Clinton turned the deadlock to his benefit in 1996 after the Republicans, having failed to force him to accept cuts in Medicare, college loans, and other social services, refused to pass a budget bill, and thereby shut down the federal government. Clinton persuaded voters that the Republicans were to blame and carried this theme into his 1996 reelection campaign. The Republican nominee, Robert Dole of Kansas, lacked Clinton's charisma and failed to shake the impression that the Republicans were flint-hearts who wanted to cut the pet programs of the American people. Clinton won decisively, even while the Republicans continued to control Congress. (see Map 32.1).

Scandal in the White House

Despite Clinton's reelection, rumors of wrongdoing clung to his presidency. The special prosecutor appointed to probe the Whitewater transactions, Kenneth Starr, turned over stone after stone in search of malfeasance, until he came across rumors that Clinton had had an affair with a White House intern, Monica Lewinsky.

Clinton initially denied the affair. "I did not have sexual relations with that woman, Miss Lewinsky," he said in January 1998. But Starr subpoenaed Lewinsky, who eventually gave a detailed account of her sexual encounters with the president and provided crucial physical evidence implicating Clinton.

Realizing that he could no longer deny the affair, the president sought to limit the damage. On August 17, 1998, he appeared before Starr's grand jury and admitted to having "inappropriate intimate contact" with Lewinsky. That evening Clinton

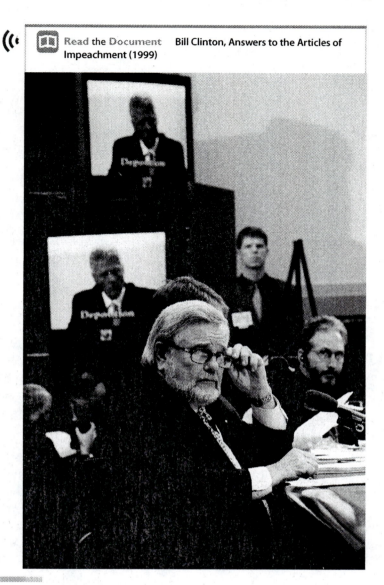

((• 📖 Read the Document   Bill Clinton, Answers to the Articles of Impeachment (1999)

CLINTON IMPEACHMENT   Chief Investigative Counsel David Schipper listens to Clinton's testimony during the hearings on the president's impeachment in December 1998. The House Judiciary Committee sent four articles of impeachment to the full House, and the House adopted two—one count of perjury and one of obstruction of justice.

spoke briefly to the nation. Claiming that he had given the grand jury "legally accurate" answers, the president admitted to a relationship with Lewinsky that was "not appropriate" and "wrong." He said he regretted misleading the people and especially his wife, but he refused to apologize for his behavior or his false denials.

But just when Clinton seemed most vulnerable, the special prosecutor inadvertently rescued him. In September, Starr sent a 452-page report to Congress outlining 11 possible impeachment charges against Clinton. The key one was perjury, and Starr provided painstakingly graphic detail on the sexual encounters between Clinton and Lewinsky to prove that the president had lied when he denied engaging in sexual relations with the intern.

Many Americans condemned Starr rather than the president. Shocked by the sordid details, they blamed the prosecutor for exposing families to distasteful sexual practices on the evening news. When Hillary Clinton stood staunchly by her husband, a majority of the public seemed to conclude that a president's conduct was a private matter to be settled between a husband and a wife, not in the public arena.

Republican leaders ignored this sentiment and pressed ahead with impeachment proceedings. In December, the House (where the 1998 midterm elections had narrowed the GOP advantage to six) approved two articles of impeachment—perjury and obstruction of justice—by nearly straight party-line votes.

The showdown in the Senate was anticlimactic. With a two-thirds vote required to find the president guilty and remove him from office, there was no chance of conviction in the highly charged partisan mood. On February 12, 1999, the GOP was unable to muster even a majority on the perjury charge, with 45 in favor and 55 opposed. After a second, closer vote, 50 to 50, on obstruction of justice, the presiding officer, Chief Justice William Rehnquist, declared, "Acquitted of the charges."

Clinton had survived the Lewinsky affair, but his presidency was damaged. His final two years in office would be devoted to a concerted effort to restore his reputation. Desperate for a legacy to mark his White House years, Clinton failed to realize that he had already created an enduring one—he would be remembered as the president who dishonored his office by his affair with a young intern.

Republicans Resurgent

32.4 How did George W. Bush become president, and what did he do in the White House?

Clinton's eight years in the White House gave Democrats hope that the conservative gains of the 1980s had been temporary. They pointed to the booming economy and the absence of a serious threat to American security as reasons for voters to leave the presidency in Democratic hands. The election of 2000 proved a bitter disappointment—all the more bitter because of how it made Republican George W. Bush president.

The Disputed Election of 2000

If history had been the guide, the prosperity of the 1990s should have guaranteed victory to Clinton's protégé, Vice President Al Gore. The state of the economy generally determines the outcome of presidential elections, and entering 2000 the American economy had never appeared stronger. The stock market soared, spreading wealth among tens of millions of Americans; the federal deficit of the Reagan years had given way to large and growing surpluses.

But Clinton's personal problems muddled the issue. Clinton had survived his impeachment trial, yet the experience tainted his record and left many voters unwilling to reward the Democrats by promoting his vice president.

Other domestic problems also unnerved voters. The 1995 bombing of a federal building in Oklahoma City by two domestic terrorists killed 168 people and suggested that irrational violence threatened ordinary Americans. This feeling was reinforced by a 1999 shooting rampage at Columbine High School near Denver, which left 12 students and a teacher dead, besides the two shooters, who killed themselves. The apparent conflict between material abundance and eroding personal values resulted in the closest election in more than a century.

The two candidates, Vice President Gore of Tennessee and Governor Bush of Texas, had little in common beyond being the sons of successful politicians. Gore had spent 18 years in Washington as a congressman, senator, and vice president. Somewhat stiff and aloof, he had mastered the intricacies of all the major policy issues and had the experience and knowledge to lead the nation. Bush, by contrast, had pursued a business career before winning the governorship of Texas in 1994. Personable and outgoing, Bush had the temperament for leadership but lacked not only experience but a full grasp of national issues. Journalists were quick to seize on the weaknesses of both men, accusing Gore of frequent and misleading exaggeration and Bush of mangling words and speaking only in generalities.

The candidacy of consumer advocate Ralph Nader, who ran on the Green party ticket, complicated the political reckoning. Nader never seemed likely to win more than a small percentage of the votes, but in a close election, a few points could make the difference. Nader's mere presence pushed Gore to the left, leaving room for Bush among independent-minded swing voters.

Election of 2000

Electoral Vote by State		Popular Vote
REPUBLICAN George W. Bush	271	50,456,167
DEMOCRATIC Al Gore	266*	50,996,064
GREEN Ralph Nader	—	2,864,810
OTHER	—	834,774
	537	105,151,815

*One District of Columbia Gore elector abstained.

ALASKA 3

HAWAII 4

WASH., D.C. 3

MAP 32.2 ELECTION OF 2000

On election night, Gore seemed the winner when the major television networks predicted a Democratic victory in Florida. They reconsidered as Bush swept the South, including the Clinton–Gore home states of Arkansas and Tennessee. After midnight, the networks again called Florida, but this time for Bush, and the vice president telephoned the governor to concede, only to recant an hour later when it became clear that the Bush margin in Florida was paper thin.

There things stuck, and for the next month all eyes were on Florida. Gore had 500,000 more popular votes nationwide than Bush, and 267 electoral votes to Bush's 246. Yet with Florida's 25 electoral votes, Bush could win the presidency. (see Map 32.2). Both sides sent lawyers to Florida. Bush's team, working with Florida's Republican secretary of state, sought to certify the results that showed the GOP candidate with a lead of 930 votes out of nearly six million cast. Citing voting problems disclosed by the media, Gore asked for a recount in three heavily Democratic counties in south Florida. All three used antiquated punch card machines that resulted in some ballots not being clearly marked for any presidential candidate when the chads, the bits of paper removed when a card is punched, were not completely detached from the cards. For weeks the results in Florida, and hence of the entire election, appeared to depend on how one divined the intent of a voter based on hanging, dimpled, or bulging chads.

The decision finally came in the courts. Democrats appealed the initial attempt to certify Bush as the victor to the Florida Supreme Court. The Florida court twice ordered recounts, the second time for all counties in the state, but Bush's lawyers appealed to the U.S. Supreme Court. On December 12, five weeks after the election, the Court overruled the state court's call for a recount in a 5 to 4 decision that reflected a long-standing ideological divide among the nine justices. The next day, Gore gracefully conceded, and Bush finally became president-elect.

✳ Explore the 2000 Election on MyHistoryLab

WHY DID DISAGREEMENT SURROUND THE 2000 PRESIDENTIAL ELECTION?

In 2000, the United States saw one of its closest presidential elections. The margin of victory between Republican George W. Bush and Democrat Al Gore was razor thin. In Florida especially, the popular vote was extremely close, and whichever candidate won the state would also win its electoral college votes and the national election itself. Numerous recounts were held in Florida and controversy ensued over what constituted a valid vote. The decision on who would be president

BUSH ON THE CAMPAIGN TRAIL Republican presidential candidate George W. Bush campaigns at this Oxnard, California, train station in 2000. Although ultimately the electoral college victor over Democrat Al Gore, Bush did not win the popular vote.

centered on questions such as whether so-called "hanging chads"—incompletely punched-through holes on punch-card ballots—should be legal votes. The results ended up before the Supreme Court, which decided in favor of Bush, who officially won Florida and the election with a majority of electoral college votes, although while his opponent Gore had more popular votes.

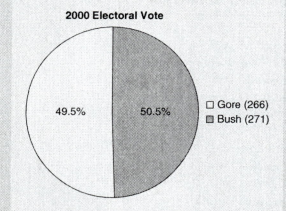

2000 Electoral Vote

49.5% | 50.5%

☐ Gore (266)
☐ Bush (271)

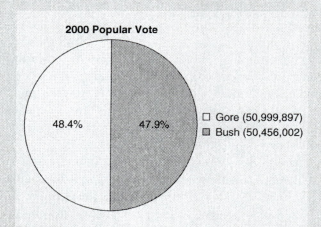

2000 Popular Vote

48.4% | 47.9%

☐ Gore (50,999,897)
☐ Bush (50,456,002)

2000 Presidential Election Results Summary

SOURCE: "2000 Presidential Electoral and Popular Vote," *FEC.gov*, http://www.fec.gov/pubrec/fe2000/elecpop.htm.

KEY QUESTIONS Use **MyHistoryLab** *Explorer* to **answer** these **questions:**

Analysis ▶▶▶ *What voting patterns influenced the 2000 election?*

Map the trends that still largely shape voting today.

Response ▶▶▶ *How did the election controversies in 2000 in Florida play out?*

Consider various socioeconomic factors and their correlations in the recounts.

Comparison ▶▶▶ *In what ways do various socioeconomic patterns correspond to American voting behavior?*

Chart such relationships to see their influence on elections.

Bush's narrow victory revealed deep divisions in American life. The rural West and South went for Bush, along with a few key Midwest and border states, while Gore won the urban states along both coasts. There was an equally strong divide along economic lines, with the poor voting for Gore, the rich for Bush, and the middle class dividing evenly between the two candidates. Gore benefited from the gender gap, winning 54 percent of the women's vote, and he won an even larger share of the black vote, 90 percent, than Clinton in 1996. Bush managed to narrow the Democratic margin among Hispanic voters, taking 35 percent, compared to only 28 percent for Dole four years earlier. The two candidates split the suburban vote evenly, while Bush reclaimed the Catholic vote for Republicans.

George W. Bush at Home

Bush's first order of business was a large tax cut, which required intense lobbying from the White House. The president had to win over enough conservative southern Democrats to compensate for losing Republican moderates who insisted on reducing the federal debt before cutting taxes. Bush managed the feat, and in June 2001, Congress slashed taxes by a staggering $1.35 trillion over a ten-year period. Many of the cuts would take effect only in future years, but Congress offered an immediate stimulus to the economy by authorizing rebates to taxpayers: $600 for couples and $300 for individuals earning more than $6000 a year. While critics saw this measure as a betrayal of the long effort to balance the budget, Bush contended that future surpluses would more than offset the loss of tax revenue.

A slowdown in the American economy, triggered by the bursting of the 1990s high-tech bubble, soon turned the projected budget surplus into annual deficits. But it failed to halt the Bush administration's tax cut momentum. In 2003, arguing that a further reduction in taxes would stimulate the stalled economy, Bush prevailed upon Congress to adopt another $350 billion in cuts. Like the 2001 cuts, the new reductions were temporary to preserve the possibility of a balanced budget by 2010. Opponents charged that if a future Congress made these tax cuts permanent, as seemed likely, the total cost would rise to nearly $1 trillion. While Clinton had favored eliminating the deficit, Bush made tax reduction the centerpiece of his economic policy.

The president also succeeded in persuading Congress to enact education reform. Borrowing the label "No Child Left Behind" from liberal Democrats, the administration pushed hard for a new policy requiring states to give annual performance tests to all elementary school students. Democrats countered with demands for increased federal funding of public education to assist states and local school boards in raising their standards. Bush shrewdly cultivated the support of Senator Edward Kennedy, a leading liberal Democrat, to forge a bipartisan consensus. The final measure increased federal aid to education by $4 billion, to a total of $22 billion annually, and mandated state tests in reading and math for all students in grades three through eight, and at least once during grades ten to twelve.

By this time the economic slowdown had become a full-blown recession, the first in ten years. A glut of unsold goods forced manufacturers to curtail production and lay off workers. Unemployment rose to six percent, despite the Federal Reserve's efforts to stem the decline by cutting interest rates. The tax rebates had boosted the economy slightly during the summer of 2001, but then the September 11 terrorist attacks led to a further decline. In 2002, the economy began to recover, only to relapse amid concern over the threat of war with Iraq.

One of the most troubling aspects of the economic downturn was the implosion of major corporations and the revelation of shocking financial practices. WorldCom, Inc., a telecommunications company, became the largest corporation in American history to declare bankruptcy, while a New York grand jury charged executives of Tyco International, an electronics company, with stealing more than $600 million from shareholders.

These scandals, however, paled before the misdeeds of Enron, a Houston energy company that failed in late 2001 as the result of astonishingly corrupt practices, including fraudulent accounting and private partnerships designed to inflate profits and hide losses. When investors began to sell their overvalued Enron stock, shares that were once worth nearly $100 fell to less than $1. Enron declared bankruptcy. The remaining share-holders lost over $50 billion, while rank-and-file employees lost not only their jobs but much of their retirement savings, invested largely in now worthless Enron stock.

The War on Terrorism

On the morning of September 11, 2001, 19 Islamic terrorists hijacked four U.S. airliners and turned them to attack targets in New York City and Washington, D.C. The hijack-ers took over two planes flying out of Boston's Logan Airport en route to California, and flew them into the World Trade Center (WTC) in New York. One plane slammed into the north tower just before 9:00 A.M., and the second hit the south tower only 20 minutes later. Within two hours, both towers had collapsed, killing nearly 3000 victims trapped in the buildings or crushed by the debris and more than 300 rescue workers who had attempted to save them.

In Washington, an American Airlines flight that left Dulles Airport for Los Angeles met a similar fate. Taken over by five terrorists, it plowed into the Pentagon, destroy-ing one wing of the building and killing 189 workers. The terrorists had seized a fourth plane, United Airlines flight 93, scheduled to fly from Newark, New Jersey, to San Francisco. Over Pennsylvania, as the hijackers attempted to turn the plane toward the nation's capital, the passengers fought to regain control of it. They failed to do so, but prevented the plane from hitting another target in Washington—perhaps the White House or the Capitol. Flight 93 crashed in southern Pennsylvania, killing all 44 pas-sengers and crew as well as the hijackers.

"None of us will forget this day," President Bush told the American people in a televised speech that evening. Bush vowed to find and punish those responsible for the attacks and any who assisted them: "We will make no distinction between those who planned these acts and those who harbor them."

Bush didn't have to look long to discover the mastermind behind the September 11 attacks. Osama bin Laden, a wealthy Saudi, released videotapes claiming responsibility on behalf of his terrorist organization, al Qaeda ("the Base" in Arabic). Bin Laden had been part of the international Muslim resistance to the Soviet invasion of Afghanistan, which had received support from the CIA in the 1980s. He turned against the United States during the Persian Gulf War, outraged by the presence of American troops in his native Saudi Arabia. Evidence linked bin Laden and al Qaeda to the bombing of two American embassies in East Africa in 1998 and to an attack on the American destroyer USS *Cole* in Yemen in 2000.

The United States had been trying to neutralize al Qaeda for a decade without suc-cess. Ordered out of Saudi Arabia in 1991, bin Laden had sought refuge in Sudan and in Afghanistan after the Taliban, another extremist Muslim group, took over that coun-try. In Afghanistan, bin Laden set up camps to train hundreds of would-be terrorists, mainly from Arab countries but including recruits from the Philippines, Indonesia, and Central Asia. After the 1998 embassy bombings, President Clinton ordered cruise missile attacks on these camps. The al Qaeda leader survived, though, leaving one of the targets only hours before the strike.

Bush's determination to go after those harboring terrorists made Afghanistan the prime target. The president ordered the Pentagon and the CIA, which already had agents on the scene, to destroy the Taliban, wipe out al Qaeda, and capture or kill Osama bin Laden.

In October 2001, the CIA and Army Special Forces began the operation, relying on the Northern Alliance, an Afghan political coalition resisting the Taliban. Using meth-ods ranging from bribes of local warlords to air strikes, American forces routed the Taliban and by December had installed a friendly regime in Kabul. Most of Afghani-stan, however, remained in chaos, and despite near misses, bin Laden avoided capture.

While waging the **war on terror** abroad, the Bush administration also focused on securing the United States from further terrorist assaults. At the president's urging, Congress approved a new Department of Homeland Security, combining the Customs

war on terror Initiated by President George W. Bush after the attacks of September 11, 2001, the broadly defined war on terror aimed to weed out terrorist operatives and their supporters throughout the world.

Bureau, the Coast Guard, the Immigration and Naturalization Service (INS), and other government bureaus.

A primary focus of homeland security was ensuring the safety of airline travel. In November 2001, Bush signed legislation replacing private companies with government employees at all airport screening stations. The airlines were required to replace cockpit doors with secure barriers and permit armed air marshals to ride among the passengers. The public fear of flying after September 11 nevertheless devastated the airline industry. Despite a $15 billion government bailout, the airlines experienced heavy losses. Several, including United Airlines, filed for bankruptcy. Although air travel began to revive in 2002, the industry, along with other forms of tourism, continued to be a drag on an already sluggish economy.

The war on terror raised an even more fundamental question than economic stagnation. Attorney General John Ashcroft, using new powers granted by Congress under the Patriot Act, conducted a broad crackdown on possible terrorists, detaining many Muslim Americans on flimsy evidence and insisting that concern for national security outweighed traditional civil liberties. Opponents argued that the terrorists would win their greatest victory if the United States violated its own historic principles of individual freedom in the name of fighting terrorism. The debate troubled many Americans who had difficulty reconciling the need for security with respect for civil liberties.

Widening the Battlefield

The terrorist attacks on the United States were the catalyst for a major change in foreign policy. The Bush administration initiated a new global policy of American preeminence. For the first time since the end of the Cold War, the United States had a clear, if controversial, blueprint for international affairs.

The new administration rejected traditional forms of international cooperation. President Bush ended U.S. participation in the Kyoto Protocol to control climate change and announced plans to terminate the 1972 Antiballistic Missile (ABM) treaty with Russia. And he was outspoken in refusing to expose American military personnel to the jurisdiction of the International Criminal Court for possible crimes committed in worldwide peacekeeping efforts.

The new direction of American foreign policy became clear on January 29, 2002, when Bush delivered his second State of the Union address. He repeated his vow to punish all nations sponsoring terrorism and denounced Iraq, Iran, and North Korea as constituting an "axis of evil." Nine months later, in September 2002, the Bush administration released a statement of its new world policy, "National Security Strategy (NSS) of the United States." The goal it declared was to "extend the peace by encouraging free and open societies on every continent."

There were two main components of the new strategy, which critics quickly called **unilateralism**. The first was to accept the role the nation had been playing since the end of the Cold War: global policeman. The United States would defend freedom anywhere in the world—with allies if possible, by itself if necessary. To implement this policy, the NSS asserted that the Bush administration would maintain "military strength beyond challenge. . . . Our forces will be strong enough to dissuade potential adversaries from pursuing a military buildup in hopes of surpassing, or equaling, the power of the United States."

As world cop, Bush and his advisers asserted the right to use preventive force. Reacting to September 11, the NSS continued, "We cannot let our enemies strike first." Although promising to seek the support of the international community before using force, "we will not hesitate to act alone, if necessary, to exercise our right of self-defense." In other words, the Bush administration, aware that the United States was far stronger militarily and economically than any other nation, asserted America's role as final arbiter of all international disputes.

Iraq quickly became the test case for this shift in American foreign policy. After his "axis of evil" speech, Bush focused on what he and his Pentagon advisers called **weapons of mass destruction (WMD)** that they claimed Saddam Hussein had been

unilateralism A national policy of acting alone without consulting others.

weapons of mass destruction (WMD) Biological, chemical, and nuclear weapons capable of widespread destruction.

Quick Check

What changes to American foreign policy were made during the War on Terror?

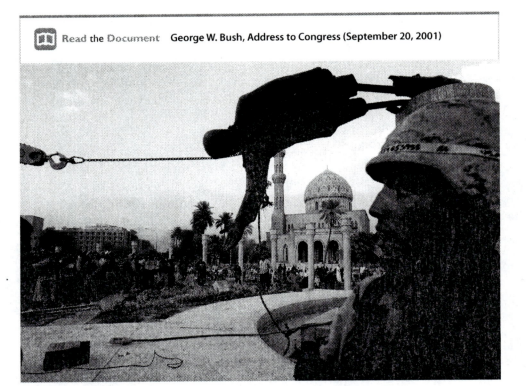

Read the Document   George W. Bush, Address to Congress (September 20, 2001)

SADDAM STATUE In a memorable image from the war in Iraq, Iraqi civilians and U.S. soldiers pull down a statue of Saddam Hussein in Baghdad on April 9, 2003.

secretly amassing. The United States demanded that Iraq permit UN inspectors (forced out of the country in 1998) to search for such weapons. Meanwhile, the Bush administration perfected plans for a unilateral American military solution to the Iraq question.

Slowly, but inexorably, the United States moved toward war with Iraq. Congress approved a resolution in October 2002 authorizing the president to use force against Saddam Hussein's regime. A month later, the UN Security Council voted unanimously to send its team of inspectors back into Iraq, warning Saddam of "severe consequences" if he failed to comply. Despite the failure of the international inspectors to find evidence of chemical, biological, or nuclear weapons in Iraq, the Bush administration kept pressing for a Security Council resolution authorizing the use of force to compel Saddam to disarm. When France and Russia vowed to veto any such measure, Bush and his advisers decided to proceed on their own. Preventive war would have its first real test.

The ensuing conflict with Iraq surprised both the backers and the critics of unilateralism. In March 2003, 65,000 American troops began to invade Iraq from Kuwait. Britain, the only major power to join the United States in the fighting, helped by besieging the city of Basra and taking control of southern Iraq. By April 8, just three weeks after the fighting had begun, marines marched virtually unopposed into the heart of Baghdad. Americans watched joyous Iraqis toppling a statue of Saddam. An Iraqi major summed up the magnitude of his country's defeat: "Losing a war is one thing, but losing Baghdad is another. It was like losing the dearest thing in life."

The rapid success seemed to confirm the wisdom of Bush's decision for war. But the subsequent failure to find weapons of mass destruction led critics to question the validity of the war. In response, the president's defenders stressed the importance of deposing Saddam by pointing to his brutal prisons and to the killing fields south of Baghdad where thousands of Shi'ite rebels had been slaughtered in 1991.

The problems of restoring order and rebuilding the shattered Iraqi economy quickly overshadowed the debate over the war's legitimacy. Daily attacks on American troops in the Sunni triangle north of Baghdad began in the summer of 2003 and increased during the fall, killing an average of three American soldiers each week. By October, more troops had died from these attacks than had been killed during combat in March and April. Looting, sabotage of oil pipelines, and difficulties in repairing and operating outdated power plants and oil facilities made economic recovery slow and halting. Efforts to involve occupation forces from other UN members yielded few troops.

The December 2003 arrest of Saddam, who had eluded capture, revived American optimism. Yet the overall situation remained troubling. Despite slow but steady progress in restoring public services such as electric power and the gradual recovery of the Iraqi oil industry, the armed insurrection continued. Mortar attacks on Baghdad hotels, roadside bombs aimed at American armored convoys, and handheld missile attacks on American helicopters made Iraq a dangerous place. Conflicts between Shi'ite and Sunni Muslims, and the Kurdish demand for autonomy, threatened the American goal of creating a stable Iraqi government.

Bush Reelected

Not surprisingly, the war in Iraq became the central issue in the 2004 presidential race. Bush cast himself as the resolute commander in the war on terror; he and his supporters contended that it would be reckless to change commanders in mid-conflict. Democrats initially favored former Vermont governor Howard Dean, who had opposed the invasion of Iraq and strongly criticized Bush's conduct of the war. But the nomination ultimately went to Senator John Kerry of Massachusetts, a decorated Vietnam War veteran who had voted for the war but later criticized Bush for misleading the country regarding the causes of the conflict, and who contended that the war in Iraq, rather than contributing to the war on terror, actually distracted from it.

The campaign was the most vitriolic in years. Democrats accused Bush of having stolen the election of 2000 (with the help of the Supreme Court) and of lying about Saddam's weapons. Republicans called Kerry's belated opposition to the war in Vietnam an insult to those Americans who had died there, and they cited his votes in the Senate as evidence of a fatal inconsistency. Both sides (following the example of Howard Dean in the primaries) employed the Internet to rally the faithful, raise money, and spread rumors.

The strong emotions produced a record turnout: 12 million more than in 2000. Bush won the popular vote by 2.5 percent, becoming the first victor since his father in 1988 to gain an absolute popular majority. The electoral race was comparably close, with 286 for Bush and 252 for Kerry. Together with the congressional elections, which increased the Republican majorities in both houses, the 2004 race confirmed a "red state/blue state" split in America, with the Republicans dominating the South, the Plains, and the Rockies, while the Democrats carried the Northeast, the Great Lakes, and the West Coast. (see Map 32.3).

Despite his modest margin of victory, Bush claimed a mandate. He proposed to privatize part of the Social Security system and promised to stay the course in Iraq. His Social Security plan went nowhere, but the situation in Iraq eventually improved. Following a new round of insurgent attacks, Bush in 2007 ordered an increase in American troop strength; this "surge," combined with a divide-and-conquer policy toward the insurgents, diminished the violence and made credible Bush's claim that Iraq had turned a corner toward democratic self-government.

Barack Obama's Triumph and Trials

32.5   What challenges faced Barack Obama and the American people during the first decade of the twenty-first century?

By then, however, Americans faced a new problem—one that looked much like an old problem. A booming real estate market in the early 2000s tempted banks and other investors to borrow and lend more than was prudent; when the real estate bubble burst in 2007, the financial markets reeled. Wall Street's panic evoked grim memories of the Great Depression of the

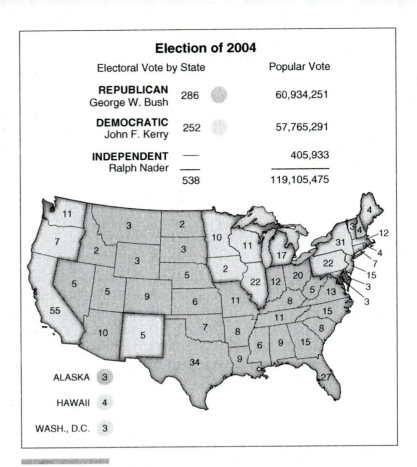

Election of 2004

	Electoral Vote by State		Popular Vote
REPUBLICAN George W. Bush	286		60,934,251
DEMOCRATIC John F. Kerry	252		57,765,291
INDEPENDENT Ralph Nader	—		405,933
	538		119,105,475

ALASKA 3

HAWAII 4

WASH., D.C. 3

MAP 32.3 ELECTION OF 2004

1930s and produced a comparable result at the ballot box: the replacement of a Republican president by a Democratic one. That this new president was the first African American to occupy the White House made his accession even more historic. But it didn't make the problems he inherited less daunting.

The Great Recession

Wall Street's troubles reached the crisis stage in the summer and autumn of 2008. Major lenders, including the government-backed twins, Federal National Mortgage Association and Federal Home Mortgage Corporation (nicknamed Fannie Mae and Freddie Mac), teetered on the brink of bankruptcy. The Bush administration, fearful of the consequences that might follow their collapse, threw the two a life-preserver of federal loans. The panic nonetheless spread, bringing down Wall Street giants Bear Stearns and Lehman Brothers and frightening the administration and Congress into crafting a broader rescue package for the financial sector, totaling hundreds of billions of dollars.

The bailout package averted chaos but left voters shaken. Until this point the Republican nominee for president, Senator John McCain of Arizona, appeared the favorite in the 2008 contest. His war-hero background from the Vietnam era reassured Americans worried about the ongoing wars in Afghanistan and Iraq. But the floundering economy neutralized McCain's advantage and made voters take a second look at the Democratic candidate, Senator Barack Obama of Illinois. Obama ran a brilliant campaign, summarized in the catchword "Hope" and the promise "Yes, We Can." More important was the fact that he was from the opposite party to that which had held the White House during the boom and bust. Obama garnered 53 percent of the popular vote and defeated McCain handily. (see Map 32.4).

Watch the Video   **The Historical Significance of the 2008 Election**

32.1
32.2
32.3
32.4
32.5

OBAMA ELECTED In 2008, Barack Obama became the country's first African American president.

Obama's supporters hoped for great things from the new president. And indeed his inauguration was historic and moving. "God calls on us to shape an uncertain destiny," Obama said. "This is the meaning of our liberty and our creed; why men and women and children of every race and every faith can join in celebration across this magnificent Mall, and why a man whose father less than 60 years ago might not have been served at a local restaurant can now stand before you to take a most sacred oath."

But the warm feeling soon wore off in the cold wind of the bleak economy. The rescue package helped stabilize the financial sector, yet unemployment rose inexorably, peaking at 10 percent in 2009 and sticking near there for the next year. Obama and the Democratic majority in Congress pushed through an economic stimulus package, which may have kept unemployment from going even higher but did little to bring it down.

Obama and the Democrats also achieved something Democratic presidents since Harry Truman had been attempting: passage of a comprehensive program of medical insurance for nearly all Americans. But the measure, passed in the face of bitter resistance from Republicans in Congress, prompted a backlash among voters. Together with the lengthening recession, it contributed to the rebuke the Democrats received in the 2010 midterm elections, in which the Republicans reclaimed control of the

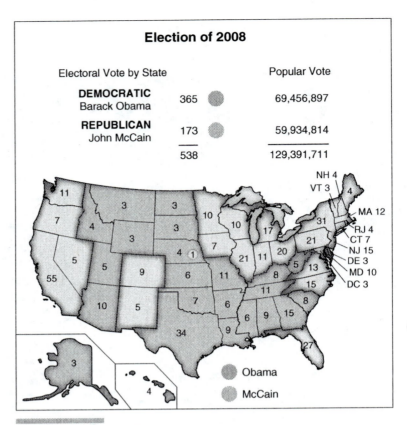

Election of 2008

Electoral Vote by State			Popular Vote
DEMOCRATIC Barack Obama	365		69,456,897
REPUBLICAN John McCain	173		59,934,814
	538		129,391,711

Obama

McCain

MAP 32.4 ELECTION OF 2008

House of Representatives, gained six seats in the Senate, and carried most of the governor's races.

Obama scored an important success when American special forces killed Osama bin Laden, the al Qaeda mastermind, in 2011. And he withdrew American troops from Iraq and scheduled the removal of troops from Afghanistan, foreshadowing a reduction of the American military role in the Middle East. But instability in Pakistan, the nuclear ambitions of Iran, and a civil war in Syria suggested that America's worries about the region were far from over.

Obama nonetheless won reelection in 2012. Republicans in Congress frustrated most of his efforts to deal with the country's economic problems, yet unemployment gradually eased and the president defeated Mitt Romney, a Republican former governor of Massachusetts. While their party's defeat chastened some Republicans, who entered 2013 appearing a bit more willing to compromise, it left the most conservative members of the party as determined as ever to hold the line against Obama's initiatives.

New Challenges and Old

Compromise seemed necessary on the federal budget, which had been knocked wildly out of balance by the Great Recession. Government revenues fell as unemployed workers no longer paid income taxes; government spending rose to cover unemployment compensation and other recession-related expenses. By 2010, the annual deficit topped $1 trillion, and it remained at that level for the next two years. Reducing the deficit seemed the first priority to many voters and elected officials, but if reducing the deficit required laying off government workers, as it seemed certain to do, it might aggravate the recession. The problem defied easy solution. As of early 2013, it defied any solution at all.

Quick Check

How did the great recession shape the Obama presidency?

770

Other problems had deeper roots but no easier solutions. The race question remained alive and contentious, despite the presence of an African American in the White House. **Affirmative action** policies—policies designed to ensure greater participation by minorities—had been under scrutiny for years. The *Bakke v. Regents of the University of California* decision of 1978 had allowed the use of race as one factor in determining admission to colleges and universities, so long as rigid racial quotas weren't employed. This dissatisfied many conservatives, who during the 1980s and 1990s attacked affirmative action politically and in the courts. In 1992, Cheryl Hopwood, an unsuccessful white applicant to the University of Texas Law School, challenged her rejection, contending that the school had admitted less-qualified African Americans. In 1996, the Fifth Circuit Court of Appeals decided in her favor, and the *Hopwood* decision raised the hopes of anti–affirmative action groups that the Supreme Court would overturn *Bakke*. But in a 2003 case involving the University of Michigan, the Supreme Court ruled that "student body diversity is a compelling state interest that can justify the use of race in university admissions." In other words, affirmative action in higher education could continue. But the narrowness of the 5–4 vote suggested that affirmative action would continue to spark controversy, as indeed it did.

Even more controversial was abortion. The issue had roiled American politics for decades, but it did so particularly after the 2005 death of Chief Justice William Rehnquist and the nearly concurrent retirement of Associate Justice Sandra Day O'Connor. The two vacancies on the Supreme Court allowed George W. Bush to nominate their replacements. Rehnquist had been a reliable conservative, but O'Connor was a swing vote, and liberals feared that a more conservative successor would tip the balance against abortion rights, among other contentious issues. Yet John Roberts, Bush's nominee for chief justice, and Samuel Alito, the nominee for associate justice, dodged Democrats' questions in hearings, and both nominations succeeded. Almost immediately, the South Dakota legislature essentially banned abortion, hoping to persuade the newly reconfigured court to revisit the 1973 *Roe* decision, which guaranteed abortion rights. South Dakota voters subsequently overturned the state law, but the issue remained highly charged.

Gay rights provoked fresh controversy as gay advocates pushed for equal marital rights. After the Massachusetts Supreme Court in 2004 struck down a state law barring same-sex marriages, gay advocates celebrated, but conservatives in dozens of states pressed for laws and constitutional amendments reaffirming traditional views on the subject and defining marriage as the union of one man and one woman. Nearly all these efforts were successful. The issue of military service proved similarly controversial. Bill Clinton had achieved a minor breakthrough with the "don't ask, don't tell" policy, which allowed gay service as long as the men and women in question kept their sexual orientation to themselves. Barack Obama campaigned to let gays come out of the military closet, but the Republican Party resisted. Finally, however, in the lame duck session of Congress in December 2010, the legislature approved and Obama signed a measure repealing the "don't ask, don't tell" policy and permitting gays to serve openly in the armed forces. Meanwhile the mood on marriage changed in certain parts of the country, till by early 2013 several states had decided to allow gay marriage. The Supreme Court, whose ranks now included Sonia Sotomayor, the first Latina justice, and Elena Kagan, took up the issue, suggesting that further changes were imminent.

Science and religion continued to battle in America's classrooms. Opponents of evolution revised their challenge to Darwin, replacing creationism with "intelligent design" and demanding that biology classes air this version of their beliefs. School board elections hinged on the issue; Ohio embraced intelligent design only to reject it following an adverse 2005 court decision in a case from the Dover school district. For the moment the evolutionists held their own, but given that public opinion polls consistently showed most Americans rejecting evolution in favor of divine creation, the fight was sure to continue.

affirmative action The use of laws or regulations to achieve racial, ethnic, gender, or other diversity, as in hiring or school admissions. Such efforts are often aimed at improving employment or educational opportunities for women and minorities.

Doubting the Future

During most of American history, every generation had been better off materially than the generation before. Events of the early twenty-first century called this implicit guarantee into question. The stubbornness of the Great Recession made Americans wonder whether the economy would ever recover its resiliency. The towering federal deficit imperiled such cherished programs as Social Security and Medicare and put the myriad other contributions the federal government had long made to American life even more at risk.

Demographics didn't help. As the baby boom generation neared retirement, the load on the Social Security system increased. Everyone realized that something would have to be done to keep the pension program afloat, but no one could figure out how to make the necessary changes politically palatable. Middle-aged Americans faced the prospect of delayed retirement, smaller pensions, or both. Not surprisingly, they objected. Younger Americans resisted the tax increases that could have spared their elders such sacrifice.

The trend in health care costs was even more alarming. For years, medical costs had grown rapidly, and as the population aged, the costs appeared certain to claim an ever-larger share of the nation's income. The health care law enacted by Congress at Obama's behest promised to rein in medical costs, but many observers doubted the promises, and the Republicans wanted to rein in or repeal the program itself.

Immigration remained controversial. Efforts to reduce the number of illegal entries—by tighter enforcement at the border, by sanctions on employers hiring undocumented aliens, by temporary visas for guest workers—stalled on the opposition of immigrant advocates, businesses, and other groups. Attempts to provide a pathway to legal status for undocumented immigrants already in the country met comparable resistance. The heavy Latino vote for Barack Obama in 2012 caused some Republicans to reconsider their position on immigration, but significant reform was slow to appear.

Environmental problems demanded attention, which they got, and solutions, which they didn't. A broad consensus emerged among the scientific community that climate change had to be addressed, but the proposed solutions—higher mileage standards for automobiles, a "carbon tax" on emissions of greenhouse gases, greater reliance on nuclear energy, among others—were costly, intrusive, unproven, or environmentally problematic in their own ways. And though the scientists mostly agreed that humans were causing climate change, the politicians did not. As on other problems facing the country, the consequence was deadlock.

Conclusion: The End of the American Future—or Not?

From before its eighteenth-century birth as an independent nation, America had been the land of the future. Immigrants to America left their pasts behind as they traveled to the new country; native-born Americans treated the future as though they owned it. And to nearly everyone in the country, the future almost invariably looked bright.

By 2013, however, the American future had dimmed. The terrorist attacks of 2001 had made Americans feel vulnerable; twelve years later they had suffered no comparable assaults, but they still felt vulnerable. They waited in long lines at airport security checkpoints and submitted to personal searches on entering public buildings and gathering places all over the country. The Great Recession darkened America's economic horizon like nothing since the Great Depression, and American officials could not agree how to restore prosperity. A 2013 poll revealed that only 15 percent of Americans believed that the next generation would enjoy a higher standard of living than the current generation.

Not everyone despaired, though. Immigrants still came to America, seeking its promise of a better life for themselves and their children. Young people went to college in search of fulfilling jobs. Young men and women got married and had children, hoping the little ones would fare well in the decades ahead.

Those who knew history tended to be the most optimistic. The country had been through difficult times in the past. The American Revolution, the Civil War, the Great Depression, and two world wars had tested Americans' mettle and faith in the future. Each time the country had survived, typically stronger for the trial. No one could guarantee that America would emerge from its twenty-first-century trial stronger than before, but Americans had never required guarantees.

Chapter Review

The First President Bush

32.1 What were the important issues in George H. W. Bush's presidency, and how were they handled? p. 748

In domestic affairs, the first President Bush focused on fixing the savings and loan industry and balancing the budget. In foreign affairs, he managed to end the Cold War peacefully and successfully. The Gulf War of 1991 liberated Kuwait and weakened the Iraqi regime of Saddam Hussein, but didn't remove Saddam from power in Baghdad.

The Changing Faces of America

32.2 How did the American population shift and grow between 1990 and 2013? p. 751

Americans continued to migrate to the Sunbelt in the 1990s and early 2000s, and immigration continued to grow. Hispanics formed the largest segment of the immigrant population and included millions of illegal immigrants. African Americans gained ground economically but still suffered from poverty, as Hurricane Katrina demonstrated.

The New Democrats

32.3 What were the accomplishments and failures of the Clinton administration? p.756

Clinton balanced the federal budget and helped revive the economy, which boomed during the 1990s. The North American Free Trade Agreement eliminated tariff barriers among the United States, Canada, and Mexico. But personal scandals led to Clinton's impeachment, which he survived, although not without damage to his own reputation and that of the Democrats.

Republicans Resurgent

32.4 How did George W. Bush become president, and what did he do in the White House? p. 760

George W. Bush became president in an election that turned on a ballot dispute in Florida, which was resolved only by the Supreme Court. As president, Bush persuaded Congress to cut taxes and, after the terrorist attacks of September 11, 2001, to authorize invasions of Afghanistan and Iraq. The war in Iraq bogged down amid an insurgency against the American-supported government in Baghdad.

Barack Obama's Triumph and Trials

32.5 What challenges faced Barack Obama and the American people during the first decade of the twenty-first century? p. 767

The culture wars between conservatives and liberals continued into the twenty-first century, with abortion, affirmative action, gay rights, and evolution provoking controversy. The Great Recession shook the economy, and Americans wondered how to deal with problems of health care, retirement, illegal immigration, and the environment.

Timeline

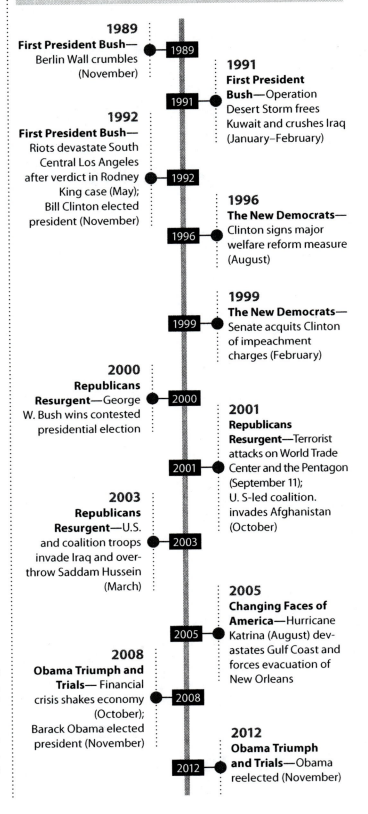

1989
First President Bush—Berlin Wall crumbles (November)

1989

1991
First President Bush—Operation Desert Storm frees Kuwait and crushes Iraq (January–February)

1991

1992
First President Bush—Riots devastate South Central Los Angeles after verdict in Rodney King case (May); Bill Clinton elected president (November)

1992

1996
The New Democrats—Clinton signs major welfare reform measure (August)

1996

1999
The New Democrats—Senate acquits Clinton of impeachment charges (February)

1999

2000
Republicans Resurgent—George W. Bush wins contested presidential election

2000

2001
Republicans Resurgent—Terrorist attacks on World Trade Center and the Pentagon (September 11); U. S-led coalition. invades Afghanistan (October)

2001

2003
Republicans Resurgent—U.S. and coalition troops invade Iraq and overthrow Saddam Hussein (March)

2003

2005
Changing Faces of America—Hurricane Katrina (August) devastates Gulf Coast and forces evacuation of New Orleans

2005

2008
Obama Triumph and Trials— Financial crisis shakes economy (October); Barack Obama elected president (November)

2008

2012
Obama Triumph and Trials—Obama reelected (November)

2012

The Declaration of Independence

In Congress, July 4, 1776

The Unanimous Declaration of the Thirteen United States of America,

When, in the course of human events, it becomes necessary for one people to dissolve the political bonds which have connected them with another, and to assume, among the powers of the earth, the separate and equal station to which the laws of nature and of nature's God entitle them, a decent respect to the opinions of mankind requires that they should declare the causes which impel them to the separation.

We hold these truths to be self-evident: That all men are created equal; that they are endowed by their Creator with certain unalienable rights; that among these are life, liberty, and the pursuit of happiness; that, to secure these rights, governments are instituted among men, deriving their just powers from the consent of the governed; that whenever any form of government becomes destructive of these ends, it is the right of the people to alter or to abolish it, and to institute new government, laying its foundation on such principles, and organizing its powers in such form, as to them shall seem most likely to effect their safety and happiness. Prudence, indeed, will dictate that governments long established should not be changed for light and transient causes; and accordingly all experience hath shown that mankind are more disposed to suffer, while evils are sufferable, than to right themselves by abolishing the forms to which they are accustomed. But when a long train of abuses and usurpations, pursuing invariably the same object, evinces a design to reduce them under absolute despotism, it is their right, it is their duty, to throw off such government, and to provide new guards for their future security. Such has been the patient sufferance of these colonies; and such is now the necessity which constrains them to alter their former systems of government. The history of the present King of Great Britain is a history of repeated injuries and usurpations, all having in direct object the establishment of an absolute tyranny over these states. To prove this, let facts be submitted to a candid world.

He has refused his assent to laws, the most wholesome and necessary for the public good.

He has forbidden his governors to pass laws of immediate and pressing importance, unless suspended in their operation till his assent should be obtained; and, when so suspended, he has utterly neglected to attend to them.

He has refused to pass other laws for the accommodation of large districts of people, unless those people would relinquish the right of representation in the legislature, a right inestimable to them, and formidable to tyrants only.

He has called together legislative bodies at places unusual, uncomfortable, and distant from the depository of their public records, for the sole purpose of fatiguing them into compliance with his measures.

He has dissolved representative houses repeatedly, for opposing, with manly firmness, his invasions on the rights of the people.

He has refused for a long time, after such dissolutions, to cause others to be elected; whereby the legislative powers, incapable of annihilation, have returned to the people at large for their exercise; the state remaining, in the mean time, exposed to all the dangers of invasions from without and convulsions within.

He has endeavored to prevent the population of these states; for that purpose obstructing the laws for naturalization of foreigners; refusing to pass others to encourage their migration hither, and raising the conditions of new appropriations of lands.

He has obstructed the administration of justice, by refusing his assent to laws for establishing judiciary powers.

He has made judges dependent on his will alone, for the tenure of their offices, and the amount and payment of their salaries.

He has erected a multitude of new offices, and sent hither swarms of officers to harass our people and eat out their substance.

He has kept among us, in times of peace, standing armies, without the consent of our legislatures.

He has affected to render the military independent of, and superior to, the civil power.

He has combined with others to subject us to a jurisdiction foreign to our constitution, and unacknowledged by our laws, giving his assent to their acts of pretended legislation:

For quartering large bodies of armed troops among us;

For protecting them, by a mock trial, from punishment for any murder which they should commit on the inhabitants of these states;

For cutting off our trade with all parts of the world;

For imposing taxes on us without our consent;

For depriving us, in many cases, of the benefits of trial by jury;

For transporting us beyond seas, to be tried for pretended offenses;

For abolishing the free system of English laws in a neighboring province, establishing therein an arbitrary government, and enlarging its boundaries, so as to render it at once an example and fit instrument for introducing the same absolute rule into these colonies;

For taking away our charters, abolishing our most valuable laws, and altering fundamentally the forms of our governments;

For suspending our own legislatures, and declaring themselves invested with power to legislate for us in all cases whatsoever.

He has abdicated government here, by declaring us out of his protection and waging war against us.

He has plundered our seas, ravaged our coasts, burned our towns, and destroyed the lives of our people.

Button Gwinnett	George Wythe	Geo. Ross	Saml. Adams
Lyman Hall	Richard Henry Lee	Caesar Rodney	John Adams
Geo. Walton	Th. Jefferson	Geo. Read	Robt. Treat Paine
Wm. Hooper	Benj. Harrison	Tho. M'kean	Elbridge Gerry
Joseph Hewes	Thos. Nelson, Jr.	Wm. Floyd	Step. Hopkins
John Penn	Francis Lightfoot Lee	Phil. Livingston	William Ellery
Edward Rutledge	Carter Braxton	Frans. Lewis	Roger Sherman
Thos. Heyward, Junr.	Robt. Morris	Lewis Morris	Sam'el Huntington
Thomas Lynch, Junr.	Benjamin Rush	Richd. Stockton	Wm. Williams
Arthur Middleton	Benja. Franklin	Jno. Witherspoon	Oliver Wolcott
Samuel Chase	John Morton	Fras. Hopkinson	Matthew Thornton
Wm. Paca	Geo. Clymer	John Hart	
Thos. Stone	Jas. Smith	Abra. Clark	
Charles Carroll of Carrollton	Geo. Taylor	Josiah Bartlett	
	James Wilson	Wm. Whipple	

He is at this time transporting large armies of foreign mercenaries to complete the works of death, desolation, and tyranny already begun with circumstances of cruelty and perfidy scarcely paralleled in the most barbarous ages, and totally unworthy the head of a civilized nation.

He has constrained our fellow-citizens, taken captive on the high seas, to bear arms against their country, to become the executioners of their friends and brethren, or to fall themselves by their hands.

He has excited domestic insurrection among us, and has endeavored to bring on the inhabitants of our frontiers the merciless Indian savages, whose known rule of warfare is an undistinguished destruction of all ages, sexes, and conditions.

In every stage of these oppressions we have petitioned for redress in the most humble terms; our repeated petitions have been answered only by repeated injury. A prince, whose character is thus marked by every act which may define a tyrant, is unfit to be the ruler of a free people.

Nor have we been wanting in our attentions to our British brethren. We have warned them, from time to time, of attempts by their legislature to extend an unwarrantable jurisdiction over us. We have reminded them of the circumstances of our emigration and settlement here. We have appealed to their native justice and magnanimity; and we have conjured them, by the ties of our common kindred, to disavow these usurpations, which would inevitably interrupt our connections and correspondence. They, too, have been deaf to the voice of justice and of consanguinity. We must, therefore, acquiesce in the necessity which denounces our separation, and hold them, as we hold the rest of mankind, enemies in war, in peace friends.

We, therefore, the representatives of the United States of America, in General Congress assembled, appealing to the Supreme Judge of the world for the rectitude of our intentions, do, in the name and by the authority of the good people of these colonies, solemnly publish and declare, that these United Colonies are, and of right ought to be, FREE AND INDEPENDENT STATES; that they are absolved from all allegiance to the British crown, and that all political connection between them and the state of Great Britain is, and ought to be, totally dissolved; and that, as free and independent states, they have full power to levy war, conclude peace, contract alliances, establish commerce, and do all other acts and things which independent states may of right do. And for the support of this declaration, with a firm reliance on the protection of Divine Providence, we mutually pledge to each other our lives, our fortunes, and our sacred honor.

The Articles of Confederation

Between the States of New Hampshire, Massachusetts Bay, Rhode Island and Providence Plantations, Connecticut, New York, New Jersey, Pennsylvania, Delaware, Maryland, Virginia, North Carolina, South Carolina, Georgia

Article 1

The stile of this confederacy shall be "The United States of America."

Article 2

Each State retains its sovereignty, freedom and independence, and every power, jurisdiction, and right, which is not by this confederation expressly delegated to the United States, in Congress assembled.

Article 3

The said states hereby severally enter into a firm league of friendship with each other for their common defence, the security of their liberties and their mutual and general welfare; binding themselves to assist each other against all force offered to, or attacks made upon them, or any of them, on account of religion, sovereignty, trade, or any other pretence whatever.

Article 4

The better to secure and perpetuate mutual friendship and intercourse among the people of the different states in this union, the free inhabitants of each of these states, paupers, vagabonds, and fugitives from justice excepted, shall be entitled to all privileges and immunities of free citizens in the several states; and the people of each State shall have free ingress and regress to and from any other State, and shall enjoy therein all the privileges of trade and commerce, subject to the same duties, impositions, and restrictions, as the inhabitants thereof respectively; provided, that such restrictions shall not extend so far as to prevent the removal of property, imported into any State, to any other State of which the owner is an inhabitant; provided also, that no imposition, duties, or restriction, shall be laid by any State on the property of the United States, or either of them.

If any person guilty of, or charged with treason, felony, or other high misdemeanor in any State, shall flee from justice and be found in any of the United States, he shall, upon demand of the governor or executive power of the State from which he fled, be delivered up and removed to the State having jurisdiction of his offence.

Full faith and credit shall be given in each of these states to the records, acts, and judicial proceedings of the courts and magistrates of every other State.

Article 5

For the more convenient management of the general interests of the United States, delegates shall be annually appointed, in such manner as the legislature of each State shall direct, to meet in Congress, on the 1st Monday in November in every year, with a power reserved to each State to recall its delegates, or any of them, at any time within the year, and to send others in their stead for the remainder of the year.

No State shall be represented in Congress by less than two, nor by more than seven members; and no person shall be capable of being a delegate for more than three years in any term of six years; nor shall any person, being a delegate, be capable of holding any office under the United States, for which he, or any other for his benefit, receives any salary, fees, or emolument of any kind.

Each State shall maintain its own delegates in a meeting of the states, and while they act as members of the committee of the states.

In determining questions in the United States, in Congress assembled, each State shall have one vote.

Freedom of speech and debate in Congress shall not be impeached or questioned in any court or place out of Congress: and the members of Congress shall be protected in their persons from arrests and imprisonments, during the time of their going to and from, and attendance on Congress, except for treason, felony, or breach of the peace.

Article 6

No State, without the consent of the United States, in Congress assembled, shall send any embassy to, or receive any embassy from, or enter into any conference, agreement, alliance, or treaty with any king, prince, or state; nor shall any person, holding any office of profit or trust under the United States, or any of them, accept of any present, emolument, office or title, of any kind whatever, from any king, prince, or foreign state; nor shall the United States, in Congress assembled, or any of them, grant any title of nobility.

No two or more states shall enter into any treaty, confederation, or alliance, whatever, between them, without the consent of the United States, in Congress assembled, specifying accurately the purposes for which the same is to be entered into, and how long it shall continue.

No State shall lay any imposts or duties which may interfere with any stipulations in treaties entered into by the United States, in Congress assembled, with any king, prince, or state, in pursuance of any treaties already proposed by Congress to the courts of France and Spain.

No vessels of war shall be kept up in time of peace by any State, except such number only as shall be deemed necessary by the United States, in Congress assembled, for the defence of

such State or its trade; nor shall any body of forces be kept up by any State, in time of peace, except such number only as, in the judgment of the United States, in Congress assembled, shall be deemed requisite to garrison the forts necessary for the defence of such State; but every State shall always keep up a well regulated and disciplined militia, sufficiently armed and accoutred, and shall provide, and constantly have ready for use, in public stores, a due number, of field pieces and tents, and a proper quantity of arms, ammunition and camp equipage.

No State shall engage in any war without the consent of the United States, in Congress assembled, unless such State be actually invaded by enemies, or shall have received certain advice of a resolution being formed by some nation of Indians to invade such State, and the danger is so imminent as not to admit of a delay till the United States, in Congress assembled, can be consulted; nor shall any State grant commissions to any ships or vessels of war, nor letters of marque or reprisal, except it be after a declaration of war by the United States, in Congress assembled, and then only against the kingdom or state, and the subjects thereof, against which war has been so declared, and under such regulations as shall be established by the United States, in Congress assembled, unless such States be infested by pirates, in which case vessels of war may be fitted out for that occasion, and kept so long as the danger shall continue, or until the United States, in Congress assembled, shall determine otherwise.

Article 7

When land forces are raised by any State for the common defence, all officers of or under the rank of colonel, shall be appointed by the legislature of each State respectively, by whom such forces shall be raised, or in such manner as such State shall direct; and all vacancies shall be filled up by the State which first made the appointment.

Article 8

All charges of war and all other expences, that shall be incurred for the common defence or general welfare, and allowed by the United States, in Congress assembled, shall be defrayed out of a common treasury, which shall be supplied by the several states, in proportion to the value of all land within each State, granted to or surveyed for any person, as such land and the buildings and improvements thereon shall be estimated according to such mode as the United States, in Congress assembled, shall, from time to time, direct and appoint.

The taxes for paying that proportion shall be laid and levied by the authority and direction of the legislatures of the several states, within the time agreed upon by the United States, in Congress assembled.

Article 9

The United States, in Congress assembled, shall have the sole and exclusive right and power of determining on peace and war, except in the cases mentioned in the 6th article; of sending and receiving ambassadors; entering into treaties and alliances, provided that no treaty of commerce shall be made, whereby the legislative power of the respective states shall be restrained from imposing such imposts and duties on foreigners as their own people are subjected to, or from prohibiting the exportation or importation of any species of goods or commodities whatsoever; of establishing rules for deciding, in all cases, what captures on land or water shall be legal, and in what manner prizes, taken by land or naval forces in the service of the United States, shall be divided or appropriated; of granting letters of marque and reprisal in times of peace; appointing courts for the trial of piracies and felonies committed on the high seas, and establishing courts for receiving and determining, finally, appeals in all cases of captures; provided, that no member of Congress shall be appointed a judge of any of the said courts.

The United States, in Congress assembled, shall also be the last resort on appeal in all disputes and differences now subsisting, or that hereafter may arise between two or more states concerning boundary, jurisdiction or any other cause whatever; which authority shall always be exercised in the manner following: whenever the legislative or executive authority, or lawful agent of any State, in controversy with another, shall present a petition to Congress, stating the matter in question, and praying for a hearing, notice thereof shall be given, by order of Congress, to the legislative or executive authority of the other State in controversy, and a day assigned for the appearance of the parties by their lawful agents, who shall then be directed to appoint, by joint consent, commissioners or judges to constitute a court for hearing and determining the matter in question; but, if they cannot agree, Congress shall name three persons out of each of the United States, and from the list of such persons each party shall alternately strike out one, in the petitioners beginning, until the number shall be reduced to thirteen; and from that number not less than seven, nor more than nine names, as Congress shall direct, shall, in the presence of Congress, be drawn out by lot; and the persons whose names shall be drawn, or any five of them, shall be commissioners or judges to hear and finally determine the controversy, so always as a major part of the judges who shall hear the cause shall agree in the determination; and if either party shall neglect to attend at the day appointed, without shewing reasons which Congress shall judge sufficient, or, being present, shall refuse to strike, the Congress shall proceed to nominate three persons out of each State, and the secretary of Congress shall strike in behalf of such party absent or refusing; and the judgment and sentence of the court to be appointed, in the manner before prescribed, shall be final and conclusive; and if any of the parties shall refuse to submit to the authority of such court, or to appear or defend their claim or cause, the court shall nevertheless proceed to pronounce sentence or judgment, which shall, in like manner, be final and decisive, the judgment or sentence and other proceedings being, in either case, transmitted to Congress, and lodged among the acts of Congress for the security of the parties concerned: provided, that every commissioner, before he sits in judgment, shall take an oath, to be administered by one of the judges of the supreme or superior court of the State where the cause shall be tried, "well and truly to hear and determine the matter in question, according to the best of his judgment, without favor, affection, or hope of reward": provided, also, that no State shall be deprived of territory for the benefit of the United States.

All controversies concerning the private right of soil, claimed under different grants of two or more states, whose jurisdictions, as they may respect such lands and the states which passed such grants, are adjusted, the said grants, or either of them, being at the same time claimed to have originated antecedent to such settlement of jurisdiction, shall, on the petition of either party to the Congress of the United States, be finally determined, as near as may be, in the same manner as is before prescribed for deciding disputes respecting territorial jurisdiction between different states.

The United States, in Congress assembled, shall also have the sole and exclusive right and power of regulating the alloy and value of coin struck by their own authority, or by that of the respective states; fixing the standard of weights and measures throughout the United States; regulating the trade and managing all affairs with the Indians not members of any of the states; provided that the legislative right of any State within its own limits be not infringed or violated; establishing and regulating post offices from one State to another throughout all the United States, and exacting such postage on the papers passing through the same as may be requisite to defray the expences of the said office; appointing all officers of the land forces in the service of the United States, excepting regimental officers; appointing all the officers of the naval forces, and commissioning all officers whatever in the service of the United States; making rules for the government and regulation of the said land and naval forces, and directing their operations.

The United States, in Congress assembled, shall have authority to appoint a committee to sit in the recess of Congress, to be denominated "a Committee of the States," and to consist of one delegate from each State, and to appoint such other committees and civil officers as may be necessary for managing the general affairs of the United States, under their direction; to appoint one of their number to preside; provided that no person be allowed to serve in the office of president more than one year in any term of three years; to ascertain the necessary sums of money to be raised for the service of the United States, and to appropriate and apply the same for defraying the public expences; to borrow money or emit bills on the credit of the United States, transmitting, every half year, to the respective states, an account of the sums of money so borrowed or emitted; to build and equip a navy; to agree upon the number of land forces, and to make requisitions from each State for its quota, in proportion to the number of white inhabitants in such State; which requisitions shall be binding; and, thereupon, the legislature of each State shall appoint the regimental officers, raise the men, and cloathe, arm, and equip them in a soldier-like manner, at the expence of the United States; and the officers and men so cloathed, armed, and equipped, shall march to the place appointed and within the time agreed on by the United States, in Congress assembled; but if the United States, in Congress assembled, shall, on consideration of circumstances, judge proper that any State should not raise men, or should raise a smaller number than its quota, and that any other State should raise a greater number of men than the quota thereof, such extra number shall be raised, officered, cloathed, armed, and equipped in the same manner as the quota of such State, unless the legislature of such State shall judge that such extra number cannot be safely spared out of the same, in which case they shall raise, officer, cloathe, arm, and equip as many of such extra number as they judge can be safely spared. And the officers and men so cloathed, armed, and equipped, shall march to the place appointed and within the time agreed on by the United States, in Congress assembled.

The United States, in Congress assembled, shall never engage in a war, nor grant letters of marque and reprisal in time of peace, nor enter into any treaties or alliances, nor coin money, nor regulate the value thereof, nor ascertain the sums and expences necessary for the defence and welfare of the United States, or any of them: nor emit bills, nor borrow money on the credit of the United States, nor appropriate money, nor agree upon the number of vessels of war to be built or purchased, or the number of land or sea forces to be raised, nor appoint a commander in chief of the army or navy, unless nine states assent to the same; nor shall a question on any other point, except for adjourning from day to day, be determined, unless by the votes of a majority of the United States, in Congress assembled.

The Congress of the United States shall have power to adjourn to any time within the year, and to any place within the United States, so that no period of adjournment be for a longer duration than the space of six months, and shall publish the journal of their proceedings monthly, except such parts thereof, relating to treaties, alliances or military operations, as, in their judgment, require secrecy; and the yeas and nays of the delegates of each State on any question shall be entered on the journal, when it is desired by any delegate; and the delegates of a State, or any of them, at his, or their request, shall be furnished with a transcript of the said journal, except such parts as are above excepted, to lay before the legislatures of the several states.

Article 10

The committee of the states, or any nine of them, shall be authorized to execute, in the recess of Congress, such of the powers of Congress as the United States, in Congress assembled, by the consent of nine states, shall, from time to time, think expedient to vest them with; provided, that no power be delegated to the said committee for the exercise of which by the articles of confederation, the voice of nine states, in the Congress of the United States assembled, is requisite.

Article 11

Canada acceding to this confederation, and joining in the measures of the United States, shall be admitted into and entitled to all the advantages of this union; but no other colony shall be admitted into the same, unless such admission be agreed to by nine states.

Article 12

All bills of credit emitted, monies borrowed and debts contracted by, or under the authority of Congress before the assembling of the United States, in pursuance of the present confederation, shall be deemed and considered as a charge against the United States, for payment and satisfaction whereof the said United States and the public faith are hereby solemnly pledged.

Article 13

Every State shall abide by the determinations of the United States, in Congress assembled, on all questions which, by this confederation, are submitted to them. And the articles of this confederation shall be inviolably observed by every State, and the union shall be perpetual; nor shall any alteration at any time hereafter be made in any of them, unless such alteration be agreed to in a Congress of the United States, and be afterwards confirmed by the legislatures of every State.

These articles shall be proposed to the legislatures of all the United States, to be considered, and if approved of by them, they are advised to authorize their delegates to ratify the same in the Congress of the United States; which being done, the same shall become conclusive.

The Constitution of the United States of America

Preamble

We the People of the United States, in Order to form a more perfect Union, establish Justice, insure domestic Tranquility, provide for the common defence, promote the general Welfare, and secure the Blessings of Liberty to ourselves and our Posterity, do ordain and establish this Constitution for the United States of America.

Article 1

Section 1

All legislative Powers herein granted shall be vested in a Congress of the United States, which shall consist of a Senate and House of Representatives.

Section 2

The House of Representatives shall be composed of Members chosen every second Year by the People of the several States, and the Electors in each State shall have the Qualifications requisite for Electors of the most numerous Branch of the State Legislature.

No Person shall be a Representative who shall not have attained to the Age of twenty five Years, and been seven Years a Citizen of the United States, and who shall not, when elected, be an inhabitant of that State in which he shall be chosen.

Representatives and direct Taxes shall be apportioned among the several States which may be included within this Union, according to their respective Numbers, *which shall be determined by adding to the whole Number of free Persons, including those bound to Service for a Term of Years, and excluding Indians not taxed, three fifths of all other Persons.** The actual Enumeration shall be made within three Years after the first Meeting of the Congress of the United States, and within every subsequent Term of ten Years, in such Manner as they shall by Law direct. The Number of Representatives shall not exceed one for every thirty Thousand, but each State shall have at Least one Representative; *and until such enumeration shall be made, the State of New Hampshire shall be entitled to chuse three, Massachusetts eight, Rhode-Island and Providence Plantations one, Connecticut five, New York six, New Jersey four, Pennsylvania eight, Delaware one, Maryland six, Virginia ten, North Carolina five, South Carolina five, and Georgia three.*

When vacancies happen in the Representation from any State, the Executive Authority thereof shall issue Writs of Election to fill such Vacancies.

The House of Representatives shall chuse their Speaker and other Officers; and shall have the sole Power of Impeachment.

Section 3

The Senate of the United States shall be composed of two Senators from each State, *chosen by the Legislature thereof,* for six Years; and each Senator shall have one Vote.

Immediately after they shall be assembled in Consequence of the first Election, they shall be divided as equally as may be into three Classes. The Seats of the Senators of the first Class shall be vacated at the Expiration of the second Year, of the second Class at the Expiration of the fourth Year, and of the third Class at the Expiration of the sixth Year so that one third may be chosen every second Year; and if Vacancies happen by Resignation, or otherwise, during the Recess of the Legislature of any state, the Executive thereof may make temporary Appointments until the next Meeting of the Legislature, which shall then fill such Vacancies.

No Person shall be a Senator who shall not have attained to the Age of thirty Years, and been nine Years a Citizen of the United States, and who shall not, when elected, be an Inhabitant of that State for which he shall be chosen.

The Vice President of the United States shall be President of the Senate, but shall have no Vote, unless they be equally divided.

The Senate shall chuse their other Officers, and also a President *pro tempore,* in the Absence of the Vice President, or when he shall exercise the Office of President of the United States.

The Senate shall have the sole Power to try all Impeachments. When sitting for that Purpose, they shall be on Oath or

---

*Passages no longer in effect are printed in italic type.

Affirmation. When the President of the United States is tried the Chief Justice shall preside: And no Person shall be convicted without the Concurrence of two thirds of the Members present.

Judgment in Cases of Impeachment shall not extend further than to removal from Office, and disqualification to hold and enjoy any Office of honor, Trust or Profit under the United States: but the Party convicted shall nevertheless be liable and subject to Indictment, Trial, Judgment and Punishment, according to Law.

Section 4

The Times, Places and Manner of holding Elections for Senators and Representatives, shall be prescribed in each State by the Legislature thereof; but the Congress may at any time by Law make or alter such Regulations, except as to the Places of chusing Senators.

The Congress shall assemble at least once in every Year, *and such Meeting shall be on the first Monday in December, unless they shall by Law appoint a different Day.*

Section 5

Each House shall be the Judge of the Elections, Returns and Qualifications of its own Members, and a Majority of each shall constitute a Quorum to do Business; but a smaller Number may adjourn from day to day, and may be authorized to compel the Attendance of absent Members, in such Manner, and under such Penalties as each House may provide.

Each House may determine the Rules of its Proceedings, punish its Members for disorderly Behaviour, and, with the Concurrence of two thirds, expel a Member.

Each House shall keep a Journal of its Proceedings, and from time to time publish the same, excepting such Parts as may in their Judgment require Secrecy; and the Yeas and Nays of the Members of either House on any question shall, at the Desire of one fifth of those Present, be entered on the Journal.

Neither House, during the Session of Congress, shall, without the Consent of the other, adjourn for more than three days, nor to any other Place than that in which the two Houses shall be sitting.

Section 6

The Senators and Representatives shall receive a Compensation for their Services, to be ascertained by Law, and paid out of the Treasury of the United States. They shall in all Cases, except Treason, Felony and Breach of the Peace, be privileged from Arrest during their Attendance at the Session of their respective Houses, and in going to and returning from the same; and for any Speech or Debate in either House, they shall not be questioned in any other Place.

No Senator or Representative shall, during the Time for which he was elected, be appointed to any civil Office under the Authority of the United States, which shall have been created, or the Emoluments whereof shall have been encreased during such time, and no Person holding any Office under the United States, shall be a Member of either House during his Continuance in Office.

Section 7

All Bills for raising Revenue shall originate in the House of Representatives; but the Senate may propose or concur with Amendments as on other Bills.

Every Bill which shall have passed the House of Representatives and the Senate, shall, before it become a Law, be presented to the President of the United States; If he approve he shall sign it, but if not he shall return it, with his Objections to the House in which it shall have originated, who shall enter the Objections at large on their Journal, and proceed to reconsider it. If after such Reconsideration two thirds of that House shall agree to pass the Bill, it shall be sent, together with the Objections, to the other House, by which it shall likewise be reconsidered, and if approved

by two thirds of that House, it shall become a Law. But in all such Cases the Votes of both Houses shall be determined by yeas and Nays, and the Names of the Persons voting for and against the Bill shall be entered on the Journal of each House respectively. If any Bill shall not be returned by the President within ten Days (Sundays excepted) after it shall have been presented to him, the Same shall be a Law, in like Manner as if he had signed it, unless the Congress by their Adjournment prevent its Return, in which Case it shall not be a Law.

Every Order, Resolution, or Vote to which the Concurrence of the Senate and House of Representatives may be necessary (except on a question of Adjournment) shall be presented to the President of the United States; and before the Same shall take Effect, shall be approved by him, or being disapproved by him, shall be repassed by two thirds of the Senate and House of Representatives, according to the Rules and Limitations prescribed in the Case of a Bill.

Section 8

The Congress shall have Power To lay and collect Taxes, Duties, Imposts and Excises, to pay the Debts and provide for the common Defence and general Welfare of the United States; but all Duties, Imposts and Excises shall be uniform throughout the United States;

To borrow Money on the credit of the United States;

To regulate Commerce with foreign Nations, and among the several States, and with the Indian Tribes;

To establish an uniform Rule of Naturalization, and uniform Laws on the subject of Bankruptcies throughout the United States;

To coin Money, regulate the Value thereof, and of foreign Coin, and fix the Standard of Weights and Measures;

To provide for the Punishment of counterfeiting the Securities and current Coin of the United States;

To establish Post Offices and post Roads;

To promote the Progress of Science and useful Arts, by securing for limited Times to Authors and Inventors the exclusive Right to their respective Writings and Discoveries;

To constitute Tribunals inferior to the supreme Court;

To define and punish Piracies and Felonies committed on the high Seas, and Offences against the Law of Nations;

To declare War, grant Letters of Marque and Reprisal, and make Rules concerning Captures on Land and Water;

To raise and support Armies, but no Appropriation of Money to that Use shall be for a longer Term than two Years;

To provide and maintain a Navy;

To make Rules for the Government and Regulation of the land and naval Forces;

To provide for calling forth the Militia to execute the Laws of the Union, suppress Insurrections and repel Invasions;

To provide for organizing, arming, and disciplining, the Militia, and for governing such Part of them as may be employed in the Service of the United States, reserving to the States respectively, the Appointment of the Officers, and the Authority of training the Militia according to the discipline prescribed by Congress;

To exercise exclusive Legislation in all Cases whatsoever, over such District (not exceeding ten Miles square) as may, by Cession of particular States, and the Acceptance of Congress, become the Seat of the Government of the United States, and to exercise like Authority over all Places purchased by the Consent of the Legislature of the State in which the Same shall be, for the Erection of Forts, Magazines, Arsenals, dock-Yards, and other needful Buildings;—And

To make all Laws which shall be necessary and proper for carrying into Execution the foregoing Powers, and all other Powers vested by this Constitution in the Government of the United States, or in any Department of Officer thereof.

Section 9

The Migration or Importation of such Persons as any of the States now existing shall think proper to admit, shall not be prohibited by the Congress prior to the Year one thousand eight hundred and eight, but a Tax or duty may be imposed on such Importation, not exceeding ten dollars for each Person.

The Privilege of the Writ of Habeas Corpus shall not be suspended, unless when in Cases of Rebellion or Invasion the public Safety may require it.

No Bill of Attainder or ex post facto Law shall be passed.

No Capitation, or other direct, Tax shall be laid, unless in Proportion to the Census or Enumeration herein before directed to be taken.

No Tax or Duty shall be laid on Articles exported from any State.

No Preference shall be given by any Regulation of Commerce or Revenue to the Ports of one State over those of another: nor shall Vessels bound to, or from, one State, be obliged to enter, clear, or pay Duties in another.

No Money shall be drawn from the Treasury, but in Consequence of Appropriations made by Law; and a regular Statement and Account of the Receipts and Expenditures of all public Money shall be published from time to time.

No Title of Nobility shall be granted by the United States: And no Person holding any Office of Profit or Trust under them, shall, without the Consent of the Congress, accept of any present, Emolument, Office, or Title, of any kind whatever, from any King, Prince, or foreign State.

Section 10

No State shall enter into any Treaty, Alliance, or Confederation; grant Letters of Marque and Reprisal; coin Money; emit Bills of Credit; make any Thing but gold and silver Coin a Tender in Payment of Debts; pass any Bill of Attainder, ex post facto Law, or Law impairing the obligation of Contracts, or grant any Title of Nobility.

No State shall, without the Consent of the Congress, lay any Imposts or Duties on Imports or Exports, except what may be absolutely necessary for executing its inspection Laws: and the net Produce of all Duties and Imposts, laid by any State on Imports or Exports, shall be for the Use of the Treasury of the United States; and all such Laws shall be subject to the Revision and Controul of the Congress.

No State shall, without the Consent of Congress, lay any Duty of Tonnage, keep Troops, or Ships of War in time of Peace, enter into any Agreement or Compact with another State, or with a foreign Power, or engage in War, unless actually invaded, or in such imminent Danger as will not admit of delay.

Article 2

Section 1

The executive Power shall be vested in a President of the United States of America. He shall hold his Office during the Term of four Years, and, together with the Vice President, chosen for the same Term, be elected, as follows:

Each State shall appoint, in such Manner as the Legislature thereof may direct, a Number of Electors, equal to the whole Number of Senators and Representatives to which the State may be entitled in the Congress: but no Senator or Representative, or Person holding an Office of Trust or Profit under the United States, shall be appointed an Elector.

The Electors shall meet in their respective States, and vote by Ballot for two Persons, of whom one at least shall not be an Inhabitant of the same State with themselves. And they shall make a List of all the Persons voted for, and of the Number of Votes for each; which List they shall sign and certify, and transmit sealed to the Seat of the Government of the United States, directed to the President of the Senate. The President of the Senate shall, in the Presence of the Senate and House of Representatives, open all the Certificates, and the Votes shall then be counted. The Person having the greatest Number of Votes shall be the President, if such Number be a Majority of the whole number of Electors appointed; and if there be more than one who have such Majority, and have an equal Number of Votes, then the House of Representatives shall immediately chuse by Ballot one of them for President; and if no Person have a Majority, then from the five highest on the List the said House shall in like Manner chuse the President. But in chusing the President, the Votes shall be taken by States, the Representation from each State having one Vote; A quorum for this Purpose shall consist of a Member or Members from two thirds of the States, and a Majority of all the States shall be necessary to a Choice. In every Case, after the Choice of the President, the Person having the greatest Number of Votes of the Electors shall be the Vice President. But if there should remain two or more who have equal Votes, the Senate shall chuse from them by Ballot the Vice President.

The Congress may determine the time of chusing the Electors, and the Day on which they shall give their Votes; which Day shall be the same throughout the United States.

No person except a natural born Citizen, *or a Citizen of the United States, at the time of the Adoption of this Constitution,* shall be eligible to the Office of President; neither shall any Person be eligible to that Office who shall not have attained to the Age of thirty five Years, and been fourteen Years a Resident within the United States.

In Case of the Removal of the President from Office, or of his Death, Resignation, or Inability to discharge the Powers and Duties of the said Office, the Same shall devolve on the Vice President, and the Congress may by Law provide for the Case of Removal, Death, Resignation or Inability, both of the President and Vice President, declaring what Officer shall then act as President, and such Officer shall act accordingly, until the Disability be removed, or a President shall be elected.

The President shall, at stated Times, receive for his Services, a Compensation, which shall neither be encreased nor diminished during the Period for which he shall have been elected, and he shall not receive within that period any other Emolument from the United States, or any of them.

Before he enter on the Execution of his Office, he shall take the following Oath or Affirmation:—"I do solemnly swear (or affirm) that I will faithfully execute the Office of President of the United States, and will to the best of my Ability, preserve, protect and defend the Constitution of the United States."

Section 2

The President shall be Commander in Chief of the Army and Navy of the United States, and of the Militia of the several States, when called into the actual Service of the United States; he may require the Opinion, in writing, of the principal Officer in each of the executive Departments, upon any Subject relating to the Duties of their respective Offices, and he shall have Power to grant Reprieves and Pardons for Offences against the United States, except in Cases of Impeachment.

He shall have Power, by and with the Advice and Consent of the Senate, to make Treaties, provided two thirds of the Senators present concur; and he shall nominate, and by and with the Advice and Consent of the Senate, shall appoint Ambassadors, other public Ministers and Consuls, Judges of the supreme Court, and all other Officers of the United States, whose Appointments are not herein otherwise provided for, and which shall be established by Law: but the Congress may by Law vest the Appointment of such inferior Officers, as they think proper in the President alone, in the Courts of Law, or in the Heads of Departments.

The President shall have Power to fill up all Vacancies that may happen during the Recess of the Senate, by granting Commissions which shall expire at the End of their next Session.

Section 3

He shall from time to time give to the Congress Information of the State of the Union, and recommend to their Consideration such Measures as he shall judge necessary and expedient; he may, on extraordinary Occasions, convene both Houses, or either of them, and in Case of disagreement between them, with Respect to the Time of Adjournment, he may adjourn them to such Time as he shall think proper; he shall receive Ambassadors and other public Ministers; he shall take Care that the Laws be faithfully executed, and shall Commission all the officers of the United States.

Section 4

The President, Vice President and all civil Officers of the United States, shall be removed from Office on Impeachment for, and Conviction of, Treason, Bribery or other high Crimes and Misdemeanors.

Article 3

Section 1

The judicial Power of the United States, shall be vested in one supreme Court, and in such inferior Courts as the Congress may from time to time ordain and establish. The Judges, both of the supreme and inferior Courts, shall hold their offices during good Behaviour, and shall, at stated Times, receive for their Services, a Compensation, which shall not be diminished during their Continuance in Office.

Section 2

The judicial Power shall extend to all Cases, in Law and Equity, arising under this Constitution, the Laws of the United States, and Treaties made, or which shall be made, under their Authority;—to all Cases affecting Ambassadors, other public Ministers and Consuls;—to all Cases of admiralty and maritime Jurisdiction;—to Controversies to which the United States shall be a Party;—to Controversies between two or more States;—*between a State and Citizens of another State;*—between Citizens of different States;—between Citizens of the same State claiming Lands under Grants of different States, and between a State, or the Citizens thereof, and foreign States, Citizens or Subjects.

In all Cases affecting Ambassadors, other public Ministers and Consuls, and those in which a State shall be Party, the supreme Court shall have original Jurisdiction. In all the other Cases before mentioned, the supreme Court shall have appellate Jurisdiction, both as to Law and Fact, with such Exceptions, and under such Regulations as the Congress shall make.

The Trial of all Crimes, except in Cases of Impeachment, shall be by Jury; and such Trial shall be held in the State where the said Crimes shall have been committed, but when not committed within any State, the Trial shall be at such Place or Places as the Congress may by Law have directed.

Section 3

Treason against the United States, shall consist only in levying War against them, or in adhering to their Enemies, giving them Aid and Comfort. No person shall be convicted of Treason unless on the Testimony of two Witnesses to the same overt Act, or on Confession in open Court.

The Congress shall have Power to declare the Punishment of Treason, but no Attainder of Treason shall work Corruption of Blood, or Forfeiture except during the Life of the Person attainted.

Article 4

Section 1

Full Faith and Credit shall be given in each State to the public Acts, Records, and judicial Proceedings of every other State. And the Congress may by general Laws prescribe the Manner in which such Acts, Records and Proceedings shall be proved, and the Effect thereof.

Section 2

The Citizens of each State shall be entitled to all Privileges and Immunities of Citizens in the several States.

A Person charged in any State with Treason, Felony, or other Crime, who shall flee from Justice, and be found in another State, shall on Demand of the executive Authority of the State from which he fled, be delivered up, to be removed to the State having Jurisdiction of the Crime.

No Person held to Service or Labour in one State, under the Laws thereof, escaping into another, shall, in Consequence of any Law or Regulation therein, be discharged from such Service or Labour, but shall be delivered up on Claim of the Party to whom such Service or Labour may be due.

Section 3

New States may be admitted by the Congress into this Union; but no new State shall be formed or erected within the Jurisdiction of any other State; nor any State be formed by the Junction of two or more States, or Parts of States, without the Consent of the Legislatures of the States concerned as well as of the Congress.

The Congress shall have Power to dispose of and make all needful Rules and Regulations respecting the Territory or other Property belonging to the United States; and nothing in this Constitution shall be so construed as to Prejudice any Claims of the United States, or of any particular States.*

Section 4

The United States shall guarantee to every State in this Union a Republican Form of Government, and shall protect each of them against Invasion; and on Application of the Legislature, or of the Executive (when the Legislature cannot be convened) against domestic violence.

Article 5

The Congress, whenever two thirds of both Houses shall deem it necessary, shall propose Amendments to this Constitution, or, on the Application of the Legislatures of two thirds of the several States, shall call a Convention for proposing Amendments, which, in either Case, shall be valid to all Intents and Purposes, as Part of this Constitution, when ratified by the Legislatures of three fourths of the several States, or by Conventions in three fourths thereof, as the one or the other Mode of Ratification may be proposed by the Congress; Provided *that no Amendment which may be made prior to the Year One thousand eight hundred and eight shall in any Manner affect the first and fourth Clauses in the Ninth Section of the first Article;* and that no State, without its Consent, shall be deprived of its equal Suffrage in the Senate.

---

*The Constitution was submitted on September 17, 1787, by the Constitutional Convention, was ratified by the Convention of several states at various dates up to May 29, 1790, and became effective on March 4, 1789.

Article 6

All Debts contracted and Engagements entered into, before the Adoption of this Constitution, shall be as valid against the United States under this Constitution, as under the Confederation.

This Constitution, and Laws of the United States which shall be made in Pursuance thereof; and all Treaties made, or which shall be made, under the Authority of the United States, shall be the supreme Law of the Land; and the Judges in every State shall be bound thereby, any Thing in the Constitution or Laws of any State to the Contrary notwithstanding.

The Senators and Representatives before mentioned, and the Members of the several State Legislatures, and all executive and Judicial Officers, both of the United States and of the several States, shall be bound by Oath or Affirmation, to support this Constitution; but no religious Test shall ever be required as a Qualification to any Office of public Trust under the United States.

Article 7

The Ratification of the Conventions of nine States, shall be sufficient for the Establishment of this Constitution between the States so ratifying the Same.

Done in Convention by the Unanimous Consent of the States present the Seventeenth Day of September in the Year of our Lord one thousand seven hundred and Eighty seven and of the Independence of the United States of America the Twelfth* IN WITNESS whereof We have hereunto subscribed our Names,

George Washington President and Deputy from Virginia

Delaware	South Carolina	New York
George Read	John Rutledge	Alexander Hamilton
Gunning Bedford, Jr.	Charles Cotesworth Pinckney	**New Jersey**
John Dickinson	Charles Pinckney	William Livingston
Richard Bassett	Pierce Butler	David Brearley
Jacob Broom	**Georgia**	William Paterson
Maryland	William Few	Jonathan Dayton
James McHenry	Abraham Baldwin	Pennsylvania
Daniel of St. Thomas Jenifer	**New Hampshire**	Benjamin Franklin
Daniel Carroll	John Langdon	Thomas Mifflin
Virginia	Nicholas Gilman	Robert Morris
John Blair	**Massachusetts**	George Clymer
James Madison, Jr	Nathaniel Gorham	Thomas FitzSimons
North Carolina	Rufus King	Jared Ingersoll
William Blount	**Connecticut**	James Wilson
Richard Dobbs Spaight	William Samuel Johnson	Gouverneur Morris
Hugh Williamson	Roger Sherman	

Amendments to the Constitution

Amendment I

Congress shall make no law respecting an establishment of religion, or prohibiting the free exercise thereof; or abridging the freedom of speech, or of the press; or the right of the people peaceably to assemble, and to petition the Government for a redress of grievances.

Amendment II

A well regulated Militia being necessary to the security of a free State, the right of the people to keep and bear Arms, shall not be infringed.

Amendment III

No Soldier shall, in time of peace be quartered in any house, without the consent of the Owner, nor in time of war, but in a manner to be prescribed by law.

Amendment IV

The right of the people to be secure in their persons, houses, papers, and effects, against unreasonable searches and seizures, shall not be violated, and no Warrants shall issue, but upon probable cause, supported by Oath or affirmation, and particularly describing the place to be searched, and the persons or things to be seized.

Amendment V

No person shall be held to answer for a capital, or otherwise infamous crime, unless on a presentment or indictment of a Grand Jury, except in cases arising in the land or naval forces, or in the Militia, when in actual service in time of War or public danger; nor shall any person be subject for the same offense to be twice put in jeopardy of life or limb; nor shall be compelled in any criminal case to be a witness against himself, nor be deprived of life, liberty, or property, without due process of law; nor shall private property be taken for public use, without just compensation.

Amendment VI

In all criminal prosecutions, the accused shall enjoy the right to a speedy and public trial, by an impartial jury of the State and district wherein the crime shall have been committed, which district shall have been previously ascertained by law, and to be informed

---

*The Constitution was submitted on September 17, 1787, by the Constitutional Convention, was ratified by the Convention of several states at various dates up to May 29, 1790, and became effective on March 4, 1789.

of the nature and cause of the accusation; to be confronted with the witnesses against him; to have compulsory process for obtaining witnesses in his favor, and to have the Assistance of Counsel for his defence.

Amendment VII

In Suits at common law, where the value in controversy shall exceed twenty dollars, the right of trial by jury shall be preserved, and no fact tried by a jury, shall be otherwise reexamined in any Court of the United States, than according to the rules of the common law.

Amendment VIII

Excessive bail shall not be required, nor excessive fines imposed, nor cruel and unusual punishments inflicted.

Amendment IX

The enumeration in the Constitution, of certain rights, shall not be construed to deny or disparage others retained by the people.

Amendment X*

The powers not delegated to the United States by the Constitution, nor prohibited by it to the States, are reserved to the States respectively, or to the people.

Amendment XI [Adopted 1798]

The Judicial power of the United States shall not be construed to extend to any suit in law or equity, commenced or prosecuted against one of the United States by Citizens of another State, or by Citizens or Subjects of any Foreign State.

Amendment XII [Adopted 1804]

The Electors shall meet in their respective states, and vote by ballot for President and Vice President, one of whom, at least, shall not be an inhabitant of the same state with themselves; they shall name in their ballots the person voted for as President, and in distinct ballots the person voted for as Vice President, and they shall make distinct lists of all persons voted for as President, and of all persons voted for as Vice President, and of the number of votes for each, which lists they shall sign and certify, and transmit sealed to the seat of the government of the United States, directed to the President of the Senate;—The President of the Senate shall, in the presence of the Senate and House of Representatives, open all the certificates and the votes shall then be counted;—The person having the greatest number of votes for President, shall be the President, if such number be a majority of the whole number of Electors appointed; and if no person have such majority, then from the persons having the highest numbers not exceeding three on the list of those voted for as President, the House of Representatives shall choose immediately, by ballot, the President. But in choosing the President, the votes shall be taken by states, the representation from each state having one vote; a quorum for this purpose shall consist of a member or members from two-thirds of the states, and a majority of all the states shall be necessary to a choice. And if the House of Representatives shall

not choose a President whenever the right of choice shall devolve upon them, before *the fourth day of March* next following, then the Vice President shall act as President, as in the case of the death or other constitutional disability of the President.—The person having the greatest number of votes as Vice President, shall be the Vice President, if such number be a majority of the whole number of Electors appointed, and if no person have a majority, then from the two highest numbers on the list, the Senate shall choose the Vice President; a quorum for the purpose shall consist of two-thirds of the whole number of Senators, and a majority of the whole number shall be necessary to a choice. But no person constitutionally ineligible to the office of President shall be eligible to that of Vice President of the United States.

Amendment XIII [Adopted 1865]

Section 1

Neither slavery nor involuntary servitude, except as a punishment for crime whereof the party shall have been duly convicted, shall exist within the United States, or any place subject to their jurisdiction.

Section 2

Congress shall have power to enforce this article by appropriate legislation.

Amendment XIV [Adopted 1868]

Section 1

All persons born or naturalized in the United States, and subject to the jurisdiction thereof, are citizens of the United States and of the State wherein they reside. No State shall make or enforce any law which shall abridge the privileges or immunities of citizens of the United States; nor shall any State deprive any person of life, liberty, or property, without due process of law; nor deny to any person within its jurisdiction the equal protection of the laws.

Section 2

Representatives shall be apportioned among the several States according to their respective numbers, counting the whole number of persons in each State, excluding Indians not taxed. But when the right to vote at any election for the choice of electors for President and Vice President of the United States, Representatives in Congress, the Executive and Judicial officers of a State, or the members of the Legislature thereof, is denied to any of the male inhabitants of such State, being twenty-one years of age, and citizens of the United States, or in any way abridged, except for participation in rebellion, or other crime, the basis of representation therein shall be reduced in the proportion which the number of such male citizens shall bear to the whole number of male citizens twenty-one years of age in such State.

Section 3

No person shall be a Senator or Representative in Congress, or elector of President and Vice President, or hold any office, civil or military, under the United States, or under any State, who, having previously taken an oath, as a member of Congress, or as an officer of the United States, or as a member of any State legislature, or as an executive or judicial officer of any State, to support the Constitution of the United States, shall have engaged in insurrection or rebellion against the same, or given aid or comfort to the enemies thereof. But Congress may by a vote of two-thirds of each House, remove such disability.

---

*The first ten amendments (the Bill of Rights) were ratified and their adoption was certified on December 15, 1791.

Section 4

The validity of the public debt of the United States, authorized by law, including debts incurred for payment of pensions and bounties for services in suppressing insurrection or rebellion, shall not be questioned. But neither the United States nor any State shall assume or pay any debt or obligation incurred in aid of insurrection or rebellion against the United States, or any claim for the loss or emancipation of any slave; but all such debts, obligations and claims shall be held illegal and void.

Section 5

The Congress shall have power to enforce, by appropriate legislation, the provisions of this article.

Amendment XV [Adopted 1870]
Section 1

The right of citizens of the United States to vote shall not be denied or abridged by the United States or by any State on account of race, color, or previous condition of servitude.

Section 2

The Congress shall have power to enforce this article by appropriate legislation.

Amendment XVI [Adopted 1913]

The Congress shall have power to lay and collect taxes on incomes, from whatever source derived, without apportionment among the several States, and without regard to any census or enumeration.

Amendment XVII [Adopted 1913]

The Senate of the United States shall be composed of two Senators from each State, elected by the people thereof, for six years; and each Senator shall have one vote. The electors in each State shall have the qualifications requisite for electors of the most numerous branch of the State legislatures.

When vacancies happen in the representation of any State in the Senate, the executive authority of such State shall issue writs of election to fill such vacancies: *Provided*, That the legislature of any State may empower the executive thereof to make temporary appointments until the people fill the vacancies by election as the legislature may direct.

This amendment shall not be so construed as to affect the election or term of any Senator chosen before it becomes valid as part of the Constitution.

Amendment XVIII [Adopted 1919, Repealed 1933]
Section 1

After one year from the ratification of this article the manufacture, sale, or transportation of intoxicating liquors within, the importation thereof into, or the exportation thereof from the United States and all territory subject to the jurisdiction thereof for beverage purposes is hereby prohibited.

Section 2

The Congress and the several States shall have concurrent power to enforce this article by appropriate legislation.

Section 3

This article shall be inoperative unless it shall have been ratified as an amendment to the Constitution by the legislatures of the several

States, as provided in the Constitution, within seven years from the date of the submission hereof to the States by the Congress.

Amendment XIX [Adopted 1920]

The right of citizens of the United States to vote shall not be denied or abridged by the United States or by any State on account of sex.

Congress shall have power to enforce this article by appropriate legislation.

Amendment XX [Adopted 1933]
Section 1

The terms of the President and Vice President shall end at noon on the 20th day of January, and the terms of Senators and Representatives at noon on the 3d day of January, of the years in which such terms would have ended if this article had not been ratified and the terms of their successors shall then begin.

Section 2

The Congress shall assemble at least once in every year, and such meeting shall begin at noon on the 3d day of January, unless they shall by law appoint a different day.

Section 3

If, at the time fixed for the beginning of the term of the President, the President elect shall have died, the Vice President elect shall become President. If a President shall not have been chosen before the time fixed for the beginning of his term, or if the President elect shall have failed to qualify, then the Vice President elect shall act as President until a President shall have qualified; and the Congress may by law provide for the case wherein neither a President elect nor a Vice President elect shall have qualified, declaring who shall then act as President, or the manner in which one who is to act shall be selected, and such person shall act accordingly until a President or Vice President shall have qualified.

Section 4

The Congress may by law provide for the case of the death of any of the persons from whom the House of Representatives may choose a President whenever the right of choice shall have devolved upon them, and for the case of the death of any of the persons from whom the Senate may choose a Vice President whenever the right of choice shall have devolved upon them.

Section 5

Sections 1 and 2 shall take effect on the 15th day of October following the ratification of this article.

Section 6

This article shall be inoperative unless it shall have been ratified as an amendment to the Constitution by the legislatures of three fourths of the several States within seven years from the date of its submission.

Amendment XXI [Adopted 1933]
Section 1

The eighteenth article of amendment to the Constitution of the United States is hereby repealed.

Section 2

The transportation or importation into any State, Territory, or possession of the United States for delivery or use therein of intoxicating liquors in violation of the laws thereof, is hereby prohibited.

Section 3

This article shall be inoperative unless it shall have been ratified as an amendment to the Constitution by conventions in the several States, as provided in the Constitution, within seven years from the date of the submission hereof to the States by the Congress.

Amendment XXII [Adopted 1951]

Section 1

No person shall be elected to the office of the President more than twice, and no person who has held the office of President, or acted as President, for more than two years of a term to which some other person was elected President shall be elected to the office of the President more than once. But this Article shall not apply to any person holding the office of President when this Article was proposed by the Congress, and shall not prevent any person who may be holding the office of President, or acting as President, during the term within which this Article becomes operative from holding the office of President or acting as President during the remainder of such term.

Section 2

This article shall be inoperative unless it shall have been ratified as an amendment to the Constitution by the legislatures of three-fourths of the several States within seven years from the date of its submission to the States by the Congress.

Amendment XXIII [Adopted 1961]

Section 1

The District constituting the seat of Government of the United States shall appoint in such manner as the Congress shall direct:

A number of electors of President and Vice President equal to the whole number of Senators and Representatives in Congress to which the District would be entitled if it were a State, but in no event more than the least populous State; they shall be in addition to those appointed by the States, but they shall be considered, for the purposes of the election of President and Vice President, to be electors appointed by a State; and they shall meet in the District and perform such duties as provided by the twelfth article of amendment.

Section 2

The Congress shall have power to enforce this article by appropriate legislation.

Amendment XXIV [Adopted 1964]

Section 1

The right of citizens of the United States to vote in any primary or other election for President or Vice President, for electors for President or Vice President, or for Senator or Representative in Congress, shall not be denied or abridged by the United States or any state by reason of failure to pay any poll tax or other tax.

Section 2

The Congress shall have the power to enforce this article by appropriate legislation.

Amendment XXV [Adopted 1967]

Section 1

In case of the removal of the President from office or his death or resignation, the Vice President shall become President.

Section 2

Whenever there is a vacancy in the office of the Vice President, the President shall nominate a Vice President who shall take the office upon confirmation by a majority vote of both houses of Congress.

Section 3

Whenever the President transmits to the President pro tempore of the Senate and the Speaker of the House of Representatives his written declaration that he is unable to discharge the powers and duties of his office, and until he transmits to them a written declaration to the contrary, such powers and duties shall be discharged by the Vice President as Acting President.

Section 4

Whenever the Vice President and a majority of either the principal officers of the executive departments or of such other body as Congress may by law provide, transmit to the President pro tempore of the Senate and the Speaker of the House of Representatives their written declaration that the President is unable to discharge the powers and duties of his office, the Vice President shall immediately assume the powers and duties of the office as Acting President.

Thereafter, when the President transmits to the President pro tempore of the Senate and the Speaker of the House of Representatives his written declaration that no inability exists, he shall resume the powers and duties of his office unless the Vice President and a majority of either the principal officers of the executive department or of such other body as Congress may by law provide, transmit within four days to the President pro tempore of the Senate and the Speaker of the House of Representatives their written declaration that the President is unable to discharge the powers and duties of his office. Thereupon Congress shall decide the issue, assembling within 48 hours for that purpose if not in session. If the Congress, within 21 days after receipt of the latter written declaration, or, if Congress is not in session, within 21 days after Congress is required to assemble, determines by two-thirds vote of both houses that the President is unable to discharge the powers and duties of his office, the Vice President shall continue to discharge the same as Acting President; otherwise, the President shall resume the powers and duties of his office.

Amendment XXVI [Adopted 1971]

Section 1

The right of citizens of the United States, who are 18 years of age or older, to vote shall not be denied or abridged by the United States or any state on account of age.

Section 2

The Congress shall have the power to enforce this article by appropriate legislation.

Amendment XXVII [Adopted 1992]

No law, varying the compensation for the services of the Senators and Representatives shall take effect, until an election of Representatives shall have intervened.

PRESIDENTIAL ELECTIONS

Year	Candidates	Parties	Popular Vote	Electoral Vote	Voter Participation
1789	George Washington		*	69	
	John Adams			34	
	Others			35	
1792	George Washington		*	132	
	John Adams			77	
	George Clinton			50	
	Others			5	
1796	John Adams	Federalist	*	71	
	Thomas Jefferson	Democratic-Republican		68	
	Thomas Pinckney	Federalist		59	
	Aaron Burr	Dem.-Rep.		30	
	Others			48	
1800	Thomas Jefferson	Dem.-Rep.	*	73	
	Aaron Burr	Dem.-Rep.		73	
	John Adams	Federalist		65	
	C. C. Pinckney	Federalist		64	
	John Jay	Federalist		1	
1804	Thomas Jefferson	Dem.-Rep.	*	162	
	C. C. Pinckney	Federalist		14	
1808	James Madison	Dem.-Rep.	*	122	
	C. C. Pinckney	Federalist		47	
	George Clinton	Dem.-Rep.		6	
1812	James Madison	Dem.-Rep.	*	128	
	De Witt Clinton	Federalist		89	
1816	James Monroe	Dem.-Rep.	*	183	
	Rufus King	Federalist		34	
1820	James Monroe	Dem.-Rep.	*	231	
	John Quincy Adams	Dem.-Rep.		1	
1824	John Quincy Adams	Dem.-Rep.	108,740 (30.5%)	84	26.9%
	Andrew Jackson	Dem.-Rep.	153,544 (43.1%)	99	
	William H. Crawford	Dem.-Rep.	46,618 (13.1%)	41	
	Henry Clay	Dem.-Rep.	47,136 (13.2%)	37	
1828	Andrew Jackson	Democratic	647,286 (56.0%)	178	57.6%
	John Quincy Adams	National Republican	508,064 (44.0%)	83	
1832	Andrew Jackson	Democratic	688,242 (54.2%)	219	55.4%
	Henry Clay	National Republican	473,462 (37.4%)	49	
	John Floyd	Independent		11	
	William Wirt	Anti-Mason	101,051 (7.8%)	7	
1836	Martin Van Buren	Democratic	762,198 (50.8%)	170	57.8%
	William Henry Harrison	Whig	549,508 (36.6%)	73	
	Hugh L. White	Whig	145,342 (9.7%)	26	
	Daniel Webster	Whig	41,287 (2.7%)	14	
	W. P. Magnum	Independent		11	
1840	William Henry Harrison	Whig	1,274,624 (53.1%)	234	80.2%
	Martin Van Buren	Democratic	1,127,781 (46.9%)	60	
	J. G. Birney	Liberty	7069	—	
1844	James K. Polk	Democratic	1,338,464 (49.6%)	170	78.9%
	Henry Clay	Whig	1,300,097 (48.1%)	105	
	J. G. Birney	Liberty	62,300 (2.3%)	—	
1848	Zachary Taylor	Whig	1,360,967 (47.4%)	163	72.7%
	Lewis Cass	Democratic	1,222,342 (42.5%)	127	
	Martin Van Buren	Free-Soil	291,263 (10.1%)	—	
1852	Franklin Pierce	Democratic	1,601,117 (50.9%)	254	69.6%
	Winfield Scott	Whig	1,385,453 (44.1%)	42	
	John P. Hale	Free-Soil	155,825 (5.0%)	—	
1856	James Buchanan	Democratic	1,832,955 (45.3%)	174	78.9%
	John C. Frémont	Republican	1,339,932 (33.1%)	114	

(continued)

Year	Candidates	Parties	Popular Vote	Electoral Vote	Voter Participation
	Millard Fillmore	American	871,731 (21.6%)	8	
1860	Abraham Lincoln	Republican	1,865,593 (39.8%)	180	81.2%
	Stephen A. Douglas	Democratic	1,382,713 (29.5%)	12	
	John C. Breckinridge	Democratic	848,356 (18.1%)	72	
	John Bell	Union	592,906 (12.6%)	39	
1864	Abraham Lincoln	Republican	2,213,655 (55.0%)	212†	73.8%
	George B. McClellan	Democratic	1,805,237 (45.0%)	21	
1868	Ulysses S. Grant	Republican	3,012,833 (52.7%)	214	78.1%
	Horatio Seymour	Democratic	2,703,249 (47.3%)	80	
1872	Ulysses S. Grant	Republican	3,597,132 (55.6%)	286	71.3%
	Horace Greeley	Dem.; Liberal Republican	2,834,125 (43.9%)	66‡	
1876	Rutherford B. Hayes§	Republican	4,036,298 (48.0%)	185	81.8%
	Samuel J. Tilden	Democratic	4,300,590 (51.0%)	184	
1880	James A. Garfield	Republican	4,454,416 (48.5%)	214	79.4%
	Winfield S. Hancock	Democratic	4,444,952 (48.1%)	155	
1884	Grover Cleveland	Democratic	4,874,986 (48.5%)	219	77.5%
	James G. Blaine	Republican	4,851,981 (48.2%)	182	
1888	Benjamin Harrison	Republican	5,439,853 (47.9%)	233	79.3%
	Grover Cleveland	Democratic	5,540,309 (48.6%)	168	
1892	Grover Cleveland	Democratic	5,556,918 (46.1%)	277	74.7%
	Benjamin Harrison	Republican	5,176,108 (43.0%)	145	
	James B. Weaver	People's	1,029,329 (8.5%)	22	
1896	William McKinley	Republican	7,104,779 (51.1%)	271	79.3%
	William Jennings Bryan	Democratic People's	6,502,925 (47.7%)	176	
1900	William McKinley	Republican	7,207,923 (51.7%)	292	73.2%
	William Jennings Bryan	Democratic	6,358,133 (45.5%)	155	
1904	Theodore Roosevelt	Republican	7,623,486 (57.9%)	336	65.2%
	Alton B. Parker	Democratic	5,077,911 (37.6%)	140	
	Eugene V. Debs	Socialist	402,400 (3.0%)	—	
1908	William H. Taft	Republican	7,678,908 (51.6%)	321	65.4%
	William Jennings Bryan	Democratic	6,409,104 (43.1%)	162	
	Eugene V. Debs	Socialist	402,820 (2.8%)	—	
1912	Woodrow Wilson	Democratic	6,293,454 (41.9%)	435	58.8%
	Theodore Roosevelt	Progressive	4,119,538 (27.4%)	88	
	William H. Taft	Republican	3,484,980 (23.2%)	8	
	Eugene V. Debs	Socialist	900,672 (6.0%)	—	
1916	Woodrow Wilson	Democratic	9,129,606 (49.4%)	277	61.6%
	Charles E. Hughes	Republican	8,538,221 (46.2%)	254	
	A. L. Benson	Socialist	585,113 (3.2%)	—	
1920	Warren G. Harding	Republican	16,152,200 (60.4%)	404	49.2%
	James M. Cox	Democratic	9,147,353 (34.2%)	127	
	Eugene V. Debs	Socialist	917,799 (3.4%)	—	
1924	Calvin Coolidge	Republican	15,725,016 (54.0%)	382	48.9%
	John W. Davis	Democratic	8,386,503 (28.8%)	136	
	Robert M. La Follette	Progressive	4,822,856 (16.6%)	13	
1928	Herbert Hoover	Republican	21,391,381 (58.2%)	444	56.9%
	Alfred E. Smith	Democratic	15,016,443 (40.9%)	87	
	Norman Thomas	Socialist	267,835 (0.7%)	—	
1932	Franklin D. Roosevelt	Democratic	22,821,857 (57.4%)	472	56.9%
	Herbert Hoover	Republican	15,761,841 (39.7%)	59	
	Norman Thomas	Socialist	884,781 (2.2%)	—	
1936	Franklin D. Roosevelt	Democratic	27,751,597 (60.8%)	523	61.0%
	Alfred M. Landon	Republican	16,679,583 (36.5%)	8	
	William Lemke	Union	882,479 (1.9%)	—	
1940	Franklin D. Roosevelt	Democratic	27,244,160 (54.8%)	449	62.5%
	Wendell L. Willkie	Republican	22,305,198 (44.8%)	82	
1944	Franklin D. Roosevelt	Democratic	25,602,504 (53.5%)	432	55.9%
	Thomas E. Dewey	Republican	22,006,285 (46.0%)	99	
1948	Harry S Truman	Democratic	24,105,695 (49.5%)	304	53.0%

Year	Candidates	Parties	Popular Vote	Electoral Vote	Voter Participation
	Thomas E. Dewey	Republican	21,969,170 (45.1%)	189	
	J. Strom Thurmond	State-Rights Democratic	1,169,021 (2.4%)	38	
	Henry A. Wallace	Progressive	1,157,326 (2.4%)	—	
1952	Dwight D. Eisenhower	Republican	33,778,963 (55.1%)	442	63.3%
	Adlai E. Stevenson	Democratic	27,314,992 (44.4%)	89	
1956	Dwight D. Eisenhower	Republican	35,575,420 (57.6%)	457	60.6%
	Adlai E. Stevenson	Democratic	26,033,066 (42.1%)	73	
	Other	—	—	1	
1960	John F. Kennedy	Democratic	34,227,096 (49.9%)	303	62.8%
	Richard M. Nixon	Republican	34,108,546 (49.6%)	219	
	Other	—	—	15	
1964	Lyndon B. Johnson	Democratic	43,126,506 (61.1%)	486	61.7%
	Barry M. Goldwater	Republican	27,176,799 (38.5%)	52	
1968	Richard M. Nixon	Republican	31,770,237 (43.4%)	301	60.6%
	Hubert H. Humphrey	Democratic	31,270,533 (42.7%)	191	
	George Wallace	American Indep.	9,906,141 (13.5%)	46	
1972	Richard M. Nixon	Republican	46,740,323 (60.7%)	520	55.2%
	George S. McGovern	Democratic	28,901,598 (37.5%)	17	
	Other	—	—	1	
1976	Jimmy Carter	Democratic	40,828,587 (50.0%)	297	53.5%
	Gerald R. Ford	Republican	39,147,613 (47.9%)	241	
	Other	—	1,575,459 (2.1%)	—	
1980	Ronald Reagan	Republican	43,901,812 (50.7%)	489	52.6%
	Jimmy Carter	Democratic	35,483,820 (41.0%)	49	
	John B. Anderson	Independent	5,719,437 (6.6%)	—	
	Ed Clark	Libertarian	921,188 (1.1%)	—	
1984	Ronald Reagan	Republican	54,455,075 (59.0%)	525	53.3%
	Walter Mondale	Democratic	37,577,185 (41.0%)	13	
1988	George H. W. Bush	Republican	48,886,097 (53.4%)	426	57.4%
	Michael S. Dukakis	Democratic	41,809,074 (45.6%)	111	
1992	William J. Clinton	Democratic	44,908,254 (43%)	370	55.0%
	George H. W. Bush	Republican	39,102,343 (37.5%)	168	
	H. Ross Perot	Independent	19,741,065 (18.9%)	—	
1996	William J. Clinton	Democratic	45,590,703 (50%)	379	48.8%
	Robert Dole	Republican	37,816,307 (41%)	159	
	Ross Perot	Reform	7,866,284	—	
2000	George W. Bush	Republican	50,456,167 (47.88%)	271	51.2%
	Al Gore	Democratic	50,996,064 (48.39%)	266"	
	Ralph Nader	Green	2,864,810 (2.72%)	—	
	Other	834,774 (less than 1%)	—		
2004	George W. Bush	Republican	60,934,251 (51.0%)	286	50.0%
	John F. Kerry	Democratic	57,765,291 (48.0%)	252	
	Ralph Nader	Independent	405,933 (less than 1%)	—	
2008	Barack Obama	Democractic	69,456,897 (52.9%)	365	62%
	John McCain	Republican	59,934,814 (45.7%)	173	
2012	Barack Obama	Democratic	65,446,032	332	57.5%
	Mitt Romney	Republican	60,589,084	206	
	Gary Johnson	Libertarian	1,273,168		
	Jill Stein	Green	464,510		

*Electors selected by state legislatures.

†Eleven secessionist states did not participate.

‡Greeley died before the electoral college met. His electoral votes were divided among the four minor candidates.

§Contested result settled by special election.

"One District of Columbia Gore elector abstained. Popular Vote

Glossary

affirmative action   The use of laws or regulations to achieve racial, ethnic, gender, or other diversity, as in hiring or school admissions. Such efforts are often aimed at improving employment or educational opportunities for women and minorities.

Agricultural Adjustment Administration (AAA)   Created by Congress in 1933 as part of the New Deal, this agency attempted to restrict agricultural production by paying farmers subsidies to take land out of production. The object was to raise farm prices, and it did, but the act did nothing for tenant farmers and sharecroppers. The Supreme Court declared it unconstitutional in 1936.

American Federation of Labor (AFL)   Founded by Samuel Gompers in 1886, the AFL organized skilled workers by craft and pursued specific practical objectives, such as higher wages, shorter hours, and better working conditions. The AFL avoided politics, and while it did not expressly forbid blacks and women from joining, it used exclusionary practices to keep them out.

Americans with Disabilities Act   Passed by Congress in 1991, this act banned discrimination against the disabled in employment and mandated easy access to all public and commercial buildings.

Anti-Imperialist League   An organization formed in 1898 to fight the Treaty of Paris ending the Spanish-American War. Members opposed acquiring overseas colonies, believing it would subvert American ideals and institutions. Membership centered in New England; the cause was less popular in the South and West.

Ashcan School   Early twentieth-century realist painters who portrayed the slums and streets of the nation's cities and the lives of ordinary urban dwellers. They often advocated political and social reform.

Axis Powers   During World War II, the alliance between Italy, Germany, and Japan was known as the "Rome–Berlin–Tokyo axis," and the three members were called the Axis Powers. They fought against the Allied Powers, led by the United States, Britain, and the Soviet Union.

baby boom   The rise in births following World War II. Children born to this generation are referred to as "baby boomers."

Baruch Plan   In 1946, Bernard Baruch presented an American plan to control and eventually outlaw nuclear weapons. The plan called for UN control of nuclear weapons in three stages before the United States gave up its stockpile. Soviet insistence on immediate nuclear disarmament without inspection doomed the Baruch Plan and led to a nuclear arms race between the United States and the Soviet Union.

Bay of Pigs   In April 1961, a group of Cuban exiles organized and supported by the CIA landed on the southern coast of Cuba in an effort to overthrow Fidel Castro. When the invasion ended in disaster, President Kennedy took full responsibility for it.

Berlin airlift   In 1948, in response to a Soviet land blockade of Berlin, the United States carried out a massive effort to supply the 2 million Berlin citizens by air. The airlift forced the Soviets to end the blockade in 1949.

birds of passage   Immigrants who came to the United States to work and save money and then returned to their native countries during the slack season.

Black Code   Laws passed by southern states immediately after the Civil War to maintain white supremacy by restricting the rights of the newly freed slaves.

Bland-Allison Silver Purchase Act   This 1878 act called for the partial coinage of silver. Those favoring silver coinage argued that it would increase the money supply and help farmers and workers repay their debts. Opponents advocated a restricted money supply based solely on gold and pointed out that few other major countries accepted silver coinage. Congress passed the bill over President Rutherford B. Hayes's veto.

Bonus Army   In June 1932, a group of 20,000 World War I veterans marched on Washington, D.C., to demand immediate payment of their "adjusted compensation" bonuses voted by Congress in 1924. Congress rejected their demands, and President Herbert Hoover had the Bonus Army forcibly dispersed.

Brown v. Board of Education of Topeka   In 1954, the Supreme Court reversed the *Plessy v. Ferguson* decision (1896), which established the "separate but equal" doctrine. The Brown decision found segregation in schools inherently unequal and initiated a long and difficult effort to integrate the nation's public schools.

Camp David Accords   In 1978, President Jimmy Carter mediated a peace agreement between the leaders of Egypt and Israel at Camp David. In 1979, Israel and Egypt signed a peace treaty based on the accords.

Chinese Exclusion Act of 1882   Legislation passed in 1882 that excluded Chinese immigrants for ten years and denied U.S. citizenship to Chinese nationals. It was the first U.S. exclusionary law aimed at a specific racial group.

Civilian Conservation Corps (CCC)   One of the most popular New Deal programs, the CCC provided 300,000 young men between the ages of 18 and 25 with government jobs in reforestation and other conservation projects.

Civil Rights Cases   A group of cases in 1883 in which the Supreme Court ruled that the Fourteenth Amendment barred state governments from discriminating on the basis of race but did not prevent private individuals or organizations from doing so. The ruling dealt a major blow to efforts to protect African Americans.

Clayton Antitrust Act   This law outlawed interlocking directorates (in which the same people served as directors for several competing companies), forbade policies that created monopolies, and made corporate officers responsible for antitrust violations. It also declared that unions were not conspiracies in restraint of trade and outlawed the use of injunctions in labor disputes unless they were necessary to protect property.

Committee on Public Information (CPI)   Created in 1917 by President Wilson and headed by progressive journalist George Creel, this organization rallied support for American involvement in World War I through art, advertising, and film. Creel worked out a system of voluntary censorship with the press and distributed posters and pamphlets.

Compromise of 1877   Compromise struck during the contested presidential election of 1876, in which Democrats accepted the election of Rutherford B. Hayes (Republican) in exchange for the withdrawal of federal troops from the South and the end of Reconstruction.

Comstock Lode   Discovered in 1859 near Virginia City, Nevada, this ore deposit was the richest discovery in the history of mining. Named after T. P. Comstock, the deposit produced silver and gold worth more than $306 million.

conservation   President Theodore Roosevelt made this principle one of his administration's top goals. Conservation in his view aimed at protecting the nation's natural resources, but called for the wise use of them rather than locking them away.

containment   First proposed by George Kennan in 1947, containment became the basic strategy of the United States throughout the Cold War. Kennan argued that firm American resistance would eventually compel Moscow to adopt more peaceful policies.

Contract with America   In the 1994 congressional elections, Congressman Newt Gingrich had Republican candidates sign a document in which they

From Glossary of *American Stories: A History of the United States,* Third Edition. H. W. Brands, R. Hal Williams, T. H. Breen and Ariela J. Gross Copyright © 2015 by Pearson Education, Inc. All rights reserved.

pledged support for such things as a balanced budget amendment, term limits for members of Congress, and a middle-class tax cut.

"Court-packing" scheme Concerned that the conservative Supreme Court might declare all his New Deal programs unconstitutional, President Franklin D. Roosevelt asked Congress to allow him to appoint additional justices to the Court. Both Congress and the public rejected this "court-packing" scheme.

Cuban missile crisis In October 1962, the United States and the Soviet Union came close to nuclear war when President John F. Kennedy insisted that Nikita Khrushchev remove the 42 missiles he had secretly deployed in Cuba. The Soviets eventually did so, and the crisis ended.

D-Day June 6, 1944, the day Allied troops crossed the English Channel and opened a second front in western Europe during World War II. The "D" stands for "disembarkation": to leave a ship and go ashore.

Dawes Severalty Act Legislation passed by Congress in 1887 that aimed to break up traditional Indian life by promoting individual land ownership. It divided tribal lands into small plots that were distributed among members of each tribe. Provisions were made for education and eventual citizenship. The law led to corruption and exploitation and weakened tribal culture.

dollar diplomacy The Taft administration's policy in the early 1900s to promote U.S. financial and business interests abroad, especially in Latin America.

détente President Richard Nixon and Henry Kissinger pursued a policy of détente, a French word meaning a relaxation of tension, with the Soviet Union to lessen the possibility of nuclear war in the 1970s.

Equal Rights Amendment (ERA) A proposed constitutional amendment passed by Congress in 1972 to guarantee women equal treatment under the law. The amendment failed to be ratified in 1982.

Espionage Act of 1917 This law, passed after the United States entered World War I, imposed sentences of up to 20 years on anyone found guilty of aiding the enemy, obstructing recruitment of soldiers, or encouraging disloyalty. It allowed the postmaster general to remove from the mail any materials that incited treason or insurrection.

Exodusters A group of about 6,000 African Americans who left Louisiana, Mississippi, and Texas in 1879, for freer lives as farmers or laborers in Kansas.

Federal Reserve Act This 1913 act created a central banking system, consisting of 12 regional banks governed by the Federal Reserve Board. It was an attempt to provide the United States with a sound yet flexible currency.

Fifteenth Amendment Ratified in 1870, it prohibits the denial or abridgment of the right to vote by the federal or state governments on the basis of race, color, or prior condition as a slave. It was intended to guarantee African Americans the right to vote in the South.

Fireside chats Radio addresses by President Franklin D. Roosevelt from 1933 to 1944, in which he spoke to the American people about such issues as the banking crisis, Social Security, and World War II. The chats enhanced Roosevelt's popularity among ordinary Americans.

Food Administration Board A government agency that encouraged Americans to save food during World War I.

Fourteen Points In January 1918, President Woodrow Wilson presented these terms for a far-reaching, nonpunitive settlement of World War I and the establishment of a League of Nations. While generous and optimistic, the Points did not satisfy wartime hunger for revenge and were largely rejected by European nations.

Fourteenth Amendment Ratified in 1868, it provided citizenship to ex-slaves after the Civil War and constitutionally protected equal rights under the law for all citizens. Radical Republicans used it to enact a congressional Reconstruction policy in the former Confederate states.

Freedmen's Bureau Agency established by Congress in March 1865 to provide freedmen with shelter, food, and medical aid and to help them establish schools and find employment. The Bureau was dissolved in 1872.

freedom ride Sponsored by the Congress of Racial Equality (CORE), freedom rides on buses by civil rights advocates in 1961 in the South were designed to test the enforcement of federal regulations that prohibited segregation in interstate public transportation.

Ghost Dances A religious movement that arose in the late nineteenth century under the prophet Wavoka, a Paiute Indian. Its followers believed that dances and rites would cause white men to disappear and restore lands to the Native Americans. The U.S. government outlawed the Ghost Dances, and army intervention to stop them led to the **Wounded Knee Massacre**.

Gold Rush of 1849 Prospectors made the first gold strikes along the Sierra Nevada Mountains in California in 1849, touching off a mining boom that set the pattern for subsequent strikes in other regions.

Gold Standard Act Passed by Congress in 1900, this law made all currency redeemable in gold. The United States remained on the gold standard until 1933.

Great Society President Lyndon Johnson's name for his version of the Democratic reform program. In 1965, Congress passed many Great Society measures, including Medicare, civil rights legislation, and federal aid to education.

Gulf of Tonkin Resolution After a North Vietnamese attack on an American destroyer in the Gulf of Tonkin in 1964, Congress gave President Lyndon Johnson authority in this resolution to use force in Vietnam.

Harlem Renaissance An African American cultural, literary, and artistic movement centered in Harlem, in New York City, in the 1920s. Harlem, the largest black community in the world outside of Africa, was considered the cultural capital of African Americans.

Hay–Bunau–Varilla Treaty This 1903 treaty with Colombia granted the United States control over a canal zone 10 miles wide across the Isthmus of Panama.

Hepburn Act A 1906 law that strengthened the power of the **Interstate Commerce Commission (ICC)** to regulate the railroads.

Homestead Act of 1862 Legislation granting 160 acres to anyone who paid a $10 fee and pledged to live on and cultivate the land for five years. Between 1862 and 1900, nearly 600,000 families claimed homesteads under its provisions.

Homestead Strike In July 1892, wage-cutting at Andrew Carnegie's Homestead Steel Plant in Pittsburgh provoked a violent strike in which three company-hired detectives and ten workers died. Using ruthless force and strikebreakers, company officials broke the strike and destroyed the union.

Imperialism The policy of extending a nation's power over other areas through military conquest, economic domination, or annexation.

Industrial Workers of the World (IWW) Founded in 1905, this radical union, also known as the Wobblies, aimed to unite the American working class into one union. It organized unskilled and foreign-born laborers, advocated social revolution, and led strikes.

Intermediate Nuclear Forces Treaty (INF) Signed by President Ronald Reagan and Soviet President Mikhail Gorbachev in late 1987, this agreement provided for the destruction of all intermediate-range nuclear missiles and permitted on-site inspection for the first time during the Cold War.

Iran-Contra affair The Iran-Contra affair involved officials in the Reagan administration secretly and illegally selling arms to Iran and using the proceeds to finance the Contra rebels in Nicaragua.

Iranian hostage crisis In 1979, Iranian fundamentalists seized the American embassy in Tehran and held 53 Americans hostage for over a year. The hostages were released on January 20, 1981, the day Ronald Reagan became president.

Iron Curtain Winston Churchill coined the phrase "Iron Curtain" to refer to the boundary in Europe that divided Soviet-dominated Eastern and Central Europe from Western Europe.

isolationism A belief that the United States should avoid entanglements with other nations.

Jim Crow laws Segregation laws enacted by southern states after Reconstruction.

Kellogg–Briand Pact Also called the Pact of Paris, this 1928 agreement was the brainchild of U.S. Secretary of State Frank B. Kellogg and French Premier Aristide Briand. Its signatories, eventually including nearly all nations, pledged to shun war as an instrument of policy. It had little effect on the conduct of world affairs.

Knights of Labor Founded in 1869, this labor organization pursued broad reform and practical issues such as improved wages and hours. The Knights welcomed all laborers regardless of race, gender, or skill.

Ku Klux Klan A secret terrorist society first organized in Tennessee in 1866. The original Klan's goals were to disfranchise African Americans, stop

Reconstruction, and restore the prewar social order of the South. The Ku Klux Klan re-formed in the twentieth century to promote white supremacy and combat aliens, Catholics, and Jews.

Lend-Lease   In 1941, Congress gave President Franklin D. Roosevelt the authority to sell, lend, lease, or transfer war materials to any country whose defense he declared vital to that of the United States.

Manhattan Project   The top-secret World War II program that produced the first atomic weapons.

March on Washington   In August 1963, civil rights leaders organized a massive rally in Washington to urge passage of President John F. Kennedy's civil rights bill. The high point was Martin Luther King, Jr.'s "I Have a Dream" speech.

Marshall Plan   A massive aid program begun in 1947 to rebuild the war-torn economies of Western Europe. The plan was motivated by both humanitarian concerns and fear of communism.

McCarthyism   A sensationalist campaign by Senator Joseph McCarthy against supposed communists in government that began in 1950 and ended when the Senate censured him in 1954.

Medicare   The 1965 Medicare Act provided Social Security funding for hospitalization insurance for people over age 65 and the disabled and a voluntary plan to cover doctor bills paid in part by the federal government.

Montgomery bus boycott   In late 1955, African Americans led by Martin Luther King, Jr., boycotted the buses in Montgomery, Alabama, after seamstress Rosa Parks was arrested for refusing to move to the back of a bus. The boycott, which ended when the Supreme Court ruled in favor of the protesters, marked the beginning of a new, activist phase of the civil rights movement.

moral diplomacy   Policy of President Woodrow Wilson that rejected "dollar diplomacy." Rather than focusing mainly on economic ties with other nations, Wilson sought to practice morality in international relations, preserve peace, and extend to other peoples the blessings of democracy.

Moral Majority   In 1979, the Reverend Jerry Falwell founded the Moral Majority to combat "amoral liberals," drug abuse, "coddling" of criminals, homosexuality, communism, and abortion. The Moral Majority represented the rise of political activism among organized religion's radical right wing.

muckrakers   Writers who made a practice between 1903 and 1909 of exposing the wrongdoings of public figures and corporations and highlighting social and political problems.

Mugwumps   Educated and upper-class reformers who crusaded for lower tariffs, limited federal government, and civil service reform. They were best known for helping elect Grover Cleveland president in 1884.

NAACP   Created in 1909, this organization became the most important civil rights organization in the country.

National American Woman Suffrage Association   Founded by Susan B. Anthony in 1890, this organization worked to secure women the right to vote. It stressed careful organization and peaceful lobbying.

National Farmers' Alliance and Industrial Union   The Alliance sought to organize farmers in the South and West to fight for reforms that would improve their lot, including measures to overcome low crop prices, burdensome mortgages, and high railroad rates. The Alliance ultimately organized the People's (Populist) party.

National Grange of the Patrons of Husbandry   Founded by Oliver H. Kelly in 1867, the Grange sought to relieve the drabness of farm life by providing a social, educational, and cultural outlet for its members. It also set up grain elevators, cooperative stores, warehouses, insurance companies, and farm machinery factories.

National Organization for Women (NOW)   Founded in 1966, NOW called for equal employment opportunity and equal pay for women. It also championed the legalization of abortion and an equal rights amendment to the Constitution.

National Origins Quota Act   This 1924 law established a quota system that restricted immigration from Asia and southern and Eastern Europe and reduced the annual total of immigrants.

National Reclamation Act (Newlands Act)   Passed in 1902, this legislation set aside most of the proceeds from the sale of public land in 16 Western states to fund irrigation projects.

National Recovery Administration (NRA)   This New Deal agency was created in 1933 to promote economic recovery and revive industry during the Great Depression. It permitted manufacturers to establish industrywide codes of "fair business practices" setting prices and production levels. It also provided for minimum wages and maximum working hours for labor and guaranteed labor the right to organize and bargain collectively (Section 7a). The Supreme Court declared it unconstitutional in 1935.

National Security Act   Congress passed the National Security Act in 1947 in response to perceived threats from the Soviet Union after World War II. It established the Department of Defense and created the Central Intelligence Agency (CIA) and National Security Council.

nativism   Hostility to things foreign.

Nazi Holocaust   The slaughter of six million Jews and other persons by Hitler's regime.

Neoconservatisim   Former liberals who advocated a strong stand against communism abroad and free market capitalism at home. These intellectuals stressed the positive values of American society in contrast to those liberals who emphasized social problems.

neutrality acts   Laws in the 1930s that forbade selling munitions or lending money to belligerents. The 1937 act required that all other trade with countries at war be conducted on a cash-and-carry basis.

New Deal   President Franklin Delano Roosevelt's program to combat the Great Depression.

New Freedom   Woodrow Wilson's program, which emphasized business competition and small government. It sought to rein in federal authority, release individual energy, and restore competition. It achieved many of the progressive social-justice objectives while pushing for a free economy rather than a planned one.

New Frontier   President John F. Kennedy's program to revitalize the stagnant economy and enact reform legislation in education, health care, and civil rights.

new immigrants   Starting in the 1880s, immigration into the United States began to shift from northern and western Europe to southern and eastern Europe. These new immigrants were mostly poor, non-Protestant, and unskilled; they tended to stay in close-knit communities and retain their language, customs, and religions. Between 1880 and 1910, approximately 8.4 million of these so-called new immigrants came to the United States.

New Nationalism   President Theodore Roosevelt's program calling for a national approach to the country's affairs and a strong president to deal with them; efficiency in government and society; and protection of children, women, and workers. It accepted "good" trusts; and exalted the expert and the executive. It also encouraged large concentrations of capital and labor.

Niagara Movement   A movement, led by W. E. B. Du Bois, that focused on equal rights for and the education of African American youth. Rejecting the gradualist approach of Booker T. Washington, it favored militant action and claimed for African Americans all the rights afforded to other Americans.

North Atlantic Treaty Organization (NATO)   In 1949, the United States, Canada, and ten European nations formed this military mutual-defense pact.

NSC-68   National Security Council planning paper No. 68 redefined America's national defense policy. Adopted in 1950, it committed the United States to a massive military buildup to meet the challenge posed by the Soviet Union.

Ocala Demands   Adopted by the Farmers' Alliance in 1890 in Ocala, Florida, these demands became the organization's main platform. They called for a sub-treasury system to allow farmers to store their crops until they could get the best price, the free coinage of silver, an end to protective tariffs and national banks, a federal income tax, the direct election of senators by voters, and tighter regulation of railroads. (see People's party).

Open Door policy   This policy established free trade between the United States and China in 1900 and attempted to induce European nations and Japan to recognize the territorial integrity of China. It marked a departure from the American tradition of isolationism and signaled the country's growing involvement in the world.

Operation Desert Storm   The American and coalition military offensive against Iraq in 1991, which liberated Kuwait and dealt a serious but not fatal blow to Saddam Hussein's regime.

Organization of the Petroleum Exporting Countries (OPEC)   A cartel of oil-exporting nations.

Overland Trail The route from the Mississippi Valley to the Pacific Coast in the last half of the nineteenth century.

Pearl Harbor On December 7, 1941, Japanese warplanes attacked the U.S. fleet at Pearl Harbor, Hawaii. The attack marked America's entrance into World War II.

Pendleton Act This 1883 law created a bipartisan Civil Service Commission to administer competitive exams for civil service jobs and appoint officeholders based on merit. It also outlawed compulsory political contributions from appointed officials.

People's (or Populist) party This political party was organized in 1892 by farm, labor, and reform leaders, mainly from the Farmers' Alliance. It offered a broad-based reform platform reflecting the Ocala Demands. After 1896, it became identified as a one-issue party focused on free silver and gradually died away.

Philippine-American War A war fought from 1899 to 1903 to quell Filipino resistance to U.S. control of the Philippine Islands.

placer mining Mining that included using a shovel and washing pan to separate gold from the ore in streams and riverbeds. Placer miners worked as individuals or in small groups.

Plessy v. Ferguson A Supreme Court case in 1896 that established the doctrine of "separate but equal." The Court applied it to schools in *Cumming v. County Board of Education* (1899). The doctrine was finally overturned in 1954, in *Brown v. Board of Education of Topeka*.

Potsdam Conference The final wartime meeting of the leaders of the United States, Britain, and the Soviet Union was held at Potsdam, outside Berlin, in July 1945. Their failure to agree about the future of Europe led to the Cold War.

pragmatism An early twentieth-century doctrine, based on the ideas of William James. Pragmatists were impatient with the concept of truth as an abstract reality. They believed that truth should work for the individual and that people were not only shaped by their environment but also helped to shape it. If an idea worked, it became truth.

Progressive (or "Bull Moose") Party This political party was formed by Theodore Roosevelt to advance progressive ideas and unseat President William Howard Taft in 1912.

progressivism Movement for social change between the late 1890s and World War I. Its origins lay in a fear of big business and corrupt government and a desire to improve living conditions. Progressives set out to cure the social ills brought about by industrialization and urbanization, social disorder, and corruption.

prohibition The ban on the manufacture, sale, and transportation of alcoholic beverages in the United States. The Eighteenth Amendment, adopted in 1919, established prohibition. It was repealed by the Twenty-First Amendment in 1933.

Pullman Strike Beginning in May 1894, this strike at the Pullman Palace Car Company near Chicago was one of the largest strikes in American history. Workers struck to protest wage cuts, high rents for company housing, and layoffs. The American Railway Union, led by Eugene V. Debs, joined the strike in June. Extending into 27 states and territories, it paralyzed the western half of the nation. President Grover Cleveland secured an injunction to break the strike on the grounds that it obstructed the mail, and sent federal troops to enforce it.

Radical Reconstruction The Reconstruction Acts of 1867 divided the South into five military districts. They required the states to guarantee black male suffrage and to ratify the Fourteenth Amendment as a condition of their readmission to the Union.

Radical Republicans Congressional Republicans who insisted on black suffrage and federal protection of civil rights of African Americans.

Redeemers A loose coalition of prewar Democrats, Confederate veterans, and Whigs who took over southern state governments in the 1870s, supposedly "redeeming" them from the corruption of Reconstruction. They shared a commitment to white supremacy and laissez-faire economics.

Red Scare A wave of anticommunist, antiforeign, and antilabor hysteria that swept over America in 1919. It resulted in the deportation of many alien residents and violated the civil liberties of many of its victims.

Roe v. Wade The 1973 Supreme Court decision that women have a constitutional right to abortion during the early stages of pregnancy.

Roosevelt Corollary A corollary to the Monroe Doctrine, which asserted that the United States would intervene in Latin American affairs if those countries could not keep their affairs in order.

Scopes Trial Also called the "monkey trial," the 1924 Scopes trial was a contest between modern liberalism and religious fundamentalism. John T. Scopes was prosecuted for teaching Darwinian evolution in defiance of Tennessee state law. He was found guilty and fined $100. Scopes's conviction was later set aside on a technicality.

Sedition Act A World War I law that imposed harsh penalties on anyone using disloyal, profane, scurrilous, or abusive language about the U.S. government, flag, or armed forces.

Selective Service Act This 1917 law required all American men between the ages of 21 and 30 to register for a military draft. The age limits were later changed to 18 and 45.

settlement houses Located in poor districts, these community centers tried to soften the impact of urban life for immigrant and other families. Often run by young, educated women, they provided social services and a political voice for their neighborhoods. Chicago's Hull House, founded by Jane Addams in 1889, was the most famous of them.

sharecropping After the Civil War, the southern states adopted a sharecropping system as a compromise between former slaves who wanted land of their own and former slave owners who needed labor. The landowners provided land, tools, and seed to a farming family, who in turn provided labor. The resulting crop was divided between them, with the farmers receiving a "share" of one-third to one-half of the crop.

Sherman Antitrust Act This 1890 act was the first major U.S. attempt to deal with the problem of the increasing size of business. It declared illegal "every contract, combination in the form of trust or otherwise, or conspiracy, in restraint of trade or commerce."

Sherman Silver Purchase Act An 1890 act that attempted to resolve the controversy over silver coinage by requiring the Treasury to purchase 4.5 million ounces of silver each month and issue legal tender (in the form of Treasury notes) for it. The act pleased opponents of silver because it did not call for free coinage; it pleased proponents of silver because it bought up most of the nation's silver production.

social-justice movement During the 1890s and after, this movement attracted followers who sought to free people from the often devastating impact of urban life. It focused on the need for housing reform, more stringent child labor regulations, and better working conditions for women.

social Darwinism Adapted by English social philosopher Herbert Spencer from Charles Darwin's theory of evolution, this theory held that the "laws" of evolution applied to human life, that change or reform therefore took centuries, and that the "fittest" would succeed in business and social relationships. It promoted competition and individualism, saw government intervention into human affairs as futile, and was used by the economic and social elite to oppose reform.

Social Gospel Preached by urban Protestant ministers, the Social Gospel focused as much on improving the conditions of life on earth as on saving souls for the hereafter. Its adherents worked for child-labor laws and measures to alleviate poverty.

Social Security Act The 1935 Social Security Act established a system of old age, unemployment, and survivors' insurance funded by wage and payroll taxes.

Southern Christian Leadership Conference An organization founded by Martin Luther King, Jr., to fight segregation through passive resistance, nonviolence, and peaceful confrontation.

Strategic Arms Limitation Talks (SALT) In 1972, the United States and the Soviet Union culminated four years of SALT by signing a treaty limiting the deployment of antiballistic missiles (ABM) and an agreement to freeze the number of offensive missiles for five years.

Strategic Defense Initiative (SDI) Popularly known as "Star Wars," President Ronald Reagan's SDI proposed to construct an elaborate computer-controlled antimissile defense system capable of destroying enemy missiles in outer space.

Student Nonviolent Coordinating Committee (SNCC) A group organized by students to work for equal rights for African Americans. It spearheaded peaceful sit-ins and marches in the early 1960s, but later grew more radical and changed its name to the Student National Coordinating Committee.

Students for a Democratic Society Founded in 1962, the SDS was a popular college student organization that protested shortcomings in American life, notably racial injustice and the Vietnam War. It led thousands of protests before it split apart in the late 1960s.

Sunbelt A broad band of states running across the South from Florida to Texas, extending west and north to include California and the Pacific Northwest. Beginning in the 1970s, it experienced rapid economic and population growth.

supply-side economics The theory that tax cuts would stimulate the economy by giving individuals more incentive to earn more money, which would lead to greater investment and eventually larger tax revenues at a lower rate.

Taft–Hartley Act This 1947 anti-union legislation outlawed the closed shop and secondary boycotts. It also authorized the president to seek injunctions to prevent strikes that threatened national security.

Teapot Dome scandal A 1924 scandal in which Secretary of the Interior Albert Fall was convicted of accepting bribes in exchange for leasing government-owned oil lands in Wyoming (Teapot Dome) and California (Elks Hill) to private businessmen.

Teller Amendment In this amendment to the declaration of war on Spain in 1898, the United States pledged that it did not intend to annex Cuba and that it would recognize Cuban independence after the Spanish-American War.

Tennessee Valley Authority (TVA) A New Deal effort created in 1933 to build dams and power plants on the Tennessee River. Its programs helped raise the standard of living for millions in the Tennessee River valley.

Ten Percent Plan Reconstruction plan proposed by President Abraham Lincoln as a quick way to readmit the former Confederate States. It called for pardon of all southerners except Confederate leaders, and readmission to the Union for any state after 10 percent of its voters signed a loyalty oath and the state abolished slavery.

Tet offensive In February 1968, the Vietcong launched a major offensive in the cities of South Vietnam. Although caught by surprise, American and South Vietnam forces quashed this attack. But the Tet offensive was a blow to American public opinion and led President Lyndon Johnson to seek a negotiated peace.

Thirteenth Amendment Ratified in 1865, it prohibits slavery and involuntary servitude.

Treaty of Paris Treaty in December 1898 ending the Spanish-American War. Under its terms, Spain recognized Cuba's independence, assumed the Cuban debt, and ceded Puerto Rico, Guam, and the Philippines to the United States.

Truman Doctrine In 1947, President Truman asked Congress for money to aid the Greek and Turkish governments that were then threatened by communist rebels. Truman asserted that the United States was committed to support free people everywhere against communist attack or rebellion.

trunk lines Four major railroad networks that emerged after the Civil War to connect the eastern seaports to the Great Lakes and western rivers. They reflected the growing integration of transportation across the country that helped spur large-scale industrialization.

trust A device to centralize and make more efficient the management of diverse and far-flung business operations. It allowed stockholders to exchange their stock certificates for trust certificates, on which dividends were paid. John D. Rockefeller organized the first major trust, the Standard Oil Trust, in 1882.

Turner's thesis Put forth by historian Frederick Jackson Turner in 1893, this thesis asserted that the existence of a frontier and its settlement had shaped American character; given rise to individualism, independence, and self-confidence; and fostered the American spirit of invention and adaptation. Later historians modified the thesis by pointing out the environmental and other consequences of frontier settlement, the federal government's role in peopling the West, and the clash of races and cultures that took place on the frontier.

Underwood Tariff Act This 1913 law reduced tariff rates and levied a graduated income tax to make up for the lost revenue.

undocumented aliens Illegal immigrants, mainly from Mexico and Central America.

unilateralism A national policy of acting alone without consulting others.

Voting Rights Act of 1965 The 1965 Voting Rights Act banned literacy tests for voting rights and provided for federal registrars to assure the franchise to minority voters.

Wade-Davis Bill In 1864, Congress passed the Wade-Davis bill to counter Lincoln's Ten Percent Plan for Reconstruction. The bill required that a majority of a former Confederate state's white male population take a loyalty oath and guarantee equality for African Americans. President Lincoln pocket-vetoed the bill.

Wagner Act The 1935 Wagner Act, formally known as the National Labor Relations Act, created the National Labor Relations Board to supervise union elections and designate winning unions as official bargaining agents. The board could also issue cease-and-desist orders to employers who dealt unfairly with their workers.

War Industries Board (WIB) This government agency oversaw the production of American factories during World War I.

war on poverty Lyndon Johnson declared war on poverty in his 1964 State of the Union address. A new Office of Economic Opportunity (OEO) oversaw programs to help the poor.

war on terror Initiated by President George W. Bush after the attacks of September 11, 2001, the broadly defined war on terror aimed to weed out terrorist operatives and their supporters throughout the world.

Watergate Scandal A break-in at the Democratic National Committee offices in the Watergate complex in Washington was carried out under the direction of White House employees. Disclosure of the White House involvement in the break-in and subsequent cover-up forced President Richard Nixon to resign in 1974.

Women's Christian Temperance Union (WCTU) This organization campaigned to end drunkenness and the social ills that accompanied it. By 1898, it had 10,000 branches and 500,000 members. The WCTU illustrated the role women played in politics and reform long before they won the right to vote.

Women's Trade Union League (WTUL) Founded in 1903, this group worked to organize women into trade unions. It also lobbied for laws to safeguard female workers and backed strikes, especially in the garment industry. While it never attracted many members, its leaders were influential enough to give the union considerable power.

Works Progress Administration (WPA) New Deal agency to provide work relief for the unemployed.

Wounded Knee Massacre In December 1890, troopers of the Seventh Cavalry, under orders to stop the **Ghost Dance** religion among the Sioux, took Chief Big Foot and his followers to a camp on Wounded Knee Creek in South Dakota. It is uncertain who fired the first shot, but 200 Native Americans were killed.

Yalta Conference A wartime conference in February 1945 in which the Allies agreed to final plans for the defeat of Germany and the terms of its occupation. The Soviets agreed to allow free elections in Poland, but these were never held.

yellow journalism To sell newspapers before and during the Spanish-American War, publishers William Randolph Hearst and Joseph Pulitzer engaged in blatant sensationalization of the news, which became known as "yellow journalism." Although it did not cause the war, it helped turn U.S. public opinion against Spain.

Credits

CHAPTER 16 Everett Collection Historical/Alamy; 354tr: Library of Congress Prints and Photographs Division[LC-DIG-cwpbh-00952]; 357tr: Library of Congress Prints and Photographs Division[LC-DIG-pga-01366]; 359t: Slavery is Dead', 1866 (engraving), Nast, Thomas (1840-1902)/Chicago History Museum, USA/The Bridgeman Art Library; 362br: Stock Montage/Getty Images; 365b: Buyenlarge/Contributor/Archive Photos/Getty Images; 368br: Valentine Richmond History Center; 370tr: North Wind Picture Archives/Alamy; 371bl: Rutherford B. Hayes Presidential Center; 375tl: Time & Life Pictures/Contributor/Getty Images

CHAPTER 17 World History Archive/Newscom; 377r: World History Archive/Newscom; 378: National Archives and Records Administration; 381t: American Museum of Natural History; 383t: The Granger Collection, NYC; 385t: Library of Congress; 386b: akg-images/Newscom; 389bl: National Archives and Records Administration; 392tr: Archive Images/Alamy; 395t: Charles M. Russell (1864-1926), "Cowboy Camp During the Roundup," oil on canvas, ca. 1885-1887, 23 1/2 x 47 1/4 inches, Amon Carter Museum of American Art, Fort Worth, Texas, 1961.186; 400tr: The Granger Collection, NYC

CHAPTER 18 Art Resource/The Metropolitan Museum of Art; 404tr: North Wind Picture Archives/Alamy; 410t: Library of Congress Prints and Photographs Division Washington, D.C. [LC-USZ62-57524]; 413c: The Granger Collection, NYC; 414t: Library of Congress; 416tr: The Print Collector/Alamy; 420c: Bettmann/Corbis; 424t: Bettmann/Corbis; 425bl: Bettmann/Corbis; 426tr: Library of Congress Prints and Photographs Division[LC-USZ62-75192]

CHAPTER 19 The Museum of the City of New York/Art Resource, NY; 430tr: Library of Congress Prints and Photographs Division [LC-DIG-fsa-8a26761]; 431b: GE Kidder Smith/Corbis; 433b: Library of Congress, Prints & Photographs Division, [LC-USZ62-50240]; 437tl: The Granger Collection, NYC; 444tr: The Granger Collection, NYC; 445b: Johnston, Frances Benjamin[Library of Congress Prints and Photographs Division/Library of Congress Prints and Photographs Division]; 448tr: Corbis; 450tr: Corbis; 452tr: Wallace Kirkland//Time Life Pictures/Getty Images

CHAPTER 20 Bettmann/Corbis; 455cr: Valentine Richmond History Center; 456tr: Library of Congress Prints and Photographs Division, [LC-DIG-cwpbh-04797]; 461t: The Granger Collection, NYC ,All rights reserved.; 462tr: Bettmann/Corbis; 463tr: Library of Congress Prints and Photographs Division [LC-DIG-ppmsca-25438]; 464b: Hulton Collection/Getty Images; 465bl: Everett Collection Inc/Alamy; 473b: The Granger Collection NYC; 476t: Everett Collection Inc/Alamy

CHAPTER 21 The Granger Collection, NYC; 480: Library of Congress Prints and Photographs Division[LC-USZ62-104479]; 483t: OpenLibrary; 486tr: akg-images/Newscom; 487t: Library of Congress Prints and Photographs Division; 490t: Historical/Corbis; 492b: Chicago History Museum, USA/Bridgeman; 493t: Ivy Close Images/Alamy; 494b: Historical/Corbis; 498t: Library of Congress Prints and Photographs Division [04183r]

CHAPTER 22 The Granger Collection, NYC; 504: Bettmann/Corbis; 506tr: Everett Collection Historical/Alamy; 507bl: Bettmann/Corbis; 510tr: Pictorial Press Ltd/Alamy; 510tl: Hulton Archive/Getty Images; 511bl: Public Domain; 513tl: Library of Congress Prints and Photographs Division; 517t: California Historical Society; 523t: PEMCO - Webster & Stevens Collection; Museum of History and Industry, Seattle/Corbis

CHAPTER 23 Library of Congress Prints and Photographs Division [LC-DIG-ppmsca-27643]; 528: National Archives and Records Administration; 529tl: Buyenlarge/Contributor/Archive Photos/Getty Images; 531tr: Library of Congress Prints and Photographs Division[LC-USZ62-30776]; 533tl: Infant Welfare Society Nurse (b/w photo), American School, (19th century)/Chicago History Museum, USA/The Bridgeman Art Library; 534tr: Beals, Jessie Tarbox/Bridgeman Art Library; 536br: Niday Picture Library/Alamy; 541t: The Granger Collection, NYC; 547tl: Library of Congress Prints and Photographs Division [LC-USZ62-84130]; 548tr: Blank Archives/Contributor/Hulton Archive/Getty Images

CHAPTER 24 Hulton Archive/Getty Images; 556tr: National Archives and Records Administration; 562br: Lordprice Collection/Alamy; 564t: akg-images/Alamy; 566br: Niday Picture Library/Alamy; 570tr: Library of Congress Prints and Photographs Division [LC-USZ62-115013]; 571bl: Chicago History Museum/Getty Images; 572br: Bettmann/Corbis; 574tr: Bettmann/Corbis; 578tr: akg-images/Newscom

CHAPTER 25 Hulton Collection/Hulton Archive/Getty Images; 582tr: Bettmann/Corbis; 584b: The Granger Collection, NYC; 587t: Stock Montage/Hulton Archive/Getty Images; 588tr: Underwood & Underwood/Historical Premium/Corbis; 589b: The Granger Collection, NYC; 591t: Bettmann/Corbis; 593t: Bettmann/Corbis; 594t: Everett Collection Inc./Alamy; 597b: The Granger Collection, NYC

CHAPTER 26 AP Images; 604tr: Carol M. Highsmith/Library of Congress Prints and Photographs Division[LC-DIG-highsm-10898]; 607t: American Stock/Hulton Archive/gettyimages; 608tr: Library of Congress Photographs and Prints Division[LC-USW33-035391-ZC]; 612br: Franklin D. Roosevelt Library; 614b: AP Images; 616r: Library of Congress Prints and Photographs Division[LC-USZC2-3731]; 619t: Hulton Archive/Archive Photos/Getty Images; 620tl: Library of Congress Prints and Photographs Division [LC-DIG-fsa-8b29516]/Dorothea Lange; 621bl: Franklin D. Roosevelt Library; 621br: World History Archive/Newscom

CHAPTER 27 Hulton-Deutsch Collection/Historical/Corbis; 626: Library of Congress Prints and Photographs Division [LC-USZ62-104520]; 628b: AP Images; 631tl: CSU Archives/Everett Collection/Alamy; 634tr: U.S. Naval Photographic Center; 637b: Bettmann/Corbis; 639tr: Library of Congress Prints and Photographs Division [LC-USZ62-36452]; 641b: Al Palmer/Bettmann/Corbis; 642br: Library of Congress Prints and Photographs Division Washington, D.C. [LC-USZ62-119496]; 646b: Underwood & Underwood/Bettmann/Corbis

CHAPTER 28 AP Images; 650tr: National Archives and Records Administration; 655t: ullstein bild/The Granger Collection, NYC; 657b: Bettmann/Corbis; 658t: Bettmann/Corbis; 660b: SSPL/Getty Images; 663tr: Scott Germain/Stocktrek Images, Inc./Alamy; 668tr: Hank Walker//Time Life Pictures/Getty Images; 669br: Julian Wasser//Time Life Pictures/Getty Images; 669bl: Ralph Morse//Time Life Pictures/Getty Images

CHAPTER 29 Cornell Capa/Magnum Photos, Inc.; 674tr: Miscellaneous Items in High Demand/Library of Congress; 678: CBS Photo Archive/Getty Images; 680tr: Allen Ginsberg/Corbis; 682tr: NYWT&S Collection/Library of Congress Prints and Photographs Division[LC-USZ62-122432]; 683t: Bettmann/Corbis; 684tr: Black parents and children demonstrating against school segregation in Saint Louis, Missouri, 1960s (b/w photo), American Photographer, (20th century)/Private Collection/Peter Newark American Pictures/The Bridgeman Art Library; 685b: Everett Collection Inc/Alamy; 687t: Gene Herrick/AP Images; 688br: Bettmann/Corbis

CHAPTER 30 AP Images; 692tr: National Archives and Records Administration; 696br: AFP/Getty Images; 699t: Black Star; 700r: Anonymous/AP Images; 702tr: Time & Life Pictures/Getty Images; 707tr: E.J. Baumeister Jr./Alamy; 709b: AP Images; 713t: Arthur Schatz//Time Life Pictures/Getty Images

CHAPTER 31 Diana Walker/ Getty Images News/Getty Images; 720tr: Library of Congress Prints and Photographs Division [LC-DIG-highsm-16601]; 723t: Bettmann/Corbis; 725bc: The Granger Collection, NYC; 727tr: Joe Sohm/Visions of America, LLC/Alamy; 731tl: Keystone/Hulton Archive/Getty Images; 732tr: Jeff Mitchell US/Reuters/Reuters/Corbis; 736tr: Everett Collection; 737t: Bettmann/Corbis; 743t: Bettmann/Corbis

CHAPTER 32 Susan Biddle/Contributor/Time & Life Pictures/Getty Images; 746tr: AP Images/Charles Bennett; 750tr: AP Images/Dominique Mollard; 752t: ROBERTO SCHMIDT/Staff/AFP/Getty Images; 754b: Marko Georgiev/Contributor/Getty Images; 756b: Stephan Savoia/AP Images; 759tc: Douglas Graham/Contributor/Congressional Quarterly/Getty Images; 762tr: Joe Sohm/Visions of America, LLC/Alamy; 766tr: AP Images/Jerome Delay; 769t: Pablo Martinez Monsivais/AP Images

Index

Note: Key terms and the text page on which the term is defined are highlighted in boldface type. Italicized page numbers indicate figures.

A

AAA. *See* Agricultural Adjustment Administration
Abbott, Grace, 513
Abilene (KS), 395
Abortion and abortion rights, 731–732, 771
Abstract expressionism, 680
"Absurd Effort to Make the World Over, The" (Sumner), 449
Acheson, Dean, 654, 656, 660, 661, 662, 668, 715
Activism. *See also specific movements and organizations*: black power movement and, 712; civil rights movement and, 686–688, *698*, 698–701, *700*, 704–705; ethnic nationalism and, 712–714; Vietnam protests and, 710–711, 722–724; women's liberation and, 714
ACT UP (AIDS Coalition to Unleash Power), 733
ADA. *See* Americans with Disabilities Act (ADA)
Adams, Charles Francis, Jr., 457
Adams, Samuel Hopkins, 543
Adamson Act (1916), 552
Addams, Jane, 451–452, *452*, 497, 514, 518, 549, 563
Adolescence, 442, 586
Adventures of Huckleberry Finn, The (Twain), 471
Adventures of Tom Sawyer, The (Twain), 471
Advertising, 417–418, 521, 583, 585, 679
AEF. *See* American Expeditionary Force (AEF)
Affirmative action, 771
Affluence: in 1920s, 583–585; in 1950s, 673–675; materialism and, 710
Afghanistan: Soviet war in, 738, 740, 742, 743, 764; U.S. war in, 764–765
AFL. *See* American Federation of Labor (AFL)
African Americans. *See also* Black power movement; Civil rights movement; Ku Klux Klan; Segregation; Civil Rights and, *447*; in Civil War, 353–355; claiming public and private rights, 368–369; education and, 442–443; farming and, 364, 365, 465–466, 512, 618; Great Depression and, 606–607, 618; Harlem Renaissance and, 588, *589*; homesteading and, 397–398;

in industrial society, 419–420, 422; in Jim Crow South, 446–448; Levittown and, 674, 675; migration (North to South) of, 754; migration (South to North) of, 430, 522, 585–586; New Deal and, 618–620; Niagara Movement and NAACP and, 513–514; progressivism and, 515, 534; in reconstruction, 353–355, 355–356, 361–362, 363–369; settlement houses and, 453; (South to North), 575, *575*; in Spanish-American War, 492–494, *494*; Theodore Roosevelt and, 539–542; in twenty-first century, 754–755; in Vietnam War, 711; women, 470, 512–513, 534; Woodrow Wilson and, 551–552; in World War I, 568, 574–575, *575*; in World War II, 643–644
African Methodist Episcopal (AME) Church, 369
Afrika Korps, 634, 638
Afro-American, use of term, 712
Age, 1990s population and, 751
Agnew, Spiro, 715, 734
Agricultural Adjustment Administration (AAA), 613
Agriculture. *See also* Farms and farming; Planters and plantations: decline of (1920s), 585, 599; post World War II, 676; settling the West and, 398–399; technology and, 398, 405
Aguinaldo, Emilio, 499
AIDS (acquired immune deficiency syndrome), 733
Air brake, 404
Air Force (U.S.), 659, 681
Airlines, September 11 and, 764–765
Airplane, invention of, 477
Alabama: Civil rights movement and, 686–688, 699–700, 704–705
Alabama, University of, 700, 750
Alamo Saloon, 395
Alaska, purchase of, 484
Alcohol and alcoholism, 434, 533–534, 587, 592
Alcott, Louisa May, 471
Aldrich, Nelson W., 545
Alger, Horatio, 421, 471
Aliens. *See* Undocumented aliens
Alito, Samuel, 771
Allen, Frederick Lewis, 588
Alliance for Progress, 694
Allies (World War I), 563, 564, 567–568, 569, 576, 578
Allies (World War II): support for, 630–634; victory of, 644–647; working coalition of, 634–638
All Quiet on the Western Front (Remarque), 628
Al Qaeda, 764–770

Aluminum industry, 585
AMA. *See* American Medical Association (AMA)
Amalgamated Copper Company, 508
Amalgamated Iron and Steel Workers, 424
Amendments, Constitutional. *See specific amendment*
America First Committee, 631
American Airlines, 764
American Empire. *See* Empire, American
American Expeditionary Force (AEF), 567
American Federation of Labor (AFL), 518, 617
American G.I. Forum, 643
American Independent Party, 716
American Indians. *See* Native Americans
Americanization programs, 515
American League, 440
American Medical Association (AMA), 532
American Protective Association, 434
American Psychiatric Association, 733
American Railway Union (ARU), 468
American Society of Composers, Authors, and Publishers (ASCAP), 523
American Sugar Refining, 415
Americans with Disabilities Act (ADA), 748
American Telephone and Telegraph Company, 416
American Tobacco Company, 540
American Union Against Militarism, 564
American Woman Suffrage Association, *534*, 535
America's Road to War, 1914–1917 (Millis), 629
Amnesty, for Confederates, 355–356
Amos 'n' Andy (radio program), 585
Anarchists and anarchism, 424
Anderson, John, 738
Anderson, Marian, 618, *619*
Anderson, Sherwood, 491
Andropov, Yuri, 742
Angel Island, California, 517, *517*
Anglo-Saxon peoples, idea of superiority of, 446, 482
Anthony, Susan B., 370, 442, 535
Antiballistic missiles (ABMs) treaty, 722, 765
Anti-Catholicism: new immigrants and, 434
Anti-Imperialist League, 497
Anti-imperialists, 497–498
Anti-Saloon League, 533, 592
Anti-Semitism, 434. *See also* Jews and Judaism

Antitrust movement, 414
Antiwar sentiment: Vietnam and, 710–711, 722–724; World War I and, 562–563; World War II and, 627–630
Apache Indians, 377, 380, 383
A&P food stores, 585
Appeal to Reason, 572
Appeasement, 629
Appliances, post World War II, 675, 676
Arab Americans, 756
Arabic (ship) and pledge, 557, 564
Arab-Israeli conflicts, 726–728
Arapaho Indians, 377, 380, 382, 383
Arbitration, labor, 519, 540–541
Architecture, urban, 432
Ardennes Forest, 644
Arizona, 751
Arizona Territory, 393
"Arkies," 619
Armed forces, 659, 681. *See also* Air Force (U.S.); National Guard; Navy (U.S.); *specific wars*
Arms control: ABMs, 722, 765; INF and, 743; SALT and, 722; START I and, 749
Arms race. *See* Nuclear arms race
Armstrong, Louis, 524
Army-McCarthy hearings, 670
Army War College, 558
Arrogance of Power, The (Fulbright), 706
Arsenal of democracy, 640
Arthur, Chester A., presidency of, 459
Art(s), 524, 679–680
ASCAP. *See* American Society of Composers, Authors, and Publishers (ASCAP)
Ashcan School, 524
Ashcroft, John, 765
Asia, 661–664; Cold War and, 661–664
Asian Americans, 517, 755
Assassination(s): Garfield, 459; Kennedy, 701; law outlawing CIA, 734; McKinley, 477, 539
Assemblies of God, 679
Assembly line, 509, 520; speed and, 509–510
Assimilation policy, Native Americans and, 385–387
Atchison, Topeka, and Santa Fe Railroad, 409, *409*
Atkinson, Ti-Grace, 714
Atlanta Compromise, 445, 446
Atomic bomb: Cold War and, 653, 659–660, *660*, 661, 667; against Japan, *646*, 647
Attlee, Clement, 651
Attorneys. *See* Legal system and profession

U.S. Map

PRESENT DAY UNITED STATES

From The American Journey, Seventh Edition. Goldfield, Abbott, Anderson, Argersinger, Argersinger and Barney.

From Maps of *American Stories: A History of the United States*, Third Edition. H. W. Brands, R. Hal Williams, T. H. Breen and Ariela J. Gross Copyright © 2015 by Pearson Education, Inc. All rights reserved.

World Map